Spatial Perspectives on
Industrial Organization
and Decision-making

Spatial Perspectives on Industrial Organization and Decision-making

Editor:

F. E. IAN HAMILTON

Lecturer in Social Studies
University of London

JOHN WILEY & SONS

LONDON · NEW YORK · SYDNEY · TORONTO

Copyright © 1974, by John Wiley & Sons, Ltd.

Library of Congress Cataloging in Publication Data:

Hamilton, F. E. Ian.
Spatial perspectives on industrial organization
and decision-making.

1. Industries, Location of. 2. Industries,
Location of—Case studies. I. Title.

HD 58.H35   658.2′1   73–14379

ISBN 0 471 34715 9

Photosetting by Thomson Press (India) Limited, New Delhi
and printed in Great Britain by Unwin Brothers Ltd.,
The Gresham Press, Old Woking, Surrey.

Contents

v

Editor's Preface

The seeds of an interest may be sown in the mind at any time in one's life. It may then lay dormant in the subconscious for an indefinite period, to be fertilized, raised and nurtured by experiences and environments to which one may be exposed. I recall that my fascination with industry began in primary school, soon after the Second World War. We had received an edition of *The British Isles* by L. Dudley Stamp. In thumbing through its pages one day a photograph of the cooling towers of a Nottinghamshire power station caught my imagination. That evening at home I set to and fashioned miniature cooling towers from my late mother's cotton reels and a power-house from my late father's matchboxes! Later, in the mid-1950s, in preparation for examinations, I was stimulated to consider more seriously some questions of industrial location by three fine teachers: Alan Nicholls, who deservedly became President of the British Geographical Association in 1972; Jack Harvey, who is now well-known for his Economics textbooks; and René Amelot, one of a number of outstanding economists who had graduated in the late 1920s from the London School of Economics and Political Science. It was in this distinguished centre of learning and scholarship, the L.S.E., that my interest in industrial location analysis broadened, deepened and gelled under the inspiring teaching of Professor R. Ogilvie Buchanan, Professor Michael Wise, Dr. Robert C. Estall and Dr. John E. Martin. It is to all these people, who have fertilized, raised and maintained my interest, that my effort in this book is dedicated.

The idea for *Spatial Perspectives on Industrial Organization and Decision-making* arose out of the demand for an original work which would examine relatively neglected, yet vitally important, aspects of industrial location analysis and impart to it new perspectives. For long there has been an apparent need to channel research effort into directions which diverge from the traditional, and hitherto dominant, mould of Weberian analysis, to explore underdeveloped avenues which might yield new insights into the problem and to give broader, more contemporary, meaning to the field of viii

industrial location analysis. This book attempts to achieve these objectives in two ways. First, the main focus is on locational behaviour by *organizations* which make decisions shaping the spatial pattern of industrial activity. Stress is laid upon the importance of corporate organizations and behaviour, not only with respect to the choice of locations for new plants or capacities but also, which is often more important, with respect to the establishment, modification, stabilization and substitution of the spatial relationships of existing industrial plants within such organizations. Key issues discussed, therefore, are, in Part I, the evolution of the corporation and its spatial production and linkage patterns; the interactions of business organization and the decision-making environment; multi-product output by firms and the problem of pollution; the interactions between information flows, multiplier effects, innovation diffusion, city systems and industrial patterns; in Part II, the investment decision process in different types of industrial firm or organization and at different geographic levels, i.e. regional, national or international; the impact of business reorganization, mergers, nationalization on locational behaviour; in Part III, the adaptation of existing and fixed, relocated or branch plants to new or changing locational environments; and, in Part IV, the effect of planning behaviour on location. To correct some of the heavy bias towards the Anglo-American or Anglo-Saxon worlds in existing research, Part V pays attention to industrial location behaviour in selected socialist states and non-Western cultures.

Second, all the chapters in this book embrace the results of recently completed or on-going and *original* research. Not only do they embody new ideas or reappraisals of traditionally-accepted ideas, but they also incorporate a range of contemporary techniques and methods pertinent to industrial location analysis. And most chapters test existing or new hypotheses in the light of empirical case studies.

In organizing the book, I have been fortunate in having been able to obtain contributions from some of the leading authorities in the field of industrial location behaviour. These include such well-known analysts as Robert McNee, Allan Pred, Michael Ray, Howard Stafford, Peter Townroe, Günter Krumme, Hisao Nishioka and John Britton. They are supported here by a group of young and enthusiastic researchers who have already begun to make a name for themselves: Brenton Barr, Anthony Blackbourn, Bill Beyers, Jim Gilmour, David Heal, Bill Lever, David North, Okezie Onyemelukwe, John Rees and Michael Turner. It is a tribute to all the contributors that, despite the heavy pressures of teaching and tight schedules to meet other research commitments, they submitted on time and were always ready to answer my queries promptly. As an editor I could not have wished for a better team. I am sure that the authors will feel their job well done if their endeavours encourage others to follow their lead, to explore more deeply the issues set out and to extend and modify our understanding of the locational behaviour of industrial organizations.

Few words can describe adequately the contribution made by people behind the scenes and without whose assistance the book would never have been published. In particular I am indebted to Gladys Cornwell, Janet Fox and Wendy Greenwood for typing and re-typing manuscripts; to Jeanne-Marie Stanton and Janet Baker for drawing the maps and diagrams; and to my family, Justyna, Bartholomew and Michael, for tolerating an edgy editor.

F. E. IAN HAMILTON
London, June 1973

The Contributors

BRENTON M. BARR, B.A., M.A., PH.D., graduated from the University of British Columbia and undertook his doctoral research work at the University of Toronto. He spent one year as an exchange scholar at Moscow State University. From his work there he wrote *The Soviet Wood Processing Industry: A Linear Programming Analysis of the Role of Transportation Costs in Location and Flow Patterns* (1970). Currently he is Associate Professor of Geography, University of Calgary, and is studying Canadian patterns of industrial linkage and location decision-making behaviour.

WILLIAM B. BEYERS, B.A., PH.D., is a graduate of the University of Washington, Seattle, where he is now Assistant Professor of Geography. He was a post-doctoral fellow in Regional Science at Harvard and Cornell Universities in 1971. His research interests in regional economics, location theory and regional development are reflected in papers which are being published currently in a number of leading North American journals.

ANTHONY BLACKBOURN, B.SC. (ECON), M.A., PH.D., graduated from the London School of Economics and Political Science and then studied for his master's degree at the University of Georgia, Athens, and for his doctorate at the University of Toronto. At present he is Associate Professor of Geography at the University of Windsor, Ontario. His current research interests focus upon regional development problems and the spatial behaviour of international corporations.

JOHN N. H. BRITTON, B.A., M.A., PH.D., studied at the Universities of Sydney and Melbourne, Australia, and the London School of Economics and Political Science. He is now Associate Professor, Department of Geography, University of Toronto. Research interests in industrial linkage and organization and regional policy are reflected in a wide range of publications in North American, British and Swedish journals and in his book *Regional Analysis and Economic Geography* (Bell, 1968).

JAMES M. GILMOUR, M.A., PH.D., studied as an undergraduate at Glasgow University in Scotland, but received his doctoral degree at the University of Toronto. He is Associate Professor of Geography at McGill University, Montreal, but during the academic year 1972–73 he has been a consultant to the Science Council of Canada in Ottawa. Author of *The Spatial Evolution of Manufacturing: Southern Ontario* 1851–1891, he has also contributed to the Economic Atlas of Ontario and written papers for the *Canadian Geographer*.

F. E. IAN HAMILTON, B.SC. (ECON), PH.D., graduated from the London School of Economics and Political Science where he is currently Lecturer in Social Studies—a post held jointly with the School of Slavonic Studies. He studied for one year at Zagreb University, Yugoslavia, under the late Professor Rudolf Bićanić, and his post-doctoral research was carried out at Institutes of Geography and Economics in Poland and the Soviet Union. Publications reflect interests in industrial location, regional economics and change and in the spatial dimensions of socialist systems: 'Models of industrial location' in *Models in Geography* (Methuen, 1967); *Yugoslavia: Patterns of Economic Activity* (Bell, 1968); *Regional Economic Analysis in Britain and the Commonwealth* (Weidenfeld and Nicolson, 1971); forthcoming are books on the spatial economic patterns and industries of Poland. In 1972, Dr. Hamilton became Chairman of a new International Geographical Union Working Group on Industrial Geography.

DAVID HEAL, B.A., is Lecturer in Economic Geography at the University College of Wales, Aberystwyth. After graduating from Oxford, he worked in the British steel industry where he gained both an interest in and an insight into locational issues. He has recently completed a book on *Postwar Experiences of the British Steel Industry* (David and Charles) to be published in 1974.

WILLIAM F. LEVER, M.A., D.PHIL. (OXON), graduated from St. Peter's College, Oxford. He is currently Lecturer in Urban Studies in the Departments of Social and Economic Research and Architecture at the University of Glasgow: his research interests include the application of social sciences to planning and the study of intra-urban industrial location and population migration. Recent and forthcoming publications include a book on planning and papers on industrial location, linkages, land use and migration in a wide range of journals.

ROBERT B. MCNEE, B.A., M.A., PH.D., graduated from Wayne State University, Detroit but gained his postgraduate degrees at Syracuse University. He has published frequently in geographic journals for two decades, especially on urban-economic and educational themes. His *Primer on*

Economic Geography (Random House, 1971) stresses the expanding role of the modern metropolis, but current research focuses on the geography of organizations. Teaching posts held include S.U.N.Y., the University of Cincinnati (Department Head, 1963–69) and many summer appointments. In July, 1973, he was named Director of the American Geographical Society of New York—the greatest challenge of his career.

HISAO NISHIOKA, B.SC. (ECON), studied at the University of Kyoto and at the School of Economics, University of Tokyo. At present he is Professor of Location Theory and Regional Economics at Aoyama Gakuin University, Tokyo. Author of many books in Japanese on location theory and planning (1959, 1963, 1968 and 1973) and on regional income differentials (1966), he has also published in English language journals, notably the *Papers of the Second Far East Regional Science Association* (1967) and *Land Economics* (1973). He has also translated leading English language books by E. M. Hoover, B. J. L. Berry, M. L. Greenhut and L. J. King into Japanese.

DAVID J. NORTH, B.A. (ECON), PH.D., graduated from the University of Sheffield and spent the years 1969–72 studying for his Ph.D. at University College, London. Currently he is Lecturer in Geography and Planning at the Middlesex Polytechnic at Enfield, London. His research interests include the perception of location problems by industrialists and planners.

J. OKEZIE C. ONYEMELUKWE, B.A., PH.D., studied at the University of Ibadan where he is a Lecturer in Geography. His post-doctoral research interests are in industrial location and commodity flow analysis. The present contribution derives from his field experience in a Rockefeller Foundation-sponsored research project on *The Cotton and Cement Industries of Nigeria: A Geographic Appraisal of Factory Location and Product Distribution*. Forthcoming publications include works on industrialization and sectoral integration of regional economies and metropolitan transport planning. In 1972–73 he was a Postdoctoral Research Fellow at the Institute of Social Studies, The Hague, Netherlands.

ALLAN R. PRED, A.B., M.SC., PH.D., is Professor of Geography at the University of California, Berkeley. He obtained his A.B. from Antioch College, his M.Sc. from Pennsylvania State University and his Ph.D. from the University of Chicago. Published works include *The Spatial Dynamics of U.S. Urban-Industrial Growth* 1800–1914 (M. I. T., 1966), *Urban Growth and the Circulation of Information: the United States System of Cities* 1790–1840 (Harvard, 1973) and 'The growth and development of systems of cities in advanced economies', in *Lund Studies in Geography*, Series B, no. 38, 1973, reflect his main research interests.

D. MICHAEL RAY, B.A., M.A., PH.D., was an undergraduate of Manchester University (England) but obtained his graduate degrees respectively at the Universities of Ottawa and Chicago. Currently he is Professor of Geography, State University of New York at Buffalo and Theme Co-ordinator, Urban Growth and Demography, Ministry of State for Urban Affairs, Canada. From September 1973 he will be Professor of Geography, University of Ottawa. He has published papers widely in North American Journals and is co-author with Brian J. L. Berry and Edgar C. Conkling of a forthcoming book *The Geography of Economic Systems.*

JOHN REES, B.A., M.A., graduated from the University College of Wales at Aberystwyth and obtained his M.A. at the University of Cincinnati, Ohio. Until 1973 he was Lecturer in Geography at the Middlesex Polytechnic at Hendon, London, but he has now taken up the position of Assistant Professor in Geography, California State University at Chico. His interests focus on the analysis of investment decisions, spatial growth patterns of firms, search behaviour and regional economics.

ROGER A. ROBERGE, B.A., M.A., PH.D., studied at Assumption College and Clark University. He is now Associate Professor, Department of Geography, University of Ottawa. At present he is engaged in research on the mid-Canadian resource town and spatial planning of technology in the pulp and paper industry. A book *The Urban Crisis,* to be published shortly, reflects a secondary interest in urban poverty.

HOWARD A. STAFFORD holds a B.S. degree from West Chester, Pennsylvania, State College and M.A. and Ph.D. degrees from the University of Iowa. He is presently Professor and Head, Department of Geography, University of Cincinnati. He has published numerous articles on aspects of economic and urban geography in journals such as *Economic Geography, Regional Studies,* and *Progress in Geography: International Reviews of Current Research.* He also was the principal author of the Manufacturing Unit of the (United States) High School Geography Project. His current research activity is focused on location theory and the implications of the study of industrial location decision-making.

PETER M. TOWNROE, B.A. (ECON), M.A., graduated from the University of Sheffield, and proceeded to research work at the Centre for Urban and Regional Studies of the University of Birmingham. There, he developed his interest in industrial movement and industrial location decisions leading to the publication of *Industrial Location Decisions: A Study in Management Behaviour* (University of Birmingham, 1971). He is presently Lecturer in Economics at the University of East Anglia and has recently been on secondment to a research programme studying industrial movement and regional development. Recent papers have appeared in *Regional Studies, Regional and Urban Economics* and *Tijdschrift voor Economische en Sociale Geografie*. A volume entitled *The Industrial Movement Process* is in preparation, and an edited collection of papers *The Social and Political Consequences of the Motor Car* (David and Charles) which will appear in 1974.

D. MICHAEL TURNER, M.A., PH.D. (CANTAB), studied at the University of Cambridge, where he is now Research Fellow in Land Economy, Magdalene College. He has published several papers on the problems of industrial land values, location economics and the interaction of urban and rural areas with special reference to eastern England.

PAUL. Y. VILLENEUVE, B.A., PH.D., studied at the Universities of Ottawa and Washington (Seattle). He is now Assistant Professor, Department of Geography, Laval University. Current research focuses on applications of allometry and the ecological conditions of ethnic groups. He has published papers in the Association of American Geographers and Les Cahiers de Géographie de Quebec.

Acknowledgements

William Beyers and Günter Krumme wish to thank Richard LeHeron and Richard Towber for their useful comments on earlier drafts of their chapter; they are grateful for generous support for their research from the U.S. National Science Foundation.

Allan Pred is indebted to Torsten Hägerstrand, Gunnar Törnqvist and Poul Ove Pedersen for the comments and stimulation they provided during the formative stages of his chapter and to Bill Alonso, John Friedmann and Risa Palm who read a draft version of the chapter.

Micheal Ray, Roger Roberge and Paul Villeneuve wish to express their gratitude for the generous support of the Science Council of Canada and the University of Ottawa.

Howard Stafford wishes to acknowledge that a major share of the credit for this work goes to his research associates, Dr. Ellin Bloch and Mr. Allan Brown. Without the cooperation of the gentlemen interviewed, Messrs. W. C. Smith, R. E. Comstock, K. D. Allen, J. Gibbs, N. Shiflett, J. Cardillo, T. Romeo and R. Earle, nothing would have been possible and their assistance is gratefully acknowledged. The research was supported by a grant from the Appalachian Regional Commission and the Ohio Department of Development and the support of Mr. Richard Darwin, Dr. David Sweet and Mr. Coder Callison is very much appreciated. Thanks are also due to Dr. Richard Symanski for helpful suggestions, and special bouquets are due to two indispensable secretaries, Miss Karen Behymer and Mrs. Alice McMahon.

John Rees would like to thank Howard Stafford and Bob McNee for encouraging his research, the University of London Central Grants

Committee for grant towards the cost of the project, and the many company executives who willingly gave their time to discuss decision-making issues.

David North is grateful for the encouragement and guidance of Peter Wood during his research at University College, London, and to firms up and down Britain that cooperated in providing information.

John Britton acknowledges support by the National Advisory Committee on Geographic Research (Canada) and by the Centre for Urban and Community Studies, University of Toronto. Important contributions to the project were made successively by Jim Stark and Tony Lea: he is indebted to them for the quality of their work.

Jim Gilmour acknowledges that the research discussed in his chapter was supported by grants from the Canada Council, the National Advisory Committee on Geographic Research and the McGill University Social Science Research Committee.

The editor is indebted to the Central Research Fund of the University of London for giving generous financial support for his research and, in particular, for financing the study of Yugoslav workers' councils and their locational decision-making behaviour.

List of Tables

List of Figures

xxiv

Introduction

1

A View of Spatial Behaviour, Industrial Organizations and Decision-Making

F. E. IAN HAMILTON

Most twentieth-century research on the problem of industrial location has pursued a dominant theme: the explanation of the choice of location of new manufacturing plants. As a very broad generalization, such research has been accomplished on two planes by two distinct groups of people using two contrasting methods. First, following the lead primarily of Alfred Weber, economists have devoted much theoretical work to the development of the partial equilibrium approach, laid down the principles governing the initial location of new plants and of industries, and have attempted to construct general equilibrium models. Second, geographers have produced largely descriptive or analytical surveys endeavouring to explain the geographic distribution of particular industries or of groups of industries at the local, regional, national and international levels. By the mid-1960s for them the study of location factors had become to industrial geography what land-use studies were to agricultural geography or service areas were to urban geography.

Of course, both economists and geographers have achieved progress and industrial location analysis has benefited from some convergence of the two approaches; this has imparted to it greater vigour and reality. That more geographers are being exposed to training in economics results in more rigorous economic analysis. Greater emphasis is placed on theory, model-building, principles and analytical techniques. Geographers have been both more willing and more able to read, understand and attempt to apply, modify or extend the works of Weber, Palander, Lösch, Hoover and Isard. Examples of significant contributions are the market potential concept (Harris, 1954) and the spatial margins of profitability concept (Smith, 1966, 1971). Economists have acquired empirical evidence, for instance, about the real nature of transport rates or business goals. This has permitted

3

4

modification of unrealistic assumptions made in earlier theoretical writings. Symptomatic of these trends is the reduced dominance of the Weberian production-function cost-minimization approach: Löschian and a market-function profit maximization approaches have been incorporated. These contrasting interpretations have been fused together to yield the minimax solution to the location problem. Innovation of input–output techniques in economics has stimulated geographers to study inter-industry linkages and spatial associations of industries, particularly at the regional and metropolitan scales. The substitution of linear programming and algorithmic procedures for geometric and graphic techniques has permitted extension of the Weberian single-plant location problem to the spatial assignment problem of allocating *m* plants or plant *sizes* among *n* locations. Descriptive and analytic writing has incorporated more elements of the 'real' industrial environment as the twentieth century has proceeded and public policy, regional planning, and social and political goals came to be appreciated as significant controls on industrial location.

If, however, the changing relationship between economics and geography have encouraged conceptual and technical progress in the understanding of the spatial economics of industrial distributions, the simultaneous shift in the relationships between economics and other social sciences has demanded reappraisal of the economic approach to location based on classical models. During the 1960s strong opinions emphasized that economic conditions and factors have been overemphasized both as variables in the interpretation of, and as aims in policies for establishing or changing, industrial production patterns. Preoccupation with the economic dimensions has reflected (1) the long-standing dominance of economics among social sciences—and hence the (economic) geographer's perception of its relevance—in combination with (2) the scientific attractiveness of the rigour and elegance of much economic analysis by comparison with those other sciences. The rise in research, the improvement in methodology and technique and the growth of information in sociology, social anthropology, psychology, social administration, government, international studies, politics and the rise of behavioural social sciences generally, have provided new conceptual frameworks, hypotheses, theories and facts which call for reappraisal of many strictly economic assumptions about entrepreneurial or business behaviour. For far too long, man—a being with varied psychological characteristics, social organization, ethnicity, political and emotional traits—has been treated either as a highly responsive, mechanistic mathematico-economic agent or, to use Adam Smith's apt term, 'an invisible hand', in making decisions. Economists have been preoccupied with processes and marginal analysis, geographers with places, so that even the very language used in their papers about industrial location 'dehumanizes' man, purging him of his behaviour traits, distorting our perception of the problem. The reaction to this situation consists in the relegation of economics to a part, but only a part, alongside social, political, national, psychological and other human elements in the complex web of society. Today, therefore, while economics preserves a basic importance among the phenomena investigated by location analysts, attention is being focused more closely upon people as decision-makers and entrepreneurs who, and upon societies as systems of organizations which, shape both the economic and non-economic dimensions of individual and aggregate industrial location patterns.

Fundamentally, until recently, the problem was still cast largely in the mould of the nineteenth-century or twentieth-century 'free market' economy. That is, the main lines of industrial location analysis were appropriate to the time when, and to the regions where, small firms with one, usually single-product, plant were economically (and not only numerically) dominant, technologies and business organization were small-scale and simple, and location decisions were made essentially in response to relatively simple economic, social, political and spatial environments external to the manufacturer. It is the developments of the past thirty years that have made traditional industrial locational analysis lose some of its utility—certainly its claim to universality—and indeed that demand our re-interpretation not only of the location of modern industry but also of the location of industry during the industrial revolution. Broadly speaking these developments are seven in number:

(1) the adoption by entrepreneurs of mass production techniques which resulted in the expansion of the scale of industrial plant, demanding:

(2) an increase in the capitalization of industry, leading to:

(3) a great growth in the size of firms, and

(4) their evolution into multi-plant, multi-functional and often multi-national corporations, forging backward and forward linkages not only with other manufacturing activities but also with primary, tertiary and quaternary (research and development) activities, necessitating:

(5) the development in each firm of a complex bureaucratic decision-making organization—often in office locations both separate from and integrated with factory (production) functions—to handle the tremendous growth of information circulation that is associated with the extension of control by the firm over more plants, more functions, more sales areas and even over other firms;

(6) as an ever-increasing number of societies and nations become industrialized, a greater share of manufacturing growth and change occurs at existing sites and within existing city systems—not in new locations; and

(7) the emergence of socialist states, embracing one-third of world population and one-quarter of world industrial output, in which key decisions are made in interacting sets of large centralized and more numerous, but smaller, decentralized organizations; and the parallel growth of bureaucracies in 'mixed societies' and 'developing economies' which are taking or influencing an expanding share of industrial location decisions.

These developments have vastly broadened the location issue. This emerges from the recent writings of a number of contributors to this book—Krumme (1969a, 1969b), McNee (1958, 1960, 1963, 1964, 1972), Pred (1967), and Hamilton (1967, 1968, 1971a, 1971b), as well as others like Dicken (1971) who attempt to interpret the significance of these developments for spatial industrial behaviour. Thus, with respect to modern location analysis and within the reference framework of this book, attention should be focused on five interrelated fields of enquiry:

first, the traditional problem of selecting the initial location of the industrial firm and its manufacturing plant;

second, the spatial forms and implications of the growth and changing organization of the firm or corporation;

third, the firm's decision-making procedures which are employed in, and the motivations for, choosing any kind of locational behaviour;

fourth, the spatial adjustment by firms to their existing or chosen environments or in changing the size or use or relative importance of existing plants or facilities within their control;

and fifth, the comparative spatial behaviour of firms of different organization and scale, of industrial organizations in contrasting economic and social systems and of firms in diverse cultural environments.

The views set forward in this introductory chapter are intended neither to be exhaustive nor to provide a comprehensive and critical review of behavioural studies of industrial location. Rather the chapter singles out significant aspects of the field and attempts, in doing so, to discuss briefly the key ideas and to synthesize the findings presented by the contributors of chapters in this volume.

Selecting a Location: Some Controversial Issues

The choice of a *location* was, and still is, often a non-issue for the small-scale entrepreneur initially establishing an industry. This applies whether one is concerned with the early industrial revolution in Europe and America, or with regions of industrial infancy in the developing world today—as both McNee (Chapter 2 below) and Onyemelukwe (Chapter 18) demonstrate. More often than not, the entrepreneur begins to operate his business in his home town or settlement. Not only is his location in effect fixed, but often the question of *any* location, let alone any *alternative* location, never enters his mind. Even if it does, good reasons explain why he usually opened his first production facility in his home town. In the environment of the developing economy—whether late eighteenth-century Britain or late twentieth-century Nigeria—communications were primitive, spatially restricted and fragmented, and slow: personal contact patterns would be thus confined to a relatively small area. Low-level technology and education combined to limit sources and modes of information flow to direct or indirect personal contacts. Information circulation concerning entrepreneurial investment or production opportunities and alternatives or locational conditions elsewhere would also have been highly restricted spatially. Uncertainty about the environment outside the home town was very great: thus entrepreneurs, insofar as they made a conscious decision, 'chose' to initiate production virtually *in situ.*

The problem, therefore, would appear to be much less one of 'given the production, where shall the entrepreneur locate?' than one of 'given the location, what and how much shall he produce?' As ever, though, it is dangerous to generalize on the basis of slender research evidence; no doubt a wealth of documents in company, city or history archives would enable historical geographers to shed light on the extent to which either or both questions were relevant in initial entrepreneurial decisions. Both are equally *location* questions, although the former, the traditional question, treats location in the more absolute sense of choosing a *place* or an area, whereas the latter treats it in the more relative sense of choosing the *spatial relationships* of a given place.

If one accepts that the entrepreneur initiated his industrial business in his home town or village, one must ask why and how did he choose to manufacture a given product or range of products? Assuming that he has the capital to invest, it is fruitful to hypothesize that his choice of productions was made in response to:

first, a personal or vested interest in a technique which he had invented himself or which he wished to use;

second, his contact with an inventor, an innovator or an adopter of an innovation who had knowledge of a particular production process and with whom he could establish a business partnership;

third, the search for the use of a local resource which the entrepreneur owned or about which he had knowledge;

fourth, the imitation of successful entrepreneurs either with whom he had regular contact or with whom he had had little or no direct contact but whom he perceived to be successful in a particular industrial activity;

and fifth, the communicated or perceived product (i.e. input) needs of local manufacturers, landowners, transport entrepreneurs and others with whom he had contact or of whom he had information.

Undoubtedly personal know-how and confidence would spur an entrepreneur on to make or apply his own or his partner's invention. Probably the shrewdness of the entrepreneur, or a chance decision, might explain why he would choose between *imitating* others, i.e. taking an essentially production-orientated decision, and serving others' needs, i.e. taking an essentially market-orientated decision. In any case, his perception of the economic and technical environments, based on his information sources, would shape his decision as to what strategy to adopt, and hence what to produce. Only possibly the second situation might involve the investing entrepreneur in a choice of place for production, particularly if the partner and inventor lived and worked elsewhere: the entrepreneur might simply confirm the partner's location by developing production there rather than where he himself lived. Once the initial decision had been taken to manufacture a given product in the 'home town', i.e. the entrepreneur had given birth to a manufacturing firm or plant, the survival and profitability of the firm became a matter of successfully adjusting or changing inputs, outputs, techniques and scales—necessitating further entrepreneurial decisions about the locational relationships of its plants. If the firm was not successful, or failed to adjust sufficiently to changing environmental conditions, and its competitiveness waned, then the manufacturer could still make a choice between locational alternatives: to close the plant and to go out of business altogether; to convert the plant to new manufacturing uses; or to sell his plant to another entrepreneur and to move to establish production in another location. Evidence presented by Stafford (Chapter 6), Rees (Chapter 7) and North (Chapter 8) indicates that these measures were, and are, usally adopted only in response to powerful stress factors.

There is, however, a sixth possible situation which could clearly shape entrepreneurial choice of production: a potential manufacturer might be in business already, perhaps in commerce or farming. Onyemelukwe (Chapter 18) emphasizes that many Nigerian entrepreneurs relate their initial manufacturing activity to their existing marketing or trading functions. From this one can infer that at any period and in any country (e.g. late eighteenth-century Britain), private entrepreneurs followed this same practice. In such situations it is logical for entrepreneurs to initiate manufacturing of the products in which they trade—both because of (1) the higher spatial and non-spatial thresholds of certainty (which accrue from superior knowledge and experience of the firm over newcomers) and (2) the savings that derive from internalizing part of the business environment. If correct, this hypothesis also points to another false generalization, but one characteristically made by traditional location theorists: that a manufacturing firm commenced its life as an industrial firm and emergent industrial firms were uni-functional. Capital for industrial investment had to be derived from *some* economic activity. Since a potential industrial entrepreneur derived his capital from farming, forestry, mining, trade, crafts or inherited land and property, those activities of which he had experience would yield two results. First it would shape his choice of manufacturing production, which to some degree then could be assumed to be *given*. Second, it would make his firm 'duo-functional' or 'multi-functional' with backward linkages into resource exploitation or forward linkages into marketing or both. A merchant trading in wool, therefore, would probably initiate woollen manufacture rather than some other industry. A landowner producing cereals would probably initiate grain milling whereas one owning large sheep runs would initiate wool manufacturing. This underlines the neglect by industrial location analysts of the *firm,* a neglect which derived from their focus on the *plant* and which has blinded them to the parallel existence, if not predominance, of simple but nevertheless *multi-functional* firms over uni-functional industrial firms *since the commencement of industrialization.*

From this, one can derive an important set of hypotheses. The entrepreneur of the multi-functional firm with business in primary or tertiary activities might have had a better developed and spatially more extensive set of regular or routine personal contacts and information sources than the uni-functional industrial firm. He may also have been exploiting resources or trading goods at several places, and hence, when he contemplated entry into manufacturing he became, or was made, more aware of the possibilities of choosing from among alternative locations. One might assume, for instance, that an eighteenth-century Liverpool merchant selling cotton to handicraft or mill spinners in the Lancashire hinterland would choose to establish a mill in a place where one or several of his customers lived and worked. If customers from two or more places made him aware of those alternative places as potential mill locations, the entrepreneur would base his selection of one location for a cotton mill on his assessment of the information feedback from those customers. However, a study of the aggregate contact patterns of the potential industrial entrepreneur would merely define the broad area within which he was aware he might locate: it would not define the precise location. Choice of that location probably derived from the merchant's more intimate contact with one particular information source: that source would influence his decision most because its information was, or was perceived to be, of greater reliability, breadth and depth than that from other sources. Intimacy of contact, however, is suggestive of the role of social, as distinct from business, contacts although the two may be clearly interrelated. This points to the underestimated role of the web of narrower and wider *family contact patterns* as a varied information source likely to influence many, though by no means all, entrepreneurial decisions—both as to what to produce and where to locate. The importance of *family action space* in shaping the initial industrial location decisions by entrepreneurs of small firms in Japan is mentioned by Nishioka (Chapter 19) and in Nigeria by Onyemelukwe (Chapter 18). There is no reason to believe that its importance during the industrialization of Europe or America was any the less: indeed its relevance continues in the current age of giant industrial corporations (Burch, 1972).

Thus the traditionally-framed location question—the choice of a *place* for given production—may always have been more relevant to the decisions by the multi-functional firms than to decisions by uni-functional industrial firms: for the uni-functional industrial firm the choice of *production,* usually *in situ,* would be more common. The entrepreneur of an emergent multi-functional 'industrial' firm already had a vested interest in a given *activity* or *commodity,* and a level of certainty connected with it, and hence for him the more likely variable would have been the choice of place for initiating manufacturing. The entrepreneur of an emergent uni-functional firm had no such vested interest nor certainty: for him uncertainty was great and the safest decision was to choose production and operate *in situ*.

If these hypotheses are correct, then the relative importance of multi- *vs* uni-functional firms may help to explain the extent to which the initial entrepreneurial problem *was* one of choosing production rather than location. Recall, however, that the information constraints on multi-functional firms—though possibly less than on uni-functional firms—were still severe: this being so, there is still a strong likelihood that entrepreneurs of such firms would initiate industrial production in their home town and that production would be vertically integrated there with non-manufacturing functions. Given that multi-functional firms began to internalize some of the environment—and that environment was less complex than that of today—they reduced some uncertainty and organizationally might be more adaptive to changing environments. They might, therefore, be expected to have a better survival rate than uni-functional firms. Such a hypothesis, however, needs empirical support, but it must be recognized that more astute entrepreneurship, better intentional or chance contacts and a better initial chance location of a uni-functional firm could ensure that the reverse be true.

The stress here on contact patterns, information sources and perception of economic environmental opportunities by the individual entrepreneur is symptomatic of a modern approach to the location problem. If the hypotheses concerning initial location decisions at the micro-level of the firm are near the truth—or at least constitute a neglected part of the truth— then they provide an important explanation of the historic emergence of specialized industrial regions at the macro-level. In other words, it is neither sufficient nor correct to argue that Lancashire in England became a specialized cotton textile manufacturing region because of its comparative economic advantages in that industry. The contact patterns of potential entrepreneurs living in the region (landowners, traders, handicraftsmen) with merchants in Liverpool who began to handle American cotton encouraged many to start cotton-spinning or weaving as their initial industrial activity, perhaps substituting the use of cotton for the traditional commodity, wool. Locally, in each area, would-be entrepreneurs might imitate the apparently successful first few cotton textile manufacturers. Undoubtedly many land-owners and craftsmen initiated production *in situ* when they had Pennine water power at hand. Others, with family or business information contacts, would have moved into valleys which offered both water power and transport connections with Liverpool. Furthermore, the limited action spaces and contacts of entrepreneurs in the early industrial revolution also explain the rise of sub-regional functional specialisms in a valley or group of settlements within the larger specialized region: in the case of Lancashire this meant the emergence of sub-areas in which entrepreneurs were concerned dominantly with spinning or with weaving cotton. Such spatial groupings of specialized endeavour knit themselves into a complex web of intra-regional contact patterns, exchanging materials, goods and ideas, forcing or stimulating technological innovation, feeding back information and, in the process, *built up* for itself cumulative advantages: these became strong enough to perpetuate regional specialization once transport improvements— particularly the railway—widened and multiplied the contact patterns of people living and working in the region and opened it to in-migration of capital and enterprise from other regions. Yet, until that time, the isolation of the region in transport and information, specialized intra-regional contact patterns and hence activities, were presumably strengthened by the relative or absolute *lack* of entrepreneurial contact patterns with people from other regions with other kinds of industrial enterprise; had those contact patterns existed they might have stimulated greater intra-regional industrial diversification.

In the case of Lancashire this meant that its specialization derived from (1) strong contacts and information linkages with the cotton import source, Liverpool, causing (2) a decline in other activities (including the wool industry) in the hinterland through entrepreneurial initiation of early progressive cotton-using industrialists and (3) the weak transport and hence information and economic links with Yorkshire or Midland England that explain why cotton did not penetrate their regional economic structures and why their specialisms (woollen, metal and pottery industries) did not penetrate Lancashire.

These views underline the strong spatial parallels between the industrial environments of early nineteenth-century Britain and those of the developing world today. The conceptual links across time are embodied in the model of an idealized pattern of transport development in an underdeveloped area evolved by Taaffe, Morrill and Gould (1963) and modified by Hamilton (1967, pp. 399–400). In the first place the model can be re-interpreted as one of idealized information flow and contact patterns: it portrays the changing patterns, through time and with economic development, of spatial biases of information circulation. In the second place, the model stresses how in the earlier development phase of a nation, its regional economies were individually linked with, were tributary to, and hence its specializations were a function of, the external ties forged by entrepreneurs with the international economy; but the regions were separated from each other by zones of very poor information access which acted as barriers to interregional contacts, innovation diffusion and hence integration with the *national* economy. It is significant in the British case that entrepreneurs began the industrial revolution in the central and interior West Midlands and, although the strong friction of distance of overland transport likewise assisted in encouraging intra-regional rather than interregional contacts and innovation diffusion, so creating a specialized industrial area, in aggregate they, either directly or indirectly through middlemen traders, enjoyed limited yet diverse contacts with entrepreneurs and traders from industrializing regions around the nation: London, South Wales, the North West (Lancashire–Cheshire) and Yorkshire. Those contacts provided the West Midland entrepreneurs with information concerning the needs of a significant proportion of the British national economy. Combined with (1) the high innovation threshold generated within the region, yielding a high innovation potential and hence adaptability, and (2) the potential diversity of the specialized industry, metalworking—entrepreneurs in the West Midlands were able to create a much more diversified and adaptable industrial economy.

In other words the West Midland industrial entrepreneur had more contact with more and with more varied innovations, and with more national demand areas and their particular needs than entrepreneurs in most other specialized industrial regions. Moreover, he worked with a material—metal—which had many more uses than cotton, wool, timber or pottery. The greater potential spatial mobility of metal industry innovations, at least in aggregate, lends itself better than more restricted innovations in other industries to Pred's thesis concerning spatial patterns of diffusion of innovation and information circulation (Chapter 4): that such patterns do not rigidly conform to a Christalleran hierarchy, emanating from the leading centre downwards, but that they may proceed (1) up or down the hierarchy from smaller to larger centres or vice versa and (2) more often laterally between centres of the same, especially the largest, size. If, for the environmental context of eighteenth-century or nineteenth-century Britain, one substitutes 'industrial settlements' for 'cities' in Pred's analysis, it would appear to explain, for instance, the interregional 'jump' of metal, metallurgical and steam-engine innovations between Cornwall, the West Midlands, Sheffield and west-central Scotland. And there is no conflict with the observation of Roberge, Ray and Villeneuve (Chapter 5) that an industry, in this case the central Canadian pulp and paper industry, may spread within a region in a hierarchical manner à la Christaller. Their analysis, using allometry, clearly demonstrates a promising field of investigation.

Thus the interpretation of the spatial pattern of information surfaces in a nation at any time must clearly take cognizance of the nature of the information, of the processes at work in using that information as well as of the spatial biases of aggregate information. In the last analysis, a comparison of the examples of Lancashire and the West Midlands points to the possibility that when entrepreneurs choose either production or location there may be an inverse relationship between innovation and imitation. The greater the exposure of entrepreneurs to inventions, to adopters of innovations or to other entrepreneurs' needs, the greater is the likelihood that their decisions will be innovative and yield greater aggregate regional diversity in production and possibly greater willingness to establish a plant in a new location. Nishioka (Chapter 19) comments on location innovation by entrepreneurs in Japan. By contrast, the lower the exposure to innovations the greater the likelihood that the entrepreneur will imitate the production and location choices of others, so yielding a narrow aggregate regional and city specialization of production. Nevertheless, one should not overlook individual entrepreneurial traits: greater innate ability or imagination is more likely to stimulate an entrepreneur to innovate than to imitate, while an entrepreneur with limited ability is more likely to 'play safe' and imitate others. One may also hypothesize that the individual firm has a greater chance of success or survival if its entrepreneur is essentially an innovator and a smaller chance if he is essentially an imitator. By inference, insofar as regional industry is dependent upon its existing entrepreneurs, that region and its industry has a better chance of survival and adaptation to changing environmental conditions if those entrepreneurs are innovators rather than imitators. Many such hypotheses alluded to in this section are relevant to industrial location behaviour generally, but clearly from observing the developing world today one can, within limits, infer entrepreneurial behaviour in industrializing Europe or America more than one or two centuries ago.

The Growth and Changing Organization of the Industrial Firm

The most outstanding single conclusion which can be drawn from the following papers is the domination of the location issue by the *industrial organization, firm* or *corporation:* its goals, growth, size, age, production profile, organization and behaviour. It is symptomatic of the neglect of this field, and hence of the novelty of much of this book, that as much as one-quarter of the terms used by McNee in (Chapter 2) and suggested by him for indexing, do not appear in David Smith's recent and comprehensive book, *Industrial Location* (Wiley, 1972). But McNee is not alone: most of the chapters embody a significant number of concepts which do not appear there either. By assuming a single-plant, single-product firm, traditional location analysts identified the firm's behaviour as a once-and-for-all location problem. The goals, size, organization and behaviour of the firm were reduced to the bald assumption that its decision-makers attempted to maximize profits or to satisfice personal and corporate needs in making their location choices. Such analysis thus tacitly assumed a static environment to which no subsequent adaptation of the firm's spatial relationships was necessary: there was no hint of studying a problem which was assumed not to exist.

In reacting generally to the economists' neglect of space in the study of economic problems, geographers became responsible for separating location from the on-going decisions or policies taken in managing and expanding a firm. That this was a mistake is abundantly clear from the ensuing chapters

GROWTH + CHANGING ORG OF THE IND FIRM

of McNee, Krumme and Beyers, North, Rees, and Stafford in particular. They demonstrate that *all* business decisions have locational implications though some have much more than others, hence firms' need to solve some spatial problem is certainly rarely a once-and-for-all affair and may be a part of relatively frequent non-routine on-going business policy decisions.

In studying the growth and organization of the firm or corporation it is essential to understand that although *all* business decisions have some locational implications firms do not necessarily, or even usually, recognize that the location aspect is important: for many firms and for many types of business decision, the location aspect is likely to be a byproduct of a particular policy to achieve some non-spatial goal. There appears rarely to be a conscious *location policy* except among very large or market-dominant corporations in which decision-makers must recognize the importance of regional or international markets and interdependencies. Some business policies and goals are likely to have greater spatial repercussions for the spatial form and growth of the firm and, hence, for industrial distributions generally. As McNee, North, Rees and Stafford stress, the goals of firms can be diverse and the spatial implications of policies for achieving those goals can be equally diverse—as further evidence by Blackbourn (Chapter 9) and Heal (Chapter 10) demonstrates. Corporate goals are rarely singular in purpose. Most firms undoubtedly seek some level of profitability and some do strive for maximum profits. However, many firms also seek to achieve other goals: growth of the firm, larger control of the market for particular products, diversification of interests, entrepreneurial satisfaction or simply self-preservation as typified British steel firms prior to nationalization (Heal: Chapter 10). Some of these goals may be incompatible, but others clearly overlap and may in practice converge. One management may decide that corporate growth, for instance, may best be achieved by diversification: the emergent pattern of plant locations within the corporation is likely to differ significantly from a corporation whose managment is bent on growth via larger control of the market for a fairly narrow range of products. Because the interrelationships between corporate goals, policies for achieving those goals and resultant plant locations ·may vary so much, it is clear that to understand plant location singly or in aggregate one should look as much at the geography and spatial economy of the firm as of an industry. Nevertheless one should not conclude that because the detailed geography of most firms is likely to differ no broad patterns emerge. From the following chapters it is clear that those general patterns do begin to emerge, and this itself raises some doubts·as to whether pleas made by contributors here and elsewhere for *more* case studies are really justified.

For instance, there is strong evidence from observations of spatial behaviour by sample firms in a regional context, south-east Ohio (Stafford: Chapter 6), and from contemporary growth industries—the British plastics industry (North: Chapter 8) and large American chemical corporations

(Rees: Chapter 7)—that rarely do industrial firms plan location decisions over a long-term or medium-term period. In most, if not all cases, a location decision of *any* kind is a response to stress conditions impinging upon the efficient operation of the firm. Stress may be generated by forces internal to the firm: by a cramped original plant site, by a vital technological innovation made within, and thus which must be used within, the firm, by militant labour action or by decisions to integrate vertically or horizontally. Stress may come from forces external to the corporation: from pressure of increasing demand, from changing political climate abroad or from increased competition from rivals. North identifies ten such stress factors, although he does not include the political factor since this is not relevant to the U.K. domestic plastics industry—but it clearly does affect international corporations as the oil industry admirably exemplifies.

Moreover, each type of stress evokes among corporate management a particular type of response. Each type of response is an explicit or an implicit location decision, but the more explicit it is the more likely is management to take account of the spatial dimensions of the problem. Overall it might seem that the options open to a firm facing stress are rather wide: expansion *in situ,* factory transfer or relocation, construction of a branch plant, acquisition of another firm, merger with another firm or closure of an existing plant. In practice it appears that the options, at least as perceived by corporate management or by industrial entrepreneurs, are far more restricted: responses to particular stresses do call forth specific location decisions. North argues that firms extend existing factories if they have planned for growth, whereas firms which relocate have to do so as a response to unplanned growth. Branch factories, as many other studies indicate, are developed to exploit untapped regional markets or labour reserves. Different goals may generate the same response: a firm seeking to overcome stress by integration, either vertically or horizontally, prefers to acquire other firms, and so will another firm whose goal is diversification. The need for rationalization of production usually leads to closures, although a large corporation may be able to substitute production and flows within its organization without actually closing facilities. Heal elaborates how drastic spatial rationalization of the British steel industry is resulting from the change in ownership and business strategy from private corporations bent on self-preservation and cooperation to a nationalized ownership seeking efficiency. This is a good example of externally imposed political stress.

Firms may view the establishment of branch plants or the acquisition of other firms as interchangeable policies in achieving growth, integration or diversification. For some this may be true. Yet Rees's work on Cincinnati firms and Blackbourn's comparison of the international expansion strategies of American firms into Western Europe show that corporate managements may have very definite policies *either* for acquisition (notably General Motors) *or* for internal corporate growth via new branch plant construction (notably Ford). One may hypothesize that a company will never deviate from that policy unless the stress factors are so great that management feels that the survival or current operations of the firm are threatened if they do not yield. Rees cites a Cincinnati firm which was forced to build a branch plant to serve buoyant markets on the eastern seaboard of the U.S.A. even though its policy was one of acquisition. More empirical evidence may be required to provide insights into why some corporations prefer acquisitions to branch plants. Managements often see acquisition as a faster and less expensive method of achieving their goals because they acquire a 'going concern', even if it has marginal profitability, with operating facilities, know-how and experience, a labour force and infrastructure—all of which must be provided, often from scratch, for a new branch plant. Moreover, the performance of a branch plant on a virgin site is shrouded in greater uncertainty. Against this must be set the possibility that opportunities for acquisition do not always match in time or in quality a corporation's need. Yet it is hard to believe, with the rapid growth of corporate size in recent years and the concomitant high rates of takeovers or deaths of firms, that at least *satisfactory* acquisition offers do not exist when required.

It would appear necessary to look more closely into business strategy and ownership to discover why corporations may take hard lines for branch plants and against acquisitions. One may hypothesize that a neglected explanation is the ownership: management relationship in a given firm. Evidence amassed by Burch (1972) heavily underlines that huge as the top 108 American industrial corporations (and the 500 top American business firms) are, *family ownership* is still significant and even dominant in terms of shareholding and executive decision-making power in 42 per cent of those industrial giants. One may thus hypothesize (and the contrasting Ford and General Motors strategies confirm the hypothesis) that it is strong family influence in a corporation which will tip the balance in favour of branch plant construction because this strengthens and does not weaken that family influence. By contrast, corporations in which such family control is absent are generally managed by professional management who seek maximum profitability for the shareholders and hence prefer acquisitions. In the case of General Motors this policy is further underscored by the corporation's 'strength through internal competition' philosophy. Given that acquisition and branch plants are largely interchangeable instruments of policy, there is no reason to believe that within the same industry emergent spatial patterns of corporations adopting each strategy would greatly differ: again Ford and G.M. are examples.

Having briefly argued why and how firms grow it is important to ask if we can generalize about the spatial form of their growth patterns. In his thought-provoking paper on the hypothetical corporation, McNee (Chapter 2) describes the corporation's spatial sphere of activities as its 'task environment'. This term is preferred to 'action space'—a term used by Dicken specifically in an industrial context, but one which has gained fairly wide acceptance among geographers who are interested in human behaviour. There is clearly a need there for standardization in the use of terminology, especially in the burgeoning field of behavioural geography with its rapid evolution along a wide front. If, however, we leave aside definitions and broadly accept that 'task environment' has many structural and spatial elements in common with 'action space', there emerges a clear link between the shape and form of the corporation's 'task environment' and Pred's observations on information flows within the context of interdependent city systems. As with the diffusion of innovations, the circulation of information may induce a fairly predictable path of corporate spatial growth which reflects the perception of, and processing of, information selected by the corporation from the environment. A processing firm may clearly pursue backward integration with resource inputs: this would result in expansion of the firm from a higher-order to a lower-order centre or perhaps from a lower to an equally low-order centre. A manufacturing firm seeking forward linkages with existing or with new markets (whether in the same products or in diversified product markets) is likely to expand from whatever rank of centre it is initially located in, to a higher or to the highest ranking and, hence, largest city in a system. Its expansion is then likely to proceed from one major city or metropolitan area to another until its 'task environment' progressively embraces various regional markets, the entire national market and overseas markets. This is supported by Nishioka (Chapter 19) who claims that interregional growth of corporations in Japan is fairly predictable and who hints that market-oriented firms tend to diffuse their new plants chronologically among regions of perceived descending economic rank. At each stage of growth, corporate management may perceive what McNee calls a 'zone of opportunity' beyond the 'task environment' in much the same way: their ideas for expansion within a nation or internationally may be led by their perceived knowledge of major metropolitan areas or, as Blackbourn (Chapter 9) observes, of the 'economic core' areas of nations.

References to the spatial distributions of major American firms by Rees and Blackbourn or of British steel firms by Heal clearly underline the existence of a 'task environment' and, what is more, support McNee's argument that each firm has a 'core region' within which the spatial inter-action between plants, offices and other facilities in terms of information, innovation, materials, components, products, services are the most intense. Central and eastern Michigan and adjacent areas form the 'core regions' of the 'big three' U.S. automobile manufacturers; the North American manu-facturing belt is the 'core region' for IBM, Procter & Gamble and many other industrial corporations; the East Midlands of Britain was the 'core region' of United Steel prior to nationalization.

However, underlying the great interregional (and international) expansion of the corporation, another set of forces is at work. Certain kinds of manufacturing industries tend to be located in certain kinds of locations with respect to the city-system hierarchy (Hamilton, 1967, pp. 389–393). Moreover, Pred (Chapter 4) observes that a corporation innovating a new technology or new product usually does so in its research and development unit which tends to be located either in the firm's initial location or at the firm's major plant and administration (the two *may be* the same place). Mass production of the product or using the new technology, however, is often initiated in a new plant in another, often lower-order, yet highly nodal, centre with good access to semiskilled labour.

Mapping the spatial and structural growth of the corporation depends upon the willingness of individual corporations to provide adequate detail about the timing, location and production profile of their plants. Without it we shall never know if McNee's hypothetical corporation, International Gismo, Inc., *is* the typical large corporation. Nevertheless, information gathered by Rees (Chapter 7) on two major American chemicals corporations (Monsanto, Procter & Gamble) can provide insights into actual corporate growth. Significant periodicity is apparent in the growth of Procter & Gamble as the corporation pursued a diversification policy. From the opening of the firm's first soap factory in Cincinnati in 1886, until 1940, there was a marked effort to expand soap (later detergent) production, with a peak of locational activity around 1930 following the firm's innovation of the first synthetic detergent. Food was a minor interest. Two spatial tendencies emerge in this period: first, material input production (cotton seed and soybean oils) in the southern U.S.A., especially along the Mississippi river system for easy supply within the midwestern states, and generally in small fourth- or lower-order settlements; and second, introduction of soap and detergent manufacture in major market nodes, usually first- or second-order cities *throughout the U.S.A.* It is significant that soap manufacture began as early as 1907 in New York, this plant being only the second to be built outside Cincinnati. It is equally significant that subsequent detergent plants were opened in other major national economic centres, namely, Dallas, St. Louis, Chicago, Baltimore, Los Angeles, Dayton (Ohio), and Quincy (Boston). This pattern was later consolidated by expansions and only in the late 1960s were new detergent plants opened, one in Lima (Ohio) and one in Alexandria (Louisiana), both of them smaller cities.

Following a break in corporate expansion in the 1940s, the firm entered a phase of vigorous diversification, entering the related fields of cellulose-pulp output and paper-products manufacture, and expanding its food production. Characteristically, cellulose-paper activities were established near raw-material sites in small towns in Florida and Michigan, but food factories were set up mainly in larger third- or fourth-order centres (e.g. Omaha). The second phase of diversification is concentrated in the early 1960s with entry into coffee production with the acquisition of a leading coffee firm with factories in major national economic centres (New Orleans, Houston,

Kansas City and San Francisco): significantly that firm was California-based, its spatial 'centre' more western and hence helped to strengthen Procter & Gamble's western interests. This pattern in the first place lends some support to McNee's hypothesis that corporate growth tends to be 'cyclical' with periods of diversification followed by concentration: there is a suggestion in a spatial context that periods of 'diffusion' of branch plants to major centres across the state is followed by reaffirmation of the 'core region' of the 'task environment', in this case by establishing new plants in the Midwest (for example the soap/detergent plants established at Dayton in 1934 and Lima in 1968, and food products at Lexington in 1955—all of them near Cincinnati). Another explanation is offered by Rees himself (Chapter 7) who suggests that it is important to distinguish between short-term growth strategies in firms towards specialization, long-term growth strategies in firms towards specialization and long-term growth strategies for diversification and rationalization. In the second place it does indicate parallels between spatial corporate growth, as expressed through plant location and extension of the 'task environment', and Pred's notions on the information diffusion and circulation that evokes corporate locational responses. That fourteen of Procter & Gamble's eighteen overseas detergents factories are located in the first- or second-order cities of states in Western Europe, Latin America and Canada lends further support to the importance of the influence of spatial biases of information in favour of larger cities or major economic regions on corporate perception of locational opportunities—certainly with increasing distance from home. Perhaps the application of allometry to corporate evaluation as Roberge, Ray and Villeneuve apply it to evolutionary patterns of single-plant Canadian pulp and paper firms will yield even greater insights into the spatial form and process of corporate growth.

In the third part of his chapter McNee raises a series of questions concerning the function, structure and evolution of the locational behaviour of the industrial corporation: many such questions are partly answered in subsequent chapters but much still remains to be learned. Structural questions will be discussed in the following section concerning decision-making. Evolutionary questions have been touched upon already and only one question need detain us briefly here: do the key nodes that evolve in a corporation become the 'growth poles' of the spatial system of the corporation? In some ways, the answers, at least at our present stage of scientific understanding, are suggested by Pred's analysis of non-local multiplier linkages and growth poles. Even though a corporate system may contain spatial groupings of plants and facilities, it is probably most fruitful to investigate multiplier effects within the corporation treated, in McNee's very words, as 'the vehicle for linkage ... with wide areas between the points linked rather than a compact metropolitan area or industrial region' (pp. 61). A corporation may innovate new technology or a new product either in existing plants or in a new plant: whichever strategy is adopted the feedback effects are most likely to affect a particular group of plants. Further diffusion of the multiplier effects may follow a wave-like pattern through the corporation's other plants according to whether they are input suppliers to the production, or purchasers, of the new product.

Functional questions pose problems relating to the interactions of organization and location. Here Krumme and Beyers (Chapter 3) make a major contribution in their re-evaluation and extension of classical location theory to incorporate the normal situations of multiple production, byproduct output and pollution by the modern firm. Preoccupation of industrial geographers with plant *location* rather than plant *size* can be highly misleading when studying the corporation. That information on plant sizes is hard to obtain from private firms, planning authorities or government agencies is one reason why few scholars have attempted, or have been able, to follow Sargent Florence's (1948) pioneering work. If we omit the rare case of the single-product, single-plant firm, the majority of firms comprise a headquarters office, other offices, a number of manufacturing plants, research laboratories, warehouses and service (e.g. transport) establishments of varying sizes and in varying (numbers of) locations which are separated by varying distances—but which are interlinked by varying scales and intensities of flows of people and commodities (materials, components, products, information, money) by varying modes of transport and communication (rail, river, road, sea, air, telephone, mail, telex, closed-circuit TV). Thus the spatial arrangement of particular *scales* of administrative, productive and service units determines the directions, scale and nature of intense linkages in the corporation: unit sizes are clearly major determinants of the spatial structure of the corporation. But there are other determinants: the *nature* of linkage—whether, for instance, linkages between groups of units comprises materials or information.

Most large corporations comprise a 'core' and a 'periphery'. Certain groupings of plants in the 'core' may be directly linked together by material flows, or there may be several sub-systems of plants similarly linked, but they will *all* be interlinked by the corporate information system and by the 'executive network'. The 'core' often embraces a large territory as McNee's observations recognize: Gilmour (Chapter 13) heavily underscores the importance of corporate organization in generating inter-metropolitan linkages (in this case Montreal–Toronto linkages) and in weakening intra-metropolitan agglomerating linkages. The 'periphery', however, is likely to be linked to the 'core' mainly by information and personnel only. Transport distance/time/cost from the core makes it necessary for the corporation to establish a regional sub-system of plants and other facilities which is highly independent in terms of material inputs. The larger the scale and complexity of this sub-system or the greater the friction of transport or social or cultural distance from the 'core', the more the sub-system is likely to be autonomous in management and information as well; but it will certainly provide useful feedbacks to the core via head office. Examples of such sub-systems are the groups of offices, research laboratories, manufacturing plants and marketing facilities of major American or Canadian corporations in Europe. Substantial autonomy not only arises in the materials sphere from excessive cost distance from the 'home country' but also in the management and information spheres because the sub-system operates in varying linguistic, legal, social and economic environments which differ from the 'home' environment of the corporation. Moreover, although levels of centralization and decentralization of management may vary among international corporations, one element is common to all corporations in their locational behaviour in developing such sub-systems overseas: they allocate their linked plants spatially among nations so that the sub-system is never entirely dependent upon any one nation and any one assembly plant must draw components from a plant in another nation (Blackbourn: Chapter 9). Pred's paper suggests answers to McNee's other functional questions concerning the diffusion of ideas and of non-local growth multipliers through the corporation.

It is not so easy at this stage to answer McNee's question as to what degree the absorbing of research functions into large corporations changes their responses to location problems: this field awaits more research. Nevertheless one suspects that research by a corporation is shaped and motivated by some compromise between (1) improving existing or innovating new products in which the corporation has a vested interest, (2) meeting technological or product challenges from competitors, (3) innovating to meet controls imposed by the external environment (e.g. state anti-pollution laws) and (4) general 'futuristic' research. Modern life is largely dominated by the need of corporations to sell the products of their often large and expensive research programmes; they do so by convincing consumers via advertising that they need the product. In other words, advertising is used as a vehicle for creating demand for products of new technologies. Internalization of research permits the corporation to 'individualize' its products— which it must to be competitive via advertising in an oligopolistic market. Short-term improvements in products may expand sales and provide feedback to expand existing plants. The most dramatic impact, however, appears to come from significant technological breakthroughs which can provide the corporation with a means of creating new markets for its products, gaining advantages over competitors and hence significant corporate expansion. Whether there is a dramatic effect in opening new plants or in reaffirming the dominance of existing centres depends upon a number of variables, not least among which is the nature of the industry. A revolution in chemicals production, for example, may require essentially the use of new inputs or new combinations of current inputs but not essentially major new processes: conversion of use of existing plant might thus be more effective than establishment of new plants. But the role of research in the end must be related to its use by decision-makers.

Decision-making

Much of the credit for stimulating geographic study of decision-making must go to Cyert, March and Simon (Cyert and March, 1963; March and Simon, 1958). However, reading the following papers reveals that the contributions of others are not inconsiderable: Aharoni (1966) Alchian (1950), Bennis (1968), Brooke and Remmers (1970), Chamberlain (1968), Chandler (1966), Dill (1958), Eells (1962), Etzioni (1964) and McNee (1960, 1963, 1972). Although business practice in making any kind of locational decision is highly divergent, little would be gained but absurd idiography if we attempted to spell out the practices of even major corporations. It is far more rewarding to expose the essentials of decision-making behaviour by references to dissimilar firms, dissimilar industries and dissimilar environments. Enough evidence is assembled in subsequent papers—from small and large firms, chemical or steel or other industries, and from the different environments of Britain, Canada, Japan, Nigeria, U.S.A., as well as of rural south-eastern Ohio or East Anglia, metropolitan Montreal or Toronto or industrial west-central Scotland—to justify the broad generalizations, concepts and hypotheses set out here.

Few firms either perceive the location problem (whether initial location of new plant or any kind of location decision) to be important enough, or have the financial and staff resources, to conduct in-depth or even any location survey prior to making a decision. Small firms rarely, if ever, do so because for them the choice of a new location is a once-and-for-all decision which is usually not premeditated prior to the impingement of stress conditions on the firm. The problem will be assigned to a person, manager or executive, or group of executives, to solve. Experience will be lacking as to what variables to investigate beyond a narrow set, and pressure of time may prevent an orderly and thorough approach to information collection and processing. However, Japanese experience shows how much can be learned and assessed in a short period if there is enough energy and initiative in a group of men who must decide a new location (Nishioka, Chapter 19). Uncertainty about performance in a new location may be high; decisions may thus be based on a hunch or on imitation of others, but it is likely that the small firm will establish a branch or relocate its plant within a safe 'short' distance of the known and existing 'task environment'. It can be argued that primitive 'rule of thumb' methods of choosing location may not at all inhibit the competitiveness and survival of the firm, *ceteris paribus,* because competitors, at least the smaller firms, will have generally chosen their locations by the same primitive procedures and because post-move satisfaction of managers with the locations chosen clearly maintains or boosts their overall business confidence. The latter point is taken up by Stafford who argues that decision-makers who were 'happiest' with their location choices were those with the lowest levels of awareness of the attributes of their choices (Stafford, p. 184). Those decision-makers who were least happy were those who had more thorough knowledge and had been able to balance the disadvantages against the advantages of the chosen location: 'the more you know, the more you can ask questions about, and the more you need to know'.

At the other end of the business spectrum, a relatively few large multi-plant, multi-product and often international firms have both a need for, and have the resources to allocate to, employment of a permanent staff to research location issues. Perhaps few of these, however, devise the sophisticated methods for location choice described by Blackbourn (pp. 248–251) or Rees (pp. 197–198).

Opinions are somewhat divided as to the frequency of the location decision among firms. In part it is a function of corporate size, complexity, growth rates, innovativeness; but in part it is a question of defining the 'location problem'. For many firms the location of a new plant is relatively rare. By contrast it may be relatively frequent among rapid growth corporations in expanding industries: for instance, Monsanto Chemicals opened 29 new plants between 1958 and 1971, an average of two per annum (Rees, p. 199). North argues from the experience of the U.K. plastics industries that broader locational decisions—relating to changes in existing capacity, in use of premises, in acquisitions or mergers, in alterations in inputs and their sources (even in small firms) and, one can add, changes in inter-plant substitutions of production within a corporation—are surprisingly frequent. On the other hand, the rate of growth and change in the industry is clearly an important variable: decision-makers managing firms in a slow-growth industry may be faced with relatively few such decisions unless major reorganization necessitates a new and far-reaching locational change, as Heal's analysis demonstrates.

The importance of the frequency of the location decision-making by a firm lies in its probable positive correlation with both the amount of personnel resources that the firm is willing to allocate to, and the amount of searching and learning experience and sophistication gained by that personnel in, the solution of location problems. The implications are that the greater the frequency of the decision, the better is their perception of the environment, the greater is their awareness of what information they require about the environment, the better the quality and the greater the quantity of information they obtain, the more thorough will be their spatial search, the greater is the likelihood that they will devise sophisticated decision procedures and criteria and the greater is their certainty of choosing a successful location. The opposite applies for infrequent location decision-making.

This broad generalization needs some modification, however.

Of central importance is the nature of the decision-maker's environment. For the small entrepreneur, who probably knows his firm's potentials and personnel very well, the main concern is to assess correctly those components of the external environment that are relevant to his firm. Larger firms, however, not only internalize segments of the environment (for example, research, transport, marketing), but are large and complex enough to constitute 'internal' corporate environments in their own right. Each intra-firm environment is a 'bundle' comprising varying: organizational structures; corporate policies and goals; role clusters; role networks; managerial, executive or owner-family personalities; corporate performance and employee morale. Given that these are complex and may be scattered among a variety of locations, it may be difficult for decision-makers to perceive and hence to assess adequately the internal environment. This should become apparent from the following generalizations.

A fairly high frequency of location decision-taking by a corporation may reflect any one or a combination of the following stress conditions: (1) corporate instability, which may express either intra-firm maladjustment or maladjustment between the firm and its external environment, or both (see Townroe, Chapter 11), for some analysis of this point; (2) radical internal (e.g. merger) or external (e.g. nationalization) environmental change, which requires far-reaching rationalization or spatial readjustment; (3) a management which is highly sensitive to changing environmental conditions and which attempts to adjust accordingly; (4) a large corporation, which has complex organization and which is operating mainly in a dynamic industry; (5) a corporation which is diversifying into growth industries. These situations, requiring location responses, will activate latent pressures which arise from vested interests within the corporate structure. Under stress, these interests generate various conflict thresholds in the decision-making process. Such conflicts are important and create a major modification of the hypothesis set out above (p. 23): they may inflate the (perceived) difficulties of the internal environment in the decision-maker's mind relative to the external environment; and they may bias the decision-maker's search of the external environment with respect to gathering, processing and ranking pertinent information and alternatives. The potential conflicts latent in a corporation become real conflicts when a choice must be made and they may involve any number of the following interest confrontations:

first, family interests *vs* shareholder interests, which may be transmitted through the structure by divided loyalties among management;

second, executives or interests who favour corporate specialization *vs* those who favour diversification;

third, those who prefer expansion of existing locations *vs* those who are 'location innovators';

fourth, inter-divisional conflicts over the share of corporate expansion or contraction, which may be conflicts between: (a) product divisions over growth/contraction rates; (b) regional divisions about where corporate growth or contraction should occur, which may also be international division conflicts (e.g. U.S. part *vs* the overseas or European part of a large corporation); or (c) between 'occupational' divisions, such as personnel *vs* supply or transport, etc., as to where economies or factor substitutions should be made, and so on;

fifth, within each division there may be conflicts between the interests of individual production or service units and their managers and personnel who may feel that their jobs, prestige or pride are threatened. These views will be communicated to the divisional office: executive management of the division will then interact with head office if the original problem arose from an intended decision by the corporation and not the division.

One can generalize, therefore, that the resolution of one or several sets of hierarchically—or laterally—arranged conflicts in the internal environment may lead the corporation to behave in a specific manner in relation to the external environment and thus to initiate a particular location decision. Conflict resolution may curtail the spatial and information search of the external environment in specific directions and stimulate it in others, so that spatial biases of types of information feedback to the corporation will result. Clearly the nature and frequency of conflict varies greatly from corporation to corporation. Some will have well-balanced divisional structures, but usually one division dominates and this may be the division assigned to solving location issues as they arise.

Almost all firms have organizational structures which have evolved in a fairly *ad hoc* manner: it is apparently rare for them to be restructured on comprehensive planning lines. Thus gaps are likely to exist in organization which may generate significant information gaps within the corporation and also between the corporation and the external environment. These gaps, moreover, will persist for two reasons. First, corporate behaviour responds primarily to stress and, although such stress may encourage responses which eliminate some gaps, no single stress-response syndrome will induce systematic identification, and hence elimination, of *all* gaps. And second, as McNee (Chapter 2) argues, following Talcott Parsons, participants in decision-making in complex corporate organizations may be primarily concerned with preserving that organization and not with attaining goals—which, on efficiency grounds, may require reorganization.

Parallel to the increased internalization of the environment by the corporation, however, there has been an increase in the dynamism, complexity and uncertainty of, and in the linkages within, the environment that still remains external. For these reasons, levels of uncertainty about that environment do not necessarily appear to be reduced, despite vastly greater circulation of information about more phenomena. Rapidity of technological change and marked short-term transformations of the international political and economic environments which have long-term implications are major reasons. Another is the fact that the external environment of corporation X includes competing corporations Y and Z with large internalized environments: to obtain enough information about *them,* the decision-makers must make prediction, bluff and espionage essential tools in their search and learning processes—otherwise they will have high uncertainty about the internal workings of rival corporations. It is often claimed that uncertainty encourages a corporation to imitate others in its location choices by choosing the same 'city type', the same region, even the same city. One may venture to suggest that the choice of the same city by oligopolistic rivals in a business and locational environment as large as the U.S.A.—Battle Creek (breakfast cereals) and Detroit (automobiles) are obvious examples—was a response designed to minimize uncertainty in growing but insecure industries by maximizing opportunities for inter-corporate information acquisition (by whatever means: cooperation, espionage, personnel contacts). Information 'leakage' among corporations enables rivals to imitate each other closely even in products which require lengthy design-to-mass-production translation periods and to define the permissible limits of 'individualism' in products.

The environment is exceedingly complex to describe: some elements of it affect all corporations in some way, such as world business climate or international political relations; other elements may affect only for a few firms, such as the exhaustion of a particular resource in one region. It is in fact many 'strata' of different environmental phenomena, of varying importance, of varying temporal or spatial incidence. It is a mosaic of the interpenetration of four environmental types (Emery and Trist, 1972): the *placid random environment* (appropriate perhaps to small firms in developing nations, or 'natural economies', for example, or to anywhere where 'perfect competition' conditions obtain), the *placid clustered environment* (to which firms can adapt providing they can pursue *goals* and can internalize parts of the environment to increase their action strategies), the *disturbed reactive environment* (a stable, oligopolistic environment in which strategies provoke rival reactions from competitors), and the *turbulent environment* (a dynamic, complex environment akin to our current one).

Limited and biased perception of the environment by decision-makers builds bias into the information sought, i.e. into the search of the environment, and hence into the actual spatial alternatives studied. There is strong conviction that corporate decisions at the macro-level, i.e. choosing a region for plant location or choosing a particular type of spatial strategy as part of the investment process in a given stress-response situation, are judgmental, but once the region or nation is chosen the micro-level decision regarding this particular town or that follows more normative lines. Decision-making sequences are discussed particularly by North, Rees and Stafford (Chapters 6–8). Thus the location of decision-makers in corporate head offices biases their perception of the environment so that their location searches tend to concentrate on areas in the vicinity of head office or spatially coterminous with the 'task environment' that surrounds head office: once a satisfactory area is defined, rigorous cost or other procedures may be used to fix the site. Intimacy of knowledge of the European environment by European firms is reflected in their more varied location of new plants in comparison with American firms which tend to cluster in or near major economic centres throughout Western Europe (see Blackbourn: Chapter 9).

Government is a growing element in the external environment of the corporation in the 'capitalist' or 'free' or 'mixed' economies of the world: it manifests itself through (1) its own internalization of environment (with research, nationalized activities etc.); (2) bureaucratic organization on a larger scale and in greater complexity than most corporations; (3) its own broad social, economic or overseas policies, its laws and its applied ideologies; (4) its own investment activity. The importance of interaction between private firms and these four aspects of the governmental environment is clearly brought out by Turner (Chapter 15), Lever (Chapter 12), Nishioka (Chapter 19) and Onyemelukwe (Chapter 18). Unfortunately, many governments of the western world still consider their major effects to be through (3) above: they often fail to grasp the tremendous modifications they introduce into the decision-making environment of the corporate industrial sector via (1), (2) and (4) above. Those modifications may stimulate positive responses from corporations—as, for example, American or other firms which locate in grant-aided development areas in Western Europe, Japanese firms which locate near new port areas or Nigerian firms locating on or near new industrial estates or roads. This often encourages agglomeration around specified nodes or along major transport arteries in a manner contrary to other 'planning' instruments for industrial dispersal. Other firms seek locations near centres of government research and information sources. Other aspects of the governmental environment may be perceived negatively, stimulating evasive action: Turner (Chapter 15) found that some British firms would rather congest the use of their current sites or make small expansions periodically rather than face the prospect of applying for an Industrial Development Certificate (I.D.C.) for one larger expansion.

Spatial Adaptation by Firms to Environments

There are basically three sets of reasons why, once located, a plant or firm must adapt to its locational environment. First, imperfections in environmental perception or spatial judgment prior to the location choice will often leave a plant, during its opening period of operation, 'maladjusted' to its real environment: in essence this is a short-term problem which may be solved in the short-term. Second, the external environment is dynamic enough to demand that even well-located plants must pursue gradual or periodic adjustment to changing conditions: this is a long-term on-going problem requiring more formalized structures and procedures. And third, the need to adapt may come from the plant itself through its own innovativeness (new products, processes etc.): this may be an intermittent, but a long-term need. As with locational issues discussed above, the stimulus to adaptation comes from some kind of stress which usually, though not necessarily, expresses itself in unused or excess capacity at the plant. This whole field has been neglected, yet it is a vital one since it is concerned with the spatial and non-spatial components of dynamic interrelationships between corporation and environment to maintain or to improve corporate viability.

Townroe (Chapter 11) analyses post-move conditions among a sample of transfer moves (relocations) and branch plants in East Anglia and Northern England. He distinguishes five processes of adaptation which are aimed at improving plant performance in a new or existing location. These processes involve changes in (1) the products manufactured, (2) the processes used, (3) linkages with input suppliers, services and consumers, (4) management, or (5) organizational structure. One might conceive of situations in which all occurred as a set of interrelated changes, although it is more common to find a clear set of interrelationships between changes in product, process and linkage and another set of interrelationships between management and organizations. However, it is conceivable that firms can adjust also by making one change at a time. Product changes appear not to be necessarily associated with poor adaptation to new locations, except insofar as labour quality was a critical factor; rather they reflected the nature of an industry and its growth characteristics. Changes in processes, however, appear to be more strongly associated with firms which are forced to relocate because of acute stress in their original location. Management problems were more often apparent in branch plants than in relocated plants. This should not be surprising since relocating firms attempt and often do take with them key personnel, especially in short-distance moves: a well-tried management 'team' has a better chance of success than a newly recruited group of individuals. Branch plants' success, however, was found to be significantly dependent upon the former experience and corporate 'involvement' of the first manager: his age was important and established managers from the firm faced fewer problems in the branch plant than newly recruited managers. Organizational changes mainly involved mergers and these, on balance, were more common among firms which had labour or technology problems and among those plants which achieved profitability quickly (in three months or under) and very slowly (in four years and over); time differences clearly explain different motives for merging.

Like the earlier discussion concerning the frequency of the location decision, Townroe's contribution is important for discussing the surprising frequency with which management makes changes of some kind in a plant in the short period—admittedly the critical 'teething' period—after its establishment in a new locational environment. Undoubtedly the chapter's major interest, however, lies in its emphasis upon managers and upon the performance of different kind of managers in different locational situations. Chapter 11's focus in Part III somewhat parallels the role of Stafford's chapter (6) in Part II. Indeed both authors are concerned with managers of recently moved plants, except that Stafford is concerned with a psychological analysis of their behaviour in choosing to locate capacity. Townroe is concerned with their behaviour in trying to 'make a go' of the location chosen. References to the behaviour of 'real people' are made also by Blackbourn, Heal, Nishioka and Rees in their chapters: the manager or director characteristics which they reveal are often very valuable in solving the real practical problems associated with adapting a firm to its new or changing environment.

Against the broad background of Townroe's chapter, the rest of Part III concentrates on the ways in which firms select and adjust their spatial linkages. Lever's chapter is concerned with both backward and forward linkages of new plants established in west-central Scotland. Gilmour (Chapter 13) stresses the difficulties involved in explaining agglomeration economies, or external economies of scale, through input linkages; his conclusions are drawn from studying sample manufacturing groups and firms in the Montreal metropolitan region. Britton (Chapter 14) underlines the importance of service-linkage patterns of manufacturing; his evidence is provided by sample firms in southern Ontario. Although the authors studied adaptation by firms in the contrasting environments of expanding Canadian metropolitan regions and of the long-industrialized and structurally retarded areas of northern Britain, significant similarities emerge in the linkage behaviour of firms located in those regions.

One conclusion which is common to all three chapters (12–14), and one which underpins the basic theme of this book, is that there are significant differences in input-linkage behaviour of *any* kind—whether of materials, of components or of higher-order services—as between branch plants of larger companies and single-plant firms. Invariably branch plant backward linkages were dominated by the corporate organization and inputs were obtained *usually* from non-local, even quite distant, parent company sources. Single-plant behaviour varied but showed somewhat greater short-distance backward linkage. With respect to material inputs, however, a divergence of opinion between Gilmour and Lever raises questions about the nature of the overall British and Canadian environments. Lever argues that branch plants located in west-central Scotland often 'inherit' linkages from the parent company but that if the branch plant is located beyond a critical transport distance from the 'inherited input supplier' then the branch plant management has generally to find nearer, alternative and less expensive sources. Gilmour observes, however, that particular production profiles of firms often require such specific inputs that they have little or no choice of input suppliers of those inputs: a given input may be available in Canada from only one producer so that, irrespective of location, a firm in Canada must buy from that one supplier. In essence there may be no conflict at all between these two views: the differences of opinion may merely reflect the differences in the industries and firms sampled. However, it could be that the spatial compactness of Britain and the spatial arrangement of her industries offers a high probability of a west-central Scottish firm being able to find an input supplier, even of a very special component, within a *relatively* short distance, whereas extensive elongation of the Canadian ecumene and the low 'density' of industry, even in Ontario and Quebec, yield low probabilities of a Montreal firm being able to find a similar supplier of a specific input within a short distance. After all, virtually the entire industry of Britain lies between London and west-central Scotland: only the Toronto–Hamilton industrial zone lies within the same distance of Montreal. Nevertheless, it would seem, from both Lever's observations of interregional links and Gilmour's interpretation of intra-metropolitan linkage behaviour contrasts, that the importance of transport and of transport costs is often *under*-estimated in studies of location or spatial adaptation.

Lever observes that firms located in west-central Scotland generally received an abnormally low proportion of inputs from suppliers within Scotland: their forward linkages with Scottish market requirements were better. This demonstrates a distinct failure for input suppliers to locate plants in west-central Scotland, i.e. to move with demand. This observation supports Townroe (Chapter 11) and Turner (Chapter 15) who argue strongly that government feels its task is complete once it has induced a firm to locate in a development area like west-central Scotland: government proceeds to let firms 'sink or swim' by not providing any follow-up assistance. That such assistance—such as inducing a firm Y which is an input supplier to firm X, a firm recently established in development area α, to locate near the new plant of firm X in area α—is never forthcoming: its absence may often cause high inefficiency of use of invested capital by firm X. The problem demonstrates clearly that Industrial Development Certificate (I. D. C.) policy is a control tool, but in no sense can it be construed as a positive, forward-looking 'planning' tool. In fact, government assistance is often *more* necessary to the relocated firm or branch plant (which was forced into a development area by government I.D.C. control initially anyway) to see it through its priod of adaptation to new environment, since this may make the difference between survival and eventual success on the one hand and unprofitability and, hence, wasted resources on the other.

Both Gilmour and Lever refer to the procedures used by corporate executives in searching the environment for input suppliers. Gilmour, who is more concerned with the selection of current input suppliers to sample firms, underlines the varying effort put by entrepreneurs into their searches and how circumscribed those searches often were. Lever is more interested in linkage *changes* and hence in the spatial search for new supply sources. His index of plant linkage change provides evidence that new plants change linkages far more often than established plants and thus that they 'take a considerable amount of time to settle down and identify a core of regular suppliers and customers after they are 'set up' (p. 328). It is perhaps significant that Lever also found indigenous, Scottish firms, more reluctant to seek new markets than were branch plants. One may suggest two possibly related explanations for this phenomenon. First, Scottish firms have operated for many years in a regional environment of severe structural maladjustment which has been expressed in above-average unemployment rates: this has conditioned their managements to be cautious or unduly pessimistic and to perceive large fields of uncertainty. This may be interrelated with the second factor, that single-plant Scottish firms have spatially narrower 'task environments' and hence less experience of either business or locational environments elsewhere. By contrast, multi-plant companies, many of which operate in, and are familiar with environments in other regions of Britain are more certain of being able to sell to new customers. Such a suggestion is not at all at odds with Lever's contention that firms look not only for new suppliers and customers in their existing areas but also in new market areas *simultaneously*.

Gilmour attacks a number of established views on industrial location. For instance, he demonstrates how the assumption that sources of the same inputs to a plant located within the same metropolis are cheaper than those which are located outside the metropolis is a product of typically Weberian thinking: in reality, differences in corporate pricing, input quality and other imperfections may well mean that longer-distance inputs are cheaper than identical ones available in the city. Moreover, scale differences may be important: intra-metropolitan suppliers may not be able to meet a firm's demand for a particular input, so that identical inputs may be procured both from within and from outside the metropolis. Plenty of evidence is also given to show how the spatial information and perception biases of entrepreneurs affect their choices of input suppliers—whether or not alternative sources exist within the metropolis. From this research Gilmour is able not only to criticize the use of standard industrial classifications in location research of any kind or the results of aggregate industry studies on spatial association or on agglomeration studies, but also to lend strong support for the observations of Pred on spatial linkages. In addition, however, he provides new insights into the differing spatial relationships and linkage patterns of manufacturing plants located in different zones of a metropolitan region, namely, the city centre, the suburbs and the periphery.

This latter theme is extended into a 'regional' context by Britton's study of the distance relationships and organizational patterns of service-linkage behaviour (Chapter 14). Some conclusions lend further support to the findings of others. The variation in behaviour between single-plant firms and branch plants emerges again in selecting sources of service inputs, the latter on balance preferring longer-distance and non-metropolitan Toronto linkages. A stronger metropolitan effect is evident for single-plant firms and this underlines Gilmour's suggestion that it is the small but cumulative advantages in the service sector in which agglomeration economies become evident. A further critical and related observation, which Britton makes, is that organizational differences appear among firms according to their distance from metropolitan service sources, especially for 'higher order' services such as auditing, certain banking services and legal services. Single-plant firms internalize more of such services with increasing distance from the metropolis. His analysis of branch-plant behaviour, however, shows a parallel trend, with the important difference that it is the parent multi-plant corporation which internalizes more services for the branch plant with increasing distance of that plant from a metropolis: thus non-metropolitan southern Ontario branch plants may derive services from head or major regional corporation offices located far away. In selecting service input sources corporate behaviour therefore, expresses 'a spatial form of organizational substitution for metropolitan access' (Britton, 1969). Management behaviour of any kind of firm varies, therefore, in response to different industrial and spatial environments, but multi-locational firms can substitute internal vs external economies of scale in the provision of higher-order service functions. Here we find evidence from service linkage patterns which in principle supports Luttrell's observations on distance as an important variable in branch-plant–parent-plant functional relationships (Luttrell, 1962).

Comparative Spatial Behaviour: Different Organizations and Contrasting Environments

From these observations on adaptive behaviour and from earlier comments on corporate organization and decision-making, it is clear that fundamental differences exist in the spatial behaviour and responses of decision-makers between the single-plant firm and the multi-plant multi-functional corporation: it confirms an observation that this author made for the second Madingley Lectures in 1965 and subsequently incorporated in *Models in Geography* (1967, pp. 365–66). However, although the division between 'single-plant' and 'multi-plant' firms may appear to be a clear one, and is obviously a very critical one in terms of the spatial dimensions of organization and decision-making, further research is necessary to establish the significance or otherwise of tremendous variations in the 'multi-plant' corporate sector. Rather than as an aggregate 'block', it might be more meaningful to consider these firms, which dominate the western world's business economies, as being arranged up a *scale* of increasing size and complexity and broadening functions from the 'two-plant' firm to the '*n*-plant' firm. And are there significant breaks within that scale, which may justify further divisions, into, say, dominantly-national and significantly-international corporations? This is clearly a problem for future research. In any case, enough has been written in this book to make it unnecessary here to labour the point concerning the comparative behaviour of firms of different size and organization.

However, from comparing the locational behaviour of firms in Japan, Nigeria and in the western world, certain significant cultural differences do emerge to differentiate behaviour. The importance of social status or acceptance and of entrepreneurial relationships within the web of community relationships, appears to be a stronger element of cultural environment in both Japan and Nigeria than in the west. Once again, however, we must beware: in European nations with strong national, cultural, religious and other divisions, one may well find significant spatial behavioural biases among industrialists which are clearly influenced by those divisions—as in Belgium, Ireland or Yugoslavia. The individualism of Japanese industrial organization is clearly influenced by cultural tradition; but until very recently very little comparative cross-cultural research had been undertaken to assess the impact of culture on business behaviour. A major source for further study of this problem is undoubtedly Dore's comparative study of British and Japanese firms (Dore, 1973). From a detailed point by point comparison of two factories making similar products in both countries, Dore concludes that the British and western 'market-oriented' employment systems were created by the peculiarities of nineteenth-century capitalism. By contrast, Japan has an 'organization-oriented' system which is neither simply an expression of her unique culture nor a remnant of the pre-industrial era. As a result, late development in Japan has enabled Japanese entrepreneurs to avoid nineteenth-century institutional straightjackets and to adopt more flexible and novel patterns of organization which are more readily adapted to the rapidly evolving requirements of modern industrial society. Dore argues that much the same is true of other non-western cultures in Asia, Africa and Latin America: time and research will tell how far his thesis assists in understanding the cross-cultural dimensions of spatial industrial behaviour.

However, a comparison of British and Japanese industrial environments does point to the greater importance of land and land values than is normally admitted in industrial location analysis. This point is stressed both by Nishioka (Chapter 10) and Turner (Chapter 15).

Attention must be focused finally upon the comparison of spatial behaviour with contrasting economic and social systems. To avoid repetition, most emphasis here will be given to the centrally-planned socialist economies:

views on spatial behaviour in these economies are spelled out in more detail elsewhere (Hamilton, 1963, 1967, 1968, 1970, 1971a, 1971b, 1973) but they must be given a more comparative slant in summary here.

The socialist firm is generally the 'enterprise' or 'plant', but as Barr (Chapter 16) observes, economic reforms and management reorganization in the U.S.S.R. (and indeed before them in East-Central Europe), are creating new forms of industrial firms and industrial associations which are not unlike western corporations in both their multi-plant and integrated character. Generally, until the 1960s, all location decisions initiating new plants and enterprises were taken by the planning authorities, although powerful individuals who were prospective managers of planned plants might have been able to influence location choices for their plants. Otherwise, enterprise management could exert an influence only on adapting the spatial relationships of the plant, once it was operating, to its environment. Prior to the economic reforms, therefore, the socialist enterprise resembled a 'single-plant firm' shorn of most of its decision-making powers—except for daily routine matters. The thus enlarged external environment of the enterprise, on the other hand, was overwhelmingly, though not completely, dominated by the bureaucratic, administrative and decision-making organization of 'the state' which owned most production factors. State ownership of the 'means of production' has combined with a high degree of planning control over non-routine decisions at all levels to create an organizational structure which virtually is 'the environment' itself. That organization shapes decision-making procedures, planning administration, economic laws and policies, social laws and policies, ideological conditions and spatial policies and, hence, 'internalizes' the interactions of decision-makers with each other and with the economic, social, political and locational 'sub-environments'. Above the organization, but interacting with it and shaping it, is the Communist Party. Frequently the western observer believes this bureaucracy to be excessive in size and complexity: yet the equivalent in his own society is the sum of the entire routine and non-routine decision-making and administrative units of all private and corporate firms as well as of public utilities, nationalized industries, and local, provincial and national governments. As Heal (Chapter 10) shows, nationalization and—as McNee claims in the corporation—centralization, are similar reorganizational processes which, in the long run, rationalize administration. In an organizational sense, corporate firms represent functionally decentralized forms vis-à-vis centralized planning administration in socialist economies; but while they perform some of the decision-making functions, which are centralized in socialist states, competing firms duplicate others. It would appear difficult in the contemporary world, therefore, to say whether one system was more 'bureaucratic' than another.

As an organization—leaving aside motivations and ideological definitions—the multi-plant, multi-locational and multi-functional corporation of the capitalist world has no equivalent in the centrally-planned economy. In the U.S.S.R., China and much of East-Central Europe, the ministry of an industry is a multi-plant, multi-locational organization, but its functions may be narrow and 'integration' in the main administratively horizontal: vertical integration is usually limited. The ministry can, and does, work out, choose and plan the rationalization of existing plant activities, changes in linkages or flows, the construction of new plants or the expansion of existing capacities like a corporation; yet the ministry is subordinate to the supreme council of ministers and must interact with the central planning organization and other ministries in order to modify and to fit its plans into the plans of the whole state before the ministry's plans are approved for central financing. In other words, the ministry does not have the independence of action which a capitalist corporation has. Moreover, because of the hierarchical organization which typifies central planning, inter-ministerial lines may be hard, certainly sharper administratively than inter-divisional lines in corporations and this inhibits both easy inter-ministerial cooperation and the shaping of 'inter-ministerial' industrial backward and forward linkages in a planned economy. By contrast the evolution of 'economic associations', following the economic reforms in East-Central Europe and the U.S.S.R., has created a form of organization which resembles more closely the multi-plant, multi-functional corporation. The economic association is a decision-making and administrative organization which often comprises vertically-integrated activities, examples of which are discussed by Barr (Chapter 16). By integrating several enterprises into one organization, such associations have been able to rationalize production, reallocate resources among plants and forge new linkage patterns. However, as is clear from Barr's research, economic associations are very varied in size, spatial form and functional structure, but like some corporations, they tend to have regional 'task environments'. If the economic association becomes an accepted organizational form in the Soviet Union, there is a possibility that economic associations might become identifiable with, and hence managements of, 'production-territorial complexes' in the newer regions. Production-territorial complexes have no administrative or decision-making significance, but they, and the economic associations, are, like the corporation, vehicles 'for linkage ... with wide areas between the points linked [which] should not blind us to the functional realities involved' (McNee, p. 61).

According to Soviet experience, it is also the economic association that resembles in the planned economy the behaviour of the corporation in the capitalist system in terms of spatial growth and evolution. For the present, the spatial extent of the task environment of the economic association, even in the U.S.S.R., is much more circumscribed than that of larger capitalist corporations. Unlike the latter they do not generally straddle international frontiers, but closer economic integration of the COMECON countries is bringing the 'international economic associations' nearer. Some striking similarities are to be observed in the growth and integration forms and processes between J. J. Gismo Corporation, Inc. (McNee) and the Ukraine Republic Everyday Chemical Goods Association (Barr). The latter since 1965 has not only functionally integrated and linked interrelated plants but also financed 'missing links' in the linkage chain and attempted to 'take over' critical plants still under ministerial control. Soviet economic associations are thus internalizing environment through 'mergers' of existing plants and building new plants. Their stimulus for doing so comes from stress of a kind not uncommon in the capitalist world, namely, the need to obviate serious unreliabilities and uncertainties in input supply. To work properly, however, the system requires conversion of plants from heterogeneous to specialized production as well as a more certain legalistic, political and economic environment.

Since an industry is administered by a ministry, one can assume that that ministry has at least some decision-making power (either directly in its plans and indirectly in convincing the central planning commission to accept its plans) over the shaping of the emerging spatial pattern of the industry. Given that assumption, ministerial planning yields a spatial pattern different from that which would evolve to serve the same market in an oligopolistic environment. First, state ministerial control will usually result in building fewer, larger-scale plants to serve the national market because corporate duplication of capacities is eliminated: this is borne out by Heal whose study suggests that centralized control in *any* economic and social system will yield fewer, bigger units of production. Not surprisingly, therefore, the socialist enterprise averages larger size than its capitalist counterpart. Second, the ministry plans for *national* or *all-Union space* (in the U.S.S.R.) and hence it will arrange its fewer larger plants somewhat differently in space within the state territory: ministerial perception of space thus differs significantly from that by management of a corporation which is spatially biased in its search behaviour by the original or headquarters location by a need to imitate or counteract rivals' spatial behaviour. Of course, other influences from the environment of the socialist economy— the socialist location principles and their application, or international division of labour and mutual aid through COMECON—may generate further contrasts with corporate location patterns.

Reference to socialist location principles and to search behaviour leads into the whole question of comparative decision-making behaviour in the capitalist and communist systems. Traditionally, the planned economy eliminated the 'market' through which the capitalist corporation competed for sales revenue and, on its economic performance, also for capital resources from investors through the stock market. This was replaced in socialist states by administrative control and by a hierarchical information flow, planning and decision-making system in which, in effect, participants bargain for investment resources and hence growth. Those participants are from the lowest level up: (1) industrial plants or local administrative areas (*rayons*, communes, etc.) which are seeking industrial plants for their territories; (2) small- or medium-sized towns and small minority peoples, for instance those living in the U.S.S.R. in the Autonomous Soviet Socialist Republics; (3) Republics (the S.S.R.s in the Soviet Union, the six republics in Yugoslavia, or Slovakia in Czechoslovakia for example) and their ministries and larger regions with their leading cities; (4) the national or all-Union ministries, specialist industrial agencies etc.; (5) the central planning commission, and (6) the supreme of decision-making organs of the state. Over time the balance has shifted in the distribution of decision-making power. Marked centralization endowed the state organizations ((4), (5), and (6) above) with significant independent discretion, but conflict of interests occurred especially among the participants of level (4). Decentralization processes have, along with the growth of many industrial plants, strengthened the interests of the lower echelons: since industry is, or has been, considered to be the means of economic development, representatives of those enterprises, local and regional interests, put pressure on the ministries and central planning authorities for new development. Conflict interdependence is thus dominant in decision-making relations and it is the central authorities' task to compromise in its location choices between local, city, enterprise, republic and ministerial interests and the national interest.

Decentralization and the growing complexity of the socialist economies has had an important impact upon information flows and supply. The more centralized the planning decisions were, as they were in the U.S.S.R. especially prior to 1953, the more the onus for searching the environment for information on resources or locations or other data fell on the central planning agency and ministries: their search would by clearly heavily influenced by their own perceptions of the problem and of the state territory. Their interpretation of information would be influenced by their abilities and by the guidelines established for location with the approval of the Communist Party. On the other hand, decentralization endows the many productive points and organizations concerned with spatial management with the ability to collect their own information and to sent it to the central authorities: the 'democratization' of information provides the central authorities with a far better idea of the locational environments of a larger part of the state territory.

Unlike either capitalist corporations or governments in most non-socialist states, the central planning authorities adopt a location policy from the outset as an integral part of their economic strategy. This is embodied in the socialist location principles discussed by Barr (Chapter 16) and elsewhere by Hamilton (1963, 1970, 1971a, and 1971b) and Koropeckyj (1967). In selecting locations for productive capacity—including expansions, conversions, closures, spatial substitution of production—the planning authorities must make a series of compromises between (1) the practical needs of the state, (2) the practical possibilities for the regions and sub-regions to satisfy those needs, (3) the demands of the Communist Party and of the socialist principles to satisfy socialist ends, particularly the above-average rate of development of underprivileged and minority-populated regions, (4) the conflicts between decision-makers over location strategies or indeed over *economic* policies which affect industrial structure and hence affect the choice of types of locations (e.g. a particular or city environment resource) or types of regions (particular regions), (5) the effects of responses by participants in planning (ministers or local officials) to particular forces at work in the environment: examples are (1) the discriminatory sector pricing policies that cause variation in economic attractiveness of particular industries, an attractiveness which is not necessarily in accord with given policy aims or plan targets, or (2) differential interregional pricing policies that endow unequal rentabilities (Hamilton, 1963, 1968) upon plants producing identical goods in different regions.

Though research is still required in this field it may be conjectured that compromise decisions are effected through the interaction of decision-makers. These interaction patterns mainly comprise normalized planning contact patterns up and down the planning and administrative hierarchy, but significant informal contact patterns are undoubtedly present outside the hierarchy. These 'deviant' contact patterns, representing interaction between particular vested interests and the final decision-makers in the central planning office, are most readily developed within the capital city where representative government and centralized functions are present. There is here clearly a need for research into what McNee terms 'role networks' or 'role clusters' within this system. Moreover, it is yet to be established how far distance decay factors influence the impact of interests which are not located in or near the capital city can have upon decision-makers located in the capital. Whatever influences are at work they do bias ultimately planners' search behaviour and choice. Till now locational strategies in planned economies have tended, therefore, to demonstrate the ascendancy of (1) industrial over agricultural interests, resulting in relative neglect of the location potentials (even for food-processing and farm-serving industries) of the dominantly rural and agricultural-resources regions; (2) supporters of heavy industry over supporters of light industry, leading to the prominence in search behaviour of mineral and energy-source locations and to lowered levels of planners' perception of labour resource locations; (3) the 'producers' over the 'servers', causing a vicious circle of lagging infrastructure provision which, in turn, encourages interests (e.g. ministers) to argue for further concentration of capacity in existing plants or industrial cities; (4) representatives of sector planning—ministers, national interest groups—over groups, chiefly local or regional authorities charged with physical planning, who support regional planning; this has stimulated further growth in developed areas and major cities to the detriment of growth elsewhere since regional needs have been subordinated to national needs; (5) major industrial plant managements over city or local governments, with resultant insufficiency of development of infrastructure which might encourage other industry, competition for use of that infrastructure or labour, into the city or area—a problem which explains why, despite pleas for balanced male/female employment provision, many towns are 'one industry' towns; (6) 'Muscovites' over 'national communists' at the international COMECON level, or of European Russian over Asiatic Soviet interests, leading to spatial biases in industrial growth patterns; (7) Communist Party or ideological leaders over economists, liberals and ecclesiastics, resulting in spatial dispersion of industry to proletarianize traditional society; (8) users of easily obtained short-term factual economic cost-profit data over users of projected social cost-benefit long-term data.

These relationships, however, are by no means either static or irreversible. A central decision, precipitated by some bottleneck or stress in the links of the industrial economy or by the results of research by the planning office or by the Academy of Sciences, can endow a neglected aspect of the environment with renewed attractiveness and give it priority among the environmental influences on search behaviour. A good example is the stress laid in the current ninth Soviet Five-Year Plan (1970–74) on locating new plant capacities of many kinds in small- or medium-sized towns and agricultural regions. Although some attention had been paid to the application of socialist principles for dispersing industry and for eliminating 'urban–rural' differences, generally such places and areas had been neglected as possible locations for industries by comparison with the mineral-resources regions and larger urban nodes. Acute shortages of male and female labour had developed in the 1960s at most existing industrial sites throughout European Russia, Siberia and the Far East. Since strong cultural distance frictions inhibit migration to those nodes by peoples from the regions of rapid population growth in Central Asia and Transcaucasia, and since all regions eastward of the Urals are short of labour, Gosplan had only one alternative: to find areas within European Russia with labour 'surplus'. Research undertaken by the newly-formed SOPS unit (Council for the Organization of Productive Forces) within Gosplan produced evidence in the latter half of the 1960s to show the extent of underemployment among rural populations in general and among the urban female population in particular. It was on the strength of this evidence that industrial strategy was shifted in favour of industrializing small- and medium-sized towns and rural regions under the ninth Five-Year Plan. Such a shift was clearly the result of a shifting balance between interests in the decision-making structure. It reflects the substantially increased influence of regional or spatial planning expertise *vis-à-vis* sector planning within Gosplan on locational behaviour which, as a result of the information collected, also strengthened the potential influence on central government of rural-regional, small town and small minority population interests.

Space prevents further treatment here of the problem, but it is necessary to compare briefly Soviet-type with 'western-type' planning behaviour as exemplified by the British system (Turner, pp. 393–410). First, Soviet planning is 'positive' in the sense that it is shaping new spatial industrial patterns deliberately, with a purpose, to satisfy defined national needs of world preeminence and maximum development of all Soviet regions. By contrast, British I.D.C. policy is a 'push–pull' control tool which is designed to steer industry to areas of above-average unemployment but which, in the process, may indiscriminately hamper growth in other regions and thus in the nation as a whole. Second, Soviet planning is concerned with all sectors of the economy, including city planning, and with the entire state. Its perception is distinctly *national* or *all-Union,* seeing the state as one unit of space and as being subdivided into interacting regional components. Two-way information flows between the thousands of industrial enterprises, cities and local government units at the bottom of the spatial hierarchy and research institutes and the central planning office at the top provides information which helps to reduce, though by no means eliminate, spatial biases in perception of environment from the capital city. Britain, however, has had partial regional policies for forty years but it appears that there is no British view of British space among either the political parties or the responsible government department, the Department of Environment (or formerly by the Board of Trade). What is more, there has been little devolution of responsibility or power to either the 'economic planning regions' or other regional units.

Local government thus remains primarily concerned with social services. Economic power is diffused among private firms or corporations, each of which has its own task environment but none of which can identify with British national interests, or among nationalized industries (coal, electricity, gas, steel) or ministries like transport and civil aviation which have their own task environments and operate more like independent corporations than as participants in even a coordinated policy. Thus intra-governmental lines are sharp and ministerial 'sector views' of the British economy are not subject to coordination by a higher body as powerful as Gosplan in the U.S.S.R. The result is that British 'planning' decisions are strongly, but vertically, centralized and central vested interests are strong: there are few mechanisms for shaping, correcting or influencing those decisions outside the central authorities. An exception is the growth of national minority interests: pressure from Scottish and Welsh, interests has succeeded in steering key industries such as steel or aluminium to their national areas. Yet many decisions taken in London—which are not necessarily directly industrial but which strongly influence both the environment in which private industry works and the logic and success of the government's own regional policies—appear to be administrative, show a high degree of independent discretion and differ little in quality or spirit from Soviet planning decisions of the 1930s. The most recent example is the Third London Airport decision. Such decisions reflect the lack of a coordinated national policy or plan and a failure to view the nation in terms of national space, its regions as an interacting and interrelated unit of national space. Concern for separate, often unrelated or conflicting policies or projects reflects the failure to view the national *economy* as a complex of interacting sectors. Planners in Britain, therefore, often do not ask themselves the right questions or do not ask questions in the right ways: governments can hardly be expected to do so either. Having asked the wrong question or a question in the wrong way, however, the information feedback reflects the spatial or other bias of the question and may be put into practice—so distorting the environment with which both government and business interact.

Third, conflicts of interest undoubtedly do occur between central and regional or local interests in both the U.S.S.R. and Britain, as they do in any nation; however, evidence from Barr and Turner would appear to indicate that local government in Britain has more independence of action in attracting industry than do Soviet local authorities.

One may ask if locational behaviour by industrial organizations and decision-makers in any other kind of socio-economic system is significantly different from that in a Soviet-type or 'mixed western' society. To examine this problem, a brief analysis of the Yugoslav case is presented in Part V (Chapter 17).

The conclusions from this are clear. Broadly speaking, the scale and organizational characteristics of industrial decision-making bodies are powerful forces shaping the interaction among participants in the decision process and the responses of those participants in their environment search and decision behaviour. Irrespective of nation or ideology, broadly similar location decision-making behaviour is apparent as a result of similar processes and particularly vertical organizational structures as between the capitalist corporation, the independent or nationalized corporation (e.g. TVA, British Steel), a government ministry in a mixed economy and ministries or other agencies in a centrally planned economy. Differences in locational behaviour would appear to be primarily the product of responses by those similar organizational structures to differences in the external political, economic and social environments. Nevertheless it is equally significant that the same kinds of behaviour can emerge as a result of different organizational decision-making structures, as for example, among the more horizontal Yugoslav self-management structures or more vertically-organized western firm. That this is so stresses the importance of the technical and economic environment of industry in general.

42

References

Aharoni, Y., 1966, *The Foreign Investment Decision Process* (Boston: Harvard Business School).

Alchian, Armen A., 1950, 'Uncertainty, evolution and economic theory', *Journal of Political Economy*, **58**, 211–221.

Argyris, C., 1967, *Integrating the Individual and the Organization* (New York: Wiley).

Bennis, W. G., 1968, *Changing Organizations* (New York: McGraw–Hill).

Britton, J. N. H., 1969, 'A geographical approach to the examination of industrial linkages', *Canadian Geographer*, **13**, 185–198.

Brooke, Michael Z. and H. Lee Remmers, 1970, *The Strategy of the Multinational Enterprise* (New York: Elsevier/London: Longmans).

Brown, A. J., 1969, 'Regional economics', *Economic Journal*, **79**, 759–796.

Burch, Philip H., Jr., 1972, *The Managerial Revolution* (Lexington, Mass.: D. C. Heath).

Carter, E. E., 1971, 'The behavioural theory of the firm and top-level corporate decisions', *Administrative Science Quarterly*, **16**, 413–428.

Chamberlain, N., 1968, *Enterprise and Environment: The Firm in Time and Place* (New York: McGraw–Hill).

Chandler, A. D., 1956, 'Management decentralization; an historical analysis', *Business History Review*, **20**, 111–175.

Chandler, A. D., 1966, *Strategy and Structure: Chapters in the History of American Industrial Enterprise* (New York: Doubleday).

Cyert, R. M. and J. G. March, 1963, *A Behavioural Theory of the Firm* (Englewood Cliffs: Prentice–Hall).

Dicken, P., 1971, 'Some aspects of the decision-making behaviour of business organizations', *Economic Geography*, **47**, 426–438.

Dill, W. R., 1958, 'Environment as an influence on managerial autonomy', *Administrative Science Quarterly*, **2**, 409–443.

Dore, Ronald, 1973, *British Factory–Japanese Factory: The Origins of National Diversity in Industrial Relations* (London: Allen & Unwin).

Eells, R., 1962, *The Government of Corporations* (New York: Free Press of Glencoe).

Emery, F. E. and Trist, E. L., 1972, *Towards a Social Ecology* (London & New York: Plenum Press).

Etzioni, A., 1964, *Modern Organizations* (Englewood Cliffs: Prentice–Hall).

Florence, P. Sargent, 1948, *Investment, Location and Size of Plant* (London: Allen & Unwin).

Forsyth, David J. C., 1972, *U.S. Investment in Scotland* (New York: Praeger).

Hamilton, F. E. Ian, 1963, *Recent Changes in Industrial Location in Yugoslavia*, unpublished Ph.D. thesis, University of London.

Hamilton, F. E. Ian, 1967, 'Models of Industrial Location', Chapter 10 in *Models in Geography*, ed. P. Haggett and R. J. Chorley (London: Methuen); also published in *Socio-Economic Models in Geography* as a paperback, 1968 (London: Methuen).

Hamilton, F. E. Ian, 1968, *Yugoslavia: Patterns of Economic Activity* (London: Bell/New York: Praeger).

Hamilton, F. E. Ian, 1969, *Regional Economic Analysis in Britain and the Commonwealth: A Bibliographic Guide* (London: Weidenfeld & Nicolson).

Hamilton, F. E. Ian, 1970, 'Aspects of spatial behaviour in planned economics', *Papers & Proceedings of the Regional Science Association*, **25**, 83–105.

Hamilton, F. E. Ian, 1971a, 'The Location of Industry in Eastern and South-Eastern Europe', Chapter 5 in *Eastern Europe: Essays in Geographical Problems*, ed. G. W. Hoffman (London: Methuen).

Hamilton, F. E. Ian, 1971b, 'Decision-making and industrial location in Eastern Europe', *Transaction & Papers, Institute of British Geographers,* **52**, 77–94.

Hamilton, F. E. Ian, 1972, 'The Nearest Neighbor Statistic: An Application to Industrial Location in East-Central Europe', in *Northwestern University Studies in Geography: Festschrift for A. E. Moodie* (Evanston: N. U. Press).

Hamilton, F. E. Ian, 1973, 'Spatial Dimensions of Soviet Economic Decision-Making', in *The Soviet Economy in Regional Perspective,* ed. V. Bandera and Z. Lew. Melnyk (New York: Praeget), pp. 235–260.

Harris, C. D. 1954, 'The market as a factor in the localization of industry in the U.S.', *Annals, Association of American Geographers,* **44**, 315–348.

Katz, D. and R. Kahn, 1967, *The Social Psychology of Organizations* (New York: Wiley).

Keeble, D. E., 1972, 'Industrial movement and regional development in the U.K.', *Town Planning Review,* **43**, 3–25.

Koropeckyj, I. S., 1967, 'The development of Soviet location theory before the Second World War', *Soviet Studies,* **19** (1), 1–28; **19** (2), pp. 232–244.

Krumme, G., 1969a, 'Toward a geography of enterprise', *Economic Geography,* **45**, 30–40.

Krumme, G., 1969b, 'The interregional corporation and the region', *Tijdschrift voor Economische en Sociale Geografie,* **61**, 318–333.

Livesey, F., 1972, 'Industrial complexity and regional economic development', *Town Planning Review,* **43**, 225–242.

Luttrell, W. F., 1962, *Factory Location and Industrial Movement* (Cambridge: National Institute for Economic and Social Research).

March, J. G. and H. A. Simon, 1958, *Organizations* (New York: Wiley).

McNee, R. B., 1958, 'Functional geography of the firm, with an illustrative case study from the petroleum industry', *Economic Geography,* **34**, 321–337.

McNee, R. B., 1960, 'Processes creating geographic patterns in managerial economy', *Annals, Association of American Geographers,* **51**, 336.

McNee, R. B., 1963, 'The spatial evolution of the Sun Oil Company', *Annals, Association of American Geographers,* **53**, 609.

McNee, R. B., 1964, 'The economic geography of an international petroleum firm', in *Focus on Geographic Activity: A Collection of Original Studies,* ed. R. Thoman and D. Patton (New York: McGraw-Hill), 98–107.

McNee, R. B., 1972, 'An inquiry into the goal or goals of the enterprise: a case study', *The Professional Geographer,* **24**, 203–210.

Pred, Allan R., 1967, *Behaviour and Location* (Lund: Gleerup).

Smith, D. M., 1966, 'A Theoretical Framework for Geographical Studies on Industrial Location', *Economic Geography,* **42**, 95–113.

Smith, D. M., 1971, *Industrial Location* (New York: Wiley).

Stafford, H. A., 1969, 'An industrial location decision model', *Proceedings, Association of American Geographers,* **1**, 141–145.

Stafford, H. A., 1972, 'The geography of manufacturers', *Progress in Geography,* **4**, 183–215.

Steed, G. P. F., 1968, 'The changing milieu of the firm', *Annals, Association of American Geographers,* **58**, 506–525.

Steed, G. P. F., 1970, 'Corporate enterprise and the location decision process', in *The Geographer and Society* (Vancouver: University of Victoria), 160–171.

Taaffe, E. J., R. L. Morrill, and P. R. Gould, 1963, 'Transport expansion in under-developed countries: a comparative analysis', *Geographical Review,* **53**, 503–529.

Townroe, P. M., 1971, *Industrial Location Decisions: A Study in Management Behaviour* (London: Research Publications).

I Towards New Hypotheses

2

A Systems Approach of Understanding the Geographic Behaviour of Organizations, Especially Large Corporations

ROBERT B. MCNEE

The Purpose and Organization of the Study

Human decisions and choices are always in the context of a society. Society is composed of both individuals and organizations. To understand the spatial behaviour of society, we must study both individual and group or organizational behaviour. In modern societies, *formal* organizations (such as corporations, trade unions, universities or governmental agencies) are of central importance, whereas in earlier societies more traditional *informal* organizations, such as the family or the tribe, were central. To date, geographers have made much more progress in studying individual spatial behaviour (as in perception studies and space preference studies) and traditional informal organizational behaviour (as in cultural geography) than they have in studying formal organizations. Indeed, study of the spatial behaviour of formal organizations has been rather fragmentary (see especially Dicken, 1971; Fleming and Krumme, 1968; Hamilton 1968, 1971; Homenuck, 1969; Kallal, 1969; Krumme, 1969a, 1970; McNee, 1958, 1960a, 1960b, 1961, 1963, 1964, 1970, 1972; Ray, 1971; Rees, 1972; Stafford, 1969, 1972; Steed, 1968a, 1968b, 1970, 1971a, 1971b, 1971c, 1971d, and 1971e).

Although Edward Ackerman is often considered one of our more perceptive guides to the 'promised land' for geography, one of his major suggestions has, in large part, gone unheeded. In 1958 Ackerman cited 'organiza-

47

tional evolution' as one of the three major cultural processes to which geographers should direct their attention. He particularly noted the rise of corporate organizations and quasi-public agencies (such as the TVA) and modern political administration as examples of such organizational evolution (Ackerman, 1958, pp. 24–25, 34). Later, he again noted that the study of the spatial behavour of formal organizations was an important research frontier (Ackerman, 1963, pp. 435, 437). More recently, the behavioural thrust in geography has encouraged more attention to organizations. Indeed, the rapid increase in research of the organizational genre in the last five years suggests that geographers may now be ready to heed Ackerman's cogent advice.

Very little in the formal training of geographers prepares them to think of organizations as something worthy of detailed geographic analysis. Hence, though many geographers now talk about becoming 'more sociological', few appear to embrace the study of organizations, a major branch of sociology. Similarly, although geographers have dealt tacitly with political organizations for a long time (as in political geography), they have tended to emphasize territory and either individual behaviour or informal group behaviour rather than formal organizational behaviour, with some recent notable exceptions (Cohen and Rosenthal, 1971; Massam, 1972). If this dimension of human decision-making and behaviour is to be adequately explored, it requires an effort of will on the part of geographers not unlike that required for the traditional economists of the early twentieth century to accept the propositions of the Institutional Economists (such as Veblen, Commons and Mitchell) when those economists first began to present their alternative mode of economic analysis. Some economists, however, did heed the institutionalists, broke out of their well-established ways of thinking, and thus greatly enriched economics (Gordon, 1963). The basic purpose of this chapter is to contribute to an analogous development in geography by presenting a detailed conceptual structure for the spatial analysis of one kind of formal organization, the large corporation.

It is essential, however to clarify further the differences between the organizational and the more established approaches in locational analysis. By the spatial behaviour of organizations such as large corporations is meant *any kind* of corporate behaviour that has a spatial dimension. Thus the problem posed here is vastly broader than the classic or Weberian locational problem, which has focused on how and why particular choices are made in *initially locating a single facility* (such as a manufacturing plant). Large corporations (or large educational systems, large trade unions, and so on) are usually multi-point phenomena. Behaviour is not just at one site (point) but rather at many sites (points) of varied nature and involves movement of flows among these points and between the points and the environment. How and why the organization chooses to add a particular point to such a spatial system is interesting indeed. But it is of not greater intrinsic interest than how particular points are used, once selected, especially since there may be a great many changes over time in the use of the points, once the initial choices, and the reasons for them, have receded into history. The longevity of large formal organizations usually greatly exceeds that of the uses initially assigned to particular site choices. The use made of the points is a dynamic, on-going, phenomenon rather than being merely a single incident in time, as the initial selection of the site necessarily is. Further, the reasons for a single locative choice by a multi-point organization are not likely to be very clear except in the context of the on-going multi-point organizational system as a whole, including the corporate growth strategy (Townroe, 1971). Likewise, the disestablishment of a point within the organizational system (or a marked downgrading in status) is conceptually at least as significant as the addition of one or more new points. Often, the two decisions are closely linked. Any change in the behaviour at any point is going to have very significant effects on the flows between the points and on the behaviour at other points in the system.

In short, established locational analysis stresses the understanding of a certain kind of real estate transfer, that related to the establishment of new production facilities, whereas the organizational approach broadens the analysis to include any kind of spatial transaction by the organization at any time. Some transactions relate to spatial behaviour within the organizational system itself, others are transactions with the environment. This certainly does not mean rejecting Weber out of hand (Smith, 1970): rather, it means persuit of an alternative path to the understanding of spatial patterns and processes, i.e. that the study of organizations may provide a means of moving toward that elusive goal of locational analysis, the provision of more direct links between the analysis of spatial process and the analysis of spatial pattern (King, 1969, pp. 593–5).

To clarify, a few questions need to be asked about any such multi-point organizational system. These questions are not meant to be exhaustive nor in the most logical order; they are meant merely to be illustrative. How and why did such a spatial system emerge? From what nucleus did it emerge? Why did it grow more in some directions than in others? Is it over-extended spatially? What holds it together? How strong are these bonds? What tends to break it into partially autonomous spatial sub-systems? What tends to promote stability and order in this spatial system? What, within the system itself and in the environment, leads to tension and conflict? How is a balance achieved between the desire for order and the desire for growth and change? What are the apparent goals of the system? If these are goals other than survival, or survival and growth, what are these goals? What kinds of information does the system collect about its own internal behaviour? To what extent is such data in a spatially coded form? What kinds of information about the environment are routinely collected and processed? How does the kind of data processing used for both internal and external information shape the kinds of conclusions reached and hence subsequent organizational behaviour? In what ways does the organization's managerial structure shape multi-point behaviour? Are there significant *similarities* as well as differences in the spatial behaviour of all organizations (McNee, 1972)? Surely these are significant questions for locational analysis. The *social relevance* of developing an understanding of the spatial behaviour of organizations, especially large organizations, is evident (McNee, 1970). But, equally, the *conceptual relevance* of organizational behaviour for a general theory of spatial behaviour should be evident from this study. In short, a focus on organizational behaviour leads to somewhat different questions from those traditionally posed by spatial analysts in geography, but to very important questions—questions we have ignored for far too long.

Perhaps the sub-title for this study should have been 'a geographic inquiry into the life and times of International Gismo, Inc.' The rest of this paper is divided into two main parts. The first, Part II, describes simply the growth and development of a hypothetical industrial corporation, 'International Gismo Inc.'; Part III provides an empirical context about which some pointed geographic questions can be raised. Instead of presenting a hypothetical case in Part II, specific data could have been used from existing corporations. However, a more general case was required that would not confuse by specific corporate characteristics. The hypothetical case of International Gismo Inc. should not be considered the 'typical case', How can we know what the 'typical case' in a geographic sense might be, until the whole subject has been explored in much greater depth, including many, many case studies? Yet this hypothetical case has not been knowingly distorted, except in the unusual choice of a bakery as the nucleus around which the organization grew and the assumed early linkages of bread-making with the matals industry.

Part III elaborates what are considered to be the key geographic questions about large corporations. In many kinds of geographic research, the basic problems posed are relatively clear because such problems have been raised for a long time. Little is gained by restating the questions, though much may be gained by efforts to frame the questions more operationally or by efforts to develop new techniques for answering them. Not so with studies of organizations such as corporations. So few geographers have examined the corporation as a geographic phenomenon that the key problems have yet to be stated. Hopefully, Part III will contribute toward the long range clarification of such key questions. By alternating the development of empirical case studies and the development of appropriate questions and concepts, it should be possible to fill gradually the great void that now exists in our understanding of spatial behaviour, that portion of total spatial behaviour which occurs within large formal organizations.

The Life and Times of International Gismo, Inc.

What's in a Name?

The imaginary corporation is a giant among corporations—indeed, among human organizations. It has assets and annual sales in billions of dollars, thousands of employees, millions of customers and hundreds of thousands of shareholders. Its operational area includes many nations and several continents and it has plans for future expansion of this operational area even further. It has hundreds of separate physical facilities (manufacturing plants, warehouses, retail outlets, mines, forests, farms, railroads, docks, local offices, regional offices, headquarters offices, research centres, recreational centres, training schools) dispersed through its operational area.

Because of past successes, its recognized ability 'to get things done', this corporation is both admired and feared by peoples and their decision-making organizations such as nation-states. Those who fear it, particularly, often refer to it as the Behemoth Corporation, likening it to the biblical beast. The corporation leaders realize that it is not enough that its behaviour be 'good' according to either its own or others' standards. It must also *seem* 'good'; the corporation (or government agency, in a mixed or socialist state) must have a favourable 'public image'. Therefore, if the name of the corporation actually were the Behemoth Corporation, it might well organize a campaign to convince everyone that 'Behemoth is beautiful'. Alternatively, it might change the name to International Unmitigated Blessings, Inc. Public imagery often obscures actual corporate behaviour (Hamill, 1963).

As investigators of organizational spatial behaviour, geographers should avoid being caught up in such games. That is why a neutral-sounding name has been chosen for the hypothetical corporation: International Gismo, Inc. As Pahl point out, a truly value-free social science is impossible and it is naive to expect one (Pahl, 1968, pp. 219–220). Still, it seems desirable to guard against bias. After organizational spatial behaviour is well understood, there will be plenty of opportunity to debate the pros and cons of the behaviour of a particular organization in relation to that of some ideal. Meanwhile, the principal effort should be to pinpoint the empirical regularities in spatial behaviour that do exist, while avoiding polemics.

The Founding and Early Growth Period

International Gismo, Inc., was not always so large or so dispersed geographically. It grew from small beginnings. In that, it was a non-typical corporation. Most corporations start relatively small but few grow to become giants like International Gismo, Inc.

In the beginning, it was a small family firm, not unlike thousands of others which together made up the main fabric of the economy a century ago.

If this family corporation, and its counterparts, had remained small, its geographic behaviour today could be explained relatively well by classical micro-economic theory and location theory largely based on that theory— the prevailing normative locational theory in economic geography today; i.e. the behaviour of the initial family firm was largely controlled by its environment. Understanding thus required primarily knowledge of the environment rather than the inner workings of the firm itself. But because of evolution to the present-day giant, International Gismo, Inc., and other giants like it, whose behaviour *does* affect the overall economic matrix quite markedly, new conceptual bases for interpretation are required.

The initial firm out of which International Gismo, Inc. grew was the J. J. Gismo Company, founded by 'Old J. J.' Gismo himself. Suppose this was a bakery on Opportunity Street in Cincinnati, Ohio. The company was a manufacturer-retailer, combining the several functions of manufacturing, warehousing, retailing and management in one small building. The portion of the environment which J. J. Gismo sought to affect directly was geographically rather small, extending a few blocks in each direction from the site on Opportunity Street. This area might be called the firm's 'activity space', but preferably *task environment,* following Dill (1958) and Thompson (1962). Beyond this small area lay a somewhat larger area that might be called the 'zone of opportunity', an area into which the task environment might possibly expand. The limits of the task environment were set by the tasks defined by the firm at a particular point in time. The limits of the zone of opportunity were rather more vague, set by J. J. Gismo's expansionist dreams. The term 'zone of opportunity' is similar to Redlich's 'ultimate horizon' (Redlich, 1951). As J. J. Gismo gradually expanded the tasks, and hence the task environment, successfully he allowed his perceptions of the zone of opportunity to expand also.

Over the years, the company grew, not only in number of employees and volume of business, but also in the size and diversity of its task environment. Put differently, the company became the organizer of a larger portion of spatial reality. It internalized more and more of the environment.

What made the company grow? Was it the opportunities in the environment, including the state of demand, supply, competition, of the business and of the industrial arts? It certainly was. But it was also the perception or state of awareness of the environment by J. J. Gismo. And, perhaps most important, it was the dreams of growth and grandeur that J. J. had for his company. No doubt profit maximization was a major goal, just as it was supposed to be according to the Occidental culture and to well-known apologists for that aggressive culture among the micro-economists of the day. But growth was somehow an important part of the goal-mix of J. J. Gismo Company too. If 'Old J. J.' had not dreamed of creating something bigger and better than just one human personality, he might not have re-invested the profits so consistently. Indeed, 'Old J. J.' had other goals besides profit maximization and growth. Some goals were at least partially contradictory. No one, not even 'Old J. J.', fully understood his goals and motivation (Baumol, 1968). But it is not necessary to try to psychoanalyse J. J. Gismo: his goals may be judged from the results. From these, growth had very high priority in his goal system; it was clearly the dominant goal.

In twenty years, operations at the initial site had expanded into adjacent buildings. Different functions (manufacturing, warehousing, retailing, management) had become spatially differentiated much more clearly. In retrospect, this was the first step in a long process of increasing spatial differentiation in the company system that today, in International Gismo, Inc., is so complex that it almost defies comprehension. But, at this point in time, the process of increasing spatial differentiation within the firm was readily comprehensible by all and, indeed, seemed the most obvious of developments. As a further step in increasing spatial differentiation, the firm had rather similar operations at three other sites in south-western Ohio and Columbus, Ohio. All four operations were linked together by flows of materials, people, ideas, funds, reports of activities. A hierarchy of decision-making channels began to form. 'Old J. J.' recognized that, unless a somewhat formalized system of channelling information flows and decision-making were developed, company growth might not continue. He had a basic antipathy for 'bureaucracy' and 'red tape'. Yet he valued growth so highly that he nevertheless laid the groundwork for the emerging channels of information and authority.

Growth continued. Forty years after its founding, the company was a far-flung enterprise with many scattered facilities. Administratively, operations were divided into three divisions. The initial activities, bakery and related activities, were grouped in the 'Central Division'. But these activities had greatly expanded in geographic scope and spatial complexity. Yet in some ways their geographic pattern was less complex than it had been earlier. Growth had permitted new locational choices which had been impracticable earlier. Various activities had been centralized into fewer and larger facilities, sometimes at old company sites, sometimes at new ones. Some old sites were abandoned in the process but not, of course, the initial shop on Opportunity Street. A new company headquarters was established in the Cincinnati CBD, near general information sources. But the complexity of the firm's geographic pattern of activities was only temporarily reduced by creating larger activity nodes. Economies of scale were associated with such concentration and spurred on further company growth and hence new site selections, yielding a net increase in the complexity of the firm's spatial form. Such oscillation between growth-induced simplification of the pattern, followed by growth-induced proliferation and increasing complexity, characterized the firm as a whole through many of the growth periods described in subsequent paragraphs.

A second division of the firm was the Grain Products Division. Initially,

'Old J. J.' had acquired a small grain-handling firm in Chicago to gain the economic advantages of backward vertical integration toward raw materials. The acquired firm had prospered and grown into a separate division. Its success resulted from the dovetailing of its information and materials flow systems with that of the Central Division. But it had also gained other customers new to the J. J. Gismo Company. Thus, this division was partly linked with the rest of the firm and partly functionally independent thereof. Hence, in raising questions about the efficiency or optimality of its locational pattern one would have to consider: optimality in relation to what? Locational optimality of flows among the sites of the Grain Products Division? Locational optimality of flows between Grain Products sites and Central Division sites? Or locational optimality relative to non-Gismo or potential customers? Profits from non-Gismo linkages flowed into the general funds of the J. J. Gismo Company: such linkages were important to all, not just to that division. Decisions relating to the Grain Products Division, including locational decisions, were necessarily compromises among differing efficiency criteria. Discussions leading to such compromises involved strategies, gamesmanship, coalitions—all aspects of internal 'company politics'. These early problems of 'divisional interest' versus overall 'company interest' were relatively easy to resolve at this stage in the company's history. But later the resolution of such problems on rational grounds became more and more difficult as the number of sub-systems within the overall corporate system of International Gismo, Inc. multiplied.

The third division of the company was the Metal Products Division. This had begun as a very modest venture, the acquisition of a small company making bread-slicing machines in Pittsburgh. 'Old J. J.' wanted the patents to the bread-slicing machines and was much impressed by the imagination of some of the employees. Soon the firm became a division of the J. J. Gismo Company and began to make a great variety of metal products, some with little connection with grains or baking. So successful was this division that its functional ties with the rest of the J. J. Gismo Company became more and more tenuous. But its overall contributions to the profits and growth of the firm were great. Thus 'Old J. J.' and his advisers had to ask themselves repeatedly, what do you want? Do you want a cohesive company, one you can understand readily, and one with a clear future? Or do you want growth, even if this means a loss in functional cohesiveness and mounting communication problems? Indeed, even if it means the great risks of getting into a business that you only partially understand? As often as not, they chose growth, and 'damn the consequences'.

Thus, by the fortieth year, the initial task environment of the J. J. Gismo Company had expanded remarkably: eastwards to Buffalo, Pittsburgh and the upper Ohio Valley towns, and to adjacent areas through the Metal Products Division; north-eastwards to Indiana, Illinois and Wisconsin through the Grain Products Division; and in nearly all directions through the Central Division. The task environments of the divisions overlapped each other, creating a company 'core area' which extended from Pittsburgh (Pennsylvania) to Decatur (Illinois) and from Cincinnati (Ohio) northward to Toledo (Ohio). Internal flows of information, people, and materials were most closely knit in this 'core area'.

However, the administrative focus for this set of flows among many dispersed activity sites remained in Cincinnati, at the southern edge of the 'core area'. The location of central administration was more inert than other sites in the company system. Perhaps it is easier to be 'rational' about the location of one's own activities than it is in planning the location of someone else's activities. Yet perhaps Cincinnati was a good location. It was not just that 'Old J. J.' liked Cincinnati. Indeed, he was probably more flexible in such matters than most employees. His senior employees, notably the administrative ones, had begun to attribute to Cincinnati some of the same characteristics of 'legitimacy' that citizens often attribute to long-lived political capitals and could have produced a long list of 'objective' and 'rational' reasons for retaining Cincinnati as the site of company headquarters. They could have, that is, if the issue had ever been raised. But it was not: a location decision (to retain Cincinnati as the headquarters site) was made by default.

As 'Old J. J.' aged, he developed rather mixed feelings about the business 'empire' he had worked so long and hard to build. He had many reasons to be proud of his handiwork and of the relatively efficient 'team' he had developed. Yet he realized that it was no longer 'his' company except in a narrow legalistic sense. In a *de facto* sense he had become simply another cog in the spatial machine that the J. J. Gismo Company had become. The biggest cog, to be sure. But he spent most of his time simply rubber-stamping decisions fed upward to him through the hierarchy. His speeches about the 'American Pioneering Spirit', 'Rugged Individualism', 'Free Enterprise', and 'Adam Smith: A Man of Vision at Chamber of Commerce luncheons were partially efforts to overcome his unconscious concern for the restraints on individualism implicit in the collective he had built.

The Gismo–Gadget Corporation

Sixty years after its founding, the company, now Gismo–Gadget Corporation, was still growing. Gismo–Gadget resulted from a merger with a New York metal products firm. A period of foundering had followed the death of 'Old J. J.', caused partly by general economic conditions in the environment and partly by a protracted struggle for control among 'Old J. J.'s' heirs and corporate bureaucrats. The internal struggle left little energy with which to search the economic environment for possible opportunities. The struggle continued after the merger with Gadget, but now no single block of stock could hope to gain control. Actual control rested in a loose alliance between professional managers and some large blocks of stock. Over time, continued dispersal of stock ownership through inheritance and a company profit-sharing plan gradually gave the professional managers more of the real decision-making power. Eventually, the stockholders, once at the very heart of the company system, became simply part of the firm's environment, outside the real system itself. Stockholders losing confidence in the management simply sold their stock, rather than trying to get back into the system by attempting to change the management. The price of the stock on the market became a kind of general indicator of how the environment perceived the company system, and hence was closely watched by the managers.

Merging involved a great many locational readjustments, particularly the 'rationalizing' of the two pre-existing locational patterns. Each had developed separately its own version of a 'rational' pattern with respect to both the environment and its own internal resources and needs. Now, though the environment had not changed so much, internally perceived needs, resources and opportunities had. So, sometimes activities at two or more old sites were simply concentrated in larger activity nodes at one old site. In other cases, two or more sites were abandoned in favour of a new one more appropriate to the new spatial pattern of Gismo–Gadget and its future plans. Such concentration was pushed because of anticipated economies of scale in production, transportation, communication and simplicity of administration. Such rationalizing was pervasive in the first years of Gismo–Gadget, but was not as radical as some efficiency experts in the firm desired. Rationalizing was constrained by the need to preserve 'morale' in the system. The leaders of Gismo–Gadget realized that the most important single asset of the merged firm was not listed at all on the company accounting books. Things listed on the books (facilities owned, supplies, accounts receivable, reserves) were less significant, really, than something rather more intangible, the reality of the 'going concern'. The phrase 'going concern' covered established decision-making channels and rules, relations with outside suppliers and customers. Therefore, though the internal geography of Gismo–Gadget differed in many ways from that either Gismo or Gadget had had previously, it retained also many resemblances to each. Such historical residues did not excire much comment either from within the company or from the environment.

Locational changes which stirred the most comment from all sources were those which were viewed as threatening. For example, Cincinnatians protested when Gismo–Gadget announced that its headquarters would move to New York City. After all, Gismo had been larger than Gadget and Gismo was definitely a 'Midwestern' firm, wasn't it? Bankers, lawyers and other sections of the downtown infrastructure felt particularly threatened by the shift of headquarters to New York (for a contemporary example, see Deutermann, 1970). What was involved was a downgrading in company status rather than actual office employment, because Cincinnati continued to be headquarters for one major division of Gismo–Gadget: in fact the divisional office employment soon exceeded that of the old J. J. Gismo Company headquarters. But the Cincinnati downtown infrastructure assumed that their functional relations with the main office would be less intense than before, an assumption which proved partially true.

By now, the task environment of the Gismo–Gadget Corporation embraced most of the United States. There were also minor foreign operations in Ontario and Britain, a heritage from some early ventures of the Gadget Company. The core area of the corporation's task environment corresponded roughly with the American Manufacturing Belt. Hence locating the headquarters offices in New York meant that the administrative focus was as peripheral to the system as a whole as the Cincinnati focus had been previously for the J. J. Gismo Company. But not for long. In the next period, rapid expansion overseas shifted New York from being a 'forward capital' to being a more 'central' capital.

International Gismo, Inc.

Eighty years on, the firm was still growing, but now as International Gismo, Inc. Re-named again, following major internal reorganization, through its various subsidiaries or divisions of subsidiaries it had gained operations in most parts of the United States and Canada. It had also flourishing subsidiaries in Western Europe, Australia and Latin America. Metal products, milling and baked goods still formed the core of company operations, in that order, but other only partially related activities had emerged also. For example, a sugar operation in Latin America had led to involvement in railroading and forestry there. Other extensions of initial economic activities had occurred in other subsidiaries. In general, the central management sought to limit such diversification to fields or geographic areas about which they felt competent, but to eschew many such trends in the company would have been to stop creativity in the system. So some rather 'oddball' extensions of activities were allowed reluctantly.

Generally, the central management in New York sought to gain as much advantage as possible from having many diverse activities included within one corporate system. Thus, they tried to integrate the varied activities, locationally and otherwise. But such integrating was not always easy to accomplish: many details had to be delegated to lower decision-making levels. Indeed, subsidiaries were large enough now for them to take many decisions including the selection of new locations. More and more the central office found itself engaged in long-range or strategic planning. This involved broad choices about which lines of productive activity might be most profitable in the long run or which geographic areas of the United States or the world would repay most handsomely initial investments, without getting down to more specific location questions. Such decisions would be assigned to the relevant existing subsidiary, or to the initial management of a new one, perhaps drawing on the accumulated expertise of some existing subsidiary or the central office. This kind of long-range corporate planning involved not only some relatively sophisticated knowledge about changing environmental conditions in various parts of the world but also about the strengths and weaknesses of the management in the various subsidiaries of the corporation. In short, it involved guesses about both 'inner' (systemic) and 'outer' (environmental) potentials for growth. In general, research seemed a consistently good gamble, even though its conclusions could upset established corporate (including locational) patterns. The central management used as much technical sophistication (linear programming, computer games, etc.) as possible to guide them in making choices. But they knew that judgment is difficult to programme, except in rather routine decision-making.

The central management was very conscious of its great decision-making power. If, over a long period, the investment policies of International Gismo, Inc. were to follow a specific geographic pattern, the firm could be a significant factor in improverishing one part of the world and enriching another. If International Gismo, Inc., invested widely in the underdeveloped world, might make respectable profits thereby and also contribute to the spread of the productive ideas or innovations of the more developed areas. Yet in so doing it would run great risks, from war, revolution and nationalization. If International Gismo, Inc. invested in areas of least political risk and greatest likelihood of significant profits—the developed countries—it would contribute to widening the gap between rich and poor countries. This would reduce international stability and create a risk to the whole corporate system. In short, the decision-making power of International Gismo, Inc., had to be used with rather more caution than that of the initial J. J. Gismo Company.

At the same time, the management of International Gismo, Inc., realized that, though powerful, it was also a 'prisoner' of the flow of information to it. In most cases, the central management could not deal with 'raw' data: it depended upon various types of secondary, tertiary and quaternary information that had been selected, sifted, weighed, tagged and organized by the vast bureaucracy that made up the skeleton of the corporation. Though largely a 'prisoner' of its own subordination in this sense, the management knew more than anyone else about the operation of the system, making it nearly impossible for any 'outsider' (a stockholder or the government) to challenge seriously its leaderhsip. The top levels of the firm became largely self-perpetuating from generation to generation.

In the hundredth year it was more of the same, except that the organization was even larger, with an expanded geographic scope, more locational complexity and more complexity in its information flows and decision-making structure.

And in the 120th year, still more of the same? Or, in the 140th year, what then? When and where would it all end? Perhaps, at some point, the internal complexities would become so great as to defeat the attempts of the management to invent new ways of coping with complexity. In that hypothetical case, International Gismo, Inc., might cease to grow, or break up into smaller, more easily comprehended systems.

Yet, for a century there had been a remarkable succession of technological innovations (improvements in transportation, communication, data storage and manipulation) permitting spatial growth that had previously seemed impracticable, if not impossible. Similarly, there had been remarkable advances in managerial concepts, a cultural transformation, indeed pioneered in the United States. For several decades this had given International Gismo, Inc., a competitive advantage internationally over its non-American rivals. Though the popular press tended to stress the 'hardware' side of technological change, it could be argued that this 'software' side (management) was really more significant. So it was difficult to foresee what the ultimate limits to the expansion of International Gismo, Inc., might be or when some hypothetical period of maturity or senescence might set in.

In any case, in the short run (as in the early 1970s), International Gismo, Inc., was too valuable as a productive 'going concern', to be allowed to founder. It might be 'saved' by support from other giants of the day, or by one or more governments. It was simply too important in the economy of too many people and too many areas to be allowed to fail. International Gismo, Inc. had begun to take on the characteristics of a long-lived social institution like the Church of the High Middle Ages. Much was expected of it; much was given to it.

Some Geographic Questions about Large Corporations

Many significant geographic questions could be raised about the modern large corporation. Some are implicit in the preceding discussion about International Gismo, Inc. Here in Part III some questions are made more pointed and specific.

The general scope of the questions that might be asked about International Gismo, Inc., or its counterparts, can be indicated by grouping them under three broad headings: function, structure, and evolution. As Rapaport (1968) has argued, any organized system can be viewed from three different perspectives: *being* (structure), *acting* (function) and *becoming* (evolution). The structure particularly includes that by which the system is able to receive, store, process and recall information. I would include also its decision-making rules and authority patterns. The functioning of the system includes particularly the way in which it responds to the environment, using the information collected, stored and processed by the structure.

Yet both functions and structures change over time, sometimes quite markedly, so the evolution of the system is important. The environment in all its complexity is involved in the analysis of all three: function, structure and evolution. Because of the great importance of the environment in geographic thinking, readers may find utility in some of the concepts presented incidently in Part II (for example, task environment and zone of opportunity) and in Part III (for example, role clusters).

The three major categories of questions may be clarified within the context of International Gismo, Inc. Thus one may ask functional questions about the real arrangement of production points in the International Gismo system at any specific time in its long development; or about the nature, volume, direction and periodicity of the flows among such production points and between such points and the environment. But examination of such point and flow patterns quickly convinces one that such patterns can only be explained in part through looking at the environment which raises questions about structure. One can query the degree to which the structure channels flows among them. For example, if International Gismo, Inc. were more highly centralized in administration, would that affect the location and relative size of the points and the volume of flows among them? But the functions and structure of International Gismo have changed significantly through time as it developed from the initial nucleus in Cincinnati. In its evolution, for example, were there observable steps, stages, thresholds or directional biases as the system grew? Hopefully, the analysis of the three categories of questions will suggest some useful paths for geographers to follow in exploring the world of the large corporation.

Functional Questions

Functionalism has a long history in geography; indeed, it is probably valid to say that the research questions most commonly pursued in urban and economic geography today are functional questions.[1] How are such questions about International Gismo, Inc. and its counterparts like, or different from, questions which have been pursued for a long time in geography?

The context of the large corporation allows a much wider range of phenomena to be considered. Rather than focusing on initial site choices, *any kind* of locational behaviour could be considered. Among major production functions, geographers have been excessively preoccupied with retailing and manufacturing, rather less with wholesaling and very little with the research and office functions (Armstrong, 1972). In the corporate context, the office function could be seen as two functions, routine control and planning, each having somewhat different locational requirements. The research function or the office function may be studied in a non-organizational context, yet growth of both functions today is so interwoven with the rise of large corporations that one cannot really be understood without the other. In any case, studies of corporate systems as functioning entities compels the interpretation of *all* points in such systems, not just those labelled 'manufacturing plants, or 'grocery stores'.

Similarly, manufacturing geography has been much more preoccupied with the location of manufacturing plants than with their size. Yet clearly, the size of each plant is closely connected with the total number that can be absorbed by a given economy: many plants of small size might call for one kind of locational pattern whereas a small number of very large plants might call for a quite different locational pattern. Generally, it has been economists rather than geographers who have considered seriously the effects of economies of scale on locational patterns. True, some geographers are now exploring the size or agglomeration economies question: Karaska (1966, 1969) for example. However, probing overall corporate investment decision-making processes (Townroe, 1971) is an essential path to understanding how facility number, facility size and facility location are interdependently related. Similarly, horizontally- or vertically-integrated corporations can be viewed as special cases of economic linkage or the industrial complex. That the *vehicle* for such linkage is a corporation with wide areas between the points linked rather than a compact metropolitan area or industrial region should not blind us to the functional realities involved. For example, the automobile assembly industry was transformed from one of many, many production sites (and many small firms) to one with far fewer sites (and a few large firms). Empirical evidence of this shift has been presented cartographically by Boas (1961).

Locational inertia of manufacturing plants becomes more significant as the advanced economies age. Considerable research attention has been paid to inertia, but primarily to the relative immobilities of production equipment and buildings. Yet the study of corporate locational systems over time shows many cases in which the site has remained as constant while the facilities and activities located there have not. Usually a whole series of locational choices have been made over the years, though since no locational shift was involved it would not be included in the Weberian type of locational analysis. Logically, decisions to maintain a particular location pattern, whether conscious or otherwise, may be just as significant as decisions to change or elaborate a location pattern.

How do ideas diffuse through a corporate system such as that of International Gismo, Inc.? In what ways is this process like, or different from, the diffusion process in general? Today, large corporations are a major vehicle for spreading technology and related ideas from more developed to less developed economies (Baranson, 1966). Yet as to what the nature of the process might be in a spatial sense, we are in the dark.

Studying locational questions in the organizational context would not only broaden locational analysis but also compel reconsideration of the assumed relationships among production functions. For example, consider the role of research and development. In established locational theory, research is usually considered exogenous to the firm making locational choices: the only control that the firm can exercise is whether or not to accept research ideas from the environment. Yet, in fact, large corporations generally have research and development divisions: part of the research factor is thus absorbed from the environment into the corporate system itself. This has sweeping implications for the solution of locational puzzles by the corporation. It means that the large corporation need not take the 'facts' of a particular locational problem (location of raw materials, method of processing, etc.) as 'realities' to which it must adapt. It has the option of trying to change the locational meaning of some or all of the variables involved through appropriate research. Rather than merely 'adapting' to an environment, the firm may seek, through research, to overcome some unwanted constraint, e.g. results of research permitted the use of low-grade Minnesota iron ores after the Second World War and hence the retention of the main part of an elaborate iron and steel location pattern in North America. The issue for geographers to explore is to what degree the absorbing of research functions into large corporations changes the ways in which they respond to locational problems.

Similarly, wholesaling in established location theory is assumed to be carried out by specialist firms, as distinct from manufacturing or retailing firms. This was indeed the case in the days of the J. J. Gismo Company, and it is still so for its counterparts today. But for International Gismo, Inc., the situation is rather more complex. Part of its wholesaling needs are performed by the corporation itself. Like most functions, wholesaling is actually a bundle of functions, not a single, highly discrete, function. So, some parts of the bundle are performed by the sales divisions, others by transport divisions, etc. The decision-makers always have the option of increasing or decreasing such direct involvement with wholesaling functions. Such absorption of part of the enviroment into the corporate system has many implications for location decision-making. For example, historically the accretion of services such as wholesaling in the cores of metropolitan or older production regions has been a significant locationally-stabilizing force for the economy. As corporate systems become accretion vehicles for such services, too, then some assumptions about the nature of metropolitan growth patterns break down. Geographers should analyse to what degree the modern corporation has become such an accretion vehicle and to what degree this changes the locational decision-making process.

The environment which must be considered in interpreting a corporate system may be rather different than that assumed in traditional locational studies. It is generally much greater territorially. In interpreting the spatial behaviour of J. J. Gismo Company (or its counterparts today), it is sensible to stress the immediate local environment, while maintaining awareness that the wider environment may also have impact, though perhaps less directly. This is what most traditional locative studies do. But the environment relevant to any single production point in the International Gismo system may well include the environment of the entire system as well as that in the immediate area of the facility itself, i.e. it is rather more complex that that for a J. J. Gismo facility. Environmental questions that may be of minor importance at the local level may become of major importance in the context of a multi-national corporation. For example, the early life of the J. J. Gismo Company was spent entirely in an area of basic legal uniformity (the United States) but International Gismo, Inc., must operate in an environment with many complex legal contradictions. That which is *required* in one country may be illegal or suspect in another. Until there is a 'world culture' and a 'world government', the environment of the international corporation will be much less predictable than that of J. J. Gismo Company. This unpredictability provides opportunities for International Gismo, but primarily poses problems. In such a situation, corporate systems become even more 'private governments' (Eells, 1962) than they otherwise would. Little wonder that Chamberlain (1968) refers to modern corporate environments as 'turbulent'. The geographic exploration of such turbulent environments is important for understanding the locational behaviour of all firms today, large or small. But such exploration requires a probing of the internal functioning of corporate systems: the firms resources and procedures and the qualities of its management (Penrose, 1959, p. 41). In short, the rise of International Gismo and its counterparts requires us to reconsider our traditional interpretations of the environments relevant to the locational decision-maker.

Structural Questions

The structure of an organizational system channels its day-by-day functioning. Perhaps the best short definition of structure is that it is a set of *roles* tied together by *communication* (Boulding, 1956). The concept of role suggests internal division of labour, lines of authority, the degree and type of centralization or decentralization in decision-making, and other aspects of the accepted 'rules' of the organization. The concept of communication, by contrast, suggests that structure involves the way in which information is received, stored, processed, recalled and used in making choices and determining action. Both concepts are important.

Asking really pointed geographic questions about organizational structures is difficult at this stage because social geography, which could provide in-depth analysis of role networks and communication networks, is in its infancy. Perhaps one day we will be able to analyse the location of 'role clusters' rather than just physical facilities such as manufacturing plants. Nevertheless, contemporary geographic studies of diffusion, perception and decision-making are of much help in interpreting organizational structures. Perhaps, too, the spatial division of labour in organizational systems can be partly understood by analogies to central place models.

Meanwhile, one can turn to those fields which have long stressed the study of organizations, particularly sociology. There are two broadly polarized approaches in sociology to the interpretation of organizational structure, the 'rational' approach versus the 'natural systems' approach. As yet, attempts to reconcile the two approaches are still embryonic.

The 'rational' approach, particularly associated with Max Weber and his followers, stresses that formal organizations and their bureaucratic structure are established precisely to interject more rationality into human affairs than might otherwise be the case. The formal organization is viewed as a consciously conceived mechanism for carrying out specific goals or objectives. One common problem a structure is posed is how efficient it is in realizing the stated goals. Rationalists are quick to note departures from rationality in organizations (for example, a less than 'perfect fit' between a corporation's goals, its location pattern and the environment) as well as evidences of rationality. However, there is probably a general tendency to view departures from rationality as occurring randomly, resulting from incorrect or inadequate information or arising from mere human error in calculation. In short, the rational approach would be the most comfortable for those geographers with strong affinities for 'economic man' and normative locational theories.

In contrast, the 'natural systems' approach, particularly associated with Talcott Parsons and his followers, puts little emphasis on goal attainment, efficiency, optimality or satisficing. Instead, the survival and development of the organization itself is considered to be of central importance: whatever the goals may have been originally, the organization will seek to survive, even if this means major modifications (or even replacement) of initial goals (Etzioni, 1964, pp. 13–14). The structure of the organization is not seen as a clearly planned mechanism for goal attainment, but rather as a spontaneous and homeostatic phenomenon. Of course, successive plans may reorder the structure (as with the various corporate reorganizations of International Gismo, Inc.) but the overall structure is viewed as the result of cumulative, basically unplanned, adaptive responses to stresses and strains in the system. These may originate either in the environment or within the system itself. Thus, the questions to be asked about the structure do not stress 'rationality' in attaining a goal but discovering what tends to produce equilibrium in the system and what tends to disrupt equilibrium (Gouldner, 1962).

Another way of describing this polarity is to call rationalism the 'closed system' view and the 'natural systems' approach the 'open system' view (Gouldner, 1959). Another categorization contrasts classical rational theory and more recent 'human relations' models (Bennis, 1962).

One of the most crucial rationalist or 'efficiency' questions one might ask about the structure of a corporate organization is whether or not the primary information system of the corporation, its accounting system, provides the kind of spatially specific data that would permit the corporation to monitor itself effectively as a spatial system. If the accounting system (which, after all, must serve many other corporate purposes as well) does not provide such data, then what kind of supplemental information of a spatial nature is routinely collected and processed? In short, to what extent does the corporation's information network reflect either rationality in day-by-day locational decision-making or departures from such rationality? Similarly, would the internal pricing system of International Gismo, almost inevitably some form of administered pricing, provide the kind of data necessary for rational locational decision-making within the system? Do the prices attached to transfers of goods or services from one division to another subtly modify the 'rationality' of locational choices? If so, how?

Alternatively, one could ask what were the advantages or disadvantages of the particular kind of decision-making patterns adopted by the organization for promoting or not promoting spatial efficiency. Chandler (1956) concluded from his study of fifty firms that (1) firms whose activities cross established industry lines tend to be administratively decentralized by product, (2) firms producing a restricted line tend to be decentralized either functionally or territorially and (3) firms oriented to the market tend to be decentralized territorially. This suggests that there is rationality in administrative centralization and decentralization patterns. Yet it remains for geographers to analyse various administrative systems to determine what kinds promote rationality in spatial decision-making and what kinds do not. An administrative system might be highly rational in many respects, yet rather weak in *spatial rationality*.

In this same context of decentralized decision-making, one could ask what provision the organization makes for resolving rationally the inevitable conflicts between 'divisional interest' and 'corporate interest.' Just as there may be spatial maladjustment in a metropolitan community (Wolpert, 1964), there may be spatial maladjustment within a corporate organization. Do the role network and the communication network tend to emphasize efficiency in a stable, static, environment or do they tend to emphasize flexibility leading toward a more long-run efficiency in a changing environment (Ausoff, 1965)? How efficient are these networks in making locational choices in crisis situations (Wolpert, 1970)?

Presumably, one principal advantage of International Gismo, Inc. over the J. J. Gismo Company is that it has more short-run options in adjusting to environmental changes. For example, temporarily it can increase a particular productive activity at point X in the system while eliminating or reducing it at point Y. Or, it can increase overall system efficiency by temporarily redirecting flows among points. Thus the principle of substitution (Etzioni, 1964, p. 3), which is usually discussed in relation to personnel or products, should also include locational substitutions. The question for geographers to explore is the nature, degree and general significance of such substitutions for location in general.

Though Goodwin (1965) made a pioneering study of the location of management centres in the United States and Armstrong (1972) has analysed the office industry of New York, the question of management locations in relation to corporate structure is yet to be explored. Are corporate management centres (including subsidiary centres and corporate headquarters) efficiently located and, if so, why? If not, why not? This is a very difficult question because the headquarters office of one firm may be much smaller than the subsidiary office or another larger, corporation. Presumably, the location needs of subsidiary or divisional management differ from those of central management. Yet this depends on the degree of decentralization in decision-making within the system. Difficult or not, the location of the decision-makers themselves is one of the most interesting aspects of corporation geography.

The importance of corporate structure for location is particularly apparent when one considers mergers and acquisitions. Corporations may choose to expand *in situ,* by branches or by acquisitions and mergers. Locational decision-making in the context of mergers and acquisitions is especially interesting because it takes on the nature of courtship and marriage. But after the union, 'rationality' may require a quite different locational pattern from before. In describing International Gismo's growth and development it was assumed that acquisition and mergers were followed by locational readjustments aimed at increasing the overall spatial efficiency of the organization. Obviously, this happens to a degree. But to what degree? How significant are *locational* rationalizations following mergers relative to other kinds of rationalizations (such as changing the product line)? To what extent are acquisitions and mergers solutions to corporate locational problems and to what extent are locational questions largely irrelevant in such forms of growth?

Thus many geographic questions flow from the rationalist view of organizational structure.

Many geographic questions can also be generated from the 'natural systems' view. To Pahl (1968, p. 230) a social system has four major functional problems: tension management and pattern maintenance, adaptation, goal attainment and integration. Such groups as the family, schools and religious bodies deal with tension management and pattern maintenance while the economy deals with adaptation, the government deals with goal attainment and lawyers or opinion leaders deal with social integration. These distinctions are valid for Pahl's purposes. However, if one views a corporation such as International Gismo, Inc. as a social system, then it is clear that its structure must be equipped to deal with all four kinds of functional problems. Thus, large corporations use company publications and other devices to create a 'family spirit', develop its own internal school system to maintain skills and communication and attribute the 'founding father' (such as J. J. Gismo) with qualities reminiscent of Moses or George Washington. Similarly, corporations periodically readjust goals to bring them into greater conformity with the beliefs of corporate personnel; for example, pressures for greater 'social responsibility' can be generated from within the organization as well as from the environment. Further, the extensive use of interlocking corporate committee structures for decision-making suggests a great concern for corporate integration, as does the practice of insisting that the directors be 'working directors' in some firms. Thus a corporation is a society as well as a highly rational production machine.

Boulding (1956, p. 8) says that, in looking at social organizations, concern must be with 'the content and meaning of messages, the nature and dimensions of value systems, the transcriptions of images into a historical record, the subtle symbolizations ... and the complex gamut of human emotions'. Such comments are reminiscent of the work of Thorstein Veblen (Ayres, 1963) who argued that all economies were best understood in the perspective of 'primitive' societies. In contemporary terms, Veblen would be talking about corporate 'cultures'. Business writers often note the importance of corporate 'personality' but the concept of a 'corporate culture' is more descriptive of the processes involved. Pahl (1968, p. 230) lists four elements in the structure of a social system, one of which is cultural values.

Other aspects of social organization are also stressed. Pages (1962, p. 173) underlines the need for a unitary conception of the firm as a 'total psychosociological field, in view of the effects of tensions within the sub-groups of an enterprise. Energy which is used in avoiding conflicts is not available to pursue officially stated goals. High tension levels restrict and distort communication by the established network within the organization (Pages, 1962, p. 174ff). Similarly, Selznick (1943) describes the common tendency for organizations to become so wrapped up in their own internal problems (tensions, conflicts, power struggles, status questions) that the organization no longer serves its original purpose. In a study of governmental administrative systems Massam (1972, p. 22) notes rather dryly that boundary values for administrative units are 'considerably stronger' than efficiency values! Not surprisingly, this problem has been known in business bureaucracies, too. Indeed many sociological concepts—such as norm, consensus, order, power, alienation and conflict (Pahl, 1968, pp. 232–3)—which could be used to advantage in interpreting a corporation as a spatial social system.

The questions that emerge if one adopts the 'natural systems' approach to organizations are rather different from those traditionally asked in locational analysis. For example, one might question the degree to which all locational decision-making in a large multi-point system such as International Gismo, Inc. is severely constrained by the desire to achieve or maintain some level of equilibrium. Thus, perhaps one locational choice might be favoured over another because it would have fewer negative side-effects in generating anxieties, tensions and conflicts within system. Or, territorial expansion by one regional division might be 'balanced' by similar expansion in another region, simultaneously or sequentially, irrespective of the true environmental opportunities.

Or, limitations or gaps in the informational network might be purposeful, following a system-protective policy of 'don't rock the boat'. Or, an organization might conceivably feel the need to express desire for social integration in a locational way. It might want to look spatially integrated on a map. One organization that I know personally marketed in two territorially separate areas: Megalopolis and Florida. A strong attempt was made to expand to fill the intervening space even though the environment indicated that this would be a disastrous policy. The effort was made and did not succeed. In this case, the wish to 'integrate' in a concrete way was strong enough to override the voices of caution. Randall (1959) would be neither surprised nor at a loss to provide other examples. But the question for geographers to explore is to what degree locational policies of corporations do reflect such thinking.

A major problem is the source of disturbance to a corporation's spatial equilibrium. The environment may, presumably, be the primary source. But since the perception of environmental opportunities or threats is so intimately connected with the role network and the communication network of the organization, the pinpointing of actual sources of disturbance of organizational equilibrium is not easy. Perhaps the source lies within the organization itself. How then is a new spatial equilibrium achieved, once there has been a disturbance? Are there geographic limits to the size and diversity of an organization seeking to achieve equilibrium? If so, what are they?

Both the rationalist and the natural systems approaches provide interesting structural questions related to comparative economic system. Are the role networks and communications networks within large 'socialist' production organizations (such as those of the Soviet Union or the East European Countries) essentially different from such networks in the 'capitalist' production systems of the West? If so, how? Mesmerized as we tend to be by nineteenth century rhetoric about 'socialism' and 'capitalism' we tend to *assume* that there are few if any similarities in the two kinds of organizations and profound differences. Yet whether or not the differences outweigh the similarities we cannot know without actual investigation. Indeed, Hamilton's (1970, 1971) studies of locational decision-making in East Europe or planned economies generally suggest that much could be clarified from comparative structural studies.

There are many opportunities also for comparative studies within the West itself. Blackbourn (Chapter 9) has investigated the locational behaviour of international firms in Europe. Such study could well be broadened to a comparative analysis of the functional flows and structure of American, European or Japanese international firms, operating anywhere on the earth. Similarly, one could examine the cultural origins of the American corporate penetration of Europe (Servan-Schreiber, 1967). Much could be learned from comparative studies of quasi-public agencies in the United States (such as the TVA, the Port of New York Authority or the Postal Service) and corporate spatial systems. Even the study of large university organizations can throw light on the locational decision-making of industrial corporations (McNee, 1972).

Questions about Spatial Evolution

The general evolutionary question is what was the process by which J. J. Gismo Company (with one set of functions and structures) was transformed into the International Gismo, Inc. (with quite a different set of functions and structures)?

One aspect is the general process of corporate growth. What made the corporate system grow, both initially and subsequently? The geographic aspects of this question might be explained by a model adapted from regional economic growth models, i.e. the corporation might be viewed as a special kind of economic region. For example, Gunnar Myrdal's concept of cumulative causation as interpreted by Keeble (1968, pp. 249–60) might be the starting point in developing such a model. One could assume a spiral of growth for International Gismo, Inc. as follows. As the longevity of the organization grew, the organization's size (measured in number of employees, quantity of output) also grew. As the firm grew, the division of labour within it increased and became more differentiated spatially. As division of labour increased, technical proficiency of the firm increased. As technical proficiency increased, more resources could be obtained from the environment. As resources increased, the longevity of the organization added employees and output, leading to further division of labour and a more complex spatial differentiation of labour, and so on in a hypothetically 'never-ending' spiral of growth. If the general process of growth for large long-lived corporations such as International Gismo, Inc. is not like that, what is it like? In short, we need to develop an acceptable model of corporate growth just as we need models for regional economic growth.

A related set of evolutionary questions involves attempts to identify steps, stages or threshold points which were crucial in the process. In describing the growth process for International Gismo, Inc. in Part II, the discussion was divided into rather arbitrary segments, each of twenty years in length. Such arbitrariness was necessary because the subject of corporate spatial evolution is as yet unexplored. I did not want to impose order when none had been perceived. Perhaps a more realistic grouping of the growth stages would have been into (1) local, Cincinnati, firm, (2) regional or

Midwestern complex, (3) U.S. Manufacturing Belt firm, (4) national (United States) firm and (5) multi-national firm. Such a set of stages stresses the increasing size of the firm's activity area. But perhaps activity area size is less significant than the nature of the functional flows and structure within that space. In that case, one might identify: (1) the initial firm, with little spatial differentiation, (2) the firm with four distinct nuclei linked to one 'head office', (3) the three separate divisions, partially overlapping each other spatially, each with many nuclei, and all focusing on one 'head office', (4) the greater complexity in functional flows and structures after the Gismo–Gadget merger and (5) the still greater complexity in the system later on, with sub-systems as large as those of stages (3) and (4). Or, possibly, latter stages were simple outgrowths of the spatial network already evident much earlier. In that case, fewer critical stages in growth might be identified. Clearly, identification of stages and thresholds in corporate spatial evolution would advance understanding of both growth and similarities in corporate functional flows and structures.

An underlying question here is the degree to which early location decisions may have conditioned all subsequent locational decisions. For example, did the nodes that emerged in the spatial system of J. J. Gismo Company persist as 'growth poles' in subsequent development? Did the existence of such 'growth poles' strongly condition the choice of the Gadget Company (over alternative spatial systems with which to merge) as a candidate for merger? Did the modified set of 'growth poles' that resulted from 'rationalization' after that merger continue throughout subsequent development, to which others were added without displacing these early 'growth poles?' In a non-corporate context, Morrill (1966) found that in simulating the development of an urban settlement system, early locational decisions had strong and lasting effects on all later locational decisions. Preliminary studies of the Sun Oil Company (Philadelphia) and Procter & Gamble Company (Cincinnati) similarly show early location decisions to have been decisive. As Dicken (1971) notes, past precedent is often the first recourse in problematic situations. Coppock (1959, pp. 353–62) describes how firms tend to lapse into historical reviews of past decisions as a way of improving on impressionistic hunches. This is particularly significant when it is difficult to obtain definitive data on demand and cost functions, which is very frequently the case for location choices.

Penrose (1959, pp. 65–87) introduces a somewhat different explanation of the importance of early decisions by pointing to the constraining effect of 'inherited resources' in determining the directions of a firm's expansion. 'Inherited resources' are those available in time period T about which decisions are made for time period $T+1$ and so on. They include the firm's assets, not least such intangibles as the accumulated experience of personnel. Though Penrose is not specifically concerned with location questions, she shows clearly how 'one thing leads to another' in nearly all aspects of corporate development. One very specific way in which inherited resources affect locational choices is in constraining the search process for new sites. Stafford (Chapter 6) shows that the location of the main office and the location of existing company-owned plants significantly influences the location of search areas. Krumme (1970) describes the process by which Siemens rearranged its internal spatial patterns after a drastic environmental change, by favouring certain existing nodes as growth poles.

But are all firms largely prisoners of their own location pasts? Radical departures from past location patterns no doubt also exist. How significant are more 'creative' responses to the location dilemma? Schumpter (1947) was much concerned with the distinction between corporate environmental responses which are nerely 'adaptive' (i.e. those following existing corporate practice) and responses which are 'creative' (i.e., those breaking new ground or involving something outside of existing corporate practice). My own unpublished studies of the Sun Oil Company suggest that throughout the history of the company there has been a kind of tension between those seeking to preserve and augment the existing spatial pattern and those wanting to create new location patterns. Thus many location decisions have tended to produce accretions around early 'growth poles' and to 'fill in' voids in company activity space. Yet, there have also been a number of spatial choices that radically upset previous locational patterns and integrations. The question of corporate spatial innovativeness must remain an open question until many firms have been studied.

Corporate spatial evolution is complicated by the need to distinguish between a sequence of small actions which comprise the system itself and more radical changes which really alter the system (Pahl, 1968, p. 235). It is the latter which must be identified for evolutionary perspective. Suppose a retailing firm (for example, the Kroger Company of Cincinnati) has a definite policy for selecting new grocery store sites and for divesting itself of old and unprofitable sites. Then opening or closing a specific grocery store would be only a small action. The 'rules' which govern the system (Eulau, 1969, p. 7) are what is important here, not each application of the rules. However, if the firm were to decide to introduce some quite new business as a sideline (say, manufacturing soup or selling drugs) with the consequent development of a locational policy and managerial structure to guide the new endeavour, this might represent a basic change in the corporate system itself.

Another way of making this distinction is to contrast tactics and strategy. Our hypothetical firm's overall retailing policy would involve a strategy, whereas specific locational choices related to implementing that strategy might be merely locational tactics. The best single treatment of the corporate tactics—corporate strategy dichotomy is by Chamberlain (1968). Historical study of several corporate strategies by Chandler (1966) yields generalizations of corporate strategy—and structure relations. Though non-spatial in orientation, his study provides a good starting point for geographic investigation. The concept of corporate strategies merges with that of corporate long-range planning. Steiner (1963) presents very interesting data on comparative long-range planning in over fifteen corporations and governmental agencies. One advantage in studying large, long-lived corporate systems is that such systems often find it necessary to articulate their strategies specifically, providing written records of the intended purpose of various location decisions, whereas the small family firm seldom feels the need.

Spatial evolution of most firms is necessarily dominated, however, by 'rationality' and carefully designed strategies: in fact, evidence lends much support to the 'natural systems' approach to corporations. The sociological concepts of *latent* function and *manifest* function discussed by Pahl (1968, p. 231) are probably crucial here. Similarly, collapse or change in particular sub-system boundaries (Loomis, 1962) would affect the *whole* system. Even if the whole system is officially dedicated to growth and expansion, significant internal barriers are likely to exist to the implementation of that policy (Bennis, 1962).

The most interesting general question concerns the ultimate limits to territorial growth. Large corporations have been expanding markedly for over a century. None has yet truly embraced the globe, though some embrace large areas of it. A series of inventions, discoveries and cultural transformations have permitted the counterparts of International Gismo, Inc. to flourish. Will similar inventions, discoveries and cultural transformations favouring the growth of ever-larger organizations continue to come, or are there spatial limits to the growth of multi-national organizations? Have such limits yet been approached, reached or exceeded? If so, what is the nature of such spatial limits to organizational growth? Are they primarily technical in nature? Or are they linked more with the character of human beings and their capacity to relate to large organizations? Careful geographic investigation of corporate spatial evolution to date would at least improve our hunches about such an important social and political problem.

Note

1. For example, central place investigations involve the question of what is the function of a set of settlement points (central places) in relation to areas and how this functional relationship affects the size, nature and distribution of the points. Similarly, Weberian analysis and Thunian analysis are functional in nature.

References

Ackerman, E. A., 1958, *Geography as a Fundamental Research Discipline* (University of Chicago).

Ackerman, E. A., 1963, 'Where is a research frontier', *Annals, Association of American Geographers,* **53**, 429–440.

Armstrong, R., 1972, *The Office Industry: Patterns of Growth and Location* (New York: Regional Plan Association).

Ausoff, I., 1965, 'The firm of the future,' *Harvard Business Review*, **43**, 162ff.

Ayres, C. E., 1963, 'The legacy of Thorstein Veblen, in' *Institutional Economics: Veblen, Commons, and Mitchell Reconsidered* (Berkeley: University of California Press).

Baranson, J., 1966, 'Transfer of technical knowledge by international corporations to developing economies,' *American Economic Review*, **56**, 259-67.

Baumol, W. J., 1968, 'Entrepreneurship in economic theory,' *American Economic Review*, **63**, 64-71.

Benne, K. D., 1962, 'Deliberate changing as the facilitation of growth,' in *The Planning of Change*, eds. W. G. Bennis, K. D. Benne and R. Chin (New York: Holt, Rinehart and Winston).

Benis, W. G., 1962, 'Leadership theory and administrative behavior,' *The Planning of Change* (New York: Holt, Rinehart and Winston).

Boas, C. W., 1961, 'Locational patterns of american automobile assembly plants, 1895-1958,' *Economic Geography*, **37**, 218-230.

Boulding, K. E., 1956, 'General systems theory—the skeleton of science,' *Management Science*, **2**, 197-208.

Chamberlain, N., 1968, *Enterprise and Environment: The Firm in Time and Place* (New York: McGraw-Hill).

Chandler, A. D., 1956, 'Management decentralization, an historical analysis', *Business History Review*, **20**, 111-175.

Chandler, A. D., 1966, *Strategy and Structure: Chapters in the History of American Industrial Enterprise* (Garden City, New York: Doubleday).

Cohen, S. B. and L. D. Rosenthal, 1971, 'A geographical model for political systems analysis,' *Geographical Review*, **61**, 5-31.

Coppock, J. D., 1959, *Economics of the Business Firm* (New York: McGraw-Hill).

Deutermann, E. P., 1970, 'Headquarters have human problems,' *Business Review, Federal Reserve Bank of Philadelphia*, 2-22.

Dicken, P., 1971, 'Some aspects of the decision making behavior of business organizations,' *Economic Geography*, **47**, 426-38.

Dill, W. R., 1958, 'Environment as an influence on managerial autonomy,' *Administrative Science Quarterly*, **2**, 409-43.

Eells, R., 1962, *The Government of Corporations* (New York: The Free Press of Glencoe).

Etzioni, A., 1964, *Modern Organizations* (Englewood Cliffs, New Jersey: Prentice-Hall).

Eulau, H., 1969, *Micro–Macro Political Analysis: Accents of Inquiry* (Chicago: Aldine).

Fleming, D. K. and G. Krumme, 1968, 'The "Royal Hoesch Union": case analysis of adjustment patterns in the european steel industry,' *Tijdschrift voor Economische en Sociale Geografie*, **59**, 177-99.

Goodwin, W., 1965, 'The management center in the United States,' *Geographical Review*, **55**, 1-15.

Gordon, R. A., 1963, 'Institutional elements in contemporary economics,' in *Institutional Economics: Veblen, Commons, and Mitchell Reconsidered* (Berkeley: University of California Press).

Gouldner, A. W., 1959, 'Organizational analysis,' in *Sociology Today*, ed. R. Merton, L. Broom and L. Cottrell (New York: Basic Books).

Gouldner, A. W., 1962, 'Organizational analysis,' in *The Planning of Change*, ed. W. Bennis, K. Benne and R. Chin (New York: Holt, Rinehart and Winston).

Hamill, L., 1963, 'Public relations programs and forest land use,' *Geographical Review*, **53**, 459-61.

74

Hamilton, F. E. Ian., 1968, 'Models of industrial location,' in *Socio-economic Models in Geography*, ed. R. Chorley and P. Haggett (London: Methuen), 361–424.

Hamilton, F. E. Ian, 1970, 'Aspects of spatial behavior in planned economies', *Papers & Proceedings Regional Science Association*, **25**, 86–108.

Hamilton, F. E. Ian., 1971, 'Decision making and industrial location in East Europe', *Transactions and Papers, Institute of British Geographer*, **52**, 77–94.

Homenuck, P., 1969, *Institutional Spatial Decision Making: A Study of the United Steel Warkers of America*, 1936–1966, unpublished Ph.D. dissertation, University of Cincinnati.

Kallal, J., 1969, *Wyoming: the Internal Organization of an Industrial Corporate Region*, unpublished M.A. thesis, University of Wyoming.

Karaska, G. J., 1966, 'Interindustry relations in the Philadelphia economy,' *The East Lakes Geographer*, **2**, 80–96.

Karaska, G. J., 1969, 'Manufacturing linkages in the Philadelphia economy: some evidence of external agglomeration forces,' *Geographical Analysis*, **1**, 354–69.

Keeble, D. E., 1968, 'Models of economic development,' in *Socio-economic Models in Geography*, ed. R. Chorley and P. Haggett (London: Methuen), 243–87.

King, L., 1969, 'The analysis of spatial form and its relation to geographic theory,' *Annals, Association of American Geographers*, **59**, 573–95.

Krumme, G., 1969a, 'Toward a geography of enterprise,' *Economic Geography*, **45**, 30–40.

Krumme, G., 1969b, 'Notes on locational adjustment patterns in industrial geography,' *Geografiska Annaler*, **51B**, 15–19.

Krumme, G., 1970, 'The interregional corporation and the region,' *Tijdschrift voor Economische en Sociale Geografie*, **61**, 318–33.

Loomis, C., 1962, 'Tentative types of directed social change involving systematic linkage,' in *The Planning of Change*, ed. W. Bennis, K. Benne and R. Chin (New York: Holt, Rinehart and Winston), 223–230.

Massam, B. H., 1972, *The Spatial Structure of Administrative Systems*, Commission on College Geography Resource Paper No. 12 (Washington: Association of American Geographers).

McNee, R. B., 1958, 'Functional geography of the firm, with an illustrative case study from the petroleum industry,' *Economic Geography*, **34**, 321–37.

McNee, R. B. 1960a, 'Towards a more humanistic economic geography: the geography of enterprise,' *Tijdschrift voor Economische en Sociale Geografie*, **51**, 201ff.

McNee, R. B., 1960b, 'Processes creating geographic patterns in the managerial economy,' *Annals, Association of American Geographers*, **51**, 336.

McNee, R. B., 1961, 'Centrifugal and centripetal forces in international petroleum company regions,' *Annals, Association of American Geographers*, **51**, 124ff.

McNee, R. B., 1963, 'The spatial evolution of the Sun Oil Company,' *Annals, Association of American Geographers*, **53**, 609.

McNee, R. B., 1964, 'The economic geography of an international petroleum firm,' in *Focus on Geographic Activity, a Collection of Original Studies*, ed. R. Thoman and D. Patton (New York: McGraw–Hill), 98–107.

McNee, R. B., 1970, 'Regional planning, bureaucracy and geography,' *Economic Geography*, **46**, 190ff.

McNee, R. B., 1972, 'An inquiry into the goal or goals of the enterprise: a case study,' *The Professional Geographer*, **24**, 203–20.

Morrill, R. L., 1966, *Migration and the Spread and Growth of Urban Settlement* (Lund).

Pages, M., 1962, 'The socio-therapy of the enterprise,' in *The Planning of Change*, ed. W. Bennis, K. Benne and R. Chin (New York: Holt, Rinehart and Winston), 168–185.

Pahl, R. E., 1968, 'Sociological models in geography,' *Socio-economic Models in Geography*, ed. R. Chorley and P. Haggett (London: Methuen), 217–242.

75

Penrose, E. T., 1959, *The Theory of the Growth of the Firm* (New York: Wiley).

Randall, C. B., 1959, *The Folklore of Management* (New York: Mentor).

Rapaport, A., 1968, 'Foreword,' to *Modern Systems Research for the Behavioral Scientist*, ed. W. Buckley (Chicago: Aldine), xiii–xxii.

Ray, D. M., 1971, 'The location of United States manufacturing subsidiaries in Canada,' *Economic Geography*, **47**, 389–400.

Redlich, F., 1951, 'Innovation in business, a systematic presentation,' *American Journal of Economics and Sociology*, **10**, 285–91.

Rees, J., 1972, 'The industrial corporation and locational analysis,' *Area*, **4**, 199–205.

Schumpter, J. A., 1947, 'The creative response in economic history,' *The Journal of Economic History*, **7**, 149–59.

Selznick, P., 1943, 'An approach to a theory of bureaucracy,' *American Sociological Review*, **8**, 49ff.

Servan-Schreiber, J. J., 1967, *Le Defi Americain* (Paris: Denoel) (later translated as *The American Challenge*).

Smith, D. M., 1970, 'On throwing out Weber with the bathwater: a note on industrial location and linkage,' *Area*, **1**, 15–18.

Stafford, H., 1969, 'An industrial location decision model,' *Proceedings, Association of American Geographers*, **1**, 141–45.

Stafford, H., 1972, 'The geography of manufacturers,' *Progress in Geography*, **4**, 183–215.

Steed, G. P. F., 1968a, 'The changing milieu of a firm,' *Annals, Association of American Geographers*, **58**, 506–525.

Steed, G. P. F., 1968b, 'Commodity flows and interindustry linkages of Northern Ireland's manufacturing industries,' *Tijdschrift voor Economische en Sociale Geografie*, **59**, 345–59.

Steed, G. P. F., 1970, 'Corporate enterprise and the location decision process,' in *The Geographer and Society* (University of Victoria, British Columbia), 160–171.

Steed, G. P. F., 1971a, 'Locational implications of corporate organization of industry,' *Canadian Geographer*, **15**, 54–56.

Steed, G. P. F., 1971b, 'Internal organization, firm integration and locational change: the Northern Ireland linen complex, 1954–1964,' *Economic Geography*, **47**, 371–83.

Steed, G. P. F., 1971c, 'Forms of corporate–environmental Adaptation,' *Tijdschrift voor Economische en Sociale Geografie*, **62**, 90–94.

Steed, G. P. F., 1971d, 'Plant adaptation, firm environments and location analysis,' *The Professional Geographer*, **23**, 324–8.

Steed, G. P. F., 1971e, 'Changing processes of corporate environmental relations,' *Area*, **3**, 207ff.

Steiner, G. A., 1963, *Managerial Long-range Planning*, New York: McGraw–Hill.

Thompson, J. D., 1962, 'Organizational management of conflict,' in *The Planning of Change*, ed. by W. Bennis, K. Benne and R. Chin (New York: Holt, Rinehart and Winston), 451–456.

Townroe, P. M., 1971, *Industrial Location Decisions: A Study in Management Behavior*, (London: Research Publications Services, Ltd.).

Wolpert, J., 1964, 'The decision process in spatial context,' *Annals, Association of American Geographers*, **54**, 536–558.

Wolpert, J., 1970, 'Departures from the usual environment in locational analysis,' *Annals, Association of American Geographers*, **60**, 220–229.

3

Multiple Products, Residuals and Location Theory

WILLIAM B. BEYERS AND GÜNTER KRUMME

Manufacturing geography has remained largely an empirically oriented field and has yet to develop satisfactory linkages with modern theories of production, markets and organization. Geographers have tended either to merely accept the body of industrial location theories developed by economists as given or to reject them on the basis of partiality and an alleged lack of explanatory power (for example, Pred, 1967). Attempts to remedy this situation and to expand and adapt this deductively derived body of theory have only recently become more frequent (Smith, 1971).

There is one significant aspect which the conventional field of manufacturing geography has in common with deductive industrial location and production theory. This is a heavy emphasis on the resource or input side of the production process with relatively little consideration given to the process by which the kind or combination of outputs is determined. Quoting Alexandersson (1967, p. 7), 'Manufacturing industry comprises two main elements, processing of raw materials and assembly of produced parts.' Analogously, in industrial location theory, the optimality problem has been formulated frequently as a minimum weighted-distance problem for a given Leontief-type production function with multiple localized inputs but only single products and a single (competitively structured) market (Weber, 1929). Considerable progress has been made in developing the single-product optimum location model by Predöhl (1925), Isard (1956), Moses (1958), Churchill (1967) and Alonso (1967); these developments have tended to move industrial location theory closer to modern production and price theory, but have still retained the single-product assumption in modelling.

This multi-resource, mono-product approach stands in sharp contrast to the typical multi-process, multi-product firm of modern industry. In view of the fact that increasing size, spatial spread and product diversification of corporations as well as multiple production on the individual plant level seem to be the rule rather than the exception, one would agree that 'no theory which assumes that only one product is in fact produced can have great practical significance' (Coase, 1937, p. 403) and that 'single-product models have been given rather more than due attention in the literature' (Danø, 1966, p. 166).

Industrial location literature has paid brief attention to the multiple-product problem. Weber (1929) treated the multi-product location problem in his agglomeration analysis but did not advance beyond his well-known isodapane-deviation approach. Hoover recognized the locational implications of multiple production patterns and possible substitution between outputs when he stated that 'in many industries, also, it is possible and profitable to vary the proportions in which various products are turned out so as to get more of those products which can be sold more profitably. Oil refineries, for instance, can vary their yields or various grades of refined products in response to changes in relative demand and price' (Hoover, 1948, p. 44). Churchill (1966, pp. 250–53) followed the tradition of many micro-economists and treated the multiple-product problem under 'Limitations [of this analysis] and Future Directions for Research'.

Industrial complex analysis does not consider many of the problems solved in a general equilibrium statement of the multiple products problem. The industrial complex technique is based largely on an extended Weberian framework and is primarily oriented towards developing an accounting system for the empirical analysis of complex industrial location decisions involving non-linear substitution, vertical integration and questions of scale. However, some useful discussions of product-mix interdependencies have been provided by empirical studies of various chemical industries (Isard, 1960).

Simple production models are based on the assumption that firms with a multitude of plants, processes and products could readily be decomposed into separate processes for individual products and that interdependencies between products could be neglected. However, in many industries, products are technologically linked in joint-production processes, or they become alternatives as soon as common capacities are fully utilized. Because of such complementarities and substitutive relationships, 'the multi-product firm cannot legitimately be regarded as a collection of single-product firms' (Pfouts, 1961, p. 651).

Economists treat the multiple-product problem in theory as an extension of the single-product problem. Hicks (1946), Carlson (1956), Frisch (1965) and other production theorists have made important contributions to the contemporary theory of multiple production. A comprehensive statement of the multiple-product problem has been provided by Mauer and Naylor (1964): their formulation is used as a basis for developing a general spatial multiple-product model.

The multiple-product location problem should not be restricted only to marketable outputs in the conventional sense, but should also extend to environmental byproducts: air, water and noise pollutants. Since increasing environmental concern of the general public and regional government is beginning to result in enforcible abatement regulations and pricing schemes for non-abated pollution, a theoretical discussion of environmentally more comprehensive production functions is appropriate (Isard and Liossatos, 1972). Owing to regional dimensions associated with pollution regulations, and spatial characteristics of pollution processes, an integration of environmental output relationships into locational models should then be more than a mere afterthought (Austin, Smith and Wolpert, 1970; Beyers, 1973).

This chapter explores certain theoretical locational characteristics of the multi-product, multi-factor firm. Locational aspects are discussed of possible continuous substitution relationships between products, between products and factors and between factors. Then extended versions of Weberian and Moses' models in situations of joint-production are presented, followed by the development of general optimality conditions on the location of a multi-factor, multi-product plant which produces multiple products of positive value as well as products which have negative effects on the production environment. The essay concludes with a discussion of algorithms and behavioural interpretations which could assist in reaching discrete and realistic solutions to these location problems.

Joint and Multiple Production Relationships

Chamberlin has been a prominent advocate of a more differentiated approach toward decision variables on the output side. Chastising microeconomic theory for its overemphasis on price–quantity relationships in market strategies for 'given products', Chamberlin (1957, p. 114) points out that 'there is literally no such thing as a given product. Products are actually the most volatile things in the economic system—much more so than prices'. Many attributes of products, such as size, quality of fabrication and functional qualities, are variables during the initial process of product specification and can be successively adapted or differentiated in the face of changing market and technological conditions.

Product variation has become increasingly important in business decision-making in the modern world where mass production combines with 'modular' or 'combinatorial' data processing capabilities and production technologies to permit the satisfaction of differentiated consumer demand through 'maximum productive variety' or maximum choice (Starr, 1970, p. 36).

However, one may imagine more or less 'continuous' product spaces from which the variables emerge that eventually determine a specific product. A variety of products may be manufactured side by side in given production processes or a given plant. Thus 'products' must be identified by their physical characteristics or by the way in which entrepreneurs or customers distinguish them. For simplicity, assume that different products are shipped separately to their respective markets; that these separate products may bear different transport rates and differ in their sensitivity to transport costs. The structure of demand for these products is assumed to be given but can be differentiated locationally.

Part of the production problem for the multi-product firm in space is to decide the optimal mix of products and output level of each product. The optimal decision is the one which maximizes profits; both revenue and cost influencing factors must be considered. More specifically, an optimal product-mix will depend on technological possibilities, a variety of inter-product relationships, factor costs, corporate organization and product market characteristics. The locations of product markets and the sources of input factors are important to the multi-product firm seeking the optimal location for its plant. Markets for some products could be quite concentrated while markets for others could be relatively dispersed. Variations in demand and product transportability mean variable influences by particular products on the location selection process. Similar forces operate with respect to input factors.

Rationales Associated with Multi-Product Production

There are many reasons why firms are forced or choose to pursue multi-product production on the plant level. In the simplest case, multi-product output is technologically determined, possibly not giving the entrepreneur even the choice of quantities. Other causes may originate in the spheres of factor procurement, plant operation, the individual production process used, marketing and transport and in the market environment for the products. Whether or not the initial reasons for establishing a multi-product plant were based on product–product relationships in production, such relationships are nevertheless likely to occur when production is concentrated on one site.

Demand Factors Favouring Multi-Product Production

If products manufactured in one plant have independent markets and demand patterns, there may still be a rationale for such production arrangements. Demand for individual products may be small, inaccessible to competitors or in other ways non-competitive, making small-scale production either mandatory or profitable for the monopolist.

Multi-product output may make it feasible for a plant to reach a sufficient threshold size. It may enable the firm to conduct a more flexible price policy (Seidenfus, 1967). Yields from selling individual products (revenues minus space-related costs) are less closely associated with the firm's overall objective function than in the single-product firm. Individual products contribute to, rather than are solely responsible for, profits and coverage of fixed costs. Thus 'margins of profitability' or 'ranges of tolerance' generated by some products may be used to 'support' the pricing strategy for other products so as to increase competitive price-responsiveness, to compensate for the non-optimality of the present location with respect to any one of the firm's products, to overcome temporary price of transport cost fluctuations without loss of markets, or to establish competitiveness in new or geographically distant markets in anticipation of future profitability or locational adjustments. The probability of finding differentiated intensity of competition among output markets probably increases with the range of a firm's product-mix.

To reduce risks, market uncertainty and dependence on any one product, an entrepreneur establishing his first plant may wish to produce more than one product from the very beginning. Limited assets may preclude production of these individual products separately at their respective optimal locations. Moreover, internal economies possibly facilitate plant diversification.

Market Interdependence

Complementary product–product relationships on the demand side are the most plausible factor behind multi-product production with respect to market factors, although competitive relationships may also play a role. Complementarity or competitiveness in a firm's inter-product relationships refers to the interdependence of prices, effective demand and revenues between the respective products. Two products can be called complementary (or competitive) 'when a given output of either product can be sold for marginal revenues which increase (decrease) with the effective demand for the other' (Weldon, 1948, p. 186).

To demonstrate complementary relationships, assume a manufacturer of photo equipment sells his cameras at product-specific marginal costs or less without regard to fixed or joint costs. Assuming that a low price will stimulate the demand for cameras, he anticipates that the expanded complementary demand for high-priced accessory equipment—for which he had experienced a relatively price-inelastic demand in the past—will enlarge overall returns and profits. Use of demand complementarity is a highly effective marketing tool; however, it often requires careful spatial and temporal tuning of the marketing effort to generate the desired effect.

For varied reasons firms may decide to produce 'self-competing' products as long as 'by introducing such new products the firm anticipates that the demand curve appertaining to all existing products in the market(s), including its own, will be shifted backward, with the net effect of increasing the total revenue from its own old and new products' (Lanzilotti, 1954, p. 467). Competitiveness among products can often be avoided or delayed by spatial separation of markets. Newly developed competitive products tend to be introduced first as a competitive response to external competitors in congested market regions regardless of their impact on previous products of the firm. In regions with lesser competition from other producers, the old and proven product may be retained and protected against the new product until its demand has sufficiently slackened. Volkswagen's lagging new-model policy in the United States is an example of this strategy.

Single and Joint Economies of Scale

Suppose that by combining the production of several different products under one plant roof the entrepreneur generates some advantage which he would not achieve by greater plant specialization, even if the same range of product variety is represented on the corporate level of the multi-plant firm. In his aim at achieving scale economies in plant operations, the entrepreneur will have to find an optimal combination of scale economies resulting from specialization and standardization on the one hand and what Robinson called 'economies of massed resources' on the other: 'The large multi-product firm shares with the large standardized firm certain economies which flow from the fact that it is large, employing large numbers of workers, with a large management, buying materials, even, if a little less standardized, on a large scale, dispatching and selling on large scale, raising capital on a large scale, and often able to use and keep busy large units of moderately versatile technical equipment on a variety of comparatively similar jobs' (Robinson, 1956, p. 190).

The equipoise between single and joint production economies will be affected by diverse factors and situations. For example, a firm's management may realize that single-product manufacture of different products in different plants may encounter diseconomies of small scale due to insufficient demand. Another firm may encounter potential diseconomies of large scale in a single product manufacturing process at the same time as it faces the dilemma that such specialized production may be inadequate for efficient plant operation. In both cases, separate production is organizationally and technically possible. However, production under one roof, possibly with additional organizational and technical integration, will yield a more optimal combination of scale economies.

Transport costs may also influence the balance of single and joint scale economies accruing to the individual firm. Joint-production often implies that output quantities of any particular product are relatively small and unable to generate significant scale economies in transport. In oil refining, for example, the volume of saleable products 'is almost as large as the volume of raw materials. This volume...costs rather more to store and to transport than crude does, because it has to be separated in separate tankage and moved in separate containers, generally smaller and less efficient than the means of transport that crude uses' (Hartshorn, 1962, p. 70). Thus, a market location would avoid diseconomies of small scale in transporting outputs (except over short distances), generate scale economies in raw material transport and, possibly, result in some economies of joint production—all compensating for the lack of single-production economies. A raw material location, however, may favour single-product output because of scale economies in both manufacturing and in transporting the single product to its markets. These economies have to compensate for the geographic separation of markets, for the higher freight rate (for outputs rather than raw materials) and for the lack of joint production economies.

Product–Product Relationships in the Production

Product–product (and factor–factor) relationships are embodied in the plant's production functions, including those of its individual processes. Relationships may also exist in the procurement environment which may influence the rate of utilization of substitutable inputs. The nature and cost of transportation, communication, warehousing, marketing and other space-related costs associated with assembling factor inputs at a specific location and distributing outputs to their respective markets are also of interests.

Figure 3.1 attempts to illustrate some of these relationships on the corporate level where there may be several plants. Each plant may produce several different outputs, and some of the output from one plant of the firm may be utilized in another plant of the same firm. Such corporate vertical integration is well illustrated in the aluminium industry where aluminium

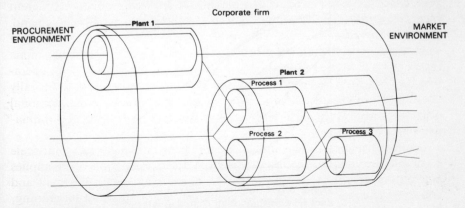

Figure 3.1. Product flows and relationships of the corporate firm.

84

producers tend to control raw material sources, refining plants for raw ores, reduction plants for refined ore and fabricating plants for reduced aluminium metal. Figure 3.1 also suggests that within a plant there may be separate stages of production in which outputs may be utilized by forward-linked stages of production in the same plant or, alternatively, shipped to other plants of the firm or sold in the market. In the pulp and paper industry, for example, the pulping process frequently not only supplies pulp for paper production in the same plant but also produces saleable pulp for paper manufacture in other plants.

Technical product–product interdependence may exist only in one sphere of plant operations (e.g., acquisition of inputs, joint use of a specific facility) or over a wider range of functions and processes. Also, inter-product relationships can be either organizational or technological. All products which are interdependent as the result of a given state of technology are linked by a single multi-product production function independent of technical production functions for other products. Additionally, products may be organizationally linked outside and between the sphere of technical production functions on the plant level.

Technically conditioned product–product relationships may be 'competitive' or 'substitutive' in the use of given resources if the output of one product can be increased only by sacrificing some amount of the other product (Heady, 1952, p. 204). Thus, production conditions for the second product may deteriorate, i.e., its marginal costs may increase as a result of the increase in output of the first product (Stackelberg, 1952, p. 70). The rate of substitution can be decreasing, constant or increasing, giving transformation curves which are, for any given resource level, convex,

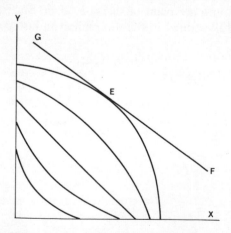

Figure 3.2. Competitive product–product relationships with changing rates of substitution.

linear or concave to the origin (Figure 3.2). For different levels of resource use, the production function may indicate different kinds of substitutive relationships; convex transformation curves close to the origin at low levels of operation due to dominant single-product scale economies might turn into concave curves with increasing input levels as joint production economies outweigh the benefits of specialization. In his graphic analysis of multiple production, Cady (1950) shows that isorevenue and transformation curves may occur in a variety of geometric configurations. Conditions may be as in Figure 3.2, where a concave transformation function is tangent to a competitive isorevenue function FG at point E. Efficient tangency conditions are also possible in more complex demand conditions. However, assuming competitive market conditions and linear isorevenue curves, we can ignore all but the concave case (or the competitive range of a transformation curve with increasing rates of substitution) for which the following explanations can be listed (Heady, 1952).

Concavity may result from diminishing marginal productivity in factor–product relationships with the supply of certain other resources held constant. As such, it may be a relatively short-run phenomenon. Thus, if we assume that certain locational commitments have been made and the use of certain resources decided upon, further shifts of resources between products would be limited. Even in the long run, when (almost) all factors of production are variable between products, diminishing returns for each product are possible due to certain technological inevitabilities or a variety of congestion phenomena on the firm level.

Non-homogeneity in resource quality may also result in product–product relationships with increasing rates of substitution. A plant's potential local labour force may be highly differentiated by education and skills and thus better be adapted to multiple production than a single, specialized activity which might suffer from shortages of a particular skill at least in expansion. Similarly, raw material quality (for example, hides and skins for the leather industry) may vary widely (and among locations) while the quality mix may change over time and possibly be difficult to predict. Thus, a multiproduct tanning and processing programme which is adjustable to different qualities will, *ceteris paribus,* be superior to a single-product activity which has to utilize or dispose of a relatively large proportion of unsuitable grades (Gutenberg, 1967).

A third reason for a concave transformation curve emerges from uneven employment and capital utilization patterns of different products through time. Seasonal employment, for example, may result in non-competitive (supplementary) relationships between a plant's two products throughout part of the year and in competitive overlaps during the rest of the year. Product substitutability will thus exist along the transitional, concave range of the transformation curve (where both products compete for the same resources) between the vertical and horizontal, supplementary ranges.

The same applies basically for changes in resource requirements during partially overlapping product life cycles in individual plants.

In addition to competitive relationships, we can identify (retaining the assumption of given inputs):

(1) 'Supplementary' product–product relationships which are characterized by the possibility of increasing the manufacture of one product without repercussions on the manufacture of the other. Suplementary relationships are likely to occur in combination with competitive relationships (with decreasing rates of substitution), each kind occupying a certain range of the transformation curve (Heady, 1952, p. 233).

(2) Inter-product relationships which are 'complementary' in the use of given resources when the increase in the output of the product cannot be accomplished without also increasing that of the other product, i.e. production conditions improve and marginal costs diminish for the second product as output of the first is increased (Stackelberg, 1952, p. 70). Resource constraint means that complementarity can occur only over a limited range before the relationship turns into a supplementary and competitive relationship.

The fixed product–product relationship is characterized by a single combination of products for any given resource level. The transformation curve is reduced to a point, no substitution being possible; both products must be produced and price relationships and comparative transport costs have no impact on the production mix.

Factorially Determined Multi-Product Production

The relationships discussed hitherto specified the type of flexibility which may (or may not) exist once the level and the proportions of resources are determined. The variability among products discussed now will not be conditioned by an adaptability of output *per se* but will rather depend on the influence which variations in factor levels and proportions may have on the product-mix. Once quantities of each of the factors are specified, the quantities of each of the outputs are also determined. These product quantities are then given functions of either the *same* factor quantities, as in the case of 'complete coupling' relationships, or of (to an extent) *separable* factor quantities (i.e., different quantities of the same factors).[1] Four cases can be distinguished:

(1) Variations in factor quantities (with given proportions) (a) may or (b) may not lead to changes in the product-mix (although the total level of output increases).

(2) Variations in factor proportions either (a) may or (b) may not lead to changes in product proportions.

The two cases listed under (a) thus identify adjustment possibilities (e.g., to changing market-related location conditions) where direct adjustments of the product-mix without recourse to the input side is not possible or feasible. Cases listed under (b) specify product-mixes which are not affected by changes in either resource quantities or proportions. Cases (1a), (1b) and (2b) represent coupling relationships leading in (1b) and (2b) to linear 'product coupling curves'. Case (2a) specifies the situation of (isoquant-) separability while in (1a) the product-mix varies with the level of operation.

A variety of special cases arise only one of which should be mentioned here. Individual outputs may be more or less directly related to inputs. Gas output, for example, may be directly related to factor quantities while the coke and tar output is a technical function of gas output (Frisch, 1965, p. 271).

Factor–factor relationships have been discussed in the literature in an almost identical fashion to product–product relationships. A detailed presentation will not be given here, therefore. Among factor–factor relationships with constant output characteristics, the substitutive relationships with a decreasing rate of technical substitution (represented by convex isoquants) has the same analytical significance as the substitutive relationships among products underlying the concave transformation (or isofactor) curve. Allowing for variability in output quantities of the individual products, the multi-product plant may or may not, under conditions similar to those discussed above, lead to changes in factor proportions. Thus, there is also the extreme case where individual inputs of a multi-product plant may be associated with either entirely separable or totally overlapping transformation curves. In the latter case, a variation of output combinations will not affect required inputs, whereas in the former, the optimal input combination will change with changing output-mix.

Merging the input and output considerations for the multi-factor, multi-product firm we could identify a large variety of possible production functions covering all possible factor–factor and product–product relationships. Now, the equivalent extreme situations would range from a production function with constant input and output coefficients on the one hand to a continuous substitution production function on the other. The latter would have the following characteristics:

(1) All factor–factor combinations could be represented by convex isoquants and all product–product combinations by concave transformation curves.

(2) All factor–product relationships would have a decreasing marginal productivity.

(3) Any specific factor combination would correspond to a specific transformation curve indicating all possible product combinations, and any specific product-mix would correspond to a specific isoquant reflecting all possible input combinations for producing this product-mix.

(4) Individual products are associated with separable sets of isoquants

and individual factors with separable sets of transformation curves (Hicks, 1946).

Ready examples for production processes allowing for 'continuous substitution' are supplied by the refining processes in the oil industry. On the input side, crude oils are differentiated not just by their spatial origins (fields) but also by their composition (e.g., paraffin-based and asphalt-based crudes; different impurities, such as sulphur). One generally refers to 'light Saharan oil' and 'heavy Venezuelan crudes'. On the output side, a variety of final product categories (e.g., gasoline, kerosene, fuel oil) are marketed in all industrialized regions, but in significantly different proportions. Consumption patterns differ between geographical markets and depend in part on levels of economic development, the significance of other energy sources and the importance of the aeroplane or the automobile as a means of transportation.

As a result of highly flexible refining processes, different crudes favour but do not rigidly determine certain output combinations. 'A wide range of conversion processes have been developed to convert those [products] of which [the refiner] gets more than he can sell into those of which he cannot get enough to satisfy the market' (Hartshorn, 1962, p. 67). Whether or not individual processes have this high degree of flexibility with respect to a response to different or changing demand requirements is not as important in this context as the fact that these processes can be differently combined to process sequences yielding products of different characteristics.

Residuals and Pollution

Most manufacturing processes produce residual materials and primary products which may be a class of factorially determined products of zero or negative value (Førsund, 1972). Primary products are those outputs which principally govern the location and production decision-making process. Residual products, such as sulphur produced in copper smelting, may also be sold (under certain conditions) and could be considered as a product subject to the same market forces as 'primary' products. Frequently, however, residuals either are not produced in locations where they can be marketed or are not captured in the production process in a marketable form.

Thus, there are differences in what should be considered 'joint-production' from a technical and an economic point of view and, one may add, from a locational point of view, depending on whether or not a technical joint product can be sold at a positive price (Danø, 1966). In situations (or at locations) where these byproducts cannot yield a positive price, the firm must dispose of residuals either in liquid form discharged into sewers and water bodies or as emissions into the atmosphere.

In many locations, the (nearly) costless traditional methods of disposal can longer be utilized; alternative disposal methods involve costs which become of importance theoretically in a manner similar to the cost of transpost or material inputs. For example, we could visualize in Figure 3.1 that process 3 in plant 2 is treating residuals produced in process 2 and that portions of these residuals would ultimately end up in the environment as useful products, as solid wastes or as pollutants. Transport costs of moving residuals to a disposal station can be treated just like other transport costs. However, environmental quality constraints, frequently part of a regional air or water quality programmes, also have spatial dimensions since it is the mutual contribution of spatially separated sources of residuals that must be controlled in an abatement programme. A decentralized plant may possibly emit a larger amount of residuals than one which is located close to a pollution monitoring station, to population concentrations or to other emitters, particularly since the absorptive capacity of the environment is limited in any specific location in space.

However, residual outputs are not always clearly identifiable as resulting from the production process of a particular plant. In these cases, externalities resulting from residuals discharges may enter the local social-cost function in a multiplicative rather than an additive manner and, thus, are not separate from the externalities created by discharges from other plants (Davis and Whinston, 1952, p. 252). Given local pollution standards, the optimal decision of one decision-maker with respect to his optimal level of production and combination of inputs and outputs including pollution outputs will depend on how other polluters might act or react. Davis and Whinston (1962, p. 255) have suggested game-theoretic approaches to this interdependence problem, but they conclude that 'non-separable externalities raise the possibility of non-existence of equilibrium'.

The relationship between production of residual products, the level of production of particular primary products and the rates and technology of utilization of particular factors is very complex in most production situations. However, one can safely assume that for most processes the rate of residual product output is positively associated with the output level of one or more primary products and the utilization levels of particular input factors in given production processes.

Although direct substitutive relationships between primary products and residuals (unless they carry a positive price) would fall into an inefficient range of the production possibility curve, substitution may be possible where primary products are linked by competitive relationships and where residuals are associated with specific primary products. The same holds for the use of inputs. The occurrence of pollution or residuals may be linked to specific inputs and thus could possibly be reduced (or increased) through input substitution. Similarly, cross-substitution elasticities between inputs and outputs in a continuous production function may be effectively used to

90

adjust pollution levels if pollution is specifically associated with one of the factors or products.

A Reinterpretation of Some Location Models

In order to introduce these production relationships into a locational framework, one must return initially to Weberian formulations and their derivatives. Weber (1929) visualized his 'transport orientation' model as being capable of extension to multiple-product situations: 'The locational figure which results has several components of consumption, their number depending upon the number of kinds of products. These components must be weighted corresponding to the kinds of products. That is all' (Weber, 1929, p. 197). Input factors would produce a constant mix of output analogous to the treatment of raw materials in the single-market Weber problem.

Weberian analysis does not admit substitution in a general manner. Isard (1956), following the suggestion by Predöhl (1925), reinterpreted location determination as a substitution problem but restricted his substitution analysis to 'transport inputs'. He did not admit general substitution among material inputs and retained the rigid technically predetermined, non-substitutable production function which underlies Weber's triangular analysis.

Moses (1958) presented the first explicit exposition of Predöhl's proposition in a more general substitution framework with regard to factor inputs and a single product market. Suppose we use Moses's analytical tools but alter certain definitions and suggest a multi-product (multi-market) one-input situation. In Figure 3.3, let M_1 and M_2 refer to markets, M_1 for product 1, M_2 for product 2. Let V refer to the single source of the localized factor used in producing M_1 and M_2. The arc IJ is a fixed distance from V.

Following Moses's assumptions, let us assume that the transport rate for the products is a known constant per unit of distance. Market prices for the products are also given and the producer is familiar with the rate of product

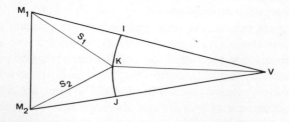

Figure 3.3. The Moses' general substitution framework.

transformation in relation to the input factor. A producer located anywhere along the arc IJ is assumed to receive net-revenues after deduction of transport cost for the shipment of the products to their respective markets M_1 and M_2. The underlying relationships can be defined as follows:

$$P'_1 = P_1 - r_1 s_1$$
$$P'_2 = P_2 - r_2 s_2,$$

where: P'_1 and P'_2 are the f.o.b. prices of products 1 and 2 respectively; P_1 and P_2 are the delivered prices of products 1 and 2 respectively, r_1 and r_2 are the transport rates on products 1 and 2 respectively; s_1 and s_2 are the distances from M_1 to K and M_2 to K respectively.

The ratio of these f.o.b. prices defines the slope of the system of iso-revenue functions for production at K. As the location of K is varied along the arc IJ this slope will change. These relationships are portrayed in Figure 3.4 where the iso-revenue function AB refers to location at I, while the iso-revenue function DE refers to location at J. In between I and J, there is a system of iso-revenue functions associated with motion along the arc IJ. These locational iso-revenue functions can be generalized in a manner similar to that described by Moses for iso-outlay functions. In Figure 3.4, the locus of optimal points corresponding to the points along the arc IJ in Figure 3.3 is shown as arc AFE.[2] A system of production possibility functions for products M_1 and M_2 also exists, and arc GH in Figure 3.4 is one of these functions. The production possibility curve which is tangential to the locational iso-revenue function AFE (at point F in Figure 3.4) indicates the optimum level of production of products M_1 and M_2 for the particular level of revenue implied by arc AFE. The tangency point F also indicates the optimal location along arc IJ with respect to this level of revenue. This system can be extended to consider many levels of revenue and output for any given arc IJ. In addition, various arc-distances from V must be considered, along with cost factors, in the process of arriving at an optimal location and production solution for this problem.[3]

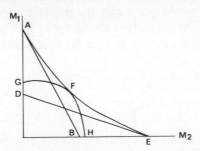

Figure 3.4. The slope of the system of iso–revenue functions for production at K.

Finally, Weber's treatment of the agglomeration problem could be interpreted as focusing on joint production. He argues that spatially 'joint' production occurs whenever the agglomeration savings exceed the increased transport costs resulting from a deviation from the single-product minimum transport cost location. Weber (1929, Chapter 5) discusses the role of plant size in allowing the existence of economies in the purchase of physical factors, labour, physical capital, and in marketing and management costs.

A Multi-Product Multi-Factor Model of Location

Limitations to such graphic analysis of general optimizing procedures in space and of along continuously substitutable production functions, require algebraic development of a more general substitution framework. Initially assumptions were stated by Mauer and Naylor (1964, p. 38): 'The objective of the firm is to maximize profit subject to the technical constraints imposed by its production function.' The latter is assumed to be continuous (with non-zero first and second order partial derivatives), relating independent factor variables to the independent product variables. These relationships have been predetermined by a set of technical decisions by the firm's engineers. The 'production function is characterized by: a decreasing marginal product for all product–factor combinations; and an increasing marginal rate of product transformation between any two products.' Factors and products are perfectly divisible and their prices are known. Neither these 'prices ... nor the parameters which determine the firm's production function will change over the time period which is being considered', nor are they 'permitted to be random variables'.

To introduce a spatial dimension into this model, assume that there is a cost associated with the movement of each factor or product and that these cost functions conform to the assumptions stated above. In addition, the space-related costs for a given factor or product are assumed to be a function of the distance between the plant and the product market or factor source location, as well as of the quantity of the factor or product shipped. We shall refer to these space-related costs as transfer costs, which include transport and communications costs.

These relationships are as follows. The product–factor transformation function is given as:

$$Q = Q(X_1, \ldots, X_i, \ldots, X_m, X_{m+1}, \ldots, X_j \ldots, X_n) = 0 \qquad (1)$$

where $X_i \geq 0$ are products and $X_j \geq 0$ are factors quantities.

The total cost function and total revenue function are denoted as C and R:

$$C = C(X_{m+1}, \ldots, X_j, \ldots, X_n, T_{m+1}, \ldots, T_j, \ldots, T_n) \qquad (2)$$

$$R = R(X_1, \ldots, X_i, \ldots, X_m, T_1, \ldots, T_m) \tag{3}$$

where T_i and T_j represent transfer costs for products and factors respectively. Costs associated with the purchase of factors at the site of the supplier (f.o.b.) are denoted as $C(X_{m+1}, \ldots X_j, \ldots X_n)$. The revenues obtained at the site of the product market are denoted as $R(X_1, \ldots, X_i, \ldots X_m)$ and, following conventional location theory, we assume that the producer of these products obtains payment for the sale of his products net of the transfer costs on their distribution. Thus, R is a net revenue function which defines the revenue obtained at the (optimal) location for the plant.

One can now proceed to identify the optimizing conditions for the plant. Assume that the plant wishes to maximize profits, π:

$$\pi = R - C \tag{4}$$

Profit maximization is constrained by the production function, Q.
Following the method of Lagrange, we form the auxiliary function Z:

$$Z = R - C + \lambda_1 Q(X_i, X_j) \tag{5}$$

where λ_1 is the Lagrangian multiplier.

Partial derivatives of the function Z with respect to the variables associated with equation 5 define the necessary conditions for profit maximization:

$$\frac{\partial Z}{\partial X_i} = \frac{\partial R}{\partial X_i} + \frac{\partial R}{\partial T_i}\frac{\partial T_i}{\partial X_i} + \lambda_1 \frac{\partial Q}{\partial X_i} = 0 \qquad i = 1, \ldots, m \tag{6}$$

$$\frac{\partial Z}{\partial X_j} = -\frac{\partial C}{\partial X_j} - \frac{\partial C}{\partial T_j}\frac{\partial T_j}{\partial X_j} + \lambda_1 \frac{\partial Q}{\partial X_j} = 0 \qquad j = m+1, \ldots, n \tag{7}$$

$$\frac{\partial Z}{\partial \lambda_1} = Q(X_i, X_j) = 0 \qquad \begin{matrix}(i = 1, \ldots, m) \\ (j = m+1 \ldots, n)\end{matrix} \tag{8}$$

If we define L^* as the optimal location for the plant, then we can state the location optimality conditions as:

$$\frac{\partial Z}{\partial L^*} = \sum_{i=1}^{m} \frac{\partial R}{\partial T_i}\frac{\partial T_i}{\partial X_i} - \sum_{j=m+1}^{n} \frac{\partial C}{\partial T_j}\frac{\partial T_j}{\partial X_j} = 0 \tag{9}$$

Transfer costs on products or factors, T_i and T_j respectively, could be defined as follows:

$$T_i = t_i d_{iL^*} X_i \tag{10}$$

$$T_j = t_j d_{jL^*} X_j \tag{11}$$

where t_i, t_j = transport rates per unit distance per unit of product i or factor j hauled
X_i and X_j = respectively the (optimal) amounts of products i being produced, and input factors j being utilized

d_{iL^*}, d_{jL^*} = the distances respectively between markets and factor locations and the optimal plant location, L^{*4}

In a cartesian coordinate system these distances would be:

$$d_{iL^*} = [(x_i - x^*)^2 + (y_i - y^*)^2]^{1/2} \qquad (12)$$

$$d_{jL^*} = [(x_j - x^*)^2 + (y_j - y^*)^2]^{1/2} \qquad (13)$$

where (x_i, y_i) = location of market of product i
(x_j, y_j) = location of source of input factor j
(x^*, y^*) = optimum location for the plant

If one considers transport costs to be of the form just stated, then optimality conditions for the location (x^*, y^*) are given as:

$$\frac{\partial Z}{\partial x^*} = \sum_{i=1}^{m} \frac{r_i X_i (x_i - x^*)}{d_{iL^*}} - \sum_{j=m+1}^{m} \frac{r_j X_j (x_j - x^*)}{d_{jL^*}} = 0 \qquad (14)$$

$$\frac{\partial Z}{\partial y^*} = \sum_{i=1}^{m} \frac{r_i X_i (y_i - y^*)}{d_{iL^*}} - \sum_{j=m+1}^{n} \frac{r_j X_j (y_j - y^*)}{d_{jL^*}} = 0 \qquad (15)$$

These conditions resemble the well-known optimization of the Weber problem as stated by Kuhn and Kuenne (1962). However, in the problem being developed here, the levels of X_i and X_j are not predetermined as in the Weber problem. Later in this paper approaches are suggested to the solution of the values X_i, X_j and the optimal location.

It is now necessary to develop the optimality conditions for relationships between products, between factors and between a product and a factor, and to interpret the conditions on optimality stated as equations (6) and (7).

First consider a product–product relationship by looking at any two partials of Z with respect to X_i, $i = (1, \ldots, i, \ldots m)$. Subscripts A and B refer to these two products. From equation (6) we have:

$$\frac{\partial R}{\partial X_A} + \frac{\partial R}{\partial T_A} \frac{\partial T_A}{\partial X_A} + \lambda_1 \frac{\partial Q}{\partial X_A} = 0 \qquad (16)$$

$$\frac{\partial R}{\partial X_B} + \frac{\partial R}{\partial T_B} \frac{\partial T_B}{\partial X_B} + \lambda_1 \frac{\partial Q}{\partial X_B} = 0 \qquad (17)$$

Rearranging and solving for λ_1, we obtain:

$$\lambda_1 = -\frac{\dfrac{\partial R}{\partial X_A} - \dfrac{\partial R}{\partial T_A} \dfrac{\partial T_A}{\partial X_A}}{\dfrac{\partial Q}{\partial X_A}} = -\frac{\dfrac{\partial R}{\partial X_B} - \dfrac{\partial R}{\partial T_B} \dfrac{\partial T_B}{\partial X_B}}{\dfrac{\partial Q}{\partial X_B}} \qquad (18)$$

or:

$$\frac{\dfrac{\partial R}{\partial X_A} + \dfrac{\partial R}{\partial T_A}\dfrac{\partial T_A}{\partial X_A}}{\dfrac{\partial R}{\partial X_B} + \dfrac{\partial R}{\partial T_B}\dfrac{\partial T}{\partial X_B}} = \frac{\dfrac{\partial Q}{\partial X_A}}{\dfrac{\partial Q}{\partial X_B}} \tag{19}$$

The right-hand side of equation (19) defines the marginal rate of product transformation and can therefore be rewritten as $-\dfrac{\partial X_B}{\partial X_A}$. The left-hand side of the equation represents the ratio of the marginal revenues of the two products, considered at the location of the plant after the deduction of transfer costs. In Figure 3.2 this relationship is indicated by the tangency point E, and the iso-revenue function GF is defined as the (iso-)revenue obtainable at the optimal plant location. Thus one can say that, at the optimal level of output, the ratio of the marginal revenue of products A and B at the producer's location must be equal to the marginal rate of transformation for the two products.

Now let us look at the relations between two factors. One may consider any two partials of Z with respect to the decision variables j, $j = (m + 1, \dots, j, \dots n)$. From equation (7) we obtain these relations, and solving for λ_1, we have:

$$\lambda_1 = \frac{\dfrac{\partial C}{\partial X_D} + \dfrac{\partial C}{\partial T_D}\dfrac{\partial T_D}{\partial X_D}}{\dfrac{\partial Q}{\partial X_D}} = \frac{\dfrac{\partial C}{\partial X_E} + \dfrac{\partial C}{\partial T_E}\dfrac{\partial T_E}{\partial X_E}}{\dfrac{\partial Q}{\partial X_E}} \tag{20}$$

In equation (20), subscripts D and E refer to the two factors. By rearrangement and substitution, we obtain:

$$\frac{\dfrac{\partial C}{\partial X_D} + \dfrac{\partial C}{\partial T_D}\dfrac{\partial T_D}{\partial X_D}}{\dfrac{\partial C}{\partial X_E} + \dfrac{\partial C}{\partial T_E}\dfrac{\partial T_E}{\partial X_E}} = -\frac{\partial X_E}{\partial X_D} \tag{21}$$

The left-hand side of equation (21) can be considered the ratio of the marginal delivered costs of the two factors, while the right hand side defines the marginal rate of substitution between factors D and E.

The point H in Figure 3.5 represents the optimality condition. The line FG represents an isoquant, while the line AB represents an iso-cost line of the delivered costs of quantities of factors D and E in the amount represented by point H. Of course, a family of isoquant and iso-cost functions exist for factors X_D and X_E such that an expansion path could be defined for this system.

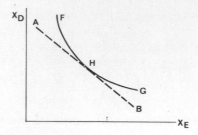

Figure 3.5. The optimality of factor–factor relationships.

Now consider the relationship between a product, A, and a factor, D. Letting A represent a product in equation (6) and D represent a factor in equation (7), by rearranging we can define λ_1 as:

$$\lambda_1 = - \frac{\left[\dfrac{\partial R}{\partial X_A} + \dfrac{\partial R}{\partial T_A} \dfrac{\partial T_A}{\partial X_A} \right]}{\dfrac{\partial Q}{\partial X_A}} = \frac{\left[\dfrac{\partial C}{\partial X_D} + \dfrac{\partial C}{\partial T_D} \dfrac{\partial T_D}{\partial X_D} \right]}{\dfrac{\partial C}{\partial X_D}} \tag{22}$$

By further rearrangement and substitution, we obtain:

$$\left[\frac{\partial C}{\partial X_D} + \frac{\partial C}{\partial T_D} \frac{\partial T_D}{\partial X_D} \right] = \left[\frac{\partial R}{\partial X_A} + \frac{\partial R}{\partial T_A} \frac{\partial T_A}{\partial X_A} \right] \frac{\partial X_A}{\partial X_D} \tag{23}$$

This relationship may be interpreted as saying that the marginal delivered cost of factor D must equal to the marginal revenue product of product A with respect to factor D. In this case the marginal revenue is a net value for product A after deduction of its transfer costs, while the marginal cost of factor D includes its transfer costs.

From equations (18), (20) and (22) it can be seen that the Lagrange multiplier λ_1 assumes a special role in the definition of optimality conditions. Substitution of appropriate values for λ_1 into equations (6) and (7) allows us to interpret these equations as the marginal revenue and cost conditions for profit maximization with respect to each product and factor. These equations also show that transfer costs enter into all of the necessary conditions for profit maximization in the multi-product, multi-factor model developed in this chapter.

Churchill (1966) defines similar relations in a very general way, while not formally specifying the conditions for optimization. But Churchill developed his model for a *given* point in space and sequentially evaluated a set of points in a grid to find the locational optimum within the set. This approach contrasts with the continuous view of space adopted in the model developed here, in which locational optimization is considered equivalent with other variables evaluated in the overall profit maximization problem. Thus, Churchill does not develop general location optimality conditions similar to those expressed in equations (14) and (15).

An Extended Model Including Residuals

In specific production situations an increase in the level of production leads to a simultaneous expansion of the output of 'coupled' products. Residual products which were already discussed as examples of coupled products shall now be introduced into our framework.[5]

Let us denote residuals as X_r and assume that X_r is subject to increasing production with respect to factors and products, i.e.,

$$\frac{\partial X_r}{\partial X_i} > 0, \ \frac{\partial X_r}{\partial X_j} > 0$$

A waste production function can be defined as:

$$X_r = X_r(X_i, X_j) \tag{24}$$

One can visualize that as X_r enters the common property environment it may become considered a pollutant. The pollution production function associated with this situation could be characterized as:

$$P = P(X_p^*, X_r, T_{rp}, X_L) = 0 \tag{25}$$

In this function X_L and T_{rp} serve to control the level of pollution at the place where pollution is measured. If we define X_p^* as a standard to be achieved and X_p as some possible level of pollution at the monitoring place, then we require that $X_p^* \geq X_p$. One must assume that X_L is an abatement good and further assume that:

$$\frac{\partial X_r}{\partial X_L} < 0$$

T_{rp} is a transfer function which relates emission of X_r at the optimal plant location L^*, and the pollution resulting at the place where X_p^* is measured. We assume that:

$$\frac{\partial X_p}{\partial T_{rp}} < 0 \text{ and } \frac{\partial X_p}{\partial X_r} > 0.$$

Assume further that there is a cost associated with the purchase of X_L for the disposal of X_r. Hence, the cost function becomes extended:

$$\bar{C} = \bar{C}(X_j, T_j, X_L) \tag{26}$$

If P acts as an additional constraint on the profit maximization process. Thus, our Lagrangian function becomes $\overline{Z}$:

$$\overline{Z} = R - \overline{C} + \lambda_1 Q + \lambda_2 P = 0 \tag{27}$$

Taking partial derivatives of $\overline{Z}$ with respect to the arguments of the problem, and setting them equal to zero, we can solve for λ_2:

$$\lambda_2 = \frac{\dfrac{\partial \overline{C}}{\partial X_L}}{\dfrac{\partial P}{\partial X_L}}, \tag{28}$$

which may be interpreted as the marginal cost of pollution reduction. These costs will enter into the marginality conditions on profits.

The locational optimality conditions may be expressed as follows:

$$\frac{\partial \overline{Z}}{\partial L^*} = \sum_i^m \frac{\partial R}{\partial T_i} - \sum_{j=m+1}^n \frac{\partial \overline{C}}{\partial T_j} + \lambda_2 \frac{\partial X_p}{\partial T_{rp}} = 0 \tag{29}$$

The first n-terms of equation (29) are similar to equation (9); the last term, however, defines the costs associated with the required pollution abatement activity.

The marginal cost of pollution reduction is λ_2 and one may interpret

$$\frac{\partial P}{\partial T_{rp}}$$

as the change in pollution with respect to the change in the transfer function T_{rp}. If the pollutant is subject to dilution with respect to distance then the distance the plant is located from the place where p is measured will influence the costs of abatement. *Ceteris paribus*, if T_{rp} increases, then the cost influence of a pollution standard X_p^* will diminish because an increase in T_{rp} would decrease X_p. If X_p^* was considered as a standard to be met by a producer at L^*, then an increase in T_{rp} would decrease residual disposal costs. However, equation (29) tells us that the plant must locate *ceteris paribus* so that the combination of transfer costs and abatement costs are minimized. This condition is rather straightforward and a simple example may help us visualize the relationship. Assume that a producer engages in a noisy production process. The producer could install noise control equipment such as soundproofing and locate where transfer costs are minimized, or he can deviate from the transfer cost minimum location and achieve a reduction in soundproofing costs as a result. All other things equal he will locate where the sum of these costs is minimized (Beyers, 1973).

We will now set forth the inter-product and inter-factor optimality conditions for the extended model. Following procedures described earlier, product relations may be defined as follows:

$$\frac{\left[\dfrac{\partial R}{\partial X_A} + \dfrac{\partial R}{\partial T_A}\dfrac{\partial T_A}{\partial X_A} + Mc_p\dfrac{\partial P}{\partial X_r}\dfrac{\partial X_r}{\partial X_A}\right]}{\left[\dfrac{\partial R}{\partial X_B} + \dfrac{\partial R}{\partial T_B}\dfrac{\partial T_B}{\partial X_B} + Mc_p\dfrac{\partial P}{\partial X_r}\dfrac{\partial X_r}{\partial X_B}\right]} = -\frac{\partial X_B}{\partial X_A} \tag{30}$$

This equation states that at the optimal level of output the marginal rate of product transformation is equal to the ratio of the marginal revenue of the products, net of marginal transfer costs to the market locations and net of the marginal costs of residual disposal attributable to the production of these products.

Factor–factor relations are defined by the following formulation:

$$\frac{\left[\dfrac{\partial C}{\partial X_D} + \dfrac{\partial C}{\partial T_D}\dfrac{\partial T_D}{\partial X_D} - Mc_p\dfrac{\partial P}{\partial X_r}\dfrac{\partial X_r}{\partial X_D}\right]}{\left[\dfrac{\partial C}{\partial X_E} + \dfrac{\partial C}{\partial T_E}\dfrac{\partial T_E}{\partial X_E} - Mc_p\dfrac{\partial P}{\partial X_r}\dfrac{\partial X_r}{\partial X_E}\right]} = -\frac{\partial X_E}{\partial X_D} \tag{31}$$

Equation (31) states that at the optimal levels of factor utilization the marginal rate of technical substitution is equal to the ratio of the marginal delivered cost of factor D plus the marginal costs of residual disposal associated with the use of factor D, with respect to the marginal delivered cost of factor E plus the marginal cost of residual disposal associated with the use of factor E.

The marginal revenue product–marginal factor cost relationship in this model can be defined as:

$$\frac{\partial C}{\partial X_D} + \frac{\partial C}{\partial T_D}\frac{\partial T_D}{\partial X_D} + Mc_p\frac{\partial P}{\partial X_r}\frac{\partial X_r}{\partial X_D}$$

$$= \left[\frac{\partial R}{\partial X_A} + \frac{\partial R}{\partial T_A}\frac{\partial T_A}{\partial X_A} - Mc_p\frac{\partial P}{\partial X_r}\frac{\partial X_r}{\partial X_A}\right]\frac{\partial X_A}{\partial X_D} \tag{32}$$

Equation (32) tells us that the marginal delivered costs of factor D plus the marginal residual disposal costs of factor D's usage must be equal to the marginal revenue product of factor D, with the marginal revenue being evaluated net of marginal transfer and residual disposal costs on product A.

The optimality conditions expressed in equations (30), (31) and (32) can be seen to be similar to equations (19), (21) and (23), with the addition of the marginal residual disposal cost terms. These residual disposal costs may influence the slopes of iso-revenue and iso-cost functions, in such a way that the mix of products and factors may be altered from our earlier formulation.

Some Interpretations of Solutions

These models are developed within the static theory framework, relying heavily upon the assumption that decision-makers have perfect knowledge about the variables contained in our models and act according to the principles set forth. These formulations are more complex than traditional location theory and yet may be more representative of actual industrial acitivities than single-product locational models with limited substitution opportunities. From the viewpoint of locational search and selection of factor and product combinations, reality tends to be less complex than is implied by continuous location and production substitutability. Heterogeneous spatial conditions, standardized products, production processes and operating procedures significantly constrain substitutability. Alternative locations and production possibilities tend to be discrete rather than continuous variables, or at least such alternatives will tend to emerge and be decided upon early or at least sequentially during the investment decision-making process (Nishioka and Krumme, 1973).

The emphasis on normative modelling does not preclude us from making behavioural interpretations. In fact, preference for a more 'adaptive' approach to the problem of locational optimization is reinforced by the lack of direct solutions to the theoretical location problem. This adaptive interpretation is aided by the existence of iterative solution techniques which involve analytical search processes and by the greater realism of sequential decision processes which do not require the complex coordination procedures of simultaneous decisions. Organizational search procedures, according to Cyert and March (1963, p. 121ff), tend to be 'simple minded' and biased heavily toward neighbourhood searches and searches along continuous performance functions rather than radical shifts. Through stepwise adaptive behaviour the decision-maker approaches the optimality conditions defined by traditional theory, but he may never actually reach them.

There is no *a priori* reason to believe in the coincidence between optima selected by normative and adaptive procedures, but this does not mean that a decision-maker may not find 'his' absolute profit maximum through a stepwise procedure. A 'local' optimum may either be optimal in view of the cost of search extensions of it may be fully satisfactory to the decision-maker relative to his aspiration levels. Hence there is no reason to downgrade the analytical value of such local optima in favour of less realistic absolute optima which may have associated with it very costly search and coordination procedures.

The search for the locational optimum for the firm wishing to produce several products will probably involve a sequence of evaluations on the part of each component of the firm's organization. Each of these components, which may be departments or separate plants representing 'procurement' (supply), 'production' and 'sales' corresponding to Figure 3.1, could be required to report its desired location decision to the plant's overall management. The manager would be than in a position of a coordinator, seeking to adjudicate the differences in locational choice on the part of each of the firm's components. His role would be to gather market and production information from each component, determine successively improving 'trial' solutions or 'partial optima' and to redistribute the pertinent, spatially corrected information to the separate departments. Situations may well develop in which the different components of the plant desire to bargain among themselves to reach acceptable solutions. However, the coordinator would be able to evaluate the overall benefits to the firm of each of the alternative locational selections and would be able to determine at what point the locational selection process would terminate. Under some circumstances game-theoretic situations may develop in which location outcomes could be dependent upon the sequence of strategies employed by the components of the firm (Isard, 1969).

The evaluation process extends to variables other than location as was implied in our model of multi-product location. The components of the firm must also decide how much of each product to produce and how to combine factors to make particular sets of products. A process by which this problem might be solved could be outlined as follows. A first-approximation location is defined by the coordinator. The firm's components would then be able to define the optimum mix of factors, products and residuals management strategies at that particular location. Given this new factor and product (including residuals management) information, and through the utilization of coordinative bargaining procedures such as suggested above, the firm could then determine an improved location. However, at this location, the firm's components could reevaluate their mix of factors and products. After making appropriate factor and product adjustments, they would agree upon a new location that represented, for that mix of factors and products, a further improved position. This procedure would continue until no further adjustments in factor-mixes, product output levels, residuals management programs or location lead to improvements in the overall values of the firm's objective functions.[6]

Once the locational decision has been made the firm may well have opportunities for adjusting factor proportions or product-mix. These factor–product adjustments may occur in the short run and decisions with regard to productive capacity may well be made to allow for this type of flexibility. For example, in the aluminium industry, producers construct about twice the capacity in the fabricating stage that they have in the aluminium reduction stage so as to be able to meet short-run changes in fabrications demand (Peck, 1961). In the medium run, we could visualize capacity and process adjustments occurring within plants at given locations, which could have implications for the plant's product- or factor-mix (Krumme, 1969).

Berry (1967) found in 1965 that 46 per cent of the 16,157 plants of the 995 largest US corporations produced more than one 4-digit product and that 'the plants of the 494 largest corporations are by no means tied to particular products even over as short a period as five years'. He concluded that at least part of the fixed capital committed to particular locations can be reallocated between different products within or between industries and that the inter-industry structure of the large industrial firms 'may be more flexible than has previously been recognized' (Berry, 1967, pp. 417–26).

The framework developed here suggests certain types of considerations which must be evaluated in the locational decision-making process in the multi-product firm that is common today. Location theory should be extended to consider multiple product situations. Not much empirical evidence has been provided for the types of process and product interdependence which were assumed in this paper. For that, the reader should refer to the evidence supplied and discussed in the literature on industrial complex analysis (see Vietorisz and Manne (1963) for further references). Evidence for the characteristics of decision processes which include the variables and interdependencies discussed here are not yet available. Case studies and location surveys focusing upon these processes in a wide spectrum of industries would be most helpful. In addition, empirical and theoretical investigations are needed to develop adequate long-range location models which match the time horizon of actual location decisions without requiring the degree of certainty implied by classical models.

Notes

1. In the case of separability, a different set of isoquants can be identified for each product, while in the case of complete coupling, the isoquants converge and coincide (Frisch, 1965, pp. 272–4). The case of complete coupling has much in common with single-product production at least in terms of its production function. On the other hand, market characteristics of coupling products can be as different as any other products produced in multi-product processes or plants (Gutenberg, 1967, p. 434).

2. See Moses (1958) for a detailed discussion of this generalization process for iso-outlay functions.

3. Under certain conditions it is likely that the output expansion path will be non-linear, which implies that the location along are IJ will shift with respect to the scale of production. However, an analysis by Churchill (1966) with respect to input factor substitution and locational variation suggests that locational shifts are unlikely under most production and market conditions.

4. Alonso (1967) has defined a similar mono-product situation.

5. It should be noted that Førsund (1972) has developed a model similar to that presented here. However, his model is primarily concerned with an extension of Lefeber's (1958) locational framework to include a residuals management programme along the lines suggested by Russell and Spofford (1972).

6. An algorithm for the solution of this problem would have to be more complex than that suggested by Kuhn and Kuenne (1962) because the weights are not known for the problem in advance. Rather, they must be developed iteratively in the process of locational selection. Churchill's (1967) model utilizes this general approach although, unlike Weberian doctrine, he treats space discontinuously. Isard's and Moses' iso-arc optimization procedures facilitate intermittent spatial solutions within the more general iteration process.

References

Alexandersson, G., 1967, *Geography of Manufacturing* (Englewood Cliffs, N.J.: Prentice–Hall).

Alonso, W., 1967, 'A reformulation of classical location theory and its relation to rent theory', *Papers, Regional Science Association*, **19**, 23–44.

Austin, M., T. E. Smith and J. Wolpert, 1970, 'The implementation of controversial facility-complex programs', *Geographical Analysis*, **2**, 315–29.

Berry, H., 1967, 'Corporate bigness and diversification in manufacturing', *Ohio State Law Journal*, **28**, 402–26.

Beyers, W., 1973, *A Model of Profit Maximizing Plant Location Subject to an Air Quality Constraint*, Unpublished manuscript, University of Washington, Department of Geography.

Cady, G. J., 1950, 'An approach to the theory of multiple production', *Southern Econ. Journ.*, **16**, 326–39.

Carlson, Sune, 1956, *A Study on the Pure Theory of Production* (New York: Kelley & Millman).

Chamberlin, H., 1957, *Towards a More General Theory of Value* (New York: Oxford University Press).

Churchill, G. A., Jr., 1966, *Plant Location Analysis: A Theoretical Formulation*, Unpublished D.B.A. Dissertation, Indiana University.

Churchill, G. A., Jr., 1967, 'Production technology, imperfect competition, and the theory of production', *Southern Econ. Journ.*, **34**, 86–100.

Coase, R. H., 1937, 'The nature of the firm', *Economica*, **4**, 386–405.

Cyert, R. M. and J. G. March, 1963, *Behavioral Theory of the Firm* (Englewood Cliffs, N.J.: Prentice–Hall).

Danø, S., 1966, *Industrial Production Models* (New York: Springer–Verlag).

Davis, O. A. and A. Whinston, 1962, 'Externalities, welfare and the theory of games', *Journal of Political Economy*, **70**, 241–62.

Førsund, Finn R., 1972, 'Allocation in space and environmental pollution', *Swedish Journal of Economics*, **74**, 19–34.

Frisch, R., 1965, *Theory of Production* (Chicago: Rand McNally).

Gutenberg, E., 1967, *Grundlagen der Betriebswirtschaftslehre: Die Produktion*, 13th Ed. (Berlin: Springer-Verlag).

Hartshorn, J. E., 1962, *Politics and World Oil Economics* (New York: Praeger).

Heady, E. O., 1952, *Economics of Agricultural Production and Resource Use* (New York: Prentice–Hall).

Hicks, J. R., 1946, *Value and Capital*, 2nd Ed. (Oxford: Clarendon Press).

Hoover, E., 1948, *The Location of Economic Activity* (New York: McGraw–Hill).

Isard, W., 1956, *Location and Space-Economy* (Cambridge, Mass.: M.I.T. Press).

Isard, W., 1960, *Methods of Regional Analysis: An Introduction to Regional Science* (New York: Wiley).

Isard, W., 1969, *General Theory* (Cambridge, Mass.: M.I.T. Press).

Isard, W. and P. Liossatos, 1972, 'On location analysis for urban and regional growth situations', *The Annals of Regional Science*, **6**, 1–27.

Krumme, G., 1969, 'Notes on locational adjustment patterns in industrial geography', *Geografiska Annaler*, **51B**, 15–19.

Kuhn, H. W. and R. E. Kuenne, 1962, 'An efficient algorithm for the numerical solution of the generalized Weber problem in spatial economics', *Journal of Regional Science*, **4**, 21–33.

Lanzillotti, R. F., 1954, 'Multiple products and oligopoly strategy: a development of Chamberlin's theory of products', *Quarterly Journal of Economics*, **68**, 461–74.

104

Lefeber, L., 1958, *Allocation in Space: Production, Transport, and Industrial Location* (Amsterdam: North-Holland).

Mauer, W. A. and T. H. Naylor, 1964, 'Monopolistic-monopsonistic competition: the multi-product, multi-factor firm', *Southern Econ. Journ.*, **31**, 38–43.

Moses, L. N., 1958, 'Location and the theory of production', *Quart. Journ. of Econ.*, **72**, 259–72.

Nishioka, H. and G. Krumme, 1973, 'Location conditions, factors and decisions: an evaluation of selected location surveys', *Land Economics*, **49**.

Peck, M. J., 1961, *Competition in the Aluminum Industry*, 1945–1958 (Cambridge, Mass.: Harvard).

Pfouts, R. W., 1961, 'The theory of cost and production in the multi-product firm', *Econometrica*, **29**, 650–58.

Pred, A. R., 1967, *Behaviour and Location*, Part I (Lund: Gleerup).

Predöhl, A., 1925, 'Das Standortsproblem in der Wirtschaftstheorie', *Weltwirtschaftliches Archiv*, **21**, 294–331.

Robinson, E. A. G., 1956, *The Structure of Competitive Industry*, Revised Ed. (Cambridge University Press).

Russell, C. S. and W. O. Spofford, Jr., 1972, 'A quantitative framework for residuals management decisions', in *Environmental Quality Analysis*, ed. A. V. Kneese and B. T. Bower (Baltimore: Johns Hopkins—Resources for the Future).

Seidenfus, H. S., 1967, 'Mehrproduktunternehmen, Preispolitischer Ausgleich und Konzentration', *Kyklos*, **20**, 208–17.

Smith, D. M., 1971, *Industrial Location* (New York: Wiley).

Stackelberg, H. V., 1952, *The Theory of the Market Economy* (New York: Oxford University Press).

Starr, M. K., 1970, 'Modular Production—A New Concept', in *Management of Production*, ed. M. K. Starr (Harmondsworth: Penguin).

Vietorisz, T. and A. S. Manne, 1963, 'Chemical processes, plant location, and economies of scale', in *Studies in Process Analysis*, ed. A. S. Manne and H. M. Markowitz (New York: Wiley), 136–58.

Weber, A., 1929, *Theory of the Location of Industries* (University of Chicago Press).

Weldon, J. C., 1948, 'The multi-product firm', *Can. J. Econ. Pol. Sc.*, **14**, 176–90.

4

Industry, Information and City-System Interdependencies[1]

ALLAN R. PRED

Problems of regional economic inequality and differential rates of city growth are virtually universal. Often government or private location policies, especially for manufacturing, are considered to be the key to ameliorating such problems. Yet classical industrial location theory and its derivatives are widely regarded as having limited applicability to problems arising from the development of regions and systems of cities (e.g., Friedmann, 1972a; Hansen, 1968; Thomas, 1972a). Alonso (1968a, p. 3) finds industrial location theory wanting because it unrealistically requires minimum transport-cost solutions and is 'poorly suited to the conditions of developing countries' because 'it assumes economic rationality, complete information, a static situation, and ignores the complexities of the broader framework of nation and region'. Their static general or partial equilibrium framework imparts to such theory 'very poor explanatory and predictive powers in a regional or urban development context' (Thomas, 1972a, p. 53). Others question the utility of a literature which is still largely confined to single-product, one-plant cases in an age when most production units in advanced economies belong to large multi-functional organizations which include a varying mix of locationally interdependent administrative, marketing, production and research facilities (Lampard, 1968).

Perhaps the most telling inadequacy of classical theory is its neglect of information as a location factor. Many recent writers claim that the locational role of transportation is declining, while information is increasingly important, especially for the location of the expanding administrative units within industrial and non-industrial organizations (e.g., Engström, 1970; Hoover, 1969; Klaassen, 1970; Törnqvist, 1962, 1968, 1970). Information costs are of growing importance to the calculus of industrial location,

105

partly because of the increasing volume of executive and clerical time allocated to intra-organizational and inter-organizational face-to-face contacts. Another factor is the mounting monetary allocation to the tasks of gathering, processing and beneficiating information for operational and innovative decision-making purposes (cf. Hedberg, 1970; Isard, 1969; Thorngren, 1970, 1972; Törnqvist, 1970). Spatial variations in the availability of information influence locational choices insofar as they bias the range of known opportunities and permit uncertainty to be reduced more easily in some places than in others (Alonso, 1968a; Webber, 1972). Furthermore, information circulation is vital both to the diffusion of new industry types and to the diffusion of other technological and organizational innovations inside and outside the manufacturing sector.

If information circulation is so intricately linked with the location of units belonging to industrial organization, and if industrial location policies are to have their desired impact on the development of systems of cities or regions, then there is need for a model or conceptual framework which adequately describes the means by which inter-urban information circulation and organizational location patterns feed back upon one another to influence both industrial growth and the process of city-system[2] development.

The model cannot be confined to purely industrial organization because of the structural shifts occurring within and the burgeoning significance of administrative activities in post-industrial societies. Much manufacturing occurs today within, and hence merely as part of, multi-functional organizations. Moreover, growth-generating interdependencies exist between increasingly specialized industrial and non-industrial activities.

Attention in the main is focused on large cities. The rationale for this is twofold. First, most perceived problems of regional economic inequality are linked in some way with the concentration of population and economic functions in large urban complexes. Second, empirical evidence indicates that there is little rank-shifting over long time periods among the largest units of city systems and, indeed, that growth concentrates largely in and around previous growth foci (Alonso and Medrich, 1972; Borchert, 1972; Robinson, 1969b; Webber, 1972). These two circumstances suggest that the process of city-system development is one wherein the largest system units repeatedly reinforce and renew their advantages after having acquired a dominant position in the urban hierarchy at some relatively early development stage (cf. Pred, 1965, 1966, 1973a).

Here an effort will be made to outline the components necessary for a model of the process of city-system growth and development. However, it is appropriate to consider why neither 'growth pole' literature nor literature which equates economic development with innovation diffusion provide sufficient insights into the process of city-based industrial development and into the part played by information circulation in that process.

Growth Pole Literature and Related Writings

Much literature on 'growth poles' and 'growth centres' has been subject to widespread criticism. This is true both of derivations from Perroux's (1950) initial formulation, which dealt with economic development in abstract rather than geographical terms and stressed interindustry linkages and the generation of sustained growth by highly dynamic and innovative 'leading propulsive industries', and also of more specifically geographical views of growth poles, as 'a set of expanding industries located in an urban area and inducing further development of economic activity throughout its zone of influence' (Boudeville, 1966, p. 11).

Hansen (1967, 1968, p. 122) has observed that growth pole theory contains 'certain ambiguities and inconsistencies in the definition and usage of terminology (particularly with reference to space); too exclusive an emphasis on the role of bigness and industry in the development process; too much emphasis on the function of propulsive firms and industries as generators of external effects; too little attention to the process of polarization as a consequence of the presence of existing external economies; and an inability to elaborate operationally feasible models capable of incorporating all of the principal concepts and relationships elaborated in the theory'.

Darwent (1969) stresses the failure to explain the location of propulsive industries in geographic space, the way in which growth is initiated, or to recognize that they are dealing with a 'limited concept which is part of a much more complex system described more realistically by the detailed input–output table on the one hand and by the notions of the central place system [sic] on the other'. By exclusive use of input–output analysis in empirical studies, growth pole scholars have ignored the process of structural change (Thomas, 1972b) and have also deprived the underlying concept of its original dynamic frame of reference, replacing it by a comparatively static approach (Hansen, 1968; Hermansen, 1970, 1972; Lasuen, 1969). Preoccupation with the notion that a growth pole 'is an urban centre of economic activity which can achieve self-sustaining growth to the point that growth is diffused outward into the pole region' (Nichols, 1969, p. 193) often results in an unrealistically narrow depiction of the non-local employment multiplier effects that transpire in an expanding economy. Growth-inducing multipliers are not only generated by industries in large cities, or metropolitan areas, for the lesser cities within their respective 'zones of influence'. Two-way interdependencies are quite typical of industries in integrated systems of cities. Expanding large cities commonly generate multiplier effects in *other large cities* by increasing their consumption of specialized goods obtained from those cities. Moreover, smaller cities, or *cities which are not 'growth centres'*, can induce growth at larger cities when the expansion of local specialized manufacturing requires the acquisition of material inputs or any of a variety of services from larger metropolitan complexes.

Although Perroux (1955) noted in passing that the 'growth of the market in space' could be the result of *communication* between 'territorially agglomerated' industrial poles, regional economists responsible for growth pole theory have neglected almost totally the significance of information circulation. While concentrating on inter-industrial linkages they have somehow ignored the fact that in both capitalist and socialist economies information flows 'are always indispensable prerequisites for flows of capital, labour and commodities' (Hermansen, 1970, p. 82).

The landmark works of Myrdal (1957) and Hirschman (1958) are often associated with growth pole theory although, technically speaking, they are interregional income inequality models and fall outside the growth pole realm. Although Myrdal talks of the principle of circular and cumulative causation, and Hirschman of the multiplier effects associated with 'backward' and 'forward' linkages, neither attempts to be very specific about the location of non-local employment multiplier effects. And, while Hirschman introduces some concern for entrepreneurial perception of where investment opportunities exist, neither is basically engrossed with the impact of information circulation of the development process. Probably the most rewarding insights into the process of city-system development are to be reaped from Friedmann's works dealing with 'core–periphery' relationships (Friedmann, 1966, 1971, 1972a, 1972c; Friedmann, McGlynn, Stuckey and Wu, 1970); but these, too, technically speaking, do not belong to the growth pole literature inasmuch as they evidence little interest in inter-industry linkages.

The Innovation-Diffusion Literature

Perroux's early papers on growth poles were plainly influenced by Schumpeter (1934) who had argued that economic development may be equated with 'the carrying out of new (manufacturing) combinations', or innovations. Perroux (1955) contended that geographic growth poles were the loci of Schumpeter's innovative industries and their linked activities. Or he contended that, 'newer industries (and cities where they are located) in which the developmental innovations take place grow at a faster pace than older industries and cities' (Lasuen, 1969, p. 139). Despite this early emphasis Perroux and his more spatially oriented French successors, had little inclination to inquire into the influence of innovation-diffusion processes upon the geographical expression of industrial and economic development.

Concentration on the vital question of innovation-diffusion (Berry, 1972; Lasuen, 1969, 1971; Pedersen, 1970, 1971a, 1971b), however, almost inevitably obscures two other major yet neglected sub-processes. First, the generation of non-local multipliers. Almost any private or public employment-providing facility or organization has direct or indirect linkages with, and hence multiplier effects on, activities in other cities—both as the outcome of existing inter-urban circulation patterns of specialized information and as contributors to subsequent patterns of specialized information circulation. Second, operational and day-to-day decision-making. The fact that a particular economic innovation diffuses through all or part of a city system does not mean it will survive or succeed on the same scale at all acceptance locations. Except possibly where a threshold or market effect operates, the degree of success of each innovation adoption will usually depend partly on the accumulation of operational decisions. In particular, the diffusion of manufacturing innovations in well-developed economies is not a catch-all for the spatial manifestation of development: in most industries diffusion is followed by the concentration of production in a more limited number of units and organizations (Bain, 1966, 1968; Nordström, 1971). Operational decision-making, which contributes to some innovation acceptances being more successful than others, is both an outcome of the existing geography of specialized information circulation and a contributor to the subsequent geography of specialized information circulation.

A further shortcoming of innovation-diffusion interpretations is that they are predominantly cast in a mould of hierarchical progress: economic innovations are supposedly first accepted in the largest unit of a city system and then descend through the urban hierarchy, the order of adoptions being determined by the size-order of cities.

A Model of City-System Industrial Development

Thus, at least three components, or interrelated sub-processes, ought to be incorporated into any large-city focused model of the process of industrial growth accompanying city-system development. In summary these are: (1) the generation of non-local multiplier effects by metropolitan activities controlled by either private and public organizations or individual entrepreneurs; (2) the diffusion of growth-inducing innovations from one city to another; (3) the accumulation of 'operational' decision-making which affects the survival and scale of manufacturing establishments and other job-providing organizational units. *In all three sub-processes information circulation is important.*

Non-local Multiplier Effects and the Spatial Structure of Organizations

Very sizeable and complex non-local multiplier effects are fostered via the consumption and production of goods and services in large cities or metropolitan complexes. For example, Artle (1965) reports that nearly every sector of the Stockholm economy has some exports, while Karaska (1969) found that most Philadelphia manufacturing activities procured their largest input from non-local sources and that very few industries were entirely dependent on local input sources.

Employment-promoting non-local multipliers associated with increases in inter-urban economic interaction may be either direct or indirect. Direct non-local employment multipliers, in turn, are of two types. First, on the demand side, the expansion of a manufacturing activity in one city may require expanded consumption of material inputs or services from another city and a consequent employment increase in those non-local employment activities. Likewise, such backward linkages may result in new non-local employment opportunities when the expansion of a tertiary or public sector activity requires the importation of services or finished goods from one or more other cities. Second, on the supply side, the expansion in one city of any industrial or service activity that does not cater exclusively for final demands may cause non-local *forward* linkages, or 'induce (non-local) attempts to utilize its outputs as inputs in some new (or existing) activities' (Hirschman, 1958, p. 100), and thereby lead to new jobs in the other urban centres involved. (If the local expansion in question also brings reduced input or service costs, or 'pecuniary external economies', the resulting induced non-local investments and multipliers will be larger than otherwise). Indirect non-local multipliers spring from the personal income expenditures created by direct non-local multipliers. That is, in those cities receiving direct non-local multipliers, the spending of new employees increases the local scale and employment level of many tertiary and other activities. Both direct and indirect non-local multipliers are frequently reflexive, or bilateral: a specific set of non-local multipliers occurring in a city may precipitate an increased demand for goods or services from other cities in the system, including the one in which the non-local multipliers originated. Finally, all types of direct and indirect non-local employment multipliers have their negative, or job-reducing, counterparts that are set in motion by a reduction in the scale of some operations in one city.

The current extent and complexity of direct and indirect non-local multiplier effects generated by large cities is—at least in highly industrialized economies—a reflection of the increasing specialization of society. It is widely recognized that: 'Industrialization and urbanization may be regarded as societal processes in which, among other things, factors, firms and localities become increasingly specialized and, within their respective market areas, more differentiated from each other' (Lampard, 1968, p. 100. Cf. Hermansen, 1970; Nordström, 1971). Or, as Hägerstrand has put it (1964, p. 3): 'Ultimately, urbanization is one aspect of the specialization of technique, and of the horizontal linkage between activities that is thereby rendered necessary ... The principle of horizontal linkage, and thus urbanization itself, is based on the art of moving materials, people and information [*between cities*]. In short, the growing intricacy of inter-city relationships and multipliers that accompanies economic growth is largely synonymous with the mounting variety of intermediate goods and services required by technologically advanced production processes (Hirschman, 1958; Lampard, 1968). In the automobile industry a final assembly plant in one city may receive components from over 17,700 firms (Johnson, 1970), mostly located in other cities. Or, in a city like Philadelphia—which resembles most major metropolitan areas in having a wide-ranging mix of fast-growing industries, middle-aged slow growing industries and a few declining industries—there is still a very extensive volume of input exchange with other cities due to 'a high degree of [production] specialization' (Isard and Langford, 1971, p. 122; Thompson, 1968).

In advanced economies the propagation of direct and indirect non-local multipliers is perhaps best depicted by the spatial structure of private and public job-providing organizations. Several Swedish geographers contend that society is an aggregation of organizations that are becoming increasingly larger. Private organizations are becoming larger via acquisitions, mergers and the formation of conglomerates, public organizations via new and expanded functions. Therefore, the future growth of urban centres is inextricably tied up with the future forms and spatial linkages of organizations (Ekström et al., 1971; Nordström, 1968, 1971; Pred, 1973b). The legitimacy of an organizational interpretation of non-local multipliers is evident from the situation prevailing in the U.S., where 70 per cent or more of the manufacturing sector of the economy is controlled by roughly 200 multi-functional business organizations, and from the conditions obtaining in socialist countries, where normally the economy is almost entirely in the hands of few state-controlled organizations.

Large organizations which economically dominate industrialized societies usually comprise functionally differentiated units that are dispersed in space. Organizations with manufacturing functions include some combination of main and branch plants, administrative offices, distributive facilities and research units. To the extent that the units of such spatially dispersed organizations are interdependent, or bound together by the flow of goods or services and information, any significant employment expansion at one unit should require the expansion of one or more other units. Or, the expansion of any organizational unit precipitates some non-local intra-organizational multiplier effect(s) (cf. Wärneryd, 1968, 1971). What, then, are the general types of inter-urban, or city-system, paths followed by intra-organizational multipliers?

Typically, organizations functioning nationally are hierarchically structured. Hence, they normally contain a permutation of units, some operating on a national basis, others on a regional or local basis (Figure 4.1). The controlling administrative unit, which allocates much of its time to making non-programmed or non-routine decisions, sits atop the hierarchy and in most cases is found in a city of national importance. Administrative units are

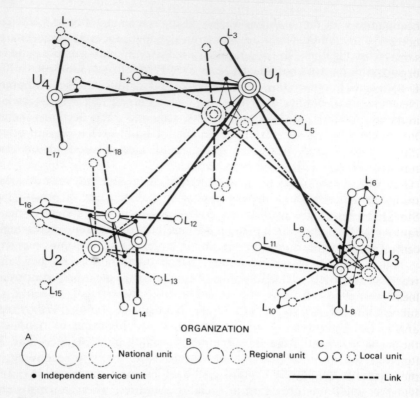

Figure 4.1. The spatial arrangement and functional character of units within three hypothetical organizations (modified from Nordström, 1968, 1971). U_1 may be thought of as the highest-ranking member of a given system of cities, U_2 as the second-ranking metropolitan area, and U_3 and U_4 as middle-ranking centres of regional importance. L_1–L_{18} are lower-order cities of varying population and local importance.

preoccupied with programmed, or routine, decision-making. This is also true of production, marketing or service units with a regional orientation, generally located in metropolitan areas of regional or national significance. Local units at the bottom of the organizational hierarchy have a greater variety of locations within the system of cities. This crudely described spatial counterpart to the hierarchical structure of organizations *should not* lead to the all too facile generalization that intra-organizational non-local multipliers and the generation of economic growth necessarily run parallel to the urban-size hierarchy.

Horizontal relationships exist sometimes at some level(s) of the organizational hierarchy. Within the same organization one regional unit may provide inputs for another regional unit located in a city of similar or larger size. More importantly, all organizations need not have their national headquarters unit in the largest complex of a system of cities. Nor is it necessary for regional units in different organizations to be located in the same cities. That is, the hierarchical structure of different private and public organizations is often asymmetrical. For example, in 1963, of the 500 largest U.S. industrial organizations, 163 had their headquarters in the first-ranking New York metropolitan area. In addition, 31 headquarters were located in the then second-ranking Chicago metropolitan area, 21 in eighth-ranking Pittsburgh, 16 each in third- and fourth-ranking Los Angeles and Philadelphia, 66 in five other centres with ranks of eleventh or higher, and the remaining 167 in metropolitan areas further down the urban-size hierarchy (Goodwin, 1965). Similarly, of 148 Swedish organizations whose stock was tradeable in 1965, 57 had their national headquarters in the first-ranking Stockholm metropolitan area, 24 in second-ranking Göteborg, 9 in third-ranking Malmö, and the remaining 58 in 31 different lower-ranking urban centres (Nordström, 1968).

Thus, an administrative decision, say, to expand operations which was reached in its high ranking headquarters city could generate a direct non-local multiplier in an even higher ranking city where an organizationally subordinate unit was located. (Note, in Figure 4.1, the linkage of a national unit in city U_2 with a regional unit in the larger U_1). Or, cities of roughly the same size and possessing the same intra-organizational production functions may cause non-local multipliers in either direction because one of the cities is also the locus of the organization's administrative headquarters. If large cities forward intra-organizational multiplier effects to urban complexes of even greater population, and if intra-organizational multipliers are shuttled between cities of the same size order, then any contention that economic growth is disseminated solely downward through the urban hierarchy is contradicted.

This viewpoint coincides with two recent observations by Borchert (1972, p. 365). In the U.S.A. 'the major metropolitan centres are less important as regional capitals than they are as major components in the national system of labour, entrepreneurship, and capital'; and: 'the overriding importance of diverse, non-hierarchical national linkages has perhaps always been a characteristic of regional social and economic systems'. The position taken is also supported by observations on the non-hierarchical attributes of the distribution of manufacturing (Duncan *et al.,* 1960; Hamilton, 1967) and by the topologically *asymmetrical* and *complex interdependencies* that arise in Dunn's (1970, 1971) flow-network descriptions of systems of cities.

Given the functional interdependencies of organizations, intra-organizational multipliers can also defy urban hierarchy interpretations of economic growth when the necessity of expanding either a regional unit in a fairly large city, or a local unit in a comparatively small city, forces employment expansion either at national headquarters, or some other unit located in a very large metropolitan area. For example, non-local multipliers were created in Toronto and major metropolitan centres of the north-eastern U.S. by the expansion of industrial activities at small cities in the southern Georgian Bay region of Ontario (Yeates and Lloyd, 1970). Frequently non-local intra-organizational multipliers result in large capital cities from the need to enlarge government agency services at regional or local centres.

Obviously, the hierarchical structure of organizations also yields many non-local multipliers which flow from larger to smaller cities, thereby generating growth according to the strict urban hierarchy proponents. Such intra-organizational multipliers very often spread from metropolitan areas of national importance (e.g., New York, Chicago, Los Angeles, Philadelphia, San Francisco–Oakland) or regionally dominant status (e.g., Denver, Minneapolis–St. Paul, Atlanta, Kansas City, Seattle) to lesser cities within their large spheres of regional influence. On a somewhat smaller scale, such multipliers spread from metropolitan cores of national, regional or sub-regional importance to the smaller urban foci within their 'urban fields', i.e., interdependent nuclei and surrounding open spaces within two hours' driving time, or 100–110 miles, of the metropolitan core itself (Friedmann and Miller, 1965; Friedman, 1972b; Berry and Horton, 1970). Implicit evidence of such larger city to smaller city intra-organizational multipliers abounds in countless regional central-place studies (Berry, 1967) in Nichols' (1969) appraisal of Atlanta's influence on the growth of less important Georgia cities and in Borchert's (1972) recent survey of the economic linkages of U.S. metropolitan areas.

Somewhat more explicit evidence is to be found in Swedish studies (Hedberg, 1970; Törnqvist, 1970) of the contact patterns of thirteen private and public organizations, and in as yet unpublished Swedish data comparing the spatial distribution of organizational contacts with that of organizational monetry flows. These materials reveal that intra-organizational and inter-organizational relationships are of three basic types: (1) those within the immediate region; (2) those within the three largest metropolitan areas (Stockholm, Göteborg, and Malmö); (3) those within contiguous regions. Since many of the organizational units studied were located in Sweden's three major urban centres, relationships (1) and (3) strongly suggest larger to smaller non-local multipliers, while (2) appears to emphasize large city specialization and interdependence.

One form of intra-organizational larger city to smaller city linkage in advanced economies is becoming especially common as organizations with manufacturing functions become associated with a growing array of products. When multi-product industrial organizations initiate production of a new item, or when new organizations begin manufacturing their first product, they often do so in the same large metropolitan area where their principal management functions are located. However, as production of any successful item becomes standardized, and as competition becomes more pronounced, the original plant frequently is replaced by one or more larger scale units in smaller cities where labour or other cost savings are available. Meanwhile, the administrative functions expand and remain in place since their day-to-day operations are so sensitive to the high information accessibility of their metropolitan locations. Consequently, new non-local multiplier relationships are set in motion between the large and small cities involved. Extensive documentation of this phenomenon exists for the U.S., Great Britain, Sweden and Denmark (see Lichtenberg, 1960; Keeble, 1971; Engström, 1970; Törnqvist, 1970; Pedersen, 1971c).

The dissemination of non-local multipliers by functionally specialized organizational units obviously occurs on an *inter*-organizational basis as well as an *intra*-organizational basis, although expanding organizations tend to internalize some of the services or production inputs previously acquired from other organizations. Technological progress often dictates that these organizations indulge in more sub-contracting and more external purchases of custom-tailored components and research, marketing and other services — all of which practices are apt to be synonymous with non-local multipliers. Since the hierarchical structure of large organizations does not coincide spatially, most organizations differ from one another in the mix of cities at which their nationally, regionally and locally oriented units are located. Because of this, and particularly because the location of national headquarters can vary, *inter-organizational multipliers not only move from larger places to smaller places, but also from large metropolitan areas to even larger metropolitan areas, between major urban complexes of the same size order, and from smaller cities to larger cities.* In fact, Friedmann (1972a, p. 97) contends that: 'For the same spatial system, any two core regions (large cities) of approximately the same level in the hierarchy will tend to have a greater and more balanced volume of mutual interaction, modified by distance, than either will have with individual lower order cores'.

Finally, despite the occurrence of major technological changes, non-local multiplier patterns generated by large spatially-dispersed organizations tend to retain some characteristics which are locationally, if not compositionally, stable. In their efforts to grow or to survive in the face of change, large organizations constantly seek to broaden their offered range of products or services they offer, and thereby guard against a decline in market demand for any single function (Starbuck, 1965). The immobility of fixed capital—large administrative buildings and costly production facilities—contributes to a situation where new organizational functions frequently inherit the locational patterns of current or previous functions (cf. Chisholm, 1968; Nordström, 1971, pp. 51–2). This should perpetuate some already existing non-local multiplier linkages, although new non-local organizational ties may appear simultaneously (cf. Thomas, 1972b, pp. 94–5).

The Inter-urban Diffusion of Growth-Inducing Innovations

Most innovations which may induce growth within industrial organizations, and thereby economic and population growth within the units of system of cities, fall into three broad categories. First, some innovations provide new products for intermediate or final markets: the diffusion of these innovations among producers or suppliers requires a simultaneous diffusion among consumers (households or firms). Second, some innovations involve the use of new production processes: their diffusion is either a concomitant of new production processes or is greatly influenced by the pattern of previously-diffused production. In highly industrialized economies the inventions behind both new products and new production processes usually occur either within the first adopting organization, i.e., within its research and development (R and D) unit, or within an organization with other manufacturing or research functions, i.e. by 'technological convergence' or 'technological invasion' (cf. Worley, 1962; Schon, 1967; Rosenberg, 1972). Third, some organizational innovations encompass one or more of the following features: new structural relationships within organizations; new operating procedures; new planning or policy-making procedures. Diffusion of this type of innovation often goes hand in hand with the diffusion of new products or production processes.

Inter-urban diffusion of such innovations greatly depends upon the circulation of *specialized* information. Clearly, patterns of specialized information circulation influence the spatial dissemination of new information regarding the existence of any specific growth-inducing innovation. However, because of the uncertainty that needs to be overcome and the risk-taking frequently involved (Strassmann, 1959, pp. 11–19; Schon, 1967), adoption of a growth-inducing innovation is not apt to be undertaken by an organization or entrepreneur immediately upon receipt of information regarding its existence. Instead, the acquisition of redundant and additional new information is necessary. Hence, the accumulation of formal personal contacts and other specialized information concerning the experience of previous adopters is often crucial to the potential adopter's, or the organization's, decision to accept or reject an innovation (cf. Rogers, 1962; Hägerstrand, 1967, pp. 263–4; Rogers and Shoemaker, 1971; Pred, 1973a).

Inasmuch as specialized information circulation is supposedly so vital to the potential adopter's knowledge and acceptance of growth-inducing innovations, existing patterns of inter-urban interaction and interdependence between job-providing establishments channel the inter-urban diffusion course of such innovations. Lasuen (1971, p. 189), similarly emphasizes 'the role of functional communication channels between firms (controlled by market-linkage intensities) in explaining diffusion and adoption patterns' (cf. Lasuen, 1969, pp. 14–15; Hermansen, 1970, pp. 11–12; Friedmann, 1972c). Existing interaction patterns, and the specialized information circulation associated with them, may influence the inter-urban diffusion paths of growth-inducing innovations by influencing what non-local innovations local potential innovators become aware of and how they react to them. Or, the inter-organizational inter-urban linkages of large organizations— which are the most active innovation acceptors under modern conditions (Starbuck, 1965; Mansfield, 1968; Dicken, 1971)—may result in the head-quarters-based 'imposition' of growth-inducing innovations at the same cities where organizational activities already exist (Anderson, 1970; Riddell, 1972). Likewise, the information funnelled into an established network of inter-organizational linkages may limit the set of cities considered as locational alternatives for a new product, service, process or organizational innovation (Ohlsson, 1972).

The assumption that existing inter-urban interdependencies channel the city-to-city diffusion of growth-inducing innovations is not at odds with currently employed Christaller-based hierarchical models which almost monopolize inter-urban diffusion literature.

Hitherto, proponents of Christaller-based models of inter-urban diffusion have not attempted to specify empirically the linkages through which infor-mation or influence passes from city to city and thereby incontrovertibly identify a hierarchical sequence. Instead, they arrive typically at a hierarchi-cal conclusion by plotting dates of acceptance against city-size and calcula-ting moderate good correlations between the two (e.g. Pyle, 1969; Pedersen, 1970). The necessary perfect correlations are never found, however, and, as a consequence, a comparison of the points falling above and below any of the obtained regression lines always shows some cities being the scene of adoption before either larger cities or other places of a comparable popula-tion. (Even a 'neighbourhood effect' in the vicinity of the largest cities would generate at least some non-hierarchical diffusion elements.)

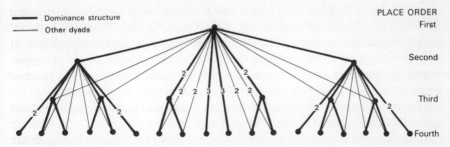

Figure 4.2. The dominance structure and other interaction linkages in a Christallerian central place system where $K = 3$ (from Pred, 1971, 1973a). The only undiagrammed linkages or flow paths involve the importation of first-order goods and services from the single first-order place by the six left-most and six right-most fourth-order places. Numbers refer to the number of orders of goods and services procured by lower-order cities from higher-order cities. Unnumbered linkages involve only one order of goods and services.

This inadequacies of hierarchical interpretations derived from Christaller's central-place theory are further illustrated by taking a glance at Figure 4.2. This diagram shows the hierarchical dominance structure and some of the other direct linkages *(information and innovation diffusion paths)* for the four highest order places in a Christallerian central place system where K 3. The dependency linkages preclude any exchange of goods and services between the second and third largest cities in the system and, for that matter, between any pair of similarly-sized cities. Nor do the linkages shown permit any larger-city procurement of goods or services from smaller cities (cf. Hermansen, 1970, p. 49; Richardson, 1972, p. 38). Hence, within this framework, there is zero probability of specialized information or growth-inducing innovations moving from large cities to even larger cities, from smaller cities to larger cities or from one city of a given size to any other city of approximately the same size—even where the separating distances are small. These severe constraints are clearly incompatible with the patterns of interdependency between cities discussed earlier and, moreover, are contradicted by much empirical evidence.

Wood (1971) found, for instance, that some flows of specialized information occurred between cities *of similar size* during the diffusion of municipally-owned electric-power systems in Canada. Simmons (1970b) notes that movement of business telephone calls in Ontario and Quebec takes place 'equally well *across the hierarchy as up and down',* commonly occurring from *large city to large city* and from *small city to small city;* and that the network of inter-urban rail shipments in these two states is considerably 'more widespread and complex than that predicted by central place or gravity models'. Boudeville observes that important *bilateral* economic interaction linkages exist between eight of France's *large and similarly-sized* regional metropolises (Boudeville, 1966; Darwent, 1969). Two decades ago, Hägerstrand (1952) noted that some innovations that have diffused in Sweden have taken 'short circuits' in passing from southern *small cities* to Stockholm and other distant *larger cities.* Dahl (1957) shows how a significant stream of business telephone calls and railroad freight shipments moves from Västerås, Sweden's fifth- or sixth-ranking urban centre, to the *higher-ranked* complexes of Stockholm, Göteborg and Malmö. Pedersen (1971c) underlines the fact that industrial innovations in Denmark neither always start their diffusion in Copenhagen, nor always gain the most widespread acceptance in that first-ranking city.

Both hierarchical and *inter-metropolitan non-hierarchical* linkages are observed to be important by Illeris and Pedersen (1968) in the overall pattern of Danish telephone traffic. In the U.S.A., a sizeable volume of specialized business information transmitted by telephone from the leading cities of Connecticut—Hartford, New Haven and Bridgeport—terminates in both New York and Boston, the *larger* metropolitan complexes which immediately 'dominate' them, as well as in more distant *larger* metropolitan areas, such as Chicago, Denver and Los Angeles (Gottman, 1961). An impressive volume of industrial and commercial goods is trucked daily to Chicago from both large metropolitan areas of *somewhat smaller* population (e.g., Detroit, St. Louis, Milwaukee, Indianapolis) and many *medium- and small-sized* cities (Helvig, 1964). During the period 1790–1840 there was very rapid growth in the volume of *two-way* flows of business information between regionally dominant U.S. cities (Pred, 1971b; 1973a), while in a variety of early nineteenth-century inter-urban diffusion processes in the U.S.A. the passage of information and influence often occurred from *one comparably sized city to another* and from *smaller places to larger places* (Pred, 1971a, 1973a). Finally, there was an absence of any hierarchical pattern in the diffusion of liquid propane gas tanks in a part of Wisconsin (Brown, 1968).

Despite this evidence, Christaller-based models may pertain to economic innovations, the successful adoption of which requires a minimum market size, a skilled labour force of given size, or some other threshold condition (Pedersen, 1970, 1971c; Pred, 1966). Yet, insofar as the minimum size requirements of threshold innovations tend to rise with economic development (Pedersen, 1970, 1971a), with time their diffusion should be characterized increasingly by spread from one large city to another. Also, where labour or resource thresholds are involved, national demand may be satisfied after a few non-hierarchically-sequenced acceptances in a small number of relatively large cities.

Some of the objections raised to strictly hierarchical diffusion models disappear if one proposes that the inter-urban flow of specialized information and innovation-adoption influence is channelled by the interdependencies existing in a Löschian central-place system where market-oriented industries as well as tertiary activities are present.

The precise set of conditions arising in such a system can be readily understood from Figure 4.3, which depicts the interaction linkages found along a cross-section passing through the system's largest city (A). The diagram reveals that, because urban-size in a Löschian system does not automatically define the array of activities locally present, there can be lateral diffusion between cities of approximately the same population. For the same reason spreading can occur from a centre of given population to another city of larger population, although in the majority of cases the linkages shown in Figure 4.2 cause specialized information circulation and innovation diffusion from a larger city to a smaller city. Despite these concessions to reality, any Lösch-based schema for interpreting the inter-urban diffusion of growth-inducing innovations would have to remain unsatisfactory on at least one very important count. A Löschian framework allows for no linkages between the largest cities present. (Notice the lack of any ties between the five largest cities in Figure 4.3.) Or, a Lösch-based model would result in a probability of zero for the movement of innovation-

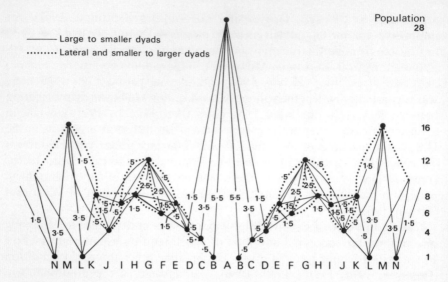

Figure 4.3. Interaction linkages for seven orders of goods and services in a cross-section through a Löschian central place system (from Pred, 1971, 1973a, as derived from Stolper, 1955). For the sake of maintaining comparability with Figure 4.2, the diagram is confined to 27 cities, each designated by a letter. The population of each city is proportional to the number of places or market area, served by each locally present order of goods and services. Numbers refer to the number of orders of goods and services procured by one city from another. Unnumbered linkages involve only one order. In accord with Stolper (1955, p. 139), it is to 'be imagined that the distribution of production schematized ... exists also in all directions'.

relevant information of influence in either direction between any pair of the system's largest cities.

Maintaining the assumption that existing patterns of inter-urban interaction channel the spread of growth-inducing innovations, it should now be evident that at least three features must be combined in any model of the diffusion sub-process of city-system development. These are:

(1) the hierarchical spread of prevailing Christallerian models;

(2) the lateral and smaller-to-larger-place dissemination allowed by a Löschian construct;

(3) a considerable volume if specialized information exchange between mutually interacting very high-order cities, or between various urban pairs within a group consisting of the largest metropolitan complex and metropolitan areas in the size class(es) just below it (Figure 4.4).

In addition, any inter-urban diffusion model aspiring to reality ought to incorporate a fourth feature. This feature would allow that normally information also flows in the direct in opposite to that of goods or services movement along any interaction linkage. That is, even if only one good or service is moving between two cities there should be bilateral information

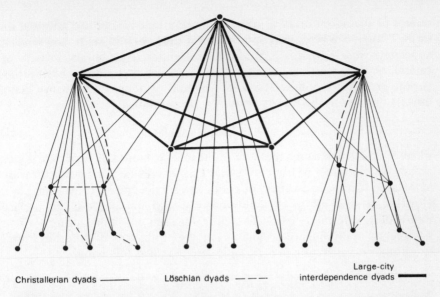

Christallerian dyads ——————   Löschian dyads — — —   Large-city interdependence dyads ▬▬▬▬

Figure 4.4. One hypothetical permutation of interaction linkages in a system of cities with Christallerian and Löschian characteristics plus large-city interdependence (modified from Pred, 1971, 1973a). In order to maintain comparability with Figures 4.2 and 4.3, the diagram is limited to 27 cities. The interaction linkages between the largest city and each of the next two highest-ranking cities would also be possible in a Christallerian system. However, unlike the conditions in a Christallerian system, here it is allowed that goods and services interaction between each pair of large cities is two-way. Also, although such interaction exists, no linkages are diagrammed between the largest city and the six left-most and six right-most cities of the smallest size-class shown.

exchange. This might be so, because information-generating monetary payments normally flow in the reverse direction of goods and service movements. Or, it might be so, for example, because information-bearing organizational representatives, or consumers, have to place orders at the good or service source before any movement of a good or service can actually occur. The need for this final feature is in part suggested by previously cited telephone-call studies. Its inclusion is also indirectly validated by two recent swedish studies. One shows that the number of trips by air to Stockholm undertaken by businessmen from other Swedish cities is roughly equal to the number of air trips undertaken by Stockholm businessmen in the opposite direction (Sahlberg, 1970). In the other instance, Hedberg's survey (1970) of thirteen private firms and public organizations indicates that the number of inter-organizational business trips and informational contacts between any pair or units tends to balance out in both directions.

Given the above requirements, a quite simple formulation is possible. It is here proposed that once a city (i) has experienced specialized information receipt or the adoption of a growth-inducing innovation, the information or innovation can be passed on in the next time period (Δt) to any *smaller, larger or similarly-sized city* (j) to which it either sends goods, services or capital, or from which it receives goods, services or capital. Thus, during Δt, the probability of specialized information or adoption influence being directly received at the jth city via i ($I_{i \to j}$) is as follows:

$$I_{i \to j} = f(T_{i \to j}, T_{j \to i}), \tag{1}$$

where $T_{i \to j}$ is some rough measure of the total volume and variety of goods and service transactions from i to j, and T_{j-i} is likewise some crude measure of the total volume and variety of goods and service transactions from j to i. However, city i is apt to be simultaneously engaging in goods and service transactions with many cities. Therefore, for each adoption during t where information and influence originates in i, the probability of diffusion from i to a firm or organization in j ($D_{i \to j}$) is describable as following:

$$D_{i \to j} = f(T_{i \to j}, T_{j-i}) / \sum_{j=1}^{n} f(T_{i \to j}, T_{j \to i}) \tag{2}$$

(Note that no distance variable is explicitly included in either of these gravity-related expressions. This is because any impact of distance on interaction is already built into each $T_{i \to j}$ and each $T_{j \to i}$).

Expression (2) states, in short, that growth-inducing innovations diffuse within a system of cities in a probabilistic manner by being passed through a succession of composite contact fields or urban information fields. Or, growth-promoting innovations are passed in a non-deterministic fashion from one city to one or more other places in its composite set of direct non-local organizational contacts, and from the recipient city (cities) to one or more other places among its often overlapping set of direct non-local organizational contacts.

Within this framework, therefore, regardless of where a growth-inducing innovation originates or initially enters a system of cities, it is soon likely to appear in some or all of the system's largest units. That is, even if an innovation did not originate or first enter a system of cities at one of a few nationally dominant metropolitan areas, those places would tend to adopt early because of their high contact probabilities with a number of other places. Clearly, within this probabilistic contact-field framework, large cities would also benefit from indirect contacts: more precisely because of their high frequency of direct contacts with one another, large cities have the potential to snap up quickly innovations originating or entering at smaller centres with which they have no direct contact, but which lie within each other's regional sphere of influence. Ironically, the high probability that large cities will predominate among early acceptors points to a total sequence of innovation adoptions that will often bear close resemblance to those sequences customarily interpreted as the outcome of a strictly hierarchical diffusion process.

If, in general, firms in large cities have the highest probabilities for the early acquisition of growth-inducing innovations, then, in many but not all instances, those same loci should have the highest probabilities for successful outcomes for their adoption decisions. This early-adoption long-run-success syndrome, which presumably helps to perpetuate the high size rank of already large cities, is usually attributable to one or more of at least three factors.

First, if a new product is innovated, then the early adopter frequently can establish competitive advantages over subsequent competitors (late adopters) as a result of temporary monopolistic or oligopolistic control over some portion of the market. In an era when the average scale or market threshold of certain types of innovations is on the rise, this kind of initial advantage is presumably all the more telling in those situations where cities at the bottom or middle of the hierarchy have difficulty in providing a large enough local market or labour supply to justify adoption (Lasuen, 1971; Mansfield, 1968; Pedersen, 1970, 1971a). (Recall, however, that once output becomes standardized, multi-functional organizations often consign production to smaller cities while retaining their principal growth-inducing administrative functions at the large-city of initial adoption.)

Second, if cost-sensitive innovations are adopted in large cities the adopting organizations can benefit competitively from the local presence of external economy-providing services and marketing channels—innovations in themselves which are less likely to be found in those smaller cities where acceptance occurs (Nordström, 1971; Webber, 1972).

Third, when manufacturing activities of the same type are clustered in the same place, and thus competitively spurred to imitate one another, the early acceptance of a process or product innovation can cause a compounding of existing advantages since it may soon necessitate additional rounds of cost-saving organizational or process innovations 'before more scattered and distant places have made the initial innovation' (Pred, 1966, p. 139).

While each of these three phenomena are occasionally important in contributing to the long-run success of early large-city adopters, a fourth more general influence, in the form of the 'operational' decision-making advantages associated with large cities, is almost always at work. For, operational, or 'day-to-day', decision-making usually has some impact on the survival or scale attained by growth-inducing innovations, regardless of how early or late adoption occurs.

The Accumulation of Organizational Operational Decisions

In advanced economies the on-going development of economic activities is largely synonomous with the accumulation of investment, resource allocation, and production decisions made by various types of job-providing private and public organizations. A small minority of those decisions involve the relatively infrequent adoption of growth-inducing innovations. Most other investment, made by organizations which are striving to survive and expand in a constantly changing environment take a great variety of forms (Danielsson, 1964; Krumme, 1969; Dicken, 1971). Only a limited number are highly relevant because of their multiplier-effect implications. Accumulation of any such decisions has clear-cut manifestations for the scale and employment total of specific activity units either inside or outside the decision-making organization.

(1) Purchase-source decisions. These price-sensitive decisions relate to the additional acquisition of: finished goods to be wholesaled or retailed; material production inputs; advertising, data processing or other business services; equipment and supplies. In a capitalist economy purchase-source decisions can be made by private *or* public organizations.

(2) Market-outlet decisions. These decisions subsume the selection of new sales targets (household or organizational consumers) either within the previously existing market area of the organization, or within a totally new area or city. Market-outlet decisions involve either products already being manufactured, wholesaled or retailed by the organization, or services already being performed by the organization.

(3) Private investment decisions. This class of decisions is restricted to investments made by private organizations in activities that are already functioning at given locations. Any investment in an activity that was not yet in operation would be equivalent to the adoption of a growth-inducing innovation.

(4) Public-organization allocation decisions. Decisions of this type require identification of those existing units that are to receive survival, or expansion-encouraging, resource allocations. These units are usually within government organization itself (e.g. nationalized industries) or are deemed to be of national importance (e.g. aerospace industries). If there was any allocation to a unit that was not yet functioning, it once again would be equivalent to the adoption of a growth-inducing innovation.

All four decision types share two important characteristics. First, whether or not the organizational decision-makers are consciously aware of it, each type has a spatial dimension, i.e. every purchase-source, market-outlet, private investment and public-organization allocation decision results in selecting places where action is to be implemented and directly and indirectly affecting some cities rather than others. Secondly, there is an information component insofar as the decision-making organization can only choose between those alternatives of which it is aware. Or, the operational decision-making of both private and public organizations is also related to the inter-urban circulation of specialized information.

Any of the four operational decision types can be made on a routine or non-routine basis. Routine or programmed decision-making is normally based on the direct operational feedback of information from on-going organizational activities (Katz and Kahn, 1966, pp. 248–9). Information coming from this closed circuit may indicate, for example, that stocks of a given item have fallen and that additional purchases from an *already identified source* are necessary. No search for alternatives is carried out in making such routine decisions since search previously carried out in a succession of similar decision situations has resulted, via information feedback, in a learning process and the identification of what is deemed a satisfactory standard solution (cf. Golledge and Brown, 1967; Dicken, 1971). Thus, routine 'day-to-day' decision-making—which probably accounts for the lion's share of organizational decision-making—by following established information-circulation channels and repeatedly choosing the same locational alternatives leads to a stabilization and expansion of existing local and non-local multiplier relationships, particularly between large cities (cf. Vance, 1970, p. 21, on routine non-local wholesaling–retailing linkages).

Non-routine, or non-programmed, organizational decision-making, relating to purchase-sources, market-outlets, investments and allocations, ordinarily requires, by definition, some search for possible alternatives. Despite the important consequences that obviously follow from most non-routine operational decision-making, when confronted with a new problem, organizations typically consider only a quite small number of decision alternatives. For example, after several case studies of organizational decision-making Cyert and March concluded (1963, p. 79) that in non-programmed situations there initially is a very limited scanning of the environment to eliminate obviously inappropriate alternatives: 'In most cases a rather firm commitment to an action (or satisfactory alternative) was taken before the search for information proceeded very far.' Likewise, an investigation of new investment decisions by private British organizations (Williams and Scott, 1970) revealed that commitments to a specific alternative were often made at an early stage in the search process. The evaluation of a limited number of alternatives in these and other non-routine circumstances is ascribable to any of a number of causes, including:

(1) the organization's recognition of the impossibility of obtaining truly optimal solutions and its consequent willingness to seek 'feasible' solutions (Cyert and March, 1963);

(2) the 'restricted cognitive range' of decision-makers (Katz and Kahn, 1966);

(3) the costs of gathering information on specific alternatives, not the least of which are the time expenditures of highly salaried administrative personnel (Isard, 1969; Hedberg, 1970; Sahlberg, 1970; Törnqvist, 1972; Webber, 1972);

(4) the refusal to process more information than seems necessary when the total activity of the organization produces or threatens information overload (Katz and Kahn, 1966).

Whatever the reason for organizations only roughly screening the environment and examining but a few alternatives, in most cases non-routine operational decision-making terminates with the selection of alternatives located in places with which the organization is already familiar: this is the most readily accessible specialized information which can be turned up by limited search, and the most readily accessible specialized information is apt to be that obtainable from *or near* the organization's already existing local and non-local contacts of both a direct and indirect (or relayed) character (cf. Golledge and Brown, 1967, p. 116). If so, then it follows that the exploitation by organizations in city *j* of non-local alternatives in any other *smaller, larger or similarly sized* city *i* is dependent upon the existing pattern of inter-urban interdependencies. Or, the probability (A_{ij}) that a non-routine operational alternative exploited in city *j* has its locus in city *i* is as follows:

$$A_{ij} = f(T_{i \to j} T_{j \to i})$$

As in expression (1), T_{ij} and $T_{j \to i}$ are rough measures of the total volume and variety of goods and service transactions respectively from *i* to *j* and *j* to *i*. Beginning from the other end, the probability *($I_{i \to j}$)* of specialized information regarding a non-routine opportunity in *i* being transmitted to *j* during a given *t* is describable by expression (1) itself. Once again, city *i* is apt to be simultaneously engaging in goods and service transactions with many cities. Therefore, the probability that organizations in the *j*th city will be early to receive or exploit opportunity-related specialized information can be portrayed by expression (2). To the extent that expression (2) actually does result in the selection of non-local alternatives situated in places with which organizations are already acquainted, it leads to a compunding of existing non-local multiplier relationships, especially those involving large cities which have a high contact probability with many places. Hence, the *non-routine operational decision-making of organizations should also tend to stabilize large-city size ranks as the process of city-system development unfolds.*

The proclivity of organizations to choose non-routine operational alternatives in or around metropolitan areas where they already have had some experience reflects some element(s) of uncertainty associated with new decisions. Organizations frequently reduce uncertainty by acting in imitation of others (e.g. by obtaining inputs or services from the same large-city source as a competitor, rather than from a physically closer but smaller city). But, uncertainty usually varies spatially because markets and organizational activities and actions are already concentrated in a limited number of relatively large cities and because face-to-face information exchange and both inter-organizational cooperation and mutual observation are more easily arranged in such cities (cf. Wolpert, 1964; Alonso, 1968b; Webber,

1972; Misra, 1971, p. 130; Klaassen, 1970; Hermansen, 1971, p. 29). The greater frequency of metropolitan area operational alternatives and the lower level of metropolitan area uncertainty combine, therefore, to encourage normally cautious multi-locational organizations to select a preponderance of large-city non-routine alternatives (cf. Borchert, 1972, p. 355). This inclination is compounded by the organizational employment of management consultants to reduce uncertainty by searching for and evaluating non-routine operational alternatives. Such consultants are mostly metropolitan-based and, because of a desire to cut the costs of data collection, their own search is likely to focus on alternatives located either nearby or in other large-city environments with which they are familiar. Moreover, consultants often hold views so similar to those of organizational decision-makers 'that they can only give the illusion of broadening the search for alternatives' (Katz and Kahn, 1966, p. 296).

Spatial Biases in the Availability of Specialized Information

Specialized information, whether or not of an economic nature, is not conveyed under normal circumstances by mass media, although it may appear in limited-circulation publications: it is not likely to be ubiquitously available. Instead, its probability of being encountered usually will be greater in some locations than others. Such *spatial biases* in specialized information availability are intimately associated with all three interrelated components of city-system development. Non-local inter-organizational and intra-organizational multiplier effects propagate specialized inter-urban information flows through their very operation. All non-local multipliers of any size spring either from the adoption of growth-inducing innovations or from routine and non-routine operational organizational decisions that affect the scale of individual activity units. Thus, inter-urban innovation diffusion and operational organizational decision-making contribute to spatial biases in the availability of specialized information. In turn, both diffusion of growth-inducing innovations and selection of operational decision-making alternatives are themselves influenced by the information generated by existing inter-urban transactions involving goods and services (or capital), i.e., by existing spatial biases in the availability of specialized information. Furthermore, highly varied non-local economic transactions of large cities should provide them with a greater probability of information receipt than lesser cities; and the sub-processes of inter-urban innovation diffusion and operational organizational decision-making ought to stabilize city-system development by helping to perpetuate the high size rank of already large cities.

There are at least three characteristics that are to be expected of specialized information circulation within systems of cities. First, spatially-biased flows of specialized information should largely parallel inter-urban flows of goods, services and capital. Second, despite their changing content, spatially-biased flows of specialized information should be fairly stable in their origins and destinations over relatively long periods of time. Third, large metropolitian areas should have the most pronounced advantages, or positive spatial biases, in accessibility to *non-local* specialized information. Support for the first expected characteristic of specialized information circulation is provided by Tolosa and Reiner (1970, p. 551) who observe that information and economic flows are interdependent, one largely generating the other, and hence their flows tend to have similar patterns (cf. Misra, 1971, p. 127; Dunn, 1970, pp. 253–4).

More conclusive evidence assumes a variety of forms. In a survey of Canadian inter-provincial interaction (dominated by inter-metropolitan interaction), Simmons (1970a) found that economic flows, as reflected by ship, rail and truck commodity flows, described 'basically the same pattern of interaction' as information flows, as measured by business telephone calls and air passenger flows. The air passenger matrix, which should mirror non-routine organizational contacts, had simple correlation co-efficients of 0·75 with the shipping matrix, 0·72 with the rail freight matrix and 0·95 with the trucking matrix. In Sweden, unpublished research pertaining to a large number of organizations located in Malmö and elsewhere unveils a high degree of correspondence between the individual organization's non-local pattern of information contacts and its non-local pattern of monetary payments. Thorngren's studies (1970, 1972) of the contact activity of Swedish organizations also point to 'both long-run and short-run connections between flows of information, physical resources, and payments' (1970, p. 420).

An extensive analysis of the inter-urban circulation of business-related information in the U.S.A. between 1790 and 1840 indicated that the most marked spatial biases in availability were attributable to the patterns of inter-urban trade existing between cities of national importance, as well as between regionally-dominant centres (Pred, 1971b, 1973a). Studies of city-system development in Spain and elsewhere enable Lasuen (1969, 1971) to propose that the acquisition of specialized information by organizations or individual entrepreneurs depends upon their 'market linkages', or the economic flows associated with them. Gould (1970, p. 169) has reported that the volume of inter-urban telephone calls in Tanzania is 'predictable to a high degree' by the level of modernization of the generating and receiving cities and the distance separating them. This too suggests that specialized information flows and economic flows share the same paths, since the 'modernization score' of a city presumably indicates its proclivity for indulging in economic transactions with other cities. Alonso (1968b, pp. 5–6) similarly shows that major ports of developing nations in Africa and elsewhere have higher levels of specialized information availability than their less import-

and export-active urban sisters located in 'remote' or 'peripheral' regions of the same countries.

Hagerstrand (1966, p. 29) has observed that 'information and influences [apparently] travel in a system of communication with a rather stable spatial configuration. The number of links between areas and places seem to remain very much the same over time, even when the acting individuals change'. Other Swedish research has shown that fairly stable information and innovation diffusion routes have emanated for at least one century from Stockholm, Malmö and Göteberg (Norborg, 1968; Gould and Törnqvist, 1971). Over an eleven-year period certain Swedish public organizations had a stable 'spatial and sectorial distribution of contacts' (Wärneryd, 1968, p. 160). In this context Wärneryd has stated (1968, p. 29) that 'the established and dominating linkages will tend to become more and more reinforced as the system is developed'. In the U.S.A., those north-eastern and Midwestern cities which were identified early in the nineteenth century as major national or regional nodes of specialized information circulation remain so today. Moreover, the principal information origins and destinations of these long dominant large-cities have been basically unchanged. The only major exceptions occur where southern and western centres that first grew to prominence in the late nineteenth and twentieth centuries have been added to a place's list of significant correspondent metropolitan areas (Pred, 1973a; cf. Borchert, 1972, p. 357). Lasuen's studies conclude that functional communications channels between firms and organizations multiply, intensify and become entrenched with the passage of time, so that (1971, p. 189): 'the stability of this communication network (together with the geographical immobility of most firms) is the central explanation for the geographical stability of (innovation) diffusion patterns'.

There is more widespread documentation on the pronounced non-local information-accessibility advantages of large metropolitan areas. Only a few pieces of evidence need be enumerated. First, the pattern of non-local business telephone messages in Ontario and Quebec is completely dominated by Montreal and Toronto, one or other participating in each of the fifteen leading information-exchange dyads while the Montreal-Toronto dyad is the most important long-distance interregional linkage (Simmons, 1970b, 1972). Moreover, the linearly distributed major cities of Canada—Montreal, Ottawa, Toronto, Winnipeg and Vancouver—have very high communications accessibility to each other: 'other places, no matter what their location, are peripheral' (Simmons, 1970b, p. 7).

Second, the contact patterns of municipal organizations in large Ontario cities are more elaborate than those of their counterparts in small Ontario cities. Large-city organizations tend to have contacts at greater distances and their greater volume of contacts *tend to involve other large cities* (Wood, 1971).

Third, air-passenger services—which are dominated on most routes by information-bearing business and government travellers—normally attain their greatest nodality and traffic volumes at the largest units of any given system of cities. This has been demonstrated to be so in the U.S.A., Western Europe and several developing countries (e.g. Taaffe, 1962; Sealy, 1968; Sahlberg, 1970; Rosenberg, 1970; Reed, 1970).

Fourth, Alonso (1968a) and Friedmann (1972a) have described how great large-city information advantages arise in developing countries due, in part, to the unreliability and relative scarcity of long-distance communications facilities at other places. These advantages are also attributable to the need for face-to-face contacts generated by non-standardized business procedures, social institutions and extremely centralized political power.

And, fifth, in highly developed economies large metropolitan areas are usually 'information rich' agglomerations (Thorngren, 1970, p. 420), mainly because of their concentration of organizational headquarters and other management and control activities. These types of activity have been cumulatively attracted to such places by external 'communications economies' and 'overview advantages' (e.g. Hoover and Vernon, 1959; Lichtenberg, 1960; Isard, 1969, pp. 84–90; Törnqvist, 1970; Engström, 1970; Thörngren, 1972; Webber, 1972). Thus, for example, while the Stockholm, Göteborg, and Malmö metropolitan areas together contained 31 per cent of Sweden's 1966 population, they answered for more than 50 per cent of the nation's 'contact intensive' employees and for 62 per cent of the 'highest level' administrative employees in public administration and other services (Engström, 1970). *Under such circumstances, a disproportionately large percentage of non-local specialized information flows within a system of cities must inevitably have their origin or destination in major metropolitan centres.* Moreover, under laissez-faire conditions, non-routine inter-urban information flows will probably remain concentrated in leading metropolitan cities during the immediate future—even if major telecommunications advances are implemented.

Conclusion

The arguments and evidence presented here have elsewhere been welded into a non-deterministic multiple feedback-loop model of city-system development. To improve that large-city focused model, and to make both that model and the conceptual framework of this chapter more powerful policy-making tools, much additional empirical research needs to be carried out. Among the matters begging further empirical inquiry, the following items seem most to deserve of attention. Although data availability problems usually occur, further studies are needed on the inter-urban flow of goods, services, specialized information and capital. Ignorance needs to be removed regarding the existing structure of interdependencies within specific systems and sub-systems of cities. For much the same reasons, studies of the recently and presently existing spatial structure of organizations should be given high priority. The reconstruction of the inter-urban diffusion of specific growth-inducing innovations is necessary because most inter-urban diffusion studies deal with other types of innovations and because almost nothing is known of the precise paths of specialized information and influence involved. Inasmuch as city-system development presumably is so much a product of the information-biased action of private and public organizations, much more needs to be known of their contact patterns and locational search procedures.

Notes

1. This chapter in large measure consists of extracts from a monograph published elsewhere. See Allan R. Pred, 'The growth and development of systems of cities in advanced economies', in Gunnar Tornqvist and Allan R. Pred, *Information Flows and Systems of Cities: Two Essays, Lund Studies in Geography,* Series B 40, 1973.
2. A 'system of cities' is here conceived as a set of cities which are interdependent in such a way that any significant change in the economic activities, employment structure, total income and/or population of one member city will directly or indirectly bring about some alteration in the economic activities, occupational structure, total income and/or population of one or more other set member (cf. Berry, 1961; Pred 1971a, 1973a; Wärneryd, 1968).

References

Alonso, W., 1968a, *Industrial Location and Regional Policy in Economic Development,* Working Paper No. 74, University of California Department of City and Regional Planning and Center for Planning and Development Research, Berkeley.
Alonso, W., 1968b, 'Urban and regional imbalances in economic development', *Economic Development and Cultural Change,* 17, 1–14.
Alonso, W., 1971, 'The economics of urban size', *Papers of the Regional Science Association* 26, 67–83.
Alonso, W. and E. Medrich, 1972, 'Spontaneous growth centers in twentieth-century American urbanization', in Hansen, 1972b, 229–65.
Andersson, L., 1970, *Rumsliga effekter av organizationsförändringar. Studier i lokalisering med exempel från skolväsendet,* Meddelanden från Göteborgs Universitets Geografiska Institutioner, Series B, 17.
Artle, R., 1965, *The Structure of the Stockholm Economy: Toward a Framework for Projecting Metropolitan Community Development* (Ithaca: Cornell University Press).
Bain, J. S., 1968, *International Differences in Industrial Structure* (New Haven: Yale University Press).
Bain, J. S., 1968, *Industrial Organization* (New York: Wiley).
Belassa, B., 1961, *The Theory of Economic Integration* (Homewood, Ill.: R. D. Irwin).
Berry, B. J. L., 1961, 'Cities as systems within systems of cities', *Economic Development and Cultural Change,* 9, 573–87.
Berry, B. J. L., 1965, *Central Place Studies: A Bibliography of Theory and Applications,* 2nd ed. (Philadelphia: Regional Science Research Institute).
Berry, B. J. L., 1966, *Essays on Commodity Flows and the Spatial Structure of the Indian Economy,* University of Chicago, Department of Geography Research Paper No. 111.

132

Berry, B. J. L., 1967, *Geography of Market Centers and Retail Distribution* (Englewood Cliffs, N.J.: Prentice-Hall).

Berry, B. J. L., 1972, 'Hierarchical diffusion: the Basis of developmental filtering and spread in a system of growth centers', in Hansen, 1972b, 108–38.

Berry, B. J. L. and F. E. Horton, 1970, *Geographic Perspectives on Urban Systems* (Englewood Cliffs, N.J.: Prentice-Hall).

Borchert, J. R., 1972, 'America's changing metropolitan regions', *Annals of the Association of American Geographers, 62*, 352–73.

Boudeville, J. R., 1966, *Problems of Regional Economic Planning* (Edinburgh: The University Press).

Boulding, K. E., 1966, 'The economics of knowledge and the knowledge of economics', *American Economic Review, 56*, no. 2, 1–13.

Bourne, L. S. and G. Gad, 1972, 'Urbanization and urban growth in Ontario and Quebec: an overview', in Bourne and MacKinnon, 1972, 7–35.

Bourne, L. S. and R. D. MacKinnon (eds.) 1972, *Urban Systems Development in Canada: Selected Papers* (Toronto: University of Toronto Press).

Brown, L. A., 1968, *Diffusion Dynamics: A Review and Revision of the Quantitative Theory of the Spatial Diffusion of Innovation,* Lund Studies in Geography, Series B, 29.

Brown, L. A. and K. R. Cox, 1971, 'Empirical regularities in the diffusion of innovation', *Annals of the Association of American Geographers, 61*, 551–9.

Bylund, E., 1972a, 'Growth centre and administrative area problems within the framework of the Swedish location policy', in Kuklinski, 1972, 231–42.

Bylund, E., 1972b, 'Promemoria concerning growth centre problems within the framework of the Swedish policy', in Kuklinski and Petrella, 1972, 113–18.

Chisholm, M., 1968, *Geography and Economics* (New York: Praeger).

Clark, C., 1967, *Population Growth and Land Use* (London: Macmillan).

Cohen, Y. S., 1972, *Diffusion of an Innovation in an Urban System: The Spread of Planned Regional Shopping Centers in the United States 1949–1968,* University of Chicago, Department of Geography Research Paper No. 140.

Cyert, R. M. and J. G. March, 1963, *A Behavioral Theory of the Firm* (Englewood Cliffs, N.J.: Prentice-Hall).

Dahl, S., 1957, 'The contacts of Västerås with the rest of Sweden', in Hannerberg, Hägerstrand and Odeving, 1957, 206–44.

Danielsson, A., 1964, 'The locational decision from the point of view of the individual company', *Ekonomisk Tidskrift, 66*, 47–87.

Darwent, D. F., 1969, 'Growth poles and growth centers in regional planning—A Review', *Environment and Planning, 1*, 5–32.

Davies, J. B., 1972, 'Behaviour of the Ontario–Quebec urban system by size distribution', in Bourne and MacKinnon, 1972, 35–49.

Dicken, P., 1971, 'Some aspects of the decision-making behavior of business organizations', *Economic Geography, 47*, 426–37.

Drewe, P., 1970, *Elementary Features of Geographical Labour Mobility,* Netherlands Economics Institute, Rotterdam (mimeo).

Duncan, O. D., W. R. Scott, S. Lieberson, B. Duncan and H. H. Winsborough, 1960, *Metropolis and Region* (Baltimore: The Johns Hopkins Press).

Dunn, E. S., 1970, 'A flow network image of urban structures', *Urban Studies, 7*, 239–58.

Dunn, E. S., 1971, *Economic and Social Development: A Process of Social Learning* (Baltimore: The Johns Hopkins Press).

Ekström, A., S. Godlund, L. Nordström, B. Sundvall, M. Williamson and O. Wärneryd, 1971, *Interregionala beroenden i Sverige,* Statens vägverk, Tekniska avdelningen, Sektionen för översiktlig vägplanering, Stockholm.

Ekström, A., S. Godlund, L. Nordström, N. Williamson and O. Wärneryd, 1969, *Nordtrans: Norden som en gemensam lokaliseringsoch kommunikationsregion*, Meddelande från Göteborgs Universitets Geografiska Institutioner, Serice B, 10.

Engström, M.-G., 1970, *Regional arbetsfördelning: Nya drag i för-värvsarbetets geografiska organisation i Sverige* (Lund: Gleerup).

Friedmann, J., 1966, *Regional Development Policy: A Case Study of Venezuela* (Cambridge, Mass.: The M.I.T. Press).

Friedmann, J., 1968, 'An information model of urbanization', *Urban Affairs Quarterly*, 4, 235–44.

Friedmann, J., 1971, *The Implementation of Urban-Regional Development Policies: Lessons of Experience*, School of Architecture and Urban Planning, University of California, Los Angeles (mimeo).

Friedmann, J., 1972a, 'A general theory of polarized development', in Hansen, 1972b, 82–107.

Friedmann, J., 1972b, *The Future of the Urban Habitat*, School of Architecture and Urban Planning, University of California, Los Angeles (mimeo).

Friedmann, J., 1972c, *The Spatial Organization of Power and the Development of Urban Systems*, School of Architecture and Urban Planning, University of California, Los Angeles (mimeo).

Friedmann, J., E. McGlynn, B. Stuckey and C.-T. Wu, 1970, *Urbanization and National Development: A Comparative Analysis*, School of Architecture and Urban Planning, University of California, Los Angeles (mimeo).

Friedmann, J. and J. Miller, 1965, 'The urban field', *Journal of the American Institute of Planners*, 31, 312–19.

Fuchs, V. R., 1967, *Differentials in Hourly Earnings by Region and City Size*, National Bureau of Economic Research, Occasional Paper no. 101, New York.

Gauthier, H. L., 1968, 'Transportation and the growth of the Sao Paulo economy', *Journal of Regional Science*, 8, 77–94.

Gauthier, H. L., 1970, 'Geography, Transportation and Regional Development', *Economic Geography*, 46, 612–19.

Godlund, S., 1969, 'Det svenska näringslivets struktur—och lägesförändringar samt betydelsen härav for hamnverksamhetens och sjöfartens omfattning och lokalisering', in *Statens offentliga utredningar* 1969: 23, *De svenska hamnarna*, 30–194.

Gohman, V. M. and L. N. Karpov, 1972, 'Growth poles and growth centres', in Kuklinski, 1972, 125–33.

Golledge, R. G. and L. A. Brown, 1967, 'Search, learning and the market decision Process', *Geografiska Annaler*, 49B, 116–24.

Gomulka, S., 1971, *Inventive Activity, Diffusion and the Stages of Economic Growth*, Skrifter fra Aarhus Universitets Okonomiske Institute, 24.

Goodwin, W., 1965, 'The management center in the United States', *Geographical Review*, 55, 1–16.

Gottmann, J., 1961, *Megalopolis: The Urbanized Northeastern Seaboard of the United States* (New York: The Twentieth Century Fund).

Gould, P. R., 1960, *The Development of the Transportation Pattern in Ghana*, Northwestern University Studies in Geography, 5.

Gould, P. R., 1966, *Space Searching Procedures in Geography and the Social Sciences*, University of Hawaii Social Science Research Institute, Working Papers, No. 1 (mimeo).

Gould, P. R., 1970, 'Tanzania 1920–1963: the spatial impress of the modernization process', *World Politics*, 22, 149–70.

Gould, P. and G. Törnqvist, 1971, 'Information, Innovation and Acceptance', in Hägerstrand and Kuklinski, 1971, 148–68.

134

Groenman, S., 1969, 'Social aspects of backwardness in developed countries', in Robinson, 1969a, 21–34.

Guteland, G. A. and L. Nordström, 1970, 'Lokaliseringsbara enheter—rapport från en arbetsgrupp inom expertgruppen för regional utredningsverksamhet', in *Statens offentliga utredningar* 1970: 15, *Regionalekonomisk utveckling,* 9: 1–9: 34.

Hägerstrand, T., 1952, *The Propagation of Innovation Waves,* Lund Studies in Geography, Series B, 4.

Hägerstrand, T., 1957, 'Migration and area: survey of a sample of Swedish migration fields and hypothetical considerations on their genesis', in Hannerberg, Hägerstrand and Odeving, 1957, 27–158.

Hägerstrand, T., 1964, 'Urbaniseringen som världsproblem: Frän vertikal till horisontell länkning', *Ingeniörsvetenskapsakadimiens meddelande,* 139, 3–16.

Hägerstrand, T., 1966, 'Aspects of the spatial structure of social communications and the diffusion of information', *Papers of the Regional Science Association,* 16, 27–42.

Hägerstrand, T., 1967, *Innovation Diffusion as a Spatial Process* (with postscript and translation by Allan Pred), (Originally published in 1953 as *Innovationsförloppet ur korologisk synpunkt* (Lund: Gleerup).

Hägerstrand, T. and A. Kuklinski (eds.), 1971, *Information Systems for Regional Development—A Seminar,* Lund Studies in Geography, Series B, 37.

Haggett, P. and R. J. Chorley, 1969, *Network Analysis in Geography* (New York: St. Martin's Press).

Hamilton, F. E. Ian, 1967, 'Models of industrial location', in *Models in Geography* (London: Methuen), 361–424.

Hannerberg, D., T. Hägerstrand and B. Odeving (eds.), 1957, *Migration in Sweden: A Symposium,* Lund Studies in Geography, Series B, 13.

Hansen, N. M., 1967, 'Development pole theory in a regional context', *Kyklos,* 20, 709–25.

Hansen, N. M., 1968, *French Regional Planning* (Edinburgh: The University Press).

Hansen, N. M., 1970, *Rural Poverty and the Urban Crisis: A Strategy for Regional Development* (Bloomington: Indiana University Press).

Hansen, N. M., 1972a, 'Criteria for a growth centre policy', in Kuklinski, 1972, 103–24.

Hansen, N. M., (ed.), 1972b, *Growth Centers in Regional Economic Development* (New York: The Free Press).

Harvey, M. E., 1972, 'The identification of development regions in developing countries', *Economic Geography,* 48, 229–43.

Hedberg, B., 1970, *Kontaktsystem inom svenskt näringsliv. En studie av organizationers externa personkontakter* (Lund: Gleerup).

Helvig, M., 1964, *Chicago's External Truck Movements: Spatial Interactions between the Chicago Area and its Hinterland,* University of Chicago, Department of Geography Research Paper No. 90.

Hermansen, T., 1970, 'Development poles and development centres in national and regional development—elements of a theoretical framework' in U.N.R.I.S.D., 1970, 1–90; and in Kuklinski, 1972, 1–67.

Hermansen, T., 1971, 'Information systems for regional development planning: issues and problems', in Hägerstrand and Kuklinski, 1971, 1–37.

Hermansen, T., 1972, 'Development poles and related theories: a synoptic review', in Hansen, 1972b, 160–203.

Hirschman, A. O., 1958, *The Strategy of Economic Development* (New Haven: Yale University Press).

Hoch, I., 1972, 'Income and city size', *Urban Studies,* 9, 299–328.

Holmstrom, J. E., 1934, *Railways and Roads in Pioneer Development Overseas: A Study of Their Comparative Economics* (London: P. S. King & Son).

135

Hoover, E. M., 1969, 'Some old and new issues in regional development', in Robinson, 1969a, 343–57.
Hoover, E. M. and R. Vernon, 1959, *Anatomy of a Metropolis: The Changing Distribution of People and Jobs within the New York Metropolitan Region* (Cambridge, Mass.: Harvard University Press).
Hudson, J. C., 1969, 'Diffusion in a central place system', *Geographical Analysis,* 1, 25–58.
Hudson, J. C., 1972, *Geographical Diffusion Theory,* Northwestern University Studies in Geography, 19.
Illeris, S. and P. O. Pedersen, 1968, *Central Places and Functional Regions in Denmark: Factor Analysis of Telephone Traffic,* Lund Studies in Geography, Series B, 31.
Isard, W., 1960, *Methods of Regional Analysis* (Cambridge, Mass.: The M.I.T. Press).
Isard, W., 1969, *General Theory: Social, Political, Economic, and Regional* (Cambridge, Mass.: The M.I.T. Press).
Isard, W. and T. W. Langford, 1971, *Regional Input–Output Study: Recollections, Reflections and Diverse Notes on the Philadelphia Experience* (Cambridge, Mass.: The M.I.T. Press).
Isard, W. and E. W. Schooler, 1959, 'Industrial complex analysis, agglomeration economies and regional development', *Journal of Regional Science,* 1, 19–33.
Isard, W., E. W. Schooler and T. Vietoriz, 1959, *Industrial Complex Analysis and Regional Development: A Case Study of Refinery-Petrochemical-Synthetic Fiber Complexes and Puerto Rice* (Cambridge, Mass.: The M.I.T. Press).
Janelle, D. G., 1968, 'Central place development in a time-space framework', *Professional Geographer,* 20, 5–10.
Janelle, D. G., 1969, 'Spatial reorganization: a model and concept', *Annals of the Association of American Geographers,* 59, 348–64.
Jansen, A. C. M., 1970, 'The value of growth pole theory for economic geography' *Tijdschrift Voor Economishe en Sociale Geografie,* 61, 67–76.
Johnson, E. A. J., 1970, *The Organization of Space in Developing Countries* (Cambridge, Mass.: Harvard University Press).
Karaska, G. J., 1969, 'Manufacturing linkages in the Philadelphia economy: some evidence of external agglomeration forces', *Geographical Analysis,* 1, 354–69.
Katz, D. and R. L. Kahn, 1966,[R] *The Social Psychology of Organizations* (New York: Wiley).
Keeble, D. E., 1967, 'Models of economic development', in R. J. Chorley and P. Haggett (eds.), *Models in Geography* (London: Methuen), 243–302.
Keeble, D. E., 1971, 'Employment mobility in Britain', in M. Chisholm and G. Manners (eds.), *Spatial Policy Problems of the British Economy* (Cambridge University Press), 24–68.
Klaassen, L. H., 1970, 'Growth poles in economic theory and policy', in U.N.R.I.S.D., 1970, 91–144; and Kuklinski and Petrella, 1972, 1–40.
Krumme, G., 1969, 'Towards a geography of enterprise', *Economic Geography,* 45, 30–40.
Kuklinski, A. R. (ed.), 1972, *Growth Poles and Growth Centres in Regional Planning* (The Hague: Mouton).
Kuklinski, A. and R. Petrella (eds.), 1972, *Growth Poles and Regional Policies* (The Hague: Mouton).
Lampard, E. E., 1968, 'The evolving system of cities in the United states: urbanization and economic development', in Perloff and Wingo, 1968, 81–139.
Lasuen, J. R., 1969, 'On growth poles', *Urban Studies,* 6, 137–61.
Lasuen, J. R., 1971, 'Multi-regional economic development: an open-system approach', in Hägerstrand and Kuklinski, 1971, 169–211.

136

Leven, C. L., 1963, *Theory and Method of Income and Product Accounts for Metropolitan Areas, including the Elgin–Dundee Area as a Case Study,* Center for Regional Economic Studies, University of Pittsburgh.

Lichtenberg, R. M., 1960, *One/Tenth of a Nation: National Forces in the Economic Growth of the New York Region* (Cambridge, Mass.: Harvard University Press).

Logan, M. I., 1970, 'The process of regional development and its implications for planning', *Journal of the Geographical Association of Nigeria,* 3, 109–20.

Lukermann, F., 1966, 'Empirical expressions of nodality and hierarchy in a circulation manifold', *East Lakes Geographer,* 2, 17–44.

Madden, C. H., 1956, 'On some indications of stability in the growth of cities in the United States', *Economic Development and Cultural Change,* 4, 236–52.

Mansfield, E., 1968, *Industrial Research and Technological Innovation* (New York: W. W. Norton).

March, J. G. and H. A. Simon, 1958, *Organizations* (New York: Wiley).

Maruyama, M., 1963, 'The second cybernetics: deviation-amplifying mutual causal processes', *American Scientist,* 51, 164–79.

Meier, R. L., 1962, *A Communications Theory of Urban Growth* (Cambridge, Mass.: The M.I.T. Press).

Misra, R. P., 1970, 'Growth pole hypothesis re-examined' in U.N.R.I.S.D., 1970, 233–53.

Misra, R. P., 1971, 'The diffusion of information in the context of development planning', in Hägerstrand and Kuklinski, 1971, 119–36.

Misra, R. P., 1972, 'Growth poles and growth centres in the context of India's urban and regional development problems', in Kuklinski, 1972, 141–68.

Myrdal, G., 1957, *Economic Theory and Under-Developed Regions* (London: Duckworth).

Neutze, G. M., 1967, *Economic Policy and the Size of Cities* (New York: Augustus M. Kelley).

Nichols, V., 1969, 'Growth poles: an evaluation of their propulsive effect', *Environment and Planning,* 1, 193–208.

Norborg, K., 1968, *Jordbruksbefolkningen i Sverige. Regional struktur och förändring under 1900–talet* (Lund: Gleerup).

Nordström, L., 1968, *Organisationer i rummet: Några reflexioner och exempel på det rumsliga samspelet—verksamheter och organizationer,* Göteborgs Universitets kultur geografiska institution (mimeo).

Nordström, L., 1971, *Rumsliga förändringar och ekonomisk utveckling,* (Göteborg: Regionkonsult Aktiebolag).

Nystuen, J. D. and M. F. Dacey, 1961, 'A graph theory interpretation of nodal regions', *Papers of the Regional Science Association* 7, 29–42.

Ohlin, B., 1933, *Interregional and International Trade* (Cambridge, Mass.: Harvard University Press).

Ohlsson, B., 1972, *Företagsservice—Urbanisering, en studie av tre konsultbyråbranscher,* Urbaniseringsprocessen, 47 (mimeo).

Olsson, G., 1967, 'Deductive and inductive approaches to model formulation', in *Proceedings of the First Scandinavian–Polish Regional Science Seminar* (Warsaw: Polish Scientific Publishers).

Pedersen, P. O., 1970, 'Innovation diffusion within and between National urban systems', *Geographical Analysis,* 2, 203–54.

Pedersen, P. O., 1971a, 'Innovation diffusion in urban systems', in Hagerstrand and Kuklinski, 1971, 137–47.

Pedersen, P. O., 1971b, *Urban-regional development in South America: a Process of diffusion and integration,* Den Polytekniske Laeranstalts Institut for Vejbyggning samt Trafikteknik og Byplanlaegning, Copenhagen (mimeo).

Pedersen, P. O., 1971c, 'Vaekstcentrer og bysystemer', Økonomi og Politik, 141–67.

Penouil, M., 1969, 'An appraisal of regional development policy in the Aquitaine region', in Robinson, 1969a, 62–112.

Penouil, M., 1972, 'Growth poles in underdeveloped regions and countries', in Kuklinski and Petrella, 1972, 119–43.

Perloff, H. S., E. S. Dunn, E. E. Lampard and R. F. Muth, 1960, Regions, Resources and Economic Growth (Baltimore: The Johns Hopkins Press).

Perloff, H. S. L. Wingo (eds.), 1968, Issues in Urban Economics (Baltimore: The Johns Hopkins Press).

Perroux, F., 1950, 'Economic space: theory and applications', Quarterly Journal of Economics, 64, 89–104.

Perroux, F., 1955, 'Note sur la notion de pole de crôissance', Economie Appliquée, 8, 307–20.

Pfouts, R. W., 1957, 'An empirical testing of the economic base theory', Journal of the American Institute of Planners, 23, 64–9.

Pottier, P., 1963, 'Axes de communication et theórie dé développement' Revue Économique, 14, 70–128.

Pred, A. R., 1965, 'Industrialization, initial advantage and American metropolitan growth', Geographical Review, 55, 158–85.

Pred, A. R., 1966, The Spatial Dynamics of U.S. Urban-Industrial Growth, 1800–1914: Interpretive and Theoretical Essays (Cambridge, Mass.: The M.I.T. Press).

Pred, A. R., 1971a, 'Large-city interdependence and the preelectronic diffusion of innovations in the U.S.', Geographical Analysis, 3, 165–81.

Pred, A. R., 1971b, 'Urban systems development and the long-distance flow of information through preelectronic U.S. newspapers', Economic Geography, 47, 498–524.

Pred, A. R., 1973a, Information Circulation and the Process of Urban Growth: The U.S. System of Cities, 1790–1840 (Cambridge, Mass.: Harvard University Press).

Pred, A. R., 1973b, 'Urbanisation, domestic planning problems and Swedish geographic research', Progress in Geography, 5, 1–76.

Pyle, G. F., 1969, 'The diffusion of cholera in the United States in the nineteenth century', Geographical Analysis, 1, 59–75.

Ray, D. M., 1971, 'The location of United State manufacturing subsidiaries in Canada', Economic Geography, 47, 389–400.

Reed, W. E., 1967, Areal Interaction in India: Commodity Flows of the Bengal-Bihar Industrial Area, University of Chicago, Department of Geography Research Paper No. 110.

Reed, W. E., 1970, 'Indirect connectivity and hierarchies of urban dominance', Annals of the Association of American Geographers, 60, 770–85.

Richardson, H. W., 1972, 'Optimality in city size, systems of cities and urban policy: a sceptic's view', Urban Studies, 9, 29–48.

Riddell, J. B., 1970, The Spatial Dynamics of Modernization in Sierra Leone (Evanston: Northwestern University Press).

Riddell, J. B., 1972, 'Mechanisms for hierarchical diffusion', Annals of the Association of American Geographers, 62, 152–3.

Rimmer, P. J., 1967, 'The changing status of New Zealand seaports, 1853–1960', Annals of the Association of American Geographers, 57, 88–100.

Robinson, E. A. G. (ed.), 1969a, Backward Areas in Advanced Countries (London: Macmillan).

Robinson, E. A. G., 1969b, 'Location theory, regional economics and backward areas', in Robinson, 1969a, 3–20.

Rodwin, L., 1970, Nations and Cities: A Comparison of Strategies for Urban Growth (Boston: Houghton Mifflin).

Rogers, E. M., 1962, Diffusion of Innovation (New York: The Free Press).

138

Rogers, E. M. and F. F. Shoemaker, 1971, *The Communication of Innovations: A Cross-Cultural Approach* (New York: The Free Press).

Rosenberg, N., 1970, *Air Travel within Europe*, Stockholm: the National Swedish Consumer Council.

Rosenberg, N., 1972, *Technology and American Economic Growth* (New York: Harper & Row).

Sahlberg, B., 1970, *Interregionala kontakt monster. Personkontakter inom svenskt näringsliv- en flygpassagerstudie.* (Lund: Gleerup).

Schon, D. A., 1967, *Technology and Change: The New Heraclitus* (New York: Dell Publishing).

Schumpeter, J. A., 1934, *The Theory of Economic Development* (translated by R. Ovie) (Cambridge, Mass.: Harvard University Press).

Sealy, K. R., 1968, *The Geography of Air Transport* (3rd ed.) (Chicago: Aldine Publishing).

Sharp, V. L., 1971, 'The 1970 Postal Strikes: Diffusion with a Behavioral Twist', *Proceedings of the Association of American Geographers*, 3, 157–61.

Simmons, J. W., 1970a, *Interprovincial Interaction Patterns in Canada*, University of Toronto Centre for Urban and Community Studies, Research Paper No. 24 (mimeo).

Simmons, J. W., 1970b, *Patterns of Interaction within Ontario and Quebec*, University of Toronto Centre for Urban and Community Studies, Research Paper No. 41 (mimeo).

Simmons, J. W., 1972, 'Interaction among the cities of Ontario and Quebec', in Bourne and MacKinnon, 1972, 198–219.

Soja, E., 1968, *The Geography of Modernization in Kenya* (Syracuse University Press).

Starbuck, W. H., 1965, 'Organizational growth and development', in J. G. March (ed.), *Handbook of Organizations* (Chicago: Rand McNally), 451–533.

Stigler, G. J., 1961, 'The economics of information', *Journal of Political Economy*, 69, 213–25.

Stolper, W., 1955, 'Spatial order and the economic growth of cities', *Economic Development and Cultural Change*, 3, 137–46.

Strassmann, W. P., 1959, *Risk and Technological Innovation: American Manufacturing Methods during the Nineteenth Century* (Ithaca: Cornell University Press).

Taaffe, E. J., 1962, 'The urban hierarchy: an air passenger definition', *Economic Geography*, 38, 1–14.

Taaffe, E. J., R. L. Morrill and P. R. Gould, 1963, 'Transport expansion in underdeveloped countries: a comparative analysis', *Geographical Review*, 53, 503–29.

Thomas, M. D., 1972a, 'Growth pole theory: an examination of some of its basic concepts' in Hansen, 1972b, 50–81.

Thomas, M. D., 1972b, 'The regional Problem, structural change and growth pole theory', in Kuklinski, 1972, 69–102.

Thompson, W. R., 1965, *A Preface to Urban Economics* (Baltimore: The Johns Hopkins Press).

Thompson, W. R., 1968, 'Internal and external factors in the development of urban economies' in Perloff and Wingo, 1968, 43–62.

Thompson, W. R., 1972, 'The national system of cities as an object of public policy', *Urban Studies*, 9, 99–116.

Thorngren, B., 1970, 'How do contact systems affect regional development?', *Environment and Planning*, 2, 409–27.

Thorngren, B., 1972, *Studier i lokalisering* (Stockholm: Beckmans).

Tiebout, C. M., 1958, 'Exports and regional economic growth', *Journal of Political Economy*, 160–69.

Tiebout, C. M., 1962, *The Community Base Study* (New York: Committee for Economic Development).

139

Tolosa, H. and T. A. Reiner, 1970, 'The economic programming of a system of planned poles', *Economic Geography*, **46**, 449–58.

Törnqvist, G., 1962, *Transport Costs as a Location Factor for Manufacturing Industry*, Lund Studies in Geography, Series B, 23.

Törnqvist, G., 1968, *Flows of Information and the Location of Economic Activity*, Lund Studies in Geography, Series B, 30.

Törnqvist, G., 1970, *Contact Systems and Regional Development*, Lund Studies in Geography, Series B, 35.

Törnqvist, G., 1972, 'Kontaktbehov och resemöjligheter—några Sverigemodeller för studier av regionala utvecklingsalternativ', in expertgruppen för regional utredningsverksamhet (1970), *Regioner att leva i. Elva forskare om regionalpolitik och välstånd* (Stockholm: Allmänna Förlaget), 245–84.

U.N.R.I.S.D. [United Nations Research Institute for Social Development] 1970, *A Review of the Concepts and Theories of Growth Poles and Growth Centres*, Geneva (mimeo).

Vance, J. E., 1970, *The Merchant's World: The Geography of Wholesaling* (Englewood Cliffs, N.J.: Prentice–Hall).

Wärneryd, O., 1968, *Interdependence in Urban Systems* (Göteborg: Regionkonsult Aktiebolag).

Wärneryd, O., 1971, 'An operational model for regional planning and development control', in Hägerstrand and Kuklinski, 1971, 230–45.

Webber, M. J., 1972, *Impact of Uncertainty on Location* (Cambridge, Mass.: The M.I.T. Press).

Whebell, C. F. J., 1969, 'Corridors: a theory of urban systems', *Annals of the Association of American Geographers*, **59**, 1–26.

Williams, B. R. and W. P. Scott, 1970, *Investment Proposals and Decisions* (London: Allen and Unwin).

Wingo, L., 1972, 'Issues in a national urban development strategy for the United States', *Urban Studies*, **9**, 3–27.

Wolpert, J., 1964, 'The decision process in spatial context', *Annals of the Association of American Geographers*, **54**, 537–58.

Wood, C. J. B., 1971, 'Some characteristics of searching by municipal governments', *Geografiska Annaler*, **53B**, 138–45.

Worley, J. S., 1962, 'The changing direction of research and development employment among firms', in National Bureau of Economic Research, *The Rate and Direction of Inventive Activity: Economic and Social Factors* (Princeton University Press), 233–251.

Yeates, M. H. and P. E. Lloyd, 1970, *Impact of Industrial Incentives: Southern Georgian Bay Region, Ontario*. Geographical Paper No. 44, Policy and Planning Branch, Department of Energy, Mines and Resources, Ottawa, Canada.

II Corporate Growth, Organization and Location Decisions

5

Invention, Diffusion and Allometry: A Study of the Growth and Form of the Pulp and Paper Industry in Central Canada

ROGER A. ROBERGE, D. MICHAEL RAY AND PAUL Y. VILLENEUVE

An Integrated Approach to the Growth and Form of Industry

The development of a dynamic theory of industrial location requires an increased understanding of the role of technological change. Griliches's path-breaking study of the invention, diffusion and rate of acceptance of hybrid corn has challenged researchers by providing an integrated view of technological change through time and space (Griliches, 1957). There are still no studies of equal scope for manufacturing activity, despite analysis of the spatial dimensions of invention, diffusion and adoption by Mansfield (1961), Morrill (1968) and Pred (1966). The objective of this chapter is to integrate the concepts of invention, diffusion and rate of acceptance, employing the concept of allometry to measure rate of acceptance for the central Canada pulp and paper industry. An invention generates large-scale change in industrial location by its spread within or between social and economic systems, inducing further adaptive inventive activity and thus accelerating social and economic change. The diffusion and allometry of inventive activity are complementary aspects of growth and form; both aspects are needed for a comprehensive understanding of system dynamics. Diffusion is the spatial dimension of absolute growth. Allometry is concerned directly with relative growth, although it has been defined more broadly as the study of size and its consequences (Gould, 1965).

Allometry

Allometry relates the size of one part of a system to the size of the total

143

144

system or other system components, either longitudinally for one system as it grows through time, or cross-sectionally for a number of comparable systems of different sizes at one point in time. The relative size of components usually changes during system growth; often, relative growth follows the law of simple allometry in which the ratio of the specific growth rate of a component to that of the entire system remains constant over the growth period (Naroll and von Bertalanffy, 1956). Moreover, if the system components are spatially defined, as in most geographic systems, the allometries may reveal growth gradients in which relative growth rates increase or decrease systematically with distance from some growth centre. The topic of allometric growth gradients—which Huxley regarded as the most important single finding of his research on relative growth—has received little attention since the publication of his seminal study. A satisfactory theory for the generality and regularity of growth gradients in either biological or geographic systems is still lacking (Huxley, 1932).

Indeed, allometry itself, remains relatively neglected in social science, despite the important insights it can yield into such problems as spatial concentration and regional disparity, the changing spatial organization of urban and regional systems with increasing size and changing technology and, more generally, the recognition of the consequences of size and the limits to growth. Enough examples of allometric growth both implicit and explicit already exist to demonstrate the pervasive consequences of size in urban and regional systems (Naroll and von Bertalanffy, 1956; Ray, 1972). Many aspects of urbanization, employment levels, occupation structure, transportation and international trade also display simple allometric growth in which the ratio of specific growth rates of a component to that of its system is a constant. But few attempts have been made to explain the allometries observed.

Hypotheses

The overriding hypothesis of this study is that a single, fundamental set of characteristics control the diffusion of innovation in industrial technology, influence the magnitude of first adoption and determine the subsequent allometries and growth gradients. Thus the date at which an innovation is adopted, the initial level of acceptance and the subsequent rate of relative growth are believed to be statistically interdependent and spatially related, as follows:

(1) A set of inventions and innovations occurs at some centre which then achieves accelerating–decelerating logistic growth in adopting and producing the innovation.

(2) Diffusion of the innovation begins, following communication channels reflecting patterns of spatial interaction and organization, and successively endowing other centres with logistic growth.

(3) The relative growth-rates or allometries at successive centres increase outward from the first innovation centre, creating growth gradients; faster peripheral growth rates compensate in part for a later start.

That is, places adopting a technology later will generally do so on a larger scale, generating faster growth from adoption. This hypothesis underlines the costs of precocious adoption. Early entrepreneurial and industrial adoption may require considerable additional reinvestments to incorporate later developments. Harvey has recently described in these terms the consequences of locational inertia:

> The trouble is that these fixed assets are invaluable to us. Yet most of them were created in a past era and reflect the technology, taste, norms, production needs, and the like, of a former society. There is thus a continuous state of tension between the spatial organization of society (which is made up of increments of assets each created in its own era) and the form of spatial organization demanded by the new social order emerging here and now. (Harvey, 1972, p. 1)

The Pulp and Paper Industry

These hypotheses are tested for the pulp and paper industry in Ontario and Quebec from 1880 to 1940. Pulp and paper manufacture, which has been concentrated historically in central Canada, is the nation's second largest export industry. Canada is the world's largest producer of newsprint (48 per cent in 1970) and second largest producer of wood-pulp (16·3 per cent in 1968).

The unit of analysis throughout is the individual pulp and paper plant. For most of the period studies, the individual plant coincided with the firm; there were few multi-plant firms of any significance. Only later, in the second technological epoch from 1915 to 1940, did firms emerge to own or control many plants. Concentration of the industry into a few firms was largely achieved during five years, 1925–1930 (Bladen, 1946, p. 184). By 1930, three corporations controlled 45 per cent of operating newsprint capacity: Consolidated Paper, Abitibi Power and Paper and Canadian International Paper (C.I.P.). In addition to these big corporations there were two other big producers: St. Lawrence Corporation and Price Brothers. Together they accounted for another 20 per cent of total capacity. Thus five corporations accounted for 65 per cent of daily capacity. According to Bladen, this concentration resulted from three sets of influences: (1) scale economies made possible by integration which lowered costs and increased profit margins; (2) the possibility of controlling competition and so maintaining higher prices in a classic oligopolistic manner; (3) the strong stock market in pulp and paper securities for multi-plant firms (Bladen, 1946, p. 184).

Dealing with separate industrial plants rather than the pulp and paper firm does not seriously affect our results until the late 1920s and early 1930s. Although new plants were built during this period and thus reflect overall corporate strategy, they nevertheless make up only a small proportion of total capacity. The multi-plant firms which arose were mainly consolidations of already existing plants. Initial location decisions, therefore, cannot be attributed to the multi-plant firms. Each corporation did reflect a certain regional concentration: the Abitibi in northern Ontario; C.I.P. on the St. Maurice; Consolidated Paper and Price Brothers on the Saguenay. Generally, the corporations took over plants which were the most efficient in each of these areas. However, the corporations had over-extended themselves by the late 1930s. Abitibi Co. was in receivership and Consolidated was already reorganized. After this experience, future capacity growth was concentrated at existing locations; few new plants opened. To differentiate diffusion and allometric patterns of the multi-plant firm from the individual firm the study would have to be extended beyond the time period selected for this analysis.

Continuing inventive activity has played a compelling role in the growth of the pulp and paper industry throughout the study period because of the need to adopt and adapt borrowed, foreign technology to domestic environmental conditions and factor proportions, and because it is primarily an export industry, competing for largely unprotected world markets. Inventive activity is thus appropriately viewed in the context of staple theory, a Canadian contribution to economic development theory.

The fundamental assumption of this theory is that staple exports are the leading sector in newly settled countries, setting the pace of economic development (Caves and Holton, 1959). General determinants of staple theory comprise the elements of spatial interaction: complementarity, transferability and the absence of intervening opportunity; the specific determinants are the characteristics of the industry itself. These help to explain the rate of inventive activity and the diffusion and the allometric growth gradients of the industry during each technological epoch.

This chapter reviews staple theory as it applies to the pulp and paper industry during the two technological epochs from 1880 to 1915 and from 1915 to 1940. Fundamental industry characteristics are then identified and applied in turn to explain the diffusion and allometric growth of the groundwood pulp industry.

Staple Theory and Inventive Activity

W. A. Mackintosh published the earliest Canadian statement urging use of the staple approach, but Harold Innis developed the theory as a particularly Canadian phenomenon (Mackintosh, 1923; Innis, 1930; Watkins, 1963). According to Innis, Canadian development did not evolve out of a non-market or subsistence economy and so does not correspond to conventional theory usually associated with nineteenth century German political economists and N. S. B. Gras in America (Gras, 1922).

Gras describes a typical sequence of development stages according to which regions are initially self-sufficient. Higher living standards are achieved as trade in agricultural products develops following reduction of transfer costs and increased specialization of production. Agricultural output in an area has an upper limit regardless of agricultural land-use intensity, so incomes cannot rise indefinitely unless agriculture is supplemented by other economic activities. Similar limitations apply to forestry and fishing but not to manufacturing. Thus continuing increases in regional income depend ultimately on industrialization. The stages theory as North points out, was formulated in the context of European development where a market-oriented economy emerged only gradually from primarily local subsistence economies (North, 1955). When the stages theory is compared with the economic history of North American and other countries settled in by Europeans, two basic objections arise: first, these stages bear little resemblance to actual development patterns and second, the stages fail to provide any insights into the processes of economic growth and change.

The staple approach, by contrast, focuses on the role of successive exports in Canadian economic history, including, first, fish and fur, then timber, wheat, pulp and paper, and finally minerals. The independent variable, assumed to initiate the development of a staple in a new country, is complementarity as indicated by the price received on world markets. Transferability sets additional constraints to the development of a staple export including the existence of an international transportation and communications network and an international power structure to keep the peace. Given these, the sole remaining determinant can then be isolated, namely the character of the export being exported (Watkins, 1963).

The character of the staple sets its production function. Succinctly defined, the production function is the technical relationship stating the amount of output capable of being produced by each and every set of inputs. Thus the possibility of factor substitution is raised such as replacing labour by capital inputs together with increasing returns as scale economies are introduced. However, what explains the manner in which production functions evolve? In answering this question, Innis was influenced by Schumpeter's critique of the then current models of economic growth (Schumpeter, 1961). Classical models failed to account for the process of economic growth because economic development is a 'distinct phenomenon entirely foreign to the tendency toward equilibrium posited by the classical model' (Schumpeter, 1961, p. 62). Economic development rather results from 'spontaneous and discontinuous change in the channels of flow, disturbance of the equilibrium stage previously existing' (Schumpeter, 1961, p. 64). Innovation destroys the equilibrium state predicted by classical models by creating a higher profit rate and reducing unit production cost. The innovation-induced rise in profit rates attracts imitators and stimulates diffusion of the innovation.

Economic development in the Schumpeterian system is a process during which the interaction of the kind described above takes place not only between two industries, but vertically and horizontally throughout the economy's input–output relationships.

Clearly Schumpeter was right in signalling technological change as a significant variable in the growth process, but he saw little dependence of innovation on the rate of invention. Rather it was the entrepreneur/innovator who held centre stage in the Schumpeterian analysis (Schumpeter, 1961, p. 66): at any one time various inventions exist and could be profitable if exploited, but it does not occur as any automatic response to favourable economic conditions but rather awaits the vision of the entrepreneur. Invention is regarded as some kind of on-going process which expresses either the laws governing the growth of knowledge or the response of individuals to intellectual stimuli.

Although Innis (1956) acknowledged the role of technological change in stimulating growth, he, like Schumpeter, maintained that technological change was exogenous. Since its occurrence was assumed to be economically unpredictable, he did not examine the conditions under which technological change occurred. Whether such an assumption stemmed from conviction or methodological convenience is unclear. In any case, the conditions under which technological change occurred in Canada were given scant attention except to say that new technology was largely borrowed from foreign sources.

Determinants of Inventive Activity

The growth rate of a nation's technological capacity has been viewed in two different ways, either the rate of production of new technology or the diffusion of already existing technology. The process implied begins with invention and culminates with a technology incorporated within a given industry. Such a distinction indicates that even where invention occurs at only one point it may still be applied at many around the world.

This distinction between invention and innovation confuses rather than enlightens. The list of important inventions compiled for any one industry indicates that few have originated in developing regions or countries. Yet invention is not an unimportant element in the economic growth of technology-importing countries. To transfer technology properly to new environments, it must be adapted to new materials, sites and scales of operation. Although some such adaptations might be obvious to those skilled in the art, they are, nevertheless, crucial if the new technology is to operate at all, or at a level of efficiency which approaches that of the donor country. Thus, the introduction of new technology to different environments requires independent invention in the recipient country or region.

The Timing of Inventive Activity

In accounting for the rate or timing of inventive activity, attention must be paid to the motivations which stimulate local inventors to adapt and possibly even to improve foreign technology. If, as Schmookler maintains, the rate of inventive activity in controlled by economic variables, then integration of inventive activity and staple theory is not only feasible but desirable (Schmookler, 1966). Clearly the staple theory approach to the investment process provides more complete determinants of the inventive activity rate than merely market size for a particular class of industrial goods.

The first determinant of the staple theory is the existence of an international demand for the commodity coupled with an international transport and communications network. It follows that if demand for a staple export increases, the quantity supplied by the new country will increase. Export expansion influences the timing of inventive activity since equipment receives its maximum use during periods of peak production. Even if problems were recognized before peak in demand were reached, motivation for seeking solutions to them is likely to be greater during this period. A time lag then occurs between the peak in invention and the peak in demand equal to the interval between the recognition of problems and of the solutions i.e. the invention (Schmookler, 1966, p. 111). Such a corresponding relationship between the lagged-rate of inventive activity and the volume of exports has been established for the central Canada pulp and paper industry, providing evidence for an endogenous view of inventive activity (Roberge, 1972, p. 34). Such a relationship, however, says nothing about types of inventive activity within an industry: that is derived from specific determinants of the staple theory which establish the production function.

Types of Inventive Activity: Technological Epochs

Production theory recognizes two major categories of technological change, neutral and non-neutral. A neutral change alters the production function but not the marginal rate of substitution. Examples include changes in the scale and efficiency of a technology. Non-neutral changes, however, involve changes in the marginal rate of substitution associated with variations in the capital-intensity and the elasticity of substitution of a technology (Brown, 1966, p. 27).

Possibilities for substitution are restricted by the capital equipment already installed, and so time must be introduced into the classification. Short-term, long-term and secular technological changes may be distinguished (Brown, 1966, p. 75). The short term is the period within which the ease of substitution between capital and labour is limited by capital equipment already installed: only minor improvements on an existing production function are possible. This limitation vanishes in the long run and is replaced by alternative capital/labour combinations under which production is feasible. The secular period in turn relaxes the limitation since the fund of technical knowledge itself changes radically, so defining a technological epoch.

Canadian staple producers adopted current foreign production functions, incorporating the best current long-term practice, when international markets opened up. Once installed, further short-term changes were likely to result from adaptations or substitution possibilities which were influenced by the relative domestic availability of production factors. However, there is a limit beyond which further substitutions of factors creates diminishing returns. A technological disequilibrium results whenever discrepancies occur in the ability of different steps to equal or exceed expected levels of performance (Rosenberg, 1963). Exploratory inventive activity is initiated and culminates in a new technological epoch.

The first technological epoch in the pulp and paper industry is defined as a non-neutral change (Roberge, 1972, p. 69). Essentially, it consisted in substituting machinery for the highly skilled labour which was required to produce paper from rags. The Canadian skilled labour supply was highly limited: development depended upon large inputs of foreign capital. Capital substitution yielded the paper machine and the mechanical and sulphite wood pulping processes. The paper machine solved the skilled labour shortage but in time created a discrepancy between productive capacity and raw material supply. Development of a commercial process to convert wood into pulp involved new machinery, such as digesters and grinders, and therefore marks the termination of the first technological epoch which extended from 1867 to 1915.

The concern of the second technological epoch (1915–1940) was a neutral change involving economies of scale. An increase in market demand is one basic prerequisite for increasing the scale of production of a commodity. Demand for newsprint and the number and size of daily newspapers varies with the literacy rate of the population served. The basic factor in increased output of newsprint, and the ground wood pulp from which it is produced, was the spread of compulsory education in the United States and Canada. Per capita consumption increased from 8 lbs in 1890 to 30 lbs in 1921 and 62 lbs in 1939 (Bladen, 1946, p. 176). In addition, depletion of spruce in the United States resulted in large-scale transfer of the industry to Canada. Evidence for larger scale operations is the increase of capital–output ratios for the Canadian pulp and paper industry relative to total manufacturing (Table 5.1). The net effect of these forces was to generate a powerful exponential growth of the industry between 1914 and 1930 (Figure 5.1); this has continued till today.

By 1940 industry growth had resulted in new plant development throughout Ontario and Quebec. Sites chosen exhibited marked differences in procurement, processing and marketing costs. Analysis of the diffusion

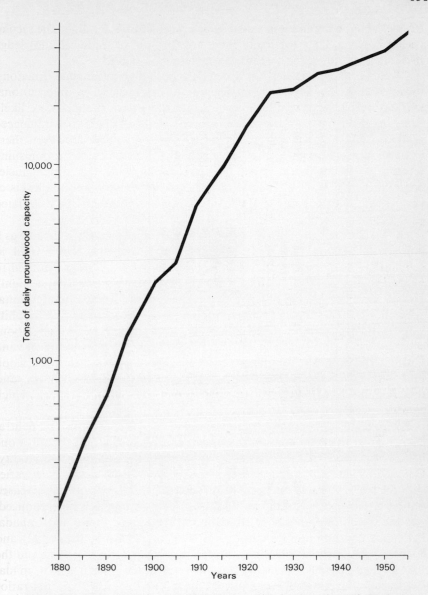

Figure 5.1. Tons of daily groundwood capacity in Ontario and Quebec: 1880–1955 (source: *Lockwood's Pulp and Paper and Allied Industries Directory*, 1875–1970 (New York: Lockwood Publishing Co.).

process therefore involves both evaluation of site characteristics and appreciation of the effects of pulp and paper industry technology on the diffusion process itself.

Table 5.1. Capital/Output Ratios for the Canadian Pulp and Paper Industry and for All Canadian Manufacturing, 1890–1939

	Canadian pulp and paper industry			All Canadian manufacturing		
	Total invested capital $	Total value of products $	Capital/output ratio	Total invested capital $	Total value of products $	Capital/output ratio
1890[1]	4,673,211	2,575,477	1·8	354,620,750	476,258,886	0·7
1901[2]	19,066,379	8,627,557	2·2	446,916,487	481,053,375	0·9
1911[3]	53,886,933	23,226,479	2·3	1,247,583,609	1,165,975,639	1·0
1921[4]	379,812,751	140,186,457	2·7	3,210,709,288	2,747,926,675	1·2
1928[4]	685,687,031	233,077,512	2·9	4,780,296,049	3,769,850,364	1·3
1939[4]	714,437,104	215,674,246	4·6	3,674,024,449	3,474,783,528	1·1

Sources. 1. *Census of Canada*, 1890–1, Vol. 3, 'Manufactures' (Ottawa: Queen's Printer)., 1894.
2. *Third Census of Canada*, 1901, Vol. 3, 'Manufactures' (Ottawa: King's Printer), 1905.
3. *Fourth Census of Canada*, 1911, Vol. 3, 'Manufactures' (Ottawa: King's Printer), 1916.
4. Dominion Bureau of Statistics, 1920–1, *General Review of Manufacturing Industries of Canada* (Ottawa: Queen's Printer).

The Diffusion of Innovations in Economic Systems

Production function theory, which explains how Canadian entrepreneurs came to use new techniques also explains their diffusion within Canada. Two broad approaches to spatial diffusion theory exist within geography (Hägerstrand, 1966). The first or neighbourhood effect suggests that in an economic system, the closer a potential adoption unit is to the place of an invention, or to another unit that has already adopted the invention, the greater is the probability that it will adopt before potential adopters who are further away. The second is that inventions diffuse through the central place hierarchy.

'A closer analysis shows that the spread along the initial "frontier" is led through the urban hierarchy. The point of introduction in a new country is its primate city; sometimes some other metropolis. Then centres next in rank follow. Soon, however, this order is broken up and replaced by one where the neighbourhood effect dominates over the pure size succession' (Hägerstrand, 1966, p. 40). Both approaches have been used to show that probable distributional change has occurred. Cohen has criticized both approaches as not being process-oriented (Cohen, 1972). Although they may explain the formal aspects of the process, they are aggregative measures which beg the question as to the actual determinants controlling the changing distribution. Cohen concludes that:

> any study of diffusion which emphasizes distance and space as major factors affecting the process of spread of a phenomenon is likely to end up with an insignificant contribution to the understanding of diffusion processes. Space and time are elements that are external to the diffusion process, while social, economic, cultural, psychological or other behavioural factors are the endogenous causes of acceptance, rejection and spread of innovations. (Cohen, 1972, p. 13)

That observation is accepted here by the attempt to identify the specific attributes which might control the diffusion of ground wood pulping technology in Ontario and Quebec. Of the two approaches, the hierarchical mode is thought to be more appropriate for the diffusion of pulping technology. Evidence for this choice lies in analogies between river and central place systems identified by Woldenberg and Berry (1967). The growth and spread of ground wood pulping in central Canada, which is so dependent on water access to raw materials and for delivery of final products should be influenced by the organization of the St. Lawrence–Great Lakes drainage system. If so, hierarchical diffusion along the existing river system should shape the location of industry and create a matching urban hierarchy. The existence of such hierarchical relationships can be tested using the formal diffusion model for the entire period and for each technological epoch separately. Each formal aspect of diffusion is associated with some part of the underlying economic process and some type of dominant cost in the pulp and paper industry (Guthrie, 1941; Roberge, 1972).

Three types of cost may be distinguished: procurement, processing and distribution costs. Procurement costs, related to raw materials assembly costs, can be expected to vary by technological epoch. Since spruce was the ideal pulping material in both technological epochs, access to raw materials can be related to the extent and density of spruce and to the size of the drainage area commanded by a location. Processing costs were reduced by scale economies in producing ground wood pulp which resulted from installation of grinders requiring large amounts of inexpensive power. One determinant likely to influence the new mills location was the existence of sites which could provide hydroelectric power. In a sense, however, procurement and processing costs were interdependent elements of cost because access to large reserves of cheap spruce was a prerequisite to large-scale operations. Another element influencing processing costs was the production efficiency accruing from vertical integration. Distribution costs depended upon distance from markets, which again related to the river system since the final product was either shipped directly to market by means of the St. Lawrence–Great Lakes system or conveyed by water and rail to eventual markets.

When viewed from the point of view of the costs which firms sought to minimize, a hierarchical form of diffusion related to the river system appears to be clearly appropriate. However, the relationships between types of cost and the elements of the formal diffusion model are neither simple nor independent. Yet, Roberge suggests that minimization of procurement and processing costs was clearly more important in the second technological

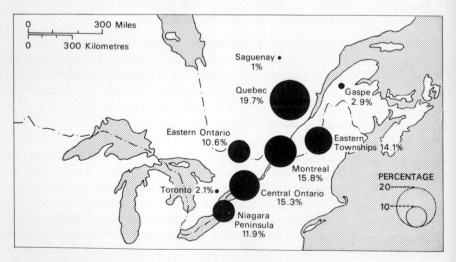

Figure 5.2. Percentage distribution of pulp and paper capacity by regions, 1890. (source: *Lockwood's Directory*).

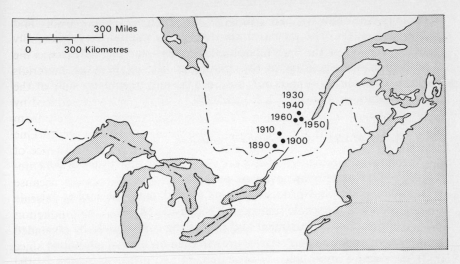

Figure 5.3. Median points of paper mill capacity, 1890–1960. (source: *Lockwood's Directory*).

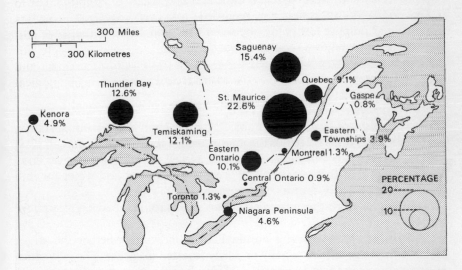

Figure 5.4. Percentage distribution of pulp and paper capacity by regions in 1930. (source: *Lockwood's Directory*).

epoch (Roberge, 1972, p. 135). The locational structure of the industry therefore can be expected to have shifted from market to more resource-oriented sites. The locational attractiveness of the market had already been reduced by the introduction of pulping technology into central Canada in the second half of the nineteenth century. Before the advent of this new technology, the industry had found its raw material—rags—at or near population centres. The increased substitution of capital for labour—the dominant concern of the first technological epoch—and the increasing scale of operations made possible by the opening in 1915 of the large American market to Canadian producers only hastened the movement from southern to northern locations (Figures 5.2, 5.3 and 5.4).

The Diffusion Model of Groundwood Production

The following specific hypotheses are suggested by this review of diffusion models and the underlying economic processes:

(1) procurement and processing costs should have the largest relative importance when the whole time period is considered;

(2) the impact of procurement and processing costs should be greater in magnitude of adoption and relative growth than on time of adoption;

(3) the relative importance of procurement and processing costs should be larger for late adopters than for early ones while delivery costs should weigh more heavily for early adopters than for late ones. This shift in relative importance should effect especially time and magnitude of adoption.

Ten indicator variables are recorded for every location adopting groundwood pulping technology between 1880 and 1940, so that each cost factor is represented by a separate set of variables.

(a) *Procurement costs* (Table 5.2)

(1) Average river discharge for the entire recorded period.

(2) Maximum river discharge: 1970.

(3) Minimum river discharge: 1970.

These variables are measured in cubic feet per second at a recording station nearest each site. This measures the importance of the river in the hierarchical system, the cost of floating logs to the mill, as well as variability in river flow. To the extent that they measure the provision of power and water for mill operations they are indicators of processing costs.

(4) Areas of drainage basin: estimates the amount of available timber supply.

(5) Spruce: measured on a nominal scale, indicates whether the larger part of a drainage basin is wholly or partly forested in spruce. The intensities of spruce, expressed as proportion of total tree cover, are: less than 31 per cent; 31–61 per cent; greater than 61 per cent.

(b) *Processing costs*

(6) Population in 1921 is a measure of available labour force and infrastructures. A single point in time was chosen to record this variable since the primary purpose was to seek a measure of the hierarchical order in the urban system.

(7) Vertical integration: presumably, degree of vertical integration in the product line of a mill indicates the degree of efficiency in the production

Table 5.2. Procurement Costs for Selected Locations, 1880/1885–1935/1940

Mill location	Period of establishment	River flow in 1000 cubic feet/second			Area of drainage basin in square miles	Spruce rating[1]
		long run average	1970 max.	1970 min.		
Valleyfield Quebec[2]	1880–1885	220,000	209,000	159,000	296,000	1
Sault Ste. Marie, Ont.[3]	1895–1900	73,600	127,000	40,900	80,000	2
Trois Rivieres, Quebec[4]	1915–1920	25,200	138,000	14,800	16,300	2
Kapuskasing, Ontario[5]	1925–1930	2,760	16,900	465	2,610	3
Baie Comeau Quebec[5]	1935–1940	36,000	47,600	8,220	17,700	3

Notes. 1. Spruce ratings are: (1) 0% to 33% of watershed in spruce
(2) 33% to 67% of watershed in spruce
(3) 67% to 100% of watershed in spruce
2. The Valleyfield mill near Montreal, was the first mill in Canada to convert from rags to groundwood pulp.
3. The Sault Ste. Marie mill was the first to be located in an area which was removed from the existing southern concentrations of population. The plant foreshadowed the large-scale shift of the industry to locations with better access to spruce.
4. The Trois Riviers mill was established to take advantage not only of proximity to the United States market but also of location with respect to wood supplies. The region in time became the largest single producer of newsprint paper in the world.
5. The last two mills sites, Kapuskasing and Baie Comeau are examples of company towns built by American newspapers (*The New York Times* and *Chicago Tribune* respectively). They illustrate the growing importance of procurement and processing costs.

process. This variable is measured on a three-point nominal scale: (i) a plant produces only groundwood pulp; (ii) a plant produces groundwood pulp and sulphite pulp or paper; (iii) a plant produces groundwood, sulphite and paper.

(8) Aluminium: this nominal variable indirectly measures power availability by indicating on a three-point scale when an aluminium plant was built in a given area. A value of two is given to sites in the St. Maurice area, where an aluminium plant was installed at Shawinigan Falls, Quebec. A value of one is given to plants in the Saguenay–Lac St. Jean area. All other sites receive zero.

(c) *Delivery costs*

Distance costs are measured by two variables:

(9) Distance from Montreal.

(10) Distance from the St. Lawrence–Great Lakes.

All the mills appearing in *Lockwood's Pulp and Paper Directory* were recorded at five-year periods beginning in 1880 and ending in 1940. Date of adoption is thus accurate to the nearest five years. Magnitude of adoption is measured by installed capacity at the nearest recorded point in time following date of adoption. Admittedly, most measurements are crude. At best they provide only clues of the mechanisms controlling diffusion. The empirical analysis, therefore, should be viewed as exploratory.

The Results: Simple Correlation

Time of adoption and magnitude at adoption are very highly inter-correlated (0·709). This confirms the initial hypothesis that larger capacity of newer mills reflected the opening of the American market to Canadian producers in the second technological epoch. The two dependent variables should have similar patterns of correlation with the independent variables (Table 5.3).

The most highly correlated single variable for the total and second technological epoch is vertical integration, a measure of processing costs. The greater efficiency which linked operations provided is reflected in this relationship. In the first technological epoch, however, date of adoption is most highly correlated with distance from Montreal (a distribution cost). These results accord well with the initial hypothesis that the early industry was tied to population concentrations which supplied both raw materials and markets. However, magnitude of adoption in the early period is identified with a procurement costs (maximum river discharge). This suggests that mills located closer to wood supplies were better placed to increase their capacities once conversion to wood pulp became technologically possible.

The largest single difference in correlations between the first and second technological epoch for date of adoption occur in the distribution cost variables. The simple correlations of these variables (distance from Montreal and from St. Lawrence) decline from 0·365 and 0·330 in the first epoch to 0·099 and 0·027 respectively in the second. In respect to magnitude of adoption, the largest is the increase in the strength of the correlations for the two processing costs variables: vertical integration (0·045 to 0·061) and aluminium (0·086 to 0·366). Clearly, these results support the hypothesis.

The Multivariate Diffusion Model

Six multiple regression analyses are presented, three with time of adoption and three with magnitude of adoption as the dependent variable. Within each set, one regression includes all 82 adopters, another the 51 early adopters, another the 31 late adopters. Logarithmic transformations are applied to most variables to stabilize residual variance.

The strong multi-collinearity exhibited among the independent variables tends to reduce the statistical significance of each of them, causing some

Table 5.3. Simple Correlations of Procurement, Processing and Delivery Costs with the Date of Plant Opening and Initial Plant Capacity, 1880–1940

Independent variable		Technological epochs					
Name	Type of Variable	Total period 1880–1950		First epoch 1880–1915		Second epoch 1915–1940	
		Date	Capacity	Date	Capacity	Date	Capacity
Procurement costs							
Average discharge		261	342	184	383	044	054
Drainage area		259	340	163	380	055	054
Maximum Discharge		209	286	214	397	−035	−037
Minimum discharge		274	306	191	345	187	029
Spruce		342	390	253	226	001	371
Processing costs							
Population 1921		−010	130	107	183	−093	198
Aluminium		161	259	096	086	−169	366
Vertical integration		513	509	089	045	346	601
Delivery costs							
Distance from Montreal		319	315	365	339	099	073
Distance from St. Lawrence–Great Lakes		073	143	330	112	027	352

Note. See text for explanation of variables and variable names. Leading decimals omitted.

interpretive difficulties in a multiple regression model. To meet the requirement in the diffusion models of a single set of independent variables, the choice is either to select a single variable to represent the group and accept the loss of the additional information in the deleted variables, or to use the complete set and accept the statistical problems. The decision made was to keep the complete set.

Results are presented in Table 5.4. For each regression, four statistics are provided: the F test for the equation as a whole indicates the accuracy of estimate; the coefficient of determination measures the proportionate importance of the explanation yielded by the equation; the standardized regression coefficients measure the amount of change due to each significant variable and allows horizontal as well as vertical comparisons; and partial F tests which measure accuracy of estimate for each regression coefficient.

The pattern displayed largely accords with the observations made in the previous section. Generally, the same pattern is revealed for both time of adoption and magnitude of adoption. This is not surprising considering the fairly high correlations between these two independent variables. Processing costs dominate the explanation when all adopters are considered. Vertical integration again emerges as the single most important variable. For plants established in the first technological epoch, delivery costs are clearly most

Table 5.4. Regression Coefficients and Partial F

	Discharge (average) (log)	Maximum discharge (log)	Minimum discharge (log)	Pop. 1921 (log)	Vertical integration	Aluminium	Distance from Montreal (log)	Distance from St. Lawrence (log)	F Test	Contributions of significant variable R
Time of adoption										
all adopters	—	—	—	—	0·47 (21·88)*	—	0·32 (7·16)	—	4·77	·402
early adopters 1880–1915	—	—	—	—	—	—	0·67 (18·72)*	0·40 (10·47)	3·60	·474
late adopters 1915–1940	—	—	0·79 (5·25)	—	0·44 (5·48)*	−0·45 (4·00)	—	—	1·40	·411
Magnitude of adoption (log)										
all adopters	—	—	—	0·22 (5·17)	0·40 (27·68)*	—	0·36 (20·55)	—	6·34	·472
early adopters 1880–1915	—	0·85	—	—	—	—	0·55 (15·26)*	—	3·04	·399
late adopters 1915–1940	2·32 (4·23)	−1·10 (4·58)	—	—	0·47 (10·06)*	0·36 (3·95)	—	—	3·40	·630

Notes. The value in parentheses is the partial F.
R^2 is based on contribution of significant variables only.
*Denotes the most important variable during each period.

important for both time of adoption as well as magnitude of adoption. Late adopters again have processing costs as the single most important category of variables with procurement costs as measured by the discharge variables also being significant. The indicator variables used to measure both types of costs were not independent of one another since integrated operations were only possible when there was access to large supplies of pulpwood. More accurate measurements would allow for a more detailed study of the weight of each factor. Yet the hypotheses formulated initially in this section can be accepted as providing some insight into the process which controlled industry diffusion in time and space. The next section will examine whether the gradients of growth at each location can also be explained by the same set of economic process variables.

Allometry

The diffusion of the pulp and paper industry across nineteenth-century Canada can be explained by regional variations in procurement, processing and delivery costs. But how fast did plant capacity grow after initial establishment? And do systematic variations occur in the growth rates that are related to the diffusion pattern and hence the economic cost structure? The traditional approach to answering such questions has been to examine the absolute growth through time of each observation unit, i.e. the individual groundwood mill. Surely, it is more appropriate to examine the growth rates of individual mills relative to aggregate industry capacity. First, absolute growth through time of any plant is subject to industry-wide fluctuations, but the relative growth rates are a direct measure of the competitiveness of each location relative to all others: more competitive plants grow faster than the industry as a whole, regardless of industry-wide trends. Second, changes in industry distribution reflect both relative growth rates at each location and diffusion of the industry to new locations. Over time, the industry concentrates in locations where it is growing fastest.

The measurement, explanation and consequences of the relative growth rates of system components, such as groundwood mills, in a system such as the central Canada pulp and paper industry, constitute allometry. Allometry focuses on relationships between growth and form and between size and organization rather than on absolute growth through time. The importance of allometry for understanding form and organization is that all form results from differential growth. Changes in form thus express differing growth rates of components during system growth so that they comprise changing proportions of the system.

The Measurement of Simple Allometry

Mathematically, the allometry of a component to some other part of a

162

system or to the total system is the ratio of their specific growth rates. Huxley's seminal study gave currency to the remarkable finding that system allometries are very often described by the power formula:

$$Y = bX$$

where: Y and X are the component and system respectively, that is mill capacity and industry capacity in this study, and b and alpha ( ) are fitted parameters. In this study, alpha is the rate at which a mill's capacity grows relative to the industry's. The significance of b, the y intercept, has remained problematic; they are not examined here (White and Gould, 1965). The logarithmic transformation of the power formula yields $\log Y = \log b - \alpha \log X$ and indicates that where this simple allometric relationship holds, the ordered pairs of values of X and Y plot along a straight line on log graph paper, the allometry indicated by the slope of the line.

Plotting the capacities of individual mills, or mills grouped by five-year period of opening, against the total groundwood capacity in central Canada from 1880 to 1940 reveals no such simple allometric relationships. Examples occur in each five-year time period of mills growing very rapidly, not at all, or closing down after a few years of operation; in any case, changes in mill capacities are discrete and abrupt rather than continuous and progressive. Simple allometric growth relationships, with increasing gradients can be observed, however, if mill capacities are aggregated into three fifteen-year sets, defined by year of mill opening, 1880–1900, 1905–1915 and 1920–1930 (Figure 5.5).

Three categories of simple allometry occur: positive allometry where the alpha value is greater than $-1 \cdot 0$ (assuming that X and Y are of equal

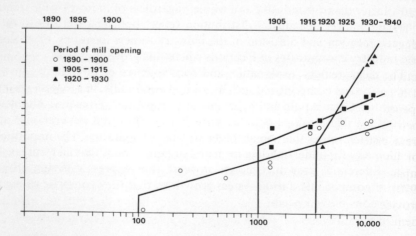

Figure 5.5. Daily capacity levels of groundwood production in Ontario and Quebec as indicated by decades, 1880–1940 (source: *Lockwood's Pulp and Paper Directory*).

dimensions, whether size and length, or area, or volume); negative allometry where alpha is less than $-1 \cdot 0$; and the special case of isometry $= 1 \cdot 0$, in which form is unchanged with growth. These definitions assume total system growth; the signs may be reversed if the system itself is declining. Thus mills that opened and increased capacity in central Canada between 1935 and 1940, when total industry capacity was falling, actually have a minus alpha value. This difficulty is evaded by computing allometries only for mills that had opened before 1935. The alpha values for the first two sets of mills opened between 1890 and 1900, and 1905 and 1915, have negative allometries ($> 1 \cdot 0$), and mills opened 1920 to 1930, during the second technological epoch, have a high positive allometry ($> 1 \cdot 0$) (Figure 5.5).

The Interpretation of Alpha

The wide diversity of phenomena whose growth is simple allometric suggests that a variety of interpretations can be given to the alpha value. It may indicate (a) merely the differences in the dimensions of two variables so that alpha value for the growth of volume to area is 3/2, or (b) a scaling adjustment required to keep the system operational at different sizes, or (c) the ability of a component to appropriate growth in competition with other components (von Bertalanffy, 1960, pp. 224–32).

Dimensional allometry follows from the laws of geometry; thus drainage basins increase as the square of river lengthens (Nordbeck, 1965). Compensatory allometry represents an adjustment to change In size required to keep a system operational. Urban examples include increasing non-basic employment and increasing diversity of manufacturing and service functions with city size. Within material firms, support staff Increase with production staff in a relationship of compensatory allometry.

The interest in allometry for this study is that it is a measure of competitive edge, or the ability of a mill to appropriate growth in competition with all other mills. The existence of allometric growth gradients in economic activity suggests that newer industrial plants, built progressively further out in a hinterland are successively more competitive. The two sets of mills opened before 1920 both of which have negative allometries are not holding their own in the competition for growth. If such allometric growth gradients are a general phenomena, then faster peripheral growth rates compensate for later start and the leadership of heartlands indeed depends on their capacity for generating and absorbing innovative change (Friedman et al., 1970). A more explicit test of the existence of allometric growth gradients is provided by computing the allometries of each individual mill and relating them to the fundamental set of industry and locational characteristics.

Computing Allometries for the Central Canada Groundwood Industry

Some fundamental problems occur in using the power formula to measure the allometries of individual groundwood mills. The mills do not have a contemporaneous existence but open, and in some cases close, at different dates. If the allometry of any mill is computed only for these years in which it is in operation, the results may not be compatible for further analysis. Half the mills opened in 1885 were closed by 1900. Can the allometries of industrial plants that had only a fleeting existence at the early stages of an industry's development be compared with the allometries of plants opening at much later dates? If so, how are the alpha values to be interpreted? If competition from the newer plants keeps production at the older plants down to zero, perhaps the allometries for older plants should be computed using zero values for years following plant closure. But alpha values cannot be defined using the power formula if zero values occur; a log-linear fit is not an appropriate description of the growth and decline of a mill. The allometry values, however obtained, would be biased in favour of the growth gradient hypothesis being tested. The allometries are computed in this study, therefore, only for the central period of major growth, disregarding early adopters in production before 1895 and the depression years from 1935 when many mills closed. Zero values, indicating that a plant was not yet in operation or has closed down, are omitted, and allometries are computed only for mills with at least three recorded years in production.

A second fundamental problem arises from concern with data accuracy. The simple power formula may not be the most appropriate model where errors of non-negligible magnitude may occur in the data. Doubts arise about the accuracy of a number of reported mill capacities, and hence of aggregate industry capacity. This concern increases because the whole system may have undergone aberrations of growth with the onset of economic depression, technical revolution and with tariff changes. In these circumstances, a simple growth model cannot be expected to comprehend the 'slippage' that occurred in the system. This 'slippage' cannot be considered as error in the moral statistical sense and calls for an alternative to the simple power formula.

An alternate 'dual-exponential' model for the computation of alpha is presented and applied which it is believed is more appropriate than the simple power formula for industrial firms. The first step is to compute $\hat{X}$, a fitted value of X, such that: $\hat{X} = f$ (time; exogenous variables; slippage). The allometric model is then $Y = bx$. The growth of groundwood production as of so many aggregate economic and population series can be accurately described by the simple exponential: $X = ce^{kt}$ where $e = 2\cdot718$, t is time and c and k are fitted parameters. Substituting the simple exponential for X into the allometric model then gives: $Y = b (ce^{kt})^{\alpha}$, which may be rewritten: $Y = re^{st}$. If this model is fitted directly as $\log y = \log r - st$ through regression analysis the estimate of α is then s/k. This estimate of alpha is not identical statistically to the direct measurement of alpha using the simple power formula $\log y = \log b + \alpha \log X$. A prior modelling step has been interposed and it must be assessed separately. Computing the alphas for all mills using both methods produces very similar results but only the results for the dual-exponential model are presented.

Allometric Growth Gradients

Strong support for the tendency for newer mills to achieve faster rates of growth in capacity is provided by multiple regression analysis of the allometries for individual mills—notwithstanding conceptual and mathematical difficulties in defining their alpha values.

The complete set of characteristics accounting for procurement, processing and distribution costs, together with date of opening and mill capacity at opening is tested; but only four prove to contribute significantly in the model to variations in mill allometries. Allometry is positively correlated with date of opening (Table 5.5). Magnitude is so highly correlated with date that both variables would not be expected to enter the multiple regression model. But for any given date of opening, the smaller the initial size, the greater the growth tends to be. Three mills, opened in 1915, had all reached capacities of 150 tons to 200 tons by 1930 but their initial capacities were 75, 100 and 150 tons, yielding allometries of 0·831, 0·634 and 0·0 (no growth at all) respectively.

Dependence of relative growth rates on two characteristics, date of opening and initial capacity, which themselves are explained by common fundamental cost characteristics, concurs with the overriding hypothesis. The diffusion of innovation, the initial level of adoption and the subsequent rate of growth are, all three, interdependent and related to a common set of economic characteristics. The explanatory contribution of the individual economic characteristics differs for diffusion and adoption level and between economic epoch. In general, processing costs become more important in the second technological epoch. The allometric growth rates can be related directly to date of opening and initial capacity though two economic characteristics make additional significant contributions. Size of drainage

Table 5.5. Multiple Regression Analysis of Allometric Growth of Individual Groundwood Mills, Central Canada, 1894–1935

Independent variables	Regression coefficient	Null t
Drainage	·494	2·44
Population 1921	·301	1·73
Capacity at opening	−·837	−2·72
Date of opening	·183	2·07
Intercept	−1·894	−2.26

Note. See text for definition of variables.

166

basin and population size in 1921, indicators of the hierarchical significance of the plant location in the river and urban systems respectively, are the two most important economic characteristics affecting growth rate. Furthermore, like date of opening, they are both positively correlated with alpha: sites at larger towns commanding larger drainage basins have grown fastest and, to the extent that they have been later developments, diffusion has progressed up, not down, the hierarchy.

Conclusion

The spatial form of economic systems is a diagram of the forces such as spatial flows of investment capital and the organization of decision-making operating during the growth of the system. Three critical aspects of growth are identified and analysed in this chapter: the diffusion of innovation, which traces the beginning of growth at a succession of new locations: the initial level of adoption; and subsequent relative growth or allometry. Diffusion contributes the spatial dimension of absolute growth. Allometry focuses on relative growth of system components. These two aspects are complementary; industrial diffusion describes the ability of locations to compete for new plants and allometry their ability to compete for growth. Diffusion, initial level of adoption and allometry display systematic spatial patterns that are interdependent and reflect a common set of underlying forces. The three dimensions of growth differ somewhat in their response to these common forces, and may change their response as new innovations usher in new technological epochs. Correspondence between them is further blurred by the difficulty of applying the concept of allometry to individual plants and the novelty of the concept itself in the social sciences. The implication of this correspondence is the existence of allometric growth gradients that parallel the diffusion pattern and which describe the changing spatial structure of location with industry growth. The date of plant opening and rate of increase of plant capacity describe a dynamic system in themselves. The thrust of this study, however, is the need to probe beyond the formal patterns of diffusion and allometry by using them as indicators of the underlying forces. Such forces operating in the pulp and paper industry are the expected components of procurement, processing and distribution costs. The analysis presented is cursory but it places industrial location within the framework of system growth and spatial dynamics and, if pursued, could contribute to a dynamic theory of the location of industry.

References

Bertalanffy, L. von, 1960, 'Principles and Theory of Growth', in *Fundamental Aspects of Normal and Malignant Growth,* ed. W. W. Nowinski (Amsterdam: Elsevier Publishing Co.), 137–259.

167

Bladen, V. W., 1946, *Introduction to Political Economy* (Toronto: University of Toronto Press).

Brown, M., 1966, *On the Theory and Measurement of Technological Change* (Cambridge University Press).

Caves, R. and R. H. Holton, 1959, *The Canadian Economy: Prospect and Restrospect,* Harvard Economic Studies, 112 (Cambridge, Mass.: Harvard University Press).

Cohen, Yehoshua S., 1972, *Diffusion of an Innovation in an Urban System,* Research Paper No. 140, Chicago, Department of Geography, The University of Chicago.

Friedmann, J. *et al.,* 1970, 'Urbanization and national development: a comparative analysis', *MS School of Architecture and Urban Planning, University of California.*

Gould, S. J., 1965, 'Allometry and size in ontogeny and phylogeny', *Biological Review,* **41,** 587–640.

Gould, S. J., 1971, 'D'Arcy Thompson and the science of form', *New Literary History,* **2,** 229–58.

Gras, N. S. B., 1922, *An Introduction to Economic History* (New York: Harper and Brothers).

Griliches, S., 1957, 'Hybrid corn: an exploration into the economics of technological change', *Econometrica,* **24,** 501–55.

Guthrie, J. A., 1941, *The Newsprint Industry: An Economic Analysis,* Harvard Economic Studies, 68 (Cambridge: Harvard University Press).

Hägerstrand, T., 1966, 'Aspects of the spatial structure of social communication and the diffusion of information', *Papers and Proceedings of the Regional Science Association,* **15,** 127–42.

Harvey, D., 1972, *Society, the City and Space-Economy of Urbanism* (Washington: Association of American Geographers), Resource Paper 18.

Huxley, J. S., 1932, *Problems of Relative Growth* (New York: The Dial Press).

Innis, H., 1930, *The Fur Trade in Canada: An Introduction to Canadian Economic History* (University of Toronto Press).

Innis, H., 1956, *Essays in Economic History* (University of Toronto Press).

Lockwood's Pulp and Allied Industries Directory, 1875–present (New York: Lockwood Publishing Company).

Mackintosh, W. A., 1923, 'Economic factors in Canadian history', *The Canadian Historical Review,* **45,** 12–25.

Mansfield, E., 1961, 'Technical change and the rate of imitation', *Econometrica,* **24,** 741–66.

Morrill, R., 1968, 'Waves of spatial diffusion', *Journal of Regional Science,* **8,** 1–18.

Naroll, R. S. and L. von Bertalanffy, 1956, 'The principle of allometry in biology and the social sciences', *General Systems,* **1,** 76–89.

Nordbeck, S., 1965, *The Law of Allometric Growth,* Michigan Inter-University Community of Mathematical Geographers Paper No. 7.

North, D. C., 1955, 'Location theory and regional economic growth', *Journal of Political Economy,* **62,** 243–58.

Pedersen, P. O., 1970, 'Innovation diffusion within and between national urban systems', *Geographical Analysis,* **2,** 203–54.

Pred, A., 1966, *The Dynamics of Urban Industrial Growth* 1820–1950 (Cambridge, Mass.: The M.I.T. Press).

Ray, D. Michael, 1971, *Dimensions of Canadian Regionalism* (Ottawa: Dept. of Energy, Mines and Resources), Ottawa.

Ray, D. Michael, 1972, *'The Allometry of Urban and Regional Growth* (Ottawa: Ministry of State for Urban Affairs Discussion Paper).

Roberge, R. A., 1972, *The Timing, Type and Location of Adaptive Inventive Activity in the Eastern Canadian Pulp and Paper Industry: 1806–1940* (Ann Arbor, Mich.: University Microfilms).

168

Rosenberg, N., 1963, 'Technological change in machine tool industry: 1840–1910', *Journal of Economic History, 33*, pp. 441–446.

Schmookler, J., 1966, *Invention and Economic Growth* (Cambridge, Mass.: Harvard University Press).

Schumpeter, J., 1961, *Theory of Economic Development* (Cambridge, Mass.: Harvard University Press).

Smith, L., 1966, 'Space for the CBD's functions', *Journal of the American Institute of Planners, 26*, No. 1, 40.

Watkins, W. H., 1963, 'A staple theory of economic growth', *Canadian Journal of Economics and Political Science, 24*, 141–50.

White, J. F. and S. J. Gould, 1965, 'Interpretation of the coefficient in allometric growth', *American Naturalists, 99*, No. 904, 5–18.

Woldenberg, M. J. and B. J. L. Berry, 1967, 'Rivers and central places; analogous systems?', *Journal of Regional Science, 7*, 129–39.

6

The Anatomy of the Location Decision: Content Analysis of Case Studies

HOWARD A. STAFFORD

The desirability, indeed necessity, of understanding the location of industries and of inductively developing theory through examination of the decision-making process has been well argued in recent years. Here, eight case studies are made of the actual manufacturing plants in south-eastern Ohio, U.S.A. The major contributions are: (1) in-depth interviews with primary decision-makers about relatively recent location decisions; (2) use of a content analysis technique to reveal and assess the internal structure of the location decision process; (3) minimization of investigator bias; (4) specification of relevant factors by decision-makers, as contrasted with the normal practice of using investigator-determined categories; (5) development of four ways to assess the relative importance of the factors, including specification of interval scale data, as contrasted with more usual ordinal scales; (6) inquiry into the location decision at four different spatial scales; (7) development of a generalized trace of the industrial location decision process.

The conduct and detailed analysis of lengthy, relatively unstructured interviews is immensely time-consuming. A deliberate choice was thus made to sacrifice a larger, more representative sample for an intense analysis of a very few in-depth interviews. Furthermore, the study includes only decisions by large firms to locate, relocate or significantly expand eight plants of modest size (50 to 200 employees) in south-eastern Ohio, i.e. the relatively underdeveloped Appalachian portion of the state. In this sense, the substantive results are more representative of a regional situation than of specific types of manufacturing. Of course, to the extent that the substantive results conform to previous research findings, they are further confirmation; and, certainly, the data and generalizations should be suggestive of hypotheses for future research.

Selection of Firms and the Conduct of the Interviews

The selection of industrial locators to be contacted required first of all the compilation of a comprehensive list of firms which had relatively recently located, or significantly expanded, manufacturing facilities in south-eastern Ohio. This involved utilization of Ohio Department of Development resources and the assistance of area utility (especially electric company) records. From the list of all new manufacturing plants built in Appalachian Ohio within the past five years, approximately 20 firms were selected for further investigation because they fitted the criteria of having at least 20 employees and making a positive location decision in south-eastern Ohio within the past five years. Then six firms with current personnel who had been involved in the south-eastern Ohio location decision were selected for in-depth interviews with management; the number was limited to six separate companies because time and resources did not permit the intensive study of more firms. These six represented eight location decisions, six of which were new plants (including two relocations) and two were significant in-site expansions of existing operations. One of the new plant relocations was of the only operating facility of a one plant firm; in each of the other seven cases the location decision was made about a non-headquarters branch plant of a multi-plant firm.

The eight sites chosen were located in the rather widely scattered small towns of Hillsboro, West Union, McConnellsville, Amelia, Caldwell, Gallipolis, Bridgeport and Waverly, Ohio. In all cases, the plants are primarily intermediate level metal fabricators of machinery or components. In addition to information on those specific location decisions, there was also an extensive interview on general principles and policy with the one firm having a specialized staff level facilities planning group; in all other firms, location decisions were made by operating management as an extra duty.

Key personnel in chosen firms were selected and contacted for interviews. This required searching of *Moody's* and *Dun & Bradstreet* directories, supplemented by personal contacts and many telephone calls. Senior managers were interviewed either at the site of the new facility or in corporate headquarters outside Appalachian Ohio.

In every case, the gentlemen interviewed were most gracious and gave freely of their time. The shortest interview lasted one hour, the longest three hours; interviews provided the basic material for the subsequent analysis. All but one of the interviews were conducted on a one-to-one basis; the exception involving three respondents. At the conclusion of each interview a subjective attempt was made to corroborate the testimony of the interviewee through a brief discussion with another senior manager involved. Although no major discrepancies were noted the fact remains that the individual interviews may not fully or accurately reflect the shared corporate opinion about the location decision. In most cases, they represent one person's perception. This is not deemed critical to the current research, given the exploratory nature of the study and the primary focus on a regional situation rather than on individual firms.

The interviews were conducted personally by the author. They proceeded by the interviewer asking the respondent to describe very briefly the general corporate situation at the time of the location decision in question, to indicate how he personally was involved in the decision process and then to describe in his own manner the actual locational decision-making process. Apart from such minimal guidance, respondents were encouraged to comment in a very free and open-ended manner. This they did. All respondents readily agreed to having the interview tape-recorded and, after the first few minutes, the presence of the recorder did not seem to inhibit candour.

Content Analysis: Data Collection and Classification

The raw material for subsequent analysis is on the interview tape-recordings. These have been dissected, using a content analysis technique (see Sundberg and Tyler, 1962). To ensure objectivity, each interview has been examined independently by three investigators: the author and two research associates, one a Ph.D. in psychology and an expert in the technique, one a graduate geography student. Interviews were listened to by the staff, then transcribed verbatim; the completed manuscripts range from 40 to 60 typed pages each. Manuscripts were analysed independently by the investigators and the results for each compared. After unanimous agreement on the resolution of discrepancies, of which there were surprisingly few, the results were recorded.

The coding system utilized for quantifying the responses involved the identification of fourteen location factors on four spatial scales and the specification for each as to whether it was a 'neutral' or 'evaluated' response. The first step, the identification of factors, was accomplished by each of the three investigators independently developing a list of all the specific location influences mentioned in the interviews. These lists were developed to achieve classificatory order out of the wide range of interview responses—parsimony being desired but not pursued to the point of excessive ambiguity. If more than three responses formed a type which did not fit easily into the already existing categories, a new category was created. This happened rarely: only fourteen factors are identified on the final composite list and the lowest total response count for any factor is nine.

While it was impossible to eliminate the preconceptions of the investigators, there was a conscious effort to allow the classification of factors to emerge from the interviews, rather than be imposed by the investigators' decree. Comparison of the three lists and emergence of a composite through the principle of unanimous agreement produced the following classification of location factors:

(1) Area personal cooperation, contacts and information (personal contacts)—the personal cooperation of the town's leading citizens and the information given to the firm; information and cooperation from state officials or power companies.

(2) Labour availability—the availability of unskilled, semi-skilled or skilled labour (number of applicants, and potential applicants).

(3) Labour productivity—an analysis by management of 'what we get for our money'; a subjective analysis based upon real productivity and the attitude of the workers.

(4) Labour rates—the hourly rates at which the shop personnel are paid; union or non-union area; competitive or non-competitive labour market.

(5) Transport facilities—the existence of adequate facilities; generally refers to truck transportation, the inter-state and major highway systems.

(6) Facilities and utilities—the availability of adequate sites or buildings with power, water, sewage and access roads.

(7) Market accessibility—the demand area for particular products; the pattern of consumption; costs and times required to service the firm's market from a location.

(8) Supplies accessibility—times and costs of assembling the materials of production at a specific location.

(9) Executive convenience—access to the plant by upper management; freedom from disruptive influences.

(10) Corporate communications—the ease with which upper management can maintain contact with the home office or other branch plants.

(11) Local amenities—the impression of the town upon the firm's decision-makers; includes shoping, housing, schools and recreation facilities.

(12) Induced amenities—special facilities (e.g., recreational) installed by the firm or by local agencies as a result, or to attract, a new manufacturing plant in a given locality.

(13) Taxes—the variable state and local tax loads.

(14) Dispersion tendencies—a measure of the degree to which firms try to locate new facilities *away* from existing plants of the same firm, or away from competitors (e.g. for labour). The converse is a tendency toward agglomeration, or inertia.

Preliminary examination of interview transcripts clearly indicated that there were distinct variations in the spatial contexts in which the locational factors were mentioned. It was possible, by noting the context of each statement, to code each factor mentioned by its spatial situation. The second stage in the development of the coding system was the identification of the spatial scales, a relatively straightforward procedure. The four scales utilized were:

(1) National: usually statements made with regard to the United States or, in some cases, broad general locational statements with no reference to a specific area.

(2) Sub-national: usually references to a two- or three-state territory. Reference to a single state which were interpreted in a broader context are also tallied at this scale.

(3) Regional: references to multi-country areas within a state, or to a single state when the comment has been interpreted as referring to the several sub-state regions.

(4) Local: statements made with reference to specific towns.

The third part of the coding system evolved from the observation that many responses are definitely positive or negative regarding a specific area in reference to a locational influence; other responses identify a factor and a spatial scale but are neutral in reference to the ability of a particular region or place to satisfy a locational requirements. This observation suggests the possibility that the directional or *evaluated* response may be the more significant since judgment is the essence of the decision process. Accordingly, each response has been coded according to whether it is neutral or evaluated.

The unit of coding is the sentence. Each has been read *in context* and judged as to the spatial scale being referred to, the location factors mentioned and whether it has been 'locationally evaluated'. Four examples, as coded, are:

	Coding
'You know, the Mexican government is offering great inducements to come in—a lot of cheap labour—but in my investigation of the border I decided this made no sense for us.'	national scale; labour rates; evaluated
'We are trying to stay away from places where we already had plants.'	sub-national scale; dispersion tendencies; evaluated
'The attitude of government to the intrusion of industry in an area is something we look at.'	regional scale; area personal cooperation, contacts, information; neutral
'Well, they had a fellow who retired from the Air Force, in his mid-forties a very vital sort of guy who headed up the industrial development corporation.'	local scale; area personal cooperation, contacts, information; evaluated

The detailed content analysis identified 1017 locational responses in the six interviews. These were classified and tallied according to the above schema and are summarized and ranked by magnitude in Tables 6.1, 6.2 and 6.3. Table 6.4 compares the relative number of evaluated to total responses for the factors at each spatial scale and for the sums of all scales.

In addition to the response counts, two other types of systematic observation were performed via the content analysis of the interviews. The first of these is extracted from the latter portion of each interview where the respondents were asked to very briefly 'recap', or 'summarize' the location decision. The maximum number of location factors mentioned by any respondent in the summary was six, while most indicated three or four; the composite is a list of ten factors. The sequence in which each factor was mentioned also can be noted. If it is assumed that the very fact of mention in a brief summary, weighted by order of mention, is an indication of the relative importance of the various factors, it is possible to construct yet another locational index south-eastern Ohio. These results are reported in Table 6.5.

The final systematic observation was to trace, both temporally and spatially, the decision process for each firm. Each decision trace summarizes both the historic sequence of events, from the time of the explicit conception of a location problem to the final location decision, and the sequential narrowing of the spatial field of search from large area considerations through to the selection of the construction site. Comparison of the traces for the eight case studies here considered shows great similarities and suggests a tentative general model of the sequence of the industrial location decision process.

Table 6.1. Response Counts For Factors

Total responses, all scales		Evaluated responses, all scales	
1. Personal contacts	(222)	Personal contacts	(117)
2. Labour productivity	(134)	Labour productivity	(108)
3. Labour rates	(101)	Labour availability	(50)
4. Labour availability	(94)	Local amenities	(49)
5. Transport facilities	(78)	Transport facilities	(42)
6. Dispersion tendencies	(71)	Labour rates	(39)
7. Market accessibility	(62)	Dispersion tendencies	(28)
8. Local amenities	(61)	Executive convenience	(27)
9. Facilities and utilities	(48)	Facilities and utilities	(25)
10. Supplies accessibility	(45)	Corporate communications	(20)
11. Executive convenience	(38)	Supplies accessibility	(17)
12. Corporate communications	(37)	Induced amenities	(13)
13. Induced amenities	(17)	Market accessibility	(12)
14. Taxes	(9)	Taxes	(1)
Totals	1917		548

Results: The Factors

The first significant result is the list of identified factors. To the extent that the preconceptions of the investigators have been neutralized, these 14 factors are those utilized by the decision-makers themselves and, thus, represent the *actual* spatial influences on the decision process. They were not assigned *a priori* by the investigators, but came directly from the interviews. Note that all of the 'normal' economic location factors—such as labour, markets and supplies accessibility, infrastructure (facilities and utilities) and taxes—are included. It is likewise interesting to note those less common factors mentioned, including: personal cooperation, contacts and information, corporate communications, executive convenience and internal dispersion tendencies of the firms. That these factors are less common in industrial location models results from the traditional academic focus on the influences of the external environment. These four factors are permitted by the ambiguities and uncertainties of the classic economic solution, and they more closely reflect the importance of the internal corporate context in which the location decision is made. The factors may partially reveal the normally 'hidden agendas' of the decision-makers: their relative importance is yet further evidence of the necessity and the rewards of in-depth analyses of actual decision-making.

For each of fourteen factors, the content analysis provides counts of the number of times each was mentioned in total responses and evaluated responses for each spatial scale (Tables 6.2 and 6.3) and for the sum of all scales (Table 6.1). Assuming that the more times a factor is mentioned the more important it is, then five separate rankings by total counts in Tables 6.1 and 6.2 provide insight into the relative importance of the various location factors for south-eastern Ohio.

It is, of course, common for industrial location surveys to produce factor rankings. Response counts, however, allow a significant advance: they provide interval scale data which measure how much more important one factor is than another. For example, it might be argued from the sum of counts for all scales (the first column of Table 6.1) that personal contacts are 13 times more important than the least mentioned factor, taxes. Labour productivity is 7·9 times as important and so on. Thus, if it is assumed that (1) the fourteen identified factors capture the essential ingredients of the location decisions and (2) the sum of response counts reflects the relative importance of the variables, the content analysis technique employed here may yield those elusive factor weightings necessary for constructing more sophisticated operational models.

Regarding the sums for all scales of total counts for individual factors, by far the most important locational factors are labour and personal contacts and information. Labour productivity, wage rates and availability rank 2, 3 and 4 singly. If they are combined, labour easily ranks as the most

Table 6.2. Counts for Factors at Each Spatial Scale by Total Responses

	National		Sub-national		Regional		Local	
1.	Labour productivity	(31)	Personal contacts	(34)	Personal contacts	(71)	Personal contacts	(109)
2.	Market accessibility	(29)	Labour productivity	(30)	Labour availability	(45)	Labour productivity	(46)
3.	Labour rates	(25)	Market accessibility	(26)	Labour rates	(38)	Local amenities	(36)
4.	Transport facilities	(22)	Labour rates	(23)	Labour productivity	(27)	Labour availability	(31)
5.	Dispersion tendencies	(14)	Dispersion tendencies	(21)	Transport facilities	(23)	Dispersion tendencies	(22)
6.	Facilities and utilities	(14)	Transport facilities	(20)	Local amenities	(22)	Facilities and utilities	(21)
7.	Supplies accessibility	(8)	Local amenities	(12)	Corporate communications	(16)	Executive convenience	(17)
8.	Personal contacts	(8)	Labour availability	(11)	Dispersion tendencies	(14)	Labour rates	(15)
9.	Labour availability	(6)	Supplies accessibility	(7)	Supplies accessibility	(14)	Transport facilities	(13)
10.	Executive convenience	(3)	Corporate communications	(5)	Executive convenience	(13)	Supplies accessibility	(13)
11.	Corporate communications	(1)	Executive convenience	(4)	Facilities and utilities	(11)	Corporate communications	(13)
12.	Local amenities	(0)	Taxes	(3)	Induced amenities	(7)	Induced amenities	(10)
13.	Induced amenities	(0)	Facilities and utilities	(2)	Market accessibility	(4)	Market accessibility	(3)
14.	Taxes	(0)	Induced amenities	(0)	Taxes	(3)	Taxes	(2)
Totals		161		198		308		350

Table 6.3. Counts for Factors at Each Spatial Scale by Evaluated Responses

	National	Sub-national	Regional	Local
1.	Labour productivity (18)	Labour productivity (25)	Labour productivity (27)	Personal contacts (66)
2.	Facilities and utilities (5)	Personal contacts (23)	Personal contacts (27)	Labour productivity (38)
3.	Labour rates (4)	Transport facilities (14)	Labour availability (19)	Local amenities (32)
4.	Transport facilities (4)	Dispersion tendencies (14)	Labour rates (18)	Labour availability (21)
5.	Market accessibility (3)	Labour availability (8)	Transport facilities (18)	Labour rates (11)
6.	Labour availability (2)	Labour rates (6)	Local amenities (15)	Executive convenience (10)
7.	Dispersion tendencies (2)	Supplies accessibility (5)	Executive convenience (12)	Facilities and utilities (10)
8.	Executive convenience (1)	Market accessibility (5)	Corporate communications (9)	Dispersion tendencies (8)
9.	Personal contacts (1)	Executive convenience (4)	Facilities and utilities (8)	Corporate communications (8)
10.	Supplies accessibility (1)	Corporate communications (3)	Induced amenities (7)	Transport facilities (6)
11.	Local Amenities (0)	Facilities and utilities (2)	Supplies accessibility (7)	Induced amenities (6)
12.	Induced amenities (0)	Local amenities (2)	Dispersion tendencies (4)	Supplies accessibility (4)
13.	Corporate communications (0)	Taxes (1)	Market accessibility (1)	Market accessibility (3)
14.	Taxes (0)	Induced amenities (0)	Taxes (0)	Taxes (0)
Totals	41	112	172	223

important factor. This is clearly an economic consideration; and the locational importance of labour is consistent with our general knowledge of Appalachian Ohio. In addition to the economic concern, there appears to be a more subtle, emotional issue: many of the labour responses reflect unionization prospects and concerns (or longings) for executive convenience.

The single most important locational factor is the nature and quality of the information and especially the personal contacts in the areas considered. Although this personal factor is always downgraded in normative economic models, it cannot be so ignored when dealing with real world decision-making. Furthermore, its significance makes sense considering that the decision is made by a very few, very human, part-time location decision-makers who must deal quite subjectively and judgementally with lack of information, uncertainty and too little time. Two quotations from the interviews capture some of the essence of this oft-mentioned factor: 'We first contact the state development agency and take their leads'; 'From my standpoint, the guy that gives me the biggest sell job, gives me the most information, is the man that I am going to look at first'. Note, also, that personal contacts are relatively unimportant at the national scale but become critical at the state, county and, especially, local scales.

The transport facilities and market accessibility variables are traditional, expected, economic concerns. They are ranked somewhat lower than might be expected for most areas. No doubt this reflects the overwhelming importance of the labour and personal contact factors. However, most decision-makers wanted to talk most about (and, presumably, were most concerned about) the within-state and local scale: thus most counts were produced at the regional and local scales, where market and market accessibility factors were often taken as given and hence not discussed much. Had discussion focused on national (or general) and sub-national scales, market accessibility should have ranked higher. Similarly, firms tended to acknowledge quickly that they would pay some transport penalty in south-eastern Ohio, but assumed they could more than offset the difference by other savings. Also, since these rather small plants ship materials in and products out by truck, their transport requirements are not exotic.

The 'dispersion tendencies' category reflects, for several firms, a desire (1) to move or locate far enough away from their own existing plants to maintain a non-union plant or at least to escape the jurisdiction of their current union and (2) to move out of the orbit of their competitors for labour. Yet one firm responded that although the original locations were dispersed, more recent decisions included one forced relocation and two expansions and they saw no reasons for moving out of their areas: in this case 'dispersion tendencies' catches the other, inertia, end of the spectrum.

The local amenities factor is really only important at the regional and local scales. However, when choosing between the few towns (usually two or three) in the final decision stage, there is an effort to select the best match

between town and firm. In addition to labour availability and local cooperation, most important are town size, shopping facilities, housing, recreation
and 'community spirit'. Most other location factors are of relatively unimportant, except occasionally in a specific instance. The two lowest ranked
factors are taxes and induced amenities. Statements indicated that, obviously,
firms do not expect a 'free ride' and they don't mind paying taxes, but they
do want to get their money's worth in public facilities. Similarly they do
not seem to expect communities to provide major new facilities and amenities
simply to attract plant location.

One may argue that evaluated responses, those in which the respondents
indicate a definite positive or negative evaluation of an area in regard to
a specific factor, are better indicators of relative factor importance than
simple totals. It can be assumed that the act of evaluation indicates an
ability to make a judgement. For this reason, the counts and rankings of
evaluated responses, the other five lists in Tables 6.1 and 6.3 are examined.

Compared with total counts, evaluated responses produce more factors
that are inconsistent at different spatial scales. Overall, however, the counts
for total and evaluated responses reveal many similarities and lead to the
same generalizations. The major exceptions are: the local amenities factor,
which occupies a significantly higher position in the evaluated list, and
market accessibility, which is much less important.

Table 6.4 expresses evaluated responses as a percentage of all responses
for each spatial scale and for the sums of all scales. The relative degree of

Table 6.4. Evaluated Responses as a Percentage of All Responses at Each Spatial
Scale and for Totals of All Scales, for Each Factor

	National	Sub-national	Regional	Local	All scales
	%	%	%	%	%
Market accessibility	10	19	25	100	19
Supplies accessibility	13	45	50	33	38
Transport facilities	18	70	78	46	54
Labour rates	16	26	47	73	39
Labour availability	33	67	42	68	53
Labour productivity	58	83	100	83	81
Dispersion tendencies	14	67	29	36	40
Executive convenience	33	80	92	59	71
Corporate communications	0	43	56	60	67
Personal contacts	13	68	38	61	53
Induced amenities	—	—	100	60	76
Local amenities	—	67	68	89	80
Facilities and utilities	36	100	73	48	52
Taxes	—	25	0	0	11
Totals	25%	56%	56%	64%	54%

certainty with which a factor is judged influences its ranking and may help to explain among-scale variations. For example, local amenities, which at 80 per cent is well above the average of 54 per cent, should be expected to rank higher on the evaluated list; likewise, the lower ranking of market accessibility might result from its share of evaluated to total responses of 19 per cent. Yet the lack of discernible trends in Table 6.4 makes it difficult to substantiate this hypothesis, or to suggest others.

The final method of evaluating the various location factors was to examine the mention and the order, or sequence, of mention in each of the interview summaries. A brief summary of the location decision process more accurately highlights the most important factors: the number of mentions, and the order of mention, indicate their relative importance. Based on these assumptions, a simple 'index of importance' was computed. The results are summarized in Table 6.5.

The major variations in Table 6.5, as compared with the listings in Tables 6.1, 6.2 and 6.3 are the relative descent of the personal contacts factor and the dramatic ascent of the executive convenience factor. The shift of the personal contacts factor may indicate that the high number of response counts in this category reflect a natural tendency for interviewees to talk overmuch about the people with whom they dealt. Perhaps the responses overstate the importance of personal contacts. Yet the number one ranking given to executive convenience in Table 6.5 conforms to the subjective impressions of the research staff from listening to the interview tapes. This suggests that this factor's moderate rankings on the response counts do not adequately reflect its critical nature in location decision-making.

Table 6.5. Factors Mentioned in 'Summaries', Ranked by Index of Importance

Rank	Index value*
1. Executive convenience	19
2. Labour availability	18
3. Labour rates	15
3. Labour productivity	15
5. Corporate communications	13
6. Personal contacts	10
6. Market accessibility	10
8. Supplies accessibility	7
8. Facilities and utilities	7
10. Taxes	3

*The 'Index of Importance' was computed by assigning a value so 6 for the first mentioned, 5 for the second mentioned and 70 so to a value of 1 for the sixth mentioned, and summing these values.

Results: Spatial Scale Variations

In addition to the observations on scale variations given above, Table 6.2 can be summarized by noting those factors which are relatively constant in rank across scales, those which tend constantly 'upward' or 'downward' (from national to local) and those which seem more erratic. These observations are made for both the total and evaluated sets.

In general, there appears to be a fair degree of stability in the rankings of factors across the scales. For total responses, the labour productivity and labour rates factors are consistently high; executive convenience, dispersion tendencies, supplies accessibility and corporate communications tend to rank in the middle; induced amenities and taxes factors are consistently ranked low. For evaluated responses, labour productivity and labour rates are again consistently high: labour availability and executive convenience tend to rank in the middle; induced amenities and taxes factors are low ranked at all scales.

It is difficult to generalize about the 'erratic' factors, that is, those which oscillate rather widely, but inconsistently, across the spatial scales. For total responses, notably variable factors are facilities and utilities, transport facilities and labour availability. For evaluated responses there are several, including facilities and utilities, transport facilities, dispersion tendencies, supplies accessibility, labour availability and corporate communications. For some they are most important in the intermediate scales and are erratic only because they do not become more or less important consistently across the spatial scales, e.g. labour availability.

That there are fewer spatially erratic factors in the total responses lists as compared to the evaluated, where judgements are required, suggests that these are the factors for which data availability is uneven or uncertainty is high. Or, since these are all intermediate in response counts, their being erratic may simply indicate that, in the 'grey' middle, precise rankings are not very significant.

Some factors significantly and consistently increase or decrease in rank across the spatial scales. For both total and evaluated sets, market accessibility shows a major downward shift with decreasing regional scale, while local amenities factor shifts significantly upward in the rankings. These shifts seem to be quite reasonable. Again for both sets, the personal contacts factor moves from a relatively low position at the national scale to a high rank at all other scales. This suggests that for the firms in question, the real locational search—which requires area personal cooperation, contacts and information—really gets started at the sub-national, rather than the national scale, and continues at the regional and local scales. This tends to substantiate the hypothesis that the spatial search process is very quickly limited in scope.

Shifting from the scale variations of the individual factors, it is significant that the sum of responses for all factors consistently increases as the scale

182

becomes larger (Tables 6.2 and 6.3). For total responses, the sum at the national scale is approximately half the sum at the local scale; for the evaluated responses the increased emphasis on the larger scales is even more dramatic. Likewise, the percentages of the sums of evaluated to total responses (Table 6.4) increases consistently as the region of search becomes more specific. These data tend to confirm the impression that most of the time, effort and judgment in decision-making is expended on relatively small areas.

Additional Observations

The examination of the interview tapes has yielded a great many other significant observations. Among these, an important one is that a very small number of management people, usually less than five, make the location decision. The decision is viewed strictly from the management side. Consequently, there is the opportunity and the tendency to maximize executive convenience, others things being roughly equal, both in the decision process and as a criterion for site selection.

Although potentially of almost infinite complexity, the location decision process is very quickly and severely simplified by the decision-makers. The temporal dimension is simplified by dealing with projections of the future of only a few years, never more than five. This despite the fact that managers seem to believe that the new facility and new location will help solve company problems for 10, 20 or 30 years. The spatial dimension is likewise severely simplified. Most areas of the world are never even thought of as potential sites. At the other extreme, the number of specific sites seriously considered is very small, usually less than six.

Managers also pay little attention to possible temporal changes in the spatial context such as shifts in supply or markets, or moves by competitors. They have few ways of dealing with such uncertainties. The relative lack of provision for future contingencies, however, is consistent with the generalization that plants are constructed to solve immediate problems. Moreover, only a very short time period is usually available for planning the new facility and selecting its new site—normally only a few months.

In the interviews, the more classic economic location factors are usually discussed first by the respondents. This priority reflects the basic importance of these factors. However, one suspects that managers like to see themselves as economically rational, and believe it is expected of them. Once the respondents are well into the interview, are relaxed, and have recalled many memories, then the subjective, judgmental and very personal nature of industrial location decision making becomes fully apparent. Hence the necessity for catching the 'open' interviews on tape and then subjecting them to content analysis.

New facilities are usually constructed to meet expanded product demand, to obtain more modern plant and facilities or to escape an unfavourable labour situation. The current findings tend to corroborate the oft-noted generalization that manufacturing firms do not establish new or expanded plants to take advantage of potential opportunities; rather, such new establishments are responses to immediate and pressing problems.

In addition to the factors analysed above, the respondents are quite well aware that a south-eastern Ohio location imposes a penalty in transport costs. In all the cases analysed in this study, materials have to be shipped in and products have to be shipped out, in contrast to locations such as Cleveland which provide local suppliers or markets, or both. Respondents are also aware of the somewhat greater odds in south-eastern Ohio in favour of non-union plant or, at least, of escaping the jurisdiction of their current union.

The manufacturers interviewed are separate and distinct, one from the other, and there seems to be no explicit element of 'following' any of these, or any other firm, in the choice of location. Of distinct importance, however, is the *internal* geography of the firm. There is a noticeable tendency to use what might be labelled a 'spatial increment' model, wherein these relatively small plants are located just beyond the firm's previous 'spatial sphere of production'. That is, located far enough away from any existing facility of that firm to gain perceived locational advantages (usually labour), but no further than necessary to facilitate inter-plant cooperation and, especially, management contact from the home office. In one case, the search area was determined by a two-hundred mile radius from headquarters—the distance the corporate jet-plane could cover in one hour. Likewise, in six of the eight cases, the decision makers were not to be personally involved in operating the new plants to such an extent that it would necessitate their living nearby; but for the two cases in which the decision-makers were designated to be also the local operators, even the then current location of their homes seemed to be a significant factor. It appears that the 'information' demands of the system are severe and the requisite information/ contacts cannot regularly be obtained/maintained too far from 'home.' This, combined with the strong desire to minimize executive inconvenience, suggests that firms will put branches as close to home as other economic conditions permit.

Of the eight plants surveyed, seven of the managements are happy with their location decision and in retrospect feel that the results confirm the wisdom of their choice; the only firm unhappy with its location decision is the firm with the resident planning group, which is contending with a decision made before the group was fully operational. With the exception of the current activities of the one in-house planning group, the decision-makers characterize their location decision process as being relatively unsophisticated. They use relatively few data, and no fancy analytic techniques. And they tend to think that other manufacturers probably are much better at the process than themselves. However, those decision-makers who confessed most readily to an 'unsophisticated' location decision process were those who (1) were most closely involved in the actual location decision, (2) could supply the most lucid and detailed retrospective analysis of the process and (3) seemed most happy with their ultimate location decisions. This point is especially interesting because it conforms to the basic psychological principle that the 'severity of the initiation' (in this case, hard work on the actual decision) is positively correlated with loyalty to the organization (or, in this case, the correctness of the location decision). This is of practical importance because it is likely that confidence in decisions leads, in part, to self-fulfilling prophecies.

The Decision Trace: A General Model

Although each locational decision differs in detail, the investigation stresses striking similarities in the decision-making *process*. In every case, there was a judgmental response, in the face of uncertainties, to an immediate need of the corporation. The decisions were made by relatively few persons in upper management, were seen as an integral part of the total financial decision process of the firm and were reached relatively quickly. Especially noteworthy were the rapidity and severity with which the scope of the spatial search was circumscribed, and relative lack of overt, detailed feedback to the decision-makers about the correctness of the location decision after the fact.

The decision processes noted tend to conform to more general models and are examples of Chamberlain's (1968) 'strategic decisions', Tiebout's (1957) 'adaptive processes' and Krumme's (1969) 'spatially active' decision-making. They fit closely Townroe's decision stages of (1) development of management policy, (2) pressure for changes in space, (3) pressures for a new site, (4) the search for a new site (1971, pp. 17–27).

Strong common denominators among the eight case studies suggest the following generalized trace of the locational decision process:

(1) Identification of *need*. New facilities are usually constructed to meet expanded product demand, to obtain more modern plant and facilities, to escape an unfavourable labour situation. The nature of corporate need influences the spatial search process.

(2) Corporate *preconditions*. The vast majority of the world's possible locations are never explicitly considered in the search process. Most are precluded by preconditions imposed by the corporate situation. These may be subdivided into:

(i) Organizational preconditions such as, 'we only consider one plant at a time' or 'we are determined to escape the jurisdiction of our present union'.

(ii) Spatial preconditions such as, 'we avoid overseas locations' or 'we have always been in Ohio' or 'we already have plants in those areas'.

(3) *The spatial search.*

(i) Selection of an area of search, at the sub-national or, more commonly, the regional scale. The preconditions provide at least vague limits to this area: it is usually centred on, or adjacent to, areas of current production and within areas of current distribution. This first spatially overt decision stage involves the rather precise, and usually arbitrary or impressionistic, delimitation of the specific area of search.

(ii) Focus on a subsection of the regional area of search. This stage is reached relatively rapidly. The decision process may involve the utilization of area development agency and utility company data, but in general it seems to be primarily based on the very limited regional knowledge and impressions of the part-time location decision-makers.

(iii) Selection of a set of towns. In this stage, a preliminary survey of the selected sub-region identifies those towns which promise to supply the minimum requirements for the plant such as sufficient population size, good labour potential or adequate accessibility. The number of towns so selected for more detailed consideration is usually very small, normally less than six.

(iv) Selection of a specific town for the plant through the analysis of objective data and the subjective impressions of the decision-makers. This, and the immediately preceding stage, consumes most time and effort in the spatial decision process. Since one criterion for selecting a town is the desirability of a specific site, the town selection process very often also determines the site selection.

(4) *Ratification* of the location decision. The location decision by the working managers normally must be ratified by the uppermost policy-makers of the firm, such as the Board of Directors and the President. So long as the location decision-makers are creditable, approval is usually routine.

(5) *Construction and operation* of the plant. After the start of production at a given site, little thought is given to the correctness of the location decision, except when a specific decision is used to model a subsequent decision. There is also a great tendency to rationalize the decision since the location chosen is recognized as permanently fixed for a long duration. Except in extreme situations, there is an effort to amortize the building and location in spite of changes in the corporate or competitive situation which may diminish the viability of the location. The plant is adapted to change.

Concluding Comments

The current study is based on a small sample of firms who have made recent location decisions regarding Appalachian Ohio. All the firms interviewed made positive moves in south-eastern Ohio; it is unknown how the results would differ if the sample had included firms which had considered, but rejected, a south-eastern Ohio location.

Obviously, there is no objective way to ascertain the validity of any generalizations coming from this study, given the small and biased sample and the open-ended, subjective interviews. There are, of course, many possibilities for refinements in future research. Among these are more careful consideration of the usefulness and implications of evaluated versus neutral statements, the utilization of information on variations in verbal emphasis (our subjective impressions are that these are in close accord with content counts, but this needs to be systematically checked) and exploration of implications of this study for space preference research (see Downs, 1970). Investigating the last point, it also seems likely that ideas from 'personal construct theory', such as the application of semantic differential techniques to the derived locational factors and spatial scales, might well be profitably borrowed (see Lundeen, 1972). Even so, the apparent success and relative objectivity of the content analysis technique, as herein used, has been gratifying and has proved useful in producing data and suggesting hypotheses. Furthermore, this study has produced results which are sufficiently well in agreement with other similar studies to suggest that the current efforts are on target.

Comparison with Townroe's British industrial location decision studies (1971) reveals many more similarities than differences in the decision-making motives or procedures. Likewise, the current analyses tend to confirm the general observations, based on a larger sample but without detailed content counts, made by Rees (1971) and Stafford (1972). Finally, the results are quite compatible with those reported for south-eastern Ohio by Hunker and Wright (1963), the major exceptions being the relative upgrading of personal contacts and labour as factors.

This investigation exemplifies several methodological and conceptual frameworks. The subjective content of interviews has been made more objective, facilitating analysis. Investigator bias has been minimized. The benefits of examining the location decision at different spatial scales has been demonstrated. Things that are common to the various decision processes have been generalized. Thus, it seems reasonable to conclude that the content analysis of tape-recorded interviews with industrial location decision-makers is a viable methodology for the more complete understanding of the geography of manufacturers.

References

Chamberlain, N. W., 1968, *Enterprise and Environment: The Firm in Time and Place* (New York: McGraw–Hill).

Downs, R. M., 1970, 'Geographic space perception: past approaches and future prospects', *Progress in Geography*, **2**.

Dun and Bradstreet Reference Book of Corporate Managements, 1971–72, 1971 (New York: Dun and Bradstreet).

Hunker, H. L. and A. J. Wright, 1963, *Factors of Industrial Location in Ohio*, Bureau of Business Research, The Ohio State University, Research Monograph 119.

Krumme, G., 1969, 'Towards a geography of enterprise', *Economic Geography*, **45**.

Lundeen, R., 1972, *The Semantic Differential Technique and Personal Construct Theory in Image Measurement*, Discussion Paper No. 5, Department of Geography, York University, Toronto.

Moody's Industrial Manual, 1971 (New York: Moody's Investors Service).

Rees, J., 1971, *Industrial Location Decision Processes: An Exploratory Empirical Analysis*, unpublished M. A. thesis, Department of Geography, University of Cincinnati.

Stafford, H. A., 1969, 'An industrial location decision model', *Proceedings of the Association of American Geographers*, **1**, 141–5.

Stafford, H. A., 1972, 'The geography of manufacturers', *Progress in Geography*, **4**, 181–215.

Sundberg, N. D. and L. E. Tyler, 1962, *Clinical Psychology* (New York: Appleton-Century-Crofts).

Tiebout, C., 1957, 'Location theory, empirical evidence and economic evaluation', *Papers and Proceedings of the Regional Science Association*, **3**.

Townroe, P. M., 1971, *Industrial Location Decisions, A Study in Management Behaviour*, University of Birmingham (U.K.) Centre for Urban and Regional Studies, Occasional Paper 15.

7
Decision-Making, the Growth of the Firm and the Business Environment

JOHN REES

The stimulus for this chapter comes from the need for studies of spatial economic behaviour to offer analytical implications either in the form of theoretical postulates about the general rules that govern industrial location behaviour at the micro- or firm level, or in the form of macro-economic spatial inferences. The construction of models is required for predicting changes in spatial behaviour as circumstances both in the firm and in the decision-making environment vary—a need to distil relationships which show the connections between real world parameters ascribed to spatial decisions of the industrial firm and the exogenous economic variables that constitute the business environment.

Initial behavioural approaches in industrial geography advocated the exploration of people and processes behind actual location decisions (Stafford, 1972; Townroe, 1971; Rees, 1972) in response to the inadequacies of traditional, normative theories of industrial location. This was not because of either the prescriptive character or the simplified sets of assumptions postulated under traditional theory but because of the constraints of the realism engendered—more particularly the uncertainty involved and the sub-optimal behaviour generated in reality. Other studies (McNee, 1958; Krumme, 1969; Steed, 1971a, 1971b) have reacted to the monopolistic postulates of past industrial location theories in light of the oligopolistic tendencies of reality, particularly by studying the multi-plant firm and interlinkages evident in spatial patterns. All such studies favour the micro-economic approach of the theory of the firm towards understanding industrial location, in the spirit of the work of Cyert and March (1963), Chandler (1966), Penrose (1968) and others in economics.

In its focus on location decisions, spatial growth and organization of the industrial firm, this chapter aspires to be complementary both to attempts at

190

explaining individual firm behaviour at the micro-spatial level and to attempts at explaining the growth of the firm and its effect on aggregated locational behaviour at the macro-scale. This will involve three stages: first, the establishment of a set of decision rules or behavioural parameters for explaining the industrial location processes of firms in both the U.S.A. and U.K.; secondly, analysing the implications of location decisions on the growth of the firm, particularly the large corporation, of examining organization structure and investment policy; thirdly, studying the interrelationships between the industrial firm and its broader economic environment.

Behavioural Parameters and a Model of the Industrial Location Decision Process

Conceptual and Empirical Model

An empirical analysis of a sample of large British and American firms provides a basis for generalizing about the location decisions of manufacturing firms in a market economy. The 20 firms examined in detail included international giants such as Procter & Gamble, Unilever, Monsanto, Formica, Imperial Chemical Industries, W.R. Grace, Shell Chemicals, British Petroleum, Courtaulds, Cincinnati Milacron and Dunlop–Pirelli, with headquarters either in Cincinnati or London. The sample represents the upper end of the firm size spectrum, simply because of the greater amount of cooperation received from these firms after 100 firms, representing a cross-section of firm sizes and industrial groups, had initially been contacted. The limitations of such a sample of firms available for analysis are recognized, but, in this exploratory study, it was only the large firms that had the resources available to cooperate at a time when industry seems to be inundated by questionnaire surveys. Two other constraints on the sample of large firms were their degree of willingness to disclose records on recent locational decisions (i.e. within the last ten years) and the degree of willingness of the decision-makers (whether owners, members of boards of directors or business managers) to discuss candidly the sequence of decision-making events as they perceived them.

Open-ended interviews with executives who were involved in capital investment location decisions confirmed the validity of a conceptual framework (Figure 7.1) of locational search, learning and choice evaluation. This is a simple stimulus–response mechanism caused by profit, growth and survival problems which Lloyd and Dicken (1972, p. 145) have since described as equivalent to exceeding a stress-tolerance threshold. The model is an adaptation of what Simon (1960, p. 2) calls a 'subjectively rational information decision system', the result of bounded optimality where people rationally but judgmentally attempt to optimize their resources while nevertheless being bounded by their own limitations.

The first phase of the decision making process seen in Figure 7.1—searching the environment—Simon (1960, p. 2) terms 'intelligence activity'. The second phase—inventing, developing and analysing possible courses of action—he calls 'design activity'. The third phase, selecting a particular course of action from those available, is labelled 'choice activity'. One can have reservations about these terms and so here they are interpreted respectively as problem perception, search behaviour and action. They are incorporated as such in Figure 7.1.

People who actually make location decisions are usually faced with an

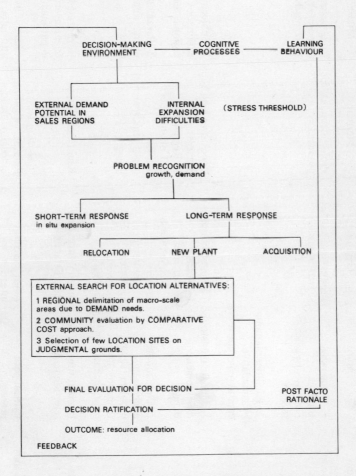

Figure 7.1. Empirical model of the industrial decision process for establishing a branch of a large corporation.

Table 7.1. Summary of Location Decision Characteristics of Ten Multi-Plant Firms (compiled from interviews)

Type of firm / Plants	Formica	Procter & Gemble	Monsanto	Cincinnati Milacron	Panacon
Response to problem	1. 'Long range' product. Forecasts by sales regions 2. Facilities planning by cumulative capital requirements	Product and market share forecasts	Project demands for product	Long range corporate plans of space needs	Customer needs in sales regions
Search process	1. Update industrial development data 2. Decision tree analysis in problem region to narrow down requirements	7 Steps: Outline: 1. Needs 2. Best area 3. Requirements survey 4. Communities 5. Screen 6. Select 7. Build	Check own land bank 3 stages: 1. Regional 2. Communities 3. Sites (strict requirements)	1. Subjective elimination on regional scale 2. Parameters restrict final choice	1. General scan and surveys of 15 locations 2. Detailed cost analyses, profit—loss statements on 2
Searchers	Internal site selection term	Internal task force, Real Estate Dept.	Real Estate Dept.	Corporate building & engineering department	Operations Dept.
Decision aids	Critical path process, Decision trees	Linear, mixed, integer programming	Relative weighting of location factors vis-a-vis requirements	Chart of locational attributes, map and tables of work residence locations	Profit and loss tabulations

Table 7.1. (Contd.)

BP	Shell	Dunlop	British Titan	Unilever
Group development plan. 1. Forecasts—regional competitors sectors 2. Facilities plan—refineries, transport	Related to corporate planning (5 stages). Capital expenditure forecasts by operating companies, regional growth centres	In context of corporate planning—competition among division for resources, search for surplus capital	Market allocation P.A. (in 5 year plan context) Market share plus sales forecasts	Capital proposals vetting system. Demand for existing/new products
Continuous search (many negative decisions) 80% investment at existing sites	1. Product allocation regional 2. Site selection		Surveys related to location requirements	Decision tree
Central Planning Department	Economics and Planning Department	Central Development Planning Department	Group Planner	Central Financial Group
Operations research L.P. models include Risk analysis. Transport flows	Linear programming	Corporate planning, L.P. Risk analysis, Profit assessments	Weighted factors, Profit statements	Sensitivity analysis and financial models, L.P. simulation

ill-defined problem which is filtered by their own motivational and perceptual distortions and by the usual operating uncertainties of the real world. The emphasis in this model is on information gathering, processing and manipulation. The very definition of strategy or policy and the instigation of decision rules are important ways in which uncertainty is avoided. There is, however, further need—as Webber (1972) recognizes—to explore conditions under which uncertainty motivates certain types of spatial responses; it is moreover essential for an operational definition of uncertainty in terms of information constraints as it limits locational choice.

The basic framework that is suggested in the model (Figure 7.1) for analysing the variables involved in the decision-making process consists in the identification of parts in the socio-economic system in which the decision-makers operate (the environment), the information available to the decision makers and the codes of behaviour used. The relationships in this decision-making system are the core of the process, summarized succinctly by the four conceptual rubrics of Cyert and March (1963, p. 116): (1) the quasi-resolution of conflict between decision-makers; (2) uncertainty avoidance; (3) a simple, problem-oriented search process; (4) organizational learning from experience. Attention is focused here on the generalizations that may be deduced from the results of the small sample of firms from both sides of the Atlantic. These enable one to specify a set of decision rules for industrial location which are discussed here with reference to specific examples. Figure 7.1 represents a summary of the location decision process for a large corporation establishing a branch plant and incorporates the stages of the conceptual model. This model emerges in all the case studies despite differences in industrial type. The implications of the various stages in the model form the basis of the decision rules elaborated upon later. Table 7.1 summarizes the characteristics of the location decision process of ten of the firms studied, compiled from responses given during the interviews, and serve as examples of the decision rules. The table categorizes the way firms respond to their expansion problems, outlines stages in the locational search process, the individuals involved in this, and the techniques they use, corresponding to the stages suggested in Figure 7.1.

Decision Rules

At least eight such guiding principles are forthcoming from this study: these should be used in developing more realistic theories of industrial location:

(1) A new plant decision is a response to a demand problem. This can arise externally from a potential market area not previously served by a company plant or internally from in-site saturation which results in stress

in the firm (Figure 7.1). A large company producing decorative laminates, for example, annually assesses its investment strategy through long-range product forecasts for marketing regions on the basis of ten-year projections. The Engineering Services department, using decision trees, then converts these marketing forecasts into cumulative capital requirements. The final stage of the operation, known as the Facilities Plan, outlines production and warehouse requirements for which the company has a rigorous set of locational constraints. These constraints are the following: that facilities should be within 24 hours trucking time of 75 per cent of the firm's customers; that no more than 5 per cent of the labour force of a single urban area be employed in the firm; strict site requirements. Figure 7.2 outlines the main stages in the decision process of this case. Another Cincinnati corporation, manufacturing construction and industrial materials, had a policy of acquiring plants by direct takeover or merger rather than building new plants. The firm did resort, however, to a new plant to meet high demand in an eastern sales region when no takeover opportunities could be found.

(2) Normally the first solution searched for is adjustment at the existing location through, for example, input substitution and, secondly, in-site expansion (Rees, 1971, p. 129). In-site locational adjustment like plant modernization to raise productivity was not the focus of this study and remains an unexplored possibility within a firms' choice of investment strategy.

(3) The demand-oriented space—whether California in the American context or the U.K. national market of regional scale in the European context—is narrowed down by the use of cost analyses of specific sites; this clearly challenges the apparent mutual intractability of Weberian cost and Löschian demand theories. Examples are cited here of the kind of location

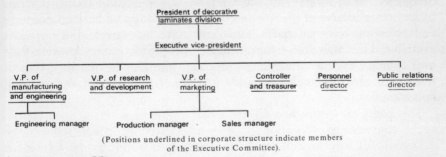

(Positions underlined in corporate structure indicate members of the Executive Committee).

Figure 7.2. The people involved in location decisions in a firm producing decorative laminates. Involvement in the decision process: 1. Production Manager develops a long-range plan of investment, product and pricing strategies. 2. Approval of strategic plan by the Executive Committee. 3. Conversion of the plan to a facilities plan by the Engineering Manager. 4. Review and approval of the facilities plan by the Executive Committee. 5. Site selection by the Engineering Department. 6. Review of the site selection conditions and recommendations by the Executive Committee. 7. To Corporate headquarters for final approval.

factors that act as constraints in the narrowing-down process when a firm makes a locational choice. Extracts are included from locational surveys carried out. The first is by a large shoe manufacturer choosing a site in Appalachian Kentucky: 'Communities were evaluated primarily on the following characteristics: liveability, labour availability, 15-acre plant sites, community leadership, financial considerations, geographic location ... Generally the type of community for which we searched was similar to those in which we are presently located'. Of the location finally chosen, it was stated: 'In appearance the community closely resembled another corporate plant location ... A strong effort to eliminate the appearance of a poverty-stricken Appalachian community was evident ... the highway system awakened them to the obvious advantage of joining the outside world economically ... the former strong influence of unionism is at a low ebb'.

The second is, by a large diversified organization that needed a new plant on the eastern seabord of the United States to relieve demand pressure on a New Jersey plant: 'For each of 15 locations, sufficient information was obtained to draw up a pro forma profit and loss statement ... In the final analysis, the three following factors most highly influenced the final net profit figures. These are: inbound freight costs on raw materials, outbound freight costs on finished products and hourly labour costs'.

For further study it is hypothesized that different factors are important at successive steps of the narrowing-down process of the location decision.

(4) The final choice (Figure 7.2) is a judgmental decision combining— in the case of Procter & Gamble (1970) for example—a number of 'economic' and 'intangible values' yardsticks. Factors measured by economic yardsticks were: costs of available industrial sites; employee availability in the desired categories; local salary and wage levels; transportation (both in terms of services available at the site and the costs of shipping finished products and receiving raw materials); local and state tax rates; utility services available. The intangible values included: people's attitudes towards their own community; the community's attitude towards new industry; type of residential areas, schools, hospitals and other recreational and cultural opportunities.

This confirms Cohen and Cyert's observations that 'many such factors as ... convenience of location ... were not viewed by firms as reducible in a meaningful way to dollars. As a result, such variables are treated as independent constraints and as irrelevant to cost estimation' (Cohen and Cyert, 1965, p. 339).

Much of the response to the location problem in reality is, therefore, a heuristic procedure, an exploratory process of trial and error; such a repeated process of searching and learning has implications for the organization's experience. As business managers face decisions which involve numerous variables and include non-quantifiable aspects, the rigorous methods suggested by operations research and decision theory lose their usefulness as decision aids. Judgment plays a more important role.

'Unfortunately the attention devoted to computational problem-solving techniques has far outstripped that devoted to judgmental considerations ... Naturally some reasonable middle-ground approach is needed so that normative, prescriptive models are outlined with realism garnered from practical experience. This appears to be a perfectly sound objective and achieving it is extremely difficult' (Kast and Rosenzweig, 1970, p. 430).

(5) A new plant decision is a long-term investment solution to the corporate growth and planning problem. No conclusive evidence was obtained of the relative importance of the new location decision as compared with other decisions such as production mix or existing plant use. But intuitively one feels that, if such a measure as personnel time devoted to location questions as a percentage of total personnel time devoted to long-term executive decisions were obtained, the location problem would rank among the highest.

Firms studied took an average of two years to decide on a location and implement their decision. Nevertheless, decision-makers use relatively short-run quantitative techniques as decision aids. As shown in Table 7.1, Procter & Gamble were experimenting with mixed-integer programming for a least-cost solution to their location investment policies: British Petroleum incorporated political risk factors as barriers in their linear programmed petroleum flows in order to formulate longer-term strategies. Longer-term uncertainty therefore, confirms that the location decision is heuristic rather than algorithmic.

The techniques used by a large producer of industrial and cleaning chemicals when choosing a plant site was elaborated on by a corporate executive and is here presented as an example:

> The plant location study was a direct outgrowth of our inventory and warehouse consolidation work. During the course of that earlier study, a linear programming of customer-demand concentrations, costed out all factors in the logistic system. This model was also used to define more efficient alternatives to the system of warehouses then in existence ...
>
> The model linear-programming took into account three entities: plants, warehouses and customer demand centres. Plants were assumed to be fixed for each linear programme run. The costs of running each plant were expressed as a series of cost curves dependent upon volume at the plant. Both fixed and variable costs were included. Transportation costs were expressed as linear functions of both distance and volume from the given plant to a specific warehouse. These costs were computed from coordinate distances thus avoiding the use of extensive rate tables ...
>
> Customer demand was expressed as area poundage concentrations, a customer demand centre being characterized by a yearly poundage and map coordinates. This data was prepared from actual sales histories and represented an extensive manual effort. Customer demand centres were fixed for each run ...
>
> Warehouses were assumed to be variable. Each warehouse was described by a series of cost curves dependent upon both volume through the warehouse and

inventory levels. Part of our earlier inventory work was to develop some of these relationships, such as expected inventory levels, as functions of warehouse demand using the technique of simulation ...

Given the preceding, the model solved the linear-programming problem in a manner equivalent to the standard transportation problem with fixed cost coefficients. This was done to provide an initial solution so that volume-dependent costs could now be included. The model was then run iteratively. After each iteration, a check was made within the programme to eliminate warehouses below a threshold volume. Thus, after each iteration, we observed a reduction in the number of warehouses in operation ...

After using this model for warehouse planning, it was determined that by changing some of the inputs, it could be extended for use in evaluating proposed plant sites equally as well. Our approach was first to extrapolate historical demand to the year of proposed plant construction. This was done using regression estimates of an exponential equation. Prior to running each case we evaluated the transportation costs from the proposed plant site to each warehouse for specified maximum distances, the assumption being that any new plant would operate at the same cost levels irrespective of location except for transportation costs to warehouses. This allowed us to sift out the most likely plant sites for each geographic area for subsequent linear-programming.

Such sophisticated mathematical techniques are used by large firms in their locational investment evaluations (Table 7.1), but in the final analysis the location decision is a judgmental one. It may be that the reason for the development of such techniques as linear programming by, in particular, international petroleum and chemical corporations, lies in the type of tangible, quantifiable information available to these firms. This also accounts for the work of Isard *et al.* (1959) on petrochemical complexes. The behaviour of firms is more difficult to predict when they are involved in manufacturing products which are subject to the more volatile trends of consumer demand (for example, detergents).

(6) Firms reduce uncertainty by seeking standard, successful solutions to their new plant problem, either by copying past successes in their own experience or by imitating competitors, thus contributing to agglomeration tendencies. For example, many American corporations have the same class of freight rates for similar products. One chemical firm admitted to locating a plant in Cincinnati to take advantage of the favourable freight rates negotiated by a larger firm. Webber (1972, p. 208) furthermore, suggests that uncertainty limits firm size and firms which have regional choices of location tend, because of uncertainty, to locate near the centre of their market. Later, when industrial patterns stabilize and when technical change is less rapid, firms get more confident as uncertainty appears reduced, external economies are internalized and the firms become less dependent on the market.

Aharoni emphasizes that 'the very essence of organizational behaviour involves routines, and rhythmical repetitions are vital components in it ... Men cannot cooperate in their activities if they have to improvise constantly under conditions of recurring stress. Organizations are adaptive in nature and they carry out search in a way that preserves existing policies at least partly because of the high cost involved in changing policies' (Aharoni, 1966, p. 302). In this vein, Procter & Gamble make the statement that: 'each new plant represents the sum of the company's manufacturing experience and engineering know-how' (Procter & Gamble, 1970, p. 1).

(7) For a large organization the location decision is comparable to what Simon (1960) calls a more frequent, habitual decision. Monsanto, for example, located an average of two new branch plants annually between 1958 and 1969. For a smaller company with less experience, however, the location problem may be a once-in-a-lifetime decision and is treated as a non-programmed strategic problem. The concept of stereotyped responses with characteristics of rigidity, repetition of success and resistance to change seems particularly relevant to the formulation of a policy for new plant investment decisions based on past experience and habitual traits (Golledge, 1969).

(8) The location decision is made by departmental or divisional managers with vested interests in the new plant. The location of a shoe plant with high labour requirements was decided upon by the personnel and manufacturing departments, while the decision of a canning firm with locational ties to specific customers was made by the sales department. In these two examples, at least, there is evidence that the location variables deemed significant affect the organizational structure of the firms so that in the first case personnel and in the second, sales, are disproportionately large and important departments when compared to others.

Spatial Growth of the Firm: Structure and Strategy

The second part of this chapter places the industrial location decision in its broader context and analyses the growth of the firm as the accumulation of numerous location decisions. This involves changes in the organizational structure of firms, the 'institutional organization of space' (McNee, 1958, p. 321), and its relation to corporate strategy and locational investment. Despite Penrose's study (1968), no comprehensive framework exists to explain the growth of the firm over space, taking account of the various organizational groups whether multi-plant, multi-form (whether regional, functional or product-line), multi-national, corporate or private, centralized or decentralized. As yet we know very little even of the functional space or task environment of the industrial enterprise, of the way it organizes itself spatially and the resulting effects, if any, of acquisition, merger and closure on spatial patterns.

An objective empirical framework for explaining the spatial extent and growth of the corporate system needs to examine a combination of internal and external stimuli to growth. These are: (1) the effect of locational expan-

200

sion and acquisition in relation to various investment thresholds, (2) the effects of corporate experience and organization structure on investment planning strategies, (3) the role of product and process innovations and (4) fluctuations in the business environment as they effect capital availability. Estall (1972, p. 195) draws on the example of science-based industries in Boston and Philadelphia to show how differences in the supply of venture capital can act as a controlling factor on the geographical pattern of industrial development. The verification of a growth formula for the various types of corporate spatial systems classified according to industrial type, organizational structure and size, would facilitate the identification of stages in the growth process of the industrial firm. Steed, following Chandler, suggests four broad stages in the growth process of the industrial firm, 'the initial expansion and accumulation of resources, the rationalization of the use of resources, the expansion into new markets and lines to help ensure the continuing full use of resources and finally the development of a new structure to make possible continuing effective mobilization of resources to meet with changing short-term market demands and long-term market demands' (Steed, 1971a, p. 55).

It is further hypothesized that the analysis of such growth stages will enable the differentiation between a short-term growth strategy of concentration and specialization and a longer term policy of diversification and rationalization. The spatial implications of diversifying and rationalizing processes have been generally ignored within the realms of location theory, though diversification alone, as Penrose (1968, p. 144) points out, can serve various purposes either as a general corporate growth policy or as a solution of problems of a decline in demand.

The growth process of the large corporate system responds to national and local fluctuations in the business cycle through implicit effects on capital availability as well as to demand factors. The growth and product history of Procter & Gamble, illustrated respectively by Figures 7.3 and 7.4, for example, shows concentrated spatial and temporal phases of investment

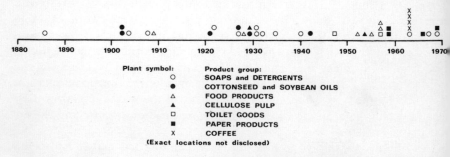

Figure 7.3. The timing and phases of new plant location and product diversification in an expanding American soap and detergents corporation.

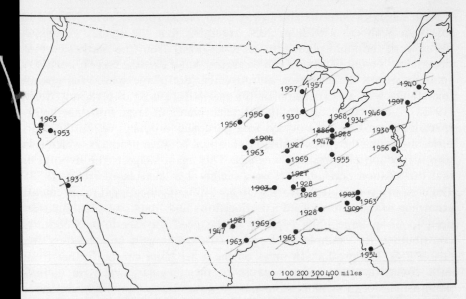

Figure 7.4. The spatial pattern of growth through time of a corporate plant system: the example of an American soap and detergents manufacturer.

expansion, obviously broken by the depression and war eras. Though this example makes it difficult to identify coincidental spatial and temporal phases of investment, the locational expansion and implicit contraction of the multi-plant enterprise remains undefined.

Intuitively one feels that the expansion of the multi-plant firm would identify location leaders and followers which would provide an empirical insight into one aspect of Perroux's concept of the 'lead firm, that which strongly influences the process of regional economic structural change' (Erikson 1972, p. 4). Thomas (1969, p. 50) suggested that a firm's spatial expansion path is usually a composite of movements along a number of possible expansion paths and that the ability of firms to innovate and change their product-mixes will condition the nature of this path.

In another context, Chandler (1961) has explored the relationship between organizational structure and strategy; and likewise one can postulate a deterministic relationship between the expansion path of the industrial enterprise and the way it organizes itself functionally. The formal structure of organizations are of four main types, each with differing spatial manifestations, be they regional, functional, product line or a combination of these. The multi-divisional structure adopted by an expanding company marks a threshold or take-off point for increasing growth and diversification, and this provides a ratchet effect to ensure further growth. Along the growth path of the firm, Steed (1971a, p. 5) advocates a distinct functional order to the spatial organization of plants where the size and functional autonomy of a plant increases with distance away from the 'corporate core'. This is in line with Webber's (1972, p. 208) argument that the spatial expansion diffusion of the multi-plant firm increases away from the market core as uncertainty is reduced. Thus it can be argued that the reduction of uncertainty spatially reflects the extension or movement out of the spatial margins of uncertainty with an expansion of the spatial threshold of certainty. Steed (1971a, p. 6) further suggests that branch plants of large firms are highly spacialized, yet they are not tied to a particular product even in the short term, suggesting the spatial liquidity of capital between products, which is in turn a function of corporate strategy. This again suggests the hypothesis that the location decision to close a facility is a 'last resort' (Rees, 1972). The units of a corporation also tend to have differing locational requirements according to the nature of information flows and functions. Headquarters need to be in large units because of the need for face-to-face contacts contributing, for example, to London's functions as a headquarters city (Table 7.4). The production units on the other hand can be further from such communication nodes because of their regular, repetitive contact patterns. The location of decision-makers, however, need not be synonymous with the location of headquarters; in numerous cases executives resident in manufacturing units are involved in location decisions, but invariably decision ratifiers (Board of Directors) are located in headquarters offices. The office location of headquarters, and location decision-makers therefore, reflects extension of a firm's activity space (task environment) and it is hypothesized that this can affect managerial spatial perception of market and alternative locations. For instance, McNee argues in this volume that the headquarters of a firm with an American Manufacturing Belt market shifted from Cincinnati to New York is shifted to a more peripheral location to the national market but becomes a 'forward capital' for international expansion. Clearly managerial perception changes from U.S. to world markets, adding to balance of payments pressures implicit in national economic growth, and this can change the scale and direction of perception of the U.S. market and further growth within it.

Assuming, therefore, that managerial spatial perception varies with the type of formal organization structure, empirical exploration of the people and process behind locations decisions discloses an informal organizational structure of paramount importance in corporate strategy. The exact role of these informal decision-makers, however, was very difficult to identify in the sample. A variety of people, with different experiences and biases at different levels in the formal hierarchical structure of an organization, were found to be involved in the location decision process (Rees, 1972). Locational research and evaluation are usually carried out at an intermediate level in the organization hierarchy by departmental or divisional managers of either critical departments or variables in the new plant decision before submitting for ratification at an executive level. This is shown in Figure 7.2.

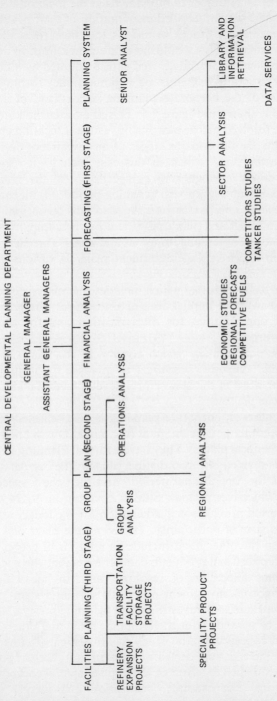

Figure 7.5. The structure of the corporate planning department of a large British petroleum firm.

The involvement of a number of individuals in the location decision process of large firms suggests that detailed examination of their position, executive power, experience and attitudes would disclose their roles and influence in the choice of location. This would facilitate generalization and prediction as to the type of locational strategy and choice adopted by different kinds of organizational structures and thus aid regional policy formulation.

The structure of the corporate planning department of a large British petroleum firm is shown in Figure 7.5. This illustrates the kinds of interests that have to be resolved before a capital investment location choice is made. It also highlights the three major stages of an investment decision process: (1) the *Forecasting stage,* which in this case includes a regional analysis and a survey of the behaviour of competitors; (2) the *group plan stage* evaluated annually for a seven-year planning period; (3) the implementation or *facilities planning stage* which puts the plan into operation. The development of such an integrated planning system by the company in 1970 called for a reorganization of planning functions and goals. Three levels in planning were defined, in which capital investment plans at various locations play only a part:

(1) *Strategic policy planning* which includes the analysis of opportunities for long-term growth, the implications of innovations within and outside the company, and opportunities for diversification and for acquisition and disposal of resources.

(2) *Developmental planning* which consists in the analysis of the future utilization of the company's resources to increase its profitability: this in fact is the major work of the new central developmental planning unit.

(3) *Operational planning.*

Current emphasis on corporate planning is also reflected in the 'gestalt' philosophy of another petroleum giant (the Royal Dutch Shell Group, with interests in 42 chemical plants). They have a formal Planning Period covering 7 years which is divided into two distinct phases: the current and following year, known as the 'operational period', and then the 5 succeeding years, known as the 'objectives period'. Studies covering up to 24 years beyond the Planning Period provide some orientation for the longer term, reflecting the increasing degree of uncertainty. The corporate plans of a large rubber manufacturer on the other hand include an analysis of group objectives to provide a geographical and product balance, reconciling these with divisional strategies and the allocation of resources and, in line with most large companies, a rigorous investment proposals vetting system.

It is in this context of total investment and planning policy that the location decision has to be viewed. Though Krumme (1969) and others have looked at this problem conceptually, no study has investigated either the relative importance of the location decision in relation to other possibilities of resource allocation open to a firm or the implicit spatial component of other business decisions. For example, acquisition and merger can have as profound an effect on the spatial organization of the firm through growth, rationalization and closure of plants as can direct locational investments in new or expanded plants. Expenditure by Courtaulds in the five financial years between 1965 and 1970 shows that $260 million was spent on new plants and machinery and only $2 million on acquisition in its fibre-*making* sector, whereas $200 million was spent on new plants and $232 million on acquisitions in its fibre-*using* divisions (Courtaulds, 1968). In this case, however, information on the trends in the total corporate pattern of plant location and in the pattern of corporate linkages in different divisions of Courtaulds was not forthcoming.

The Firm and its Environment

The way a firm allocates its resources, directly or indirectly, over space is but one way it responds to the general economic environment: over time such responses result cumulatively in a dynamic economy. In analysing spatial economic patterns through the decision-making behaviour of individual firms, a variety of spatial responses—or what Steed (1971b) calls corporate–environment relations—are evident.

(1) An on-going study of post-war changes in the spatial organization and behaviour of one sector of the British chemical industry has disclosed a spatial response to the minimal growth rates experienced by British industry. Manufacturers' investment in new plant and equipment usually exhibits a strong tendency to lag behind the cyclical pattern of the economy. Increases in spending on new facilities tend to slow down in a recession and these capital outlays actually decline as the economy begins to recover. Only after the recovery has been under way for some time does spending on new plant and equipment begin to increase again. If one examines capital invest-

Table 7.2. U.K. Chemical and Allied Industries: Regional Investment, 1970–71

	1971 £m	No.	1970 £m	No.
North West	337·8	86	355·6	91
Wales	190·5	36	109·0	37
North East	173·1	61	179·9	60
Midlands	115·9	48	140·9	61
Scotland	114·8	31	147·6	42
East	78·5	19	46·1	26
N. Ireland	63·1	11	35·0	40
South East	41·8	30	43·0	40
South West	9·9	4	15·1	16
Unspecified	8·9	3	51·4	11
Totals	1134·3	329	1143·6	399

Source: *Chemical Age*, September, 1971.

ment in new building work and plant, machinery and other equipment in the U.K. chemical industry between 1963 and 1971 there emerges a close correlation between investment in plant and machinery and total investment (a surrogate for the business cycle) which in this instance, suggests that investment in plant machinery closely reflects the general economic cycle. Yet, the steadier curve for new building investment does not reflect variations in the business cycle. The shallowness of the curve, however, does reflect the lack of investment and growth in British industry generally.

This aggregated pattern of chemical investment also has varying regional impact. Table 7.2 shows total regional investment projects in the U.K. chemical industry in 1970–1 as compiled by *Chemical Age International*. The ten leading companies in terms of investment totals is given in Table 7.3. In 1971 heavy organic chemicals had displaced petroleum refining and was followed in descending order of importance by town gas, plastics, man-made fibres, fertilizers, pharmaceuticals, inorganic chemicals, industrial gases, chemical coal and rubber. The North West remained the most important region, accounting for nearly 30 per cent of the survey total but Wales (particularly because of BP investments) had displaced the North East as the second most important area. Scotland had fallen from third to fifth place, with a fall of 22 per cent in 1971 compared to 1970.

Between 1958 and 1963 the U.K. Census of Production shows that the number of firms producing heavy and fine chemicals in the U.K. as a whole declined from 618 to 557 and the number of establishments (plants) decreased from 871 to 857, while output rose from £603 million to £876 million, disclosing a rationalization factor in the number of firms and plants. Capital expenditure in new buildings (and machinery) in the same period was down from £19·1 million in 1958 to £8·8 million in 1963, and in 1963 the cost of

Table 7.3. Leading Companies in Terms of Investment Totals, 1970–71

	1971 £m	1970 £m
Shell	269	272
BP	210	183
ICI	162	175
Conoco	55	52
Gas Council	44	74
Burmah Oil	36	25
ENI/Marco	35	46
Esso	27	34
Amoco	26	30
Courtaulds	20	22
Monsanto	20	25

Source: *Chemical Age*, September, 1971.

disposing land and existing buildings was double that of acquisition (Census of Production, 1963). Though the number of firms employing over 100 people decreased from 186 to 140 in these years, the number of those firms with interests in other industrial groups increased, disclosing a horizontal, diversifying process.

Out of a sample of 152 firms listed under heavy and fine chemical products, 54 were affiliated to other corporate groups and holding companies, 18 of which had their headquarters in the U.S.A. and another 6 in continental Europe (Dun and Bradstreet Directory, 1971). This form of spatial organization is typical of the U.K. chemical industry's current problems, where over-capacity on a world scale has meant rising imports of low-priced products in the U.K., particularly from the staturated markets of the U.S.A. It is perhaps an unfortunate policy implication of such a highly developed international industry that chemical producers aggravate each others' problems by exporting their difficulties to other countries through selling surpluses at low prices, thus exaggerating balance of payments and world currency problems. Thus international investment flows affect production and capacity use at various locations.

It is not surprising, therefore, that one response to this trend within the chemical industry has been a strong lobby for agreements between producers. Moves towards this include an information exchange agreement to phase investments in ethylene by ICI, Shell and Fison's and an agreement to phase investments in ethylene by ICI, Shell and BP. Both these agreements are allowed within the context of current Restrictive Practices legislation in the U.K., even though it encourages permanent barriers to competition. The spatial significance of the latter virtually implies companies taking turns over the introduction of vast new naphtha crackers and associated their complexes of downstream plants. General supply and demand trends in the economy, therefore, cause individual firms to respond through their capital investment policies, and these have significant temporo-spatial implications.

(2) A second response to detrimental conditions in the economy with implications for the spatial organization of firms takes the form of mergers and acquisition. In October 1926 the merger of British Dyestuffs, Brunner Mond, Nobell Industries and United Alkali to 'develop their business on broad imperial lines' saw the birth of ICI as a British response to aggressive commercial competition from the great German chemical trust and to the potential threat from large scale American chemical organizations like Du Pont, Union Carbide or Grace ICI (1967). Similarly, the 1970 union of Dunlop and Pirelli was a response to increasing competition from the large American firms, Goodyear and Firestone; but the union is also complementary geographically, with Pirelli strongest in southern Europe and Dunlop in the former British colonial territories. Economic difficulties have, however, put the future of this union in jeopardy. Indeed, of the 2126 manufacturing firms quoted on the U.K. stock exchange in 1954, more than

400 had been acquired by 1960, and of the 41 chemical firms which 'died between 1948 and 1960, 28 disappeared through acquisition (Singh, 1971 p. 20). Mergers are largely a function of the legal and institutional environment, where the strong anti-trust legislation in the U.S.A. provides a contras to the U.K. The role of mergers, however, as instruments of rationalizing the spatial pattern of British industry, still remains unexplored. Yet, according to *The Times* (April, 1972) merger activity in Britain reached such a peak in 1967–8 that, if maintained on a projected trend, it could lead to the fina merger into one firm, U.K. Amalgamated Ltd., as early as 1978!

   (3) A third feature of firm-environment relationships is the impact of the large organization on the regional economic growth process through multiplier processes, follow-the-leader effects, 'seed-bed' growth pattern and the advantages of industrial linkages (Thomas, 1972; Moore, 1972) The distribution of headquarters is markedly concentrated in the tradition ally favoured growth areas, the manufacturing belts of both countrie (Table 7.4). New York City alone houses 137 corporate headquarter of the 500 largest American firms *(Fortune* 500, 1968), although this i a decrease from the 1963 number of 163 (Goodwin, 1965), probabl because of micro-scale decentralization of firms from the metropoli itself but to locations within the metropolitan region. Because sheer number may in fact reduce the apparent concentration of economic power in a large city, the importance of management centres, as Goodwin points out has to take account of total assets, sales, profits and employment size Detroit, for example, may rank only fifth in the U.S. as far as numbers o headquarters are concerned, but the assets of one corporation in particula (General Motors) raise that rank to second only to New York City in term of control over total assets. Though the number of headquarters is merel a crude surrogate for managerial status and decision-making power mapping then distribution effectively points out areas without any head quarters. In this respect the British position is more exaggerated than the American, with London housing 446 headquarters out of the 1000 larges British firms and 81 out of the largest 100; Wales on the other hand, has a mere 8 headquarters *(The Times* 1000, 1971).

   It is significant that there is less correlation of city rank with the importance of industrial corporation headquarters in the U.S.A. than in the U.K. This may reflect the greater size variation of U.S. companies, the greate variety of their choice of national economic centres, the greater size o nation and the fact that federal structure means that no city is economicall and administratively dominant as London is in Britain.

   Spatial search behaviour is a two-way process, comparable to Cyert and March's (1963, p. 80) mating theory of search, with areas looking fo industries as well as firms searching for locations. Regional economi equality, therefore, may be enhanced if such headquarters, rather that manufacturing plants, were directed to less developed growth centres to

Table 7.4. Headquarters Locations of the Largest 500 Industrial Firms in the U.S.A. (1967) and the U.K. (1971)

U.S.A. 1967		U.K. 1971	
	No. of offices	Assets (billion $)		No. of offices	Assets (£'000)

U.S.A. 1967	No. of offices	Assets (billion $)	U.K. 1971	No. of offices	Assets (£'000)
New York	137	120·342	London	295	25,605
Chicago	38	16·553	Glasgow	10	1,140
Pittsburgh	18	16·677	Birmingham	8	487
Cleveland	18	6·386	Sheffield	8	215
Detroit	11	20·386	Liverpool	7	256
St. Louis	11	5·763	Manchester	6	320
St. Paul and Minneapolis	11	3·645	Leeds	5	107
Los Angeles	10	7·268	Edinburgh	4	533
Philadelphia	10	5·886	Nottingham	2	137
San Francisco	6	7·202	Bradford	2	40
Toledo	6	2·322	Wolverhampton	1	52
Boston	5	1·283	Leicester	1	37

Sources: *Fortune*, May, 1968; *Times 1000*, 1972.

help generate and attract regional economic growth. Since the role of manufacturing firms in regional development seems ambiguous (Parsons, 1972; Watts and Barlow, 1972) loosening the ties of the large firm with the metropolis remains currently impracticable as a result of the overwhelming inertial advantage of corporate contact patterns in large urban units (Goddard, 1972).

Location decisions such as those described in this chapter, therefore, have important implications for regional equality as well as for economic growth. Yet the role of the investment strategies of the multi-plant industrial enterprise remains undefined in the idealistic world of location theory.

References

Aharoni, Y., 1966, *The Foreign Investment Decision Process* (Boston: Harvard Business School).

Chandler, A. D., 1966, *Strategy and Structure* (Cambridge, Mass.: M.I.T. Press).

Cohen, K. S. and R. M. Cyert, 1965, *Theory of the Firm: Resource Allocation in a Market Economy* (Englewood Cliffs: Prentice–Hall).

Courtaulds, Statement by the Chairman, 1968.

Cyert, R. M. and J. G. March, 1963, *A Behavioural Theory of the Firm* (Englewood Cliffs: Prentice–Hall).

Dun and Bradstreet Reference Book of Corporate Managements, 1971–72, 1971 (New York: Dun and Bradstreet).

Erikson, R. A., 1972, *The lead firm concept: an analysis of theoretical elements*, Working paper, University of Washington, Seatle.

Estall, R. C., 1972, 'Some observations on the internal mobility of investment', *Area*, **4**, 193–8.

Goddard, J., 1972, *Contact systems and regional development in Britain*, Working paper, Department of Geography, London School of Economics (mimeo).

Golledge, R. G., 1969, 'The geographical relevance of some learning theories', in *Behavioural Problems in Geography: A Symposium*, ed. K. Cox and R. G. Golledge (Evanston: Northwestern University).

Goodwin, W., 1965, 'The management center in the United States', *Geographical Review*, **55**.

Imperial Chemical Industries, 1967, *ICI in Focus* (London: ICI).

Isard, W., E. W. Schooler, and T. Vietonsz, 1969, *Industrial Complex Analysis and Regional Development* (Cambridge, Mass.: M.I.T. Press).

Kast, E. and J. Rosenzweig, 1970, *Organization and Management—A System Approach* (New York: McGrew–Hill).

Krumme, G., 1969, 'Notes on locational adjustment patterns in industrial geography', *Geografiska Annaler*, Series B. **51**, 15.

Lloyd, P. E. and P. Dicken, 1972, *Location in space: a theoretical approach to economic geography* (Evanston: Harper and Row).

McNee, R. B., 1958, 'The functional geography of the firm', *Economic Geography*, **34**, 321.

Moore, C. W., 1972, 'Industrial linkage development paths in growth poles: a research methodology', *Environment and Planning*, **4**, 253–71.

Parsons, G. F., 1972, 'The giant manufacturing corporations and balanced regional quarter in Britain', *Area*, **4** (2), 99–103.

Penrose, E. T., 1968, *Growth of the firm* (Oxford: Blackwell).

Procter & Gamble Co., 1970, *Blueprint for growth,* (mimeo).

Rees, J., 1971, *Industrial Location Decision Processes: an Exploratory Empirical Analysis,* unpublished M.A. thesis, University of Cincinnati.

Rees, J., 1972, 'Organization theory and corporate decisions: some implications for industrial location analysis', *Regional Science Perspectives,* 2, 126–35.

Simon, H. A., 1960, *The New Science of Management Decisions* (New York: MacMillan).

Singh, A., 1971, *Take-overs* (Cambridge University Press).

Stafford, H. A., 1972, 'The geography of manufacturers', *Progress in Geography,* 4.

Steed, G. P. F., 1971a, 'Locational implications of corporate organizations of industry, *Canadian Geographer,* 15–54.

Steed, G. P. F., 1971b, *Growth Centres and Organizational Space,* Working paper, Simon Fraser University.

Thomas, M. D., 1969, 'Regional economic growth: some conceptual aspects', *Land Economics,* 40 (4), 421–32.

Thomas, M. D., 1972, The regional problem, structural change and growth pole theory', in *Growth Poles and Growth Centres in Regional Planning,* ed. A. R. Kuklinski (Mouton), 69–102.

Townroe, P., 1971, *Industrial Location Decisions,* Occasional Paper 15, University of Birmingham Centre for Urban and Regional Studies.

U. K. Census of Production, (London: Honso), annually.

Watts, H. D., A. T. Barlow, 1972, 'Comment on giant manufacturing corporations', *Area,* 4 (14), 269–75.

Webber, M. S., 1972, *Impact of Uncertainty on Location* (Cambridge, Mass.: M.I.T. Press).

8

The Process of Locational Change in Different Manufacturing Organizations

D. J. NORTH

Despite numerous, recent empirical studies of industrial locational behaviour, several gaps remain in our understanding of the process of locational change in firms. Wood (1969) has drawn attention to these in a series of questions: 'How does the pattern of decision and action with respect to location vary between different types of firm?'; 'At what point in the general process of making decisions does plant location become a significant factor in relation, for instance, to the growth phase of the business cycle?'; 'When are transport costs, labour availability, or site factors regarded as significant determinants of location?'; 'Can simplified models of existing situations, constructed by 'boundedly rational' industrial managers making decisions about location be identified?' (Wood, 1969, p. 37). This chapter attempts to answer some of these questions. At the same time, it provides either support for or confutation of the conclusions of recent empirical studies. Recent workers have made a plea for more 'in-depth' empirical work. Townroe calls for more intensive studies of the location decision-making process. Stafford stresses that systematic research into this process is long overdue, whilst Krumme argues that more case studies of corporate behaviour were needed before aggregate analyses could result in generalizations or the creation of realistic simulation models (Townroe, 1971, p. 126; Stafford, 1972, p. 255; Krumme, 1970, p. 321).

The present chapter has five aims. The first is to analyse in detail the entire process of locational change in manufacturing organizations. This involves studying all those decisions that amount to a change in the locational arrangement of a firm's activities. Factory extensions, factory closures and company takeovers and mergers are included, besides the more commonly treated location decisions—relocations, branches and initial location decisions. The second is to regard locational change as an intrinsic part of a firm's investment and development process so that locational considerations are viewed in proper perspective and not given exaggerated significance by being divorced from associated decisions. Hence the survey investigates firms over a twelve-year period of their development instead of adopting a cross-sectional approach of studying a recent location decision for each sample firm. The third is to examine in detail the locational search and selection activity of firms. This involves research into decision objectives and constraints, previous experience of location decisions, levels of decision responsibility, information contacts, evaluation methods and the reasons behind the final location selection. The fourth is to study the process of locational change for a large sample of differently organized manufacturing firms, ranging from the small owner-manager concern to the large multiplant, multi-enterprise, multi-national corporation. A growth industry with a heterogeneous range of firms is ideal for the purposes of the study since investment activity and its resultant locational changes are likely to be of greater significance in an expanding industry than in a stagnant or declining one. And the fifth aim is to produce a conceptual framework of the firm and its decision process, both to give greater precision to the survey design and to form a basis for the ultimate aim of developing models of typical forms of locational behaviour. The conceptual framework also serves as a source of hypothesis creation.

The Conceptual Framework

In this chapter firms are conceptualized as administrative and productive organizations making decisions in conditions of uncertainty arising from their interactions with complex and dynamic environments (Figure 8.1). At any one time, a firm's management faces a number of stresses, some being the direct result of changes in the firm's environment, others stemming from the intentional and unintentional processes operating within the firm. Management, therefore, is often confronted by a dilemma (Chamberlain, 1968, p. 10). Despite having goals that express the firm's desired course of development, environmental changes threaten to put the plans seriously off-course. If the firm is to survive, then management has to react and adjust to the environment changes (Cyert and March, 1963, p. 100; Loasby, 1967, p. 248). But at the same time management can take action through striving after goals to influence part of the firm's environment, although this usually necessitates elaborate decision-making machinery and long-range planning.

It is crucial that the whole process of locational change is viewed in the context of the interdependence between a firm and its environment and as part of the stress and response process. Thus internally and externally generated stresses may result in specific location problems for a firm that

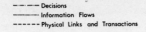

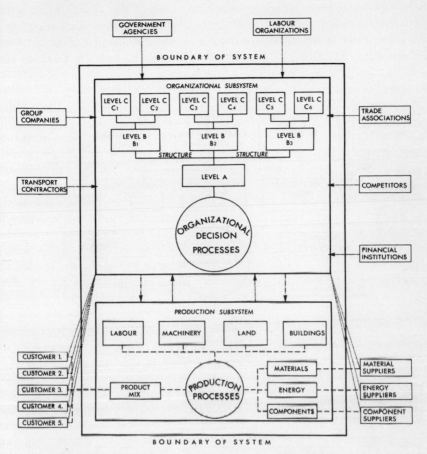

Figure 8.1. Production and organizational subsystems of the firm.

require a change in the locational arrangement of its activities if disruption to its progress is to be minimized. Invariably, location decisions result directly from internally generated stresses embodied in the investment strategies of firms. A simple four-stage decision model is proposed to show the relationship between the location decision and the investment process (Figure 8.2). The first stage is the product policy decision. The production policy is essentially the 'raison de'être' of a firm and forms the central part of its planning activity. Other policies, such as marketing, financial and technological policies, tend to be subordinate to the main production policy. There are several alternative kinds of production policies open to a firm and,

216

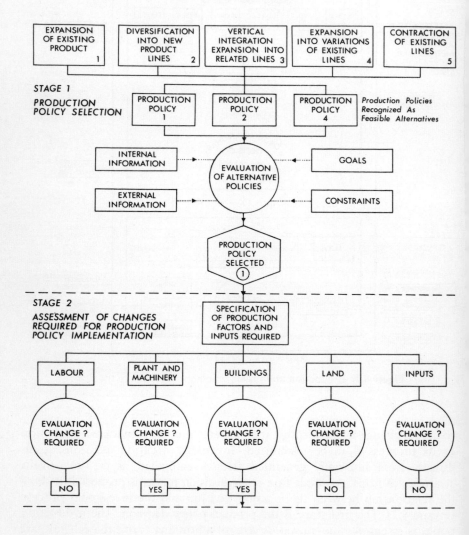

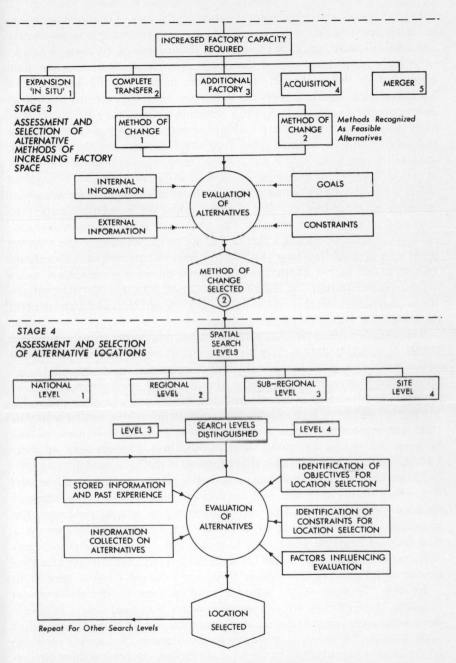

Figure 8.2. Locational change as part of the investment process of the firm.

at any one time, it may recognize more than one of these as being feasible alternatives. Evaluation of alternative production policies is made in the light of the goals and constraints imposed by the firm. The implementation of the chosen production policy will possibly involve changes in productive and administrative factors of production: the analysis of the changes required in these forms stage two of the model. This stage constitutes the main investment or disinvestment decision since it involves the allocation of liquid resources on fixed assets or, in the case of disinvestment, the sale or destruction of fixed assets. Again a selection process may be involved as more than one way may exist of making the necessary changes in productive and administrative systems. The third stage focuses on the alternative ways of making quantitative and qualitative changes in a particular factor of production. If, for example, an increase in factory capacity is required before a particular production policy can be implemented, then this may be achieved by extending existing premises, opening a branch factory, or acquiring an established concern. The final stage is the location decision. Having for example chosen a branch factory as the solution to the capacity problem, a firm will then have to search for and evaluate alternative locations. This stage can have a number of substages if different geographical scales are recognized for selecting the ultimate location. The decision may initially aim at choosing a suitable region for the branch and then concentrate upon the choice of a site within the selected region.

It is possible to propose several variations on this simple decision sequence model. In certain instances there may be a direct link between the production policy decision and the location decision, cutting out the intermediate step of evaluating alternative changes in the factors of production. This may happen where there is an established method of carrying out a particular production policy such as setting up a separate branch factory to manufacture each major innovation in product type. In other instances the link between the production policy and the location decision may be more circuitous and less obvious than that proposed in the basic model.

At any stage in the decision sequence environmental stresses of one kind or another are likely to influence the decision process and in that sense no decision will be the result of solely internally generated processes. But sometimes the link between an externally generated stress and the location decision response will be a direct one. For example, the compulsory purchase of a firm's land by the local authorities, the termination of a lease or the withdrawal of the labour force are external stresses specific to a location. Because of the strategic consequences to the development of a firm, these external stresses interfere with the normal course of investment decision-making and lead to a concentration of management effort upon considering ways of overcoming the stresses. A location decision of one kind or another may be the kind of reaction adopted in these circumstances.

The United Kingdom Plastics Industry

The study is based on a detailed survey of 100 firms in the U.K. plastics industry—an industry having one of the fastest growth rates in the manufacturing sector during the post-war period. Between 1958 and 1967 the plastics industry's average annual growth rate in value of production was 11·0 per cent compared with 7·0 per cent and 3·0 per cent respectively for chemicals as a whole and total manufacturing industry (Chemicals EDC, 1970). Technological breakthroughs in the oil and petrochemical industries after the Second World War initiated the rapid expansion in the production of an enormous variety of different types and grades of plastic materials. Consequently, plastic is now a multi-functional material, its uses ranging from highly specialized technical applications to simple domestic products.

A growth industry like plastics enjoys the repeated entry of new firms and the rapid expansion of existing ones. Nevertheless, even though the plastics industry itself has grown rapidly many firms within it have not experienced rapid development. The growth reputation of plastics products frequently encourages firms to exaggerate the market potential for their products and services and hence to over-invest in production capacity, so that later planned or enforced contraction may ensue. As well as possessing a high birth-rate of new firms, a growth industry often suffers from highly competitive conditions which shrink profit margins, causing the death or withdrawal of weaker firms from it. A growth industry therefore permits consideration of the locational consequences of contraction and rationalization. The plastics industry contains a heterogeneous range of firms and enables the process of locational change to be examined in firms that vary according to their size, growth, profitability, factory organization, manufacturing activities, market structure and conditions, decision-making procedures, and other organizational features.

Two main production sectors of the plastics industry are usually identified:

(1) *The material manufacturing sector:* this comprises firms which are concerned with the manufacture of synthetic resins and thermoplastics from various petrochemicals made available from oil refineries. Because this requires heavy investment in chemical process plant, research facilities and affiliated services, the preponderant part of the activity in Britain is in the hands of fewer than 10 home-based firms (such as Shell, British Petroleum and Imperial Chemical Industries), although several foreign firms (such as Monsanto and Ciba-Geigy) have a substantial share of the market and have established their own production subsidiaries in this country.

(2) *The plastics processing sector:* this comprises firms that manufacture semi-finished or finished products from plastics materials and is generally divided into three distinctive categories according to the nature of the relationship between producer and consumer:

(i) *Trade converters* manufacture components or finished products designed by the consumer rather than by themselves. Close liaison exists therefore with the customer. Trade converters are typically very small, independently-owned firms, although recent developments in both the manufacture of very large and very intricate components have encouraged firms to become public companies and to take over or amalgamate with competitors. Several large corporations have moved into the trade conversion business, among them Guinness and Imperial Tobacco.

(ii) *Proprietary converters* manufacture products to their own design for direct sale and thereby have very little direct connection with the consumer. Usually they are larger than most trade converters, have more capital-intensive production processes and are either independent public companies or subsidiaries of public companies. Examples include Metal Box (packaging products), Marley (building products) and Fothergill and Harvey (textiles).

(iii) *Service converters* have an expertise in providing a range of services associated with a fairly complex type of process, such as polyurethane foam conversion or plastics lamination. They do not produce a standardized range of products but instead vary the final product according to the customer's specifications. They are normally medium- or large-scale firms.

Because of the tremendous number of firms engaged in the plastics processing sector (in excess of 1,200), a sample survey was necessary. The processors were sampled from two contrasting regions of Britain, the South East and the North West. Nearly all the firms in the material manufacturing sector of the industry were included. Wherever possible, senior executives were interviewed who had first-hand experience of the development of the company during the twelve-year study period beginning in 1960 and ending at 1971. The interviews covered the history of the company during the twelve-year period, the nature of the pressures and decision sequences that led to location decisions being taken, the manner in which alternative solutions were evaluated and the character of the locational selection process. Factual information was collected on measures of the scale, growth, profitability, degree of capital intensification, decision-making organization, and manufacturing characteristics, and also details of the major investments that had been made during the twelve years. This information was obtained both from direct contact with the firms, using a printed questionnaire, and from their accounts which were filed at Companies House of the Department of Trade and Industry.

Characteristics of Different Types of Location Decisions

One of the conclusions of several recent works on industrial location is that

Table 8.1. The Number of Firms Making Each Type of Location Decision at Specified Numbers of Times during the Period 1960 to 1971

No. times decision made:	1		2		3		4		5		
Decision type	No. of firms	% of total	No. of firms	% of total	No. of firms	% of total	No. of firms	% of total	No. of firms	% of total	Total
Complete transfer	26	83·9	5	16·1	—	—	—	—	—	—	31
Branch establishment	19	70·4	7	25·9	—	—	—	—	1	3·7	27
Acquisition	17	63·0	3	11·1	4	14·8	—	—	—	—	24
Extension	20	51·8	10	18·5	7	12·9	3	5·5	6	11·1	54
Closure	3	60·0	2	40·0	—	—	—	—	—	—	5
Initial location decision	24										24
No decision	11										11

location decisions occur relatively infrequently during the life of a firm compared with many other types of investment decisions (Townroe, 1971 p. 35; Krumme, 1969, p. 32; Needleman and Scott, 1964, p. 157). For most firms in this study location decisions were not routine investment decisions made every year or two, although a few notable firms made a succession of branch decisions. Nevertheless, the majority of firms did make at least one location decision during the twelve years. Sixty-nine per cent of the firms made at least one decision involving the choice of a new location, i.e. a transfer, branch or initial location decision; when extensions, takeovers and closures are included, 89 per cent of the firms made one or more decisions affecting the location of their manufacturing operations (Table 8.1). In terms of the number of firms making one decision of a particular type, extensions proved to be the most common decision, and this was followed successively by transfers, branches, takeovers, initial locations and, finally, closures. This order is changed slightly when the total number of decisions of each kind is considered. The number of extensions is then more than double any of the other decisions and is followed successively by branches, takeovers, transfers, initial locations and closures. The change in ranking is due to more firms having made two or more branch and takeover decisions than transfer decisions. Extensions, takeovers and, to a lesser extent, branches are decisions which tended to be repeated every few years, whereas transfers were normally once-and-for-all decisions.

The North West plastics processors accounted for the highest proportion of transfers both in terms of the number of decisions taken and the number

222

Table 8.2. The Location Decisions Made by Material Manufacturers, South East Processors and North West Processors

	Material manufacturers			South East processors			North West processors		
	No. of firms	No. of decisions	% of total material mfrs.	No. of firms	No. of decisions	% of total SE processors	No. of firms	No. of decisions	% of total NW processors
Complete transfer	1	1	8·3	12	12	25·0	17	21	42·5
Branch establishment	5	5	41·7	14	22	29·2	8	11	20.0
Acquisition	4	5	33·3	13	17	27·1	7	13	17·5
Extension	8	11	66·7	28	38	58·3	22	29	55·0
Closure	9	0	—	5	7	14·6	—	—	—
New firm	—	—	—	9	9	19·6	15	15	37·5

of firms that made at least one relocation during the study period (Table 8.2). This can partly be attributed to the higher proportion of young, small firms in the North West sample, since small firms had a higher propensity to relocate their factories than did larger firms. Another contributory factor was the nature of much factory building in the North West region. Many firms had taken advantage of the very cheap factory space which was available in converted textile mills. Because of the space limitations of both the sites and buildings, *in situ* expansion was often rendered impossible and more production space could only be achieved by moving to a larger building, usually another mill. New firms set up since 1960 constituted a higher proportion of the North West firms than the South East ones. Branch, acquisition and closure decisions, on the other hand, were slightly more common among the firms that had their headquarters in the South East, this being partly a reflection of the tendency for the parent factories and head offices of multi-plan and multi-enterprise firms to be located in the South East (Parsons, 1972, pp. 99–103).

Most relocations occurred over short distances, the mean and median distances for all the moves being 45·9 and 13·1 miles respectively (Tables 8.3 and 8.4). The discrepancy between the two figures shows that the mean value has been distorted by a few long transfers. Most relocations were under 25 miles, but in four cases exceeded 100 miles. In contrast, branch factories were established at greater distances from the parent factory, the mean distance being 190·2 miles and the median 178·5 miles. However, eight firms set up branches less than 10 miles from their main factory; of these six were North West firms overcoming the space restrictions of old mills

Table 8.3. Summary Statistics of the Distance of Move (in Miles) for the Different Types of Location Decisions

Decision type	Mean	Median	Standard deviation	Maximum	Minimum
Complete transfer	45·9	13·1	84·4	331·7	0·5
Branch establishment	190·2	178·5	172·8	597·0	0·5
Acquisition	155·3	128·0	112·6	368·4	0·0
Closure	219·6	109·6		597·0	50·2

Table 8.4. Results of the Mann-Whitney Test of Difference Applied to the Distance of Move for Each Pair of Location Decision Types

	·01 significance level
Transfer/branch	x
Transfer/acquisition	x
Transfer/closure	x
Branch/acquisition	—
Branch/closure	—
Acquisition/closure	—

Note. x indicates a signmicant difference.

by starting additional factories nearby. The mean and median figures for the takeover distances were similar to those for branches; 15 of the acquired firms were located over 200 miles from the main factory of their new parent company. The very high mean figure for the distance between closed factories and their parent plants resulted from 4 of the 7 closures being of factories which were over 400 miles from the parent factory.

Characteristics of Firms Making Different Types of Location Decisions

The hypothesis that there is a relationship between the type of location decision taken and the type of firm making that decision was tested for the hundred firms. Each of seven company attributes was taken in turn and summary statistics calculated for all the firms that made each type of decision. The attributes were age, size (measured by employment and turnover), growth (measured by the average annual change in turnover), profitability (measured by profits as a percentage of total assets), ownership/management type, manufacturing type and capital/labour ratio. All the attributes were measured at the time of the decision. The Kruskal–Wallis analysis of variance test was used to test for a difference between the firms over the five types of

Table 8.5. Summary Statistics of the Attributes of the Firms Maming Each Type of Location Decision

	Mean	Median	Standard deviation	Maximum	Minimum
Complete transfer					
Age (years)	17·7	9·0	25·2	102·0	1·0
Employment	238·2	60·0	557·6	2900·0	7·0
Turnover (£ thousand)	1379·7	160·0	4172·9	22912·5	30·0
Change in turnover (%/annum)	53·8	29·0	74·8	316·7	−9·8
Profit as % total assets	2·7	8·3	23·2	36·1	−97·6
Plant + equipment/ employee (£/employee)	1076·1	808·2	905·9	3429·0	121·2
Branch establishment					
Age (years)	22·2	15·0	15·8	70·0	3·0
Employment	1014·4	450·0	1855·2	9000·0	60·0
Turnover (£ thousand)	5235·0	2440·0	8751·8	48000·0	140·0
Change in turnover (%/annum)	24·7	20·0	20·7	77·9	3·1
Profit as % total assets	11·5	10·0	10·0	41·9	−3·5
Plant + equipment/ employee (£/employee)	1302·5	1094·0	909·1	3717·9	185·1
Acquisition					
Age (years)	18·3	16·0	11·3	37·0	1·0
Employment	816·2	300·0	2029·9	10000·0	12·0
Turnover (£ thousand)	5703·1	1275·6		86000·0	60·0
Change in turnover (%/annum)	23·3	22·4	13·9	57·5	2·4
Profits as % total assets	13·8	15·5	13·5	38·8	−18·7
Plant + equipment/ employee (£/employee)	1275·3	1072·4	783·5	3717·9	139·8
Extension					
Age (years)	28·2	22·0	24·1	125·0	1·0
Employment	526·1	310·0	772·2	4249·0	6·0
Turnover (£/thousand)	4364·0	1372·0	1233·3	18166·9	20·0
Change in turnover	27·7	17·3	52·5	391·0	−7·9
Profits as % total assets	11·5	11·7	13·5	49·0	−24·0
Plant + equipment/ employee (£/employee)	1541·2	942·9	1869·0	9865·4	170·2

decision, taking each attribute in turn (for the two attributes measured on a nominal scale the chi-square test was used). Where a significant overall difference existed for the five kinds of decision then there was justification in testing for a significant difference between each pair of decision types, the Mann–Whitney 'U' test being used for this purpose. The results of the

Table 8.6. Percentage of Firms in Each Ownership/Management Category

Ownership/ management category	Transfer	Branch	Acquisition	Extension	Closure
	%	%	%	%	%
Public/corporate management	6·45	14·81	8·33	15·52	0·00
Independent, privately-owned entrepreneur	38·71	7·41	16·67	24·14	0·00
Subsidiary of public company/corporate management	35·48	59·26	58·33	41·38	100·00
Subsidiary of private company/corporate management	9·68	0·00	0·00	0·00	0·00
Subsidiary of private company/entrepreneur	9·68	18·52	16·67	18·97	0·00
	100·00	100·00	100·00	100·00	100·00

Table 8.7. Percentage of Firms in Each Manufacturing Category

Manufacturing category	Transfer	Branch	Acquisition	Extension	Closure
	%	%	%	%	%
Material manufacturer	3·33	18·52	16·67	14·04	0·00
Trade converter	50·00	14·81	25·00	22·81	37·50
Proprietary converter	26·67	33·33	16·67	33·33	50·00
Trade/proprietary converter	10·00	11·11	20·83	21·05	0·00
Service converter	10·00	22·22	20·83	8·77	12·5
	100·00	100·00	100·00	100·00	100·00

Kruskal–Wallis test indicated that firms making the different types of decisions differed significantly with respect to age, size, growth, profitability and ownership/management characteristics. The characteristics of the firms making each type of location decision will now be summarized (Tables 8.5, 8.6 and 8.7).

Complete Transfers

In general, relocating firms were both younger and smaller than those making the other types of decisions. Nearly all of them had less than one hundred employees, an annual turnover of under £500,000 and 85 per cent of them were single-plant firms. The majority had high growth rates (in excess of 30 per cent per annum), this being particularly the case with those in their first years of trading. A large range of profitability levels existed for the transfer decision firms, some having incurred heavy losses prior to making the relocation decision whereas others had made substantial profits. Most of the newly established firms incurred losses in their first few years of production because of heavy expenditure on plant, machinery and buildings, this being particularly the case for those investing large sums in product or process development. Such firms often had the financial backing of large parent companies and could withstand high initial expenditures. Relocation decisions were commonly made by firms in these circumstances. Privately-owned companies run by entrepreneurs accounted for a far higher proportion of all the firms making transfer decisions than of those making other types of decisions.

The main exceptions to the above characteristics were five long established, large-scale, corporately-owned firms that relocated one of their branch factories.

Branch Establishments

Firms that made branch decisions were significantly older and larger than transfer decision ones. Forty-eight per cent of them were already multi-plant firms at the time of the decision. Most were growing at more than 10 per cent a year although a few had very slow growth rates prior to setting up branches. Some had already outgrown their existing factory capacity with a consequent delay in production growth; for others the establishment of a branch factory presented a possible solution to a slow growth problem, particularly when the factory was to serve a previously untapped market. Branch decision firms had significantly higher profitability levels than those making transfer or closure decisions. A high proportion, 75 per cent, were either subsidiaries of public companies or themselves publicly owned and hence run by professional managers. The branch decision was the most common form of location decision for the service converters since their type of activity requires regular contact with the customers, making it advantageous to have separate factories serving each market concentration.

Acquisitions

For all the attributes the firms that made takeover decisions were very similar to those which made branch decisions. This is not entirely surprising since firms often regarded acquisitions and branches as alternative methods of achieving the same objective and many of those firms establishing branch factories during the study period also acquired other companies. In brief, takeover decision firms had generally been established for at least ten years, were of medium or large scale, had experienced high growth rates and profitability levels and were subsidiaries of public companies run by professional managers.

Extensions

Extensions to existing factories were usually made by old firms, only 10 of the 58 firms having been established for less than ten years. Young firms making extension decisions were nearly all subsidiaries operating on sites belonging to their parent companies. Most newly-formed firms, especially those run by entrepreneurs, had insufficient capital in their early years of operation to purchase a large site to accommodate years of expansion. In contrast, older firms had often been able to purchase large sites before the post-war escalation in land prices and the increase in planning restrictions, and these sites were of sufficient extent to facilitate much of their subsequent expansions. Most extension firms were of medium or large scale, but they varied with respect to their profitability and growth rates. Neither did they show any marked similarity in ownership/management characteristics. Extensions were the most common of all location decisions for the firms concerned with material manufacture and proprietary conversion, but not for those concerned with trade and service conversion activities. Material manufacturers and proprietary converters were generally capital-intensive firms and produced materials and products to their own design for distribution to a national market. These two features encouraged the concentration of production on large sites at a restricted number of locations, i.e. these industries have lower propensities for mobility and higher propensities for inertia.

Closures

Only 5 of the sample firms made at least one factory closure during the twelve-year period. This would seem to be an insufficient number for making reliable conclusions. However, the five firms were markedly similar in several respects. They were long-established firms, four of them having been in existence for between 25 and 46 years at the time of the closure decision. They were all medium- or large-scale firms and subsidiaries of public companies. They had significantly lower growth rates and profitability levels than firms making other kinds of decisions, several having suffered repeated losses. Factory closure was in part a consequence of these circumstances.

Types of Stresses Leading to Location Decisions

Ten types of stresses leading to decision sequences incorporating a location decision were identified for the sample firms: (1) planned growth of existing product lines; (2) development of regional markets for existing products and services; (3) unplanned growth of existing product lines; (4) diversification into new product lines; (5) vertical integration; (6) horizontal integration; (7) externally generated stresses; (8) stresses exerted by the pattern of the market distribution; (9) a decision imposed by the parent company; (10) rationalization of operations. Space does not permit a detailed consideration of each of these decision sequences here; instead five conclusions will be discussed.

First, factory transfers were mainly a response to the pressure of unplanned production growth on factory capacity whereas both factory extensions and branch establishments were generally responses to planned production growth. When transfer and branch decisions were made for either of these reasons then they were usually a second-best solution to the problem since extensions would have been the preferred course of action.

A lack of long-term planning led to many firms making investment decisions on an *ad hoc* basis. The multi-functional role of the entrepreneur in smaller firms meant that time could not be spent on market forecasting and the estimation of future requirements of fixed assets. Furthermore, such firms had very little market control and operated in conditions of great uncertainty. Despite high sales growth rates, marked fluctuations in sales were frequently experienced: a new sales contract could double a firm's sales in the short run and exert tremendous pressures on factory capacity. The limited financial resources of newly established, privately-owned companies meant that capital expenditure well in advance of production requirements was impossible. Thus these firms could only effectively plan for the short term. Thirteen firms made a transfer, nine an extension and five a branch decision in this sort of situation.

In complete contrast were the firms that made location decisions as part of a decision sequence linked to the planned growth of existing products. Production targets were incorporated in long-term investment plans in several ways: some firms carried out market research surveys and produced demand forecasts, others projected recent growth trends to arrive at a target figure and some specified a rate of output growth as one of their goals. Having set production targets, firms prepared estimates of changes in technology, machine capacity, size of labour force and factory capacity required to meet the production forecasts. Discounted cash flow techniques, or similar methods, were used to calculate the return on the proposed capital investment, the length of the payback period and any other financial measures needed for making the decision. Space needs and their costs formed part of the total investment plan which could cover anything from two to ten years.

Extensions to existing factories were by far the most common solutions to the need for factory space to accommodate planned production growth, 38 firms making at least one extension decision for this reason. For the majority, extensions took the form of erecting purpose-built premises on land which was already owned by the firm or its parent company. Large sites were gradually filled over several decades and extra space was sometimes made available by adapting or demolishing obsolescent premises. So the fundamental question was not *where* increases to factory space should be located but *when* the increases should be made. Some firms engaged in as many as six such extensions during the twelve-year study period. Planned production growth was also the most common pressure leading to branch decisions being taken, 11 firms opening a branch for this reason. Only 3 firms made a transfer decision to accommodate planned production growth.

Second, the complete transfer decision was the only type of locational response which was the direct result of externally generated stresses operating on organizations. All the large-scale, publicly-owned companies that made a transfer decision did so to combat external stresses.

Seven of the sample firms made a relocation decision to overcome externally generated stresses. They were much older than firms making transfers for other reasons and in four cases they were also much larger. In fact, all four were concerned with relocating a branch factory. Most of the moves were over a short distance. The severity of the stresses varied. For 3 firms the impetus to move was the destruction of the previous premises by fire, this being a very dramatic stress which, for two single-plant firms, threatened their entire existence. A change in the insurance premium for a factory without a sprinkler system resulted in one firm making a relocation. The other three firms all transferred their factories becuase of a number of stresses acting in combination and impeding the efficient functioning of the firm. These stresses included congestion in large urban areas with consequent delays in communication and distribution, a high labour turnover and low labour productivity.

Third, for those firms which had a defined aim of expansion through developing regional markets for their goods and services, the opening of branch factories was central to the investment policy. This was the only reason leading firms to make two or more branch decisions during the study period.

Seven firms made branch decision of this kind. The decision sequences were similar to those resulting from planned production growth except that the stipulation was made to achieve growth by creating a specific regional market for the firm's products. The setting up of a branch factory to serve the chosen regional market was the accepted way of providing the increased production capacity. These firms either produced a bulky product which was costly to transport or carried out a service type of activity that

230

required close liaison with customers and speedy delivery of output. The geographical distribution of production units was considered to be of primary significance to the firm's development and a succession of branch decisions was the normal method of expansion. One of the firms made as many as five such branch decisions during the twelve-year period. Having selected the region for market development, customers were initially supplied from one of the existing factories and the branch factory opened when sufficient demand had been generated to support it.

Fourth, for policies of diversification, vertical integration and horizontal integration, the takeover of a firm already engaged in the proposed line of activity was much preferred by firms to indigenous forms of expansion.

Diversification, vertical integration and horizontal integration policies usually resulted from two kinds of stresses. First, changes in a firm's external environment, such as the appearance of a new competitor, led to pressures which threatened the attainment of its objectives. Secondly, some firms had the self-imposed force of 'empire building' to spread their risks and increase their growth prospects by moving into several different productive operations. For firms pursuing a policy of diversification the establishment of a branch factory often presented an alternative to the takeover of an existing firm, but both vertical and horizontal integration were carried out only by acquisition. Five firms made at least one takeover as part of a diversification decision, 12 as part of a vertical integration policy and 9 because of horizontal integration. The acquisition of an established concern was preferred to indigenous forms of expansion because management and operative expertise, regular customers and an entire physical and information linkage network were inherited, so that there was no need to invest in machinery, land and buildings; and a takeover was the quickest and least disruptive form of expansion.

Fifth, factory closures directly resulted from a policy concerned with the rationalization of operations which, in turn, was a response to conditions of low growth and profitability.

Stresses in the form of low growth rates and profitability levels were imposed on firms because of previous bad decisions or environmental changes. In these circumstances firms had surplus manpower, machinery and factory capacity. Inflow of capital from large parent companies enabled them to withstand financial difficulties for a time, but no parent was prepared to tolerate the low return indefinitely. Strong pressures were therefore exerted upon firm managements to find ways of regaining profitability and discovering new growth courses. Sometimes a new management team was put into a company precisely for this purpose. Since production capacity exceeded sales volume, higher profits could be achieved in the short term by planned contraction of capacity and a reduction of overheads, thereby enabling more intensive use of capital assets. This frequently involved 'hiving off' the unprofitable production lines and concentrating on more promising products. The outcome was a smaller firm with fewer factories ready to start a new programme of expansion into production lines with higher financial returns.

The Locational Search and Selection Process

Once the decision had been taken to go ahead with a particular type of locational response to internally- or externally-generated stress, firms were usually confronted with another choice. For relocation, branch and initial decisions a search had to be made for a satisfactory location and possible alternatives had to be compared. Extension and closure decisions could also involve a choice between two or more of the firm's existing sites.

Table 8.8. The Main Correlations between the Locational Search and Selection Process Variables

Pair of variables	Correlation coefficient
Formalized objectives/Take advantage of Development Area benefits	0·6333
Formalized objectives/Reduce transport costs	0·6327
Formalized objectives/Detailed cost comparisons	0·5718
Formalized objectives/Search between regions	0·5706
Formalized objectives/Contact with trade unions	0·5706
Formalized objectives/Contact with Department of Trade and Industry	0·7245
Formalized objectives/Contact with Development Corporations	0·6764
Retain existing labour/Local move	0·7562
Take advantage of Development Area benefits/Contact with Department of Trade and Industry	0·6545
Take advantage of Development Area benefits/Contact with Development Corporations	0·8767
Select location close to new market area/Policy of developing regional markets	0·8220
Reduce transport costs/Search within prespecified region	0·6327
Reduce transport costs/Contact with trade unions	0·5812
Reduce transport costs/Distance of move	0·5818
Detailed cost comparison/Search between regions	0·7545
Discounted cash flow/Plot of market distribution	0·5000
Discounted cash flow/Contact with trade unions	0·6083
Plot of market distribution/Contact with trade unions	0·6247
Plot of market distribution/Distance of move	0·7169
Search in prespecified region/Distance of move	0·6675
Search in prespecified region/Transport costs form over 5% of total costs	0·5933
Search in prespecified region/Development of regional Markets	0·5706
Contact with trade unions/Distance of move	0·5222
Contact with Department of Trade and Industry/Contact with Development Corporations	0·6554

For acquisitions the search and evaluation focused on alternative companies rather than locations.

A test of association was made between different aspects of the search and selection process for the firms making transfer and branch decisions. Forty-eight variables were included in the analysis and a list of the main correlations is contained in Table 8.8. With the exception of the movement distance and the size of the new factory all the variables were measured on a dichotomous, nominal scale (i.e. presence/absence). If a particular objective or technique did apply then a score of 1 was assigned; if not, a score of 0. The correlation between each pair of dichotomous, nominal scale variables was measured by means of the phi-coefficient, and the correlation between the two interval scale variables and the dichotomous nominal scale variables used the point biserial coefficient. Both are directly comparable to the product-moment correlation coefficient and range between $+1\cdot0$ and $-1\cdot0$. There is no point in describing the correlation matrix; the main correlations support the following description of the characteristics of the transfer and branch decisions.

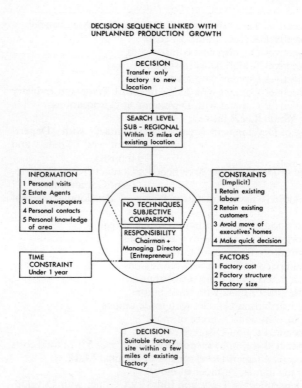

Figure 8.3. The search and selection process at the local level for a factory relocation decision (10 firms).

Transfer Decisions

For all but four of the firms that relocated a factory, the search for a suitable location was confined to the region of their existing factories. Two dominant types were identified. First, very small, privately-owned firms, usually concerned with trade conversion, confined their search to a radius of no more than ten miles about their present factory (Figure 8.3: 10 firms). Normally the search was unsystematic, discontinuous and made without specified objectives or requirements for the new location. Dominating the search was the constraint of retaining most of the existing workers since it often took a small firm several years to build up a loyal labour force: the loss of key workers could be disasterous to the firm's development. The avoidance of moving executives' homes and familiarity with the local business environment were added inducements for a short distance transfer.

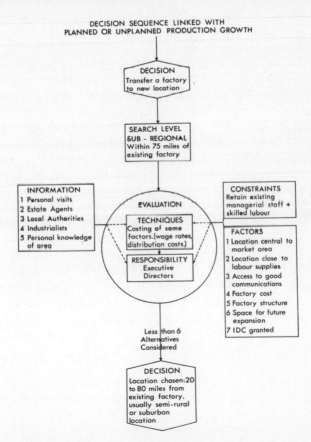

Figure 8.4. The search and selection process at the intra-regional level for factory relocation decisions (10 firms).

The location decision relied heavily on the impressions, preconceived notions and local knowledge of management; very few contacts were made with outside agencies apart from estate agents. The urgency of the decision in those firms experiencing the pressure of unplanned growth resulted in the first satisfactory site being selected.

The second main type comprised slightly larger, corporately-owned firms that conducted their search further afield, particularly in the South East region, because of the difficulty of finding a sufficiently large site locally (Figure 8.4: 10 firms). Unlike the smaller firms, they were confident that skilled workers could be persuaded to stay with the firm, either because the firm could afford to help workers find a house in the new area or because it could provide a bus service from the old location. Furthermore, they were in a position to offer competitive wage rates for less-skilled labour in the new location. A number of outside contacts were made to assist the search, especially with local authorities, and a few of the firms laid down specific requirements for the new location.

For those firms moving to overcome externally generated stresses at a particular location, the need to alienate the existing difficulties strongly influenced the search for a suitable location. For example, a firm moving from South London because of its proximity to a major competitor was determined to find a location close to an untapped market area and, similarly, firms experiencing high labour turnover and absenteeism rates were resolved to find a location with reserves of readily trainable, good quality labour.

The four firms moving factories over distances greater than one hundred miles were significant anomalies here. One of them made a choice between locations in different regions and used comparative cost analysis and factor weighting procedures on data collected from a variety of sources to find that location with the highest financial return from among the alternatives considered. The benefits of a particular Development Area swayed the balance in favour of the chosen location. The other three firms moved factories from one region to another to be nearer the hub of the market distribution. The region for the new factory was usually pre-specified and site criteria determined the selection of the precise place for development.

Branch Decisions

Three distinctive types of branch decisions were identified according to the geographical scale at which the search and selection process was performed.

Only four firms evaluated alternative regions before looking for a suitable site (Figure 8.5). They were fairly large, publicly-owned companies and each had previously expanded at one site. Restrictions upon future *in situ* development led to the decision to start a second factory. Since all four served a national market for their products they decided to split the market into two areas by having a southern and a northern factory. Thus alternative northern regions were considered. Each firm adopted a systematic approach to the problem: explicit objectives were laid down for the new location, techniques such as comparative cost methods and plotting the actual and potential customer distribution were used to handle much of the information, financial assessment using discounted cash flow was performed either to aid the selection of a location or as a check once the selection had been made, and numerous information contacts were made, notably with Government departments, trade unions, local authorities, other companies in the proposed region and development associations. They all had a strong desire to take advantage of Development Area benefits. For one of the firms, objective analysis was adhered to throughout the entire decision process. Eight sub-regions were designated and evaluated according to a comprehensive range of factors to select that which most satisfied the objectives of attaining the maximum financial return and the minimum distribution costs. However, for the other three firms personal considerations in the end had an overriding influence despite the attempt at objective evaluation. The reputation of the group in, and the familiarity of senior directors with, a particular region imposed a marked bias upon the search process from the outset. These companies had little confidence in their calculations because so many vital factors, such as labour quality, defied quantification. Once the region of the additional factory had been chosen, attention was focused on the selection of a suitable site and here a different set of factors came into play. In two cases site evaluation was unnecessary since the parent company had a vacant site in the chosen region. For the other two the availability and quality of labour, access to good communications, adequate supplies of water and electricity, facilities for waste disposal and the size and cost of sites influenced the ultimate location decision.

For the firms that grew by developing new regional markets served by market-located production plants, the evaluation of alternative regions was made on the basis of sales potential in the market expansion decision (Figure 8.6: 7 firms). Thus locational search was only really carried out within a prespecified region. Normally the chief objective influencing the search was the need to find a site central to the spatial arrangement of the market to minimize the time and cost of transport. Plotting the customer distribution frequently aided the search. Other factors included labour availability, industrial infrastructure and, not least, site considerations. Because these firms had little previous knowledge of the new region, government agencies, trade unions, industrialists and local authorities were normally contacted. It was common for these firms to make a succession of branch decisions, so their management showed an acumen for location decisions and had mental if not written procedures for the search. Most of them considered there to be little need for sophisticated techniques since not only were many factors unquantifiable, but also few factors were spatially variable between sites within a region.

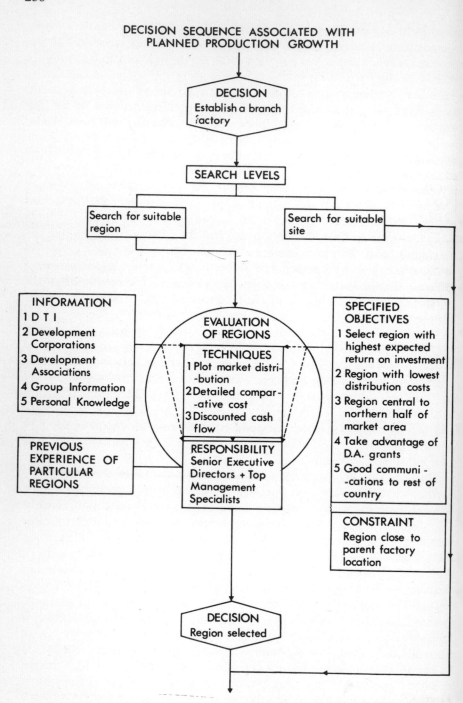

DECISION SEQUENCE ASSOCIATED WITH
PLANNED PRODUCTION GROWTH

DECISION
Establish a branch
factory

SEARCH LEVELS

Search for suitable region

Search for suitable site

INFORMATION
1 D T I
2 Development Corporations
3 Development Associations
4 Group Information
5 Personal Knowledge

PREVIOUS EXPERIENCE OF PARTICULAR REGIONS

EVALUATION OF REGIONS

TECHNIQUES
1 Plot market distri--bution
2 Detailed compar--ative cost
3 Discounted cash flow

RESPONSIBILITY
Senior Executive Directors + Top Management Specialists

SPECIFIED OBJECTIVES
1 Select region with highest expected return on investment
2 Region with lowest distribution costs
3 Region central to northern half of market area
4 Take advantage of D.A. grants
5 Good communi--cations to rest of country

CONSTRAINT
Region close to parent factory location

DECISION
Region selected

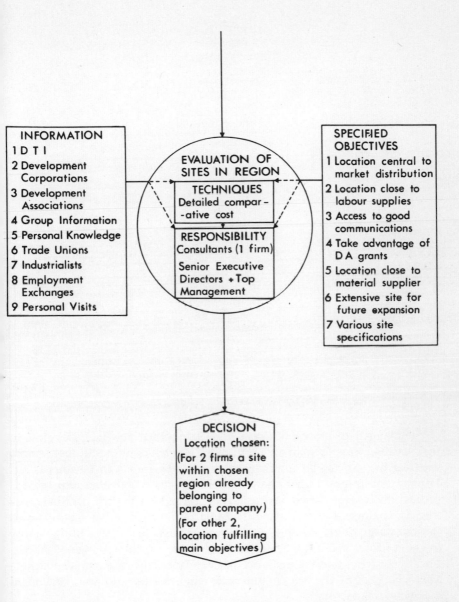

Figure 8.5. The search and selection process at the interregional level for a branch factory decision (4 firms).

238

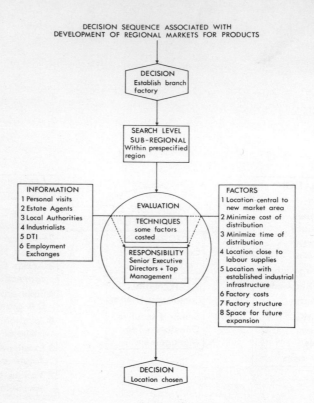

Figure 8.6. The search and selection process within a prespecified region for a branch factory decision (7 firms).

The majority of branch decision firms set up their new factories close to their existing ones (Figure 8.7: 9 firms). The idea of an additional factory was usually resorted to after an extension was found to be impossible. Implicit constraints rather than explicit objectives influenced the search process. Since these firms were reluctant to make a branch decision, they tried to minimize the cost and disruption of having another factory; thus the aim was to find a suitable site as close as possible to the existing factory to avoid management duplication and facilitate the interchange of labour. Local knowledge and the guidance of newspaper advertisements and estate agents influenced the search and site requirements and were the main discriminating factors.

Initial Location Decisions

Most new firms (16) were set up as subsidiaries of existing companies

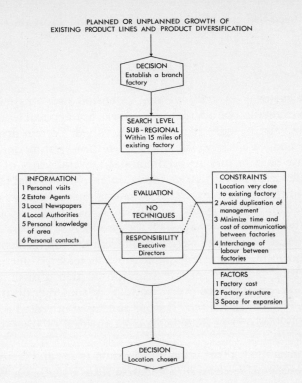

PLANNED OR UNPLANNED GROWTH OF
EXISTING PRODUCT LINES AND PRODUCT DIVERSIFICATION

DECISION
Establish a branch
factory

SEARCH LEVEL
SUB - REGIONAL
Within 15 miles of
existing factory

INFORMATION
1 Personal visits
2 Estate Agents
3 Local Newspapers
4 Local Authorities
5 Personal knowledge
of area
6 Personal contacts

EVALUATION

NO
TECHNIQUES

RESPONSIBILITY
Executive
Directors

CONSTRAINTS
1 Location very close
to existing factory
2 Avoid duplication of
management
3 Minimize time and
cost of communication
between factories
4 Interchange of
labour between
factories

FACTORS
1 Factory cost
2 Factory structure
3 Space for expansion

DECISION
Location chosen

Figure 8.7. The search and selection process at the
local level for a branch factory decision.

nd either started their lives in a vacant building belonging to the group or
shared one of their parents' factories. A fresh location decision, therefore,
was not concomitant with the birth of a new company. Strong physical
ies often existed between the new company and its parent, especially where
he former was a captive processor providing its parent with components.

Firms created by new entrepreneurs (9) invariably located in the areas
where their founders previously lived and worked. The new entrepreneurs
usually gained managerial and technical experience in a plastics manufactur-
ng or processing company and an inventive spirit or the spark of an original
production idea prompted the decision to set up their own business once
hey had amassed sufficient capital for the initial investments. It was not
unusual for the original business to be entirely concerned with marketing,
he production side coming as the second phase of business creation. A
familiar environment and long standing contacts were considered to be
crucial to the initial success of a new firm, so the possibility of opening a
factory in another region was rarely considered. New firms were therefore
created from and located near established firms, thereby supporting the

concept of 'seed-bed growth' (see also Mueller and Morgan, 1962; Taylo
1969).

Extension Decisions

Since the majority of firms making extension decisions had only on
factory, the evaluation of alternative sites was not applicable, but both th
frequency and size of individual extensions varied. Certain firms preferre
to purchase and lease a large site adjacent to their existing one and erect
large purpose-built factory to accommodate several years of productio
growth; these were generally large, capital-intensive firms that had complex
integrated production layouts. Plastics material manufacturers for exampl
made tremendous investments in site infrastructures; strong physica
linkages between different stages of the production process meant tha
considerable scale economies were derived from the enlargement of existin
sites. Investment in one ethylene plant could increase production capacit
by 250,000 tons and cater for five years production growth, resulting i
large extensions being phased every five years or so. Other firms engaged i
a succession of small extensions. Having purchased or rented a site *en bloc*
they gradually made small increments over a period of several years unti
the site was filled.

Even for most multi-plant firms, the decision to expand factory capacit
did not lead to an assessment of alternative sites. Usually each site had it
own production process or product specialization, consequently the sit
decision was an intrinsic part of the decision to increase the output of a
particular product. Thus in a multi-plant firm with distinctive operation
for each location the expansion of a factory reflected the demand for it
products. Firms with a policy of developing a regional network of market
located branch factories sometimes had to make an evaluation betweer
alternative sites before deciding where the expansion funds should go
In this situation, the profitability record of each factory was usually the mair
criteria for allocating the investment funds. In the larger firms a discounted
cash flow assessment incorporating sensitivity analysis was performed to
select that site with the quickest or best return on capital. An evaluation of
different locations was also included in an extension decision when a multi-
plant firm invested in a completely new production process which did not
fit into the operations at any one of the existing production locations.

Closure Decisions

Factory closures were a direct result of a policy of rationalization
associated with falling profit margins and excess production capacity.
The scale of production no longer justified so many factories and resulted
in the decision to close one or more of them. Normally there was an obvious

candidate for closure since one factory suffered fundamental disadvantages relative to the others, such as low labour productivity, poor access to market areas or low profitability. In all cases it was the most geographically peripheral factory relative to the market distribution that had these problems and was closed.

Acquisitions

Locational considerations were relatively unimportant in the search for a suitable company for takeover compared with such factors as a company's profitability performance, management quality and market share. Especially when an acquisition was being made as part of a diversification policy the number of companies fulfilling the requirements was so few that the expanding company could not afford to take account of locational considerations. However, some firms did restrict their search for a suitable company to a specified geographical area. In the first place there were several privately-owned firms supplying a small market concentration that looked for a suitable company in the vicinity of their existing factory. This spatially confined search process was typical of the small trade converter intent upon acquiring a toolmaking subsidiary. Second, some firms pursuing a policy of horizontal integration were interested in a particular regional market; rather than set up a branch factory, they favoured acquiring the company that had the largest share of that market. Finally, one firm with a policy of 'empire building' through vertical and horizontal integration had a strong preference for taking over firms located near its headquarters not only to prevent spreading its management resources too thinly, but also to create a strong feeling of physical and organizational interdependence between the group factories. A closely knit empire was preferred to one spread all over the country, even though the group served an international market.

Occasionally, the decision to take over a company was followed by a decision to close one or more of its factories and move plant, machinery, management and skilled labour to the parent company's plants. It was the size, profitability and assets of the new company which were important, not its factory or location. Rationalization plans were drawn up to concentrate production activities at a restricted number of sites and so reduce expenditure on overheads, minimize management and administrative duplication and produce a tightly coordinated, efficiently run company (see also Keeble, 1971, p. 33.)

Conclusions

At this juncture the following general conclusions regarding the locational behaviour of firms in this study can be made. First, although they were not programmed investment decisions made every year or two, location decisions were more common occurrences in the lives of firms than other writers have suggested. Seventy per cent of the sample firms experienced at least one decision involving the selection of a new location during the study period; and when extensions, acquisitions and factory closures are included as part of the location change process, ninety per cent of the firms made one or more location decisions. Extensions and, to a lesser extent, takeovers and branches were decisions that were repeated by many firms whereas factory relocations tended to be once-and-for-all decisions.

Second, firms making the different kinds of location decisions had distinctive characteristics. Transfer decisions were typically made by either young, small-scale firms run by entrepreneurs or by recently created members of groups. Both types were experiencing rapid growth. Branch and takeover decisions were normally made by medium- or large-scale companies enjoying fairly high growth and profitability rates. Extensions were usually made by long established, medium- or large-scale companies with capital-intensive production processes. Factory closures were typified by old, publicly-owned, large companies suffering from low growth and profitability.

Third, each type of location decision was more likely to be a response to certain kinds of stresses than to others. Relocation decisions were associated with pressures resulting from unplanned production growth and environmental stresses experienced at a particular location. Branch decisions usually resulted from pressures exerted on factory capacity by the planned growth of production if *in situ* expansion was impossible and the policy of expansion was by developing regional markets. Acquisitions were normally related to policies of diversification and vertical or horizontal integration. Extensions invariably resulted from the planned growth of existing product lines. Factory closures formed part of a rationalization programme to reduce production capacity and attain profitability.

Fourth, as far as the locational search and selection process is concerned, two things are abundantly clear. In the first place, it was very rare for firms to perform a strictly objective analysis of alternative locations. The speed with which location decisions had to be made, the many imponderables in the choice and the inevitable personal and emotional involvement of individuals making the decision led to the neglect of many economic criteria. Even where firms did employ objective methods and tried to quantify as many relevant factors as possible, the ultimate decision was often made on the basis of hunch, personal preference, and previous experience of an area. Whilst many of the classic locational factors such as transfer costs and labour costs were taken into account at the regional level, the precise location was normally determined by personal preferences and site considerations such as factory cost and structure and opportunities for future expansion. Apart from the firms that produced plans incorporating locational considerations for several years ahead, time was a major constraint on the location decision.

The pressure of time meant that only a few alternative locations could be assessed and that one which appeared to be the most suitable for the present needs was usually selected.

In the second place, firms displayed a tremendous inertia for their existing locations. Initial location decisions were themselves often the outcome of the forces of inertia. For nearly all the relocations and many of the branches the aim was to keep the distance of move to a minimum, this being partly a reflection of firms' reluctance to move and their preference for *in situ* expansion. The pull of self-generated externalities and the desire to prevent the duplication of plant and services were key factors restricting the distance of moves. In general, only those firms which had a bold concept of developing a network of regional markets supplied by separate branch plants were geographically mobile.

The author has used the information on the attributes of the firms, the decision sequence leading to location decisions and the characteristics of the locational search and selection process to classify the sample firms into distinctive groups according to their locational behaviour. The model types of behaviour resulting from the classification are presented elsewhere. (North, 1973).

References

Chamberlain, N., 1968, *Enterprise and Environment* (New York: McGraw–Hill).

Chemicals Economic Development Council, 1970, *Economic Assessment to 1972* (London: National Economic Development Office).

Cyert, R. and J. G. March, 1963, *A Behavioural Theory of the Firm* (Englewood cliffs: Prentice–Hall).

Economic Consultants Ltd., 1971, *Strategic Plan for the South East*, 5 (HMSO).

Keeble, D., 1971, 'Employment mobility in Britain', In *Spatial Policy Problems in the British Economy*, ed. M. Chisholm and G. Manner (Cambridge: University Press).

Krumme, G., 1969, 'Toward a geography of enterprise', *Economic Geography*, **45**, 30–40.

Krumme, G., 1970, 'The interregional corporation and the region', *Tijdschrift voor Economische en Sociate Geographie*, **61**, 318–33.

Loasby, B., 1967, 'Managerial decision processes', *Scottish Journal of Political Economy*, **14**, 243–55.

Mueller, E. and J. Morgan, 1962, 'Location decisions of manufacturers', *American Economic Review, Papers and Proceedings*, **502**, 204–17.

Needleman, L. and B. Scott, 1964, 'Regional problems and location of industry policy in Britain', *Urban Studies*, **1**, 153–73.

North, D., 1973, *Locational Change in the Development of the Firm. A Study of the U.K. Plastics Industry since 1960*, Ph.D. thesis, University of London, unpublished.

Parsons, G., 1972, 'The giant manufacturing corporations and balanced regional growth in Britain' *Area*, **4** (2), 99–103.

Stafford H., 1972, 'The geography of manufacturers', *Progress in Geography*, **4**, 181–215.

Taylor M., 1969, *Industrial Linkage, Seed-bed Growth and the Location of Firms,* Occasional Paper 3, Department of Geography, University College, London.

Townroe P., 1971, *Industrial Location Decisions—A Study in Management Behaviour,* University of Birmingham, Centre of Urban and Regional Studies, Occasional Papers 15.

Wood P., 1969, 'Industrial location and linkage', *Area,* **1** (2), 32–9.

9

The Spatial Behaviour of American Firms in Western Europe

ANTHONY BLACKBOURN

The most important form of business today is the multi-plant corporation operating on a national or international scale. In industries such as oil it is no longer possible to be a major producer without operating as a multinational corporation and competitive forces are likely to make multinational operations essential in a wider range of industries. These corporations differ both qualitatively and quantitatively from the traditional single-plant manufacturer (Galbraith, 1967, p. 21); their locational problems are much greater. The small company, owned and managed by one family, normally manufactured in the owner's home town. This location might limit the growth of the business or even be so unsatisfactory that the firm goes bankrupt. Yet, it is often an optimum location for a small business since it minimizes uncertainty about the business environment (Webber, 1972, pp. 106–7). The decision process involved is simple, subjective and satisfactory.

A corporation expanding abroad faces a much more complex problem. Decision-makers selecting a location for an overseas plant will normally be unfamiliar with local business conditions and may be easily influenced by non-economic considerations. Mackenzie quotes a U.S. company president who was influenced by his wife's preference for the cultural attractions of Madrid. The plant there suffered such high transport costs that the company could not compete in the Spanish market and was forced to sell its plant (Mackenzie, 1972, p. 38). Henry Ford's emotional attachment to his ancestral homeland induced him to establish the disastrous Cork (Ireland) plant in 1917 (Wilkins and Hill, 1964, p. 70). Such mistakes can be avoided by adopting proper procedures for handling overseas locational decisions.

Few businesses expand fast enough to require frequent location choices for new plants. Consequently, in most companies such a decision is not routine and does not fit into existing procedures. *Ad hoc* procedures of varying degrees of sophistication are likely to be used. Some companies may use primitive procedures; others may seek expert advice by engaging locational consultants or by careful study of the location experiences of other firms in their industry. Companies whose *ad hoc* procedures derive experience from others successfully are more likely to survive and grow than those with poor information or poor ability to use that information (Pred, 1967, pp. 21–64 and 90–5).

Companies with the best information on foreign plant location are those corporations who make foreign plant location facilities frequently enough to have developed a routine to handle such decisions.

The Development of Multi-National Corporations

Multi-national corporations operating on a global scale make investment, as opposed to locational, decisions relatively frequently. Most decisions involve a dialogue between a local branch, affiliate or representative and the head office. This discussion will concentrate on an example of multi-national corporations with head offices in the U.S.A. and investments in Europe. Since the majority of multi-national firms are American-owned and since Europe is the region with the greatest amount of U.S. investment, this study concentrates on the most important international business operations *(Survey of Current Business,* 1971).

Multi-national corporations are normally companies with both a large domestic business in the home country (the U.S.A.) and a large foreign operation. Their development is related to the product cycle (Vernon, 1966): an innovation or new product is likely to be exploited earliest in a rich country like the U.S.A. with a large domestic market. Once a company establishes a strong position in the American market it has a strong competitive advantage if it produces its product in smaller countries where local producers are still experimenting with the product. The foreign plant is likely to be established by an industry leader (e.g. Singer, N.C.R., Ford, IBM) anxious to protect business in a large export market threatened by tariffs. The OECD report on electronic computers refines this model to give a three-stage model of overseas expansions:

Stage   I is characterized by the transfer of *products* by export of either the basic product or parts to licensees and assembly plants.

Stage   II is distinguished by the transfer of *technology* by licensing, assembly plants and manufacturing.

Stage III involves the *creation of local technology* by local research and development work (OECD, 1969, p. 81).

The crucial stage for locational decision-making in this model is the second stage when assembly or manufacture commences.

The organization of an international company will be determined by its size, type of business, stage of development, and by the preferences of its management. The common divisions are by product group, area, function (central services) or some combination of the above (Table 9.1). Brooke and Remmers found functional division (e.g., Finance, Production, Marketing) to be best suited to small multi-national corporations and likely to be replaced by product or area divisions when the corporations grew (Brooke and Remmers, 1970, p. 27). Product group organization was normally developed for the domestic market and continued as foreign operations developed from exporting to foreign production. Product groups at head office often tend to ignore foreign operations and the resulting communications problems may lead either to an areal organization or a mixture of area and product organization. Area organization either alone or combined with product group organization is used by the largest international businesses (Brooke and Remmers, 1970, p. 28). With this form of organization the most serious communications problems are often between the International Division at Head Office in the U.S.A., and product groups of the domestic operation (Brooke and Remmers, 1970, p. 32). An International Division organization tends to be more aggressive in its attitude towards foreign operations than companies organized by products or functions.

A questionnaire survey of American companies with investments in Europe in May and June 1972 produced usable replies from 105 companies with 288 European plants (*Survey*, 1972). Area organization was used by the majority of companies and these companies had more European plants per company than companies using other types or organization (Table 9.1). Product group organization was most common in the fabricating industries, a type of manufacture where a wide variety of products is likely to be more common than in the simpler processing and service industries.

Table 9.1. The Organization of American Companies in Europe

Organization of divisions according to:	Function	Product	Area	Other*	Total
Companies in processing industries	3	3	24	4	34
Companies in fabricating industries	7	11	29	8	55
Companies in service industries	3	1	8	4	16
No. of companies	13	15	61	16	105
No. of plants	17	40	194	37	288
Plants per company	1·31	2·67	3·18	2·31	2·74

*Other represents combinations of the three basic groups.
Source: *Survey*, May and June, 1972.

The Decision-Making Process

Area organization can be taken as the standard form, with product and function groupings being regarded as deviations necessary to suit the needs of some corporations. An International Division in a large multi-national corporation may make locational decisions frequently enough to have developed a routine for handling such decisions. The procedure developed by International Business Machines World Trade Corporation (IBMWTC) is described here as an example of the best contemporary practice. This corporation represents an extreme example of the use of area organization since IBMWTC is a separate corporation from the parent American IBM company. It has headquarters in New York and is licensed by the American IBM corporation to manufacture IBM computers in Canada, France, U.K., Germany, Italy, Japan and Sweden (OECD, 1969, p. 45). It also operates assembly plants in other countries and engages in its own research and development work in Europe. The company is the leader in the international computer market, controlling two-thirds of computer markets in France, West Germany, Netherlands, Belgium, Italy, Scandinavia and Switzerland, and two-fifths of the British market (OECD, 1969, pp. 161–70). IBM also produces a full line of business equipment, including electric typewriters. The OECD report treats IBMWTC as an organizational model for a multinational company producing a sophisticated product. Their routines are supplemented here, however, also by reference to procedures in other companies.

The first stage in location decision-making is the identification of possible investment opportunities. A strong initiating force must be present before a company will investigate the possibility of overseas investment (Aharoni, 1966, p. 49). Aharoni's discussion relates primarily to the decision to establish the first overseas plant and he recognizes that multi-national corporations such as IBMWTC may undertake an active search for new investment opportunities (Aharoni, 1966, pp. 192–4). The major initiating forces are often defensive strategies to prevent loss of overseas sales built up during the stage of transfer of products. Head offices react to pressures from competitors, governments and overseas managements saddled with a product not suited to the local market. Brooke and Remmers' study of expansion strategies also emphasizes defensive strategies and justifies this emphasis by estimates of the frequency with which the various strategies are used (Brooke and Remmers, 1970, pp. 227–9). More than half of their small sample mentioned tariffs, nationalism, transport costs or delays, difficulties with agents, resources and the 'bandwaggon effect'. The only aggressive strategy mentioned frequently was more profitable use of capital. Six of the nine defensive strategies were important but only one of four aggressive strategies was important.

At IBMWTC the initiating force may be either the management of a

European subsidiary, IBM Europe or a head office research group. A flexible planning model allows IBMWTC to simulate operations under different conditions (Rippe, 1966, pp. 21–7). This model can operate at country, plant or laboratory level and is capable of identifying problems in the existing organization and optimizing existing operations in terms of plant location, customer assignment to plant, purchasing planning and financial allocation (Rippe, 1966, p. 21). The model is an input–output model based on existing facilities and, as such, deals primarily with optimizing use of these facilities. However, if the model identifies a problem that might be solved by investment in a new plant, it would be possible to simulate the corporation's operations with a new plant at an assigned location. The model is not a location model enabling the corporation to select a minimum production cost site: it enables planners to estimate the impact of a new facility on the corporation's other operations. It may indicate the need for new facilities and thus provide the initiating force. The input to the head office from either a local manager or the model of the corporation's operations operated by the head office research group would be essentially similar and stresses market factors.

The next stage for IBM Europe (one of two operating groups within IBMWTC) would be for several European country managers to compete for the new plant (Groo, 1972). The competing country managers would present briefs to the presidents of IBM Europe, stressing sales volume versus IBM investments in their country. No set formula for these briefs exists but market conditions and government attitudes 'to IBM would dominate the presentation. IBM Europe evaluates the proposals from the various country managements and recommends that head office in New York approve one of the proposals. At this stage, no specific locations are considered and the basic aim is to select a country in which to invest: the main criterion used is market size.

The corporation never produces a full product line in any country and consequently it both exports and imports products from all countries (Turner, 1970, pp. 19–24). Plants are located to balance corporate investments with sales in a country rather than to operate a miniature version of American IBM behind a tariff wall. The European Economic Community has made this policy easy but the British IBM company was a part of the integrated European operation before Britain joined the Common Market. The motivation for a policy of balancing sales in a country and investment in that country is basically political. The company has the public relations advantage of being able to claim that it manufactures in all its major markets but because it does not manufacture a full line of products cannot easily be expropriated. This type of balancing investment with local sales is not confined to IBMWTC but is also used by Ford of Europe (Anon, 1972, pp. 24–6). Ford's automatic transmission plant was located in France because Ford had large investments in Britain, Germany and Belgium but nothing in the large French market. Ford produces each of its European car lines in at least two countries and uses parts from its plants in other nations so that plants could not be run on a national basis.

After a country has been selected by IBMWTC the search for a location within that country begins. Local management is expected to select about half a dozen locations for evaluation (Groo, 1972). The selection is a judgmental one but selections are evaluated on a standard rating scheme at head office. Webber has stressed the importance of local knowledge in location selection under conditions of uncertainty in which search procedures are expensive (Webber, 1972, pp. 110–14). The reliance on local managers satisfies this condition even though it often involves using people who have never tackled a locational decision of this magnitude before. The use of standardized ratings schemes can eliminate very poor choices while a man with local knowledge may be able to select an excellent site that would be overlooked by an experienced outsider.

The sites selected are evaluated by head office under the weighted criteria method. The criteria used by IBMWTC are: living conditions (100 points), accessibility (75 points), industrialization (60 points), labour availability (35 points), economics (including construction costs and local taxes) (35 points), prestige effect on company reputation (35 points), community capability and attitude (30 points), for a total of 370 points (Groo, 1972, p. 77). Of this total amenity factors (living conditions, community capability and prestige) account for 165 points (45 per cent) and economic factors for 205 points (55 per cent). The high weight given to amenities results from (1) the need to consider multi-lingual facilities in a multi-national company and (2) the footloose nature of the industry. The rating scheme includes a comprehensive list of factors to be considered. Head office assigns scores to each location on each criterion and picks the locations (normally two or three) with the highest aggregate scores for detailed investigation.

The final stage is a full-scale feasibility study on the locations chosen by the weighted criteria method. These studies are expensive (Aharoni estimated $100,000 as a normal figure in the mid-1960s) and cover legal, engineering and economic aspects of the sites (Aharoni, 1966, p. 109; Groo, 1972, p. 77). Thus a complete comparative cost study is carried out on a small number of sites which have been vetted thoroughly to make certain that they have no major disadvantages. The sequential process of decision-making leaves the expensive surveys to last and used a routine which is intended to minimize the amount of senior executive time devoted to the decision. The process can take a few weeks or a couple of years, depending on the urgency of the decision.

When the feasibility studies are completed, head office consults with local management on the final decision. Groo claims that it is unusual for local management to be overruled (Groo, 1972, p. 75).

The routine developed by IBMWTC for location decision-making is more complex than that described by Rees or Stafford (Rees, 1972; Stafford, 1972). It is a sequential process in which market size is considered before cost considerations. However, it gives greater and earlier consideration to amenities and psychic income than Stafford's model and has more screens to weed out unsuitable choices. Multi-national organization allows a dialogue between local management and head office staff which would be difficult to achieve in the sample of companies studied by Rees and Stafford. The cost factors discussed in location theory only enter into the decision process at a late stage after the preliminary judgmental selection has taken place. Cost and time constraints rule out a comprehensive search covering all possible locations so the decision is reduced to a choice among attractive alternatives. The procedure is sparing of head office executive time and gives the local office considerable responsibility.

The IBMWTC decision-making process is more complex than that used by most companies, yet it represents best conventional practice and probably will be copied by other companies. Aharoni describes a typical three stage investigation, consisting of: (1) examination of general indicators (a wide evaluation of the political and economic climate in a country), (2) on-the-spot investigation involving fieldwork (sometimes using a questionnaire or check list) to establish capital requirements, costs of production, and sales and price estimates, and (3) a decision by head office on the investment on the basis of the field report (Aharoni, 1966, pp. 76–121). This represents normal practice for careful medium-sized businesses, but is *ad hoc* and can be very subjective. The sequence of investigating market before costs is preserved in this procedure.

Selection of a Country for Operations

The decision-making process emphasizes the importance of market size in selecting a country for operations. Table 9.2, based on a survey of U.S. companies with European operations, shows that almost two-thirds of the respondents rated market size as the decisive factor; only one-eighth did not consider it a location factor.

Although no other factor was mentioned by more than half the respondents, labour cost was clearly the second most important factor. Taxation policies, considered by almost 80 per cent of the respondents, were rated decisive by only 27 per cent of the respondents. Materials or parts availability, tariffs and labour relations were considered by most companies. Despite the high weighting of amenity factors on IBMWTC's criteria, social factors were not considered important by over half of the companies, only five considering them decisive. Government grant schemes and communications with the U.S.A. were rarely considered. Despite this claim, evidence for Britain and Belgium indicates that regional grants may, in practice, have

Table 9.2. Factors Considered by Respondents in Selecting a Country of Operation

Decisive Responses

Factor	Res-ponses	% Decisive responses	% Res-pondents	Pro-cessing	Fabri-cating	Other
Market size	69	26·2	65·7	23	34	12
Labour cost	39	14·8	37·1	10	24	5
Material or parts availability	29	11·0	27·6	12	15	2
Taxation policies	28	10·7	26·7	10	13	5
Tariffs	26	9·8	24·8	10	14	2
Labour relations	24	9·2	22·9	10	12	2
Other factors	20	7·6	19·0	7	9	4
Communications with U.S.A.	14	5·3	13·3	5	7	2
Government grants	9	3·4	8·6	3	5	1
Social (e.g. education services, etc.	5	2·0	4·8	3	2	0
Total	263	100·0		93	135	35

Not Considered Responses

Factor	Res-ponses	% Not consi-dered responses	% Res-pondents	Pro-cessing	Fabri-cating	Other
Labour pool	15	3·1	14·3	2	7	6
Access to market	18	3·8	17·1	2	11	5
Labour cost	18	3·8	17·1	2	8	8
Communications network	38	7·9	36·2	8	22	8
Services available locally	34	7·1	32·4	6	17	11
Local industrial structure	40	8.4	38·1	8	22	10
Grants from national government	53	11·1	50·5	11	28	14
Grants from local government	55	11.5	52·4	11	30	14
City size	52	10·9	49·5	10	31	11
Other factors	93	19·5	87·0	31	47	15
Social factors	62	13·0	37·1	14	35	13
Total	478	100·1		105	258	115

Table 9.2. (Contd.)

Not Considered Responses

Factor	Res-ponses	% Not consi-dered responses	% Res-pondents	Pro-cessing	Fabri-cating	Other
Market size	14	3·5	13·3	3	7	4
Labour cost	22	5·6	21·0	5	10	7
Material or parts availability	36	9·1	34·2	6	19	11
Taxation policies	23	5·9	21·9	6	11	6
Tariffs	34	8·6	32·4	5	15	14
Labour relations	36	9·1	34·2	6	19	11
Other factors	76	19·3	72·4	24	40	12
Communications with U.S.A.	42	10·7	40·0	9	24	9
Government grants	51	12·9	48·6	11	26	14
Social (e.g. education services, etc.)	60	15·2	57·1	12	35	13
Total	394	99·9		86	206	101

Source: *Survey,* 1972.

Table 9.3. U.S. Investments in European Manufacturing, 1929, 1958 and 1970

Countries ranked by GNP, 1970	No. of plants	1929* Value	1958 Value	1970 Book value	Growth (1958 = 100)
		U.S. $ millions			
Germany	78	139	410	2812	686
France	86	91	279	1867	669
United Kingdom	169	268	1361	7126	524
Italy	24	13	104	801	770
Spain	18	12	21	402	1914
Netherlands	10	27	48	790	1646
Sweden	8	7	30	163	543
Belgium	17	38	129	855	663
Switzerland	6	6	41	463	1130
Total	453	629	2475	13703	

*The categories used in the 1929 survey differ from those used in 1958 and 1970 so the values may not be strictly comparable. Compiled from Southard, 1931, p. 193; U.S. Department of Commerce 1960, p. 89; *Survey of Current Business,* 1971, p. 33.

been more important in influencing American corporation choices of location in Europe. If the distribution of U.S. investment in Europe is examined, the importance of market is confirmed. A. Spearman's rank correlation value of 0·667 (significant at the 5% level) is found if book value of U.S. investment in 1970 is correlated with Gross National Product.

American investment in all time periods was especially high in Britain and Belgium (Table 9.3). The lack of a language barrier and Britain's high relative level of income in the pre- Common Market period explain the great inflow of investment into Britain. The high value for Belgium is harder to understand, but it may be the result of an open doors policy towards foreign investment and a role as gateway to continental Europe. Spain is the outstanding example of a country with little U.S. investment. Underdevelopment and politics explain why until recently American investment avoided Spain. Table 9.3 confirms not only the importance of market size in determining the choice of a country but also the secondary role of labour. The low wage countries of Europe have not attracted a disproportionate share of American investment. However, of countries with index values for growth over 700, only one, Switzerland, is a high wage country and Swiss growth may be due to its stable currency and low interest rates. The advent of the European Economic Community does not seem to have ruled out national markets as a factor in the selection of a particular country.

Selection of a Location within a Country

The company survey of factors considered in selecting a region or city of operation revealed that labour pool, labour costs and access to market were the primary considerations (Table 9.4). Local communications, services, industrial structure and social factors were also considered (although rarely rated decisive) by many respondents. Surprisingly, grants from both local and national governments were ignored by over half the companies. Obviously, therefore, existing regional development grant schemes have not made much impact on Americans investing in Europe.

Upon examination, it appears difficult to classify the actual locations selected. Table 9.5 deals with only three classes of location and suggests that national capital locations have great appeal for American investment in many European countries. A high percentage of the plants shown in the 'metropolitan areas' column for Switzerland were in Zurich—the main economic centre. In Italy, Milan, the main economic centre, was chosen by most manufacturers. The distribution of American-owned plants in Europe is very similar to the distribution of European-owned industry. The major industrial cities in all countries are the major centres of American investment. Few American manufacturers locate in remote areas eligible for regional development grants. The small number of plants in the individual countries of Europe makes further analysis of location within the nation difficult if individual companies are not discussed.

In addition to information on factors influencing their choice of country

Table 9.4. Factors Considered by Respondents in Selecting the Region or City of Operation

Decisive Responses

Factor	Responses	% Decisive responses	% Respondents	Processing	Fabricating	Other
Labour pool	57	23·4	54·3	17	32	8
Access to market	52	21·3	49·5	18	24	10
Labour costs	45	18·4	42·9	14	26	5
Communications network	21	8·6	20·0	8	8	5
Services available locally	16	6·6	15·2	6	10	0
Local industrial structure	13	5·3	12·4	4	7	2
Grants from national government	13	5·3	12·4	7	5	1
Grants from local government	9	3·7	8·6	5	3	1
City size	8	3·3	7·6	3	2	3
Other factors	6	2·5	5·7	2	3	1
Social factors	4	1·6	3·8	2	2	0
Total	244	100·0		86	122	36

Table 9.5. Locations Selected by Region

	National capital	Other metropolitan areas	Other areas	Total
Germany*	n/a	21	14	45
France	15	7	15	37
Britain	17	15	36	68
Italy	0	27	7	34
Spain	6	6	6	18
Netherlands	1	8	11	20
Sweden	3	1	1	5
Belgium	11	9	12	32
Switzerland	0	7	2	9

*No national capital was given for Germany since both Berlin and Bonn functioned as capitals during the period of American investment in Germany.
Source. *Survey*, 1972.

and region or city within a country, corporations were also asked to indicate whether they had encountered problems relating to access to market, labour, communications with the parent plant, and parts or material supply.

This, together with data on numbers of plant expansions, was used a𝗌 evidence of satisfaction with the location selected (Table 9.6).

Labour problems were most common: the strongly-unionized Britisℎ and Italian labour forces created as many problems as the booming Dutc𝗁 and German economies with their labour shortages. The only other frequent‧ ly occurring problem was the remoteness of northern Italy from the centr𝖾 of the EEC.

Statistics of numbers of plant expansions (indicating that the locatio𝗇 was at least satisfactory) and of lack of problems revealed that America𝗇 were very satisfied with plants in Belgium. The Belgians were also the onl𝗒 people to have attracted large numbers of plants to grant-aided developmen𝗍 areas except the remote Ardennes region. Brussels, the Belgian capital shared with London the distinction of being the most popular location fo𝗋 European regional head-offices because of its 'capital' function for EEC 21 offices compared with 29 in London (Williams, 1967, p. 91). Paris, with 𝟨

Table 9.6. Problems Encountered by American Corporations in Europe: Numbers of Plants by Country

	Pro-cessing (P)	Fabri-cating (F)	Others (O)	Companies without plants in country	Market			Labour			Communication		
					P	F	O	P	F	O	P	F	O
Germany	14	26	5	74	0	1	0	3	7	0	1	0	0
France	15	17	5	72	1	1	2	1	1	0	1	1	0
Britain	19	42	7	51	1	1	1	2	0	1	1	1	0
Italy	15	16	3	73	2	3	0	1	5	0	0	2	0
Spain	11	4	3	90	0	0	1	0	0	0	0	1	0
Netherlands	7	12	1	85	0	1	0	3	4	0	0	0	0
Sweden	1	4	0	100	0	0	0	0	0	0	0	0	0
Belgium	14	15	3	74	0	1	0	0	0	1	0	0	0
Switzerland	2	7	0	97	0	0	0	1	1	0	0	0	0
Denmark	2	2	0	101	2	0	0	0	1	0	0	0	0
Austria	0	0	0	105	0	0	0	0	0	0	0	0	0
Norway	3	0	0	101	0	0	0	0	0	0	0	0	0
Finland	1	0	0	104	0	0	0	0	0	0	0	0	0
Greece	1	0	0	104	0	0	0	0	0	0	0	0	0
Protugal	1	2	0	102	0	0	0	0	0	0	0	0	0
Ireland	2	3	0	101	0	0	0	0	0	0	0	0	0
Luxembourg	0	1	0	104	0	0	0	0	0	0	0	0	0
Iceland	0	0	0	105	0	0	0	0	0	0	0	0	0
Tax havens	0	1	0	104	1	1	0	0	0	0	0	0	0
Total					7	9	4	10	26	2	3	5	0

Table 9.6. (Contd.)

Parts and materials	Number of plants expanded	Number of plants receiving development grants	Total number of plants in country	Percentage of total number of problems
P F O				
0 0 0	7	3	45	11
1 1 0	7	3	37	10
0 2 0	25	6	68	18
1 0 0	11	6	34	14
1 1 0	2	1	18	4
0 0 0	11	2	20	8
0 0 0	2	0	5	0
0 1 0	14	10	32	3
0 0 0	2	0	9	2
0 1 0	0	0	4	2
0 0 0	0	0	0	0
0 0 0	3	1	4	1
0 0 0	1	0	1	0
0 1 0	0	1	1	1
0 0 0	0	0	3	0
0 1 0	2	1	5	1
0 0 0	0	0	1	0
0 0 0	0	0	0	0
0 0 0	0	0	1	2
3 8 0	87	34	288	77

head offices, was the only other centre of significance: some 29 American companies had no European regional head office.

Locations in Britain and Benelux

Evidence of the types of locations preferred by American firms investing in Europe is available from detailed studies of locations selected in the British Isles and Benelux countries. Dunning compared a sample of 300 American-owned firms in Britain in 1953 with the distribution of all British industry. The locational preferences of the two groups were generally similar but London, eastern England and Scotland had major concentrations of American-owned plants (Dunning, 1958, pp. 83–90). The major attractions seemed to be (1) the London market especially in the pre-1939 period before the introduction of controls on industrial location, (2) industrial estates (parks) dating back to before World War I when Ford, Westinghouse and six smaller U.S. companies all based their British operations on Trafford Park industrial estate, and (3) Scotland after 1945 when regional development grants became attractive.

Excellent statistics about foreign-owned factories established in Ireland between 1955 and 1969 (Irish Development Authority, 1970) reveal similar orientations. These show locations preferred by all foreign companies permitting a comparison between the behaviour of American and other foreign investors. Firms from three nations invested heavily in Ireland: from Britain, the United States and West Germany. British firms preferred sites with close economic ties with England, so that locations of American plants are more readily compared with those of German firms. American firms developed in the capital (Dublin had 25 per cent of all American plants, but only 4 per cent of German plants) and industrial estates (35 per cent of U.S. plants; only 10 per cent of German plants). From among development areas, American firms have shown a preference for Shannon airport locations (15 out of 27 plants in development areas of Ireland) whereas two-thirds of German firms located in other development areas.

Mingret found that in Belgium the national capital, industrial estates and areas eligible for development grants were the most attractive locations (Mingret, 1970). Of the 103 American-owned plants established between 1960 and 1968, Brussels received only 14, but the Brussel–Antwerp–Ghent triangle attracted 65 of them. The most popular locations were small centres near the inter-city autoroutes like St. Niklaas near Antwerp, an area eligible for regional development grants, which attracted 23 of the 65 plants. Haute-Sarts illustrates the attraction of industrial parks. A centre for transforming the whole Liège area into a modern industrial region, Haute-Sarts attracted 12 of the 23 American-owned plants in Liege province. These stand beside 12 Belgian and 3 British companies which have generally smaller plants on the same site.

American-owned plants in the Netherlands localize (de Smidt, 1966) in the western Amsterdam–Rotterdam–Utrecht areas with 63 per cent of all American-owned plants established between 1945 and 1964 as compared with 58 per cent of British and only 35 per cent of the plants established in the Netherlands by continental European companies. Only 18 per cent of the growth in industrial employment in the Netherlands between 1950 and 1963 was in the Western provinces, yet 54 per cent of the growth in numbers of employees working for foreign-owned plants occurred there: 100 of the 199 foreign-owned plants were American (de Smidt, 1966, pp. 6–15). These firms, however, were attracted neither to peripheral development areas nor to industrial parks in the Netherlands.

The general conclusion on locational preferences within nations is greatly influenced by the sample of nations selected. However, there is an obvious preference for major manufacturing regions, a tendency which seems stronger among American-owned than among either locally-owned or other foreign firms. This may reflect less familiarity among American firms with Europe, stimulating them to attempt to reduce uncertainty and eliminate unacceptable risks by selecting apparently safe locations among many other plants (Aharoni, 1966, pp. 279–82). Preferences for industrial parks is explained by the speed with which a company can obtain factory premises, by risk avoidance and 'psychological agglomeration'. The latter is de Smidt's term for the tendency for foreign companies to form national industrial 'ghettos' once links with companies in the homeland are

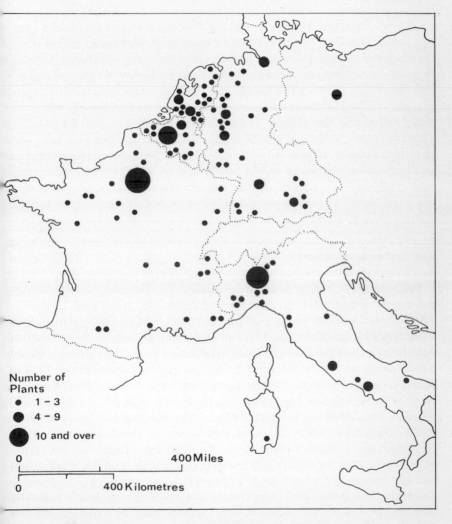

Figure 9.1. The distribution of American-owned electronics plants in the European Economic Community in 1969.

transferred to foreign subsidiaries. The apparent influence of regional development grants is exaggerated here because Britain, Eire and Belgium all have elaborate programmes.

The Electronics Industry

The electronics industry exemplifies recent trends in the location of an advanced technology industry in the European Economic Community. Industry distribution shown in Figure 9.1 reveals a concentration in the major urban centres of each nation (European Economic Community, 1969, pp. 43–4). Paris has 55 per cent of the American-owned electronics plants in France. However, 75 per cent of *all* electronics plants and 57 per cent of the employment in electronics in France is concentrated in Paris, so American firms are in fact less concentrated in the capital than other electronics plants (Michel, 1972). In other EEC lands also, the political and economic capitals are the leading electronics centres: Brussels and Antwerp (Belgium), Amsterdam and the Hague (Netherlands), Frankfurt and Berlin (West Germany) and Milan and Rome (Italy). Other large cities also have some electronics plants. IBMWTC's French plant at Montpelier (Riviera) is one of the few locations which would rate highly on an amenities (recreational) scale. However, if amenities include also strong cultural traditions many of the cities chosen emerge as desirable locations according to Groo's criteria (Groo, 1972, p. 77).

The Automobile Industry

This industry is much older than electronics. Hence it better illustrates the stages in historical development of American investment in Europe. Today American firms produce 25 per cent of all vehicles manufactured in the Common Market (Hellman, 1970, p. 60). Ford was the pioneer American entrepreneur to enter Europe: mass production gave him a strong competitive position which yielded good European export opportunities. In 1907, James Couzens—who was in charge of Ford sales—toured most European capitals to set up sales organizations: these were coordinated by a branch office in Paris (Wilkins and Hill, 1964, p. 31). Sales of Ford cars in Britain had expanded by 1909 to the point where local assembly was justified. The local manager selected a plant in the Trafford Park Industrial Estate near Manchester; this decision was approved in Detroit. Trafford Park, a port on the Manchester Ship Canal, appeared to be a desirable location for assembly. This British plant was treated as just another assembly plant (like those in the U.S.A.) and it was falsely assumed that the Ford management system would succeed in avoiding the labour problems of the Manchester area (Wilkins and Hill, 1964, pp. 49–50).

World War I saw Ford establish an assembly plant at Bordeaux (France) and a tractor plant at Cork (Ireland). Both were rather remote locations, useful in wartime, but far from peacetime markets. Cork typified the sentimental ties of an entrepreneur in selecting a country for investment. After the war a small assembly plant was opened in Hamburg before German inflation made new investment undesirable (Wilkins and Hill, 1966, pp. 96–7). Knudsen of the Detroit office drew up a comprehensive European plan, dividing Europe into marketing regions, but sales problems prevented its smooth innovation.

Ford's European operations in the 1920s thus consisted of a large assembly plant at Manchester, one at Cork which had no market for its products after Irish Independence, and a bewildering array of short-lived continental assembly plants—successful at Copenhagen, Rotterdam and Antwerp, mainly unsuccessful at Fiume and Cadiz. Capital city locations in Paris and Berlin replaced port assembly plants in Bordeaux and Hamburg, but Ford was of minor significance there.

The major event of the inter-war years was development of full-scale integrated manufacture in Britain and Germany. A plant was located at Dagenham near London against the advice of the English management which wanted a plant at Southampton (Wilkins and Hill, 1964, pp. 59, 34–5). The decisive location factors were proximity to the London market, access to its labour pool and to water transport. The German plant was on the Rhine at Cologne because of transport nodality and the tax concessions granted by Mayor Adenauer. Both Dagenham and Cologne were part of a plan for Ford in Europe prepared in 1928 by Ford's Sorensen of the Detroit branch. The market was then buoyant and growth prospects good; thus the plan proposed plants at Livorno (vetoed by the Italian government), Gdynia (Poland) and eventually in Barcelona (Spain) and Romania (Wilkins and Hill, 1964, p. 200). By this time Ford realized that the European market demanded smaller cars than the American; accordingly he relaxed opposition to purchasing local firms which might be inefficient producers. This led to disastrous joint operations with the French Mathis company at Strasbourg, while an Italian merger was prohibited by the Italian government. The break-up of the Mathis enterprise in 1938 led Ford to establish a Paris manufacturing plant which was eventually sold off to Simca in 1954.

Post-1945 expansion has consisted of establishing large manufacturing or components plants in Britain (Liverpool), Germany (Saarlouis), Belgium (Genk) and France (Bordeaux). All are sited in development areas for which government grants were obtained (Anon, 1972, Wilkins and Hill, 1964, p. 207).

General Motors expansion into Europe occurred later and followed a different path. Between 1923 and 1928 assembly plants were establishment at Berlin, Antwerp and Copenhagen (all existing locations of Ford assembly plants); in 1936 a Swiss assembly plant near Bern was added. (Donner, 1967, p. 15). Experience showed that European-size cars must be produced for the company to succeed. Consequently, the corporation negotiated for the purchase of most leading European producers—Austin, Citroen, Peugeo and Fiat (Southard, 1931, pp. 70–4)—but unsuccessfully. However, in 1925 they did purchase Vauxhall of Luton (England) and in 1926 added Opel o. Frankfurt (Germany). Alfred Sloan, who negotiated these agreements describes the purchases, in his autobiography, as part of corporate policy but not the locations (Sloan, 1964, pp. 313–27).

Since World War II expansion (Donner, 1967, p. 59) has been in Britain (near Liverpool), Germany (at Bochum in the Ruhr) and France (a trans mission plant at Strasbourg): the first two are both in depressed areas but close to major markets.

Chrysler operated assembly plants in Europe in the 1920s but has entered the European market only recently by purchasing French Simca and British Rootes Corporation in the 1960s.

The location of American automobile plants in Europe differs from that of local manufacturers in that they are generally located closer to the economic centre of each nation and away from the traditional engineering centres where local producers operate. This is especially true in Britain and Germany, but less so in France where most French production—like the Chrysler Simca—comes from Paris.

The decision-making processes used by the auto-makers differed according to their conception of the market. Ford's philosophy of standardization centralized decision-making in Detroit, with relatively little local input, and resulted in several mistakes, including a failure to investigate site engineering problems at the successful Dagenham plant—a site approved by an American official after one day in London (Wilkins and Hill, 1964, p. 135). American officials (including Ford himself) frequently visited Europe and made elaborate plans in 1923 and 1928 for European development. However they treated Europe as another mass market which could be organized similarly to the U.S. market. Local management did not succeed in persuading the American management that political problems could restrict corporate freedom of action (as in Italy and Spain) and local advice on site selection was sometimes ignored or overruled (e.g. Southampton and Cork).

General Motors and Chrysler usually avoided the pitfalls of initial locational decision-making by purchasing subsidiaries. In no case did a small assembly plant grow into a manufacturing operation. The change of scale in switching from assembly to manufacture was great enough to make a completely new location normal. No sequence of development from sales outlet to assembly plant to manufacturing plant at the same location could be seen.

Conclusion

Decision-making by American firms locating plant in Europe often involved a rational sequential process involving a dialogue between local management and the American head office. Market and labour considerations are of primary concern. Locations selected are generally near the economic centres of European and national markets, though there are site preferences for industrial parks. The arrival of the EEC does not seem to have made nation states obsolete as units in corporate decision-making. Our knowledge of the locational patterns is at present scanty and statistics for the entire EEC are long overdue. The locational orientations and location factors considered by American companies locating in Europe are what location theory would lead us to expect. Yet corporate organization and strategy, and political considerations, are of great moment: neither is adequately handled by current location theory. Multi-national corporate locational problems are as much political as economic and theories must embody them.

References

Aharoni, Y., 1966, *The Foreign Investment Decision Process* (Boston: Harvard Business School).

Anon, 1972, 'Common marketing for the Common Market', *Forbes*, July 1, 22–6.

Brooke, M. Z. and H. L. Remmers, 1970, *The Strategy of the Multi-national Enterprise* (New York: American Elsevier).

de Smidt, M., 1966, 'Foreign industrial establishments located in the Netherlands', *Tijdschrift voor Economische en Sociale Geoagrafie,* 1–19.

Donner, F., 1967, *The World Wide Enterprise* (New York: McGraw–Hill).

Dunning, J. H., 1958, *American Investment in British Manufacturing* (London: Allen & Unwin).

European Economic Community, 1969, *Die Elektronische Industrie der Gemeinschafts- Lander und der Amerikanischer Investitionen* (Brussels).

Galbraith, J. K., 1967, *The New Industrial State* (Boston: Houghton Mifflin).

Groo, E. S., 1972, 'Choosing foreign locations: one company's experience', *Columbia Journal for World Business,* Sept.–Oct., 71–8.

Hellman, R., 1970, *The Challenge of U.S. Dominance of the International Corporation* (New York: Dunnellen).

Irish Development Authority, 1970, *Principal New Industries with Foreign Participation* (Dublin).

Mackenzie, E., 1972, 'Finding the ideal plant location', *International Management,* Aug., 38–41.

Michel, M., 1972, 'Les industries electroniques en France,' *L'Information Geographique,* Jan.–Feb., 35–47.

Mingret, P., 1970, 'Les investissements Americains en Belgique,' *Revue de Geographie de Lyon,* **45**, 243–78.

Organization for Economic cooperation and Development, 1960, *Gaps in Technology— Electronic Computers* (Paris: OECD).

Pred, A., 1967, *Behaviour and Location: Part I* (Lund: Gleerup).

Rees, J., 1972, 'Implications of modelling the industrial location decision process', *International Geography* 1972 (Toronto University Press).

Rippe, D. D., 1966, 'Mechanized and integrated planning in IBMWTC', *European Business,* 21–7.

Sloan, A. P., 1964, *My Years with General Motors* (Garden City, New York: Doubleday).

Southard, F. A., 1931, *American Industry in Europe* (Boston: Houghton Mifflin).

Stafford, H. A., 1972, 'Industrial location decision-making', *International Geography* 1972 (Toronto University Press).

Survey 1972: Questionnaires were sent to 1735 companies with European investments listed in Juvenal L. Angel, *Directory of American Firms Operating in Foreign Countries* (New York: World Trade Academy Press, 1969); 89 questionnaires were returned as undeliverable, 13 companies wrote to say that they received so many questionnaires company policy was to answer no questionnaires, 56 replies were unusable because overseas operations were very small; only 105 companies completed the questionnaire in sufficient detail for it to be usable.

Survey of Current Business, Oct., 1971, **51** (10), 32–6.

Turner, L., 1970, *Invisible Empires* (London: Hamish Hamilton).

U.S. Department of Commerce, 1960, *U.S. Business Investments in Foreign Countries* (Washington, D.C.).

Vernon, R., 1966, 'International investment and international trade in the product cycle', *Quarterly Journal of Economics,* 190–204.

Webber, M. J., 1972, *Impact of Uncertainty on Location* (Cambridge, Mass.: M.I.T.).

Wilkins, M. and Hill, F. E., 1964, *American Business* (Detroit: Wayne State University Press).

Williams, C. R., 1967, 'Regional management overseas', *Harvard Business Review,* 87–91.

10

Ownership, Control and Location Decisions: The Case of the British Steel Industry Since 1945

DAVID HEAL

Normative location models are built on the assumption that firms within an industry engage in intense competition with each other to maximize their individual profits. It has been suggested recently that the behaviour of mature corporations is better understood in terms of maximizing the growth rate of revenue, but it is again assumed that inter-corporation competition and rivalry persist. Both models, have areas of application, but neither model provides an adequate conceptual framework for explaining the locational decisions of firms in mature industries in which competition is *not* intense. The presence or absence of competition is critical. If competition is absent, the industry, and its constituent firms, can exercise discretion in the choice of goals. Attainment of these goals can be guaranteed subject to the two provisos that the firms must be able to generate or attract finance for future capital investment and that the ground rules of not actively competing are continuously observed by all. Discretionary goals are legion, but among the foremost is that of preserving the individual identity of the firm. It can be argued that self-preservation is the first aim of firms in competitive and non-competitive industries alike, but in non-competitive industries firms can work together to attain that aim: to exchange the lonely concern of the individual firm for self-preservation for a collective concern to achieve the preservation of all. A location model built on the assumption of cooperation for survival would not be of universal applicability, but—by providing a framework for examining the behaviour of those industries for which it is thought to be appropriate—it relieves the profit-maximizing and growth-maximizing models of some of the pressures to which they are currently subjected.

This chapter examines, within the framework of cooperation and company preservation, the pattern of capital investment in the British steel industry since 1945. In 1967 the 14 largest companies were nationalized. This political act, which created the British Steel Corporation, reduced those 14 decision-making centres to one and provided an opportunity to formulate and implement a unified plan to cover 90 per cent of British steel production.[1] One consequence of nationalization is a fresh emphasis on the external factors which separate the British bulk steel industry and its overseas counterparts, and a reduction of the internal differences which were previously dominant. Another is a change in the ground rules for locating new investment within the British bulk steel industry.

Decision-making under Private Ownership, 1945–67

In 1945 the industry produced 11.8 million ingot tons.[2] More than 95 per cent of this came from 23 companies whose individual outputs exceeded 0.1 million ingot tons. The median and maximum levels of output for these companies was 0.22 million ingot tons and 1.55 million ingot tons respectively.[3] They operated 52 steel plants (Figure 10.1) whose median and maximum capacites were 0.2 million and 0.65 million ingot tons respectively. Fourteen companies each operated one plant, the remaining nine operated between two and ten plants. By 1965, the year of record output under private control, total production had increased by 129 per cent to 27.1 million ingot tons. In contrast, the original twenty-three companies, and the number of plants which they operated, had been reduced to 19 and 41 respectively. The median level of plant and company outputs had risen to 0.4 million tons and 1.0 million tons; the maximum levels were 2.7 million tons and 3.3 million tons. In twenty years, therefore, the industry had added more capacity than had been installed in the previous eighty years; the output of the largest plant had been multiplied more than four times and the largest company had more than doubled its capacity.[4] These accomplishments are insignificant, but the manner in which they were achieved need not be accepted uncritically. Although the total level of output achieved in 1965 fell short of the industry's own ambitions, it was only marginally short of national requirements, Criticisms of the industry's performance centre more appropriately upon the issues of plant size and the duplication of effort which accompanied the fragmented ownership pattern rather than upon the total level of output *per se*.

The structure and shape of the industry for 1945 and 1965 are summarized in Figure 10.2. Each square, scaled in proportion to the company outputs, contains a symbol for each of the plants belonging to each company. The position of the major squares within the diagrams roughly follows the geographical position of the largest companies in Britain. Thus Colvilles (1A), who dominated the Scottish industry, are found at the top of the diagram, and Richard Thomas (1K), whose main centre of activity was in South Wales, occupy the lower left-hand corner.

Figure 10.1. The location of the major British steel plants in 1945.

Each company tended to concentrate its production in one of the six clusters identified in Figure 10.1, but since four major companies deviated from this pattern it is not possible to perfectly match the diagrams in Figure 10.2 with the geographical pattern of production. Although the problem of matching cartographical and diagrammatic representations of the production pattern may appear trivial, it reflects the major obstacle which frustrated

268

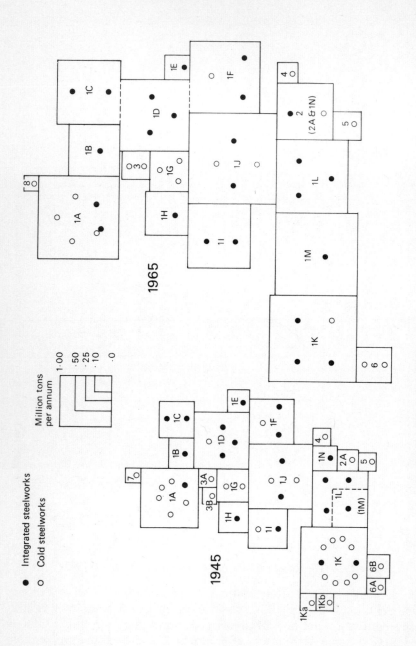

Figure 10.2. Ingot steel production by major companies, 1945 and 1965.

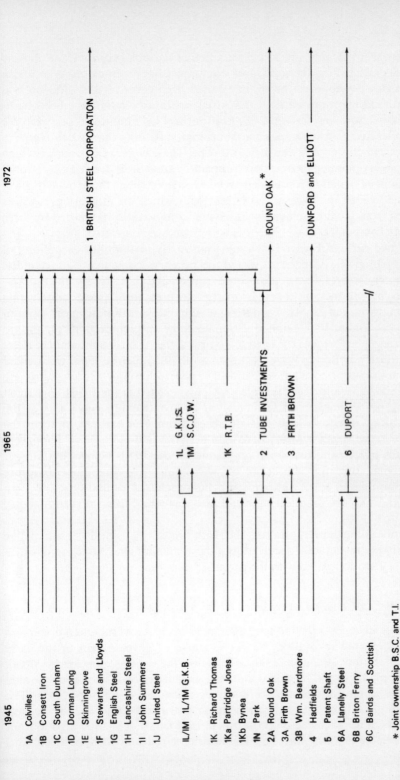

Figure 10.3. Changes in the pattern of ownership, 1945–72.

all attempts to rationalize the industry before nationalization. If the clusters of plants rather than the individual companies had been the units of which the various development programmes had been composed, a different and almost certainly more efficient industrial structure would have been built. The reality, however, was that The United Steel Companies, as one example only, operated an isolated plant at Workington (Cumberland), two plants in the Sheffield cluster, and one in Scunthorpe. These were the basis upon which the company planned its own development. United Steel derived operational and financial benefits from wide spread of interests, but those benefits have to be set against the lower levels of efficiency which the industry as a whole suffered from having a cluster of three plants in Scunthorpe owned by three separate companies.

The two parts of Figure 10.2 show that, firstly, with minor exceptions all the companies shared in the growth of the industry up to 1965, that, secondly, only minor changes were made in organization and that, thirdly, the rationalization of production through works closures took place only *within* company boundaries. The progress of company rationalization is summarized in Figure 10.3. Limited rationalization was achieved in response to two forces. The first was the need to complete the reconstruction of the sheet steel industry in South Wales, following the introduction from the United States of the continuous hot strip mill. The new technology rendered obsolete the 50-odd sheet and tinplate mills which had existed in the 1930s. This most pressing post-war problem was resolved by constructing a new mill at the Port Talbot works—which was detached from Guest Keen to form the nucleus of the Steel Company of Wales in 1947—and by Richard Thomas & Baldwins purchasing two small companies in the 1950s before they closed. The second force was the desire of two engineering companies to secure captive sources of steel. Tube Investments purchased Round Oak and Park Gate, and Duport Engineering purchased Llanelly Steel and Briton Ferry during the 1950s.

The preceding paragraphs, together with Figures 10.2 and 10.3, summarize the changes that actually occurred, but these changes pale into insignificance when they are compared with the promises that were made in 1946.

Prosperity: A Common Acceptance of the Status Quo

In December 1945 the industry presented to the Government a document which purported to outline the likely course of development in the early post-war period (*Reports*, 1946). A major theme was that many small, obsolete plants would be closed and that production would be concentrated in larger plants located on the coast or upon the inland ore fields. The potential gains from rationalization were illustrated by reference to the steel plants which were clustered on the North East Coast. The total ingot output of the region in 1945 was 2.35 million ingot tons, divided between four

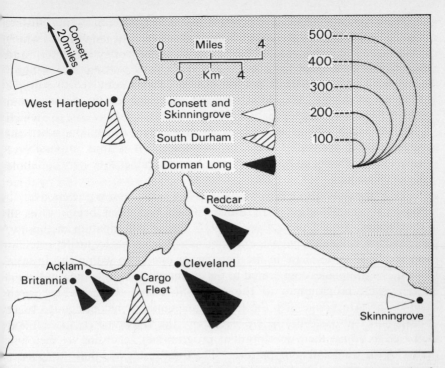

Figure 10.4. The North-East Coast: steel production by plants in 1945 (thousands of tons per annum).

companies operating eight plants (Figure 10.4). The proposals were: that Dorman Long would close the Acklam and Britannia works and concentrate production at Cleveland-Lackenby and Redcar; that South Durham would close West Hartlepool; that Consett Iron would leave the steel billet trade, and specialize in plate production; that Skinningrove would be closed; that Dorman Long, South Durham and Consett Iron would cooperate to construct a new billet mill. The report implied that this mill would be built at Cargo Fleet and that South Durham and Dorman long would merge. Similar changes were promised for other regions.

The report was composed by the British Iron and Steel Federation. This organization, to which all the steel companies belonged, had been created in 1934. By 1945 the Federation included among its many functions an elaborate system for controlling steel prices and for equalizing the raw material costs of different producers. This latter, important, aim was achieved through the Industry Fund. The Fund obtained its income from a levy imposed upon the companies according to their ingot output. It was supplemented by a further levy imposed on the tonnage of scrap metal purchased by each company. The major payments from the Fund were then made, firstly to minimize the differences in iron production costs between users of cheap home ore and of expensive foreign ore and secondly to minimize variations in steel production costs between the cheap scrap metal consumers and expensive pig iron consumers. The Fund was publicly justified in terms of its benefits to the nation, but it also had the consciously recognized purpose of keeping in business all who so wished: the low-cost producers connived to subsidize high-cost producers. The details of the operation of the Fund remain obscure. It seems probable that in 1952, for example, the net cost to Stewarts & Lloyds–a low cost producer–was approximately £3 million, when that company's pre-tax profits were £13.4 million.[5] It is thus impossible to consider the different companies as competitors; rather they were collaborators or colleagues.

The Federation also enjoyed advisory but not coercive powers over the industry's reconstruction programme which had been begun after the introduction of tariff protection in 1932. Active participation in this programme was voluntary, but was expected as a *quid pro quo* for tariff protection and the freedom to share in the benefits of operating within the Industry Fund. The companies cooperated to the extent of submitting their individual development programmes to the Federation, and these became public knowledge. Amendments to the programme could be recommended by the Federation, but could not be enforced, and the individual companies were left free to adjust their development programmes according to their own views of the total emerging pattern.[6] The total result was that the low-cost producers protected the high-cost producers, but lacked the power to force through a radical programme of reform. Yet no evidence exists to suggest that low-cost producers desired radical reformation, so the absence of such powers went unnoticed. Thus on the North East Coast, as elsewhere, the proposals contained within the Federation's report were ignored. South Durham and Dorman Long did not merge and by 1965 annual capacity at West Hartlepool—which according to the development report had been scheduled for closure—had been expanded to 1.0 million ingot tons. Consett grew to a similar size and the company expanded its interests in both plates *and* billets. Skinningrove continued to operate as a profitable producer of specialized sections. Rationalization was restricted to Dorman Long alone: Acklam and Britannia were closed as planned, progressive closure of Redcar followed.[7] This was made possible by technological developments which permitted the continuous growth of output at Cleveland-Lackenby. Here, as elsewhere, it was the company identity and not plant identity which was thought to be worth preserving.

The 1945 development report promised cautious growth within a rationalized industrial structure. In due course, production targets, which were progressively raised throughout the 1950s, were consistently exceeded, but rationalization remained elusive because the executive powers were not persuaded of its necessity. The collective aims and attitudes of the industry's leaders were well expressed by Sir Andrew McCance in a lecture delivered in Middlesbrough in 1950 (McCance, 1950). Sir Andrew argued that there was an approximately constant relationship between total industry output and the largest plant which should produce 5 per cent of total output) and that there was a 'natural limit of size' to individual plants. Furthermore, the largest plant was the apex of a broad-based pyramid containing all the plants within the industry. The closure of many small plants and the concentration of production in large plants would destroy this relationship, and the construction of a tower-like industrial structure in the place of the pyramid might 'well be [to court] failure'. The McCance doctrine, which was an accepted truth throughout the industry, implied that growth should be allowed at most, if not all, locations.

A second and extended statement of industry aims was presented in 1952 by a team reporting its findings on a comparative study of the American and British steel industries (Anglo-American Council on Productivity, 1952). It showed that the average size of American bulk steel plants in the larger American industry was two-and-a-half times greater than the British average and concluded that British plant size should be increased, but not to the level already attained at Sparrows Point (3.4 million tons) in Maryland. Recognizing that 'Britain is a land of old traditions' and that the British possessed a 'passion for equity and compromise', they concluded that the pyramidal structure should be retained in a modified form technical requirements should be tempered by social expectations. This 1952 report, based on a realistic assessment of what the industry wanted as opposed to what it needed, was a more accurate prognostication of real trends than the 1945 report had been.

The 1950s were a decade of increased output, higher profitability and growing optimism. In 1960 the industry produced 24 million ingot tons but was planning an annual capacity of 34 million ingot tons by 1965. The first attempts were being made to accommodate the oxygen steel-making processes and to provide a suitable infrastructure for the efficient use of a larger tonnage of foreign ore. Significantly all these attempts continued to be made *within* existing company boundaries.[8] In 1959–60 development schemes estimated to cost a record £423 million were proposed. Characteristically, they related to almost every plant in Britain, the absentees being the plants which had been recently expanded. Increased profits, regular payments of larger dividends by all companies and the ability to finance further development were all evidence that the chosen policy of mutual tolerance and co-operation was practicable. No one noticed that such a policy had been tested only under the indulgent conditions of prosperity.

Adversity: Initiatives for Change

The early 1960s brought new and severe tests. The industry anticipated an average annual demand of 30 million ingot tons equivalent, but the maximum level achieved was 28.3 million tons in 1964 and the 1960 level was surpassed only in 1964 and 1965. The financial performance was even worse: combined trading profits after depreciation of the companies later incorporated within the British Steel Corporation fell from £104 million in 1960 to £23 million in 1967 (British Steel Corporation, 1968). Their associated return on capital invested plummeted from 18.8 per cent to 1.9 per cent over the same period. Attention to cost-cutting and improved efficiency, which had earlier appeared to be merely desirable, became essential. Yet even that policy could not provide the investment funds needed to keep the industry abreast of the technological changes which were affecting the steel industries of the world.

It appears that the scales which impaired the vision of the industry had been partially removed by 1967, but the evidence does not compel the belief that the need for radical action was universally recognized. Major development programmes were announced in 1965–66 for Port Talbot, for Cleveland-Lackenby and for United Steel's Scunthorpe plant, but the success of these ventures depended upon the willingness of other companies to forgo expansion. This was a minimum requirement, which was second-best to their leaving the primary stages of steel production completely. Instead, the directors of Consett Iron, for example, gave their opinion that expansion of ingot output from their plant to a level of 3.5 million was entirely feasible. The post-war record of the company indicated that its conviction in its own abilities to overcome the physical problems associated with its inland, hilltop plant should by no means be discounted. This type of issue had not been resolved by 1967, but one attempt to simplify the ownership map of the industry was made by Stewarts & Lloyds in 1965.

The Federation provided a focus for industry-wide discussion and cooperation, but closer ties between certain companies were also secured through a number of cross-directorships. The most important of these linked United Steel with Stewarts & Lloyds on the one hand and John Summers on the other. In 1965 Nial Macdiarmid, Managing Director of Stewarts & Lloyds, and as such a director of United Steel, took advantage of this arrangement to propose secretly that the two companies act together to take over South Durham (Peddie, 1969). His object was the purchase and further expansion of the wide diameter steel pipe capacity already installed at West Hartlepool. Stewarts & Lloyds were already in this trade and Macdiarmid was intent on a rationalization programme which would also provide his company with a plant located on the coast. United Steel, he argued, would benefit from the joint venture by the ability to close South Durham's unprofitable Cargo Fleet plant and by the consolidation of the order books for steel rails, sections and billets. United Steel, however, were already planning for Scunthorpe the initial stages of a plant which could be expanded to 5·0 million tons on a new 50 : 50, home ore: foreign ore, iron-making basis. They could not pretend that Scunthorpe was a coastal location, but they were convinced that the proposed ore-mix would provide cheap iron over the short and long term. They, therefore, attempted to interest Stewarts & Lloyds in this venture. This conservative counter-proposal was unacceptable to the radical Macdiarmid, who thereupon opened direct negotiations with South Durham. By the autumn of 1966 the range of talks had been extended to include Dorman Long and it was agreed to merge the three companies if the Government's nationalization proposals were rejected by Parliament.[9] With Dorman Long in the scheme it was possible to make maximum use of Stewarts & Lloyds' financial powers in rationalizing all stages of steel production at West Hartlepool and on the south bank of the Tees.

British Steel & Tubes, as the new company was to have been called, was created through a rare combination of circumstances. Dorman Long, which possessed the lowest cost location of the foreign ore consumers, needed additional financial resources to develop that location and assured access to a wider range of markets for the larger tonnage of steel which development would produce. South Durham, dominated since the 1920s by the Talbot family, needed fresh direction after the sudden death of Chetwynd Talbot in July 1966. Stewarts & Lloyds, driven by Nial Macdiarmid, needed a long-term profitable venture for their large financial resources. Macdiarmid played the essential role of a catalyst and the financial contribution of Stewarts & Lloyds was sufficient to assure him the controlling position in the new venture which was justified by his initiative.[10] In no other part of the industry was a similar combination of human, financial and location factors to be found. Neither the large sheet steel producers in South Wales nor Colvilles in Scotland had the incentive to rationalize the English industry, hopes for which, therefore, lay in persuading United Steel to extend the range of its interests. Subsequent events were to show that United Steel had the requisite managerial resources in depth to play a larger role, but in the 1960s the board was still adhering to the policy, laid down by Gerald Steel in the 1950s, of limited vertical as opposed to horizontal growth. Furthermore, the decision to invest £80 million at Scunthorpe fully absorbed the company's financial resources. The growth of United Steel in the post-war years had been cautious, persistent and profitable; there was no evidence that the board could be tempted into the uncharted course of rationalizing a large share of the English industry outside British Steel & Tubes. United Steel could afford to continue its cherished policy of tending its own affairs; Stewarts & Lloyds, at any rate with Macdiarmid in control, could not.

The New Structure since 1967

Planning the Nationalized Industry

Although strong economic and technological arguments favoured unifying the planning of a British industry whose total capacity was smaller than the

276

United States Steel Corporation, the opportunity to do so originated in the political arena with the election of a large socialist majority to Parliament in 1966. The 1967 nationalization act short-circuited all tentative moves towards a new corporate structure and imposed upon an unwilling industry a degree of internal coherence which it would otherwise not have obtained. The resultant shape and structure of the industry is presented diagrammatically in Figure 10.5, which uses the same principles of construction on 1970 production data as were used in Figure 10.2. By 1970, the British Steel Corporation had obliterated the old company boundaries and had organized its steel-making activities into four product divisions, the component parts of which are widely scattered. Thus the General Steels Division, with its headquarters in Glasgow, operates works in South Wales and the Midlands, although its production focus is on Teesside and in Scunthorpe. The headquarters of the Strip Mills Division in Cardiff—a neutral location between Newport and Port Talbot, the focuses of Richard Thomas & Baldwins and the Steel Company of Wales—also supervises

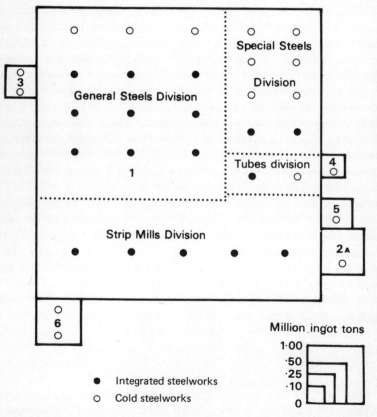

Figure 10.5. Ingot steel production by major British companies in 1970.

production in North Wales and Scotland. Production of tubes in Scotland and the North East Coast is controlled from Corby. The Special Steels Division, focused on Sheffield, has its administrative headquarters in the old head office of United Steel in Sheffield. An earlier attempt to organize the Corporation according to a less radical regional model had foundered on the rock of vestigial company and regional jealousies which that model tended to preserve. By 1970 however, the central organization, located in London, had established complete control over its empire by means of a policy of divide and rule.

The Product Divisions were set up in 1970, but the internal structure of the London head office was not stabilized until the end of 1971. This now consists of two main groups—Staff Units who report to the Chairman and Head Office Divisions who report to the Deputy Chairman and Chief Executive. Corporate strategy, planning and organization are among the responsibilities of the Staff Units and it was at this level that the development plants for the 1970s were designed. There has, therefore, been a deliberate policy (1) to free management of the Product Divisions from the responsibility of formulating development strategy and (2) to remove this function from the steel-making regions while ensuring that that strategy should be designed to benefit the Corporation as a whole, subject only to social and political restraints imposed by the Government. Other Staff Units are responsible for the Corporation's relationships with government and for formulating commercial policies. The role of the Head Office Divisions is to ensure that the Corporation's policies and procedures are carried out and to provide coordination and specialist support for the Product Divisions. Although there appears to be overlap between some Staff Units and Head Office Divisions—for example, each group has a component labelled Personnel, Social and Regional Policy—the planning function has been firmly assigned to a Staff Unit responsible to the Chairman.

Changes in the organization of the Corporation have been paralleled by changes in personnel. Lord Melchett, the Chairman, and Dr. H. M. Finniston, one of the three Deputy Chairmen in the original organizational framework, were recruited from merchant banking and electrical engineering, but the other two Deputy Chairmen were the former Chairmen of Richard Thomas & Baldwins and United Steel, Mr. M. Milne-Watson and Mr. A. J. Peech. Mr. Peech also served as managing director of the Midland Steel Group, the largest of the regional groups, dissolved in 1970. The other three regional groups were led by Mr. W. F. Cartwright from the Steel Company of Wales, Mr. T. R. Craig from Colvilles and Mr. Macdiarmid. The majority of senior staff positions were filled by men from the former companies or from the British Iron and Steel Federation and the Iron and Steel Board. There was, therefore, continuity of personnel at all levels as well as a broad continuity in the pattern of organization. Undoubtedly this facilitated the act of transition, but it also delayed the creation of a new identity as each man brought his own accumulated loyalties into the new organization.

By 1973 the majority of senior positions in London had been filled by men recruited from outside the industry—there were exceptions, like Lord Layton formerly of the Steel Company of Wales—or by men who had been trained by the former companies, but who generally had not reached company director status. Former employees of United Steel now lead three of the four Product Divisions, including the Strip Mills Division in which that company had had no interests, while two of the six Head office divisions have been led by men from the same source. There is irony in the fact that the managing director and the senior group directors of the General Steels Division, whose major development is scheduled for Teesside, were trained by United Steel whose board had declined to take an interest in that area at Mr. Macdiarmid's invitation. At lower levels there has been more interchange of personnel between the divisions than there had been between companies. Important accomplishments of the years since nationalization have, therefore, been the injection of personnel trained in a more competitive business environment than the steel industry, the provision of wider horizons for the able men within the old companies—administrators, accountants and commercial men as well as those from production—and the gradual establishment of loyalties to the new, larger organization. This was essential if nationalization was to yield a commercially successful operation. In five years a variety of management structures, some of which were only suitable for single-plant companies, have been welded into an organization suited to the control of a nationwide enterprise: planning has been systematized in the same way as accounting procedures have been standardized.

The other problems for the Corporation concerned its financial structure and its freedom to operate independently of close government intervention. The former was solved in 1971–72 and, in theory, the Corporation will have greater commercial freedom under the rules of the European Coal and Steel Community than the old companies had under the Iron and Steel Board. The capital development programme could not be finalized until these issues had been resolved. Accordingly, it was not until the end of 1972 that the Corporation, after 18 months of intense discussions with the government, produced an outline plan to expand its capacity to a possible 36 million ingot tons by 1980. This target is lower than the original ambition of 40 million tons by 1980 and precludes the possibility of building on a greenfield site. Early optimism had prompted many outside suggestions for the location of such a plant, ranging from Hunterston on the Ayrshire coast (near Glasgow), through Teesside, Humberside and the Thames estuary, to Southampton Water on the south coast. The arguments were variously couched in terms of minimizing raw material assembly costs, minimizing total costs, improving employment in depressed areas and even sympolizing national prestige—Welsh, Scottish and British—but the costs were never quantified. It was a minority which believed that 'a new integrated works based on present-day techniques [would] be a financial disaster wherever the location' (Busby, 1971). In the new era of modified optimism, and cautious expansion, the viability of such a works will not be put to the test.

Under the new plan there will be five major integrated plants— Ravenscraig, mid-Lanarkshire (3·2 million tons); Lackenby-Redcar on at South Teesside (12·0 million tons); Scunthorpe (6·35 million tons); Port Talbot (6·0 million tons) and Newport (3·5 million tons) in South Wales— and one large cold metal complex in Rotherham, near Sheffield (2·0 million tons). In addition, the Corporation will continue to operate seven small cold metal works and the integrated works at Corby (1·0 million tons). It seems probable that Brymbo will be sold back to Guest, Keen & Nettlefold. Between 1968, when the first closure occurred, and 1980 the number of ingot steel producing plants operated by the Corporation will have been reduced by 15.[11] Following a decision not to build greenfield plants, rationalization within the Corporation will follow the same policies that were practised by the private companies—closures, within expansion at the best locations already available—but with the important difference that the entire ingot steel capacity of *no fewer than five of the old companies will be closed.*

Between 1967 and 1972 the Corporation reviewed the strengths and weaknesses of its inherited structure. The review gave birth to the so-called 'heritage programme' which was characterized by the mutually interacting policies of integrating previously separated plants, consolidating production at fewer locations and judicious expansion at selected locations. The Park Gare and Steel, Peech & Tozer plants in Rotherham (Sheffield area), for example, were combined into a total cold metal complex of 2·0 million tons under one management. Similarly, the production of medium plates was consolidated on Lackely and duplicate facilities at West Hartlepool and Scunthorpe were colsed. In the Strip Mills Division the range of products rolled by each hot mill has been reduced and cold mills are specializing within the range of finished steel; Ebbw Vale, in South Wales, and Shotton, on Deeside, are to become cold rollers only. The importing of iron ore for South Wales is to be concentrated at Port Talbot. Newport, built in sight of the sea, will then be effectively 50 miles inland. These and many other acts of integration and consolidation were designed to reduce operating costs without adding to the Corporation's production capacity.

The major expansions of capacity under the 'heritage programme' were at Lackenby and Teesside in the General Steel Division. In 1969, the Corporation decided to add a third vessel to the oxygen plant started by Dorman Long at Lackenby and to build a continuous casting plant for blooms. This was completed in 1971–72, permitting closure of open-hearth furnaces at Cargo Fleet, Skinningrove and Lackenby. Mills at the outlying plants, together with the rail mill at Workington (Cumberland) are now supplied with blooms from Lackenby. Ironworks at Cargo Fleet and Skinningrove have also been closed and the Lackenby plant is supplied by the three modernized blast furnaces at nearby Clay Lane.[12] At Scunthorpe the Corporation took the £80 million United Steel scheme for Appleby-Frodingham and developed it into a £230 million programme to also include Redbourn (formerly Richard Thomas & Baldwins) and Normanby Park (formerly Guest, Keen & Nettlefold). The open-hearth capacity at Appleby Frodingham and Redbourn (2·0 million tons) will be closed in 1973 as a three-vessel oxygen plant (4·4 million tons) is phased in. The total capacity of the three-plants-in-one will be 5·5 million tons. Three mills in the town have been closed, three have been modernized and the new scheme includes a continuous casting plant for slabs and a new bloom, billet and medium section mill. The base of this reconstructed and rejuvenated plant is a new ore preparation plant to process the 6 million tons of foreign and local ores needed by the ten modernized blast furnaces located in three ironworks. This amalgam of the old and the new—new ore preparation, modernized blast furnaces, new steel plant, modernized and new rolling mills—will create operational difficulties and will produce higher operational costs than would be found in a planned greenfield plant.[13] Nevertheless, the mixing of old and new to reduce capital costs is traditional in the industry. Dissolution of the companies has not changed that tradition, it has merely allowed a greater freedom of choice and facilitated the transition of local loyalties, in this case from three companies to one.

The other plants chosen for expansion under the heritage programme were Ravenscraig and Newport where, together with Port Talbot, Teesside and Scunthorpe, all major developments prior to 1980 will now also take place (see above). The details of these developments have not been revealed, but a new integrated plant of 7·0 million tons is to be built in two stages at Redcar, a third oxygen vessel, plus ironmaking capacity, will be built at Port Talbot and production at Scunthorpe will be 'substantially increased'. Redcar will be operated in conjuction with Lackenby-Cleveland, giving a total BOS and electric arc output of over 12·0 million tons.

With ownership vested in the nation, the identity of the British Steel Corporation is proof against direct attacks which might otherwise originate from commercial sources—its future will be influenced by political decisions and by its international competitiveness. Politically motivated changes seemed likely in 1970 after the election of the Conservative Government, but these are now discounted.[14] Nevertheless, there still remains limited scope for tidying the so-called 'ragged frontier' between the public and private sectors, but this could yield only minor modifications.[15] The possibility of a joint venture with a continental company in the construction of a greenfield plant in the 1980s should not be ignored, but future changes in the pattern of ownership of the British steel industry are more likely to be found, if at all, within the private sector.

The Private Sector

Nationalization, which broke up the Federation, also drove a wedge between the Corporation and the private companies that now form the British Independent Steel Producers Association. Attempts to rationalize ownership and control within the private sector have, however, taken place outside this body, whose main function is to challenge the pricing policy of the Corporation. In 1969 the state-owned Industrial Reorganization Corporation acquired a 50·1 per cent holding in Brown Bayley, a Sheffield special steel producer.[16] This move was interpreted as a first step towards further rationalization, but negotiations towards a merger with Dunford & Elliott, who had acquired Hadfields in 1968, were inconclusive. The separate revival of these two companies makes a merger seem unlikely and other companies have declared their intentions of remaining independent.[17] In 1971 Brown Bayley purchased Rotherham-Tinsley rolling mill from Leeds Assets and has subsequently expanded its own ingot output to 0·13 million tons—the first company since the 1930s the join the ranks of those who produce over 0·1 million tons.[18] In the winter of 1972–73 Dunford & Elliott attempted to take over the larger Firth Brown, but the approach was opposed on financial grounds and on claims of superior industrial logic. The evidence in all cases is that the companies remain jealous of their independence, and the low profitability of the industry has not attracted interference from outside.[19] Rationalization of production has continued to take place only *within* company boundaries.[20] Given the reluctance to merge, the only alternative agent for change is the formation of new steel producing companies. The 'mini-mill' concept has provided a means for avoiding the earlier capital obstacles to entry and has resulted in one new plant at Sheerness in Kent and firm proposals for similar mills at Dudley and Birkenhead; but in each case the new plants are subsidiaries of existing organizations. The Birkenhead and Sheerness mills are to produce reinforcing steels for the construction industry in competition with the British Steel Corporation rather than with the other private companies; output from the Dudley mill is destined for engineering companies which provided the capital. None of these projects impinge upon the structure of the special steels industry, the immutability of which lies in the determination of the companies to preserve their identities and in the reluctance or inability of larger members to impose a solution through financial pressure. Without a change in these attitudes the locational pattern of steel production outside the British Steel Corporation will remain inert.

Conclusion

During the twentieth century the British steel industry shared in the industrial evolutionary trend away from the single-plant firm posited by classical economics and location theory towards the multi-plant corporation. Movement along this trend occurred at different rates so that by 1945 there was a wide range of organizational forms. In single-plant companies all forward planning and decisions were taken at boardroom level—the administrative overheads were minimal—whereas the multi-plant companies had established a sophisticated range of central research, advisory and administrative offices. Between 1945 and 1967, however, the institutional framework of the industry displayed a rigidity which was in no way imposed upon it by outside controls designed to prohibit mergers and consolidation. The threat of nationalization possibly acted as an inhibiting factor, but the third consecutive electoral victory of the Conservative Party in 1959 together with changes in Labour Party composition which appeared to remove the likelihood of state ownership also failed to produce any immediate changes in the ideas of the leaders of the industry.[21] Control of steel prices, which prevented the generation of exceptional profits, similarly served to inhibit exceptional action. But the principal reasons for perpetuating the *status quo* appear to have been company individualism—sometimes fortified by intense local loyalties, which were an obstacle to voluntary mergers—and absence of the dominating personalities needed for a campaign of takeovers backed by financial strength. By common agreement future needs were to be satisfied by changes within existing boundaries. The formation of the British Steel Corporation has not, in itself, changed this philosophy, but in principle it has produced greater planning flexibility. There is no *a priori* reason for supposing that the Corporation will not extend the realm of its internally planned economy and take the next step on the evolutionary path towards the multi-national corporation. It is the only British steel company which has the financial and managerial resources and the administrative structure to do so.

Notes

1. Only those companies whose individual output in the year ending June 1964 exceeded 0·475 million tons were nationalized. The private sector, composed of about 160 companies many of which are subsidiaries of engineering firms, contribute 10% to the total tonnage, but 30% of the total value of British steel. These private companies are concentrated in the special steels trades.

2. The long ton (2240 lbs) is the unit of measurement used throughout this chapter.

3. A plant is defined as a centre of ingot steel production. It can, but need not, contain ironworks, rolling mills and more than one melting shop. For historical reasons, and the perpetuation of the names of sometime independent concerns, the definition on the ground is not always clear. The key to the present is the management structure.

4. The largest company in both years was The United Steel Companies Limited. The largest plant in 1945 was Appleby-Frodingham at Scunthorpe (United Steel). The largest plant in 1965 was Port Talbot (Steel Company of Wales (S.C.O.W.)).

5. In 1952 the values were: Ingot levy £5·60 per ton; Scrap levy £1·00 per ton; Pig iron remission £1·75 per ton. These figures were adjusted from year to year but always operated

against the interests of the home ore-field steel producers. For a fuller discussion see Burn (1961) from which these values were obtained.

6. For example, when Dorman Long announced their intention to build the first British universal beam mill at Lackenby, United Steel shelved its proposals for a similar mill at Appleby-Frodingham, Scunthorpe.

7. The timing of the closures was not as scheduled. Acklam was not closed until 1963, whereas the 1945 plan had looked no further forward than 1953.

8. These attempts are discussed in detail in Heal (in press).

9. The initial proposal was that South Durham and Stewarts & Lloyds should build a jointly owned mill at West Hartlepool.

10. Stewarts & Lloyds: authorized capital £60 million; trading profit £15·3 million.
South Durham plus Dorman Long: authorized capital £68 million; trading profit £11·6 million.

11. If either Shelton, in Stock-on-Trent, Bilston, in Wolverhampton, or Irlam, in Lancashire, are rebuilt to the 'mini-mill' concept the number of plant closures will be 14.

12. Weekly output from two of the three blast furnaces at Clay Lane has been raised from 12,000 to 18,000 tons. Nevertheless, this is insufficient to support the planned annual output of 4·5 million tons from the BOS plant. Further blast furnace capacity will be required.

13. Such a plant would require only two blast furnaces (plus one as standby capacity) and the units of plant would be located logically within the works. At Scunthorpe the Normanby Park ironworks is four miles from the ore preparation plant.

14. There is mention of denationalizing the Special Steels Division and of breaking the Corporation into four multi-product companies. The case for returning Brymbo and possibly Cardiff to G.K.N. rests on the fact that that former owner still takes about 80% of their output.

15. The Corporation and Firth Brown have reached agreement on the ownership of the Shepcote Lane stainless steel sheet mill in Sheffield. The Corporation has sold its tool steels business to Edgar Allen & Co., but is still a joint owner of Templeborough Rolling Mills, Sheffield Rolling Mills and Alloy Steel Rods.

16. The I.R.C. was dissolved by the Conservative Government in 1971 and the share-holding is now vested in the Department of Trade and Industry.

17. Viz. Sir Wilton Lee, Chairman of Arthur Lee & Sons Ltd., in his 1970 statement to shareholders. Similarly the attempted merger of Spear & Jackson and Edgar Allen in 1971 failed.

18. Brown Bayley's Managing Director, Mr. T. S. Kilpatrick, is another product of the old United Steel stable.

19. Dunford & Elliott have the financial backing of William Brandt, merchant bankers. The injection of this source of finance which has procured a threefold increase in profits since 1968 indicates that there is scope for interference.

20. Major rationalization programmes have been completed by Duport Engineering, Samuel Osborn and Arthur Lee.

21. The industry was nationalized in February 1951, but the Conservative Government, elected in October 1951, suspended all central functions of the state-owned company and progressively returned the industry to private ownership. This was largely completed by 1957, although R.T.B. was never denationalized.

References

Anglo-American Council on Productivity, 1952, *Iron and Steel,* June 1952; in particular, Chapter 9, 'Works size, layout and transport'.

British Steel Corporation, 1968, *Annual Report and Accounts* 1967–68.

Burn, D., 1961, *The Steel Industry* 1939–1959 (Cambridge University Press).

Busby, J., 1971, *The British Steel Industry and its Expansion Plans in Scotland* (North Ayrshire Coastal Development Committee).

Heal, D. W., (in press), *The Steel Industry in Post-War Britain* (Newton Abbott: David & Charles).

284

McCance, Sir Andrew, 1950, 'Production in the steel industry, its growth, distribution and future course', *Third Harold Wright Lecture to Cleveland Scientific and Technical Institute*.

Peddie, R., 1969, *The United Steel Companies* 1918–1968. *A History* (Manchester: C. Nicholls & Co. Ltd.).

Reports, 1946, by the British Iron and Steel Federation and the Joint Iron Council to the Ministry of Supply (Cmnd, 6811).

III Adaptation to Environment

11

Post-Move Stability and the Location Decision

PETER M. TOWNROE

Empirical studies of location choice and decision-making procedures in manufacturing industry have indicated that decisions tend to be non-optimal in a strict economic sense.[1] They suggest that the character of the location decision for the average firm requires a higher subjective or judgmental element, based on incomplete or uncertain information than other decisions involved in evaluating prospective new investments. Although the choice of a new location is of strategic and essentially long-term concern, and hence an important financial commitment, such a choice is undertaken relatively rarely in the majority of manufacturing companies. There thus tends to be a lack of experience and precedent to fall back on in the decision-making procedure. Decision-makers are not aware of the full extent of the relevant information field and there is uncertainty about the applicability of criteria for choice. The most important single pressure on firms to choose new locations away from existing facilities is the pressure of internal growth. This pressure urges speed, which further encourages search for the acceptable rather than the optimal site. Relatively simple decision rules may then govern that acceptance.

The methodology of the various interview or postal questionnaire surveys on which this picture of location decision-making is based is open to criticism if each investigator ignores the limitations inherent in asking questions both of fact and of opinion about decisions which lie in the past, decisions in which the respondent may have been only indirectly involved. However, there seems no reason to dispute the general characterization of locational decision-making in manufacturing industry shown by these studies. If the portrait is broadly correct, it raises a number of awkward questions, both for the evolution and evaluation of policies designed to encourage industrial movement and for theories of industrial location. Recent literature shows evidence of considerable confusion and uncertainty among those writing and researching in the field as to the nature of the alternative theoretical approaches to location problems. At the same time both industry and public planning agencies are seeking guidance: for them *ad hoc* empirical studies are clearly inadequate. Where are the main areas of confusion?

Mainstream location theory is a direct descendant of the neo-classical economic theory of resource allocation: the deductively derived marginalist theory, successively elaborated since the late nineteenth century. Ignoring the caution of the founding fathers, this theory has been interpreted as a theory of company behaviour. This has led to a number of problems, both in the relationship of the theory with observed behaviour and in its internal coherence and generality. Discussions in the 1930s, leading to the theories of imperfect competition from Joan Robinson and of monopolistic competition from Edward Chamberlain, reflected professional unease with the theory, when seen both as a theory of the firm and, more correctly, as a theory of market form. This unease has continued (Loasby, 1971; Machlup 1967). However, the investment in the conceptual apparatus has been considerable, making it difficult to discard. The general suitability of marginalist theory for many applications, both direct and as a conceptual framework and heuristic, has meant that the difference in its function as a theory of resource allocation, as opposed to a theory of the firm, has been blurred (likewise, the distinction between its use as a positive theory and as a normative theory). Competing theories of company behaviour have been found inadequate when judged by the degree of formality and generality attained and by their predictive power. There has thus been little inclination to accept the need for a paradigm change.

This is not the place to rehearse the full range of arguments put forward attacking, and in defence of, the marginalist theory of the firm. But in the application of interest here, location decisions, there is a strong case for arguing that the role of deductively derived classical theory must be closely circumscribed. As a positive theory, the degree of necessary abstraction for formulating a quantifiable model detracts from a true understanding of the forces actually at work. As a normative theory, it suffers for the 'second-best' objections of partial equilibrium analysis and from its essentially static formulation. This suggests that it is wholly right of Chisholm to be asking 'what do we want a location theory for?' and to accept that there may be a place for more than one type of theory in the study of this aspect of industrial behaviour (Chisholm, 1971). Moreover, the explanation and prediction of industrial location decisions may require an approach rather different from that of industrial location patterns.

Consideration of the functions of location theory indicates that most stress on the 'unreality' of the assumptions in marginal theory, when applied to locational behaviour, shows a misunderstanding of what that theory is trying to do and perhaps an unthinking attraction to the realist position on the role of a scientific theory, rather than the more flexible operationalist stance. If we agree that decision-makers, in choosing a new site for industrial investment, are unlikely to 'optimize' in the conventional sense (i.e. that they will search until they find all plans or alternatives which satisfy an exhaustive list of pre-specifications and then will choose the most economic), we need to be aware of the reasons for such non-optimal behaviour (e.g. lack of information, the existence of uncertainty, organizational compromise). This leads to four alternatives for constructing theories of industrial location behaviour. We can redefine the maximand to include either extra-economic factors, such as growth of turnover or market domination, or extra non-economic factors, such as managerial utility. Or we can do away with the idea of a maximand, either partially, by introducing the idea of satisficing, or wholly, as in a behavioural model. Or we can retain the profit maximizing objective, modified by uncertainty into the context of a probabilistic model or a gaming model. Or we can accept that it is the viability and efficiency of the longer-term patterns of industrial location in which both industry and public policy agencies are interested, and so agree not to worry too much about competing theories of decision-making behaviour but rather to concern ourselves with the results of that behaviour.

Each of these alternatives poses problems in conceptualization and in generating suitable hypotheses for empirical testing. Each, in its own way, restricts the generality, of purpose and of application, of the resulting theory or model. What follows takes the last of the four alternative routes away from the dissatisfaction with location theory as currently formulated and applied. Remembering the longer-term policy concern, this chapter explores the notion of response by companies in the post-location decision period to the consequences of that decision as experience is gained at the new site.

The Adaption[2] Process

Both within the organization of a firm and within its wider network of spatial relationships, there is a system learning process. The context of the operations of the whole firm and of the individual plant undergoes continual change. The firm or plant reacts to these changes in its particular context and in so doing establishes new forces for reaction by other participants in the system. The system 'learns' and adjusts. Within the firm there are three dimensions to this idea: current operational policies, current objectives and appreciation of constraints, and current views of how situations (whether generated internally or externally) should be classified and manipulated. Externally, the firm operates within both an economic and legal system and also within a social system against which the roles of individuals within the company have to be set. Both internal and external environments provide expectations to those in decision-making positions, expectations upon which the criteria for exercising judgment are based.

Changes in these dimensions internally constitute a process of response by the economic unit to its environment. Put forward originally by Alchain (Alchian, 1950), the idea of response was taken up by Tiebout (Tiebout, 1957), who suggested the use of the polar types of 'adaptive' and 'adoptive' behaviour in a location theory. If the high degree of uncertainty that is involved in a long-term location decision is accepted as inevitable by the company management involved (because some uncertainty must be accepted in any future commitment, then there is a corollary that (even if only partially) those same decision-makers must be prepared to modify their positions in the light of actual experience. A locational choice which results in 'bad' long-term returns on capital will require a firm to counter-act. In the very long term, the 'survival of the fittest' principle must apply, but the speed and rigour with which it does so depends upon the degree of competition and upon the technology involved. The 'better' the location choice, the less the need for counter-action.

Empirically, it is extremely difficult to isolate those forces requiring action by a given firm which relate only to its specific choice of location, from those forces which are operating completely independently of location or which have an effect irrespective of the specific locational choice. There may well be overlap, the need to choose a new location and to be involved in the process of industrial movement strengthening latent non-locationally specific forces within a company to a point where action is required. Thus, an empirical view of the adaption process must be somewhat oblique. The need to adapt may be sparked off by a wide range of factors. In terms of the location decision, we need to distinguish conceptually between: (1) a change in conditions not foreseeable at the time of the decision; (2) the inadequacy of information, available or sought for; (3) an inadequate appreciation of the relevance and relative importance of each factor; (4) poor judgment and insufficient evaluation.

If plant performance in a new location is inadequate according to a firm's own internal standards, what can be done? Clearly, this depends upon which factors are contributing to poor performance and the ease with which they can be identified. Poor performance could be accepted on an interim basis in the hope that in time environmental changes will justify the judgments made in the location choice.

Alternatively, changes can be made in management or other personnel, in product lines or in processes used, or the growth rate may be reduced to allow breathing space, or in any combination of these. Each alternative involves a financial or an opportunity cost. If none of these alternatives, alone or in combination, is enough, there remain the locational alternatives of complete closure, of closure and relocation or of partial closure. Despite inadequate evidence, these last alternatives will probably not come into play until after the others have been at least considered, if not tried.

Location inertia is often regarded as evidence of some imperfection in the economic system, a delay in making desirable responses to a new equilibrium position. For the individual firm, however, location inertia may be highly rational. This non-spatial reaction to spatial forces is important when studying plant location patterns. In maximizing profits and returns on capital, there are clearly costs of moving or of closing a plant. Furthermore, a location sub-optimal in operating expenses may still be optimal in returns on capital, especially when locational incentives from a governmental agency are accounted for at least in the short-run amortization period of the initial investment. Short-run benefit is accepted rather than a prospective long-run benefit, which may be greater but is associated with a high degree of uncertainty. The personal utility function of either a proprietor of a salaried manager, those factors, such as golf courses, schools, like-minded neighbours, the local social ambience—often regarded as 'irrational' in the location decision—will seem highly pertinent. While there is a danger of overplaying factors which cannot be quantified, such factors cannot be ignored. As an important locational process, adaption can be analysed in economic terms, while remembering some social and organizational factors, and has important implications for both location theories and policy. The degree of adaption required in response to poor locational decision-making involves a general social welfare loss. More particularly, policies for regional development will be made more costly and will be slower to reach their objectives if the growth rates of newly located plants are slowed or if there is plant closure. Few figures have been published on the closure rate of mobile plants. However, Table 11.1 shows rates of closure up to the end of 1971 of between 2·2 per cent per annum and 4 per cent per annum for the total interregional moves in the United Kingdom that occurred in

Table 11.1. Manufacturing Establishments Opened in 1966–68 after Interregional Movement and Recorded as Closed as at the End of 1971 (provisional figures)

Regions	1966 Recorded	Closed	1967 Recorded	Closed	1968 Recorded	Closed
Principal assisted	75	7	67	5	108	8
Partially assisted	35	2	25	2	35	4
Non-assisted	36	6	39	3	46	2
U.K. Total	146	15	131	10	189	14

Source. Department of Trade and Industry unpublished figures.
Notes. 1. Establishments recorded: Holders of Industrial Development Certificates for 5,000 square feet or more, and occupiers of other premises employing at least 100 at some time in the period.
2. Principal assisted : N. Ireland, Scotland, Wales, Northern Standard regions.
   Partially assisted : North West, South West regions.
   Non-assisted : Yorkshire and Humberside, East and West Midlands, East Anglia, South East Regions.

the period 1966–68. Policies focused upon particular post-move problems
might be able to reduce the risk of closure.

The Survey

In 1972 over 200 manufacturing plants which had been opened within the
previous six-year period—the majority of them between six and four years
previously—were visited and asked a limited number of questions about
post-move stability and change. Of these, 74 plants had moved into or
within the Northern Economic Planning Region, 84 in the East Anglian
Planning Region and 51 within Greater London. As many firms as possible
in all sectors of manufacturing industry, which had moved in either 1966
or 1967, were contacted in each area; five years was judged sufficient time
for initial problems in the new location to be resolved. Coverage in the
Northern Region and East Anglia was as complete as possible and a response
of over 80 per cent was obtained to requests for interviews. A small propor
tion of the total included here moved after 1967 (and one or two before)
in general, this resulted because the sampling frame obtained from the local
planning authorities did not tally with information received from the firm
at the time of the interview. In Greater London coverage was much less
over half the London boroughs contacted had no record of either industrial
movement or commencement of operations by firms within existing premises
Therefore, there was no way of knowing the full extent of movement *within*
London. A response of 35 per cent was obtained on the basis of lists of
names provided by 12 boroughs.

Within the East Anglia and Northern Region groups, there are local
short-distance moves as well as longer interregional moves. The Greater
London group were all local moves. Of the 191 moves, 100 were transfer
moves: either independent plants or establishments acting as the parent
unit to branches elsewhere. The remainder were branch plant moves: either
subsidiary companies or operating sub-units, being established in locations
different from the parent plant. Information was collected about the growth
cost and personnel experience of each plant since it opened. The data is
used to illustrate and evaluate the processes of adaption.

Product Changes

Table 11.2 relates changes in product lines to employment in the firm
at the time of the move in the case of transfer moves and to employment in
the parent plant at the time of the move in the case of branch moves. The
 high proportion (62·5 per cent) of plants changing products so soon after
a move is perhaps surprising, even when one removes the 48 plants which
simply added extra product lines. Some 37 per cent reduced the number of

Table 11.2. Changes in Products by Employment in the Firm or Parent Plant at the Time of Move in 98[1]Transfer Moves and 91 Branch Plants

Employment	No change	Change	Of those changing More products[2]	New designs[3]	Other
Transfer moves		(%)			
No answer	11	4 (27)	3	1	0
0–49	21	42 (67)	18	14	10
50–99	4	6 (60)	2	4	0
over 99	2	8 (80)	4	4	0
Total	38	60 (61)	27	23	10
Branch plants					
No answer	5	3 (27)	1	1	1
0–99	2	12 (86)	3	7	2
100–499	8	12 (60)	4	6	2
over 499	18	31 (63)	13	10	8
Total	33	58 (64)	21	24	13

Notes. (1) 2 non-respondents.
(2) Products additional to original set.
(3) Replacement of existing product.

products, or innovated new designs or new materials. If these changes are evidence of adaption or of instability in recently moved plants, few strong patterns of relationships emerge between these changes and the characteristics of the move. Yet some significant differences are evident.

For example, strongly growing transfer moves (more than doubling

Table 11.3. χ^2 of Product Changes by Process Used for 94 Transfers and 91 Branch Moves

Process used	Transfer moves Change v. No change	Of those changing More products	New designs	Branch moves Change v. No change	Of those changing More products	New designs
Non-routine [1]	2·634	5·730*	3·677	—	2·723	—
Non-routine [2] and batch	2·027	—	—	5·663*	—	—

Notes. * = significant at 2·5 per cent.
(1) Using the Woodward distinction (Woodward, 1965):

Customers' requirements	cf.	Intermittent production of chemicals
Production of prototypes		Production of large batches
Fabrication of large equipment		Mass production
		Continuous flow production
		Production of small batches

(2) As (1), with 'Small batch, and 'Large batch' changing sides.

turnover since the first year of operation) were more likely to change product $\chi^2 = 4.83$, significant at 5 per cent) than either slow-growing transfers or an branch moves. Plant size at the time of the move, or at the time interviewed did not seem to affect product changes. This was contrary to the expectation that smaller plants would be more likely to be changing than larger plants However, there is a weak relationship between change and type of industry engineering firms are more likely to change than firms in other industrie in their branch operations, but less likely in transfer; and both transfers an branches in engineering are more likely to introduce new designs and us new materials than firms in other industries (57 per cent compared with 2 per cent, and 61 per cent compared with 33 per cent). This reflects the jobbin nature of the output of many engineering firms (see Table 11.3). Thus many firms in new locations change their products, add to or reduce thei product lines, because of the nature of their industry, irrespective of an problems associated with the move. Does the survey therefore indicat any links between product changes and the characteristics of the move?

No support could be found for the hypothesis that firms forced to move fo reasons of compulsory purchase, lease termination or deteriorating labou in the old location would be more unstable than firms moving for the mor 'positive' reasons of expansion and growth. In the post-move experience o transfer moves, 5 of the 16 firms with problems in labour training introduce new designs, as did 5 of the 17 firms which had difficulties in labour supply However, only one firm dropped a product line: no relationship was foun between product changes and various other problems (e.g. managemen problems, technical difficulties, marketing and finance problems, etc. cited by transferring companies as restraining growth or as putting pressur on unit costs. Rather more suggestive relationships between product change and post-move problems exist among branch plants. Of the 37 plants makin changes other than adding extra products, and still having problems whic were restraining growth after the first two years of operation, 6 made change because of internal difficulties ($\chi^2 = 3.85$, significant at 5 per cent). Labou problems were also strongly associated ($\chi^2 = 4.73$, singnificant at 5 per cent with the addition of extra products. Problems in using labour and problem affecting costs were associated with product changes after the firs two years.

Another indication that product changes are part of a process of adaptio to locational difficulties may be the relationship between product change an the time taken for new plant to run up to capacity, break even financiall and make an 'adequate' profit. Just over half of those transfer move firm failing to reach full capacity within twelve months of opening, change products. Only 28 per cent reached full capacity within 12 months. Howeve this contrast is not maintained in transfer moves in the time taken to brea even financially or to achieve profitable operation. Although those branc moves not reaching full capacity in 12 months are more likely to add ne product lines $\chi^2 = 5.94$, significant at 2.5 per cent) if they are making changes, no strong relationship emerges between delays in the time taken to reach successful operation and changes in products other than additions. In fact, in both transfer and branch moves a significant number of the firms breaking even and reaching profitability in under three months were firms which subsequently introduced new designs into their product range.

Finally, do longer distance moves yield adaptation problems which are reflected in product changes other than additions? The evidence is weak but positive.

Process Changes

The above results are somewhat ambiguous, mainly because of the many reasons for changing product lines and the lack of identification of the relative ease with which products could be changed in the plants surveyed. It may be more satisfactory to relate changes in production processes used in the plants to the moves and the subsequent problems. Changes in process involve most firms in greater commitments than product changes, although it is difficult to compare degrees of change. Table 11.4 shows the proportion of new plants changing the processes used.

No pattern relating changes in process to the initial size of plant and

Table 11.4. Changes in Processes by Employment in the Firm or Parent Plant at the Time of Move in 95 Transfers[1] and 88 Branch Plants[2]

Employment	No change	Change	Of those changing Using new technology[3]	Other
		(%)		
Transfer moves				
No answer	10	4 (29)	0	4
0–49	25	38 (60)	29	9
50–99	3	6 (67)	4	2
over 99	3	6 (67)	1	5
Total	41	54 (57)	34	20
Branch plants				
No answer	4	4 (50)	2	2
0–99	6	8 (57)	2	2
100–499	9	10 (53)	8	2
Over 499	20	27 (57)	21	6
Total	39	49 (56)	37	12

Notes. (1) 5 non-respondents.
(2) 3 non-respondents.
(3) Including increased automation.

parent at the time of the move emerges, except the high number of small transfer moves using new technology and increasing automation. Perhaps those small firms which are technological innovators or are flexible in their technology are the ones making a large enough return on capital to finance a transfer move satisfactorily. These are also the firms with the high growth rates: 43 of the transfer moves, initially employing under 50, more than doubled their employment and 48 their turnover by the time of the interview. Of these, 47 per cent and 46 per cent respectively had introduced new technology or more automation, compared with 34 per cent of all transfer moves. Faster growing branch plants, however, are not more likely to change processes than the slow growers.

As with products, engineering plants are more likely to change processes than plants in other industries, especially the branch plants. For example 18 of the 22 branches in S.I.C. Orders VII, VIII and IX (Mechanical, Industrial and Electrical Engineering) changed processes compared with only 32 of the 64 branches in other industries $\chi^2 = 5\cdot55$, significant at $2\cdot5$ per cent). Changes in process do not relate as strongly to the nature of processes used in the plants as changes in product. How do changes in process relate to the characteristics of the move?

The hypothesis that 'forced' movers are more likely to have to engage in subsequent adaption in the new location is supported here. Some 75 per cent of the 32 transfer moves which resulted from factors exogenous to the firm concerned changed processes after the move, compared with 50 per cent of the non-forced movers ($\chi^2 = 4\cdot45$, significant at 5 per cent). Of plants with problems hindering growth in the post-move period, changes in the process used in branches were more often associated with internal than with external problems (markets, finance, government policy measures): 77 per cent of those with internal problems in the first two years changed processes compared with 44 per cent of those claiming a restraint on growth from external factors. After the first two years, 86 per cent of those with internal problems changed processes compared with 41 per cent of those with external problems. This contrast was not found in the transfer moves. No pattern was found relating changes in processes to the problems cited in interviewed companies in relation to costs. The use made of labour was the most frequent cost problem referred to in 39 plants, but this was associated in just under half the cases with the absence of change of processes.

Nothing indicated that delays in reaching full capacity and breaking even financially resulted in changes in process in either transfer moves or branches. In view of the more suggestive results obtained for product changes this is a disappointing blow to the original hypothesis of adaption. That expensive alterations in the processes and technology used cannot be indulged in until the original installation has been made to work profitably reflects firm's attitude. The survey results show a near constant proportion of process changers among the various groupings of times taken to reach viability.

Changes in Linkage Patterns

A further form of adaption by companies with plants in new location is to change their linkage patterns. *A priori,* a certain reorientation of links is expected among transferring plants. New branch plants usually experiment with new outlets and suppliers. The degree to which changing linkage patterns occurs over and above that anticipated at the time of the location choice is very difficult to judge. It is an adaption, in part by the economic environment of the new plant, in part by the plant to the environment. The companies interviewed were asked to detail their linkage changes after the first year of operations, the answers thus reflecting adaption after the initial patterns had been established.

In each of the three groups of companies interviewed, only a minority changed either their suppliers, their markets or the services used (legal and financial services, technical services and subcontracting facilities). Table 11.5 shows these minorities for the three groups, as well as for a sub-group of all moves in excess of 25 miles, a sub-group for which the retention and use of pre-move linkages might be difficult. The table shows the very low propensity to change of the movers within Greater London and the greater use of local links within East Anglia than within the Northern Region, especially for services, and reflects the tendency for the larger longer distance movers to be those which are increasing exports.

The pattern of supply linkages has been examined in more detail elsewhere (Moseley and Townroe, 1973). Is there any evidence to support the adaption thesis from these linkage changes? That is, adaption according to experience of operation in the new location, and in the face of problems encountered. Table 11.5 shows considerable ability in the linkage patterns of the majority of firms interviewed. But are those changing the firms encountering problems in the new location?

Table 11.6 shows that, outside Greater London—where numbers of firms citing internal and labour problems as factors hindering their growth rate is very small—the proportion of firms with these problems that change their linkages after the first year of operation is higher than the proportion of companies changing their links in general. Differences are barely significant in most groups, however, except in firms in East Anglia with both internal problems after the first two years of operation and labour problems.

Evidence that linkage change is a form of post-move adaption encouraged by post-move problems is rather inconclusive. Changes in supply linkages are important in a group of small plants involved in non-routine or batch production in engineering, moving over relatively small distances (25–100 miles) and moving reluctantly because of a push from their old location (Moseley and Townroe, 1973). If no definite pattern emerges of linkage changes as part of an adaptation process, but rather as part of an adoption process, then evidence of adaption must be sought in the managerial structure of recently moved plants.

Table 11.5. Percentages of Migrant Firms Changing Links with Suppliers, Markets and Services

	Greater London			East Anglia			Northern Region			All moves >25 miles		
	S	M	V	S	M	V	S	M	V	S	M	V
Firms establishing more 'local' ties	0	0	0	1607	9·5	35·7	11·1	5·6	3·7	16·2	6·0	27·4
Increased exports	—	7·8	—	—	13·1	—	—	27·8	—	—	20·5	—
Other changes	35·2	39·2	17·7	32·2	29·8	11·9	20·4	25·9	18·5	25·6	26·5	12·8
No change	64·7	49·0	80·4	48·8	45·2	50·0	66·6	38·9	74·1	55·6	44·4	56·4
No answer	0	3·9	2·0	2·4	2·4	2·4	1·9	1·9	3·7	2·6	2·6	3·4
Total interviewed	51	(100%)		84	(100%)		54	(100%)		117	(100%)	

S = Percentage changing suppliers
M = Percentage changing markets
V = Percentage changing services

Table 11.6. Numbers of Migrant Firms with Growth Problems Changing Links with Suppliers, Markets and Services

Problems hindering growth	Greater London				East Anglia				Northern Region				All moves 25 miles			
	S	M	V	T	S	M	V	T	S	M	V	T	S	M	V	T
Internal																
in 1st 2 years	2	3	1	7	15	16	16	29	3	5	5	1	15	19	20	37
subsequently	0	0	0	1	5	7	6	9	0	0	0	1	4	7	6	10
Labour																
in 1st 2 years	2	1	0	4	9	10	9	17	1	3	1	5	10	13	10	22
subsequently	3	4	0	6	12	11	9	20	0	0	0	1	12	11	0	21
Total number changing links as percentage of total number interviewed	35·3	47·1	17·6		48·8	52·4	47·6		31·5	57·4	22·2		41·9	53·0	40·2	

S = Number changing suppliers
M = Number changing markets
V = Number changing services
T = Total number citing problem

Changes in Management

Earlier work (Townroe, 1971, pp. 91–2 and 97–100) shows that many initial post-move problems are exacerbated by inadequate management in the new plant. Branch plants tend to be administered by relatively junior or inexperienced managers and yet 'many firms considered the quality of the manager to be the key to success in a new venture of this sort' (Luttrell, 1962, p. 149). Although managerial problems are found most frequently in branch plants, some transfer moves also face management problems. A move which generates too many problems for the owner-manager will result in a slowing of the growth rate or in closure. In transfer moves not run by owner-manager there will be the same problems of appointing a manager as in a branch (and of removing him if he is not successful). Thus, part of the adaption process will involve changes in management personnel and in management structures. Inadequacies in the location decision process will emerge as problems for management which can perhaps be solved only by changing the management. The personality of the first chief resident manager in the new plant may be crucial in solving these problems.

The Appointment of the First Manager: One difficulty voiced by managers in an earlier survey (Townroe 1971, p. 91) was having to live with the results of someone else's choice of site for the new plant and hence with any inadequacies of the location decision-making procedure. From the 202 replies to this question in this survey, 38 chief managers had been appointed *after* the choice of location had been made. Understandably, this was much more common in branch plant (26·6 per cent) than in transfer moves (11·8 per cent). It was also more common in larger moves, in moves with the larger parent company at the time of the move and in longer distance (150 miles) moves. These are the kinds of moves for which (1) a team approach to locational choice is most usual and (2) evaluation is wider, more detailed and involves consultation with both in-house and external specialists (Townroe, 1972). With good planning, especially if the new plant is mainly a subsidiary operational unit to an existing factory, involvement of the eventual manager in locational choice may be unnecessary. But also, existing decision-making management in larger concerns may be little inclined to move to establish the new plant. That appointment after the choice is more common for plants being established in the Northern Region, even allowing for different move characteristics, reinforces this impression. Luttrell also notices that existing senior managers avoided appointments to a new but distant plant. Does late appointment of the first manager have any subsequent repercussions? The survey results contain no suggestion that appointment of managers after the choice of location is associated with greater difficulties in expanding the new plant and only a tentative suggestion that they have greater problems with costs. In fact, more later appointees (63 per cent) were associated with plants doubling their turnover since opening than early appointees (49 per cent); this reflected the tendency for later appointments to be made in larger companies for larger new plants.

Firms concerned with the high degree of uncertainty which may surround a new plant in a new location, or aware of their own managerial inexperience in starting up new plant, may appoint the first chief manager on a temporary basis. A short-term contract (2–5 years) may also be attractive to professional managers who specialize in establishing new plants. Foreign companies, in particular, may find it useful to hire the relevant experience in this way. Yet only 7 of the 196 companies replying to the question had made such temporary appointments. Four of these temporary managers were appointed into companies with a turnover exceeding £5 million, and five in new units initially employing more than 50 people. In three cases, the appointment was of a 'prove thyself' nature for a younger man; the remaining four used the temporary 'company doctor' type of manager.

The Experience of the First Manager: Evolution of the degree of managerial experience of the first manager of the plant before his appointment is extremely difficult, especially if the interview is with his successor or with a fellow manager. However, the origin of the manager indicates the extent to which a company has to, or is willing to, look outside itself for recruits. Fifty-two plants were run initially by the owner-proprietors, in four cases a partner going off to establish a new branch; 38 transfer moves and 51 branch moves required an appointment from outside the company. As expected *a priori,* owner managers dominated smaller companies and smaller moves. They also had more problems recruiting and training labour than other managers. Externally-recruited managers in branch plants had proportionally fewer problems with factors hindering growth than managers from within the company, especially with internal and labour supply problems. No strong differences emerge in the cost problems listed.

Does the appointment of a younger man result in more problems from inexperience, or in greater success from greater energy and a desire to justify and sustain promotion? Although no clear distinction between branch and transfer moves emerges, younger men seem prepared to move further from the original location than older men (Table 11.7). The survey gives no evidence of younger men being appointed only to smaller plants, but they do tend to be appointed in industries where competition is 'weak' or 'very weak' and into plants using mass production techniques (where perhaps there is less room for managerial discretion). Conversely, managers over the age of 50 were proportionally over-represented in plants concerned with specialized one-off designs to customers' designs and with fabricating large equipment items. Younger men were more commonly appointed to branch plants being established for marketing reasons, whereas, as expected, older men were more heavily represented among those moves 'forced' by

Table 11.7. Age on Appointment of First Manager by Distance of Move

Distance (miles)	No answer	Age (years) over 50	41–50	31–40	under 31	Total (= 100%)
	%	%	%	%	%	
under 25	—	30	33	26	7	27
25–150	10	24	37	22	7	83
over 150	—	9	46	26	20	46
	5·8	20·5	39·1	23·7	10·9	156

problems of labour, original buildings or compulsory clearance. No distinct pattern emerges between industries, except the fairly strong preference for younger men by the chemical industry.

Younger men seem to be associated with faster-growing, larger plants, employing over 50 people initially. This is not just a function of young managers being appointed to the branch establishments of larger firms; figures for branch plants alone do not differ markedly from the overall picture. Younger men in smaller transfer moves are often, of course, younger members of a family firm trying to push the company ahead, a move being part of an expansion strategy.

Do different age groups run into different sorts of problems in the early years of the new plant? In transfer moves a higher proportion of younger men (80 per cent) admitted to problems which hindered growth than the group over 40 years of age (67 per cent), but older men were nearly twice as likely to have labour problems. This pattern is repeated in branch plant moves, only 12 per cent of younger men having no problems compared with 25 per cent of the older group, but again older men had labour problems. Labour was the principal cost problem of 25 per cent of the older group, but of only 15 per cent of the younger men in the first two years; and subsequently labour was still a problem for 20 per cent of the older and 13 per cent of the younger men. Problems of finance and developing new markets were proportionally greater for younger than older managers, both in transfer and in branch moves.

Tenure of the First Manager: In measuring the degree to which problems mentioned by survey respondents really do restrict growth which would have otherwise occurred or do result in some kind of adaption, there is one strong test for the effectiveness of the first manager: whether he remains in his job at the plant. In 209 cases, 68 first managers had moved on by the time of the interview. Of these, 10 went in the first year, 18 in the second, 17 in the third, the remainder subsequently. The reasons for their going were varied.

In only 12 cases did interviewees state that the first manager had left for reasons of direct inadequacy, although organizational changes and takeovers accounted for a further 14 cases. Only one man left because he personally disliked the new location. Some left for further promotion, and seven because they were on temporary contracts anyway. Fifty-four per cent of the branch and subsidiary managers left, but only 16 per cent of the chief executives in transfer moves.

A significant relationship exists between slow growth rates of both turnover and employment and rapid replacement of first managers. This is especially so in branch plant moves: 60 per cent of those recording a less than doubling of turnover replaced the first manager, compared with only 27 per cent in plants recording a turnover increase of more than five times. Replacement rates of managers are also higher in those firms giving labour as the principal cost problem in the first two years (49 per cent) of an overall rate of 33 per cent. This rate was 77 per cent in branch plants compared with 54 per cent overall. These findings support the argument that in many location decisions, preparation for the labour function is the weakest area of planning. Previous work (Townroe, 1972) has shown the lack of consultation in the location decision-making process on labour affairs, resulting in problems of both labour recruitment and labour relations. Yet there is no evidence that problems of labour supply, training and cost are worse for longer distance movers. For example, in the Northern Region group of interviewed companies, labour supply was regarded as a problem by 3·1 per cent of the 74 firms (cf. 13·8 per cent overall), labour training by 10·2 per cent (cf. 14·2 per cent) and labour costs by 15·6 per cent (cf. 26·2 per cent).

Of the 68 first managers who had lost their position by the time of the interview, 25 stayed with the company in another capacity. Those (12) who went because of their inexperience, were in plants associated either with very large or with very small parent firms at the time of the move, thus perhaps reflecting the appointment policies of such firms. Rates of leaving overall were proportionally much higher in plants associated with parent firms employing over 500 people (58 per cent, compared with 25 per cent for those employing under 500). Managers leaving because of organizational change all worked in plants employing fewer than 250 people initially. Seven of the 12 inexperienced managers left plants with problems of labour or 'managerial efficiency' which affected both growth rates and costs. Eight of these men worked in branch plants more than 100 miles from the original location, perhaps reflecting inadequate liaison and supervision. Approximately half the changes in chief managers associated with organizational changes were in plants which recorded 'no problems' with labour or growth in the first two years: thus a change of manager may not indicate the existence of a problem, but rather that changes in overall company strategy affect plant performance irrespective of individual success or failure.

Changes in Organizational Structure

One further mechanism of adaption in the post-move situation which may need to be considered as a result of poor locational decision-making and planning is a change in the organizational structure of new plant management. Steed (1971b) has shown how internal company structure may both respond to changes in its environment and increase flexibility of response to exogenous change. Although it is very difficult to distinguish between changes which result, directly or indirectly, from locational choice and those changes brought about by other factors, the survey results are suggestive of adaption processes.

Plant managers were asked how plant organization and its relations with the parent company had changed since opening. Thirty-one per cent of transfers and 49 per cent of branch plant moves cited changes: mergers in 7 transfers and 9 branches increased delegation to 11 branches with full subsidiary status to a further 3, formalization of management structure in one branch and 7 transfers and 'other' changes in a further 9 transfers and 19 branches. Among transfer moves, forced movers were more likely to change their structure than the remainder. No significant relationships, however, could be found between management structure changes and company problems. Those transfers taking over 12 months to break even and to make an adequate profit were twice as likely to formalize their management structures, perhaps reflecting a tightening of control after a period of poor performance. Increases in delegated responsibility in branches went to plants with large batch and continuous flow processes and to those which had moved for growth or marketing reasons. Mergers affected most of those plants with problems of labour or technology. No pattern emerged between organizational change and delays in reaching profitability, except that mergers were divided between those plants breaking even in under three months and in more than four years, thus reflecting two different motives for merging.

Seventeen branch plants were involved in switches of products with other plants in the firm. In six cases, interviewees attributed switches to problems of management or of new locality (other changes resulting from rationalization schemes or exploitation of scale economies). These reasons for switching were especially important in the long distance moves, in plants taking a long time to work up to full capacity and in plants with labour cost problems. The larger the parent company, the greater propensity for switching product lines between plants.

Conclusion

Tiebout (Tiebout, 1957) suggests that 'adaption' by the firm to its locational environment is a process contained within the choice of a 'proper' location, a view also taken by Pred (Pred, 1967). The firm looks at its locational economic environment and adapts to it. The polar opposite to adaption is then 'adoption'. In the extreme, because of uncertainty, firms act locationally in a random manner and the economic system 'adopts' those which fit the economic environment. Tiebout suggests that 'while location of economic activities represents a combination of both views of economic behaviour (adaptive and adoptive), the Alchian view (adoptive) is a major factor' (Tiebout, 1957). Unfortunately, in stressing adoption, Tiebout fails to consider the implications for locational behaviour of the two forms of adaptive behaviour suggested by Alchian: imitation and trial-and-error (Alchian, 1950). Alchian argues that firms will consciously imitate patterns of action observable in past successes, especially when uncertainty is high. 'Imitation affords relief from the necessity of really making decisions innovations, which, if wrong, become "inexcusable"' (Alchian, 1950). Trial-and-error also occurs but requires two conditions: that a trial must be classifiable as a success or failure and that the process induces convergence towards an optimum. Although changing a location is both expensive and time-consuming for an industrial company, changing the use made of any given location need not be difficult. Therefore, both processes, of imitation and trial-and-error, are invoked in response to a new locational environment, once firms realize that uncertainty may be reduced and profits increased by change. Thus, in Alchian's interpretation, adaption continues after locational choice. Tiebout used the polar types of 'adoption' and 'adaption' in a static sense, missing Alchian's dynamic interpretation.

Empirical results in this paper lend limited support to the concept of environmental adaption as a corporate movement towards a changing equilibrium of locational forces (Steed, 1971a). This movement is important in both the evolution of industrial location patterns and the survival and success of individual plants. A number of changes within a plant in the first few years of its life in a new location form part of an adaption process. But difficulties remain in distinguishing between those changes resulting from normal trading problems and from company growth processes, and those resulting from the choice of location and the adequacy of company response to the full process of movement and establishment of a new plant more detailed case-study treatment is thus still required.

The survey shows, however, that many changes do occur in the early lives of new industrial plants. These changes can often be related to the teething troubles of bringing the plant up to profitable and secure operation. Although results relate to one end of a rather crude dichotomy between adaptive and adoptive behaviour, they support both Smith's idea of spatial margins in location theory (Smith, 1971) and Alchian's contention that economic behaviour is closely akin to the theory of biological behaviour. Behavioural theories of industrial location should look beyond the information conditions of the decision itself and concern with the profit maximization assumption, using the adaption process as one mechanism for treating uncertainty.

The results have obvious implications for regional development policies. Those regional incentives which ease cash flows during the early life of a mobile plant are important in attracting the plant to a given area; but they also affect significantly subsequent plant survival and growth. Thus, the full cost effectiveness of rent-free periods in government factories, training grants or limited time-span operational grants may exceed investment allowances or investment grants paid in arrears. Intervention by regional development agencies in the locational decision process—either advisory, in providing advice and information, or compulsory (as with the British industrial development certificate system (see Chapter 15)), in licensing locations for new investment—becomes critical in preventing avoidable and costly post-move adaption. This may affect, therefore, both the choice of firms and localities to receive assistance. The adaption process also suggests that follow-up by regional development agencies after the move may be as important for a minority of movers as the initial effort of attraction. In the United Kingdom, this is something the 1972 Industry Act equips the regional offices of the Department of Trade and Industry and the new Industrial Development Executive to undertake.

Notes

1. See reviews in Keeble (1971), Krumme (1969), Smith (1971) and Townroe (1971).
2. The word 'adaption', rather than the word 'adaptation', has been used in this chapter to denote the particular usage.

References

Alchian, A., 1950, 'Uncertainty, evolution and economic theory', *Journal of Political Economy,* **58** (2), 211–21.

Behran, J. N., 1969, *Some Patterns in the Rise of the Multi-National Enterprise* (North Carolina: Chapel Hill).

Chisholm, M., 1971, 'In search of a basis for location theory: micro-economics or welfare economics?', *Progress in Geography,* **3**.

Keeble, D. E., 1971, 'Employment mobility in Britain', Chapter 2 in *Spatial Policy Problems of the British Economy,* ed. M. Chisholm and G. Manners (Cambridge University Press).

Krumme, G., 1969, 'Towards a geography of enterprise', *Economic Geography,* **45**, 30–40.

Loasby, B. J., 1971, 'Hypothesis and paradigm in the theory of the firm', *Economic Journal,* **81** (324) 863–85.

Luttrell, W. F., 1962, *Factory Location and Industrial Movement* (London: National Institute of Economic and Social Research).

Machlup, F., 1967, 'Theories of the firm: marginalist, behavioural, managerial', *American Economic Review,* **57** (1), 1–33.

Moseley, M. J. and P. M. Townroe, 1973, 'Linkage adjustment following industrial movement', *Tijdschrift voor Economische en Social Geografie* (forthcoming).

Pred, A., 1967, *Behaviour and Location: Foundations for a Geographic and Dynamic Location Theory,* Part 1, Lund Studies in Geography, Series B, **27**.

Smith, D. M., 1971, *Industrial Location: An Economic Geographical Analysis* (New York: Wiley).

Steed, G. P. F., 1971a, 'Forms of corporate environmental adaptation', *Tijdschrift voor Economische en Sociale Geografie,* **62**, 90–4.

Steed, G. P. F., 1971b, 'Internal organization, firm integration and locational change: the Northern Ireland linen complex, 1954–64', *Economic Geography,* **47** (3), 371–83.

Tiebout, C. M., 1957, 'Location theory, empirical evidence and economic evolution', *Papers and Proceedings of the Regional Science Association,* **3**, 74–86.

Townroe, P. M., 1971, *Industrial Location Decisions: A Study in Management Behaviour,* Occasional Paper, 15, Centre for Urban and Regional Studies, University of Birmingham.

Townroe, P. M., 1972, 'Some behavioural considerations in the industrial location decision', *Regional Studies,* **6** (3), 261–72.

Woodward, J., 1965, *Industrial Organizations: Theory and Practice* (Oxford University Press).

12

Manufacturing Linkages and the Search for Suppliers and Markets

WILLIAM LEVER

Most studies of industrial decision-making have concentrated upon either the initial locational decision, or subsequent decisions to relocate or establish branch plants. Such a cross-sectional approach relies upon equilibrium theories, whereas industrial decision-making is clearly a continuous process of evaluation in a dynamic situation. The search and learning processes of manufacturers, therefore, are more appropriately studied in everyday decisions about the choice of suppliers and markets rather than in the often once-and-for-all decision about location. Access to suppliers and customers has been central to much of location theory in, firstly, minimizing aggregate costs of assembling inputs and, secondly, maximizing profits by trading off input transport costs against access to potential markets. Since the early 1950s, however, profit-maximizing models of location have been criticized because they make no allowance for either the entrepreneur's information deficiences or the possibility that he may trade off part of his theoretical maximum profit against psychosocial gains such as risk minimization or environmental amenity (Katona and Morgan, 1951; Simon, 1957; Eversley, 1965). Nevertheless, once the locational decision is taken, on whatever basis, the entrepreneur must then make decisions concerning possible suppliers of inputs and possible customers.

Studies of industrial location in the 1950s and early 1960s tended to stress the unimportance of transport costs as a location factor, compared with costs of labour, premises and land and external economies frequently associated with major urban centres (Hague and Dunning, 1952; Hill, 1954; Luttrell, 1962). More recent work has demonstrated that transport costs have been consistently underestimated (Frost, 1969; Edwards, 1970). The increasing availability of data, much of it from the Census of Production, led Edwards to conclude that 'it is probable that transport accounts for at least 9 per cent of the total costs of producing and distributing'. In addition to this 9 per cent—which represents the cost of maintaining a firm's transport fleet and payments made to other carriers and to the distributive trades— other distance costs may also be incurred. These include the costs of information transfer (post, telephone) and personal travel, higher levels of stock-holding necessitated by remoteness from suppliers and costs incurred by the loss of face-to-face contact between suppliers and customers in industries such as castings, subcontracted metalworking, chemicals and construction were the customer's specifications dictate the nature of the product. Thus, although the costs of access to suppliers and customers represent only a small proportion of all production costs in a highly competitive situation where labour, space and capital costs are fairly uniform, a manufacturing firm's profitability is critically dependent upon the minimization of these access costs.

If access costs are important to manufacturers they clearly constrain both the location and the subsequent decisions about suppliers and markets: if they are relatively unimportant the manufacturer will stress other factor costs, such as wages, and there will be less reason to seek to minimize aggregate access costs or to reevaluate suppliers and markets at frequent intervals.

Most assessments of the importance of transport costs have taken data aggregated to industrial group level. Recent studies comparing interregional distributions of industrial employment have found a general tendency for industries (which are known from input-output analysis to be functionally linked) to be similarly located (McCarty, Hook and Knos, 1956; Richter, 1969; Streit, 1969; Lever, 1972). This appears to be true not only for industries located during the nineteenth century and handling bulky, low value goods, but also for lighter, higher value goods handled by industries with the most rapid recent rates of growth. Such research indicates that transport costs are important and that peripheral regions of Britain are at a transport cost disadvantage in relation to national markets—for which they attempt to compensate by establishing relatively self-sufficient regional economic structures (Chisholm and O'Sullivan, 1973).

In looking at the decision process as it concerns the selection of suppliers and customers, however, research at the level of industrial type is clearly inappropriate. It was Wood who pointed out that

> the behaviour of firms may perhaps be explained more effectively with reference to a multi-variate classification ... A more useful differentiation (than by industry) might categorize plants according to their position within the chain of production, their organizational status or their ownership background. The performance of these categories may well be more predictable than the traditional division of manufacturing into, for instance, metals, textile or wood-based industries. (Wood, 1969)

Analysis of the backward and forward linkages of the individual manufacturing plant is very time-consuming. Some analysts, notably Salt and James, limited their enquiry to questioning the managers of only one or two establishments (James, 1964; Salt, 1967). More commonly, people in a larger number of establishments are asked general questions about linkages, usually to facilitate comparisons between contributions made to a regional economy through the income multiplier by various industries (Steed, 1968; Britton, 1969). This chapter takes the former approach, using the collection of detailed data from officials, usually purchasing and sales managers, of a relatively small number of manufacturing establishments: firstly, to assess how industry, or rather the type of goods handled, affects managerial decisions about linkage length, secondly, to test whether characteristics of the establishment such as size, organizational structure and growth rate affect the linkage length of plants within an industry and, thirdly, to use data over time to relate changes in linkages to type of plant and managerial strategy.

The Selection of Establishments for Survey

As an intensive study of a comparatively small number of plants was proposed, the plants were chosen carefully in order to test hypotheses about the variables which affect managerial decision on linkages. If the relative importance of industrial type and plant type are to be tested as variables explaining linkage length, the selection of establishments becomes a two-stage process. Firstly, a number of industries are chosen which, hypothetically, should provide a range of linkage characteristics. Secondly, within those industries plants are chosen in which different purchasing and sales strategies are likely to occur. For several reasons the choice of industrial type is important in explaining linkages. The national distribution of plants engaged in any industry varies widely. Foodstuffs and clothing manufacture are widely dispersed, while oil refining and woollen textiles manufacture are concentrated in a few locations. Industries of the first type are likely to be located near their markets and thus to have short forward linkages. The length of their backward linkages will depend upon the spatial distribution of plants in the industry supplying them with inputs. Foodstuffs based on grain milling products will have short backward linkages as grain milling is relatively ubiquitous. The clothing industry, however, draws the bulk of its supplies from the highly concentrated cotton and woollen textile industries and therefore has long backward linkages. Industries which, spatially, are highly concentrated tend to have long forward linkages when they supply the national market, as for example, oil refinery products and soap manufacture. Short forward linkages occur where sales managers can identify a single concentrated market for their product, as in the textile machinery industry.

In order to compare the degree of dispersion or concentration of employment in industries a coefficient of localization (L) was devised based on Florence's similarly named measure (Florence, 1944), with the formula

$$L_i = \frac{1X_i - X_a 1}{2}$$

where X_i is the proportion of employment in industry i in region X, and X_a is the proportion of all manufacturing employment in region X. The coefficient has the disadvantage of being affected by the number of regions over which the comparison is made: as the number of regions was held constant for all industries it does not affect the validity of the measure, however, in this instance. A value of $L_i = 100$ represents the unlikely case in which all employment in industry i is located in one region and that region has no other employment, whereas a value of $L_i = 0$ represents the case in which employment in industry i is distributed amongst the regions in exactly the same proportions as employment in all manufacturing. Using data from the 1966 Sample Census Economic Activity Tables, the coefficient was calculated over 62 sub-regions for Minimum List Headings 211–499 of the 1958 Standard Industrial Classification that in turn was grouped into 57 industrial types on the lines of the 1953 Input–output Tables for the United Kingdom.

Table 12.1 lists the coefficients of localization for each of the 57 industries, from 21·1 for woollen spinning and weaving to 0·9 for timber and miscellaneous wooden products. Manufacturing processes which depend upon the import of bulky raw materials such as soap, oil refining and sugar are found to have high coefficients as are those industries such as coke ovens and cement manufacture which are dependent upon particular limited geological resources. Low coefficients are recorded by those industries such as confectionery, miscellaneous foodstuffs and drink whose products are widely demanded but difficult to transport over long distances. Such industries as leather, agricultural machinery and grain milling tend to be widely dispersed as they are linked with dispersed agricultural production. Industries involving heavy materials with low values such as miscellaneous building materials and timber have the lowest coefficient of all. Lastly, there is a tendency for miscellaneous and residual industrial groups (i.e. those whose Minimum List Heading number ends in 9) to have low coefficient as the aggregation of specialist industries into heterogeneous industrial groups may conceal their regional concentration.

If a single explanatory variable is to be found to account for differing degrees of spatial concentration then the value/weight ratio of product appears, intuitively, to be the most promising. Data on the value/weight ratio is difficult to obtain: the New York Metropolitan Region study offers the most comprehensive list and this, supplemented by data from the British 1963 Census of Production, forms the basis of the cents per pound values in Table 12.1 (Chinitz, 1970). A rank correlation test between the coefficient of

Table 12.1. Coefficients of Localization and Value/Weight Ratios for 57 Industries in the U.K. in 1966

Industry	L	Value cents/lb	Industry	L	Value cents/lb
Wool	21·1	543	Motor vehicles	4·3	51
* Soap, oil, fats	11·8	15	Aircraft	4·2	722
* Textile machiney	11·4	116	Industrial plant	4·2	83
Hosiery, lace	10·6	912	* Other vehicles	4·2	51
Pottery, glass	10·6	225	Pharmaceuticals	3·9	168
Footwear	9·7	422	* Chocolate, confectionery	3·8	70
* Oil refining	7·8	3	Radio, telecommunica-		
* Manmade fibre	7·8	44	tions	3·7	155
* Sugar	7·6	8	Paper, board	3·6	48
* Cotton	7·6	280	* Synthetic resin, plastic	3·5	112
† Other metal goods	7·6	50	Electrical machiney	3·5	59
* Coke ovens	7·5	10	Machine tools	3·4	102
† Non-ferrous metals	7·3	95	Contractor's plant	3·4	36
* Wire, cable	7·0	45	Paper products	3·2	13
* Texile finishing	6·8	67	† Other chemicals	2·7	22
Industrial engineering	6·7	116	Rubber	2·6	49
* Cement	6·2	2	† Miscellaneous		
Shipbuilding	6·2	—	manufactures	2·5	51
Scientific instruments	6·2	4047	Clothing	2·4	108
* Office machiney	6·0	174	* Leather	2·4	37
Engineer's tools	6·0	59	* Agricultural machinery	2·3	—
Tobacco	5·9	—	† Other food	1·7	31
Furniture	5·4	33	† Miscellaneous		
Printing	5·4	55	mechanical engineering	1·6	—
* Other textiles	5·1	67	† Non-electrical machiney	1·5	—
Iron, steel	4·9	41	Drink	1·5	6
Paint, ink	4·9	22	* Grain milling	1·4	5
Light metals	4·7	95	* Other cereals	1·2	15
* Cans, metal boxes	4·5	17	† Other building materials	1·1	4
Electrical goods	4·4	140	Timber	0·9	—

* Eliminated because of insufficient plants in study area.
† Eliminated becuase of residual category.

localization and the value per pound of output yields a value of $R = +0.3$ where $n = 51$ is significant at the 5.0% level. It does therefore seem probable that industrial processes which involve goods with high value/weight ratios are concentrated in relatively few locations as their high value products can support high transport costs incurred by long linkages. Conversely, industries involving low value/weight goods are widely distributed to minimize linkage lengths. Empirical evidence to support this conclusion can be drawn from Table 12.2 compiled from the New York Metropolitan Region study. Industries producing low value goods such as petroleum, fertilizers, concrete, building materials and grains products sell more than twice as much within

Table 12.2. Flows of Goods from Firms in the New York Metropolitan Region, 1956

	NYMR	200–500 miles	500–800 miles	800 miles
Low value/weight	74%	15%	8%	3%
High value/weight	36%	24%	27%	13%

the New York Region as do those producing high value goods such as scientific instruments, aircraft, tailored clothing, footwear and electrical equipment which sell up to 40% of their product to customers more than 500 miles distant. Comparable data for Britain is not available but the Ministry of Transport Survey of Road Goods Traffic in 1964 suggests similar conclusions. Of thirty commodities listed only four have average journey lengths exceeding 50 miles—animal and vegetable fats and oils, plastics, iron and steel finished products, and electrical and non-electrical machinery. Similarly, only four have a average journey lengths of less than 25 miles—coal, crude minerals, iron ore, and diary and poultry produce.

A plant's position in the chain of production will influence plant management in their choice of linkages. Industries which are heavily dependent upon bulky, low value raw materials will have their backward linkages shaped by the distribution of indigenous raw material sources and ports. At the other end of the chain of production are plants whose managers located close to large urban markets as their forward linkages are shaped by the location of final demand (Pred, 1964). As most chains of production involve additions in value to the product and reduction in weight, access to market should be less important to firms than access to suppliers—except where special conditions, such as processes which increase the bulk, fragility or perishability of the product or which require face-to-face contact with the customer, apply. The proportion of inputs from the primary sector (agriculture, forestry, mining and quarrying) purchased by each industry was calculated from the input–output tables as was the proportion of sales going to final demand. These values were also used in the selection of industries for study.

Of the 57 industries, only 37 had sufficient establishments in the study area—West Central Scotland—to offer a wide enough choice of establishment. Of these 37, nine were residual industrial categories which were eliminated from the list because of the difficulty of generalizing about product types and linkage decisions in such categories. From the remaining 21 industrial groups, six were selected for study (Table 12.3). These provide a wide range of localization values, from glass (with the fourth highest) to light clothing (with the tenth lowest), and a wide range of value/weight ratios, from glass (with the seventh highest) to paper products (with the eighth lowest). One industry, glass, depends quite heavily upon raw material inputs and one, light clothing, upon sales to the public. Finally, the glass

Table 12.3. Industrial Groups Selected for Study in West Central Scotland: Their Localization Coefficients, their Output, Inputs and Sales Values

Industry	Minimum List Headings classification	Coefficient of localization	Output value cents/lb	% Raw material input	% Sales to final demand
Glass	463	10·6	225	15·9	27·0
Engineer's small tools	333	6·0	59	8·3	24·3
Paint	274	4·9	22	1·0	27·4
Electrical machinery	361	3·5	59	0·7	64·7
Paper products	482/3	3·2	13	0·4	19·5
Light clothing	444/5	2·4	108	0·2	96·4
Median, all industries		4·1	54	1·0	52·7

and paper products (predominantly cardboard or corrugated paper boxes) industries should offer some insight into the effect of increases in product fragility upon linkage lengths.

Having selected the industries for study, consistent manufacturing plants should be chosen to test further hypotheses about linkage lengths and search procedures. Two variables might explain differences between manufacturing establishments (in the same area and engaged in the same industrial process: in the choice of suppliers and customers size and organizational structure. There are several reasons why, within a given Industry, large plants will on average have longer backward and foward linkages than small ones. Stigler, describing the economics of information, asserted that the range of prices of any uniform good represented a measure of the level of ignorance in the market (Stigler, 1961). Economies of scale are available to managers of large firms in their search for cheap suppliers, whereas those of small firms may be either unaware of the range of prices prevailing for a uniform good or unwilling or unable to finance a search for lower input prices. Although Stigler was concerned only with the costs of inputs into any given establishment, the same argument can be applied to management's search for better markets for its plant's products. Chinitz emphasized that production costs, rather than transport costs, were becoming increasingly important and that large firms would tend to internalize economies to reduce production costs: thus they were less likely to have short distance linkages with firms performing ancillary roles such as the supply of specialized components (Chinitz, 1961). This contrasts with small firms which tend to have short linkages with highly specialized firms in segmented production sequences such as those in the furniture and clothing industries which are characteristic of many major British city centres (Martin, 1964). There is also evidence that large firms are able to force concessionary freight rates from hauliers because they generate more freight, whereas small establishments cannot (Elliot, 1948;

316

Taylor, 1970). Hill suggests that small firms are likely to be locally-owned and located near the residence of the manager/owner who already knows potential suppliers and customers before he sets up business. His initial linkages are therefore likely to be short and he is unlikely to extend them to find cheaper inputs or a better price for his product. He is likely to be a satisficer rather than a profit maximizer, preferring to be satisfied with a reasonable profit rather than attempting to achieve a maximum profit. Such attitudes were commonly found in the recent British Committee of Inquiry into Small Firms and were typified by the owner of a small printing firm saying, 'You want a reasonable return on your capital, but basically it's not the money, you do it for personal satisfaction (Bolton Committee, 1971, p. 24).

Little evidence exists by which to test the hypothesis that mean linkage length varies directly with plant size. Keeble's findings on 114 firms in north-west London, shown in Table 12.4, present some supporting evidence but a test on the data is not very conclusive, finding that the difference between establishments with fewer than 50 employees and those with more than 50 employees is significant only at the 10 per cent level (Keeble, 1969). Small firms, however, were more likely to have more than 25 per cent of their linkages with other firms in north-west London than were large ones.

Linkages patterns of plants in any given industry are affected by the organizational structure of that plant within the parent company. It is possible to define three types of plant: (1) the indigenously-owned single plant firm, (2) the branch plant of a non-locally (i.e. non-Scottish in this case) owned and controlled company and (3) a single plant company formerly located outside Scotland and now located in Scotland. Intuitively, indigenous firms are probably more dependent upon local suppliers and local customers than branch plants or mover firms. The managers of mover firms have, by definition, generally experienced input costs and output prices in an alternative location and may therefore choose to maintain some of their former, longer, linkages. Managers of branch plants may be subject to centralized

Table 12.4. Size of Plant and Linkages: North-West London

Employees	Percentage of local linkages			Number of plants
	> 25%	25%–1%	0%	
	%	%	%	
10–24	55	10	35	20
25–49	29	19	52	21
50–99	19	23	58	26
100–249	16	33	51	27
250–499	40	10	50	10
500–999	20	30	50	10
Total	27%	23%	50%	114

corporate purchasing and sales controls operated from outside the region in which the branch plant has been located.

Fulton and Hoch suggested that parent companies often set up branch plants to capture, or make more certain, markets distant from their main manufacturing plants—providing that the cost of transporting inputs to the new branch did not become prohibitive (Fulton and Hoch, 1959). If this market capture theory of branch location is correct, it implies that branch plants tend to have long backward linkages and short forward linkages. Regional development policies in Britain, however, have maintained the hope that where large companies can be induced to set up branch plants in the more depressed areas these branch plants may develop short backward linkages as component suppliers locate close to the branch plant or as supplies are purchased from pre-existing indigenous plants. Studies of the dispersal of branch plants of motor vehicle companies from the Midlands to Scotland and Merseyside found, in fact, that a set of short backward linkages failed to develop. Less information exists on mover firms, possibly because they are much fewer in number. Keeble, however, did find that when large engineering firms moved from London to the New Towns, small subcontracting firms were unwilling to accompany them, thereby lengthening the linkages of the larger firms. A parallel example may be drawn from Friedley's work in which he demonstrates that mover households make a higher proportion of their domestic purchases at non-local shops because they are aware of a wider range (both spatially and economically) of alternatives. Hague and Dunning suggest that the linkages of branch plants remain longer than those of mover firms as the latter turn more readily to local suppliers.

Thus, within the six selected industries the establishments selected for study should cover these two parameters of size and organizational structure. Unfortunately the number of mover firms available for study is so small and the individuals form such a heterogeneous group that this group had to be excluded. The Howard Report lists 307 mover firms and branch plants locating in Scotland between 1945 and 1965, but of these only 40 are movers and the remaining 267 are branches of non-Scottish firms. Data on indigenous single-plant firms were drawn from the Glasgow University Register of Industrial Establishments. From these two sources, four establishments in each of the six industries were selected—one large local, one large branch, one small local and one small branch—a total of twenty-four. As far as possible the four establishments in each industry were identical in their processes, inputs and products and, where possible, were established about 1964–5.

Data were collected from their purchases and sales records for either the calendar years 1966 and 1970 or the financial years 1966–7, 1968–9 and 1970–1. It has been suggested that such an approach often fails as many manufacturers purchase their inputs from stockholders rather than manufacturers; but this was rarely so in this case. The only instances of purchase records failing to show the geographical location of the previous stage in the production chain were (1) the purchase of some specialized toolmakers' steels from the British Steel Corporation which did not specify which BSC plant actually made the steel and (2) some imported raw materials for glass manufacture which were listed under the importing agent's addresses in London. In both cases the manufacturers concerned knew the actual location of the supply sources, i.e. in steel-making and mining. On the output side some problems were encountered where manufacturers sold finished goods to national retail chains which owned large regional warehouses. In these cases, relatively few in number, the forward linkages were recorded as terminating at these regional warehouses although clearly the actual locations of final demand were spread more widely than was implied by the locations of the few major distribution centres.

Linkages 1970–71

The 24 plants' purchases for the year 1970 or 1970–71 totalled fractionally less than £6 million of which only 14·9 per cent was spent in West Central Scotland and a further 5·1 per cent was spent in the rest of Scotland. Thus by value, one-fifth of all backward linkages were with suppliers in Scotland as compared to 20·5 per cent with South East England, 17·1 per cent with North West England, 12·0 per cent with the West Midlands and 20·7 per cent with abroad. Other British regions, as Table 12.5 shows, were rarely linked with the Scottish manufacturing plants (e.g. a range from Yorkshire, 3·7 per cent, to Northern Ireland, 0·02 per cent).

If these general figures do not suggest that entrepreneurs chose to locate in West Central Scotland for reasons of access to suppliers, the figures for sales do suggest a reason (Table 12.6). Sales by the 24 establishments in 1970 or 1970–1 totalled £12·4 million of which 59·0 per cent went to customers in West Central Scotland, while a further 16·7 per cent went to customers in the remainder of Scotland. Elsewhere, the North West (6·4 per cent of all sales), the South East (4·6 per cent) and exports (4·1 per cent) formed the more important markets. Other British regions each took between 2·6 per cent (West Midlands) and 0·02 per cent (Wales) of sales.

Table 12.7 also demonstrates the difference between the regional distribution of backward and forward linked firms. Of the 1328 firms which supplied inputs to the 24 plants in 1970, 630 or 43·9 per cent were located in Scotland, while 17·0 per cent were in the South East, 13·4 per cent in the North West and 9·1 per cent were in the West Midlands. The fact that the 43·9 per cent of linked firms in Scotland provided only 20·0 per cent of the inputs reflects the low average value of backward linkages with local firms. Whereas each supplier sold an average of £4,000 worth of inputs to the study establishments, firms in Scotland sold on average only £1,900 worth

Table 12.5. Purchases by 24 Selected Plants in West Central Scotland, 1970–71, by Region and Industry

	Glass	Electrical machinery	Paper products	Engineers' small tools	Paint	Light clothing	Total
	%	%	%	%	%	%	%
Scotland	7·68	25·16	13·87	53·63	37·05	18·83	19·98
North England	1·71	3·72	0·07	0·22	4·83	1·43	1·96
North West	37·91	10·52	1·96	1·25	12·58	48·83	17·71
Yorks/Humberside	3·02	5·90	0·40	12·82	2·84	11·03	3·69
East Midlands	2·44	0·95	0·05	4·03	0·02	8·35	1·34
West Midlands	6·41	28·23	5·51	12·27	5·26	1·15	11·96
East Anglia	—	—	—	0·37	0·75	—	0·10
South West	0·22	0·91	0·70	0·62	—	0·18	0·58
South East	11·06	25·15	37·27	10·65	25·84	9·54	20·50
Wales	—	0·23	1·02	—	9·62	0·08	1·53
Northern Ireland	—	—	—	—	—	0·38	0·02
Total U.K.	70·48	100·00	60·85	100·00	98·80	99·82	79·30
Rest of world	29·52	—	39·15	—	1·20	0·18	20·70

Table 12.6. Sales by 24 Selected Plants in West Central Scotland, 1970–71, by Region and Industry

	Glass	Electrical machinery	Paper products	Engineers' small tools	Paint	Light clothing	Total
	%	%	%	%	%	%	%
Scotland	95·39	14·15	91·11	76·17	77·96	43·37	75·68
North England	1·03	0·58	5·88	2·58	8·06	5·61	2·28
North West	0·72	23·76	0·86	5·10	1·80	16·40	6·41
Yorks/Humberside	1·18	10·35	0·17	5·01	0·40	11·59	1·25
East Midlands	—	0·99	0·05	1·05	0·33	0·58	0·33
West Midlands	0·06	13·25	0·42	4·41	3·69	1·15	2·61
East Anglia	—	0·05	—	1·46	—	—	0·07
South West	—	0·15	0·14	—	—	1·27	0·81
South East	0·06	16·97	0·81	2·94	5·97	16·35	5·56
Wales	0·06	—	—	—	—	—	0·02
Northern Ireland	1·17	0·15	0·53	—	1·79	2·12	0·83
Total U.K.	99·65	80·41	99·99	98·74	100·00	98·42	95·95
Rest of world	0·35	19·59	0·01	1·26	—	1·58	4·05

Table 12.7. Linkages by 24 Selected Plants in West Central Scotland, 1970–71

| | Backward linkages | | Forward linkages | |
	Number	Percentage	Number	Percentage
		%		%
Scotland	630	43·9	1543	66·3
North England	28	1·9	124	5·3
North West	193	13·4	201	8·7
Yorks/Humberside	80	5·6	99	4·2
East Midlands	65	4·4	21	0·9
West Midlands	130	9·1	52	2·2
East Anglia	3	0·2	7	0·3
South West	12	1·3	14	0·6
South East	244	17·0	169	7·4
Wales	12	0·8	5	0·2
Northern Ireland	3	0·2	63	2·7
Total U.K.	1407	97·8	2298	98·8
Rest of world	31	2·2	29	1·2

of inputs and firms in West Central Scotland sold only £1,650 worth. By contrast, suppliers in South Lancashire averaged sales of £21,000, those in South West Wales averaged £16,000, those on Merseyside averaged £14,600 and those in the outer metropolitan London region averaged £11,000. On the sales side, however, average sales per forward linkage in 1970 were £5,330, but £6,070 for Scottish and £6,630 for West Central Scottish linkages. These figures support the initial impression that a wide range of plants were located in the area to serve local markets and were consequently willing to haul most inputs over considerable distances to Scotland whilst relying upon the local economy for minor inputs. This is strengthened if input linkages are divided into four types—inputs to (1) the manufacturing process, (2) capital equipment, (3) subcontracting and (4) overheads. The proportion of inputs purchased in Central Scotland (West Central, Central and Edinburgh) is only 16·0 per cent compared with 46·5 per cent of expenditure on overheads, 49·7 per cent of expenditure on capital equipment and 89·7 per cent of subcontracting.

Against this general background, Tables 12.5 and 12.6 demonstrate that there are considerable differences between the linkages of the six industries selected for study. The glass industry buys sands from the North West and South East England and sheet glass from France and Belgium. Sales, among which whisky bottles make up a prominent part, go predominantly to Scotland, while window glass is distributed more widely to Northern Ireland and the northern English regions. The electrical machinery industry buys its inputs almost equally from Scotland, the West Midlands and the South East; its sales are widespread, almost 20 per cent going for exports and the

North West being the largest single British regional market. The paper products industry buys almost 40 per cent of its paper input from both the South East (i.e. the Thamesside paper mills) and abroad (Scandinavia and Canada) as Scottish-made paper is largely used for newsprint; sales of the bulky paper products such as corrugated boxes go mainly to Scotland and the North East. Establishments manufacturing engineers' small tools have the shortest backward linkages of the six industries since they rely on Scottish steel, supplemented by special steels available only from Sheffield. Moreover, three-quarters of their output is sold to Scottish engineering industries. The paint industry buys most inputs from chemical industries in Scotland, the North West and the South East and sells almost four-fifths of its output within Scotland. Lastly, the light clothing industry buys almost half of its inputs from the Lancashire cotton and synthetic textile industry, plus small amounts from the other textile-producing regions— Scotland, Yorkshire and the East Midlands; sales are widely distributed, with Scotland (43 per cent), the North West (16 per cent), the South East (16 per cent) and Yorkshire (12 per cent) being the main markets.

It was hypothesized earlier that value/weight ratios of goods handled might provide the best explanatory variable for inter-industry comparisons of linkage patterns. Initially, the relationship between linkage length and value seems poor. The glass and clothing industries produce high value goods which theoretically can bear the high cost of long linkages while tools and electrical machinery are of medium value and paint and paper products are of low value. Although the high value industries buy few of their inputs locally, the medium value industries buy more locally than do the low value industries (Table 12.8). Moreover, while the low value industries sell the highest proportion of their output locally the high value industries sell more locally than do the medium value industries. The initial hypothesis however does stand up better if two of the twelve sets of linkages are removed. Whilst glass products do have a high value/weight ratio their bulk and fragility make it unsurprising that most of their forward linkages are short. Whilst raw paper has a low value/weight ratio the unsuitability of the Scottish

Table 12.8. Value/Weight Ratios and Scottish Linkages, 1970–71

	Value cents/lb	Scottish purchases	Scottish sales
		%	%
Glass	225	7·7	(95·4)
Clothing	108	18·8	43·4
Electric machinery	59	25·2	14·1
Small tools	59	53·6	76·2
Paint	22	37·1	78·0
Paper products	13	(13·9)	91·1

paper industry for the manufacturer of cartons forces the paper products industry to accept long backward linkages to Canadian, Scandinavian and Thamesside suppliers—particularly as the bulky nature of the product, even in knockdown form, necessitates the minimization of forward linkage lengths. With these two sets of linkages removed, rank correlations tests, between value/weight ratio of goods and proportions of local purchases and sales, yield values which are significant at the 5 per cent level. The general truth that high value/weight goods travel longer distances, both as backward and forward linkages, does seem to be borne out by Table 12.9. Of all linkages involving goods worth less than £50 per ton 75·0 per cent were with Scottish firms and 6·8 per cent were with firms in North England, of those involving goods worth between £50 and £500 per ton the proportions were 64·3 per cent and 2·7 per cent respectively, and of those involving goods with more than £500 per ton the proportions were 48·5 per cent and 4·6 per cent respectively. By contrast, linkages both backward and forward with the more distant regions were much more common amongst high and medium value goods. Some 7·2 per cent of high value linkages and 8·0 per cent of medium value linkages were with firms in the Midlands compared with only 3·2 per cent of low value linkages; for the South East respective figures were 12·1 per cent, 10·2 per cent and 3·8 per cent.

Whilst it is therefore possible to identify some regularities between the spatial distribution of plants in an industry, the value and type of goods handled and the length of both forward and backward linkages, it is debatable to what extent findings at the industry level hold good for all plants within that industry. Differences between plants within an industry may be as,

Table 12.9. Value/Weight Ratios and All Linkages, 1970–71

	< £50 per ton		£50–£500 per ton		> £500 per ton	
	Number	Percentage %	Number	Percentage %	Number	Percentage %
Scotland	300	75·0	988	64·3	885	48·5
North England	27	6·8	42	2·7	83	4·6
North West	27	6·8	84	5·5	285	15·5
Yorks/Humberside	12	3·0	53	3·5	114	6·3
East Midlands	5	1·2	17	1·1	64	3·5
West Midlands	8	2·0	106	6·9	68	3·7
East Anglia	—	—	5	0·3	5	0·3
South West	4	1·0	9	0·6	20	1·1
South East	15	3·8	156	10·2	221	12·1
Wales	—	—	12	0·8	5	0·3
North Ireland	2	0·5	34	2·2	30	1·6
Total U.K.	400	100·0	1506	98·2	1790	98·3
Rest of world	—	—	28	1·8	31	1·7

324

or more, important than differences between industries in explaining the choice of suppliers and customers and the resultant linkage lengths. It was hypothesized that if inter-plant differences were significant then the two best explanatory variables could be the size of plant and organizational structures of plant.

Table 12.10 compares the regional distribution of purchases and sales of the twelve larger plants averaging 200 employees and the twelve smaller plants averaging 50 employees in the survey. There is a tendency for the managers of small plants to purchase more of their inputs from Scottish firms than those of large ones (27·5 per cent; 18·4 per cent) though the difference is accounted for by more purchases from the rest of Scotland (11·2 per cent; 3·9 per cent) than by purchases from West Central Scotland (16·3 per cent; 14·5 per cent). There is little difference in the percentage of purchases made from suppliers in the northern English regions (North, North West, Yorkshire, East Midlands) but large plants are much more likely to buy inputs from the West Midlands (2·1 per cent; 14·3 per cent) and the South East (6·4 per cent; 23·9 per cent). If large plants do enjoy economies of scale in transport costs, as hypothesized, then these economies only appear to affect linkage lengths significantly at distances exceeding about 300 miles. Curiously, a larger proportion of inputs for small plants come from abroad than for large plants (34·4 per cent; 16·9 per cent). This is largely due to the dependence of the glass and paper product industries upon imported supplies and the fact that the small plants in these industries were considerably larger (average =70 employees) than the small plants of the other four industries (average =25 employees) thereby weighting the average proportion of purchases from abroad. The differences between the

Table 12.10. Purchases and Sales, 1970–71, by Size of Plant

	Purchases Large	Small	Sales Large	Small
	%	%	%	%
Scotland	18·42	27·46	69·41	85·25
North England	1·98	1·98	1·90	5·41
North West	17·37	19·74	7·60	1·76
Yorks/Humberside	3·55	4·41	4·09	0·33
East Midlands	1·43	2·06	0·39	0·14
West Midlands	14·31	2·07	3·96	1·74
East Anglia	0·12	—	0·12	—
South West	0·65	0·32	0·17	0·09
South East	23·89	6·40	6·36	2·22
Wales	1·39	2·10	0·02	0·01
Northern Ireland	0·02	0·02	0·87	0·58
Total U.K.	83·15	66·57	94·86	99·99
Rest of world	16·85	34·43	5·14	0·01

input linkages of large and small plants were compared with the null hypothesis and the difference was found to be significant at the 5 per cent level. The difference between the forward linkage patterns of large and small plants is less significant but there is a tendency, as the original hypothesis suggested, for small plants to sell more of their output locally than large plants. Insofar as the sales managers of manufacturing firms 'select' their customers by directing their advertising material and sales representatives at potential customers it does seem that those of small manufacturing establishments do concentrate more single-mindedly upon the local market whereas economies of scale in information dispersal allow those of larger manufacturers to look to more distant potential markets.

Table 12.11 compares the regional distribution of the purchases and sales of the twelve indigenous single-plant companies and of the twelve branches of non-Scottish companies. An χ^2 test on the regional distribution of purchases finds the difference to be significant at the 1 per cent level. There is, therefore, a high probability of a real difference between the backward linkages of the two types of plant. The significant difference, however, is not in their relative dependence upon Scottish suppliers for whilst local firms took 23·7 per cent of their inputs from Scotland, branch plants took 18·5 per cent of their inputs from Scotland. The major difference is that local firms took 33·1 per cent of their inputs from the North West compared with branch plants which took only 11·8 per cent. The branch plants were more dependent upon supplies from the West Midlands and the South East (36·7 per cent) than were local firms (21·5 per cent) and upon supplies from abroad (26·5 per cent; 5·8 per cent).

It is difficult to estimate the effect that the location of the branch plant's

Table 12.11. Purchases and Sales, 1970–71, by Type of Plant

	Purchases Branch	Indigenous	Sales Branch	Indigenous
	%	%	%	%
Scotland	18·52	23·70	65·07	87·89
North England	1·77	2·40	5·04	0·72
North West	11·75	33·12	8·47	1·99
Yorks/Humberside	3·78	3·44	4·57	0·71
East Midlands	0·50	3·51	0·37	0·26
West Midlands	14·30	5·91	4·17	1·56
East Anglia	0·13	—	—	0·23
South West	0·05	1·94	0·06	0·29
South East	22·38	15·58	5·76	4·74
Wales	0·33	4·58	0·02	—
Northern Ireland	—	0·08	0·66	1·07
Total U.K.	73·52	94·25	94·24	99·48
Rest of world	26·48	5·75	5·76	0·52

Table 12.12. Backward Linkages of Branch Plants by Headquarters Location

Purchases from	Headquarters located in		
	North West and Yorks	Midlands	South East
	%	%	%
Scotland	26·79	48·42	24·79
N.W. and Yorks.	17·47	8·62	28·56
Midlands	10·40	28·84	7·70
South East	13·48	13·64	13·28
Other	31·85*	0·48	25·67*

* Mostly imports.

main manufacturing unit has on decisions made by the branch plant about subsequent purchasing patterns. Of the twelve branch plants, three had headquarters in Yorkshire or Lancashire, two were based in the Midlands and six were based in the South East. Table 12.12 suggests that the firms based in Yorkshire and Lancashire are more likely to purchase inputs from those regions than they are from any other non-Scottish region. Similarly the branches of firms based in the Midlands buy considerably more inputs from that region than from any other. The branches of firms based in the South East however are no more likely to buy inputs from that region than any of the other branches. It may be possible to infer from this that linkages can be 'inherited' by branch plants from parent companies. Beyond a certain critical distance, however, branch plants are forced to find alternative suppliers either in their own region or regions relatively close to it like the North West.

The distribution of sales demonstrates that whilst branch plants may be drawn to areas such as Scotland by local markets, local firms are considerably more dependent upon Scottish markets (65·1 per cent; 87·9 per cent) and upon West Central Scotland customers in particular (46·6 per cent; 70·1 per cent). Branch plants sell proportionately more of their output to all the British regions except the negligible cases of East Anglia, Northern Ireland and the South West, and more to customers abroad than do local

Table 12.13. Forward Linkages of Branch Plants by Headquarters Location

Sales to	Headquarters located in		
	North West and Yorks	Midlands	South East
	%	%	%
Scotland	83·0	90·0	58·7
N.W. and Yorks.	7·7	1·5	15·5
Midlands	2·0	2·0	1·7
South East	1·3	5·5	7·5
Other	6·0	1·0	16·6*

*15·9% of which = sales to Northern England.

firms. Table 12.13 presents evidence that different branch plants established to serve 'the regional market' mean different things by 'region'. Branch plants of companies based in the North West and in Yorkshire, and in the Midlands, are established to serve the Scottish market which take 83·0 per cent and 90·0 per cent of their product respectively. Branch plants of companies based in the South East however sell a lower proportion to Scotland (58·7 per cent) but also serve the North West and Yorkshire (15·5 per cent) and Northern Ireland and North England (most of the 16·6 per cent listed under 'other regions') from their Scottish branches.

Linkages 1966–70

From the cross-sectional analysis of 1970 data it has been possible to identify inter-industry differences in patterns of backward and forward linkages and to examine differences in the decision parameters between plants within industries in terms of plant characteristics. Changes in linkage patterns over time should throw further light on the decision-making process by which businessmen select suppliers and customers. A number of firms made data available for two previous years, 1966 and 1968: this forms the basis of the final section of the study. The managerial decision to purchase inputs from a different supplier or to seek out alternative or additional customers may be taken for a number of reasons. Growth of production may force a manufacturer to find additional suppliers and customers when existing suppliers and customers are unwilling or unable to increase sales and purchases proportionately. Particularly in times of economic difficulties, manufacturers may seek to reduce production costs by finding cheaper, closer or more efficient suppliers and to increase sales by finding higher prices for their goods or reducing transport costs by replacing distant customers with more local ones. Manufacturers may be forced to change suppliers or customers either by the closure of suppliers or by the cancellation of orders by customers. Lastly, changes in product by manufacturers may necessitate changing suppliers and customers. Some of these pressures for linkage change result from decisions by the firm or plant itself—a product change, or increase in output—but some result from exogenous forces such as the loss of orders or closure of suppliers.

Whatever the cause of the decision to alter suppliers or customers, the search procedure described by Cyert and March (1963) has a relevance to the selection process. The three stages are:

(1) the search in the neighbourhood of the problem situation;
(2) the search in the neighbourhood of the current alternative;
(3) if the neighbourhood search process does not provide an adequate solution, then successively the use of 'more distant' search procedures.

Golledge and Brown (1967) have pointed out the unmistakable spatial bias of search procedures formulated in this way. The three stages in the current study would be:

(1) the attempt to retain current linkages by changing the volume or type of goods involved;

(2) the searching for similar suppliers or customers within the same market area;

(3) the search for similar suppliers or customers in areas previously not searched.

The data available to the study does not fully cover stage (1) of the process, although where increased production by an establishment is matched by a proportionate increase in purchases from the same set of suppliers and a proportionate increase in sales to the same set of customers this could be inferred. Yet data does permit calculation of indices of linkage change both on an establishment basis and on a spatial basis. These indices were then used to test three hypotheses: (1) that old-established plants are less likely to change suppliers and customers than recently-established plants, (2) that indigenously-owned plants are less likely to change suppliers and customers than non-locally owned branch plants and (3) rapidly growing plants are more likely to change their suppliers and customers than slow growing or stagnant plants.

The index of establishment linkage change was calculated simply by the proportion of suppliers or customers in 1970 who had not been suppliers or customers in 1968, and the proportion in 1968 who had not been in 1966. Table 12.14 indicates that roughly between 20 and 30 per cent of all linkages changed in each two-year period with input linkages slightly more likely to change (26·7 per cent and 28·9 per cent) than output linkages (22·8 per cent and 18·9 per cent). If the aggregate figures are broken down by age of plant into new plants (all founded in the period 1961–64) and old plants (founded between 1880 and 1940) then there is always a tendency for new plants to change linkages more than old plants. This difference is more noticeable in changes in customers than in suppliers. The implication of this is that new plants take a considerable amount of time to settle down and identify a core of regular suppliers and customers after they are set up.

Table 12.14. Index of Plant Linkage Change, 1966–68 and 1968–70

| | 1966–68 | | 1968–70 | |
	Input	Output	Input	Outpu
All plants	26·7	22·8	28·9	18·9
New plants	27·9	28·9	32·9	24·9
Old plants	25·5	16·7	24·9	12·9
Branch plants	26·3	29·9	29·3	25·9
Indigenous plants	27·1	15·7	28·5	11·9
Rapidly growing plants	45·3	34·8	44·5	26·4
Slow or no growth plants	8·3	10·9	13·3	11·6

If the branch plants are compared with indigenous firms, irrespective of age, there appears to be little difference in the rate of input linkage change, but indigenous firms were a great deal more reluctant to find new customers than were branch plants. The most significant distinction, however, is that between rapidly growing plants (sales increased between 34 per cent and 67 per cent at constant prices in the period 1966–70) and slow growing or stagnant plants (sales changed by +7 per cent to −22 per cent). The difference is most marked in the case of inputs, implying that the rapidly growing firms in the survey grew by expanding sales to existing customers and finding new customers but having to rely very largely on new suppliers to provide the additional inputs required.

The index of spatial linkage change is calculated by

$$C = \frac{(X_{a1} - X_{a2}) + (X_{b1} - X_{b2}) - (X_{n1} - X_{n2})}{2}$$

where X_{a1} is the proportion of all purchases (or sales) in region a in year 1 and X_{a2} is the proportion in year 2 and n is the number of regions (in this case 65). Like most indices of this sort the value depends upon the size of n but as the size of n is held constant the index does provide a meaningful base for comparison. The index would take a value of zero where the proportion of purchases or sales from each of the 65 regions remained the same between the year 1 and year 2 and 100·0 where all purchases or sales were transferred from a set of regions in year 1 to a second set in year 2 where no regions are common ot both sets. Table 12.15 presents findings which are broadly similar to those of Table 12.14. The firms in the sample had altered the spatial distribution of suppliers more than that of customers in the period 1966–70 and in almost every case old plants changed the spatial pattern of both backward and forward linkages less frequently than did new plants, branches made more changes than did indigenously-owned plants and again the greatest distinction was between fast growing plants and slow growing plants.

Table 12.15. Index of Spatial Linkage Change, 1966–68 and 1968–70

	1966–68		1968–70	
	Input	Output	Input	Output
All plants	19·92	16·01	27·74	13·92
New plants	21·38	20·16	36·33	17·80
Old plants	18·37	12·61	19·14	10·03
Branch plants	18·84	20·01	27·03	19·27
Indigenous plants	20·99	12·02	28·44	8·57
Rapidly growing plants	21·21	23·26	36·97	18·94
Slow or no growth plants	17·36	8·77	18·50	8·89

Comparison of the two indices, of plant change and of spatial change, at the level of the individual firms showed that firms tended to have high values on both indices or low values on both indices. This tends to suggest that, when plants set out to look for new customers or new suppliers, stages (2) and (3) of Cyert and March's search procedure, rather than being sequential, are simultaneous and that firms look not only for new suppliers or customers in their existing market areas but in new areas at the same time. In only a few examples did a manufacturing plant have very different scores on the plant and spatial change indices, in both cases on the input side. The plant which had a high establishment change index but a low spatial change index was an old established glass-making firm which still had a policy of putting out to tender all subcontracting jobs and suppliers of capital equipment rather than maintaining links with a few regular suppliers but who tended only to request tenders from local firms. There was, therefore, a high rate of change of input linkages from year to year, but only between firms within the Glasgow area. The plant which had a low establishment change index but a high spatial change index was a recently formed tool-making company which, having built up a number of suppliers in its first few years of operation, had decided that further expansion of production should be achieved by finding new suppliers away from central Scotland whilst at the same time continuing to purchase inputs from the earlier set of suppliers.

Whilst the index of spatial linkage change measures change in the spatial distribution of suppliers or customers it does not indicate whether backward or forward linkages are on average becoming shorter or longer. At the level of the individual plant many firms demonstrate a remarkable stability in the proportion of purchases or sales made in Scotland. Table 12.16, though, provides data on three branch plants all set up in 1964–5 which exemplify very different strategies of branch plant operation. *Plant A* is the branch of a Birmingham-based toolmaking firm set up in Scotland largely to supply the Scottish engineering industry. The proportion of sales to Scottish customers remained steady at the 89–90 per cent level over the 1966–70 period although sales increased by 34 per cent during that time. Local suppliers had little impact on the original decision to set up the branch plant but gradually local suppliers were used so that their proportion rose from 38 per cent in 1965 to 51 per cent in 1966 and to 57 per cent in 1968. In late 1968 however experiences with local suppliers led the firm to think that it had relied too heavily on short backward linkages and by 1970 local purchases had fallen to 34 per cent and the proportion of purchases from the Midlands and the South East rose accordingly. *Plant B* is the branch of a London company engaged in the manufacture of paint and the coating of boards. Initially the plant was set up to serve only the Scottish market as the high percentage of sales figures for 1966 indicates, but the success of the plant led to work being transferred to it from the Surrey factory for customers in the Northern

Table 12.16. Change in Scottish Sales and Purchases, 1966–68 and 1968–70 by Three Plants

	Percentage Scottish purchases			Percentage Scottish sales		
	1966	1968	1970	1966	1968	1970
	%	%	%	%	%	%
Plant A	51	57	34	90	89	89
Plant B	14	32	56	89	73	46
Plant C	10	14	20	0	12	18

region and particularly Tyneside: hence the fall in percentage of local sales to 73 per cent in 1968 and to 46 per cent in 1970. Initially the plant brought most of its inputs, mostly chemicals, from the southern suppliers who served the Surrey factory but it rapidly replaced these linkages with much shorter ones to local suppliers. *Plant C* manufacturing light clothing, was drawn to the region by ample reserves of female labour, which was scarce close to its original location in Essex. As an industry handling high value/weight goods the plant was quite prepared to accept costs incurred by both long backward and long forward linkages. By 1970, however, five years after its establishment the branch was, almost despite its original policies, buying about one-fifth of its inputs from and selling one-fifth of its output to the Scottish market.

Conclusion

In contrast to the study of the location decision, relatively little emphasis has been placed on linkage decisions by manufactures despite the on-going controversy about the relative importance or unimportance of transport and distance costs as a proportion of all manufacturing costs. Aggregate studies of several developed industrial economies have suggested that transport costs are sufficiently important to have an industrial agglomerative effect with some attempt to keep transport costs down to a viable level. Using data from a small but carefully chosen sample of manufacturing establishments in the West Central Scotland region it has been possible to demonstrate the importance of the value, bulk and fragility of goods handled in determining the backward and forward linkages of plants engaged in six industrial processes. Almost equally important as inter-industry comparisons however are contrasts within an industry. Economies of scale in transport and information collection give larger firms an advantage in identifying and using more distant suppliers and customers. Branch plants of non-Scottish companies do have a tendency to retain links with suppliers and customers in their base region where this is less than approximately 300 miles from the Scottish branch plant but at a distance exceeding this figure linkages are rarely inherited from the headquarters location. When forced, either through internal decisions about volume or nature of output, or by external circumstances, to change linkage patterns, there is evidence that new plants and, especially, rapidly expanding plants pursue a more vigorous policy of linkage change than older and slower growing plants. Lastly, although the search process has been conceptualized as a sequence in which an intensive search for solutions in existing market and supply areas is, if unsuccessful, then followed by a search for more distant suppliers, and customers, the evidence from this sample of manufacturing establishments suggests that if forced to find new suppliers or customers they pursue both strategies simultaneously.

References

Board of Trade (Howard Report), 1968, *Movement of Manufacturing in the U.K., 1945–1965* (London: HMSO).

Bolton Committee (Committee of Enquiry on Small Firms), 1971, Report: *Small Firms* (London: HMSO).

Britton, J. N. H., 1969, 'A geographical approach to the study of industrial linkages', *Canadian Geographer,* **13**, 185–95.

Chinitz, B., 1960, *Freight and the Metropolis* (Cambridge, Mass.: M.I.T.).

Chinitz, B., 1961, 'Contrasts in agglomeration: New York and Pittsburgh', *American Economic Review,* **51**, 279–89.

Chisholm, M. and P. O'Sullivan, 1973, *Freight Flows and Spatial Aspects of the British Economy* (Cambridge University Press).

Cyert, R. M., and J. G. March, 1963, *A Behavioural Theory of the Firm* (Englewood Cliffs: Prentice–Hall).

Edwards, S. L., 1970, 'Transport costs in British industry', *Journal of Transport Economics,* **4**, 265–85.

Elliot, F. E., 1948, 'Location factors affecting industrial plants', *Economic Geography,* **24**, 283–5.

Eversley, D. E. C., 1965, 'Social and psychological factors in the determination of industrial location', in *Papers on Regional Development,* ed. T. Wilson (Oxford: Blackwell).

Florence, P. Sargent, 1944, 'The selection of industries suitable for dispersal to rural areas', *Journal Royal Statistical Society,* **107**, 93–116.

Frost, M., 1969, 'Distribution costs as a factor in a location of industry policy', *London School of Economics Department of Geography Discussion Paper,* 34.

Fulton, M. and L. C. Hoch, 1959, 'Transportation factors affecting location decisions', *Economic Geography,* **35**, 51–9.

Hague, D. C. and J. H. Dunning, 1952, *Costs in Alternative Locations* (Cambridge: National Institute for Economic and Social Reserach).

Hill, C., 1954, 'Some aspects of industrial location', *Journal of Industrial Economics,* **2**, 184–92.

James, B. G. S., 1964, 'The incompatibility of industrial and trading cultures', *Journal Industrial Economics,* **13**, 90–4.

Katona, G. and J. N. Morgan, 1951, 'The quantitative study of factors determining business decisions', *Quarterly Journal of Economics,* **66**, 67–90.

Keeble, D. E., 1969, 'Local industrial linkage and manufacturing growth in outer London', *Town Planning Review,* **40**, 163–88.

Lever, W. F., 1972, 'Industrial movement, spatial association and functional linkages', *Regional Studies,* **6**, 371–84.

Luttrell, W. F., 1962, *Factory Location and Industrial Movement* (London: National Institute for Economic and Social Research).

McCarty, H. H., J. C. Hook, and D. S. Knos, 1956, *The Measurement of Association in Industrial Geography* (Iowa City: University of Iowa).

Martin, J. E., 1964, 'Three elements in industrial geography of Greater London', in J. T. Coppock and H. C. Prince, *Greater London* (London: Faber).

Ministry of Transport, 1964, *Survey of Road Goods Transport, 1962: Statistical Paper 2* (London: HMSO).

Pred, A., 1964, 'Towards a typology of manufacturing flows', *Geographical Review,* **54**, 65–84.

Richter, C. E., 1969, 'The impact of industrial linkages on Geographical association', *Journal of Regional Science,* **9**, 19–28.

Salt, J., 1967, 'The impact of the Ford and Vauxhall, plants on employment on Merseyside 1962–65', *Tijdschrift voor Economische en Sociale Geografie,* **58**, 255–63.

Steed, G. P. F., 1968, 'Commodity flows and inter-industry linkages of Northern Ireland's manufacturing industries', *Tijdschrift voor Economische en Social Geografie,* **50**, 245–58.

Streit, M. E., 1969, 'Spatial association and economic linkages between industries', *Journal of Regional Science,* **9**, 177–88.

Taylor, M. J., 1970, 'Location decisions of small firms', *Area,* **2**, 51–4.

Wood, P., 1969, 'Industrial location and linkage', *Area,* **2**, 32–9.

13

External Economies of Scale, Inter-Industrial Linkages and Decision Making in Manufacturing

JAMES M. GILMOUR

Since the inception of the 'industrial revolution' in Britain, manufacturing industry has experienced almost continuous growth matched by incessant change in structure and form. Production units, processes, products, organization and indeed almost all aspects of manufacturing have been evolving and changing at an accelerating rate such that a world of difference separates the Lancashire cotton spinning mill of 1820—the archetype of early British industrialism—and the salient manufacturing concern of our time—the multi-national corporation embracing horizontally and vertically linked firms and production units in many countries. No less than structure and organization, the distribution of manufacturing has altered greatly through time. On a world scale, factory-organized manufacturing has diffused from its British coalfield hearths and enjoyed enthusiastic adoption, first in other European countries and later in other continents. But while manifesting these spatially dispersive tendencies at a global scale, manufacturing has tended consistently to concentrate in space at the national and regional level. Its distribution is characterized by large agglomerations in and around large cities and by clusters of these agglomerations. In other words, manufacturing centralizes and there is little or no evidence to suggest a diminution in this spatial proclivity. Decentralization there certainly has been; but it has not taken the form of redistribution between regions and urban centres, rather it has been a matter of spatial reallocations within the major agglomerations, more especially, expansion and growth at the peripheries of industrial agglomerations in association with relative, and at times absolute, decline in their original cores.

335

This tendency of manufacturing establishments to cluster together in space has shown none of the ephemerality so common amongst other attributes of manufacturing: if anything, it grows in strength and proves to be rather impervious to the variety of incentive schemes and legislative measures designed by a number of governments for the purpose of weakening it. A majority of manufacturing firms are located in agglomerations and most location decisions take the form of choosing between alternative industrial regions and agglomerations, and, at a finer detail, choosing between alternative locations or sites within agglomerations.

This chapter is not concerned directly with how firms resolve this problem of selection, rather it aims to elucidate how firms utilize their locations. An attempt to understand the behaviour of firms once their locations have been chosen is a valid, although infrequently tried, means of understanding the locational attractiveness of agglomerations. In pursuit of its objectives this chapter explores some aspects of industrial location theory, examines some approaches to the study of agglomeration economies and inter-industrial linkages, and, with particular reference to the selection of input suppliers, probes aspects of the operational behaviour of firms located within agglomerations.

External Economies of Scale

The phenomenon of agglomeration has not been wanting in scholarly attention, although, regrettably, returns have not corresponded to effort. There have been many approaches, both theoretical and empirical, but pride of place, for both relevance and importance, falls to industrial location theory and its attendant concept of external economies of scale. Location theory purports to explain the continuing locational attraction of industrial agglomerations in the following manner. Agglomerations, regardless of the reasons for their many and varied origins, offer firms located in them the advantages of agglomeration economies, or, more appropriately, external economies of scale that are not available to firms in locational isolation. Firms in agglomerations, therefore, enjoy savings in costs, the net result of which, in the long run, is to favour the growth of manufacturing in the agglomeration at the expense of other locations, multiply the availability of external economies of scale and further augment the agglomeration's locational attractivness. There are a number of noteworthy aspects of this theory of which the above is a very crude caricature. First, the theory was deductively derived. Second, it has never been shown to be completely valid. Third, it has generally been assumed to be valid and for pedagogical purposes has provided the explanatory basis of agglomeration absorbed by several generations of university students. This last circumstance has arisen presumably because no one has succeeded in dethroning the theory and in replacing it with a better one. However, it is also the case that this explanation of agglomeration is so intellectually appealing as to cause us to assume it must be right (it probably is). The theory has enjoyed a long life. It has never been demonstrated that it is completely invalid, but neither has the converse been demonstrated. More than anything else this note-worthy state of affairs reflects the theory's difficulty of verification.

The credit for the theoretical explanation of agglomeration must go to Weber (1929). Others have laboured in this field but their contributions have largely embellished rather than replaced his ideas. It is unfortunate that Weber was never able to carry out his intention of verifying his theory, for it was not until comparatively recently that serious efforts were made to establish empirically the existence of the postulated external economies by such means as identifying the various contributory components and by measuring the strength of their agglomerative attraction.

External economies of scale refer to economies external to the individual firms, which are available to them in their transactions with other firms and organizations both inside and outside the manufacturing sector. They are postulated to be more readily available in spatial concentrations (agglo-merations) of firms in manufacturing and related economic activities, it being held that it is the presence of many firms in spatial proximity to one another that permits the realization of large scale economies in their many transactions. For example, it is believed that it is only when there are many customers in close proximity to one another that specialist service industries can emerge to supply services at lower costs than the customer firms could provide for themselves. One important benefit of the spatial proximity of linked industrial activities is the possibility of economizing on transfer and communication costs. This relates not only to the short distances involved within agglomerations but also to the rapidity with which transportation and communication can be effected.

In all probability the only infallible means of establishing the existence and magnitude of external economies of scale is to ascertain the total costs of each firm located in an agglomeration and compare these costs against the total costs which would be incurred at all alternative locations outside the agglomeration. If agglomerations offer external economies of scale, firms located in them would be able to achieve lower total costs than at any alternative locations. However, the practical difficulties involved in carrying out this approach are insurmountable and some easier, if less rigorous, means must be used to identify and measure external economies of scale.

A number of researchers believe they have found an acceptable alternative means in the study of industrial linkages. It not all, then at least many external economies of scale can be thought of as expressing themselves in the transactions between firms. These transactions are translated into tangible or non-tangible flows, consisting of the spatial transfer of informa-tion, people and materials, and, as such, link firms and industries together.

It is only through the study of linkages between firms and industries that the presence of external economies of scale may be detected; and if, for example, it can be demonstrated that linkages confined within the agglomeration are of greater relative importance than those extending beyond the agglomeration, there would be reason to suspect that external economies of scale, expressing themselves in transactions, exert an important locational attraction.

Of course, it bears repeating that not all external economies of scale need reside in inter-firm or inter-industrial transactions. It is conceivable, although most unlikely, that a firm may have no interactions at all with other firms in the same agglomeration as itself, yet enjoy the external economies of scale deriving from a large and varied labour force. Consequently, it should be understood from the outset that the study of industrial linkages cannot by itself provide a total approach towards the understanding of agglomeration.

The Spatial Association Approach

Since 'intra-agglomeration' linkages are the only readily available, or measurable, indication of the possible presence of external economies, it is perplexing indeed to find that most efforts aimed at elucidating agglomeration and external economies of scale have ignored linkages in favour of an approach which, regardless of how well it is handled, cannot contribute significantly to the problem. This is the spatial association approach to the study of agglomeration, and it is one of the many subdivisions of the 'have computer, will travel' school of geography which led many to revere technique before relevance during its halcyon days, the 1960s. Its basic method consists in finding the degree of spatial association between pairs of industries by correlating their employment, or some other magnitude figures, for areal units. In its earlier uses spatial association analysis proceeded no further than this. In its more recent manifestations it has been taken a stage further with a search for relationships between spatial association and economic linkage. One way in which this has been accomplished is by correlating coefficients of spatial association and indices of economic linkage (Streit, 1969). Much can be said about the technical problems and pitfalls lying in wait for the user of the technique, but this chapter refrains from consideration of technical problems and how their treatment may influence results, on the grounds that the approach is of little value to the study of agglomeration or to the quest for industries constrained in locational choice, regardless of how well or badly it is carried out.

If there are intrinsic economic advantages arising from the spatial proximity of firms in the same or different industries, they will be detected only by examining the behaviour of firms and not by examining the behaviour of industries, which is the sum of the behaviour of the firms composing them. For example, economic advantages may accrue to firms if they procure materials from nearby firms as opposed to distant firms. To verify this we must as a *sine qua non* establish that neighbouring firms do in fact buy materials from one another. The spatial association approach ignores this necessity and in so doing becomes an exercise in futility. Its methodology may be enlisted to show that two industries, A and B, are spatially associated. It may also be shown that industries A and B are functionally related, selling and buying materials to and from one another. But this knowledge cannot permit or support any inferences regarding the behaviour and resultant spatial linkages of the production units composing industries A and B. Unfortunately, several researchers have ignored this self-evident truth and crossed the uncrossable gap to draw inferences about firm behaviour on the basis of the analysis of data that does not describe the behaviour of the firm.

It is often forgotten that the indices describing the functional linkages between industries have no spatial attributes. They describe no spatial reality. They are the aggregates of tens of thousands of inter-firm linkages and it is these and these only which have real spatial existence. No amount of statistical manipulations of inter-industry linkage data will lead to knowledge or understanding of the transactions or spatial linkages at the level of the firm. More particularly, therefore, we cannot conclude that the firms of industry A deal with the nearest firms of industry B and vice versa simply because A and B are spatially associated and functionally related; nor can we assume that firms of functionally related industries in the same agglomeration buy and sell from one another. Only examination of *real* inter-firm linkages will tell us how firms in agglomerations behave and only the knowledge of that behaviour will enable us to understand the economic advantages apparently offered by agglomerations, or tell us which industries are spatially constrained by the nature of their interactions with other industries.

At a very fundamental level, therefore, serious objections are raised against the spatial association approach. But the matter does not end there; there are other difficulties relating to the approach which are not inherent in it but which almost always occur. This approach is not normally employed unless an abundance of statistical data describing manufacturing is available. Data abundance, coupled with the presence and availability of computers, has not always been a blessing in geography or other social sciences; and this is probably a case in point, for it has encouraged indifference to the relevance of data and significance of the questions asked of it. Too often a problem has been shaped to find use for data or a data manipulating technique. The spatial association approach may be just such an example. The data employed in such analyses have not usually been collected for the purpose of facilitating spatial analysis of manufacturing Often, for example, the level of industry aggregation is so great as to render any analysis virtually worthless in terms of elucidating the spatial characteristics of manufacturing activity. Streit (1969) used only 26 industrial activities and Lever (1972) used 61 industrial groups. To talk in terms of functional linkages between such large groups, composed of many heterogeneous activities, with different inputs, products, processes, markets and therefore linkages, subjects reality to such abstraction as to cause the researcher to study relationships which have only a statistical existence. Streit, for example, deals with a group called the food, beverages and tobacco industry. One can appreciate the reasons for treating these industries as one group. Unfortunately, a grouping such as this contains industries with fundamentally different patters of spatial linkage.

Analysis of Aggregate Linkages

Having made the case for an approach which emphasizes the examination of inter-industrial linkages, it behoves the writer to demonstrate its power to provide meaningful insights into agglomeration economies. The rest of this chapter is devoted to some exemplifications of the inter-industrial linkage approach and to examination of some questions raised by applying it.

The manufacturing complex employed to illustrate this approach is that of Metropolitan Montreal and its surrounding area. This is a particularly good test area for the study of inter-industrial linkages. In the first place, the manufacturing complex is of a size—over 5000 manufacturing establishments and a quarter of a million employees in Metropolitan Montreal alone in 1967—to permit the reasonable anticipation that it offers significant external economies of scale. Second, the complex is in relative isolation from other major manufacturing cities. The closest centres are all at least 80 miles from the centre of Montreal and of comparatively small importance. There is no danger, therefore, that short inter-metropolitan linkages will obscure the agglomerative force of the Montreal economy.

As a first step in trying to detect the assumed external economies of scale, a simple test was made of the hypothesis used by Karaska (1969) in his study of inter-industrial linkages in Philadelphia. Karaska (1969, p. 354) reasoned as follows: 'We postulate that the agglomeration forces may in part be described by procurement actions between local manufacturing firms. The strength of the linkage with the local manufacturing system is a measure of the agglomerative force exerted by the size of the local metropolitan industrial complex.' For the purposes of testing this hypothesis, linkage data were obtained from a sample of manufacturing establishments located within 40 miles of downtown Montreal. The data described only the material linkages of manufacturing and were not on a firm-to-firm basis because such detailed information was not necessary at this preliminary phase of enquiry. For the same reason material inputs and outputs were each treated as aggregates and no attempt was made to collect information on separate inputs or outputs. In any case, since the plants were drawn from a wide range of industries, meaningful comparisons could be made only for aggregated inputs and outputs. A stratified random sample took cognizance of the following characteristics of manufacturing establishments—size (by employment), industry type (20 groups at the 2-digit level of the Standard Industrial Classification used in Canada) and distance from the centre of Montreal—yielded linkage data from 198 separate establishments (approximately 3 per cent of all establishments in the study area).

As far as material linkages are concerned the agglomerative force of the Montreal economy for these 198 establishments appears to be rather weak. Linkages extending beyond the agglomeration are far more important than linkages wholly contained within it. More than two-thirds of all purchases and sales (when establishments are weighted by size) are made outside Metropolitan Montreal. Only 27·3 per cent of sales (weighted) and 31·6 per cent of purchases (weighted) are made in Metropolitan Montreal. However, limited findings from other cities indicate that Montreal is not unusual in this regard. It was found by Field and Kerr (1968, p. 50) that firms in Toronto's periphery made only 26 per cent (weighted) of their sales to Metropolitan Toronto. Their estimate of suburban sales (weighted) to Toronto was 35 per cent. For Philadelphia firms, Karaska's estimate of local purchases was 37 per cent (1969, p. 359). The situation in Montreal, therefore, may be a rather typical one.

This very slim evidence suggests that external economies of scale in the procurement of inputs from and the distribution of outputs to other firms in the same industrial complex do not play a prominent role in explaining the high locational preference of Canadian firms for the Montreal area. This in turn inclines one to anticipate that if external economies of scale are available to manufacturing firms in Montreal, and, for that matter, in all industrial complexes, they reside in the transactions related to non-material connections. That is, the agglomerative force of the complex may be more strongly expressed in the attractions of the labour force and in the strength of linkage with firms which are involved in service, financial and commercial transactions than with firms which are directly involved in the interchange of material inputs and outputs.

The picture changes somewhat, however, if the aggregate situation is subjected to some dissection. First of all, there is the question of the size of manufacturing establishments. Theory and intuition suggest that the behaviour of firms within industrial complexes may have some relationship to size. It was thus postulated that the agglomerative force of the industrial complex is inversely related to the size of manufacturing establishments. In other words, it is anticipated that the external economies of scale available in an agglomeration are increasingly used as the size of establishment falls. The basis of this postulate lies in an assumption that small establishments in general cannot be as self-sufficient as large establishments and that, with

Table 13.1. Sales Areas, Source Areas of Materials and Total Linkage by Size of Plant

Size of establishment (employees)	No. of plants			Metropolitan Montreal	Quebec and Montreal	Elsewhere
				%	%	%
1–25	53	%		41·4	70·0	30·0
26–100	71	%	of sales made to	35·1	55·9	44·1
101+	74	%		26·6	45·8	54·2
1–25	53	%		46·7	67·6	32·4
26–100	71	%	of purchases from	41·2	54·7	45·3
101+	74	%		30·0	47·8	52·2
1–25	53	%		44·1	68·8	31·2
26–100	71	%	of total linkage with	38·1	55·3	44·7
101+	74	%		28·3	46·8	53·2

increasing size, establishments are likely to 'internalize' their linkages and, as a consequence of their increasing scale of output, are likely to extend spatially their external linkages. Conversely, reduction in the scale of the manufacturing establishment implies a reduction in its self-sufficiency, 'externalization' of linkages and an increasing reliance on other firms in the industrial complex.

The linkage data largely speak for themselves (Table 13.1). The smallest establishments have the strongest connections with the local economy, and with the Province of Quebec as a whole, in sales, purchases and therefore in total linkage (derived by averaging the percentages for the other two linkages). Almost 70 per cent of their total linkage is with the Quebec economy and less than a third with the rest of Canada and other parts of the world. Their input linkages with the local industrial complex are especially strong, constituting nearly 50 per cent of purchases by value. Among larger establishments the strength of linkage with the Montreal economy and the Province of Quebec becomes weaker. The largest establishments, those with over 100 employees, have the weakest linkages with the region in which they are located. Less than a third of their sales and purchases are made in Metropolitan Montreal, and over half of all their transactions are made outside the Province. Small establishments appear to have stronger connections with the local industrial economy and this suggests that external economies of scale exert a weakening locational pull as the size of establishment increases. More extended analysis of these data can be found in Brooks, Gilmour and Murricane (1973).

With a diameter of 80 miles, the study area is large; and the spatial patterns of inter-industrial linkages might be expected to vary considerably within it. Accordingly, to consider the effects of location, the study area was divided

Table 13.2. Linkage to Metropolitan Montreal by Size of Plant and Location

Size of plant (employees)	Location of plant	No. of plants	Sales	Purchases	Total linkage
			%	%	%
1–25	centre	20	54·1	45·2	49·6
1–25	suburbs	17	38·3	40·5	39·4
1–25	periphery	16	31·9	54·3	43·1
26–100	centre	31	37·3	34·5	35·9
26–100	suburbs	25	32·1	36·1	34·1
26–100	periphery	15	35·8	52·8	44·3
101 +	centre	29	27·1	27·4	27·2
101 +	subsurbs	32	27·1	30·1	28·6
101 +	periphery	13	25·8	32·6	29·2

into three zones: the metropolitan centre, the metropolitan suburbs and the metropolitan periphery. Although a certain arbitrariness attaches to the boundaries of those zones, they approximately distinguish between the older manufacturing districts of the strongly urbanized central city, the newer industrial areas of the suburbs and, last, the old and new manufacturing in many small and medium-sized communities in Montreals's immediate hinterland. This crude classification of locations is more suited to the particular spatial configuration of Montreal than a more rigorous classification based on distance measures.

Several interesting and (some quite unexpected) findings emerge from this finer examination (Table 13.2). The most significant is the divergence in the spatial patterns of input and output linkages. In outputs, plants in the central city are more strongly connected to Metropolitan Montreal than establishments in the periphery. This is most marked in the plants with 1 to 25 employees. Establishments of this size in the central city sell 54 per cent of their output to customers in Metropolitan Montreal: the corresponding figure for the peripheral plants of this size class is only 32 per cent. This difference in sales orientation between central and peripheral establishments is much less pronounced in the other two size classes.

Examination of inputs reveals an opposite and unexpected tendency. In every size class the strongest linkage with Metropolitan Montreal occurs in the peripheral establishments. With the exception of the smallest size class, the central city establishments have the weakest linkage with Metropolitan Montreal. This represents almost a complete reversal of what our theoretical writings on agglomeration economies would lead us to expect, and, like earlier findings, suggests that external economies of scale, as they relate to the procurement of materials within industrial agglomerations, are relatively insignificant. However, there are no immediately obvious explanations as to why this should be so; any interpretations can only be exceedingly tentative.

Plants in the small communities of the periphery can acquire practically none of their inputs from other establishments in their respective communities, whereas, it may be anticipated that plants in the industrial complex (in this case Metropolitan Montreal) can, if they so wish, procure a large proportion of their inputs from firms in that complex. For the peripheral establishments, Montreal is the closest large industrial centre from which many of their inputs may be obtained. For the establishments in Montreal, alternative sources for inputs are found in other large industrial complexes that are comparable to Montreal. Such complexes also represent alternatives to Montreal for the peripheral establishments, but it is less likely that peripheral establishments will go beyond Montreal for the procurement of materials than the establishments located in Montreal. This should be qualified, however, to take account of the size of establishments. As plant size increases the dependence upon Montreal for inputs diminishes, so that it is the small- and medium-sized peripheral establishments which have a particularly high dependence upon Montreal for their inputs.

There are probably several reasons why the smaller peripheral plants rely more heavily on the local industrial complex than plants located within it. First, there may be a time and distance factor in the transportation of inputs to the periphery from industrial centres other than Montreal; a factor which would unnecessarily add to the costs of peripheral firms. There is, for example, a likelihood that shipments would be routed through Montreal and then channelled to the peripheral towns, thus causing transhipment costs not experienced by firms within the complex itself, and increasing the length of time required for completion of deliveries.

Second, it is possible that manufacturing in the periphery tends to be of such a nature that it can more easily procure its inputs within the regional economy than can manufacturing in Montreal. This factor, or consideration of it, may have guided the locational choice between the city and the periphery in the first place. One suspects that firms which have need of inter-regional linkages are more likely to locate within an industrial complex than firms which can procure most of their inputs within the local region. If this point could be verified by means of empirical investigation it would be of considerable significance, because it conflicts with some of our long held ideas about external economies of scale, and agrees with others. For example, it is generally believed that an important locational attraction of spatial concentrations of manufacturing is the existence of economies in the interchange of materials between firms in the same industrial complex. The evidence of this chapter casts some dubiety on that notion. Yet industrial complexes are generally cited as offering external economies of scale in transportation and communications. Since the establishments in the metropolitan area have weaker linkage with the metropolitan area than firms located in the surrounding area, it seems reasonable to assume that the metropolitan establishments are partly drawn to the complex because of the economies it offers in inter-metropolitan transportation and communication.

Third, the spatial pattern of input linkages is related to the knowledge about potential input supplies possessed by establishments. Smaller establishments in the periphery may have less information on suppliers than smaller establishments within the industrial complex and larger establishments both within the complex and in the periphery. Their knowledge may be largely confined to Montreal suppliers. This is a very conjectural point but it could conceivably play a role in affecting the spatial pattern of purchase linkages.

Inter-Firm Linkages

The linkages described above still represent a high degree of aggregation and abstraction. They are aggregates first of the values of different inputs and second of the inputs of different industries. As they are organized neither on an inter-firm nor an individual input basis, they are in several senses spatial abstractions of the tangible material flows which are the life-blood of firms. It is only through an examination of these real linkages that the spatial patterns of the abstract and aggregate linkages can be explained. Accordingly, this section examines several aspects of inter-firm linkages, including the decision-making behind them, with a view to adding some substance to the conjectures given above and, more particularly, to understanding why such a small proportion of linkages is contained within the agglomeration. For the most part, discussion is concerned with purchases and empirical evidence is derived from a very small number of industries, firms and linkages. This reflects the many difficulties involved in obtaining inter-firm linkage data.

Limited Choice of Suppliers

There is no point in approaching the study of inter-firm linkages in an abstract manner. The focus of attention must be the needs and circumstances confronting those who have to choose the firms which will furnish inputs. As soon as this practical approach is adopted, certain fundamental characteristics of manufacturing have to be considered because of their vital bearing on the decisions to choose input suppliers. One such characteristic is extremely high product heterogeneity. Far too many researchers have been blinded to this fact by the various classifications of manufacturing employed by governmental statistical agencies. It is generally assumed that titles such as the 'paints and varnish industry' or 'hosiery mills industry' (much more finely delineated industries than those normally used in the spatial association approach) describe collections of manufacturing plants which, while probably differing in scale, age, organization, production methods and other aspects, are fairly uniform in their outputs and, by inference, in their inputs. In terms of complying with their generic titles they are uniform in product but the diversity embraced by such titles can be quite remarkable. This diversity occurs because there is a general tendency for firms to strive to create a monopoly in unique products and because a modern industrial society requires an astonishing array of products designed for very specific purposes: the result is that the number of products is so great that any particular one is manufactured by only a small number of firms. In view of this diversity, even our most detailed classifications of manufacturing group together establishments which are remarkably heterogeneous in their products and, by inference, equally heterogeneous in their input requirements.

There is a much narrower choice of suppliers of any particular input than has been tacitly assumed in our studies of agglomeration; most firms are much more 'particularistic' in their products than is generally realized. The 'hosiery mills industry', for example, appears to be a fairly simple industry with a clearly defined and easily recognizable product; but closer examination quickly reveals that even this uncomplicated industry produces many different and unalike products. Each firm has its own product range and therefore its own input range, with the result that different establishments are linked to different industries. The Directory of Manufacturing Establish- of Quebec produced by the Quebec Bureau of Statistics (1970) recognizes 31 major product categories in this industry. These include: 'men's socks, work, wool and wool mixtures (over 50 per cent wool)'; 'men's socks, fine, cotton and cotton mixtures'; 'women's hosiery, full length and knee high, nylon and nylon mixtures (over 50 per cent nylon)'; sheer, mesh and plain greige hosiery (all types)' and so on. Of the 95 hosiery mills in the Province of Quebec, none manufactures all product categories, many produce several, but just as many produce only one type.

The product range of the 'Paints and Varnish' industry is at least as large and heterogeneous. Quebec has 42 firms in this industry and their output is classified into 27 major product categories, such as paste paints, semi-paste paints, ready-mixed paints and enamels (exterior type), lacquers—cellulose type, lacquers—non-cellulose type, and so on. All firms produce only some of these categories with the result that the number of Quebec suppliers of any particular type of paint is usually very limited. There are for example, 29 establishments in Quebec manufacturing ready-mixed paints and enamels for exterior use. However, semi-paste paints (exclusive of water-thinned types) are manufactured in only 5 Quebec establishments. Should a firm's requirements be so particular that a calcimine based, water-thinned paste or enamel is required, it is confined to one Quebec producer or the choice of going beyond the provincial boundaries. Firms requiring lacquers as an input have the choice of 8 producers in Quebec and if they need stains they will find 10 producers. Of course, the fact that there are ten producers does not necessarily mean that any one of them can meet a firm's particular requirements.

The paints and varnish industry requires an amazing number of inputs. Excluding containers and packaging materials, the D.B.S. publication 'Paints and Varnish Manufacturers' (1972) listed 300 separate commodities which are inputs to the industry. It is highly unlikely that any one plant requires all 300 inputs. The range of each plant's products will determine its particular input requirements. For most inputs, the number of alternative suppliers, even in Canada as a whole, is very limited. The number of suppliers in Quebec is even smaller and in the Montreal agglomeration smaller still. Urea and formaldehyde resins have the greatest number of Canadian producers. There are 25 and seven of these are in Quebec. There are 10 suppliers of alkyds, two of which are in Quebec. In the case of most inputs, the number of domestic producers is very small. For example, there are only three Canadian producers of epoxy resins (1 in Quebec), four of polyvinyl chloride emulsions (1 in Quebec) and one producer of methyl amyl acetate (none in Quebec). For many inputs there are no Canadian producers at all, e.g., methyl acetate, silicone oils, vinyl toluene, acrylic acid, phenolic resins and many others. In short, the chances of a paint and varnish producer in Montreal finding a local supplier of an input are not high and his chances of having a choice between local producers is poor.

A limited number of suppliers restricts the possible variation in the spatial pattern of inter-industrial linkages. An examination of the soft drinks industry provides ample support for this point. This may well be the world's most ubiquitous industry and, as far as its production processes and number of input requirements are concerned, may also be the least complicated industry. It is the epitome of the market-oriented industry: the major product is bulky, of low value and costly to transport so that establishments are widely distributed throughout the market area and located centrally in the local markets they serve. In the Province of Quebec there are 165 plants in this industry and these are found throughout the length and breadth of the populated area.

The industry is remarkable for its low product diversity—the major reason for examining this industry in more detail. A majority of inputs are used by all firms, thus enabling meaningful comparisons to be made between firms. All plants produce some form of soft drink, with the product varying according to sugar content and the way in which it is packaged. Some firms 'can' their product, some 'bottle', while others market it in bulk containers such as barrels and tanks. Such variations cause dissimilarities in the inter-industrial linkages of the industry's firms. There is another product variation which is more important and serves to divide the industry into two types of plants and to create an important industrial linkage which is largely internal to the industry. Soft drink manufacturers perform two distinct industrial operations: they (1) manufacture concentrates or syrups for use in making soft drinks and (2) combine concentrates or syrup with carbon dioxide gas and water to produce the beverages which are bottled or canned for distribution. All plants in Quebec engage in the latter operation, but only a minority (usually bigger firms with larger plants) manufacture syrup and concentrates. This minority, therefore, has a set of linkages not possessed by the majority. These are linkages connecting them with the industries producing inputs required for the production of concentrates and syrups. The greater part of concentrate and syrup output is used by its manufacturers but a significant proportion is sold to the firms which do not manufacture their own, thus creating a linkage internal to the industry. However, there are some concentrate and syrup producers in other industries. For example, in Quebec there are 48 soft drinks plants making concentrates or syrups, but there are 9 other producers in the industry described as 'Miscellaneous Food Industries'.

Despite these variations in processes, products, input requirements and linkages, a number of inputs are required by almost all establishments. Some were selected for study: metal closures (bottle caps), granulated and liquid sugar (most firms use granulated), concentrates, glass bottles and carbon dioxide. Together these account for over 90 per cent of the input costs of soft drink bottling plants. In all cases except that of concentrates there is a very limited choice of suppliers in Quebec.

Metal closures are fabricated by plants in the industry described as the 'Metal Stamping, Pressing and Coating Industry'. This is a typical type of census industry and one which is defined on the basis of process rather than use of final product or materials. It manufactures a great diversity of objects, including such items as magnesium castings, culvert pipe, curtain rods, galvanized sheet, lockers, parking meters and metal window frames (71 major product categories). In Quebec there are 181 firms classified into this industry. Each firm specializes in only a few of the industry's many products. Only four firms make metal closures and, of these, only two (both in Montreal) make the type of closures required by the soft drinks industry. (It is respectfully submitted that analysis of the spatial association between the 'metal, stamping, pressing and coating industry' and the 'soft drinks industry' would be an exercise in sheer nonsense.) Sugar is obtained from the 'sugar refineries industry' which has six plants in Quebec. Five of these can meet the soft drinks industry requirements. There are 47 producers of concentrates and these are widely distributed. Bottles are obtained from establishments listed as belonging to the 'Glass and Glass Products Industry', but of 60 establishments in this group only two manufacture the types of bottles required by the soft drinks industry. Finally, there is carbon dioxide. This emanates from 'Manufacturers of Industrial Chemicals'. There are 33 Quebec establishments in this industry, but only two of them supply the soft drinks industry with carbon dioxide gas.

With the exception of concentrate manufacturers almost all the producers which can supply the soft drinks industry with the inputs considered above are located in Metropolitan Montreal. This causes most linkages to originate in Montreal regardless of the location of a soft drink plant and results, therefore, in a spatial lengthening of linkages with increasing distance of plants from Montreal. An establishment located one hundred miles from Montreal obtains its supplies from the same few sources as an establishment located only five miles from Montreal. Obviously, there is no diminution in the degree of dependence upon Montreal for materials as distance from the city increases.

The Role of Wholesalers

The product heterogeneity, which so typifies manufacturing, militates strongly against the confinement of linkages to the local agglomerations. However, manufacturers do not necessarily have to buy their inputs directly from their producers. They may have recourse to that intermediate economic institution—the wholesaler—the presence of whom in the agglomeration may represent an external economy of scale and, therefore, act as a significant locational factor. The wholesaler, purchasing in large lots beyond the needs of any individual small purchaser can bring together inputs from many producers at different locations and sell at short notice to industrial firms in the agglomeration and its surrounding area. Various economies can be expected to accrue to the industrial firm, as, for example, in the cost of the material, in smaller inventories and in delivery reliability, to name but a few. But such economies may be expected to become less significant as firm size increases, because the larger firm, purchasing in larger lots, is likely to suffer no economic disbenefits by dealing directly with the producer. Indeed, beyond a certain size of firm, purchasing from wholesalers may increase costs rather than decrease them. Data from the 198 Montreal establishments (Table 13.3) whose linkages were considered earlier in this paper, suggest that small manufacturing establishments may be less dependent on manufacturers

Table 13.3. Type of Material Sources by Size of Plant

Size of plant (employees)	No. of plants	Precentage distribution of purchases		
		Manufacturing	Wholesale/ Retail	Other
		%	%	%
1–25	53	62·6	30·5	6·8
26–100	71	72·1	23·3	4·6
100 +	74	70·3	25·1	4·6

for their inputs and more dependent on other sectors than large establishments. The evidence provided by Table 13.3 is very weak, but examination of more detailed inter-firm linkage data from the 'metal stamping, pressing and coating industry' lends some corroborative evidence. The Quebec (1970) Industrial Directory listed 119 Montreal establishments as belonging to this industry in 1970. Attempts were made to obtain information from all of them. It was found that approximately 10 per cent had gone out of production between 1970 and 1972 (a 'death' rate matched by most other industries in Quebec). Of the remaining firms, only 12 agreed to provide detailed information on their inputs—a strong indication of the difficulties involved in getting the necessary information for this type of work.

Some descriptive details of these firms are contained in Table 13.4. Clearly, they are highly varied. In fact, one wonders at the wisdom of a classification which can allow a manufacturer of window frames and a manufacturer of jewellery settings to be allocated to the same industry. The major inputs of each firm are noted in Table 13.5. In most cases the inputs

Table 13.4. Some Characteristics of 12 Montreal Firms in the 'Metal Stamping, Pressing and Coating Industry'

Firm	Employees	Sales in 1971	Major products
		$000	
A	230	5,000	pipes and elbows, pressure and vacuum tanks, ventilators, parts for paper-making machinery
B	65	1,000	kitchen equipment for cafeterias and restaurants, range hoods, tanks
C	10	300	kitchen equipment for cafeterias and restaurants
D	600	18,000	castings in aluminum, copper alloy and magnesium, kitchen equipment for cafeterias and restaurants, aluminum windows
E	20	500	metal stampings, all metals
F	14	235	pipes and elbows, storage and processing tanks, ventilators
G	50	1,500	garbage and ash cans, pipes elbows
H	50	1,000	shower stalls, contract work
I	25	500	custom work
J	50	700	plating—custom work only
K	50	700	dies, metal-working, metal settings for jewellery, jewellery boxes
L	15	350	plating—custom work only

account for 90 per cent or more of the value of each firm's purchases. There is almost always a residual that is unaccounted for: its size for any firm is determined by the industrial manager's patience in answering detailed questions about the confidential affairs of his firm.

In procuring the inputs listed in Table 13.5, the 12 firms maintained 94 separate linkages. These can be viewed in several ways. Intra-agglomeration linkages were numerically dominant; 67 linkages (71 per cent) were with

Table 13.5. Inputs of 12 Montreal Firms in the 'Metal Stamping, Pressing and Coating Industry'

			Sources			
		Value of input in 1971	Wholesalers in Montreal	outside Montreal	Manufacturers in Montreal	outside Montreal
Firm	Input					
		$000				
A	Stainless steel	1,750				5
	mild steel and galvanized sheet	500				2
	aluminium sheet	75	3			
	welding rods	5	3			
B	Stainless steel sheets	165	1			
	aluminium sheet	50	1			
	iron plates	25	1			
C	stainless steel sheets	70	2			
	aluminium sheet	3	2			
	hardware components	7	11			
D	aluminium—various forms	1,000	1			
	steel plate	1,500				1
	iron and steel bars	200	5			
	stainless steel sheets	6,000				4
E	Steel sheet	170	4			1
	roll formed steel	20			1	
	ball bearings	n.a.				2
F	black sheets	65	4			
	stainless steel sheets	20	3			
	aluminium sheet	5	3			
	paints and varnish	2			1	
G	galvanized steel sheets	650				2
	chrome plated sheet metals	20				1
	aluminium sheet	30				1
	cardboard cartons	24			1	
H	cold rolled steel	135	1		1	
	brass plumbing accessories	81				1
	paints and varnish	60	1			
	corrugated boxes	46			1	

Table 13.5. (Contd.)

Firm	Input	Value of input in 1971	Wholesalers in Montreal	Wholesalers outside Montreal	Manufacturers in Montreal	Manufacturers outside Montreal
	plastic extrusions	26				1
I	stainless steel sheet	100	2			
	drive equipment	40	(varies from job to job)			
	welding rods	3.6			1	
J	solution for plating	180	5			
K	brass coils	80			1	
	steel coils	45	1			
	satin cloth	n.a.			1	
	velvet	n.a.				2
	leatherette and vinyl covering materials	n.a.				1
L	anodes—zinc copper nickel	45		1		
	solution for plating	5	4	1		
	various chemicals, e.g. caustic soda, boric acid, chromates, metal cleaner	n.a.	1			

firms in the local complex. Linkages with local manufacturing firms were weak. Only 8 linkages (approximately 8 per cent) were with manufacturers in the local complex. The local linkages were dominated by purchases from wholesalers (59 linkages, approximately 78 per cent of all local linkages). Linkages to manufacturers outside the local complex were numerically more important than linkages to local manufacturers. Only two links were made to non-local wholesalers. In short, local linkages were more numerous than external linkages; linkages to wholesalers outnumbered links to manufacturers; and purchases from wholesalers were dominant in the local linkages, while purchases from manufacturers were dominant in the external linkages.

The situation assumes a very different character when the values of the inputs are considered. The two large firms (A and D) completely controlled the linkage pattern. Linkages to manufacturing were valued at approximately $11 million, whereas those to wholesaling were approximately $2·5 million. That is 81 per cent of the value of purchases was from the former and only 19 per cent from the latter. Similarly, despite the clear numerical superiority of intra-agglomeration linkages, about 80 per cent ($10,852,000) of all expenditures on inputs were made outside the local economy. Purchases made in Montreal totalled only \$2,611,500 (20 per cent of the total). Purchases from local manufacturers were only \$176,000: less than 1·5 per cent of value of all purchases. Obviously, links to other manufacturers in the same industrial complex are of no locational significance.

This example provides further reinforcement of a point made several times already. Manufacturing is so heterogeneous that only one or a few firms produce any particular product; and it is highly probable that the industrial city or complex in which a firm is located will have no producers of many particular input requirements. The most important input to the 'metal stamping, pressing and coating industry' is steel, especially steel sheet. There is no production of this commodity in Montreal and the primary iron and steel industry as a whole is very weakly represented in the vicinity of Montreal. This is hardly a remarkable fact; in Canada, as in all countries, there are few primary producers of iron and steel and, therefore, only a small number of locations from which these commodities emanate. Heavy users of iron and steel, except when located in iron and steel production centres, will inevitably have weak linkages with other manufacturers in the same industrial complex as themselves. No doubt this is why this sample of firms has a greater external orientation in its procurement patterns than the larger more broadly based Montreal firms considered earlier.

Confronted with the situation of having no local producers, firms can procure their inputs from wholesalers in the local complex or purchase directly from producers in other cities or complexes. From this example it appears that smaller firms prefer the former alternative while larger firms prefer the latter. But, it would be wrong to think in terms of a dichotomy based on the size of firms. The limited evidence of this small and biased sample of industries suggests that larger establishments are making their largest purchases from manufacturers outside the local complex, but their smaller purchases from wholesalers inside it. In all probability, therefore, it is not so much the size of firm, *per se,* which determines purchasing behaviour, rather it is the size of the firm's requirement; and naturally it is only the larger firms which have need of a large volume of any particular input. In satisfying their larger needs by purchasing directly from external manufacturers the large firms exert a dominant influence on the spatial patterns of inter-industrial linkages even though the linkages of small firms to local suppliers are much more numerous. The wholesalers are obviously important in meeting the more modest input requirements of small and large producers alike; they enable many firms to procure all their inputs from the local complex and are thus responsible for the plethora of short, small intra-urban movements which greatly outnumber inter-urban or 'inter-complex' movements. The latter, however, are much greater in volume and their spatial patterns completely overshadow those of intra-urban linkages. From his examination of Philadelphia's manufacturing Karaska arrived at substantially the same conclusion.

Some Effects of Corporate Organization

When Weber was trying to provide a theoretical explanation of agglomeration early in this century the organization of manufacturing was characterized by the single-plant firm. While these are still important, a very significant proportion of manufacturing throughout the world has been organized into large or huge multi-plant firms which may be national or multi-national in character. Weber made no allowance for these sprawling corporate entities that embrace both horizontally and vertically linked plants as well as, in many cases, primary extractive activities and a variety of service and exchange functions. It is hardly surprising if this type of organization leads to material interchanges between establishments in the same firm. Often these interchanges are international and, like other activities practised by these organizations, a cause for serious governmental concern. In view of their spatial expansiveness and their use of intra-firm linkages, the large corporations can be expected to reduce the importance of intra-agglomeration linkages. Some data collected from four Montreal plants in the paints and varnish industry permits some examination of this point.

The corporate affiliations of these four plants are highly representative of the wider scene in Canadian manufacturing. Plant A is owned by an American firm which confines itself to the manufacture of paints and varnishes. It has 12 factories: 9 of them are in the United States and 3 are in Canada. The Canadian headquarters are in Toronto. Plant B is owned by a very large European chemicals company which, amongst other interests, has 4 plants for paints and varnishes manufacture in Canada. The headquarters of the Canadian paints division is the Montreal plant. Plant C is the smallest and is the one and only plant of a small Canadian firm. Plant D is one of at least 20 plants coming under the control of a Canadian corporation which manufactures a wide range of chemical products, including paints and varnishes.

As pointed out earlier, this industry displays a certain amount of product variation from firm to firm. Accordingly there is a matching variation in inputs. To avoid the difficulties this presents for the making of comparisons between plants a small number of inputs which are essential to virtually all types of paint were selected for study.

In all four plants the biggest single input both in value and volume is titanium dioxide. For example, Firm B uses 3·5 million pounds per annum at a cost of $924,000, which is about 40 per cent of the total value of its inputs. In all Canada there are only three producers of titanium dioxide; all are located in Quebec within a hundred miles of Montreal; and each firm buys from one or more of them. Thus, for this input all plants purchase outside the local complex and all react to the situation in the same way.

The linkages of the second input are confined to the local complex and again the behaviour of all plants is identical. For the most part the finished product of this industry is sold in metal containers. Only two firms in Quebec, both located in Montreal, produce the requisite containers and all four firms purchase supplies from both firms. The closest alternative producers are in Toronto. Since their product is exactly the same as is obtainable in Montreal and their selling price is identical, but delivery price on this bulky product is higher, it would be economic nonsense for the paint companies to consider any suppliers other than the two in Montreal.

Calcium carbonate was the third input to be examined. In value, if not in volume, it is a minor input. Firm D uses approximately one million pounds per annum at a cost of only $20,000. This is about 2 per cent of D's total purchases. Canada has two sources of calcium carbonate, but both of them are a long distance from Quebec which has no production. However, in the neighbouring American State of Vermont there is one producer from whom all the Montreal plants purchase this input.

The fourth input was linseed oil. This is used by the paints and varnish industry in a variety of forms, including raw, boiled, acid refined, alkali refined, heat bodied and blown. Small quantities of linseed oil fatty acid are also used. It is not an important input and accounts for only about 2 per cent of total purchases. There are two sources in Canada for this product in its various forms. One is in Toronto, the other is in Montreal. Two of the Montreal plants buy from both suppliers, that is, bring part of their supply a distance of about ten miles and the rest of their supply a distance of approximately 350 miles. The other two plants buy only from the Montreal supplier.

The final input reveals significant differences in the behaviour of the four firms. It is really a number of separate smaller inputs which can all be described as alkyd resins; these account for 15–25 per cent of the total value of each firm's inputs. In Canada there are 15 firms making alkyd resins in 17 establishments. Not all, however, are producing them for sale; some are producing solely for consumption internal to the firm. Only 9 firms with 10 plants sell this commodity; two firms with two establishments are in the Montreal industrial complex and most of the rest are in southern Ontario, mainly in and around Toronto.

Plant A is part of one of the firms which produces alkyd resins solely for its own consumption. They are manufactured in the Toronto plant and from there some are shipped to the Montreal plant. Both Montreal plants which produce alkyds are perfectly capable of meeting Plant A's needs in this commodity and, indeed, at one time, one of them was the supplier to Plant A; but once Plant A's firm entered into the production of alkyd resins, this linkage was severed and, for almost twenty years now, Plant A has obtained its supplies from Toronto. Only in an emergency, arising, say, from strikes in the Toronto plant or in the transportation industries, does Plant A turn to one of the alternative local sources. The European firm which owns Plant B has no production facilities for alkyd resins in North America and Plant B at present obtains its supplies from the Montreal firm which used to supply Plant A. The small single-plant firm—Plant C—buys some of its supplies from the same firm supplying Plant B, but it also purchases from an Ontario producer which maintains a storage and distribution facility in Montreal. Plant D is similar to Plant A. The firm owning Plant D manufactures its own alkyd resins in its Toronto factory. Supplies are shipped from there to the Montreal plant, which, acting in accord with company policy, must obtain its supplies from this source.

This example is not a spectacular illustration of the effect of corporate organization on linkage patterns. Nevertheless, it does provide in its own modest way, through the example of the fifth input, another important reason why linkages extend beyond an industrial agglomeration even when suitable suppliers are present perhaps a mile or less away. *The achievement of economies within the firm can be more important economies deriving from the proximity of suppliers in the same agglomeration.* All the evidence indicates, moreover, that intra-corporation economies will become increasingly important during the next several decades.

Perception and Attitude of Decision-Makers

In Montreal, manufacturing in the aggregate buys the greater part of its input requirements from suppliers that are not located in the local industrial complex. Similar findings have been made for other industrial complexes. Some suggestions have been made in this paper to explain why this situation arises. These have related entirely to the circumstances confronting firms in their search for suppliers. Regardless of the attitudes, perceptions and goals of firms' decision-makers, it seems as if a framework of circumstances predetermines that linkages with the world beyond the agglomeration will be stronger than those within the agglomeration. This statement does not imply, however, that the human element is of no significance in influencing the outcome of events or that the decision-maker has no choice worthy of consideration.

The range of choice open to the decision-maker is much narrower than has been commonly supposed, or implicitly inferred, by location theory. The alternatives are very limited more often than they are numerous. At least, in practical terms they are usually very limited; but the knowledge most purchasers have about suppliers is very limited and it is this limited knowledge which describes the real world in which a choice has to be made. Yet, in many cases, as far as the decision-maker is concerned there is no choice at all.

Location theorists would have us believe that firms congregate in agglomerations because their costs, including their input costs are lower there than in alternative locations. This raises two questions about inputs.

Is it really the case that firms are concerned to minimize their input costs? In general, are costs lower if inputs are obtained from the agglomerations in which the firm is located? If either of these questions receives a negative answer, there is even less reason to anticipate that the input linkages of firms located in an agglomeration will be mainly confined to the agglomeration.

A partial answer to both questions is provided through an examination of information obtained from firms in the 'metal stamping, pressing and coating industry'. For every input for which a respondent was prepared to volunteer information, the following question was asked: 'In selecting your present supplier of this input did you select the one which offered the lowest delivered price?' Answers were obtained for 46 procurement actions, most of which are described in Table 13.5. In only 18 cases (40 per cent of the total) did the respondent claim to be obtaining the input from the source which he knew to be offering the lowest delivered price. (In considering this result it must be borne in mind that knowledge of suppliers varied amongst the respondents.) However, for 6 of the 18 positive answers, the respondents claimed they either did not know of an alternative supplier or all the suppliers known to them provided the input at the same delivered price. There were, therfore, only twelve (24 per cent) unequivocal cases when there was a choice between delivered prices and the firm offering the lowest price was chosen. Of these 12 input transactions, 7 were made with firms in the local complex and 5 were made with firms outside it. In 19 cases (41 per cent) the respondent claimed the lowest price known to him was not taken. In the remaining 9 cases the respondent did not know if the lowest delivered price had been chosen. It appears as if there is no strong concern with obtaining the lowest price; and if the lowest price is taken, the supplier is almost as likely to be outside the agglomeration as within it.

Respondents were provided with a check list of factors which may be important in determining their choice of supplier for any particular input. Three factors were indicated as important in determining the choice of suppliers (Table 13.6). These were, delivery reliability (the only factor regarded as important for every transaction), delivered price and quality of product. Most respondents would not or could not rank these three factors and regarded them all as being equally important. Even when they were asked to name the single most important factor influencing their choice of supplier, most respondents referred to a combination of factors (Table 13.7).

It is interesting to note that proximity to supplier was almost unanimously considered to be unimportant. Probably this arises because delivered price was rarely regarded as the single decisive factor. One can appreciate that, if it is considered to be no more important than quality of product or delivery reliability, then proximity to suppliers is no longer decisive in choosing suppliers or, for that matter, in the firm's choice of

Table 13.6. 'Metal Stamping, Pressing and Coating Industry': The Relative Importance of Factors Influencing the Choice of Suppliers for 26 Inputs

	Important	Moderately important	Unimportant
1. Proximity to the supplier	0	1	25
2. Ease of communication with supplier	6	10	10
3. Quality of product	23	2	1
4. Delivered price	23	2	1
5. Delivery reliability	26	0	0
6. The volume of your requirements	3	1	22
7. No alternative suppliers	3	1	22
8. Other	5		

location. This is an interesting speculation because proximity to suppliers has long been regarded as one of the key locational attractions of industrial agglomerations. Its probably exaggerated importance was an inevitable consequence of the 'rational economic man' paradigm to which our location

Table 13.7. 'Metal Stamping, Processing and Coating Industry': The Single Most Important Factors Influencing Choice of Suppliers for 42 Inputs

1. Price and quality
2. Price and quality
3. Quality and delivery reliability
4. Price and delivery reliability
5. Ease of communication
6. Can fill our specifications
7. Quality
8. Quality and delivery reliability
9. Price, delivery, reliability and quality
10. Price and quality
11. Price, reliability and quality
12. Quality, price, reliability
13. No alternate supplier
14. Quality, price, reliability and knowledge of supplier
15. Previous dealings and reliability
16. Quality and previous dealings
17. Ease of communication
18. An arrangement mutual to buyer and seller
19. Price
20. Price
21. Comparable price
22. Price
23. Variety and past credit help
24. Keeps their sizes in stock
25. No other supplier
26. No other supplier
27. Speed of delivery, price and quality
28. Could satisfy our design requirements
29. They are all the same
30. Quality of service
31. No alternative supplier
32. Price
33. No alternative supplier
34. Delivery and reliability and technical service
35. Speed of delivery
36. Service
37. Special arrangement
38. Quality and reliability
39. Service
40. Quality and technical service
41. Quality and technical service
42. Quality and technical service

models belong. Weber, for example, threw the whole weight of his argument onto the minimization of costs; and, logically and inevitably, proximity to suppliers assumed a great importance in explaining agglomeration insofar as distance minimization should promote (freight rate structures permitting) transport cost minimization. But the moment an entrepreneur allows considerations of quality to enter the equation, the proximity factor immediately loses a great deal of its importance.

Quality of product has been completely neglected in the research on linkages. It obviously has some influence on the decision to choose a particular supplier; although its importance seems to vary according to the nature of the input. Significantly, several respondents, when discussing an input which varies little in quality from one firm to another, substituted the phrase 'quality of service' for 'quality of product'. This was particularly noticeable with regard to those inputs of soft drink bottlers which are very uniform in quality and price and available from only two or three suppliers. On occasion, a respondent would claim he could find no differences between suppliers in price, quality or service and had chosen his present supplier because of the personality of the salesman.

Ease of communication with suppliers was not ranked highly by the respondents. Thus, another factor long considered to be a locational attraction of agglomerations is brought into question. Finally, it should be noted that delivery reliability was regarded as important regardless of the location of the supplier and did not emerge as a competitive advantage of local suppliers. Even when supplies were obtained from abroad, delivery reliability was named as having been an important consideration in choosing the supplier concerned.

If delivered price is a consideration of lesser importance than has usually been assumed, there thus emerges another reason, to be added to those already detected, for industry being only lightly dependent upon the local complex for its inputs. There appears to be at least one other factor to consider.

For many inputs, it may be just as cheap, if not cheaper, to buy inputs from suppliers located outside the agglomeration. Provided an entrepreneur is concerned to minimize the cost of an input and is prepared to search widely for the lowest price, he will eventually find a lower delivered price from an outside supplier than is obtainable from a local supplier. This was exemplified in all industries examined. Of course, whether or not a businessman is prepared to search out a cheaper price in more distant areas depends partly on his temperament, partly on the relative importance of the input to his business and partly on the nature of the input. Most of the businessmen contacted freely admitted to being 'satisficers' as opposed to 'optimizers'. Many agreed that they could probably get an input more cheaply from another supplier and they would say something like, 'I don't believe in shopping around', or 'we've been doing business with this supplier for 15 years, they give us good service and they know our needs'. As a general rule the reliance on local suppliers is inversely proportional to the size of the purchaser's needs. When the purchaser's requirements are modest, he is content to buy from a local producer or wholesaler. Suppliers outside the city are often not known or considered. However, the purchaser is more likely to look for alternative and cheaper sources inside or outside the local agglomeration if an input is of greater relative importance to his business.

The firms which agreed to detailed interviews about their purchasing behaviour exhibited great variety in attitude, knowledge, perception and actual behaviour. As a general rule large firms were more knowledgeable about suppliers and more inclined to purchase from distant sources. For example, in the 'metal stamping, pressing and coating industry', seven firms were using stainless steel sheet (see Table 13.5). Of these, five were small and buying from local wholesalers. Only one of them claimed to be buying at the lowest price known to him. On the other hand, the two larger firms both claimed to be buying at the lowest prices known to them. One was purchasing directly from producers in Japan and Sweden; the other was obtaining supplies from Ontario, England and Sweden.

However, even among the small firms there are differences in attitude and behaviour which, if anything, reflect the personalities of their owners or managers. The same industry provides exemplification of the point. Six firms were using aluminium sheet. Five of them were getting their supplies from Montreal wholesalers. The sixth, who was acquainted with all the local sources, was getting his supply from a source in Taiwan. His only reason for buying from Taiwan was that it was the cheapest source known to him. He had no explanation as to why it was cheaper: in fact, he was quite puzzled about it. He had learned about this source from a business friend.

This section was oriented towards two central questions. The first was 'Is it really the case that firms are concerned to minimize their input costs?' The answer appears to be that firms seek to obtain their inputs at 'reasonable' costs. Cost is certainly not their only major concern and it is very seldom their prime concern. It has to be balanced against other considerations such as quality of product, quality of service and delivery reliability. The second question was, 'In general, are costs lower if inputs are obtained from the agglomeration in which the firm is located?'. This research indicates that costs are nearly always 'reasonable' if local suppliers are used; but a cheaper source can often be found outside the local complex. Whether or not a firm searches for cheaper sources outside the agglomeration depends on the nature of the input, the size of the firm, the absolute and relative importance of the input to the firm, the personal attributes of the decision-maker, and probably a host of other factors which have not been considered in this chapter.

Conclusion

The major objective of this paper was to understand some aspects of the operational behaviour of firms in a large industrial complex in the hope that such understanding would provide some insights into the locational attractiveness of agglomerations. Towards this objective the paper has presented evidence on the aggregate material input and output linkages for industry as a whole in the major industrial complex of Montreal. For a much smaller number of industries and firms the paper has explored in detail the nature of input linkages: the decisions which establish these linkages, some of the external circumstances impinging on these decisions and some attitudes of the decision-makers to the selection process.

Agglomeration forces are complex and this paper has concentrated on only one of their aspects. However, the idea that firms are drawn to agglomerations because of the ease with which they can interact with other manufacturing firms in the same agglomeration has long occupied an important place in the speculative explanations of industrial agglomeration. The evidence of this chapter undermines the validity of that supposed component of agglomeration economies.

At least for aggregate manufacturing—if not always for individual firms, which naturally enough vary in their needs, attitudes and motivations—the local industrial complex is neither the major source of materials nor the major sales area. This result, which corroborates the findings of other studies does not invalidate the notion of external economies of scale or deny their postulated strong locational attraction. However, it does suggest strongly that, as far as material linkages are concerned, the general effect of the industrial complex upon manufacturing location, within the context of external agglomeration economies, is weak.

This apparent weakness of the industrial complex is probed here and several reasons are provided, admittedly based on flimsy evidence, as to why linkages are weaker within the complex than they are with the world beyond it. Circumstances external to the establishment, as well as certain attitudes, perceptions and motivations of decision-makers, work against the existence of strong local linkages. This is less the case with small single-plant firms: these appear to function within the agglomeration in a manner more closely approximating the postulated behaviour patterns of manufacturing as a whole. But, while small firms and their transactions are numerically significant, they exert a comparatively small influence on the aggregate linkage patterns of the agglomeration.

Evidence of strong agglomerative forces will have to be sought in other directions. Linkages to services, to the labour force, public and private amenities, and other aspects of urban complexes for which linkage analysis is not appropriate, should be examined. But one begins to suspect that isolation of any particular agglomeration component may bring disappointing results. It may be that many little advantages, none of which is significant by itself, combine to form one large composite advantage which forms the basis of manufacturing's marked locational preference for industrial agglomerations.

References

Brooks, S., J. M. Gilmour, and K. Murricane, 1973, 'The spatial linkages of manufacturing in Montreal and its surroundings', *Les cahiers de Geographie de Quebec* (forthcoming).

Canada, Statistics Canada, 1972, *Soft Drink Manufacturers,* Cat. No. CS32–208/1972 (Ottawa: Queen's Printer).

Field, N. C. and D. P. Kerr, 1968, *Geographical Aspects of Industrial Growth in the Metropolitan Toronto Region* (Toronto: Government of Ontario, Regional Development Branch, Department of Treasury and Economics).

Karaska, G. T., 1969, 'Manufacturing linkages in the Philadelphia economy: some evidence of external agglomeration forces', *Geographical Analysis,* 1 (4), 354–69.

Lever, W. F., 1972, 'Industrial movement, spatial association and functional linkages', *Regional Studies,* 6, 371–84.

Quebec, Ministere de l'industrie et du commerce, 1970, *Repertoire des Manufactures de la Province de Quebec* (Quebec: L'Imprimeur de la reine).

Streit, M. E., 1969, 'Spatial associations and economic linkages between industries', *Journal of Regional Science,* 9, 177–88.

Weber, A., 1929, *Theory of the Location of Industries* (Chicago: University of Chicago Press). An English translation of *Uber den Standort der Industrien,* with introduction and notes by Carl J. Friedrich.

14

Environmental Adaptation of Industrial Plants: Service Linkages, Locational Environment and Organization

J. N. H. BRITTON

The empirical research tradition of industrial geography has always sat rather uncomfortably with the intellectual rigour of location theory. The former approach, however, has yielded to 'explanatory' treatment by 'testing' or elaborating hypotheses derived from location and regional economic theory. But now, another source of uneasiness affecting the field is social science theory. For example, organization theory has generated substantial interest in the value of models of non-normative decision-making, in learning by firms. To absorb new questions, concepts and models of industrial behaviour and integrate them with, and to the benefit of, established geographic problems is a major difficulty for industrial geography. This chapter stems from an ultimate interest in regional and industrial policy and is aimed at interpreting actual industrial 'behaviour'. In establishing a conceptual basis, however, it reflects much recent thinking in industrial geography by recognizing some inhibiting aspects of location theory.

Initially, four general research problems are defined to clarify the focus of the paper. First, locational choice (particularly locational search) and decision-making by firms has been relatively well developed as a field of enquiry, but at the expense of other types of industrial 'behaviour' that have geographic significance, especially when the location of a firm is 'given'. Second, too little attention has been paid to organizational differences between industrial plants: single-plant firm, domestic branch plant, subsidiary of foreign corporation all crudely embody some potentially important distinctions. Because location theory assumes occupational (though not production) homogeneity for industrial plants, substantive work has recognized but poorly analysed varying degrees of functional complexity. Third, the varying functional mix of plants is ignored by the production focus of theory and most analysis. Much location theory is structured around the influence exercised by material spatial-economic linkages, but it is argued here that service connections are locationally much more significant than such theory allows. Similarly the impact of new industrial development upon urban and regional economies is determined greatly by the types of service linkages generated. As the relative costs of materials movement decline, as organizations and business services become more complex, as technology and information exchanges become more important to the viability of many firms—then service linkages demand more critical attention in industrial geography. Fourth, the clustering tendency of many industrial plants in like and different industries, and intraregional or intra-urban material and service linkages, are treated in a manner inconsistent with the remainder of location theory. The argument has been developed that external economies may be earned by plants in industrial agglomerations and hence the tendency to clustering is 'explained'. But this aspect of theory would require specific information on agglomeration diseconomies be available like labour costs; theory demands plants use information in the location problem to which they have access only after the plant is already operating in an agglomeration.

These views on the limitations of location theory are explored in a systematic review and integration of work on industrial behaviour (adaptation), the locational environment of firms, and economic linkages (particularly service linkages) and their geographic mobility. Subsequently, key ideas from this discussion are implemented in the design of enquiry and pilot analysis of service linkages of manufacturing plants in southern Ontario.

Adaptive Behaviour

While the location problem is an important issue, recent published work on manufacturing focuses excessively on that problem. Even immobility is a locational decision. This view is useful in a *post facto* sense but a richer basis for analysis of industrial behaviour is to accept that in their decision-making firms demonstrate an ability to adapt (adjust) to a changing (business) environment but do so against a background of the long and short run history of interaction of the firm with its environment (Alchian, 1950; Murphy, 1965). Some firms generate branches, some relocate with or without expansion, some re-site, but others establish new input and output connections with other firms, with or without changes in the production functions of plants in the firm. The arguments for this are that at any time most industrial plants are fully functioning and must accept their location: only a small proportion of plants engage in relocation. This view is supported by the 'strategic' nature of the location decision (owing particularly to the substantial capital involved), the locational inertia experienced by management and the lack of easily obtained information on comparable locations. Furthermore, firms maintain complex decision apparatus which, via a search procedure, allows improvements in information (quantity and quality) on locational and production choices to be related to goals of the firm by a feedback (learning) process.

The form of adaptation considered here focuses on the functional economic linkages of industrial plants. Business service linkages reflect the way a plant adjusts its interaction with other economic units. While adaptation embodies learning and, therefore, change in the arrangement of economic linkages, in this chapter adaptive behaviour is examined in a cross-sectional manner—it focuses on differences in the service arrangements that plants make depending on:

(1) the particular industrial environment of the plant (location) and
(2) the organizational structure of the firm (organization)

Multi-Locational Firms

Although the organizational differences that may exist between plant and firm are generally recognized, the multi-locational character of the most important industrial firms is poorly represented in location theory. The development of ideas on this subject has depended on a more empirical tradition. It is understood that branch plants may be sustained by the parent plant under a variety of administrative arrangements and this points to the need to recognize more formally the substitutability of (a) interdependence of branches with other firms in the local urban-industrial environment and (b) dependence of branches on the parent firm, particularly for the supply of a wide range of inputs from all economic sectors. Early work by Luttrell (1962) is well known in this connection but his types of branches appear to be particularly relevant to the British geographic context. In North America a macro-geographic focus has been favoured but has not contributed to the understanding of the way branches are located or choose linkage arrangements from different locations (Ray, 1965).

The substantial literature on business, especially corporate, behaviour has provided some impetus to geographic inquiry; but this has been mainly sifting relevant works for aspects of product and locational diversity, corporate organization and response to technical, economic and political changes and the like which have geographic significance. Most geographic work which follows the lead of business economics, administration and management strategy, however, concentrates on general aspects of corporate adaptation to environmental conditions or on aspects of a particular corporation's operations (Krumme, 1969; Steed, 1971). In that sense there is 'geography of enterprise' but focus on the individual 'business' weakens the geographic output of this approach because an integrated view of the behaviour of industry (i.e. many firms) within different economic environments cannot be derived directly. Nevertheless, the traditional problem of locational choice has also been cast in the business frame (Townroe, 1971).

Possibly the most productive matter that can be tackled in 'business geography' is that of organizational structures since these have a geographic dimension. There is much conceptual work to be completed here, but contributions such as that of Brooke and Remmers (1970) on the multi-national corporation are instructive on the complexities of corporate structure. In their work, four types of structure are recognized, but the geographic implications of those organizational forms are either not immediately apparent or not easily described.

The recognition of the general geographic significance of the multi-locational nature of firms is almost solely confined to Swedish writing. Törnqvist is the main contributor and although his view of organizations is highly generalized and simple, especially when compared with writings in business, it has the advantages of emphasizing the research and administrative as well as productive functions of firms (Törnqvist, 1970). These are combined in various proportions in different locations thus giving rise to an important influence on the goods–service linkage patterns of any locational unit. But single-plant firms also vary in their occupational structure and hence in their contact patterns; more important for the branch is that, in addition to some provision of services within the *plant,* there is the complication that scale economies may be generated if services of various types are provided from within the *firm* to various manufacturing locations. This dimension to enquiry, while elementary in theoretical origin, has been relatively ignored in terms of geographic interpretations. Nevertheless, intra-firm linkages between locationally distinct units contain information essential for examining the autonomy/dependence of branches in terms of investment, production and personnel.

Törnqvist's work is particularly significant since he attributes changes in Sweden's interregional (interurban) structure and distribution of economic activities to the multi-locational nature of many firms in the economy. Units with production as a primary function, can be accommodated in non-metropolitan centres while the organization as a whole enjoys 'central' research, financial and other tertiary and quaternary contact arrangements in Stockholm by virtue of its head office location. Kristensson, working primarily on the problem of optimal allocation of different types of economic activities (within and between firms) in the Stockholm region from the standpoint of contact accessibility has produced related ideas that apply at the regional scale and which cast useful conceptual light on the operation of various agglomeration economies within metropolitan areas like Stockholm (Kristensson, 1967). Thorngren's examinations of contacts within large organizations are related to Kristensson's work but are stimulated

nore directly by organization theory and ultimately may provide a basis
'or explaining urban growth and agglomeration that is less dependent on
·conomic theory and more concerned with business behaviour (Thorngren,
1970).

The functional and locational division of a firm ensures that intra-firm
inkages of information and materials are of critical geographic importance
und this is particularly significant if the relationship between plants and the
urban system is to be understood. But alongside this seemingly innocuous
statement must be placed the fact that the deductive derivation of a hierarchically structured urban system (from economic units to the system level)
hat incorporates manufacturing activity has proved impossible (Lösch),
ulthough it is readily accepted that the locational forces bearing on manu-
'acturing activities support the form of urban systems as strongly as do
central place functions. (Lösch, 1954). In addition, the literature on the
theory of agglomeration economies (see below), so vital to understanding
the structure of an urban system, is most highly developed in the context
of manufacturing activity. There is, however, no general acceptance in
substantive research, of the importance of the multi-locational nature of
firms!

The importance of intra-firm linkages is illustrated if, to sustain the
argument, it is assumed initially that manufacturing plants (of uni- or
multi-locational firms)—whose locations have been previously determined
obtain necessary tertiary and quaternary functions (externally) from the
nearest appropriate urban centres whose structure reflects the various
thresholds applying to the provision of different business services. If this
arrangement is subsequently modified, however, to allow multi-plant firms
to earn internal scale economies by centrally providing some services from
either within the company (e.g. accounting) or outside (e.g. legal services),
short circuits will be created within the urban system. Some firms contain
plants which interact at a low level with service firms in their particular
regions while substantial volumes of business may be created in the urban
centre where the company head office is located. It is evident, some geographic implications of a 'branch-plant national economy' may be evaluated
by considering such short-circuits from a domestic urban system.

Linkage

Three distinctive themes may be identified in the literature on economic
linkages that includes not only statements from location theory and practice but also works on urban economic structure and growth.

(1) Inputs (or outputs), being transportable, incur transfer costs and
there are associated inventory costs and internal scale choices which can

be placed in perspective in a total cost minimizing treatment of *the location problem.*

(2) Through the clustering of economic activities, firms benefit economically from being located in an agglomeration; the skilled labour pool, well developed transport and utilities systems and the great potential for a wide variety of alternative opportunities for informational, service and material linkage are all aspects of the external economies (of scale) that are thought to be available. Recently emphasis has been given to costless 'side flows' of information, for example, rather than direct commercial relations that may occur within a limited area (Thorngren). In this way the view developed by Marshall is re-presented to conform with a changed structure of economic activities (Jansen, 1970; Marshall, 1946). While Thorngren is concerned with 'spontaneous cooperation', other writers indicate the importance of primacy in communications media to an explanation of the advantages of agglomerations: *infrastructural urbanization economies* (Bergsman *et al.,* 1972).

(3) It is argued, in association with the latter view, that the agglomeration of industry also allows specific local input–output relations to develop, juxtaposition permits complex connection systems to function so that external economies *(linkage economies of localization and urbanization)* are earned through a variety of arrangements including that of the highly structured industrial complex.

Perhaps the best known statement on agglomeration is that of Weber (1929). While he outlined only some of the arguments indicated above (2 and 3) he did specify one way in which agglomeration economies could be absorbed into the location problem as solved by cost minimization; sixty years later Isard elaborated upon the decision-making and planning significance of Weber's view of agglomeration (Isard, *et al.,* 1969). Agglomeration has also been incorporated by Lösch into a spatial-market approach to theory, but it is in the context of costs of production that relevant external economies attain their main theoretical development. Yet, it may be argued, location theory is here at its weakest as it demands information in the form of prior production experience (see above). The aims of the theory of Weber and others are generally considered reasonable; but only a *post facto* interpretation may be given to problems using their approach: this means external economies are to be gauged from an assessment of existing linkages, for example. This is extended to its maximum when agglomeration economies are inferred from spatially associated industries.

Location theory is no complete guide to geographic action. Rather than the Weberian argument it is suggested that industrial plants tend to agglomerate because of their managements' limited knowledge about less visible but feasible alternative locations; choice is exercised often by imitation in order to minimize uncertainty about competitive conditions, costs and demand (Tiebout, 1957). In essence, it can be argued, a behaviourist 'explanation' can be made of agglomerative location selection that is more reasonable for a wide range of plants (industries) than the purely economic argument. In the development of location theory, the 'spatial margin' concept allows an uneasy coexistence with this type of thinking (Pred, 1967 and 1969; Smith, 1971).

Ideas on agglomeration and linkage, however, are not limited to location theory *per se:* from the adaptation standpoint, other economic geography literature is important:

(1) Support for the economic concept of agglomeration has been provided by particular regional investigations: using detailed field evidence external economies have been inferred from the interconnections between plants and the generally favourable conditions for production in 'industrial quarters'—the New York garment district, jewellery and gun trades in Birmingham, clothing, furniture and some engineering industries in London —and in urban regions—metal trades and engineering in Birmingham and the West Midlands (Chinitz, 1960; Hall, 1959; Wise, 1949; Martin, 1966; West Midland Group, 1948).

(2) In macro-economic models of urban/regional structure and growth, a variety of linkages are of major significance. At an applied level, 'industrial complexes' are defined for planning purposes as 'a set of industrial activities ... subject to important production, marketing, technological, energy or other interrelations and their location ... constrained by these relations' (Hodge and Wong, 1970; Luttrell, 1972) and clearly exemplify contemporary support for an old idea: urban growth is supported by activities that generate their own external economies. Similarly growth pole (centre) 'theory' assigns a key role to linkages by which polarization takes place. Darwent, however, appropriately takes issue very strongly with the 'inadequate treatment of the whole of external economies and the pronounced tendencies towards agglomeration' in the literature on growth poles and centres (Darwent, 1969).

(3) Darwent reacts strongly against discussions of external economies which do not admit explicitly the importance of the geographic context (in a national economy) in which interaction occurs (Scitovsky, 1954). He argues, that without space, *agglomerations* cannot be derived from external economies, and particular spatial situations producing external economies would be ignored. Generally an areal limitation is involved in defining the urban/industrial environment in which linkages convey external economies. The 'economy-wide' and areal views of external economies may be reconciled if a variety of geographic scales is employed in considering linkages.

In spite of the theoretical development of the field, there are major unresolved applied problems with concepts of agglomeration and external economies and of particular importance is the difficulty of measurement.

(1) The view of Chinitz (1960) is, 'the savings, the external economies, ... are difficult to measure quantitatively, but they are nonetheless real and significant ...'. Nevertheless, that there 'is almost no quantitative evidence as to the role of external economies in the agglomerating process' (U.S. Department of Agriculture, 1966) is worrying and imposes a major difficulty in even *post facto* use of location theory. Of the aspects of agglomeration described previously, linkage economies are the more tractable: there is less variability in definitions. These direct linkages between economic units are individually more 'visible' (hence easier to identify) and, therefore, more amenable to study.

(2) Not all identifiable firm-to-firm linkages necessarily earn external economies as conventionally defined: some industrial inputs may be so widely available that it is unlikely they will generate external economies. This means a plant in a metropolitan centre may discover no locational advantages compared with a smaller community. Also, some linkages within or between regions occur within companies (organizations) and thus may demonstrate the way internal economies are earned.

(3) In addition to geographically constrained (immobile) external economies, a *mobile* variety is defined by Robinson (1937; see also Britton, 1969) concerned with conditions of information diffusion (new equipment, research results, but also marketing arrangements) which extends the general scale advantages of large agglomerations (infrastructural urbanization economies). This idea may be generalized to cover direct economic linkages, and the immediate implications would be the following:

(a) Intermediate-goods suppliers and industrial and commercial services may achieve their thresholds for viability by maintaining contacts over a variety of *ranges*.

(b) The size of possible ranges depends on the location and 'transportability' of the particular good or service, the efficiency of ancillary communications which allow distribution of information, and the relative decline in costs of (goods, personnel and information) movement (see below) that increases the effective range over which linkages may occur.

(c) The ranges for some linkages in the past have been limited to industrial quarters; increasingly, however, the urban area, conurbation and urban region are becoming the more common scale at which intense interaction occurs.

(d) Once 'mobility' is admitted to the discussion of linkages, the distance over which connections are established becomes the important variable and displaces consideration of 'externalities' attached to connections. In this way industrial linkages are identified as another instance where the basic concept of *interaction field,* already applied to a wide range of functions to describe the urban sphere of influence, allows consideration of geographic differences in the organization of various categories of linkages.

Although the term external economy is defined to have the wide application described above, in practical terms there are major problems. The breadth of the definition is illustrated by an argument developed by Chinitz (1960) in the context of the New York apparel industry. He argues: 'the nature of transport facilities determines in part how close a plant must be to the Region in order to enjoy the advantages of external economies ... the geographic boundaries of the Region present no insuperable barrier to the firm that attempts to enjoy at a distance some of the advantages of the cluster'. But to accept such an explosion in number of economic linkages that might transmit external economies is for practical research without value, given the existing difficulties of movement. The most useful argument would suggest that:

(1) the term 'external economy' has significance only in that type of economic-geographic *theory* which attempts *economic rationalization* of the locational choice of the firm and an explanation of urban growth;
(2) the concept probably has no *operational* value in the study of the interactive behaviour of individual firms.

Service Linkages and Linkages Mobility

Industrial complex analysis and related work has shown that there are powerful forces behind the geographic concentration of some linked activities that reflect economies of sequential operation involving the solution of scheduling, inventory, energy and movement problems. Nevertheless, modern techology applied in production and transport has allowed locational disassociaton to increase in some production sequences: generally increased transportability of materials has led to a reduced significance of transfer costs in locational choice.

Are there spatial parallels in the way 'service' inputs (personal and informational contacts) are arranged by manufacturing plants? Since many services involve the use of skilled workers they represent relatively high value 'goods' ; furhermore, improved communication systems, particularly telephone and telex, have reduced the effect distance may have on some forms of interaction; many services are so widely available they would not attract plants using them to form agglomerations. Four problems, however, limit the generalization of patterns of service linkages that can be derived from these considerations.

(1) While substantial information has been considered on material linkages 'we have only a scanty knowlege of the contact linkages between differnt activities in society' (Gad, 1973; Goddard, 1971).

(2) While there is great variation in the 'value' of services, from the payroll service provided by a local bank branch to the international patent lawyer, contrasting circumstances possibly inhibit development of greater variability in the 'range' over which services are obtained. At the former end of the sale of services, ranges are probably small, not so much because of communication costs acting in a frictional sense, as rather because firms supplying low 'value' services are relatively widespread in location. This is probably attributable both to low thresholds and to the broad market structure (range of functions) served by these service firms. Proximity of economic units to clusters of higher 'value' services, however, might be encouraged by the desire to reduce personal travel time and allow face-to-face contact: thus 'ranges' for this category of function might be smaller than otherwise expected.

(3) Different purposes of contact between firms will be reflected in the way linkages are arranged. Distinctions between programmed, planning and orientation activities, for example, are useful since they are associated with increasing concern over information inputs and face-to-face contacts and since different methods of research enquiry must be developed in association with the various types of linkage. The geographic implications of the classification are not clear: most face-to-face contacts generate short distance linkages (see above), but, by contrast, increased *personal* transportation is substitutable for locational proximity in achieving face-to-face contacts.

(4) The major proportion of research on goods linkages has used aggregate flow data because of its availability and its suitability for analysis by means of the gravity model; but special surveys must always be undertaken to obtain data for analysis of *various types* of service interaction. External personal contacts of organizations and business airline trips have been studied in order to investigate functional and spatial patterns of personal contact; studies of office linkages by Gad and Goddard and Thorngren depend on hitherto impossibly large volumes of data assembled by compilation of personal contact diaries of sample executives.

A Case Study of the Service Linkages of Manufacturing Plants

The investigation and analysis reported in the remainder of this chapter is structured around the issues for industrial geography described above. While the case study focuses on the behaviour of individual plants—in the sense of service linkages—emphasis is given to differences in connections of each plant associated with the different urban-industrial environments in which the plants in the study are located. More specifically, the aims of the investigation are to identify:

(1) differences in the ways single-plant firms and branches of multi-locational firms establish linkages with activities supplying service inputs. The differences may be gauged in terms of:
(a) services provided within the plants, within the firm or externally to the firm, i.e. *organizational* differences;
(b) service connections being developed over short or long *distances*—within the plant, or two, within the region (possibly in a larger city), in Toronto (the metropolitan centre), another region, or another country;
(2) differences in (1) that are associated with different urban-industrial environments, industries and plant sizes.

The study differs in orientation from those reviewed above in that it is concerned only with non-material (service) links of the *programmed* and *planning* variety. Even the latter category of contacts is characterized by well established relations, 'you know whom you are going to talk to about what'. This characteristic has been used to design an enquiry which has produced nominal data capable to supporting simple tests of relationships but which was relatively undemanding of business executives.

Survey Data

Managements of manufacturing plants were asked a series of questions about the dominant or 'usual' source from which a service was obtained

Table 14.1. Services in the Questionnaire Enquiry

Office Services	
Bookkeeping	— bookkeeping and accounting
Auditing	
Legal	— e.g. patents
Banking 1	— banking services used for plant operations, e.g. payroll
Banking 2	— loans for capital equipment or expansion
Other financial services	— e.g. brokers
Plant Services	
Maintenance	— plant machinery maintenance
Electrical	— industrial electrical installation and repair
Janitor	— janitorial services

Note. It was found impossible to obtain from the sample plants *systematic* data on a wider range of plant services, particularly those which would be expected to be 'higher order' plant services such as drafting, polishing, grinding, heat treating, toolmaking and so on. All of these latter services would have been involved directly in the production process.

during the preceding year. This mode of enquiry was used so that, by means of interviews, plant managers or other executives could describe, wherever appropriate, that type of regular contact which accounted for the majority of a particular type of business linkage. With industrial plants as observations this type of information was processed in an incidence form.

The questonnaire examined the way a number of services was arranged for each plant (Table 14.1) so that 'organizational' and 'distance' patterns of connection could be derived. The enquiry included *plant services* that were expected to be provided either within the factory or from its town/ city location. Similarly it was expected that bookkeeping—in the *office service* category—would be undertaken by the plant's office staff (however small). Banking 1, Banking 2, Other financial services, Legal and Auditing would demonstrate the ability of plants to arrange 'higher order' services in various, and more interesting, ways depending upon the complexity and policy of the firm, opportunities for linkage in the plant's location (or region) and location of the plant relative to the metropolitan focus of the region.

The Sample Industries

The sample was not designed to be representative of all industry in southern Ontario. Initially four 2-digit S.I.C. industry groups were selected (Metal Fabricating, Machinery, Transportation Equipment, and Electrical Products) using the following criteria: each is well developed in Ontario (none employing less than 5% of the province's manufacturing workforce in 1966), is distributed widely throughout southern Ontario, has at least two-thirds of the plants belonging to multi-locational firms (represented crudely by the proportion of plants in incorporated companies), and maintains notable inter-industry connections (characteristic of the engineering/ metal fabricating industries. From within this 'engineering' industry group Wire and Wire Products (Canadian S.I.C. 305), Motor Vehicle Parts (S.I.C. 325), Electrical Appliances (S.I.C. 331, 332, 334) and Machinery (all 3-digit groups) manufacturers were selected for intensive study on the basis of number of plants (for sampling), homogeneity of class, and expected well developed industrial linkage patterns (pertinent for other purposes of the enquiry).

The Sample Locations

Several environmentally different locations in southern Ontario were defined for the study:

Toronto   1. Metropolitan Toronto, the metropolitan focus of the Province.

Horseshoe	2.	Hamilton (the second ranking urban area in southern Ontario) and the 'Golden Horseshoe': the area stretching along Lake Ontario from Oshawa to Hamilton and extending to the north and north-west of the lakeshore to include towns such as Aurora and Georgetown that have similar access to suppliers and consumer markets in metropolitan Toronto or Hamilton, to which they are tributary. Hamilton and the Horseshoe have been combined in the preparation of the sample rather than kept separate.
London–St. Catharines	3.	The London–St. Thomas–Stratford–Woodstock and St. Catharines–Niagara Falls–Welland groups of towns. While these represent significant urban concentrations in south-western Ontario—and thus possess the urban and industrial infrastructure required to sustain a large number of industrial enterprises—they are geographically separated from Toronto so as to have a lower order of accessibility to this centre than locations in the Golden Horseshoe. This, it is hypothesized, will affect marketing, supplies and labour competition for industries located here, thus requiring these locations to be classified as examples of another type of industrial environment.
Other urban	4.	Towns to the north and east of Toronto. Urban development of a lower order is characteristic of these towns—which are generally remote from their suppliers, their markets, and many external services. Thus, firms found in such areas are posited to adapt their behaviour, including their organizational structures, in yet again different ways to those chosen by firms in other situations.

(The Kitchener–Waterloo–Galt–Guelph group of towns was excluded from the study because their location makes them intermediate in type between environmental groups (2) and (3) above. The areas beyond London to the south-west, beyond Kingston to the east, and beyond Midland–Orillia to the north were excluded by virtue of cost considerations in collecting data.)

Plant Sizes

The size distribution of plants by industry for the selected locations, when roughly tabulated by quartiles according to multi-locational and single-unit firms, (employment and organizational characteristics may be gauged from commercial directory sources) prompted exclusion of the smallest size category because of the preponderance of single-unit firms—a less interesting group from the study viewpoint.

The Sampling Technique

Industry, location and size were used as strata, but by using different sampling fractions for industries and locations some economy was introduced into the procedure of selecting plants for the interviews. Nevertheless, in the sample, the ranking of industry-location cells is similar to that in the population of plants. Sample plants were obtained by random selection; 79 per cent of the sample produced usable interview data.

The Pattern of Responses

The arrangement of responses is described in Tables 14.2 and 14.3: 63 branch plants and 24 plants of single-unit firms comprise the completed sample. Lack of 'control' over the representation of the two organizational types of plants is evident in Table 2 but the roughly 3:1 proportion is an effective division of the responses, given the interest in the branch-plants. The majority of single-plant firms are private corporations; the importance of *wholly*-owned subsidiaries among the branch-plants is paramount.

Analytical Technique

Although several methods of analysing the data were considered, that which proved most suitable was evaluating all hypothesized relationships and response patterns by the chi-square test. Statements of fact are derived only from significant chi-square tests that were run using geographical and organizational linkage data as classified by branch-plant versus single-plant firm, industry, location, locational combinations, plant size and nationality of parent firm.

Analysis of Distance Patterns of Service Linkages

Analysis of service linkages separated 'distance' relationships from 'organizational' patterns and then attempted a joint examination of these aspects. The initial assumption is that services may be classified in aggregate 'range' differences. Subsequently, enquiry was made into the behaviour of *individual* branches and single-plant firms—particularly whether comparable services were obtained in similar manner. The 'distance' over which

Table 14.2. The Sample: All Plants–Basic Structure

Industry	Toronto		Horseshoe		London–St. Catharines		Other urban		Total	
	Single-plant firms	Branch-plants	Single-plant firms	Branch-plants	Single-plant firms	Branch-plants	Single-plant firms	Branch-plants	Single-plant firms	Branch-plants
Wire	6	2	5	6	3	2	1	1	15	11
Machinery	3	4	2	6	1	4	1	4	7	18
Auto	0	4	1	6	1	8	0	3	2	21
Electrical	0	5	0	3	0	1	0	4	0	13
Total	9	15	8	21	5	15	2	12	24	63

Table 14.3. Sample Branch-Plants: Nationality of Parent Firm and Industry

Industry	Canadian	American	British	Other European	Total
Wire	3	5	1	2	11
Machinery	7	10	0	1	18
Auto	4	17	0	0	21
Electrical	4	9	0	0	13
Total	18	41	1	3	63

a service linkage is maintained has been coded according to the following categories—not at all used, in the plant, in the town or city of location, elsewhere in the region (i.e. in other neighbouring towns), in Toronto, in another region, and in another country—of alternative origins of a service linkage. In the strict sense of the word, 'range' cannot be applied to such data, but it is probably no less meaningful than 'distance'.

The assumption that an ordered set of services was chosen for enquiry was well founded:

(1) Low-order plant services are distinguished by low 'range' i.e. plant and town responses predominate.

(2) The patterns of office services vary from Bookkeeping—'linkages' concentrated in the plant—through Banking 1 (town linkages) to Banking 2, Other financial services, Legal and Auditing which are divided in the way major contact is made either in the town or in Toronto.

A division of the data into branches and single-plant firms, however, allows for organizational differences that may occur in the geographic distribution of linkages. A second sample split, Toronto versus other regions, seems warranted on grounds of the differences in industrial environment.

Consistency in Geographic Linkage

The data in Table 14.4 show the extent to which in aggregate related, but different, services are obtained in geographically similar manner, by branches or firms. The linkage patterns are similar for the Maintenance–Janitor, Banking 2–Other financial services and Auditing–Legal pairs, for example, but this apparent agreement must be checked to see if *individual* branches and firms obtain the paired services in identical manner. Is there *consistency* in geographic linkage? Investigation shows there is less 'consistency' for the pairs of higher-order functions. For example, 68 per cent of

Table A.4 Location of Service Linkages: Sample

| | Used in (Non-Toronto) | | | | | | | Used in (Toronto) | | | | | |
	Not used	(a) Plant	(b) Town	(c) Region	(d) Toronto	(e) Another region	(f) Another country	Not used	(a) Plant	(b) Toronto town	(c) Region	(d) Another region	(e) Another country
Non-Toronto branches								**Toronto branches**					
Bookkeeping		37	1	1	4	2	3		14	10	1		1
Auditing		3	7	2	20	7	9		2	13	1		2
Legal			9	2	21	5	11			14	1		1
Banking 1			37	4	4	3							
Banking 2	1	1	16	3	12	5	10			13			1
Other financial services	9	2	13	2	19	1	2	2		11	1	1	
Maintenance	1	38	6		3	3			11	4			
Electrical	1	25	18	1	3	1	1	1	8	5	1		
Janitor		16	27	1	3	1			4	11			
Non-Toronto single-plant firms								**Toronto single-plant firms**					
Bookkeeping		13	1	1					8	1			
Auditing			2	7	5				1	8			
Legal		1	3	4	4		3			7		1	
Banking 1			10	1	3		1			9			
Banking 2			7		3		5			8			
Other financial services	3		5	2	3	1	1	4		4		1	
Maintenance		11	1	2	2		1		5	4			
Electrical		6	5	2	1		1		1	8			
Janitor		10	3	1	1				7	2			

380

branches obtain Auditing and Legal in identical geographic arrangements compared with 83 per cent for Maintenance–Janitor. This may be attributed to the greater variety of feasible geographic alternatives for linkage. Similarly, there is greater 'consistency' in the way single-plant firms obtain higher-order services than is true for branch-plants where various intra-company options may be exercised. Overall, however, this check at the level of *individual* plants seems to indicate the *aggregate* patterns of similarity in geographic linkage of pairs of services are meaningful.

Toronto–Other Regions: Low-Order Functions

The patterns of service linkage by *branches* in the cases of Bookkeeping, Maintenance, Electrical, Janitor and Banking 1 are simple in that: (1) there is no significant[1] difference in the way Toronto branches assemble service inputs compared with subsidiaries in other locations; (2) the plant services and three office functions are shown to be relatively low-order activities by the dominant proportions of linkages organized within the plant or the town; (3) while the analysis of the connections of *single-plant firms* is made very difficult by the sample size there is only minor deviation from the proportional arrangement described for branches (Table 14.4).

Toronto–Other Regions: Higher-Order Office Functions

Branches

There is a pronounced metropolitan effect in the manner in which Legal, Auditing, Other financial and Banking 2 services are arranged by branches. The abstract of the data shown in Table 14.5 shows not only the expected preponderance in local linkages of Toronto branches but also the substantial proportion of Toronto contracts made by non-Toronto branches.

Table 14.5. Branch-Plants: Location of Service Linkage (Table 14.4 abstract)

Location of linkage	Non-Toronto branches			Toronto branches	
	In town (and region)	In Toronto	Other locations	In Toronto (and region)	Other locations
Legal	9(11)	21	16	13(14)	1
Auditing	7(9)	20	19	10(11)	4
Other financial services	13(15)	19	5	11(12)	3
Banking 2	16(19)	12	16	13(13)	2
		$n = 48$		$n = 15$	

Evaluating the linkage arrangements of Toronto and non-Toronto branches is made difficult by the unequal number of locational categories (Toronto = town for Toronto branches). In the case of Banking 2, however, the following combination

Location of service Linkage	Location of branch	
	Non-Toronto	Toronto
Town + Toronto	31	13
Other	16	2

is insignificant showing that the branches in non-metropolitan locations do substitute Toronto links for local ones. But rearrangement of the data, viz.,

Location of service linkage	Location of branch	
	Non-Toronto	Toronto
Town	19	13
All other	28	2

reveals, by the significance of chi-square, the importance (for non-Toronto branches) of not only Toronto connections but also all non-local links. Two related questions emerge: (1) Do single-plant firms maintain similar patterns of connections to those described for branches? (2) If not, is the explanation of difference dependent on the arrangements made by the parent organization of the branch?

Single-Plant Firms

There is evidence in Table 14.6 that plants establish broadly similar connections to those of branches in that the metropolitan effect is demonstrated; but the connection of non-Toronto plants with Toronto appears relatively less well developed. This may reflect the more limited operations of some of the plants, causing them to require less specialized Legal, Auditing and Other financial services and also the development of intra-firm linkages by branches.

Table 14.6. Single-Plant Firms: Location of Service Linkage (Table 14.3 abstract)

	Non-Toronto firms			Toronto firms	
	In Toronto	In town	Other	Toronto	Other
Legal	4	3(7)	4	7	1
Auditing	5	2(9)	1	8	1
Other financial services	3	5(7)	2	4	1
Banking 2	3	7(7)	5	8	0
		$n = 15$		$n = 9$	

The Metropolitan Influence

While service linkages of the sample plants located in metropolitan Toronto differ from those in other locations it is not clear whether this applies also to the group of towns and cities in the Golden Horseshoe (including Hamilton). Bearing in mind the overall 'distance' patterns for each service, and after general screening and specific tests the following conclusions emerge:

(1) Service demands of Toronto plants are satisfied mainly in Toronto— this establishes a distinct pattern.

(2) A substantial proportion of linkages of plants in the Horseshoe are with service firms in Toronto but only in the case of Legal services is the pattern significantly different from that of the other non-Toronto regions combined.

(3) Local connections are not well developed in London–St. Catharines and are much like those for the Horseshoe but longer distance connections seem substituted for those which would otherwise be with Toronto.

(4) An even smaller proportion of local linkages is made by cases in the 'other urban' category but there is no agreement in pattern with London–St. Catharines arrangements.

While the connections by branches and single-plant firms have a fair measure of agreement, in the former case company organization is probably reflected in the greater proportion of longer-distance (non-Toronto) linkages. When the data for branches alone are evaluated the following results emerge:

(1) For all four services, branches demonstrate spatial substitution in

Table 14.7. Auditing Linkages: Branch-Plants

Location of auditing linkage	Toronto (1)	Horseshoe (2)	London–St. Catharines (3)	Other urban (4)
Another region or country	2	5	7	10
Toronto	0	8	5	0
Plant, town or region	13	9	3	0

χ^2columns 1234 = 36·3* χ^2columns 234 = 17·1*
6 degrees of freedom   4 degrees of freedom
χ^2columns 123 + 4 = 28·1* χ^2columns 12 + 3 + 4 = 18·0*
3 degrees of freedom   2 degrees of freedom

N.B. No corrections for continuity have been made in these calculations.
*Significant at ·05 probability or better, one tail test.

inkage arrangements that is not characteristic of single-plant firms which by comparison show a local linkage bias.

(2) The substitution takes the form of proportionally greater importance of long-distance connections ('another country' and 'another region' versus 'Toronto' links), for branches in the 'London–St. Catharines' and 'other urban' categories compared with Horseshoe and Toronto branches.

(3) For Auditing and Legal services connection patterns are significantly different for Toronto, Horseshoe and Other regions (Table 14.7); in the case of Banking 2 and Other financial services, however, there are virtually no non-metropolitan connections by Toronto's branches.

Analysis of the Organizational Basis of Service Linkages

From the analysis above it is evident that an explanation of long-distance contacts may lie in the way branches' demands for services are met by other units within the company. This organizational basis of service connection was hypothesized at the inception of the study. To analyse the importance of organizationl factors directly, linkages have been coded according to whether a service that is used is obtained in the plant, elsewhere in the company (for branches only) or outside the organization and plant.

Because of the distinctly different options available to single-plant firms as compared with branches, the analysis has been divided. Services may be categorized as follows:

(1) Bookkeeping is undertaken principally *within* single-plant firms and branches (Table 14.8).

(2) Plant services are separated from all other office functions by their 'plant' or 'external' linkages. Some different connection patterns of this group are found to be statistically significant, but not easily explained in terms of industry, location, nationality or size.

(3) The greater importance of external connections of branches when obtaining Banking 1 sets that service apart from Auditing. Unfortunately, some poor quality responses for the latter reduces the value of audit information for branches.

(4) Legal and Banking 2 establish dominant 'company' or 'external' linkages in the case of branches; Other Financial and Auditing services are very similar. There are intriguing differences, however, between industries. Banking 2 services, for example, are obtained 'externally' by almost all Wire and Machinery branches while, significantly, more than half Auto and Electrical branches have 'company' arrangements ($\chi^2 = 16 \cdot 9(1)$). These latter industries include well-developed multi-locational firms providing central services for administrative and economic reasons. There is, it should be noted, an 'external' bias in the way Legal and Banking 2 linkages are

maintained for Toronto and Horseshoe regions: there are significant differences but the two patterns tested may not be independent (see below).

Supplementary data, related to the 'processing of inventory, payroll, accounting and sales' data were examined to reveal significantly more Auto-plants depending on a head office to undertake part of these functions; the proportion, however, is less than 50 per cent. Thus substantial independence is exercised by branches in this sample and small proportions (1/3 to 1/2) of computer use in each of the functions listed above reinforce this interpretation as there is an association between computer use and involvement of head office.

The salient information derived from Table 14.8 is:

(1) The hypothesis of 'order' among the services is supported on organizational, in addition to geographical, grounds. There are pronounced differences in the willingness of managements of single plant firms and branches to undertake certain tasks within the unit, i.e., to internalize.

(2) The possibility of providing branches with services from or via a centralized company office is realized in a substantial proportion of cases for higher-order services.

(3) Possibly, the substitution of within-company service links for external connections is influenced by proximity to Toronto—this metropolitan effect must be examined in the organizational context just as it was for 'distance'.

Consistency

While services can be grouped, as above, by the proportional incidence of links in different organizational categories, the question remains whether there is 'consistency' in the way individual branches or single-plant firms arrange service connections. Consistency is of importance since its presence in 'company' linkages by branches may be interpreted as reflecting 'control' over the branch by the parent head office. Furthermore, reduction in branch autonomy creates substantially greater chance that service arrangements will not follow the urban system hierarchy of southern Ontario.

To a large degree interest must focus on connections *within the company*. There is some apparent variability in the way services are arranged (Table 14.8) but for Banking 2 and Legal—which have similar numbers of in-company and external connections—there is a fair measure of consistency. Furthermore, in this case, Toronto–Horseshoe branches and those in other regions have significantly different connection patterns. Branches in or near Toronto are more likely to establish local contacts external to the company, and the metropolitan effect identified in distance terms is again encountered. 'Company' linkages are relevant to only one-third of the branches at most (Table 14.8) and while there are regional differences in the incidence of 'control', direct evidence of its existence is not strong.

Table 14.8. Organization Patterns of Service Connection

(a) *Branches*

	Not used	Plant	Company	External
Bookkeeping		50	10	3
Auditing		5*	17	41
Legal			22	41
Banking 1			4	59
Banking 2	1		20	42
Other financial services	11	2	8	42
Maintenance	1	49		13
Electrical	2	33		28
Janitor		20		43

(b) *Single-Plant Firms*

	Not used	Plant	External
Bookkeeping		21	3
Auditing		1*	23
Legal	1	1*	22
Banking 1			24
Banking 2	1		23
Other financial services	8		16
Maintenance		15	9
Electrical		7	17
Janitor	1	17	6

*Presumably interview recording errors.

Joint Organizational–Distance Patterns

The separate examinations that have been made of distance and organizational patterns allow inferences to be made of joint patterns.

Low-order plant services. There is very little meaningful differentiation between single-plant firms and branches in the way these items are obtained: it is a plant–town choice with which location, industry and plant size variables are not associated.

Low-order office services.[2] Banking 1 service does not discriminate between type of plant—the bulk of contacts are made locally. For Bookkeeping only slightly more direct company involvement occurs.

High-order office services. It is with Legal, Banking 2, Auditing and Other financial services that the distinction between single-plant firms and branches emerges. The single-plant firms connect with service suppliers in the local

386

town and in a secondary capacity Toronto (for non-metropolitan plants) as do roughly two-thirds of the branches. The remaining third of branches, however, are sustained by linkages within the company—divided between Toronto and 'another country' as the primary origins.

The evidence is sufficient, therefore, to warrant exploring the manner in which branch-plant service linkages reflect the exercise of company 'control' over the plant's operations.

Direct and Indirect Control of Branch Arrangement of Office Services

Two broad groups of service linkages were examined—those developed *within the company* and occurring in 'another country', 'another region', Toronto, 'region' and 'town', and *external* connections occurring in 'another country' or 'another region'. These groups were scrutinized very carefully. In all cases checks were made of the location of Canadian or foreign head offices or operations that provided the potential for an (indirect) *company-organized* link developed outside the company. Several external connections in the 'another region' category were deleted since they could not be attributed reasonably to head office influence and since they appeared to represent a choice of service origin based on the largest-nearest principle, or were related to other input–output linkages. Toronto branches were also excluded from subsequent consideration if their external service connections were within Toronto.

Non-Toronto branches were checked for the 'another region' response that showed connection with Toronto, but in no case was there also a Canadian or general head office in Toronto: thus no arrangement within the company could be inferred. Similarly, external 'another region' linkages were checked and only those where an obvious company influence emerged were retained for analysis.

Results

More than half (36) the branches in the sample obtain some of their high-order service linkages in such a manner that the location of other company offices is reflected directly (Table 14.9). Functions supplied within and by the company and services arranged with outside firms (e.g. auditors) who supply the company (at various locations) are included in the total set of linkages, Of the 36 branches, 32 have in-company connections of some type related to office services but Auditing, Legal and Banking 2 are principally involved; 6 branches obtain services externally in another region; 6 branches satisfy some service demands in an other country.

These various 'control' or 'dependence' linkages are examined as one

Table 14.9. Joint Distribution of Service Linkages: In-Company, Company 'Controlled' External Links

	Audit	Legal	Banking 2	Bookkeeping	Other financial services	Banking 1
Company Linkages						
Another country	9	9	7	2	2	2
Another region	2	3	3	3		1
Toronto	2	8	6	3	2	1
Town	2	2	1	1		
Region	1	1	1			
Sub-total	16	23	18	9	4	4
External Linkages						
Another country	2	2	4		2*	1
Another region	3	1	2		2	1
Sub-total	5	3	6		6	5
Total	21	26	24	9	6	5

*External Toronto

category. There is a significant relative incidence of these linkages among American subsidiaries. In terms of industrial occurrence control linkages are concentrated in the Auto parts industry (absolutely and relatively) while Machinery branches have such a small share that their relative autonomy is thrown into relief.

The regional incidence of 'control' linkages follows an urbanization gradient—Toronto having the lowest proportion (partly a consequence of the limiting definition used?) and 'other urban' areas, furthest removed from the metropolitan centre, experiencing company 'dependence' in every case. These significant arrangements illustrate a spatial form of organizational substitution for metropolitan access and is evidence of (i) dissimilarity in the management of branch plants operated in different industrial environments, (ii) the ability of multi-locational companies to substitute internal versus external scale economies in high order service functions, (iii) the possibility of development of non-metropolitan regions (in advanced economies) by supporting the location and expansion of *branch*-plants, and (iv) the manner in which leakages occur from the main channels of hierarchical connection within an urban system: leakages occur by means of intra- and inter-firm service linkages.

Conclusion

The rewards from increased understanding of industrial behaviour are small given the effort required to assemble and analyse pertinent data. Nevertheless, the organizational and distance ordering of service inputs has been supported by the study and it is useful that it is demonstrated in a clear systematic way. Future work can focus on the way high-order office functions are arranged by plants under various ownership and organizational systems. The study confirms the attractive power of metropolitan nodes for all manner of manufacturing plants. There is evidence, however, that substitution of company for metropolitan service connections is not only feasible but a type of industrial behaviour some Governments may be prepared to encourage because of its locational, hence regional development, implications. Two consequences of a policy of limiting metropolitan growth, but encouraging urban development in a smaller number of other locations are: first, the need to concentrate public and private investment in these 'growth centres' so as to provide necessary plant services and infrastructure to permit production units to be established and expand; and, second, the inevitable population of these centres with branch plants which guarantees intra-company leakages of high-order service demands to other larger, probably metropolitan, centres. Within a closed economic system the latter result would lead to some strengthening of backwash effects supporting the main urban centres. In an economy like that of Canada, however, there is justifiable concern about a substantial volume of economic linkages of this type being exported in an involuntary manner, primarily to the U.S.A. The absolute magnitude of such leakages should be gauged to consider adequately the economic importance for the economy of 'foreign ownership'. The substantive results discussed here are important also for the economic geography of industries and firms. Complexity in patterns of service linkage for manufacturing plants is attributed particularly to the multi-locational nature of many firms. This aspect can no longer remain peripheral to enquiry in industrial geography. The indirect and direct manner in which management 'control' is exercised over branch-plant operations located in other regions and economies affirms that the behaviour of multi-locational firms is of ultimate significance in an understanding of the functional structure of industrial regions.

Notes

1. In this instance only the Banking 1 test achieved a meaningful chi-square result at ·05 probability, suggesting a weak Toronto orientation effect—see higher-order functions.
2. It is noted at the foot of Table 14.1 that it was found impossible to overcome variation in the incidence of high-order plant services to permit their evaluation in this enquiry.

References

Alchian, A. A., 1950, 'Uncertainty, evolution and economic theory', *Journal of Political Economy*, **58**, 211–21.
Bergsman, J., *et al.*, 1972, 'The agglomeration process in urban growth', *Urban Studies*, **9**, 264.
Britton, J. N. H., 1969, 'A geographical approach to the examination of industrial linkages', *Canadian Geographer*, **13**, 185–98.
Brooke, M. Z. and H. L. Remmers, 1970, *The Strategy of the Multi-National Enterprise* (London: Longmans).
Chinitz, B., 1960, *Freight and the Metropolis* (Cambridge, Mass.: Harvard University Press).
Darwent, D. F., 1969, 'Growth poles and growth centres in regional planning—a review', *Environment and Planning*, **1**, 5–32.
Gad, D., 1973, 'Office Location and Office Linkages', Toronto Ph.D. dessertation, in progress.
Goddard, J. B., 1971, 'Office communications and office location: a review of current research', *Regional Studies*, **5**, 263–80.
Hall, M., 1959, *Made in New York* (Cambridge, Mass.: Harvard University Press).
Hodge, G. and C. Wong, 1970, 'Prospects for an expanded non-ferrous metals industrial complex for northern Ontario', *Report to the Department of Treasury and Economics, Ontario*.
Isard, W., *et al.*, 1969, *General Theory: Social, Political, Economic and Regional* (Cambridge, Mass.: M.I.T.).
Jansen, A. C. M., 1970, 'The value of the growth pole theory for economic geography', *Tijdschrift voor Economische en Sociale Geografie*, **61**, 72.

Kristensson, F., 1967, *People, Firms and Regions* (Stockholm: Stockholm School of Economics).

Krumme, G., 1969, 'Toward a geography of enterprise', *Econ. Geogr.*, **45**.

Lösch, A., 1954, *The Economics of Location* (New Haven: Yale University Press).

Luttrell, W. F., 1962, *Factory Location and Industrial Movement* (London: National Institute of Economic and Social Research).

Luttrell, W. F., 1972, 'Industrial complexes and regional economic development in Canada', in *Growth Poles and Growth Centres in Regional Planning*, ed. Antoni Kuklinski (The Hague: Mouton).

Marshall, A., 1946, *Principles of Economics* (London: MacMillan).

Martin, J. E., 1966, *Greater London—An Industrial Geography* (London: Bell).

Murphy, R. E., Jr., 1965, *Adaptive Processes in Economic Systems* (New York: Academic Press).

Pred, Allan, 1967 and 1969, *Behaviour and Location* (Lund: Gleerup).

Ray, D. M., 1965, *Market Potential and Economic Shadow: A Quantitative Analysis of Industrial Location in Southern Ontario* (University of Chicago Department of Geography Research Paper 101).

Robinson, E. A. G., 1937, *The Structure of Competitive Industry* (Cambridge University Press).

Scitovsky, T., 1954, 'Two concepts of external economies', *Journal of Political Economy*, **62**, 143–54.

Smith, D. M., 1971, *Industrial Location* (Toronto: Wiley).

Steed, G. P. F., 1971, 'Locational implications of corporate organization of industry', *Canadian Geographer*, **15**, 54–7.

Thorngren, B., 1970, 'How do contact systems affect regional development?', *Environment and Planning*, **2**, 409–27.

Tiebout, C., 1957, 'Location theory, empirical evidence and economic evolution', *Papers and Proceedings of the Regional Science Association*, **3**, 74–86.

Törnqvist, G., 1970, *Contact Systems and Regional Development*, Lund Studies in Geography, Series B, 35.

Townroe, P. M., 1971, *Industrial Location Decisions* (University of Birmingham, Centre for Urban and Regional Studies, Occasional Paper, 15).

U.S. Dept. of Agriculture, Economic Research Service, 1966, 'Analysis of urban agglomeration', *Agricultural Economics Report*, **96**, June.

Weber, A., 1929, *Theory of the Location of Industries* (Chicago University Press).

West Midland Group on Post-War Reconstruction and Planning, 1948, *Conurbation*, (a planning survey of Birmingham and the Black Country) (London).

Wise, M. J., 1949, 'On the evolution of the gun and jewellery quarters in Birmingham', *Transactions and Papers, Institute of British Geographers*, **15**, 57–72.

IV Planning Environments: Two Contrasts

15

Location Decisions and Industrial Development Certificate Policy in the United Kingdom

D. Michael Turner

The Early Years

The Industrial Development Certificate (IDC) procedure owes its existence to the Report of the Royal Commission on the Distribution of Industrial Population (the Barlow Report, 1939). Prior to this date the only measures taken by central government in Britain to influence industrial location decisions were directed to the financing of schemes for retraining and re-settling labour (1928), and to identifying Special Areas of heavy structural unemployment where industrialists could purchase or lease premises and negotiate rent, rate and tax subsidies with the appointed Commissioners (Special Areas Act 1934).

The Barlow Report considered the industrial location problem within a framework which included strategic issues, increasing congestion in the Birmingham and London conurbations, and wide interregional variations in unemployment levels within the United Kindom. The Report envisaged direct control over industrial location to re-route mobile industry to those peripheral regions of the United Kingdom which has suffered, at least since the early twentieth century, from dependence on industries with falling manpower requirement. Barlow drew attention to the need for a positive policy of steering industry away from the Midlands and South East and towards Scotland, Wales, Northern Ireland and the declining industrial areas of Lancashire, Yorkshire and Northumberland to alleviate the related problems of unemployment in outlying regions and congestion in central regions. A White Paper of 1944 referred to the need for a 'proper industrial balance', but the powers necessary to compel industrialists to comply with the requirements of the kind of regional policy envisaged by Barlow were not introduced until the Labour Government took office after the war. The discretionary tradition of the 1934 Act was continued under the Distribution of Industry Act 1945, which required an industrialist proposing to construct new industrial premises exceeding 10,000 square feet in area, simply to notify the Board of Trade of his intention to build. The Board of Trade, which took over the powers of the Commissioners for the Special Areas at this time, were given larger and more numerous regions, renamed Development Areas, in which they were able to offer industrialists a modified set of inducements. They retained the Commissioners' powers to purchase and develop sites for industrial use. These Development Areas included most of the outlying parts of the United Kingdom, being centred on those densely pupulated areas where the traditional industries of coal mining, iron and steel manufacture and shipbuilding were in decline.

It was not until the Town and Country Planning Act of 1947, however, that direct powers of control over industrial location were finally vested in central government. The 1947 Act laid down that any planning application to develop manufacturing premises of over 5,000 square feet in area must be accompained by an Industrial Development Certificate issued by the Board of Trade (BoT) and stating that the proposed development was in accordance with 'the proper distribution of industry'. The proper distribution of industry was not defined.

The Post-War Period, 1945–58

The period of reconstruction after the Second World War was followed by a decade of relatively lax use by central government of the available industrial location inducements and policy instruments (Brown, 1972). The Development Areas enjoyed a period of substantial growth immediately after the war, capturing half of the total factory floor space notified to the Board of Trade in 1949. The initial success of the Development Areas, which was due partly to the availability of surplus munitions factories and partly to building licence control, operated against their best long-term interests for, as time passed, their employment problems seemed relatively less important when measured against other threats to the national economy, such as the successive balance of trade deficits (Loasby, 1965).

In 1954 increasing pressure on land resources in the growth regions of the South East and Midlands followed the removal of the 100 per cent development charge, which had been imposed in 1947, and the abolition of building licences. The resulting boom in property development brought sharply into focus the problem of congestion in these prosperous areas and led to a greater flexibility in the use of IDC control, as the Board of

Trade sought to encourage overspill schemes designed to relieve these pressures. Industrialists prepared to relocate or set up branch plants in new and expanding towns (New Towns Act 1946; Town Development Act 1952) found no great difficulty at this time in persuading the BoT to issue IDCs for sites in towns within commuting distance of their original location. The first ring of New Towns was established at a radius of roughly 25 miles from central London, and though the Expanding Towns have generally been at greater distances, the range of facilities available and the cooperation of the Greater London Council, County Councils and local authorities have compensated, to a greater or lesser extent, for the distance factor.

The Change in Emphasis, 1958–63

The Distribution of Industry (Industrial Finance) Act of 1958, however, removed the flexibility of IDC control procedure and put location policy sharply into reverse. Unemployment once again became the key issue as far as the BoT was concerned and there was a tightening of IDC policy in relation to the expanding areas. The Act introduced a list of small new Development Districts selected on the basis of their having suffered from a high and persistent level of unemployment in the immediate past. The BoT took this to mean an average unemployment rate of 4·5 per cent for the preceding twelve months. Regional strategy was forgotten and policy became a tactical exercise in the elimination of highly localized pockets of unemployment. The 1958 Act and the Local Employment Acts which followed in 1960 and 1963 represent what Loasby (1965) has called 'the dead end of policy', the furthest retreat from a policy aimed at a proper distribution of industry.

The local Employment Act of 1960, which explicitly adopted the 4·5 per cent unemployment criterion, replaced the previous Areas and Districts with a new List of Development Districts, many of them with fewer than a hundred unemployed. The consequences of this change of policy can scarcely have been considered by the legislature, for in certain circumstances the arrival of even a single factory was sufficient to remove the cause of so-called high and persistent unemployment as defined in the Act.

In one small urban district in the rural south of Norfolk, for instance, a manufacturer of agricultural machinery sought planning permission and an IDC for the relocation of part of his factory which had been hemmed in for a number of years on a congested site in north London. The closure of a nearby military aerodrome and the gradual decline in demand for agricultural manpower had resulted in the level of unemployment in the Norfolk town temporarily exceeding the 4·5 per cent level. Since the town had achieved Development District status, the necessary approvals were granted and the industrialist immediately requested twenty-five men from the register of unemployed to assist in constructing the factory and installing the machinery. With the industrialist's arrival, the level of unemployment dropped below the statutory minimum and remained so subsequently (Turner, 1966).

Had the policy of 1958–63 been extended for a longer period of time, factories would no doubt have been springing up at practically every rural crossroads in the south-east of England, as the advantages of industrial jobs in areas where agricultural employment was declining were being widely recognized by local planning authorites eager to take advantage of the financial inducements of the Local Employment Acts and the Greater London Council's overspill programme.

Towards a Regional Policy—1963 and Onwards

A growing awareness of the wider implicatons of industrial location policy was, however, apparent even while the narrow definition of areas of need was being applied under the Local Employment Acts and while government expenditure on factory building, loans and grants leaped from £5 million a year in the 1950s to £37 million in the early 1960s as a result of the Local Employment Acts of 1960 and 1963 (Brown, 1972).

White Papers reevaluated the problems of the North East and Scotland (Board of Trade, 1963a and 1963b) and considered which parts of the two regions might be the most suitable for promoting economic growth. Growth areas were suggested, not simply on the basis of their high level of unemployment, but mainly according to whether or not they could eventually generate zones of self-sustaining growth.

The demand for regional economic strategies was recognized officially with the establishment of Economic Planning Councils in 1965 and from this point a clear change of attitude is apparent, both in official reports, such as that of the National Economic Development Council in 1966, and in the legislation which followed. Development Districts were abolished by the Industrial Development Act 1966 and replaced by geographically wider Development Areas selected on much the same criteria as applied in 1945, namely, the state of employment and unemployment, population changes, migration and the objectives of regional policy. Within these areas certain places, hard hit by the accelerating rate of colliery closures at that time, were later designated Special Development Areas.

In 1967 came the first legislative attempt to solve the problem of heavy unemployment by means of a direct subsidy on the employment of labour. The Regional Employment Premium provided for an exchequer payment of £1·50 per week for each adult male worker employed in a Development Area. This measure was introduced in part no doubt to counter the criticisms of those who saw capital intensive industry moving out to those Development Areas where labour intensive industry was the primary need.

The demand for wider recognition of regional problems has led recently to ever finer distinctions of areas of need. The Development Areas of 1966 incorporated Special Development Areas in 1967, and Intermediate Areas were introduced in 1969 (Department of Economic Affairs, 1969). The Intermediate Areas and the Special Development Areas were themselves added to in 1970. The result is that the Assisted Areas (Industry Act 1972) now cover half the total area of Great Britain. Within them, however, the scale of assistance still depends on historical chance as much as on economic need. The Assisted Areas now include the Northern Region, Merseyside and Furness, Northern Ireland, Wales and Scotland, and most of Cornwall and North Devon. They contain about one-fifth of the country's employees, one-third of its unemployed, have a preponderence of decling industries and a less than proportionate share of dynamic growth industries. Growth in employment and incomes is slow, earnings are below average outward migration continues to be substantial (Department of Economic Affairs, 1969).

The IDC Procedure as an Instrument of Regional Policy

Thus the IDC procedure has been used as an economic planning instrument designed to raise the nation's industrial efficiency and to achieve a high rate of employment in the Assisted Areas. It has also been used as a tactical measure in the field of town and country planning since an IDC can operate only when supported by planning consent.

In considering the effectiveness of the IDC procedure in reducing unemployment and achieving a proper industrial balance it has been commonplace to adopt the view that without controls, congestion would be several degrees worse in the South East, the rate of unemployment would be higher than it is in the Assisted Areas and the nations industrial efficiency would be impaired by the existence of under-utilized resources.

The support for this argument is that the total effect of financial incentives, infra-structural improvements and IDC control has been to divert industrial growth away from the Midlands and South East and towards the Assisted Areas. The measures of assistance, which started with the provision of factories and general purpose loans and grants in 1934, have been extended recently (e.g. in 1958, 1960, 1963, 1966, 1967 and 1972) to include assistance with the transfer to key workers and re-training grants, a wide range of tax, rate and rent subsidies, and direct subsidies for the employment of labour. The total expenditure on incentives to firms moving into the Development Areas in the late 1960s was calculated by the Hunt Committee as £182 million on investment grants (Industrial Development Act 1966), £38 million on grants and loans (Local Employment Acts 1960 and 1963). £13·5 million on factory buildings constructed in advance by the Industrial Estates Corporations, £25 million on Regional Employment Premium (REP) and Selective Employment Tax (SET) and £2·8 million on training grants—an annual figure in excess of £260 million.

The Hunt Committee (Department of Economic Affairs, 1969) were in no doubt that the level of assistance had had a marked effect in persuading firms to move to the Development Areas, and they quoted evidence to indicate that the capital grants available might reduce a firm's costs of production in the Development Areas by about 2·5 per cent and that REP/ SET might reduce costs by a further 2·5–3 per cent as compared with firms locating elsewhere in the United Kingdom. Wilson (1967) arrived at a similar conclusion, though he attacked both the capital grant system, as applied, and also the unconditional nature of the regional employment premium: he pointed out that permanent subventions inevitably lead to a conflict of policy objectives because of the weakening of the links between financial assistance and industrial performance.

It does seem, therefore, that one policy objective at least has been achieved by the strengthening of regional policies. Howard's analysis (Board of Trade 1968) of industrial moves since the war showed that after 1960 there was a significant rise in the Development Areas' share of employment in mobile manufacturing industry. Between 1952–59 and 1960–65 their share of the United Kingdom toal of IDC approvals rose from 29 per cent to 55 per cent and, in estimated additional employment generated, their share rose from 22 per cent in 1956–58 to 53 per cent in 1965–67. Whether this objective was achieved by tighter IDC control or more generous inducements is a matter of doubt.

Brown (1972) found it exceedingly difficult to disentangle the effects of the positive and negative aspects of industrial location policy. He failed to find any way of measuring the effectiveness of the positive financial inducements as compared with negative IDC restrictions. On balance he favoured the view that without Development Area incentives far more of the firms faced with the probability of an IDC refusal would not have bothered to examine the possibilities of a Development Area site. The combination of financial incentives and negative IDC control in the early 1960s, according to his calculations, probably diverted something like 25 per cent of the factory schemes requiring Board of Trade approval in the South East and West Midlands to other areas of Britain. Brown estimated that the flow of job opportunities in manufacturing industry to the Development Areas from elsewhere had at least trebled since the 1950s under the influence of policy changes (Brown, 1972). Since one aspect of policy is to promote the flow of jobs from regions of low unemployment to those of high, some success for official policy may be claimed. There is a strong body of opinion, however, which feels that the additional employment created which, in he first round, probably averages 30,000 new jobs per annum in the Development Areas, is simply not sufficient to enable the Assisted Areas to catch up with the more prosperous regions and can only maintain the existing mbalance. What is required is a policy geared to creating 80,000 new jobs annually in the Assisted Areas (Regional Studies Association, 1972).

The Effect of IDC Policy on the Location Decisions of Industrial Firms

The Board of Trade survey of 1964–67, quoted in the Hunt Report and again by Brown (1972), covered 116 firms initially, of which half set up plants in Development Areas and half elsewhere. The firms were asked to indicate whether such factors as proximity to markets and suppliers, availability of labour, government inducements and IDC controls were of major or minor importance in determining their choice of location. Table 15.1 indicates the relative importance of these factors for firms locating in Development Areas. Availability of labour was the key factor, as other surveys have indicated (Luttrell, 1962; Cameron and Clark, 1966), though, outside the Development Areas, access to existing plants or markets ran it a close second. Financial inducements, particularly machinery and building grants and assistance with the training of labour, were of major importance for 70 per cent of the firms surveyed.

The influence of the IDC factor was probably more important than the table reveals, since the precise location chosen by half the firms in the survey was determined by the availability of existing premises, usually privately owned, to which IDC controls do not apply.

Table 15.1. Factors Influencing Location Decisions by Firms Establishing New Plants in Development Areas 1964–67

Factor	Percentage regarding Factor as of Major Importance
Availability of labour	86
Government inducements	70
Likelihood of IDC being issued	43
Access to markets	40
Assistance of local authority	40
Availability of premises	25
Good local amenities	23
Access to raw materials	neg.
Access to existing location	neg.

Source. *Hunt Report,* Cmnd. 3998, paras. 113–120.

Townroe (1971) found a similar situation in his survey of 59 firms in the West Midlands and North East in 1969. The refusal of the Board of Trade to grant an IDC provided a major impetus to movement in 17 cases and was a subsidiary factor in 3 others. For over half the firms, the availability of buildings was an important factor, being particularly vital for small firms in a hurry to get into production, for whom the possibility of negotiating a lease on a government-owned factory was a strong incentive to move.

The situation is succinctly summarized in the Hunt Report. On the one hand the Government have committed themselves to a policy of moving out population and employment from the congested areas; on the other hand, under Government policies of industrial location, industrialists considering moving from the congested areas are asked first to consider movement to a Development Area. If they are unable to contemplate such a move the possibility of location in a new or expanded town is suggested. Finally, consideration is given to the possibility of their being given permission to develop on a site of their own choosing. By the time an industrialist has considered and rejected a location in the Assisted Areas he has not infrequently, decided as a result of frustration, to develop in or on the periphery of a congested area, possibly in second-hand premises or, in many cases, to abandon plans for expansion altogether. Statistics cannot show how far firms are deterred from even a preliminary approach to the Department of Trade and Industry (previously the Board of Trade) for an IDC and how much growth is lost in this way. However, special surveys conducted during the period 1963–68 by the Birmingham Chamber of Commerce and the Confederation of British Industry (CBI) considered this point. In the Birmingham survey, in which roughly half the respondents were small firms with fewer than 50 employees, 13 per cent of the respondents claimed to have been deterred from even applying for an IDC. In the CBI survey, in which half the firms who responded employed between 50 and 500 and only one firm in seven had fewer than 50 employees, 5 per cent said they had been wholly deterred from applying, 9 per cent modified their schemes, 6 per cent abandoned them and 5 per cent deferred them because of IDC requirements—in addition to the 8 per cent of firms which were refused IDCs altogether.

The Hunt Committee were persuaded that IDC control had resulted in a loss of industrial growth which would otherwise have taken place, particularly in the South East and West Midlands and 'especially among smaller and medium-sized firms that are unused to, and sometimes wary of, dealing with officialdom'. Brown (1972) estimates the total reduction of expansion as a result of formal refusals at about 5 per cent of the employment content of all applications. One has to bear in mind, however, that despite the deterrent effect of the policy, relatively few IDC applications in the congested areas of the South East and West Midlands are in fact turned down. Between

1964 and 1967, for example, *only* 17 *per cent of the floor space applied for in these two regions was refused,* and four-fifths of the firms whose applications were refused subsequently undertook some form of expansion, many in development or overspill areas. The Department of Trade and Industry has considerable leeway in the congested areas, as the proportion of IDCs granted that are not subsequently taken up averages about 20 per cent. The Hunt Committee found widespread misconceptions about IDC control and a belief that it was rigidly applied. They recommended that the Government should widely publicize the considerations determining the exercise of IDC control, so that it 'should ... be seen to be in the service of a positive location policy ... as a tool for long-term planning of the proper distribution of industry'.

In a survey of recent industrial location literature, Townroe (1971) draws attention to the need to view locational choice in an organizational context and as part of an investment decision. The danger of asking industrialists 'why did you move here?' in an interview is that there is a temptation for them to argue that the actual choice was the correct one. The influences on the choice, he argues, can only be revealed by a close study of the processes of decision-making itself. Frequently this will indicate that a firm was not looking for a profit-maximizing solution but simply for a suitable site which satisfied certain minimum criteria in a particular area. Cameron and Clark (1966) and Seeley (1967) found, like Townroe, that the vast majority of firms did not evaluate alternative locations on explicit cost grounds and that the financial assessment, if any, came after the locational choice had been made. Within the average firm there was simply no formula which could usefully be employed to assist in costing alternative locations. The need to find new accommodation presented a unique problem for that particular decision-making unit. Invariably, when a Development Area site was being considered, the Board of Trade would be consulted but, outside the Assisted Areas, information was sought firstly from estate agents, newspaper advertisements and by local searches. The Board of Trade was approached for advice only by a minority of firms seeking sites outside the Assisted Areas.

Clearly for any firm contemplating a move there are two distinct problems to be solved. The first relates to the choice of the general area to which the firm is prepared to move and the second relates to the choice of a particular site. In relation to both area and site the Department of Trade and Industry (formerly the Board of Trade) exercises considerable influence, not only by operating IDC policy to give the highest priority to the Assisted Areas and afterwards to the New Towns and Expanding Towns, but also by actively encouraging and advertising the advance factory building programme of the English, Welsh and Scottish Industrial Estates Corporations. Townroe considers the advance factory building programme to be the most important single aspect of public policy in the United Kingdom.

Despite the publicity given to the financial advantages of the Assisted Areas and the activities of the Department of Trade and Industry, however, half of the industrial moves occurring recently have still been to sites in the unassisted areas of the South East and West Midlands (Department of Economic Affairs, 1969). The forces of supply and demand continue to exercise a predominant influence on the operations of the industrial land market as they have since the start of the industrial revolution. In this century the pressures of demand were concentrated initially in two areas: in the London (Greater London Council) region where a sharp rise in industrial land values occurred immediately after the last war, with more modest growth subsequently, and in the South East Region, which enjoyed a dramatic growth in land values during the last decade. The Midlands and North enjoyed a marked post-war boom, albeit at a lower level than that experienced in the London region, but have recently experienced slower than average growth rates (Table 15.2).

Table 15.2. Industrial Land Prices (Median Values) 1892–1969 in £1000 Per Acre

Year	London (GLC area)	South East	Midlands and North	South West and Wales	All England
1892–1916	3·30	0·35	0·50	0·30	1·33
1917–1930	1·03	0·28	0·14	0·12	0·28
1931–1945	3·60	0·90	0·50	0·26	1·27
1946–1963	26·10	1·40	7·60	1·40	4·15
1964–1969	50·00	20·00	9·10	5·00	11·90

Source. E. A. Vallis, 1972, 'Urban land and building prices 1892–1969, *Estates Gazette*, **222**, 1406, Table 3.

The figures in Table 15.2 reveal broad regional differences in industrial land values but conceal the land value peaks associated with certain densely populated urban centres within each region. Figure 15.1 illustrates the familiar concave slope of the land value gradient from the centre of London; Figure 15.2. shows the distribution of industrial land sites sampled. Similarly shaped curves will be found for other major centres where adequate data is available. The situation within the London (GLC) region is an interesting one, with the highest industrial building values being historically associated with the City's eastern end. The steep increase in values in the western quadrant of the city is of very recent origin, as Table 15.3. illustrates.

A recent investigation of the prices paid for land with planning permission for industrial development in two years during the 1960s, for which adequate data were available, confirm the phenomenon of peaking land values within densely populated urban areas. The twin factors of accessibility to London and the population of the town in which the industrial site lay, were found to be of paramount importance in explaining variations in the price of

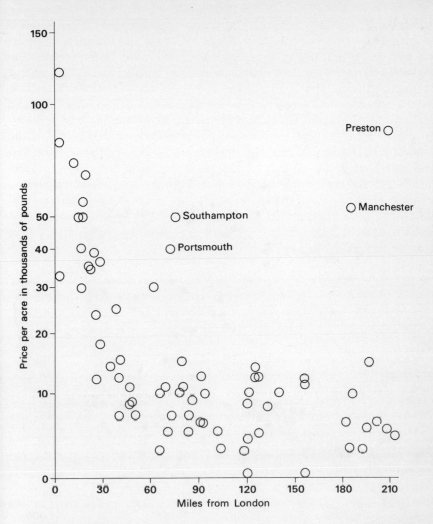

Figure 15.1. The relationship between industrial land values and distance from London in 1968 (source: published auction data).

industrial land. Using the data from 71 observations in each year it was found that the two factors of population size and accessibility to London (Figure 15.1), in association with proximity to other large centres of population, accounted for up to half of the variation in prices paid.

The proportion of the variation in prices explained by distance, population and site area is indicated in Table 15.4. In 1964 almost half of the variation in prices is explained by the five variables considered and in 1968 roughly 40 per cent is so explained.

The industrial land market introduces an objective measure of the

404

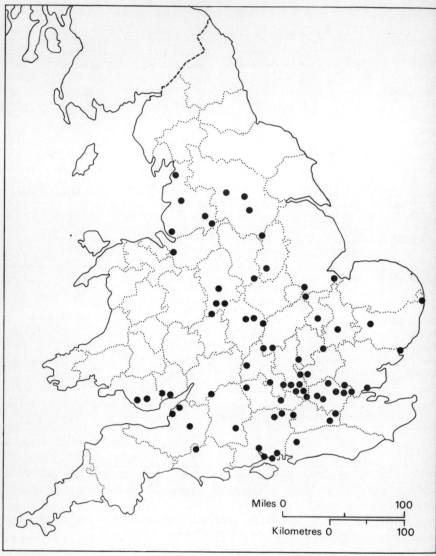

Figure 15.2. Industrial land values, 1968: the location of the 71 sites surveyed.

essentially subjective processes of industrial location decision-making. Market analysis indicates that industrialists continue to bid for sites in the prosperous regions with easy access to the major population centres of central and South-East England. A glance at the motorway map, the inter-city rail networks and the within-Britain airline system provides convincing evidence of the advantages to industrialists of the Midlands and South East in both accessibility of goods to markets and personal contacts between

Table 15.3. Industrial Building Prices (Median Values) in New Pence Per Square foot, 1892–1969

Year	E.C.	S.E.	North and East	W.C., S.W.1 and W.1.	W., N.W. and Middlesex	S.W.
1892–1916	290	78	25	90	30	20
1917–1930	91	45	49	65	40	50
1931–1945	82	52	42	73	43	47
1946–1963	240	140	190	320	200	220
1964–1969	480	280	380	430	460	450

Source. E. A. Vallis, 1972, 'Urban land and building prices 1892–1969', *Estates Gazette,* **222,** 1406, Table 4.
Abbreviations denote postal districts within Greater London: e.g. E.C. = East Central: S.E. = South East: W.C. = West Central: S.W. = South West, etc.

Table 15.4. Variation in Industrial Land Prices Explained by Selected Independent Variables 1964 and 1968

Independent variable	Recent variation explained 1964	Recent variation explained 1968
Distance to London	27·0	8·2
Population of city or town	12·6	28·0
Site area	6·6	1·7
Distance to town of 200,000	2·8	2·8
Distance to town of 100,000	neg.	neg.

Note. All the coefficients relating to independent variables were found to be significant at the 95 per cent confidence level.
Source. D. M. Turner, from published auction sales data collected by E. A. Vallis (1972).

manufacturer and customer. In addition there are, of course, the industrial linkages existing in these regions and the relatively high quality of the environment, to which Hunt and others have drawn attention. Evidence presented to the Board of Trade as to the motives and experience of firms which undertook industrial moves in the middle 1960s confirms the empirical evidence of Cameron and Clark (1966) and Townroe (1971) that industrial location decisions are, however, also affected by a wide range of non-economic, subjective and chance factors. Attitudes to reports of industrial unrest and the opinions of industrial managers who have undertaken previous moves can be strong influences against the selection of certain regions as possible areas to search. Ignorance of the way the Department of Trade and Industry operates the IDC procedure may limit choice, while, on the other hand, the assistance of local authorities in finding suitable premises may extend it. Imponderable forces operate on the market and little enough is known of the mechanics of the decision-making process.

The relative weigh that economic forces have on the choice of a site is difficult to determine. One can conclude, however, that public policy, especially the operation of IDC procedure, produces a conflict between the legitimate aims of manufacturers seeking to maximize corporate profits and the social objectives of governments determined to achieve a high level of employment. The end result of the decision-making process is a compromise. In times of prosperity and high employment, the United Kingdom appears to operate more or less as a single market-place and a flexible IDC policy ensures that practically every region provides satisfactory sites for mobile manufacturing industry. In times of depression there is a greater awareness of locational advantages, so that access to the buoyant markets of the Midlands and South East has a higher priority for mobile firms than access to the under-utilized resources, particularly of labour, in the Assisted Areas. Current policy at such times is, however, to attempt to use the IDC procedure to try to solve regional unemployment problems—which it is manifestly not capable of doing. What is required at these times is a general re-stimulus of industrial activity.

Town and Country Planning Objectives and IDC Policy

One further matter which deserves attention is the conflict which arises between central government, as represented by the Department of Trade and Industry, and local government, as represented by the town and country planning authority. In the planning of industrial location, as has been indicated above, lip service is frequently paid to the concept of the 'proper distribution of industry', a term which is enshrined in statute but is nowhere defined. A similar situation exists in town and country planning where the Minister has never really had effective machinery for guiding land-use planning in a positive direction and yet, in legal terms, has had the responsibility for achieving consistency and continuity.

As regards broad planning strategies, central Government appears to have been convinced that a philosophy of containment is the best solution and the preventative side of policy has been stressed. Greater weight is placed on land-use controls operated by local planning authorities than on a range of central government measures designed to disperse employment and to develop job opportunities in particular centres. This was as true in the 1950s, under successive Conservative governments, as in the changed political climate of the Labour administration of the 1960s (Harrison, 1972).

Land-use control is only one facet of planning, but exaggerated claims are often being made for its effectiveness in changing social and economic conditions. Both major political parties are agreed upon the need for planning, but neither attempts to define the broad concepts associated with it. There has been a tendency, possibly to ensure a consensus about planning, to rely upon established methods and accepted definitions. Although a town plan may have many social and economic implications, when the planner comes to day-to-day decisions he is careful how we imposes costs and distributes benefits, because his task is to deal with *land* alone and not with people. In the real political system one would expect the administrator to exercise his influence in favour of particular groups, but it is difficult for him to do so publicly. Even a policy of restricting sites to firms from particular locations may be hotly disputed.

Because he deals with land alone, the planner must consider land use in idealized terms, largely in disregard of factors such as ownership and tenure. He is, in effect, discouraged from interfering directly in the market or working with property owners. There is inevitably a conflict, in which a private definition of the optimum solution is opposed by the planner's notion of the public interest. This is precisely the same problem, one stage removed, faced by the Department of Trade and Industry when considering the merits of an application for an IDC. In the case of the local planning authority, however, there is the additional problem that the decision-makers are non-professional elected representatives, who may or may not accept a planner's decision on the merits of a particular planning application, especially if they can see how a development would benefit some interest with which they are in sympathy. In such circumstances financial pressures or political considerations may affect land-use decisions.

It is easy to appreciate the attitude of the town clerk or municipal treasurer of a town undertaking an expansion programme. Incoming industry means additional revenue, an opportunity to improve social amenities and to undertake comprehensive town centre redevelopment, and enhanced prestige. A study of two pioneer expansion schemes in East Anglia illustrates some of the financial consequences of the introduction of overspill industry and new jobs (Table 15.5).

Since the inception of the two town expansion schemes, the available local revenue has risen nearly twenty times and the annual budgets now

Table 15.5. Local Revenue and Rateable Values in Two Expanding Towns, Haverhill and Thetford, 1957–1972

Haverhill	Rateable Value	Industrial percentage rateable Value	Rate Call	Thetford	Rateable Value	Industrial percentage rateable Value	Rate Call
	£000	%	£		£000	%	£
1957–58	34·1	2·9	29·400	1957–58	40·1	6·4	39·100
1963–64	193·0	26·9	89·490	1963–64	231·5	22·6	106·600
1972–73	516·2	30·6	550·937	1972–73	761·7	41·0	649·800

Source. *Rates and Rateable Values in England and Wales,* HMSO, London, annual series.

408

exceed £500,000. In both cases it is the incoming industrialist who has shouldered the rate burden and the domestic ratepayer is in a more fortunate position than the average residential occupier in other urban districts and non-county boroughs where industry has not settled so readily (Wallace and Turner, 1963). Ten years before expansion began Eastwood (1951) considered that there was little possibility of any significant industrial growth in either town owing to their disadvantages of location and for other historical reasons.

The beneficial consequences of expansion for the towns concerned include a wider variety of employment opportunities, greater choice in the shops and improved educational facilities. The stated objective of the Town Development Act is, however, not economic stimulus for local authorities but the relief of congestion in metropolitan areas, and current planning philosophy no longer favours decentralization by this particular method. The demands of the local authorities for more industry to help meet target population projections agreed with the Greater London Council, therefore, meet strong resistance from the Department of Trade and Industry which, for strategic reasons, is unwilling to issue IDCs so freely in these areas.

The nub of the conflict lies in the fact that it is the Minister's job to achieve consistency and continuity in planning but it is the local planning authority that acts as 'agent' for the Minister and has only the most general indication of Ministerial policy. In addition, the authority has a certain need to attain consistency in its own local political terms. Dependence on rates may not necessarily be a rational reason for giving an approval but it may influence the local political climate.

With proper Ministerial guidance, IDC policy and land-use planning could exert a powerful influence on industrial location decision-making and operate as effectively as financial incentives in inducing industrial movement. Without a satisfactory definition of the 'proper distribution of industry', however, it is likely that they will remain as rather ineffective tactical implements rather than the tools of strategic planning.

References

Board of Trade, 1963a, *Central Scotland. A programme for development and growth,* Cmnd. 2188 (London: HMSO).
Board of Trade, 1963b, *The North East. A programme for regional development and growth,* Cmnd. 2206 (London: HMSO).
Board of Trade, 1968, *The Movement of Manufacturing Industry in the United Kingdom, 1945–65* (London: HMSO).
Brown, A. J., 1972, *The Framework of Regional Economics in the United Kingdom* (Cambridge University Press).
Cameron, G. C. and B. D. Clark, 1966, *Industrial Movement and the Regional Problem,* University of Glasgow Social and Economic Studies, Occasional Paper, 5 (Edinburzh: Oliver and Boyd).

Department of Economic Affairs (Hunt Report), 1969, *The Intermediate Areas*, Cmnd. 3998 (London: HMSO).

Eastwood, T., 1951, *Industry in the Country Towns of Norfolk and Suffolk* (Oxford University Press).

Harrison, M. L., 1972, 'Development control—the Influence of Political, Legal and Idealogical Factors', *Town Planning Review*, **43** (3), 254–74.

Loasby, B. J., 1965, 'Location of Industry: Thirty Years of Planning', *District Bank Review*, 28–52.

Luttrell, W. F., 1962, *Factory Location and Industrial Movement* (London: National Institute of Economic and Social Research).

Regional Studies Association, 1972, *Regional and Local Perspectives on Industrial Development Policy* (Conference at Sheffield).

Royal Commission on the Distribution of Industrial Population (Bowlow Report), 1939, Cmnd. 6153 (London: HMSO).

Seeley, I. H., 1967, 'Planned dispersal by town development schemes', *Chartered Surveyor*, **100**, 188.

Townroe, P. M., 1971, *Industrial Location Decisions*, University of Birmingham, Centre for Urban and Regional Studies, Occasional Paper 15.

Turner, D. M., 1966, *The Inter-relationship of Urban and Rural Communities*, unpublished Ph.D. thesis, University of Cambridge, Department of Land Economy.

Vallis, E. A., 1972, 'Urban land and building prices 1892–1969', *Estates Gazette*, **222**.

Wallace, D. B. and D. M. Turner, 1963, 'Agriculture in an Industrial Community', *Westminister Bank Review*, August 1963.

Wilson, T., 1967, 'Finance for regional industrial development', *The Three Banks Review*, September 1967, 3–23.

16

The Changing Impact of Industrial Management and Decision-Making on the Locational Behaviour of the Soviet Firm

BRENTON M. BARR

If earth space presents similar frictions of distance and locational costs in countries with different means of spatially allocating resources (Clark, 1957; Holzman, 1957; Hunter, 1957; Hutchings, 1971; Hamilton, 1973) then the goals and motivations of locational decision-makers also must have elements in common among different economic systems. Evidence strongly suggests that perceptual limitations, goals, motivation, behaviour, conflicts, milieux, education and expectations found among decision-makers in the USSR are reasonably similar to those observed in complex western industrial societies (Berliner, 1957; Dicken, 1971; Granick, 1954, 1961). The role of committees, the desire for personal advancement and prestige, the attraction of material rewards, and the number of people involved in complex decisions in the USSR often resemble similar features in western corporations. While there are important differences in personal belief, distribution of power, social and economic institutions and political organization, the economic and political 'tycoons' or 'bosses' of the communist world are not fundamentally different organizers from their counterparts in large western corporations (Granick, 1961, Chapters 3, 4, 11 and 18). The similarities between the technical and organizational problems faced by management of a pulp and paper mill in North America and the USSR are greater than the differences: coordinating procurement of raw materials, manufacture of products and efficient delivery of finished goods is a universal spatial problem. The manner of solving problems and establishing responsibility, however, is apparently quite different between

411

412

Soviet administration and capitalist corporations; yet some aspects of their respective internal structures are quite similar.

Locational decisions usually involve some conflict among different levels of management within *any* decision-making body. Although unanimity among ruling Soviet circles is a fundamental tenet of democratic centralism, neither all official programmes nor spatial decisions are welcomed by all managers and administrators. In the 1950s, for example, Khrushchev's 'virgin lands scheme' and *sovnarkhoz* administration were neither enthusiastically accepted nor universally adopted. The 'economic reform' of the 1960s revealed that individuals and groups were ready to propose alternative methods of central planning and resource allocation (e.g., the debate triggered by E. Liberman, see Sharpe, 1966.) The Lake Baykal controversy shows that supposedly harmonious groups within Soviet society have different perceptions of territorial space and natural environment. Responsible groups of intellectuals, scientists and laymen are informed and, within limits, are prepared to become vituperative. Such criticism or partisanship would surprise people in the West who do not believe that social action groups can exert pressure on the Soviet Communist Party.

Compromise in spatial behaviour is probably contained in many Soviet location decisions. Study of capitalist firm and industrial organization has been partially facilitated by access to both business records and managerial personnel. Such access in the Soviet Union has been more restricted; opportunities to penetrate the information curtain are fewer. Behaviour usually has to be inferred from a wide variety of published sources: the study of the Smolensk archive (Fainsod, 1958; Narkiewicz, 1970) or analysis of the previous behaviour of managerial war refugees (Berliner, 1957, 1962) result only from unusual circumstances. Conflicting objectives must usually be analysed from material in the Soviet press and academic literature. Consequently, geographical interpretations of Soviet locational patterns have suffered from informational limitations (plus the limitation of high costs required to consider all fragmentary evidence in the press) and have usually been confined to analysis of aggregate regional production statistics. Books by Cole and German (1970), Dewdney (1965), Hooson (1966), Mellor (1964), Parker (1969) and Shabad (1969) are examples where official production statistics have been supported by additional press information. These texts provide useful information on the location of particular industries: here the interrelationships are considered between industrial organization, planning and location.

The Soviet Location Problem

Soviet Location Principles: The Substitute for Location Theory

The location problem has usually been treated in the USSR in aggregated

413

form, without much concern for the individual enterprise, firm or decision-maker. The first fifty years of Soviet industrial management involved attempts to develop criteria which would facilitate practical solutions to the location problem (Koropeckyj, 1967). These criteria do not comprise a location theory since they contain diverse and some non-economic elements: (1) the need for eliminating differences between urban and rural environments, (2) reduction of transportation flows to ease freight burdens, (3) industrialization of backward regions to facilitate economic and social development of ethnic minorities, (4) preparation for defence, (5) regional specialization to satisfy national demand, (6) regional autarky to satisfy regional market demand, (7) international specialization within COMECON and (8) the need for distributing industrial production to utilize effectively all regional human and material resources (Koropeckyj, 1967; Hamilton, 1970, 1971; Bor, 1967). Their relative importance varies with the changing goals of the Communist Party, but most have been significant throughout the Soviet industrialization period and reflect solutions to pragmatic problems rather than application of location theory (Koropeckyj, 1967, p. 23).

The head of the Gosplan USSR prestigious Council for the Study of Productive Forces (SOPS), N. N. Nekrasov, noted in 1970 that, even with completion of the 'General outline for the development and location of productive forces up to 1980', the Soviet Union still needs to develop location theory and methodology (Nekrasov, 1971, p. 225). Problems of defence and backward national ethnic regions are now of minor concern; more important are environmental degradation and economic modelling to form new economic regions and production complexes. The objective of developing new regions to sustain materials supplies also now embodies greater flexibility and efficiency of the technology used. Concern for differences between town and country has diminished as the Soviet Union has become more urbanized; indeed, location policy now focuses more on eliminating differences between large cities and small towns because large concentrations have not minimized social overhead capital needs (Nekrasov, 1971; Mikhailov and Solov'ev, 1969; Vilenskii, 1969).

Regional Locational Analysis

The location problem figures prominently in literature pertaining to resource use and to developing primary manufacturing complexes. Holzman (1957) analysed the locational conflicts and alternatives involved in the Urals–Kuznetsk Combine in the 1930s, relying heavily on Clark's (1957) empirical evidence for the iron and steel industry. In analysing regional energy production mixes, Dienes introduces a behavioural element by referring to 'pro-Europeans' and 'pro-Siberians' among Soviet planners (Dienes, 1971, p. 54). Identification of such broad interest groups among planning officials is also possible from recent conflicts over the location of new steel plants. Kistanov and Epshteyn (1972) favour a Siberian whereas Gladkevich (1971) favours a European location. Hutchings also observed that location policy comprised distinct eastern and western components (Hutchings, 1971, p. 225).

Classification of planners' behaviour into broad groups suggests that their goals and attitudes are not uniform throughout either all levels of Soviet administration or all economic regions. Planners are required to make general plans and recommendations. Their schemes are highly influenced (Hamilton, 1970, 1973) by the quality of information they select from the economic environment, by their own location and spatial experience, education and training and by their interpretation of the general locational expectations of the two major bodies to whom he is ultimately responsible— the Communist Party and the Council of Ministers. Similarly, outlines prepared by planners will be further disaggregated and interpreted according to the behaviour patterns of industrial decision-makers. Works of Kosmachev (1970), Maslov (1970), Meshcheryakova (1967), Movchan (1970) and Rostovtsev (1970) stress the clear need still to base planning of primary manufacturing complexes on general objectives.

The Soviet locational problem is most frequently analysed by Soviet and western scholars alike in terms of regional economic behaviour. Soviet studies prefer to delimit and analyse regional production complexes. Western studies deal with regional aggregations of enterprises and not with the firm. The firm seems to be an insignificant unit when compared with the broad locational considerations which have traditionally been cited as factors in Soviet regional industrial development. Hutchings' work is representative of this broad approach:

> Though to some extent the authorities can shift consuming districts, in practice mobility is limited by the hostile climatic conditions in Siberia, the absence of east to west waterway communications, the need to create social capital in proximity to producing works which are removed from inhabited places, and the ingrained preference of the ministries to build nearer to Moscow or other large cities in European Russia. Following the re-creation of the ministries in 1965, there is also every reason to suppose that their typical vices will again be manifested. (Hutchings, 1971, p. 224)

His general prediction that the ministries would reassert their pre-1957 predilection for autocratic centralism must now be modified in the light of experience with the economic reforms launched when the ministries were recreated. While the outcome of experiments with new forms of lower and middle management agencies is still uncertain, the indications are that the Soviet firm is gaining considerable independence in its economic behaviour and becoming important in the spatial behaviour and locational decision-making of Soviet industry.

Old versus New Locations

It is useful to distinguish between decision-making prior to the location of a new firm and that following the firm's existence and operation. Larger-scale issues of regional development, optimum location, location orientation, interdependencies and economic linkages might be assessed prior to location of the individual economic unit, the firm. Yet, in many ways, the existence today of so many Soviet firms and enterprises automatically limits the choices open to Soviet decision-makers. While the location of major new investments are a matter of national priority and control, many less spectacular—but nevertheless significant aggregate—location decisions are heavily influenced by local officials with the chief administrators of their respective ministries. The predilection of managerial personnel for expansion in existing locations and regions creates inertia in spatial industrial patterns. Large new resource-using industries receive most attention from the Soviet press: enterprises like the Krasnoyarsk hydroelectric plant or Bratsk aluminium plant show how capital-intensive energy and primary manufacturing projects are often associated with developing virgin territory in peripheral economic regions. Yet, much basic growth in the Soviet economy does not accrue to spectacular projects: it occurs with little fanfare at sites of existing manufacturing.

Issues associated with regional development policies are well documented in many Soviet sources and will not be restated here. Instead, most attention is paid to the spatial behaviour of the Soviet firm in relation to both centralized and decentralized locational decisions. This is consistent with Townroe's observation that a firm's decision-makers are influenced by external and internal forces (Townroe, 1969, p. 16).

Location and Behaviour

Berliner has been prominent among economists for his behavioural analysis of the Soviet firm. He stresses the need 'to pierce the official facade' of Soviet literature and 'to sketch out the informal features of the system' (Berliner, 1957, p. 408). He criticized western observers who relied solely upon superficially sterile literature and claimed that, without some access to individuals and some means of evaluating their behaviour, such methods were more appropriate to economic history than to the study of institutions.

Major examples of successful behavioural analyses of Soviet institutions according to the criterion of behaviour are works by Bienstock, Schwarz, and Yugow (1944), Gerschenkron (1950), Granick (1954), Berliner (1957) and Kornai (1959). Nove's comprehensive analysis of the Soviet economy (Nove, 1968) combines normative expectations with actual behaviour. Behavioural interpretations by Bergson (1964), Bornstein and Fusfeld (1966), Campbell (1966), Feiwel (1967), Felker (1966), Goldman (1968) and Wiles

(1963) confirm that analysis of the Soviet system must recognize differences between official economic theory (or doctrine) and operational reality. However, the problem of Soviet *spatial* behaviour has still not received sufficient attention by western economists, partly because they have neglected spatial economics generally (Hamilton, 1973).

Thus an important avenue of research is the interpretation of interactions between the locational behaviour and the informal organization of the Soviet firm. Berliner employed a very simple and rudimentary model to interviews with émigré Soviet industrial managers. His objective however, to obtain more than 'occasional glimpses of those personal and *informal* relations which are the meat on the bones of a social system' (Berliner, 1962, p.408) is consistent with analytical frameworks being used increasingly by geographers for analysis of western locational behaviour.

Behaviour and the Firm

Analysis of decision-making must consider the structure of the organizations making decisions (Dicken, 1971). This also pertains to location decisions, although Dicken interprets location in a much wider and more meaningful context than traditional analysis. Location decisions are made infrequently, being only a minor set of all decisions made by a firm in its attempt to survive and expand within its economic environment: 'Spatial the expansion or contraction of a firm, changes in inputs and outputs, the operation of spatial pricing policies, rationalization of operations, adoption of innovations of certain kinds, and so on'. (Dicken, 1971, p.427). Furthermore, the decision-maker is boundedly rational, possesses limited knowledge, is conditioned by his relative access to information systems and usually selects sub-optimal solutions (Dicken, 1971, p. 433).

Dicken designed a model, inspired by Huff (1960), of the coding mechanism by which decision-makers receive and interpret information signals to form their behavioural environment ('action space'). This model also contains elements which Berliner incorporated into his classic interpretation of the Soviet firm: for example, the goals of Soviet managerial behaviour could be evaluated by considering bonuses *(premia)*, profits (really output plan fulfilment) and the 'quiet life' *(chtoby zhit' spokoino)*. Having accepted these goals, Soviet management seeks to attain them by adopting concomitant principles of economic behaviour including the 'safety factor' or insurance *(strakhovka)*, simulation *(ochkovtiratel' stvo)*, or 'rubbing-in someone's eye-glasses' and pull or graft *(blat)*. These principles suggest that Soviet management expects its members to foster mutual support *(krugovaya poruka)*. (Berliner, 1962, pp. 413–426).

If Dicken's claim that 'phenomena, places, or events outside the behavioural environment have no relevance to, and no influence upon, conscious decision-making' (p. 428) is true, then there is no reason why the perception mechanism of locational decision-makers in a Soviet-type economy should not contain elements similar to those of management in other highly complex industrial societies. Soviet social scientists suggest that the spatial planning and operating processes analysed by Berliner and Holzman have become exponentially more severe as the economy has grown and diversified since 1955. Gertrude Schroeder describes this situation as 'the curse of complexity', adding that 'each successive change in the rules [of the economy] has only added to complexity and confusion' (Schroeder, 1971, p. 41).

The Economic Environment of the Soviet Firm

The behavioural environment, or geographic action space, of the Soviet decision-maker is created by the response of elements within his own coding system to the objective Soviet environment or milieu. Berliner concluded from interviews, that the behaviour of the Soviet firm reflects five factors: (1) the relative priority of each firm, (2) the short tenure of office of plant directors, (3) the firm's recent performance record, (4) the peculiar combination of informal and personal relations within the bureaucratic system and (5) the lack of full control by management over the firm.

The firm's objective economic environment includes factors common to many economies (Steed, 1971; Townroe, 1969):

(i) Spatial shape, size and distance.

(ii) Turbulence, which is associated with production plans and conflicts within related administrative chains; pressure for change is generated by disaggregation of annual and quinquennial national economic plans.

(iii) Cost and supply conditions, which are related to physical conditions, technical levels, changing material locations due to discoveries, establishment of new supply links, capital supply and delivery bottlenecks.

(iv) Demand conditions, which are related to output and sales plans and to instability caused by technological changing among consumers.

(v) Influences from similar and associated industries.

(vi) Labour quality and performance, which are related to the industrialization of a peasant society.

(vii) National ideology.

(viii) National stress and spatial goals of the military planners.

(ix) Social, cultural and economic relations among decision-makers.

Berliner's behavioural categories relate specifically to the operation of *Soviet* firms. Their rearrangement, however, can provide general utility. The relative priority of each firm (1) suggests conditions of size, reputation and perceived importance. This characteristic can be included under (v) above since it contains relatively important elements which relate to the opportunities and performance of other firms and institutions. The short

Table 16.1. Personnel Turnover in the USSR, 1966–1971 (Percentage of 1966 officials not in the same positions in 1971)

Party apparatus: Position	Turnover
	%
Full Members, CPSU Politburo	0
Full Members, CPSU Central Committee	24
CPSU Central Committee Secretaries	27
CPSU Central Committee Department Heads	46
Republic Party First Secretaries	14
Full Members, Republic Party Bureau	37
Full Members, Republic Party Central Committee	41
Republic Central Committee Secretaries (except First Secretaries)	58
Republic Central Committee Department Heads	65
Oblast Committee First Secretaries	44
Oblast Committee Second Secretaries	67
City Committee First Secretaries (50 largest cities)	61
District Committee First Secretaries (in 10 republics)	57

State apparatus: Position	Turnover
	%
Deputy Chairmen, USSR Council of Ministers	0
Ministers and Chairmen of State Committees sitting on the USSR Council of Ministers	12
USSR Deputy Ministers of Defence	55
Commanders, Military Districts	100
USSR Deputy Ministers	35
Chairmen, Republic Councils of Ministers	60
Deputy Chairmen, Republic Councils of Ministers	45
Republic Ministers and Chairmen of State Committees	41
Oblast Executive Committee Chairmen	56
Directors, 170 largest factories	44

Source. Jerry F. Hough, 'The Soviet system: petrification or pluralism?', *Problems of Communism,* March–April, 1972, pp. 25–45, p. 6.

tenure of plant directors (2) is a condition of turbulence (ii). In fact, all levels of party and state administration are in a constant state of flux (Table 16.1), although top positions actually change abruptly. The firm's recent record (3) applies both to (iv) and (v) in such items as credit rating, reliability and ability to effect output plans. Lack of full control (5)—resulting from production enthusiasm by over-zealous workers or information leaks to higher authorities by informers—appears to be another case of turbulence (ii). Informal and personal relations (4) occur in most social and economic organizations and are not limited to the Soviet bureaucracy. American businessmen often identify with each other when problems are overcome by illegal means: some will not testify against each other because the economic community of which they are part might disapprove and collectively disrupt delivery of supplies (Berliner, 1968, p, 196). Failure by Soviet managers to prosecute those suppliers who fail to honour delivery contracts is also a response to the possibility of future reprisals. Consequently, it is meaningful to incorporate evidence of personal and informal relations into (ix).

Modification of the Objective Economic Environment

Their own personal coding mechanism encourages Soviet decision-makers to select elements from the (objective) economic environment and thereby to create a behavioural environment in which they attain locational goals (see Figure 16.1). Obviously that environment varies among decision-makers, in the same decision-maker for each set of decisions, and for similar decisions at different time periods, as learning and feedback modify the components of the coding mechanism. The Soviet location decision-maker, like his western counterpart, suffers from imperfect understanding and knowledge of elements in the changing objective environment of the firm: he is neither superhuman, super-rational, super-totalitarian nor an automated cog in the wheel of a monolithic totalitarian economic and political system. He pursues centralized and decentralized spatial goals by (1) perceiving the need for decisions and indentifying problems, (2) preparing alternative satisfactory solutions and (3) selecting acceptable solutions from among alternatives. This suggests that there is considerable divergence between the objective and behavioural economic environments of Soviet decision-makers.

Decision-Making and the Firm

General location principles which guide Soviet decision-makers are first formalized into general planning guidelines by central authorities. In preparing the 'General Outline for Developing and Locating the Productive Forces of the USSR up to 1980', the major territorial forward planning group of the USSR Gosplan—the Council for the Study of Productive Forces (SOPS)—for the first time in Soviet history set out major planning guidelines for the regional location of industrial investment. The General Outline was shaped by over 20,000 scholars and specialists working in 560 research and planning organizations under the supervision of the Territorial Planning Division of Gosplan and the Soviet Academy of Sciences.

The specialized roles of centralized and decentralized decision-makers lead to disfunctional behaviour, reducing decision-making efficiency. In 1966, 1290 project and survey organizations worked on capital construction projects. Some were small, local, insignificant; others were large design organizations engaged in technical surveys, research and development and in creating regional and industrial development plans (Jackson, 1971

420

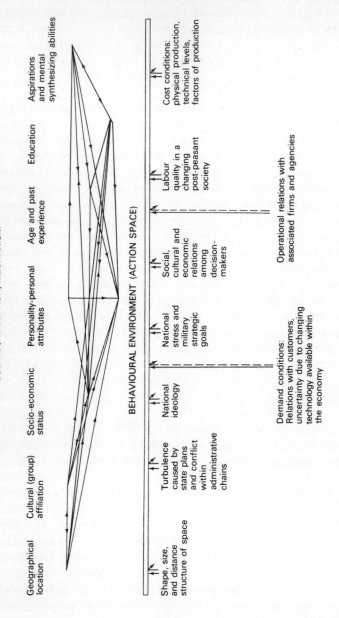

CODING (PERCEPTION) MECHANISM

Geographical location

Cultural (group) affiliation

Socio-economic status

Personality-personal attributes

Age and past experience

Education

Aspirations and mental synthesizing abilities

BEHAVIOURAL ENVIRONMENT (ACTION SPACE)

Shape, size, and distance structure of space

Turbulence caused by state plans and conflict within administrative chains

National ideology

National stress and military strategic goals

Social, cultural and economic relations among decision-makers

Labour quality in a changing post-peasant society

Cost conditions: physical production, technical levels, factors of production

Demand conditions: Relations with customers, uncertainty due to changing technology available within the economy

Operational relations with associated firms and agencies

OBJECTIVE (ECONOMIC) ENVIRONMENT

Figure 16.1. The behavioural modification of the objective economic environment of the Soviet firm (after Dicken).

p.4). More were responsible to particular ministries and *Glavki* and were highly specialized. As many as 20 such institutes cooperate on a single project. Enterprises purchase services for small-sclae modernization and expansion, while *Glavki* are clients for larger-scale reconstruction and construction of new enterprises. In 1967, more than 48,000 firms were in operation in the USSR, of which 5,500 each employed more than 1,000 workers (Keefe, 1971, p. 636). Detailed project proposals prepared by project organizations and clients are evaluated by perhapas 15 to 20 different agencies (Jackson, 1971, p. 6). New projects which cost over one million roubles, use complex imported equipment, or constitute 'especially important projects', are examined by Gosplan USSR and Gosstroi USSR (Jackson, 1971, p. 6). Once the *technical* nature of a project has been successfully evaluated by the pertinent administrative bodies, it becomes an *investment* project: a feasibility study is then initiated by Gosplan or the appropriate industrial ministry. If successful through the evaluation stage, it becomes an 'assignment for project-making' eligible for inclusion either in future annual investment plans or in research and development plans. Approval of assignments permits clients and project organizations to conclude formal legal contracts.

Rules for designing and evaluating projects vary according to their complexity and implementation costs. Administrative procedures for planning defined by Soviet law do not facilitate selection of optima from among alternatives. Most projects are designed by reference to centrally-authorized norms, not cost. Costs, estimated in an *ex post* manner, facilitate accounting within aggregate investment and construction plans but do not serve as criteria for selecting alternatives (Hamilton, 1970; Jackson, 1971). Between 1963 and 1965 the central annual capital investment plan accounted for approximately 90 per cent of Soviet investment; the remainder were decentralized funds. National plans prepared by Gosplan USSR and approved by the Council of Ministers contain aggregate allocations among major industrial branches and regions. Each subordinate planning agency then relates invesment allocation from above to sums for projects requested from below. To balance funds with requests, some projects are modified or excluded. Decisions must choose among (1) projects by industrial branches or regions and (2) projects of different branches or regions. Considerable flexibility and room for manoeuvre exist in the process of disaggregating allocation plans: the spatial significance of this form of behaviour is important although difficult to monitor.

One reason is the poor flow of information between decision-makers. Any incorrect information originating from a decentralized source (e.g. factory) will become incorporated in an aggregate plan and then be fed back of the decentralized agency. If both agencies are engaged in a continuous feedback process, final allocations and decisions could contain compounded errors (Jackson, 1971, pp. 16–17). Such information flows in the planning process mean that rules and operational techniques for determining and selecting the best alternative plans become difficult to apply. Moreover, selection procedures often contain criteria which both conflict and defy objective measurement. Jackson, for example, cites Soviet sources which claim either that optimal solutions are decided subjectively according to many criteria, some of which support while others reject a project, or that the Soviet system of indices can prove any case. Ellman demonstrates that economic planning criteria have led to location choices which do not offer the lowest costs even when cost considerations were of prime concern (Ellman, p. 299). The final selection of industrial projects, and hence the location of investment, can reflect the ability of persons engaged in the planning process to sustain certain interests, i.e. location decisions may reflect both the different behavioural attributes of the decision-maker and the relationship of the firm to the entire structure of industrial management in the USSR.

The Firm within the Structure of Soviet Industrial Organization

Industrial Management

Traditionally, the physical structure of the Soviet economic environment has been organized in industrial sectors within a hierarchical set of administrative and political organizations. Ultimate control over more industries rests at the centre, in Moscow, in the Central Committee of the Communist Party of the Soviet Union (CPSU) and the Council of Ministers. The latter is the supreme coordinating body for union ministries which administer individual industrial sectors. Each ministry is further divided into several departments *(glavnye upravleniya,* or *glavki)* which in turn supervise enterprises and service agencies. The individual enterprise is the basic operational unit of the industrial economy. Some enterprises have become increasingly grouped into associations *(ob'edineniya)* which are administrative units intermediate between the individual enterprise and the *Glavk,* or which replace the *Glavk* and are subordinate directly to the ministry.

Ministerial organization was interrupted between 1957 and 1965 when the Khrushchev regime attempted to administer industry on territorial *(sovnarkhoz)* principles, initially with 105, but later 47, regions (Dewdney, 1967, pp. 28–9). Evidence shows, however, that recentralization processes began almost immediately in 1958 (Berliner, 1968, p. 180), indicating the ability of the Soviet system to resist major decentralization processes. The most persistent form of semi-decentralized industrial administration is the union–republic ministerial organization, which duplicates functions of all-Union ministries and has jurisdiction over industries of local or regional significance: in 1968, of 37 industrial ministries, 19 were all-Union and 18 were union-republic (Nove, 1968, p. 110). The Soviet Council of Ministers is the supreme body of the state's chief industrial and management representatives—virtually an 'all-Union board of directors'—and composed of ministers from each central ministry and chairmen of the major central state committees. The chairman of each republic's Council of Ministers is an *ex officio* member of the USSR Council of Ministers. The chairman of the USSR Council of Ministers is equivalent to a Minister in the West (Keefe, 1971, p. 391).

The Council of Ministers is constitutionally responsible to the Soviet elected government, the Supreme Soviet. In reality, it is responsible to the CPSU in which many senior government officials hold office and by which all major government administrative appointments are approved. At all levels of industrial administration, there are parallel organizations of government and Communist party. The party supervises, monitors and regulates government administration from the Central Council of Ministers down to the individual enterprise. This dual structure is crucial in analysing decision-making; it complicates the decision process and prevents economic forces operating free from Party political objectives. Those engaged in making decisions have been approved by the political apparatus via the *nomenklatura* mechanism, party-controlled lists of appointments or of those eligible to hold responsible positions in the government. The *nomenklatura* is implemented at each level by at least one appropriate party committee (Nove, 1968, p. 109). The party strives to control formation and execution of policy, being involved in basic planning decisions, the appointment and supervision of ministers and the choice of alternative projects by industrial and agricultural managers. The party, therefore, cannot be omitted from detailed analyses of managerial behaviour.

The 'firm' consists of factories or plants and, traditionally, has been synonymous with the enterprise *(predpriyatiya)*; it is owned by the state. However, since 1962, the firm or company *(firma)* has also taken the form of amalgamations of enterprises (with former enterprises becoming sub-units of the firma) and of federations in which enterprises retain degrees of autonomy. Since restoration of the ministerial system in 1965, some firms have been broken up and subordinated to ministries. Within the ministerial system a similar organization, the *ob'edineniye* (association or corporation), also referred to as a *firma,* has been tested since 1965. Experiments with such firms continue as the Soviet government attempts to achieve economies of scale in administration, planning and operation: grouping smaller enterprises under one organizational body can reduce the firm's administrative overheads and strengthen its production linkages without weakening the administrative and planning authority of the *Glavk* or the ministry.

The enterprise, still the official and *de facto* basic operational unit of activity within the Soviet economy, is governed by statutory laws and goals. To date the same cannot be said for the association since administrative decrees alone regulate its operation. Some economists suggest that the association be given the same rules and legal status as the enterprise so that suppliers and sub-component manufacturers can be legally bound together in a single production plan. When the same range of decisions officially permitted to the enterprise is extended to the association,

> decisions on strategic questions of production, the distribution of capital investments, the utilization of sources of finance for capital investment, the determination of long-term contract orders for scientific institutions, the study and shaping of demand for the final product—are concentrated in the hands of the general board of directors (*CDSP*, **22**, no. 6, pp. 8, 10)

The enterprise is 'a single production-economic unit concerned with fulfilling the national plan for producing industrial goods, characterized by united production technology, organization and economic structure, and by operational independence' (Aleksandrov, 1965, p. 10). This definition does not include any provision for the enterprise to achieve efficient spatial location.

The enterprise is also a plant or works (*zavod* for heavy industries), factory or mill (*fabrika* for light industries). A major production subdivision of the enterprise is the shop *(Tsekh)* that may be spatially separated from related activities of the firm, because of specific resource-processing needs or space problems. Such division is at a very local level and does not significantly influence location behaviour.

Throughout Soviet industrial history, the individual enterprise has been responsible to some form of chief administration within an industrial ministry, or commissariat, or VSNKH (Nove, 1961, pp. 62–63). However, the problems of coordinating the enterprise and its suppliers and customers have led Soviet authorities to experiment with intermediate organizations. Prior to 1932, the Trust *(Trest)* was a horizontally integrated organization consisting of larger-scale enterprises operating within some limited spatial framework. The Trust ceased to play a dominant role when the ministerial system was introduced in 1932. It was replaced by the vertically integrated Combine *(Kombinat)*, which persists today as a multi-functional large firm (Nove, 1961, pp. 62–4). The *Kombinat* implies geographically localized production to minimize product transfer among related processing stages. Distance is not specifically mentioned in the most common form of *Kombinat* but is recognized as being important in interregional organizations like the Urals-Kuznetsk Combine. Early Combines tended toward integrated production from raw materials through successive stages of manufacture to the finished product: e.g. mining iron ore, producing pig iron, steel, rolled metal, and manufacturing metal products and tools (Aleksandrov, 1965, p. 9). Others comprised sawmilling, kiln drying, wood processing and furniture manufacture. Some Combines were established to use waste materials and sub-components from various industries, e.g. chemical pulp rom sawmill residues. More recently, Combines have been innovated to ise raw materials and recycle component materials to maximize efficiency, :.g. a pulp and paper mill which uses chips for chemical pulp, the bark, dges and slabs for hog fuel, residues from cooking tall oil, a chemical 'urnace to recover liquors used in the digesters, and garbage pulp or paper rimmings to produce wrappings paper, egg cartons and roofing felts. 5oviet sources claim that Combines (1) reduce administrative expenses >y integrating similar shops and departments, (2) reduce production costs, 3) increase output-mix and volume, (4) facilitate process integration, (5) 'educe the length of production periods and (6) reduce transport costs.

Neither the ministerial system nor the short-lived *sovnarkhozy* system 'acilitated efficient production relationships between suppliers and whole- ;alers on the one hand and manufacturers on the other. To the extent that nuch mechanical and electronic equipment is purchased by enterprises in ill industrial sectors, the complicated relationships between the firm, its *Glavk,* and planning and administration tends to restrict efficiency and >revent specialization: it encourages auxiliary production. Most Soviet :ritics of the present management system conclude that middle management nust be revamped and firms permitted to vary their output-mixes to serve ndustry-wide consumers. If relationships and linkages among industrial >roducers become more direct and efficient through the association then he Secretary of the Byelorussian Communist Party Central Committee, A. Smirnov, has noted that the chief administration *(Glavki)* may become ;uperfluous *(CDSP, 22,* no. 42, p. 10).

Some Spatial Effects of Current Organization Changes in the Soviet Firm

Reform of management

The need to improve economic performance and to organize associations has received widespread attention since a Plenary Session of the CPSU Central Committee in September 1965. By 1970, the first phase of the reform had been largely completed and new planning methods and incentives introduced in 42,000 industrial enterprises. In phase two, planners are attempting to accomplish six major objectives by reforms which include making the association (or *firma*) the major operational unit. Although explicit provisions for spatial change are not contained in the reform, most proposed management changes imply locational adaptation. Current objectives of the economic reform are to:

(1) reduce superfluous managerial functions and create effective mana- gerial and operational systems;

(2) create large production units which will contain integrated research, design and production facilities for applying new technology and improving existing operating functions;

426

(3) relate science and production by improving the interface between innovation and construction of experimental models;

(4) facilitate production specialization and industrial independence

(5) improve managerial functions by applying computer technology

(6) generate long-term relations among producers for more effective realization of five-year planning objectives.

These changes relate to the role of the *association as an enterprise,* or a a major replacement of the *Glavki* in middle management. The association becomes directly subordinate to the ministry, either as an industrial complex or as an all-Union (or republic-wide) association where enterprises are united in territorial complexes. For example, enterprises producing bearing or lumber or plywood in many widely separated regions would be grouped in their respective national or republic associations (*CDSP,* 23, no. 4, pp. 6–8).

These six objectives now serve as general goals for decision-makers, but the way in which they perceive the objectives and the economic and political environment shapes the information which they pass along the lines of management (according to the principle of democratic socialism; *CDSP* 23, no. 36, pp. 5–7). Until recently managerial science received a low priority despite the apparent awareness of the utility of computer technology for information processing. If the thirty billion (i.e. 30×10) sheets of documents which flow in and out of Soviet institutions each year were pasted together, the paper ribbon could be wrapped around the equator 200 times. Thus 'it is physically impossible to give all of this information high-quality processing by the usual methods'. *(CDSP,* 23, no. 36, p. 7). Furthermore much slack exists in the economic system, permitting great variation in behaviour. Common methods and rules of decision-making have not been adopted by such basic institutions as the local Soviets *(CDSP,* 23, no. 36 p. 6). Administrative organization of meat procurement, for example, varies among union republics: in some it is accomplished by the republic ministry of agriculture, in others by the ministry of meat and dairy industry, and in one (Uzbekistan) by the chief administration of the Uzbek Council of Ministers *(CDSP,* 23, no. 42, p. 24). *Pravda,* in 1971, noted that the behaviour of individual firms and ministries has a widespread effect on the efficiency of the entire Soviet economy:

> The people in the All-Union Office Equipment Association under the Ministry of Instrument-Making, Automation and Control Systems explain the modest scale of the production of managerial equipment by citing the plants' limited opportunities for amalgamation and the fact that planning agencies have not given proper attention to the reconstruction of old enterprises or the construction of new ones. (*CDSP* 23, no. 42, p. 7)

This suggests that both the institutional framework and the insufficiency of applied computer technology are strangling the firm's attempts and opportunities to produce efficiently the goods needed by the economy.

The *association* represents the latest Soviet attempt to achieve specialization within, and interdependence among, enterprises which, until now, have themselves produced many general items because of the uncertain and irregular supply of components:

> The special characteristics of associations are the large-scale concentration of general services, the simplification of the managerial apparatus and the reduction of its cost. Now, according to selective-sample data, out of every 100 machine-building plants, 99 manufacture gear wheels, 65 make metal fastenings, 71 make iron castings, 84 make forgings and 57 make non-ferrous castings. By unifying the small auxiliary production lines, it is possible to create large and well-equipped services for repairs, transportation and the manufacture of billets, tools, fittings, non-standard equipment and packing materials, and to unite scientific laboratories in the same speciality, to centralize the training of cadres, to concentrate reserves. (*CDSP*, **22**, no. 6, p. 10)

The chairman of the Lithuanian Republic Council of Ministers, J. Maniusis, claimed in 1970 that 'the economically accountable production association that is endowed with the rights of a chief administration, [i.e. *Glavk*] can combine branch and territorial planning, and this is very important for improving the elaboration of plans for the integrated developments of the national economy of the Union republics and the economic regions' *(CDSP,* **22**, no. 7, p. 5).

The association is being developed because of its ability both to strengthen inter-plant linkages and to create more efficient linkages between project and design institutes on the one hand and manufacturing plants on the other. Blyakhaman notes that the most effective life of new machine operation in the USSR, from the date of invention until technical obsolescence, is only seven years in many growth industries. Because long periods are necessary to introduce new inventions into production, more than half the scientific development 'never enter production or enter it with their last gasp' *(CDSP,* **23**, no. 48, p. 1). Blyakhaman argues that integrated research and production associations are the best mechanism hitherto known in the USSR to propel new ideas and projects from research through to production in technological industries. Information links, which are currently external for isolated research, design and production agencies, are internalized in the association. However, he cautions against creating a standard type of association: reform must discourage stereotypes and avoid the rigidity of previous governmental agencies. Blyakhaman identifies seven types of research-and-production or scientific-technical associations which are distinguished from each other by their types of linkages and might overcome institutional inflexibility:

(1) *Scientific and technical associations,* include general science institutes, an experimental plant, a design bureau, and a labour training centre.

(2) *Educational, scientific, and technical associations,* resembling type (1) but more interdisciplinary and academic.

(3) *Research and production associations* are problem solving organizations responsible for making innovations operational. They comprise a scientific institute, design bureau, technological bureau, a start-up and adjustment organization an experimental department and an enterprise for mass production of new equipment. This organization would then provide its ministerial branch with both prototypes and auxiliary equipment and specially trained labour to operate new equipment (e.g. The Food Industry Automatic Machinery Association in Odessa).

(4) *Technical associations* are headed by a large design bureau which is integrated with research institutes and production enterprises (e.g. The Soviet Aviation Industry).

(5) *Production and technical associations* which ensure that new technology is made operational at the enterprise level. This is now the weakest link between research and production in the USSR *(CDSP, 23,* no. 48, p. 2). Such associations contain a start-up and installation organizations, enterprises, information services divisions, labour research branches and project evaluation centres. These associations are particularly valuable to small enterprises especially in consumer and light industries which do not have adequate engineering subdivisions of their own.

(6) *Production and scientific associations* are important in branches where models of new equipment are both experimental and industrial e.g. custom-building machinery. These associations link research institutes primarily with one enterprise (e.g. Leningrad Optical Mechanical Association; Urals Machine Building Plant; Moscow Likhachev Motor Vehicle Plant).

(7) *Associations providing scientific services to enterprises and other organizations* offer consulting services and do not appear to have permanent ties with their customers *(CDSP, 23,* no. 48, pp. 1–3).

These associations relate to the applied factory side of science, not to theoretical work. To be effective they must be free to modify their internal linkages through time as demand by their customers and technology itself changes. Evaluation of the potential of the association has obviously led Soviet economists, engineers, managers, politicians and planners to consider the fundamental defects of the present industrial system and behaviour of the enterprise.[1]

The association will have, hopefully, suitable procedures for fulfilling central production plans and flexibility in using incentive funds, determining and manipulaing labour requirements, substituting materials and sources of supply, and designating the location and structure of linked industries and organizations. Hence, its potential spatial significance for Soviet locational decision-making cannot be overstated. Currently, adoption of the association as a permanent industrial production unit is proceeding cautiously as the performance of experiments must be evaluated. The associations do not yet have special legal status; their power and prestige varies from one case to another apparently as a function of the wisdom, responsibility, prestige and behaviour of related officials.

Each ministry has also to work out the nature of relations among component enterprises and agencies: the form and function of association—if and when they become recognized legally—will thus vary according to industry and the innovative skills of each ministry (see *CDSP*, **22**, no. 50, p. 37). The association exemplifies the dilemma of attempting to introduce flexibility into economic and spatial behaviour without reducing all-Union centralized control.

One avenue of current experimentation is to instil the association with the chief attributes of a large-scale (and often capital-intensive) resource-converting *Kombinat*: spatially separated, small, secondary manufacturing plants are often combined with related tertiary industries, the vertical linkages resembling those of the *Kombinat*, horizontal linkages those of the *Trest*. Enthusiasm for the association stems from the success of large-scale Soviet enterprises. Boldyrev claims that in 1969 plants employing more than 1000 workers produced 62·4 per cent of Soviet output and earned 63·3 per cent of profits *(CDSP*, **23**, no. 22, p. 11). Fedorenko and Bunich claim that many enterprises are below optimum size, but they do not define optimum size. Approximately three quarters of Soviet enterprises employ fewer than 500 people and produce only one quarter of industrial output; half employ fewer than 200 people and produce only 9 per cent of output *(CDSP*, **22**, no. 6, p. 8). Many enterprises, which should be grouped together because of similar product lines, are in fact organizationally separate and subordinated to different industries.

By bringing small and physically-separated enterprises together administratively, planners hope to change locational patterns by increasing plant specialization and by achieving economies of scale through the introduction of more flexibility into supply systems and production linkages. For example, in 1970, four separate agencies—the Plastic Materials Polymerization Research Institute, a design institute, an experimental plant, and the Okhta Combine, all of which are located in the Leningrad region,—were combined into the Leningrad Plastic and Polymerization Materials Association: this was the first chemical association combining research and production *(CDSP*, **22**, no. 5, p. 24). The Byelorussian Communist Party Central Committee Secretary claims that one-third of Byelorussian industrial output in 1970 came from two basic types of associations *(CDSP*, **22**, no. 42, p. 10): in one type an existing enterprise becomes dominant, all other production units in the association losing their economic and judicial independence; in the other type, known as territorial-branch associations, enterprises retain much of their independence. The first is common in consumer-goods industries, the second in food industries *(CDSP,* **22**, no. 42, p. 10).

The association has replaced chief administrations *(Glavki)* in some ministries where experiments with managerial reform have been completed successfully *(CDSP,* **22**, no. 19, pp. 16–17). In other cases, however, demands by the central leadership for reform in management have been ignored: 'the process of creating associations is slow progress, and their number has not increased in recent years; the main blame here rests with the ministries and department's *(CDSP,* **22**, no. 9, p. 3). Two recent Soviet experiences illustrate the dilemma of middle management relationships with the association.

The Ukrainian Chemical Industry: The Ukraine Republic Ministry of Chemical Industries has recently achieved noteworthy breakthroughs in production by reorganizing *Glavki* into associations. From the Chief Chlorine Industry Administration, the ministry created the Ukraine Republic Everyday Chemical Goods Association and the Ukraine Republic Plastics Association *(CDSP,* **22**, no. 19, p. 16). This replaced bureaucratic departments by economically accountable production associations which would act like large independent firms directly responsible to the ministry. By integrating enterprises into one large firm and removing the previous administrative division between related producers, the association has been able to organize the specialization of its sub-unit enterprises, rationalize productive capacity, redirect raw materials and supplies without reference to outside control agencies and transfer personnel from one enterprise to another. *The chief administration which the association replaced did not have these capabilities.*

Among its many achievements, the Ukraine Republic Everyday Chemical Goods Association created two experimental production units for developing technology and shipping containers. Their location is related to the association's production requirements and is, therefore, a function of the association's decision-making processes. Such decentralized behaviour by individual firms and associations may thus encourage spatial agglomeration. Since the association has the power to move factors of production among its sub-units, it can also attempt to gather unto itself as many related productive units as possible. In this case the goal is to reduce uncertainty in physical production and material supply and to control the turbulence of the economic system through control of related facilities. The Ukraine Republic Everyday Chemical Goods Association has recently attempted to expand its sphere of operations by requesting control over certain branches of all-Union ministry research institutes to internalize a subordinate scientific research base. This request has been cautiously received by the ministry since it implies that certain departments and chief administrations within it are redundant. However, should the Soviet industrial administrative system expect to survive in a rigid form within the environment of such an advanced industrial state?

The Soviet government is both pleased by, and afraid of, the productive and spatial behaviour of the association. Since the rights and duties of the association are not regulated by official statutes, it is guided by the principle, 'we'll do it if we choose to; if we refuse, no one will compel us' (*CDSP*, **22**, no. 19, p. 17).

Soviet machine-tool production: Potential conflict of interest between an association and another administrative unit is common. If the association replaces the *Glavk*, the points of friction within the industrial branch system are reduced but not eliminated. However, if the *Glavk* feels threatened, no statutes can compel it to allow the association to live and prosper. Association management has no recourse to legal action if the *Glavk* makes its existence unbearable. An example is the Kharkov association. 'Union Industrial Equipment' *(Soyuztekhosnastka)*, created by Government fiat in April 1971 within the Ministry of Machine-Tools and Instruments (Selyunin, 1972, p. 2) as a leading inter-industry technical design bureau with experimental production facilities. The association was made subordinate to the Equipment *Glavk* of the Ministry. Relations between the association and the *Glavk* indicate that 'a cold war has raged between the *Glavk* director and the association management. There has not been one item on which both sides have been able to agree'. Selyunin (1972), reporting in *Sotsialisticheskaya Industriya*, suggests that the *Glavk* director is the villain, the Association management being responsible individuals helping government efforts to increase efficiency and economic growth.[2] The director of the *Glavk* behaved antagonistically to both the association and the central government, but with the support of the Minister of Machine-Tools and Instruments. The director, aware that the association is not protected by law, chose to force the association management to resort to illegal means to secure finance for new capacity and the labour required to fulfil its production goals. The director's letters to the association management were high-handed and contemptuous, suggesting that higher output goals could be met by far fewer workers. Yet he admitted to the newspaper that targets set for the association by the government were unrealistic. The reporter could draw only one meaningful conculsion: 'very soon the association will fulfil one-third of all industrial programmes of the *Glavk*. Given another two such associations and the *Glavk* will be able to celebrate its own redundancy!'

Problems in Middle Management

The general problem is one of multi-stage management in which any one administrative branch has insufficient legal independence. The associations are clearly in an unstable position. For example, although in Lvov the drive to create associations was apparently initiated by the Lvov Oblast Party organization, some ministries have recently dissolved associations. Related enterprises of some associations, located in different Ukrainian cities, have been reconverted independent enterprises or transformed into trusts subordinate to the ministries. When the ministries were reinstituted, firms set up under the old *sovnarkhozy* system were converted to trusts to protect many of the local specialists who had worked in the *sovnarkhozy* (*CDSP*, **22**, no, 20, p. 15). *Pravda* in 1970 reported that 'the firms were abolished to set up trusts and administrations, which the ministries needed to provide jobs for their administrators' (*CDSP*, **22**, no. 20, p. 15). Since the association is supposed to reduce management costs through specialization of enterprise production functions, management would often become redundant and either have to find less remunerative employment or relocate expanding enterprises possibly in more peripheral growth regions. Some ministers complain about the *centrifugal* effect of Party desires to create specialized production facilities within the associations. With reintroduction of trusts and independent enterprises, managerial staff has grown faster than either the number of workers or physical output. *Pravda* concluded that *Glavki* strongly opposed associations as they tend to 'eat up' trusts, leaving the *Glavki* without work.

Some enterprise managers fear loss of independence and personal prestige if they enter an association. Apparently the initial impetus for creating many associations comes from Party organizations, some of which probably contain members from industry who can transmit the fears of reluctant managers and restrain Party enthusiasm for the association. Moreover, the *oblast*, and possibly the *kray* or *ASSR* as well, may lose deductions from profits which accrue to their budgets if the output from one enterprise leaves the province and is sent to a related firm in another region (*CDSP*, **22**, no. 32, pp. 9, 31). Thus, resistance to the association occurs in both centralized and decentralized organizations. This is important as spatial flows of commodities and information can change in direction and form when associations are created.

Middle Management in Resource-Converting Industries

The feeling by middle management in the *Glavki* that the association poses a special threat is supported by experience with managerial reform in the all-Union Petroleum Ministry which controls 98 per cent of Soviet oil output (*CDSP*, **22**, no. 39, pp. 5, 7). This ministry is completely reorganized on a three-tier management structure: ministry, association, enterprise. This large resource-intensive ministry must be aware of spatial differences in production, research and development because of inherent spatial variations in resources. The association replaced the former territorial-production administrations (which had greater spatial awareness than most *Glavki*). In 1970, the Soviet petroleum ministry was reorganized into 21 associations which each employ between 15,000 and 50,000 persons.

In 1971 the Soviet Minister of the Lumber and Wood-Processing Industry reported that his ministry had been similarly reorganized on a three-tier basis, replacing the former pattern of management of combines, trusts and chief administrations which was 'clumsy and insufficiently flexible' (*CDSP*, **23**, no. 13, p. 24). This ministry, with 2,000 enterprises and 2,000,000 workers, evaluated its new firms and associations over a four year period through its own research organizations. The ministry concluded, in 1971, that 'it seems desirable to adopt statutes for the new industrial economic accountability associations and to amend the existing statutes on socialist enterprises as soon as possible' (*CDSP,* **23**, no. 13, p. 25). The ministry partly eliminated middle management organizations by removing more than 20 combines and trusts. Their managerial functions are being shifted to associations which encompass the concept of 'management by product' (*CDSP*, **23**, no. 13, p. 25). There are three forms of association in this ministry:

(1) *The branch association* operates at an all-Union or republic scale, and includes an entire production line or a specialized service, e.g. Plywood and Match Association; the Logging Machinery Repair Association.

(2) *Associations of enterprises of and economic region* are based on the branch principle, including the Kirov Lumber Trust, Karelian Lumber Export Trust and Moscow Furniture Trust.

(3) *Associations of enterprises of a single speciality extending over the boundaries of economic regions*, including the Southern Furniture Trust, the Volga Furniture and Lumber Trust.

The Ministry itself is being reorganized according to specific products, particular types of processing and will also include agencies responsible entirely for supply or planning. Five new production management structures have been introduced into the ministry to deal with logging, rafting, milling, furniture making and board production. At present, they are concerned with 'control' functions—supervision and checking—not operation. Traditionally, the ministry has not held complete authority over timber production and sawmilling in the USSR since one-third of the timber and one-half of sawmill products come from enterprises subordinate to other departments in the government. This defect has still not been overcome. The Minister of the Lumber and Wood-Processing Industry, N. Timofeyev, is seeking more central control over logging and sawmilling, because of the conflict between planned timber production and so-called 'independent loggers' which has become (*CDSP*, **24**, no. 19, pp. 26–27; **23**, no. 51, p. 17) a major problem in some regions. In Irkutsk oblast, 140 lumber camps established by various construction (hence, the term, 'independent loggers') organizations outnumber those of the USSR Ministry of Lumber and Wood-

Processing Industry by more than two to one. Most timber in the region is officially allotted to the Bratsk timber processing complex but independent loggers cut for their own agencies with impunity, ignoring proper conservation measures, overloading roads and burning waste wood which could help satisfy the large local firewood market. This necessitating long-distance railroad transport of roundwood for official wood-processing complexes where reserves are now exhausted.

Some ambiguity exists in the new managerial system of this ministry since not all middle management structures (*Glavki*) have been eliminated. Furthermore, organizations which overlap economic-regional boundaries encompass different local party organizations: some conflict of interest may arise here as workers in one association will have allegiance to different provincial party organizations. Smirnov, Secretary of the Byelorussian Communist Party Central Committee stressed in 1970 that:

> The experience of Leningraders and other Party committees confirms that we should be more active in setting up single primary Party organizations for entire associations, regardless of the administrative region in which any particular branch enterprise and its primary Party organization are located. This refers especially to the primary Party organizations of associations that are made up of branch enterprises that have lost their juridical and production independence. (*CDSP*, **22**, no. 42, p. 23)

In view of the party's close supervision of economic activity, new industrial management structures must be similar to that of the party hierarchy if the new system of management is to function effectively and still be consistent with the goals of democratic socialism. Khrushchev made a similar mistake when his reforms in 1962 violated boundaries of existing administrative and political units.

The spatial behaviour of the association in the Soviet Lumber and Wood-Processing industry combines many attributes of branch decision-making with a territorial distribution of individual firms and enterprises. This industry processes a major raw material which is widely distributed throughout territorial space, especially in the northern European and Asiatic USSR. Regional administration is effected through provinces, territories and ASSRs within a system of Union republics. Existing forest inventories and many other social and administrative operations within the ministry are organized according to this spatial administration system. Unlike engineering and equipment-manufacturing, the organization of raw material extraction and resource management has a definite spatial bias which cannot be overcome without major administrative readjustments. The Ministry of Lumber and Wood-Processing has, therefore, tailored many of its locational decisions to create patterns of industrial linkages within firms which will correspond to the existing political and administrative territories of the USSR. Their heaviest concentration is in these major forest resource regions because this industry, like major segments of pulp and paper manufacturing, is highly influenced by processing relationships which encourage locational-orientation toward the primary raw material (Barr, 1970, 1971).

Another type of association is the agro-industrial complex which integrates agricultural production with industrial processing. Most are in the southern USSR in the North Caucasus, Moldavia and the Crimea (*CDSP*, **24**, no. 11, p. 11) and process perishable fruits and vegetables (for example, the Moldavian Fruit and Vegetable Industry Association). This is subordinate to the republic Council of Ministers and the USSR Ministry of the Food Industry. It absorbed 30 canneries, 26 state farms and their industrial units, 35 procurement offices, a packaging-materials plant, a printing plant manufacturing labels, several trucking companies, a technical school and laboratories; and employs 50,000 people. The basic industrial unit within this structure is the territorial association consisting of various combinations of state farms, canneries and procurement offices (*CDSP*, **24**, no. 30, p. 23). In regions where animal husbandry is important, agro-industrial associations integrate mixed-feed plants, livestock operations, meat-packing and dairy facilities (*CDSP*, **24**, no. 11, p. 11).

Locational Behaviour of the Soviet Firm

Western location and spatial behavioural theory assume that the decision-maker is independent and acts by evaluating forces in the objective environment. Behavioural postulates range from assumptions of economic to satisficer man. An independent unit in a democratic system, the Soviet firm, however, is enmeshed in a state ideology which assumes (1) a unity of economics and politics, (2) the precedence of politics over economics, (3) a correct political approach to all economic questions, (4) the dominance of Soviet Communist Party policy over economic decisions, (5) a national approach to all economic problems, (6) democratic centralism in economic management, (7) a centrally-planned and centrally-managed economy, (8) balanced and integrated development of economic regions (*CDSP*, **22**, no. 9, pp. 3–5). These assumptions are incorporated into Soviet locational principles. The major problem of the Soviet economy—indeed one inherited from Czarist Russia—is to strike a balance between centralism and independence (Gerschenkron, 1960).

A recent evaluation of the enterprise and centralism recognized that there are limits to the extent to which central agencies can control day-to-day operation of an enterprise, application of material incentives and implementation of central decisions. Even advocates of rigid centralism realize that enterprise management must bear the responsibility for making the items required by the central plan. However, these same advocates insist that enterprise management is controlled by a large number of laws, decrees and rules which make freedom of action for enterprise management a relative matter:

> There can be no complete independence for an enterprise, in the sense that it would determine independently its production speciality, the list of items it produces and their prices. This would contradict the requirements of the rational division of labour and would signify a voluntary refusal to exploit the advantages of socialism. ... Any attempts to bring about unlimited independence for enterprises, to carry the principle of self-management as far as in fact to undermine the economic foundations of the centralized management of the economy, would contradict the interests of the state, and, consequently, the interests of the enterprises themselves.
>
> Autarky, leaving each enterprise to its own devices; or the isolation of enterprises from one another—all these are incompatible with the principles of socialism, with the nature of production relations in our society .... The expansion of the independence of enterprises is not an end in itself but a means for creating the most favourable conditions for the efficient management of the economy. If we accept this initial premise, we must admit that not all enterprises have equal opportunities for the effective utilization of their rights. (*CDSP*, **22**, no. 9, p. 3)

This quotation is reminiscent of George Orwell: all enterprises are equal but some are more equal in opportunity than others. We are told that 'in most branches, larger enterprises have better opportunities for ensuring high efficiency in utilizing materials, labour and finance ... and for developing creative initiative in economic management' (*CDSP*, **22**, no. 9, p. 3). The reasons for greater probability of success among larger firms are not hard to infer. Current preference for large plants derives from the need to control sub-component suppliers. Where these are not under the purchaser's control, delivery schedules become a major bottleneck. Larger enterprises can meet exigencies under the production plan more easily and also have greater access to material incentive funds—a cornerstone of the new reformed economic system—and in particular to the production development fund (*CDSP*, **22**, no. 9, p. 4). Advocates of the association, like the Chairman of the Lithuanian Republic Council of Ministers support the creation of large associations with the powers of *Glavki* because this reduces the levels of management, brings management closer to production, frees Ministry staff both from deciding day-to-day questions on enterprise operation *and from the avalanche of superfluous information* (*CDSP*, **22**, no. 7, p. 5). Soviet leaders, having reaffirmed their belief in the principles of Soviet democratic centralism, continue to 'meddle' in the operations of the individual firm while also offering enterprise management more material incentives for correcting mistakes made by supervising agencies. The problem of red tape and conflicting messages from higher, central authorities has existed since planning the great industrialization. The problem subsided with the temporary demise of the ministries in 1957 but has since reappeared.

Most operational and production problems appear to have their immediate origin from central agencies:

Ministries and departments frequently continue to use the same methods of management as they did before the reform. Planning according to the achieved level,
repeated changes in the plans, the tardy presentation of plan assignments to enterprises, the distribution of part of the list of items to be produced without consideration for the actual possibilities of the enterprises, underestimation of the enterprise's
role in drawing up plans—all these shortcomings in the work of the individual
ministries have still not been fully eliminated. (*CDSP*, **22,** no. 9, p. 4)

Despite the economic reforms under the Brezhnev and Kosygin administration, the firm and enterprise continue to be the victims of institutional
uncertainty and *turbulence* without having the necessary independence to
take proper corrective measures. For location studies this highlights the
interaction of decision-makers between the enterprises and the state's
complex of administrative and planning organizations. (Hamilton, 1970).

The objective spatial environment is modified into numerous behavioural
environments at each stage of project-making and selection of investment
projects. Each behaviour environment influences successive environments
until, as Jackson suggested for general investment plans, the patterns of
spatial behaviour and industrial location become distorted. If project costs
usually seem to exceed planning estimates by a wide margin (Jackson,
1971, p. 18), then the spatial efficiency of industrial location is distorted.
Excessive costs lead to incorrect spatial flows, delays in commissioning
regionally, integrated producers and non-minimum cost location patterns
of new industrial capacity. For example, a location could become uneconomic if actual project costs exceed those which would have been incurred
by a rejected, but more accurately prepared, alternative project with slightly
higher original cost estimates (Barr and Smillie, 1973).

Advocates of a behavioural approach to consumer and industrial space
preferences assume that consumers and locators are acting according to
their perception of supposedly rational objective information. Most deviation in behaviour is measured with reference to some expected pattern,
whether normative or stochastic: Koropeckyj (1967) has reviewed Soviet
attempts to apply Weber's model of industrial location. However, basic
information used by Soviet decision-makers is sub-optimal. Plans contain
many defects. Norms and standards may be obsolete, conflicting or even
unavailable. The basic book *Construction Norms and Rules* is not made
available automatically to all project organizations by its central publisher
and is not published in large numbers (Jackson, 1971, p. 20). The prices of
equipment, supplies and materials frequently vary for the same good,
depending on the official classification of the purchaser. These elements of
uncertainty and turbulence mean that project organizations have traditionally not evaluated alternative proposals. Hence, basic procedure for decision-
making is frequently violated in locating new Soviet industrial capacity.
Jackson has concluded that 'confused information about the way to prepare
projects and about preferred project parameters undoubtedly reinforced

otherwise existing propensities of project-makers to neglect examinations of alternatives and emphasize technological considerations in project elaborations' (Jackson, 1971, p. 22). These structural defects in the economic and planning system account for many problems of investment location.

Soviet locational behaviour reflects many, often conflicting national objectives. Prime among them, however, has been the central allocation of resources to create large manufacturing complexes and spatially-extensive, resource-extracting industries. In primary manufacturing operations, for example, the enterprise or firm has taken the form of a *Trest* or *Kombinat* to ensure coordinated operation of resources extraction and primary processing. Location of Combines in coal, petroleum, iron and steel, and wood-processing, non-ferrous metals, and heavy engineering has been part of the all-Union goal of industrialization. Although the location of many firms has been hotly debated, like the Urals-Kuznetsk Combine, the need to achieve this goal by physical planning has meant that application of economic criteria in analyses of existing industrial locations was usually academic and devoid of operational significance unless the results of analysis were incorporated into locational adjustments in subsequent planning periods.

The chief locational tool for major primary manufacturing industries has been some form of Weberian locational analysis in which physical properties of materials and products were assessed in relation to transportation costs (Koropeckyj, 1967; Holzman 1957; Clark, 1957). The location of secondary manufacturing industries has tended to favour pre-Soviet industrial regions such as the Donbass, Moscow, Leningrad and the Urals or to develop concentrations with access to energy and transport in the Voga–Kama region, urban regions of the Caucasus, the Baltic States, Central Asia or southern Siberia. The purpose of secondary manufacturing has been to strengthen the Soviet industrial base, not to serve the population with consumer durables. Hence, there has been a clear spatial preference by machinery and equipment industries for locations accessible to the all-Union industrial market of the Donbass–Moscow-Urals axis. Manufacturing has been established also in regional and administrative centres to utilize existing social overhead investment and provide employment for the population. In this way, ideology has influenced the regional allocation of industry. This allocation has encouraged manufacturing growth within existing populated regions with access to industrial markets and industrial suppliers. Some Soviet transportation and equipment industries are oriented toward agricultural machinery requirements, but since the major population distribution has been traditionally associated with agriculture, industry could be oriented simultaneously to urban population concentrations, rural labour, final demand for agricultural products and major sources of metal and engineering equipment. Associated with ideology is the Soviet desire for greater integration of producers within COMECON. Some

Soviet firms which produce goods for sale to, or purchase commodities from eastern Europe derive locational advantages from locations in the western Soviet Union.

Many authors note the locational importance of strategic factors (Holzman, 1957; Hutchings, 1971; Koropeckyj, 1967) yet none can demonstrate any dominance or even the existence of defence considerations. Their significance is now harder to understand when long-range bombers, intercontinental missiles and super-spy satellites have radically altered geopolitical relationships. Defence is more likely to influence location through efficient inter-industry relationships and research and development agencies, mostly located in a few complex Soviet urban/industrial nodes, mostly in European USSR and not in the eastern regions. Defence is unimportant in the General Outline for Development in the 1970s, yet central military strategists may well have been consulted during its preparation and there are probably geographically-based plans for converting peacetime industrial plants to military uses.

During the early Soviet industrialization, the qualities, quantities and locations of many raw materials were poorly understood or unknown. Those Czarist industrial nodes which were still located in the USSR after Russian territorial losses from World War provided the base for industrial recovery (Hooson, 1968). National transport nodes supported industrial expansion and provided some inertia in locational experiments and regional development. Thus, to this day, Leningrad retains leadership in many engineering sectors, The Donbass and Kharkov still occupies a leading place in ferrous metallurgy and engineering. The Urals' industrial role was greatly revitalized after the revolution. Baku, another Czarist industrial node based on foreign capital, has retained some importance in petroleum extraction and research, though its relative contribution to Soviet energy supply is now minuscule in comparison even with its role in 1950.

Thus the Soviet manufacturing belt, chiefly confined within the Leningrad–Odessa–Chita triangle, has continued to dominate the spatial structure of Soviet industry. To the north and east, the environment significantly raises costs of development and operation, favouring punctiform resource-extraction and processing linked to centres within the manufacturing belt. To the south, two major concentrations of non-Slavic populations exist in the Caucasus and Central Asia. Industrialization there has been based on local resources and the need to develop local cultural and economic opportunities. These objectives have probably been achieved more satisfactorily in the Caucasus because of its greater accessibility to the Soviet manufacturing belt than in Central Asia which is both distant and less developed in education, skills and infrastructure. Given centralized investment allocation, the economic opportunities of Central Asia are probably less understood by Russian planners than are those of regions nearer Moscow (Hamilton, 1973).

One major objective of location behaviour since 1928 has been to ease tightening bottlenecks in freight movements on Soviet railways. Materials moved to manufacturing centres—metals, fuels and timber—came from more accessible central, northern and eastern regions rather than from the Caucasus or Central Asia. As the creation of major manufacturing concentrations in regional complexes has characterized Soviet industrialization, the professed but often neglected objective of uniform spatial industrial development would have weakened realization of this major goal. Thus, the objective Soviet economic environment includes large spaces and long distances, leaving many 'unknowns' for the central planner. He tends, therefore, using restricted information, to select only those locations and locational strategies which can facilitate rapid industrialization: nonferrous metals from Kazakhstan, cotton from Central Asia, timber from Siberia to fulfil physical production goals in manufacturing at more central and hence better understood, locations in the manufacturing belt.

The objective environment also comprises formal relationships with suppliers, government agencies, and customers. If relations with certain, and not other, suppliers facilitate greater efficiency in production, then those linkages should determine spatial input movements. However, the Soviet behavioural environment has been established traditionally by central agencies, not by the firm. Production linkages have not been determined by those responsible for fulfilling industrial plans. Reliability of contracts with component manufacturers has been chaotic, supported by *blat* and the *tolkach* (expediter, pusher). Relations with other firms have not been based on spatial proximity or association but have been fitted during the planning process into the general system of material balances. Costs of delivered materials and their supply routes have not been the concern of enterprise managements: the cost of procuring raw materials is a planned cost, not affecting the direct locational profitability of the firm. Yet tenuous supply links effect the operational behaviour of the firm if transport bottlenecks develop or if the distance between producer and supplier prohibits closer understanding. Operational links with banks, material suppliers, and research organizations are neglected in official organization of the firm.

The economic reforms of 1965 were expected to give greater freedom to enterprise managements to determine the location of material supply and, perhaps, of the destination for manufactured products: in effect, the latter would form part of another plant's inputs, and hence the customer's, not the producer's concern. However, the reform has failed to permit this. Planning continues to be based on technical coefficients and nominal consumption rates: these do not encourage firms to experiment with input and hence input-source substitution. Moreover, security of supply of centrally-planned inputs is a continuing operational problem. The firm's external relations have been conducted through an administrative chain consisting of middle management *(Glavk),* central authorities of the related ministry, central and middle authorities of another ministry or commission and, finally, the individual supplier or customer. The nature of material linkages resembles that of Christaller's $K = 7$ distribution of central places and not the $K = 3$ scheme whereby each consumer (here, producer) is as close as possible to the available source of the good (material input).

Consequently, contemporary locational behaviour of the Soviet firm is geared primarily to establishing direct control over the operation of related input suppliers through the formation of associations. The association has great spatial significance in organizational performance because component suppliers are tied to a final producer. Establishment of association in Lvov, Riga and Leningrad confirms that production associations will probably have a regional or nodal character. As associations grow, they require additional operating facilities, more inputs from related suppliers and better research facilities. Their managements establish new operations or expand contacts with existing establishments within general geographical proximity to minimize costs of administration, travelling time between units and misunderstandings resulting from infrequent liaison with related operators.

The association is particularly important in integrated and complex equipment industries or in manufacturing with strong links with tertiary and quaternary services. The latter industries are heavily localized in the manufacturing belt and derive benefit from contact and exchanges among themselves. The freedom of those associations linked with research and development to locate outside large or medium-sized urban nodes remains restricted by the general preference of scientific personnel for cultural and scientific amenities. Associations in timber processing, food processing or consumer light industry do not have the same operational limitations imposed by technological linkages with services and research on their locational freedom. Their behaviour is more constrained by the friction of freight movement of their inputs tying them to supply sources. Consumer-oriented industries manufacturing furniture and household utensils continue to form associations with a strong regional element of sub-suppliers in order to achieve regional self-sufficiency.

Resistance by many middle management personnel to the challenge of the association suggests that much of the firm's behavioural environment is shaped by the actions of middle management. The Soviet press often reports cases where middle management has reacted uniformly in different regions to the greater independence of the firm. Dissolution of associations by management in the western Ukraine proceeded in concert with middle management from disparate ministries. Reaction by middle and upper management in some *key* ministries is duplicated by decision-makers in less important ministries. Hence, the Ministry of Wood-Processing enthusiastically introduced the new form of management (while retaining much central control) after its successful adoption by the prestigious Ministry of Petroleum.

Thus decision-makers' behaviour expresses their coding mechanisms which reflect their experience, education and ethnic affinity (Fig 16.1), and determine the information they adopt from the environment. For example, between 64 and 80 per cent of Tatars in different occupations believe that managers in the Tatar ASSR should be of Tatar nationality (Katz, 1971).

Current industrial management reform aims at improving control over labour and equipment using computer technology, particularly in large production organizations such as combines or associations of specialized producers. Although the association facilitates automated control, its introduction depends upon the availability of skilled labour and this is still scarce in some regions. Planners suggest that labour-intensive firms locate in regions with a relatively large primary sector to tap undergraduate or female labour. Yet, Soviet industry is not sufficiently automated that it can ignore labour pools in developing regions like Central Asia, the European south-west or the Caucasus. Decision-makers are under pressure from central political authorities to pay more attention to surplus labour particularly since interregional movements of additional population will not alleviate present urban crowding or reduce current environmental degradation within the manufacturing belt.

Many conditions associated with processing production factors and establishing markets which are within the decision-making realm of the Western firm, are managed in the USSR by central planning agencies and industrial ministries. Spatial problems associated with marketing do not concern the individual firm that is under no obligation to achieve spatial monopoly or to out-sell another producer. Spatial linkages generated by central allocation, however, are being modified by the associations. Yet cost and demand conditions do affect the Soviet firm when planned supply and marketing procedures fail as they have in Irkutsk province, where timber procurement patterns for the pulp and paper industry are being disrupted by anarchic felling by various construction Trusts. Demand conditions are most commonly met among large manufacturers by creating Combines, among smaller producers by establishing associations. One major contribution these associations might make is product specialization and differentiation within economic sectors according to the location of product demand. Greater spatial specialization in producing various types of plywood might result if supply to the national economy is organized effectively by the new territorial associations under the Ministry of Wood-Processing. Thus, if some new middle management associations are able to coordinate regional production functions and output-mixes of subordinate manufacturing firms, then other firms which buy these products may be able to increase their own specialization and eliminate the need for auxiliary manufacturing shops.

Conclusions

Soviet decision-makers operate within a behavioural environment which is similar to, but not identical with, that of decision-makers in other industrial societies. Some elements of the objective economic environment are analysed for the Soviet firm by central authorites. All decision-makers pattern their own behaviour according to the qay in which individually, or collectively, they perceive the economic environment. Such perception may vary among management levels. At higher levels, especially the centre, greater bonuses might be earned by deriving more reliable linkages among producers. Improvement of the economic performance and spatial organization of the firm by establishing production associations is meeting mixed reactions from lower and intermediate levels of management. In some regions, management is enthusiastic about change whereas in other regions change spells the loss of local prestigious jobs or an established way of life. In resource-oriented industries, the location of new associations generates production linkages similar to those of the *Kombinat* and *Trest*. The new reforms mean little in primary manufacturing and capital-intensive industries, where production has been organized traditionally in Combines or Trusts. However, in secondary manufacturing and assembly industries the association can bring about functional (hence, place) specialization of plants by creating reliable linkages among producers and obviating the need for self-sufficient plants. Experiments with the association suggest that the spatial pattern of Soviet industry cannot be considered independently either of the locational behaviour of the firm or of the behavioural environment of the decision-makers.

Notes

1. Another type of firm, the 'intermediary firm', which carries out specialized tasks in research and development on a rather *ad hoc* basis and does not appear to have a permanent existence, has appeared in various cities in the past few years—Novosibirsk, Baku, Leningrad, Tomsk, Kiev, Krasnoyarsk, Riga, Vilnius, Sverdlovsk and Severodonetsk. This firm fills a gap between science and production when application of new technology is under way in a ministry of enterprise, or when unplanned work must be undertaken by two uncooperative ministries etc. These firms are a mechanism for individuals to participate in legal, but extra-curricular, consulting work such as that done by personnel from business, government and university in the West. Some of these firms are organized by agencies such as the republic council of trade union (*CDSP*, 23, no. 29, pp. 13, 28). A major advantage of the intermediary firm, its flexibility, could obviously be provided by 'Associations for scientific services to enterprises and other organizations'.

2. Soviet newspapers have the habit of acting as judge, jury and legal counsel for opposing interests by sending special correspondents into government organizations to investigate alleged complaints. Hence there is always the possibility that the final product, an article assessing the problem, in a national newspaper may contain some bias. However, the newspapers themselves can be reprimanded if the material they publish is proved to be biased or incorrect.

References

Aleksandrov, A., 1965, *Slovar'-Spravochnik Ekonomista Promyshlennogo Predpriyatiya* (Moscow: Politicheskaya Literatura).

Barr, B. M., 1970, *The Soviet Wood-Processing Industry* (Toronto: University of Toronto Press).

Barr, B. M., 1971, 'Regional variation in Soviet pulp and paper production', *Annals, A.A.G.*, **61**, no. 1, 45–64.

Barr, B. M. and K. W. Smillie, 1973, 'Some spatial interpretations of alternative optimal and sub-optimal solutions to the transportation problem', *Canadian Geographer*, **16**, no. 4.

Bergson, A., 1964, *The Economies of Soviet Planning* (New Haven: Yale University Press).

Berliner, J. S., 1957, *Factory and Manager in the USSR* (Cambridge, Mass.: Harvard University Press).

Berliner, J. S., 1962, 'The informal organization of the Soviet firm', in *Readings on The Soviet Economy*, ed. F. D. Holzman (Chicago: Rand McNally), 408–31.

Berliner, J. S., 1968, 'Managerial incentives and decision-making: a comparison of the United States and the Soviet Union', in *New Currents in Soviet-Type Economies*, ed. G. R. Feiwel (Scranton, Pa.: International Textbook Co.), 167–98.

Bienstock, G., S. Schwarz, and A. Yugow, 1944, *Management in Russian Industry and Agriculture* (New York: Cornell University Press).

Bor, M., 1967, *Aims and Methods of Soviet Planning* (New York: International Publishers).

Bornstein, M. and D. Fusfeld, 1966, *The Soviet Economy. A Book of Readings*, revised Edition (Homewood, Ill.: Richard D. Irwin).

Campbell, R. W., 1966, *Soviet Economic Power* (Boston: Houghton Mifflin).

Clark, M. G., 1957, *The Economics of Soviet Steel* (Cambridge, Mass.: Harvard University Press).

Cole, J. P. and F. C. German, 1970, *A Geography of the USSR*, 2nd ed. (London: Butterworths).

Current Digest of the Soviet Press (abbreviated as *CDSP*), **22**, 5, 24; **22**, 6, 8, 10; **22**, 7, 5, 8; **22**, 9, 3–5; **22**, 19, 16–17; **22**, 20, 15; **22**, 31, 6–7; **22**, 32, 9, 31; **22**, 35, 8–9; **22**, 39, 5, 7; **22**, 42, 10, 23; **22**, 47, 9–10, 10–11, 11, 18; **22**, 50, 37; **23**, 4, 6–8; **23**, 13, 19; **23**, 13, 24–25; **23**, 22, 11; **23**, 22, 11–12; **23**, 29, 13, 28; **23**, 36, 5–7; **23**, 42, 23–24; **23**, 48, 1–3; **23**, 51, 17; **24**, 11, 10–11; **24**, 19, 26–27; **24**, 27, 21; **24**, 30, 23.

Dewdney, J. C., 1965, *A Geography of the Soviet Union* (Oxford: Pergamon).

Dewdney, J. C., 1967, *Patterns and Problems of Regionalization in the USSR*, Research Papers Series, No. 8, Dept. of Geography, University of Durham.

Dicken, P., 1971, 'Some aspects of the decision-making behavior of business organizations', *Economic Geography*, **47**, no. 3, 426–37.

Dienes, L., 1971, 'Issues in Soviet energy policy and conflict over fuel development', *Soviet Studies*, **23**, no. 1, 26–58.

Ellman, M., 1969, *Economic Reform in the Soviet Union*, PEP, 'Broadsheet', No. 509, April.

Fainsod, M., 1958, *Smolensk Under Soviet Rule* (Cambridge, Mass.: Harvard University Press).

Feiwel, G. R., 1967, *The Soviet Quest for Economic Efficiency. Issues, Controversies, and Reforms* (New York: Praeger).

Feiwel, G. R., 1968, *New Currents in Soviet-type Economies: A Reader* (Scranton, Pa.: International Textbook Co.).

Felker, J. L., 1966, *Soviet Economic Controversies* (Cambridge, Mass.: MIT Press).

Gerschenkron, A., 1950, 'A neglected source of economic information on Soviet Russia', *The American Slavic and East European Review*, **9**, February, 1–19.

Gerschenkron, A., 1960, 'Problems and patterns of Russian economic development', in *The Transformation of Russian Society*, ed. C. E. Black (Cambridge, Mass.: Harvard University Press), 42–72.

Gladkevich, G. I., 1971, 'Determination of an optimal location for an iron and steel plant based on iron ore of the Kursk Magnetic Anomaly', *Soviet Geography*, **12**, no. 9, 604–10.

Goldman, M. I., 1968, *The Soviet Economy: Myth and Reality* (Englewood Cliffs: Prentice–Hall).

Granick, D., 1954, *Management of the Industrial Firm in the USSR* (New York: Columbia University Press).

Granick, D., 1961, *The Red Executive. A Study of the Organization Man in Russian Industry* (Garden City, N.Y.: Doubleday).

Hamilton, F. E. Ian, 1968, *Yugoslavia: Patterns of Economic Activity* (London: Bell).

Hamilton, F. E. Ian, 1970, 'Aspects of spatial behavior in planned economies', *Papers, Regional Science Association*, **XXV**, 86–103.

Hamilton, F. E. Ian, 1971, 'The location of industry in East-Central and South-East Europe', in *Eastern Europe: Essays in Geographical Problems*, ed. G. W. Hoffman (London: Methuen), 173–213.

Hamilton, F. E. Ian, 1973, 'Spatial dimensions of Soviet economic decision-making', in *The Soviet Economy in Regional Perspective*, ed. V. Bandera and Z. Lew Melnyk (New York: Praeger), pp. 235–260.

Holzman, F. D., 1957, 'The Soviet Ural-Kuznetsk Combine', *Quarterly Journal of Economics*, August, 368–405.

Hooson, D. J. M., 1966, *The Soviet Union* (London: University of London Press).

Hooson, D. J. M., 1968, 'The growth of cities in pre-Soviet Russia', in *Urbanization and its Problems: Essays in Honour of E. W. Gilbert*, ed. R. P. Beckinsale and J. M. Houston (Oxford: Blackwell), 254–76.

Hough, J. F., 1972, 'The Soviet system, petrification or pluralism?', *Problems of Communism*, **21**, no. 2, 25–45.

Huff, D. L., 1960, 'A topographical model of consumer space preferences', *Papers and Proceedings, Regional Science Association*, **6**, 159–73.

Hunter, H., 1957, *Soviet Transportation Policy* (Cambridge, Mass.: Harvard University Press).

Hutchings, R., 1971, *Soviet Economic Development* (Oxford: Blackwell).

Jackson, M. R., 1971, 'Information and incentives in planning Soviet investment projects', *Soviet Studies*, **23**, no. 1, 3–25.

Katz, Z., 1971, 'Sociology in the Soviet Union', *Problems of Communism*, **20**, no. 3, 22–40.

Keefe, E. K., *et al.*, 1971, *Area Handbook for the Soviet Union* (Washington, D.C.: U.S. Government Printing Office).

Kistanov, V. V. and A. S. Epshteyn, 1972, 'Problems of optimal location of an industrial complex (with reference to an iron and steel plant and related establishments)', *Soviet Geography*, **13**, no. 3, 141–52.

Kornai, J., 1959, *Overcentralization in Economic Administration* (London: Oxford U.P.)

Koropeckyj, I. S., 1967, 'The development of Soviet location theory before the Second World War', *Soviet Studies*, **19**, Part 1: no. 1, 1–28; Part 2: no. 2, 232–44.

Kosmachev, K. P., 1970, 'Economic-geographic prediction of the process of economic development of an area (with particular reference to Irkutsk Oblast)', *Soviet Geography*, **11**, no. 8, 660–71.

Maslov, Ye. P., 1970, 'The significance and role of sectoral-production complexes in the formation and evolution of economic regions', *Soviet Geography*, **11**, no. 9, 746–54.

Mellor, R. E. H., 1964, *Geography of the USSR* (London: Macmillan).

Meshcheryakova, M. N., 1967, 'The integrated development and location of the petro-chemical industry in industrial nodes of the Middle Volga Region", *Soviet Geography*, **8**, no. 2, 81–7.

Mikhailov, S. and N. Solov'ev, 1969, 'Small and medium-size cities and the location of industry in the USSR', in *Contemporary Soviet Economics, Vol. II*, ed. M. Yanowitch (White Plains, N.Y.: International Arts and Science Press), 129–36.

Movchan, B. S., 1970, 'Use of the mathematical method in the solution of a location problem', *Soviet Geography*, **11**, no. 8, 649–54.

Narkiewicz, O. A., 1970, *The Making of the Soviet State Apparatus* (Manchester: Manchester University Press).

Nekrasov, N. N., 1971, 'Scientific principles of the general outline for the location of productive forces of the USSR for the period up to 1980', *Soviet Geography*, **12**, no. 4, 219–26.

Nove, A., 1961, *The Soviet Economy* (New York: Praeger).

Nove, A., 1968, *The Soviet Economy*, 3rd ed. (London: George Allen and Unwin).

Parker, W. H., 1969, *The Soviet Union* (London: Longman).

Rostovtsev, M. I., 1970, 'Geographical approaches to the study of extractive industries', *Soviet Geography*, **11**, no. 8, 616–28.

Schroeder, G. E., 1971, 'Soviet economic reform at an impasse', *Problems of Communism*, **20**, no. 4, 36–46.

Selyunin, V., 1972, 'The logic of an illogical decision', *Sotsialisticheskaya Industriya*, p. 2.

Shabad, T., 1969, *Basic Industrial Resources of the USSR* (New York: Columbia University Press).

Sharpe, M. E., (ed.), 1966, *Planning, Profit, and Incentives in the USSR: Vol. I: The Liberman Discussion, a New Phase in Soviet Economic Thought; Vol. II; Reform of Soviet Economic Management* (White Plains, N.Y.; International Arts and Sciences Press).

Statisticheskiy Slovar', 1965 (Moscow: Statistika).

Steed, G. P. F., 1971, 'Plant adaptation, firm environments and location analysis', *Professional Geographer*, **23**, no. 4, 324–8.

Townroe, P. M., 1969, 'Locational choice and the individual firm', *Regional Studies*, **3**, 15–24.

Vilenskii, M., 1969, 'Determining the efficiency of territorial distribution of production', in *Contemporary Soviet Economics, Vol. II*, ed. M. Yanowitch (White Plains, N.Y.: International Arts and Science Press), 117–28.

Wiles, P., 1963, *The Political Economy of Communism* (Oxford: Blackwell).

Zaleski, E., 1967, *Planning Reforms in the Soviet Union, 1962–66: An Analysis of Recent Trends in Economic Organization and Management* (Chapel Hill: University of North Carolina Press).

V Experience in Three Nations

17

Self-Management: The Yugoslav Case

F. E. IAN HAMILTON

Until 1952 industrial location decision-making in Yugoslavia broadly resembled in miniature the hierarchical structure of the Soviet system. Yugoslav planning behaviour during the First Five-Year Plan (1947–51) differed from Soviet practice mainly as a response to the specific problems of the local environment, namely: the absence of a dominant ethnic group and, hence, strong national conflicts for scarce resources which were formalized through the federal structure; the localization of a poor and incomplete infrastructure in the north and north-west (mainly Slovenia, Croatia and Vojvodina); a lack of modern infrastructure elsewhere and the desperate need to develop backward central and south-eastern regions to supply materials and energy to the federation and to eliminate great inter-regional socio-economic differentials (Hamilton, 1968). From 1948, Cominform blockade stress conditions strengthened industrial development in the centre.

Towards Workers' Control of Spatial Decisions

More fundamentally, that blockade caused a reappraisal of Marxist ideology which precipitated Yugoslav experimentation with new forms of decentralized socialist management. The evolution of these forms, generally termed 'self-management', has occupied the centre of Yugoslav attention in the quarter-century since 1948. Progressively 'state' ownership has been 'withered away' and industrial (like all other socialized) enterprises are managed by their workers through workers' councils: hence the term self-management. But self-management also applies in local and regional government since these organizations collect their own budgetary resources from their territories and, resources permitting, invest in their own industrial enterprise. Self-management (*samoupravljenje*) has been subject to continual experimentation and policy changes. However, for purposes of studying locational behaviour, three broad periods may be distinguished: the early period, 1950–57; the middle period, 1957–64; and the current period since 1964.

Change began in 1950 when laws replaced centralized 'state capitalist' by polycentric 'social' ownership which vested economic management of the industrial enterprise (*preduzeća*) in the workers' council (Radnički Savet). In 1952 the 'new economic system' based on the 'market principle' was introduced. More flexible pricing and bonus schemes for workers encouraged the workers' councils to take decisions to improve the spatial relationships of their plants with input suppliers and customers and to achieve 'profitability' in order to bolster meagre wages. Their efforts, however, were heavily circumscribed by (1) continued central control of investment until 1956 so that workers' councils had little or no influence on location of capacity and (2) inertia in the power structure and conservatism in behaviour which enabled enterprise directors to continue authoritarian relationships and often to run, or overrule, the workers' councils. From 1965, however, changes in the method of allocating industrial investment began to permit workers' councils to participate in spatial planning, if not to influence it.

These changes crystallized as a two-way polycentric planning process which operated during the Second and Third Five-Year Plans 1957–64. This constitutes the 'middle period' of self-management and was characterized by three major developments. First, local government self-management was more formally crystallized through the peoples' council *(narodni odbor)* of the commune *(općina* or *opština)* which, from 1957 to 1964, had its own budget and could compete for republic and federal resources. Second, a unique system was introduced whereby workers' councils of existing industrial plants (or where appropriate, of socialized farms) and peoples' councils of communes competed through the federal investment bank for investment funds which had been allocated broadly among sectors and industries by the federal budget (Hamilton, 1968, pp.106–15, 244–54). Third, and less important, there was an increase in the proportion of revenue which industrial enterprises were allowed to retain: this did mean, however, somewhat greater managerial flexibility in allocating profits to wages or to investment.

Production profiles of Yugoslav plants in 1957 had been determined within the central planning environment, generally prior to 1952, and had been incorporated in the First Five-Year Plan 1947–51, the Annual Plans 1952–56 (for existing plants) and the 'key projects' plan 1952–56 (for new plants). The ability of managements to adapt their enterprises to the new 'semi-market' environment varied, however, from plant to plant. Managements of heavy industrial plants often had little option in modifying either production or the spatial relationships with input suppliers and customers— unless these had been irrational prior to 1957—for three reasons: federal government control of such industries was tight; low fixed prices for their products restricted revenue and hence the enterprise's autonomous budget resources; the nature of production could not be altered in the short term. Managements of consumer goods and manufacturing enterprises, especially those which had been built after 1945 and were reasonably modern, were better placed: high prices for their scarce products yielded them bigger profits which they were free to invest. Many did so in response to stress conditions generated by rising demand at home, and from the Third World markets which Yugoslavia was penetrating at this time. Workers' councils were, however, often faced with a choice of growth strategies. Under the old centralized system there would have been no choice, as in the USSR: capacity growth would have been decided in Belgrade or, possibly, in a Republic capital like Zagreb or Sarajevo. Under the decentralized system, however, enterprise managements could choose one, or a combination, of the following strategies: first, to expand the existing plant; second, to modernize or innovate new technology in the plant, often using product licences from West European or American firms (e.g. Fiat, Citroën. CAV, Erickson, Siemens, ICI, etc.); and third, to establish in separate locations branch plants which would be managed by their own workers' councils—rather like Japanese practice *vis-a-vis* branches. If the financial resources of the enterprise were insufficient for any of these purposes, as they usually were, its management could compete for federal funds through the investment bank, provided that the federation had budgeted for expansion in the enterprise's line of production. If it had, and the federation granted investment to the enterprise, then the workers' council put its growth strategy into practice. *For the first time, therefore, workers' councils of existing plants could decide, and obtain funding for, the establishment of new plants in new locations.* They could begin to shape locational changes other than altering the sizes and relative importance of their *existing* plants. If the federation had not budgeted for expansion in that industry or if the project for expansion submitted by the enterprise had been rejected by the investment bank, then the management could only rationalize its production relationships within the limits of its own capital resources. In this case workers' councils could adapt production and alter forward and backward linkages; however, the limited degree of industrialization within Yugoslavia placed severe constraints on the choices of domestic input suppliers and foreign currency shortages often ruled out overseas input sources *unless the enterprise was a good exporter* and hence earner of foreign currency.

In choosing growth strategies, enterprise managements behaved broadly in a manner similar to their Western corporate decision-making counterparts. Where plant expansion *in situ* was possible, this was often preferred; where it was not possible, then branch plants were established elsewhere. Another possibility was cooperation or merger with nearby enterprises: this was a management response to mounting pressure from the federation for greater plant specialization of production as well as for vertical or horizontal integration between enterprises. This pressure was necessary because many firms, as in all centrally-planned economies (see p. 441 above), tended to manufacture many products to reduce the uncertainties of input-supply; that was a direct legacy of the vertical organization and administration system of the central planning era.

There are, however, two significant divergencies from Western practice. First, pressure for cooperation met resistance from workers' councils and reflected worker participatory power. This resulted from their involvement and pride in the enterprise and its products and from a feeling that newly-gained power and independence in managing 'their' plant might be placed in jeopardy, especially if cooperation had to be with a larger plant. On grounds of prestige and primitive pride—after all, most workers had strong peasant backgrounds—they also objected strongly to sacrificing finished product lines for component product lines in such cooperation schemes. Thus retention of management authority by the workers of the enterprise often restricted integration of production and hence linkage flows between enterprises. The second important difference is evident in management behaviour connected with choosing between expansion *in situ* and branch-plant establishment. Except in mountainous Slovenia or Dalmatia or in small and older industrial districts of Belgrade or Zagreb or Ljubliana, there were very few sites in a developing nation like Yugoslavia where expansion could *not* take place *in situ*. Many more enterprise managements than one would expect, however, did choose to establish branch plants in small towns or villages, usually within a radius of 35 miles of the 'parent' enterprise. This behaviour represents a response to the specific conditions of the Yugoslav environment and, particularly, to: (1) the strong socialistic conscience among working people and the continuing influence of the League of Communists which stimulated managements *almost invariably* to establish branch plants in nearby 'backward areas' of high rural under-employment; (2) the widespread problem of underdevelopment, even in peripheral areas of Slovenia; (3) the underdevelopment of the nation as a whole and its expression through scarce resources for improvement of a poor infrastructure, with the result that neither could housing for the new labour force required by expansion be provided near the parent plant, nor could transport for carrying commuters from the villages to the parent plant be improved; (4) lastly, but by no means least, strong 'national' con-science often led workers' councils to search for branch plant locations only within their own republics. Thus the 'Iskra' cinematographic equipment plant at Kranj (Slovenia) established four branches in west and central Slovenia; the 'Rade Končar' electronics factory in Zagreb (Croatia) estab-lished component production in western Croatia; radio and textile industrial enterprises in Belgrade set up branches in northern Serbia; the 'FAP' bus and truck factory at Priboj in the Serbian Sandjak established a branch at Prijepolje, also in Sandjak.

Like Western firms, however, Yugoslav enterprises did tend to concentrate more complex, finished or assembled output in the parent plant and move their components manufacture or simpler manufacturing processes to the branches; yet in this way, of course, 'parents' were able to obviate workers' potential objections to such 'lower' type of manufacturing activity, because branches could not choose their workers' councils until they had a work force and were operative.

Such degrees of decentralization were unknown elsewhere in the socialist world in the early 1960s, but the 1964 economic reform that began the 'current period' was radical even in Yugoslavia. Federal investment control virtually disappeared and enterprises were permitted to retain all their revenue (after taxation). Industrial investment decisions were thus completely decentralized to the enterprise. Moreover, the government drastically altered the environment of the enterprise: it swept away controls on prices and initiated an almost free market situation. This new environment replaced the former dominantly political uncertainties of constantly changing administrative organization with the dominantly economic uncertainties of operating in fully competitive home and overseas markets. Adaptation of enterprise managements, whether of directors or of workers' councils, to this changed environment has proved to be a traumatic experience of trial-and-error, learning, success and failure. Given more investment decision-making power, enterprise managements could, of course, pursue even more vigorously the strategies described above for the previous period, namely, expansion, modernization or branch-plant establishment. However, the reform so changed the economic environment that decisions of spatial economic behaviour of a new kind were necessary. It exposed the production irrationalities and poor internal organization of firms, their excess capacities and their poor management abilities—all of which had been protected throughout the decentralization trends of the 1950s by central government risk-taking and subsidies. It also permitted foreign investment in Yugoslav firms, provided that Yugoslavia retained 51 per cent ownership.

Radical environmental change called for radical responses from workers' councils. These have taken several forms. First, varying degrees of change in production profiles have been effected: from complete changes—discarding unwanted or out-dated products and substituting new equipment to produce goods saleable in Yugoslavia or abroad—to modification of production to improve the design or quality or content of production. The concomitant search for new input suppliers and markets proceeds as in a Western corporation, though with earlier biases still apparent. Second, the search has been undertaken for opportunities to cooperate with foreign firms which might be willing to invest in Yugoslavia and hence partially overcome the difficulties faced by the 'environmental revolution'. This has been particularly true of enterprises exploiting and processing natural resources. Such firms have inherited serious economic penalties from the former environment which, by maintaining fixed or controlled prices on basic products, restricted their indigenous capital resources—indeed often caused losses; and, moreover, the new environment imposes severe competitive penalties on such firms because many are located in backward areas with relatively poor transport and market access. Enterprises engaging in labour-intensive activities have also been able to attract foreign capital, technology and business because of the competitive advantage cheap Yugoslav labour offers to those firms in overseas markets, e.g. shoe-manufacture, printing, textiles, metal wares.

Third, managements of buoyant Yugoslav firms have been able to reach agreements with other domestic firms of varying economic performance to invest in capacity expansions for raw materials, components or other inputs from those firms or in the development of markets in other firms for their products, i.e. to develop inter-enterprise backward and forward linkages. Horizontal cooperation or integration has also increased.

Fourth, workers' councils of Yugoslav enterprises have shown increasing interest in 'internalizing' environment within their own management control. This has taken many forms. Some firms have integrated backwards into raw material supply by investing in mines or energy sources, for example, the cellulose-pulp and viscose factory at Banja Luka, Bosnia, has extended its fir and poplar plantations to ensure raw material supplies for the next 25 years. Others, like the 'Zlatorog' pharmaceuticlas, chemicals and cosmetics combine in Maribor, Slovenia, have opened their own research, marketing and transport units to reduce their dependence upon an uncertain environment which includes the changing and adaptive behaviour of firms in industry and other economic sectors with which they formerly did business. A few firms have been able to establish an international reputation of sufficient stature to set up overseas branches, for example, 'Tomos', Kopar (Slovenia), producing motorcycles, has opened an assembly plant in Amsterdam.

Fifth, closure of firms—indeed even the reduction of the labour force in existing enterprises—is impossible in Yugoslavia for social reasons: labour cannot be unemployed. Enterprises in difficult situations have thus sought assistance from other enterprises, by 'merging' production and management with them, or from banks or from their communes. An example is the timber-processing and furniture factory at Čačak, Serbia, which was able to solicit financial help from other diversified enterprises in the town, and from the town peoples' council, in order to modernize and change its production profile to meet new external environmental conditions—changes which it could not afford and without which it would have been bankrupt. An increasing tendency which is observable in Yugoslavia over the past decade has been the increase in cooperation and investment flows among enterprises located in different republics and ethnic regions—a tendency which expresses the rising strength of economic responses over ethnic responses among managements to environmental conditions.

Energoinvest: An Expanding Enterprise

A good example of the evolution and behaviour of a large Yugoslav self-managed enterprise today is 'Energoinvest' of Sarajevo. Established during the First Five-Year Plan (1948) to produce heavy electrical equipment, the enterprise amalgamated in 1954 and 1955 with two physically adjacent plants in Sarajevo Polje—'Elektroremont' and 'Stup'—which had been established simultaneously to manufacture related equipment: pylons and porcelain insulators. (This adjacency was an example of the success of integrated spatial economic planning during the centralized planning period.) Production was now rationalized and integrated physically and administratively so that in 1956 'Energoinvest' as a whole produced a wide range of high- and low-voltage electricity transmission equipment. But a major link—production of transformers—was missing: uncertainties in transformer supply had by 1961 caused sufficient stress in 'Energoinvest' operations for the workers' council to take a decision on future growth policy which recognized the necessity to control transformer supply. The alternatives were to build a branch plant or to amalgamate with a trans-former-producing enterprise. The latter path was chosen and 'Energoinvest' integrated backwards with 'Elektroinvest' of Črnuče near Ljubljana, Slovenia—the first time enterprise linkage crossed republic frontiers. Mergers continued and today 'Energoinvest' comprises 16 production units. Its core is still in Bosnia, focused on Sarajevo, with 12 plants, but its other backward linkages integrate it with 4 plants in four other regions, namely in Črnuče (Slovenia) Makarska (Croatia), Danilovgrad (Montenegro) and Priština (Kosovo-Metohija). In the same period, from 1954 to 1972, the gross product of the enterprise rose from 165 million to 20,500 million dinars, employment from 125 to 4,800 workers. By merging with other plants, 'Energoinvest' has internalized part of its production environment. It has also endeavoured to internalize other segments of the environment by establishing (1) four research units (respectively for electrical engineering, power and nuclear energy, automation, and electronics) in Sarajevo and other major urban nodes and (2) sales offices in the Republic capitals of Yugoslavia, i.e. all the major cities excepting only Rijeka.

Each production unit has its own workers' council, while the head office and plant in Sarajevo contains the central workers' council. In the Yugoslav system mergers do not eliminate control of the production units by the workers themselves. The function of the central workers' council is to coordinate the plans of the workers' councils of the member production units of the enterprise, but it has no right to impose any decisions on the workers' councils of the production units: differences must be hammered out by democratic discussion. This much more 'horizontal' management structure of the multi-plant Yugoslav enterprise generates far more two-way flows of information, decisions and personal contacts, much greater decision-making interaction among the units of the enterprise, than does the more vertical capitalist corporate structure, or the more vertical centralized planning system of the USSR and other East European states.

The Decision Process and Workers' Participation

To conclude this study of the Yugoslav case, however, it is necessary to establish briefly the extent to which workers' councils *are* effective in making decisions enumerated above. Till now I have been careful to refer to 'enterprise management' in assessing spatial responses by Yugoslav enterprises to external environmental change. This is deliberate. Research by Adizes (1971) and by this author (as yet unpublished) establishes that although all Yugoslav enterprises have workers' councils, the actual power of the workers *vis-à-vis* the power of the directors or technocrats to make decisions is highly variable. In practice the degree of autonomy of workers' councils ranges from the advisory only to competent executive decision-making. There is some spatial explanation of such variation. Evidence points to greater workers' participation and influence in areas where people have higher levels of education or where they have been exposed for longer periods to 'commercialized' as opposed to 'peasant or subsistence' environments, i.e. in the more developed regions or cities. But even in the cities, plant labour forces can comprise high percentages of commuters from the peasant countryside. From an analysis of workers' council agendas, Bićanić established that in less developed areas workers were more concerned to improve basic working conditions in the factory (e.g. provision of canteens, washing facilities)—and thus directors would have a freer hand on policy matters—whereas those in more developed areas spent more time discussing enterprise *policy,* such as plant expansion, rationalization, mergers, branches or prices. 'Internal' enterprise management environments are thus in part a function of their external environments: the socio-economic and cultural environments and experience of their labour forces. This clearly contrasts with Western corporate managements, and sometimes with socialist enterprise managements in centrally-planned economies, which tend to be an 'elite' separate from, and occupationally or interregionally more mobile than, the plant labour forces.

Equally, however, there are non-spatial dimensions to variation in workers' council influence on decision-making. Workers' management is apparently more effective in more profitable and often larger enterprises, but profitability levels may also be long-term results of past decentralized economic policies which were regionally discriminatory (Hamilton, 1968). However, Danilović argues that part of the problem lies in the sociological environment of the worker: that workers' self-management is ideally adapted to the pre-industrial world of the peasant (i.e. the majority of workers' backgrounds) but that there is a time-lag in the converting of the 'social-space' to 'work-space' in his mentality that is necessary to encourage his involvement in the self-management of modern industry (Danilović, 1968). In other words, once the peasant begins work in a factory, a period of adjustment is necessary during which he ceases to behave as if workers' councils were social 'club-like' contact organizations and to behave as if they are tools for changing and improving the technical and economic world in which he works. For now, however, one must be content to generalize that, in aggregate, Yugoslav enterprises can be grouped into three categories, namely, those enterprises with (1) well-developed and properly functioning workers' councils, (2) well-regulated workers' councils, the decisions of which are only partially implemented and (3) powerful central self-management elements—the director who, or technocratic caucus or a central workers' council in a multi-plant enterprise which, decide everything. Internal and external environments tend to make these characteristics self-perpetuating in each enterprise unless the rotation system brings a strong group together which can initiate changes in power.

That types (1) and (3) can be found in virtually adjacent enterprises of the same size which manufacture similar products and draw labour from identical villages is demonstrated by Adizes' survey of two Belgrade textile firms. Yugoslav enterprises in category (3) approximate most closely to Western corporate practice although their workers' councils, even if relatively passive, still mean greater horizontal segmentation in decision-making organization than in Western firms; in Adizes' study the Belgrade enterprise of this type was designated ABC. From 1962 the new director of this enterprise dominated decision-making. He was young, energetic, full of ideas; he explored alternatives, drew definite conclusions and derived power from technical competence and from personal connections with the local bank (useful for finance) and the Party (useful to obtain social support). He drew up agendas for workers' councils and got his way by persuasion at the workers' councils and at meetings and by removing or overruling 'obstructionsts'—like the production manager who supported the use of cotton, opposed the use of synthetics and held up modernization, and was thus directly responsible for the loss of markets to imported Italian nylon fabrics. The director overcame these inherited problems by modernization throughout the spinning, weaving, dyeing and finishing units and by cooperation with Italian firms in producing synthetic fabrics. 'Top–bottom' strategies dominated decision-making behaviour in ABC.

The second enterprise, designated XYZ by Adizes, approximates to the ideal or model of Yugoslav self-management. This enterprise upholds the self-management system, the principles of industrial democracy, by distinguishing administrative (*rukovodjenje*) and governing (*upravljenje*) functions. The administrators are the elected Workers' Council which in turn elects their executive body (the Governing Board) and nominates the Director (who stands for re-election every four years) and the top executives of the enterprise. Their task is to *suggest* decisions to the government of the enterprise and to *implement* them, while the government *makes* the decisions. The government is the total membership (employees and workers) of the enterprise and it governs through referenda or meetings (*zbor*). Each economic sub-unit of an enterprise (e.g. weaving, spinning, printing, transport etc.) has its own self-management organization which is a microcosm of that of the entire enterprise. Each workers' council and governing board may organize specialized committees of its members as well as other *ad hoc* committees. Adizes concludes that the plethora of workers' councils and committees in enterprise XYZ make 'representative decision-making positions available to about 40 per cent of the membership. Since there is rotation in each position, virtually no member of the organization can escape confrontation with the company's problems and participation in the decision process' (Adizes, 1971, p. 36). Decisions in XYZ were made through both 'top–bottom strategies' for modernization and 'bottom–up strategies' for organizational change. The initiative, purpose and determination of the Director of the Research and Development department was the main force in achieving the modernization of the enterprise's two plants, the introduction of new technology and the substitution of mixed synthetic fibre-wool (*kamgarn*) products for 100 per cent wool (*štrajgan*) products. Since the latter had been produced for 40 years and change could affect jobs, opposition came from both workers and production managers. However, financial, technical and marketing elements in the enterprise did support the R and D Director because they saw that his suggestions would save money in production, modernize technology and increase sales and revenues. The two opposing groups, operative at many levels throughout the enterprise, discussed and argued the issue at many, often voluntary, *ad hoc* group meetings during several weeks until a *ripple effect* achieved a consensus to change to *kamgarn*. 'Deliberations' took place as long as the arguments of each side were strong. Each side employed more and more convincing data—UN statistics, Russian statistics—until one side ceased to resist. The time factor served as a variable: if the decision had to be made in a hurry, and the expected value was high, an individual was likely to yield more rapidly to another's arguments. Consensus was arrived at through increasing pressure on the individual to conform to the group ... discussion always continued in each group until a unanimous vote developed' (Adizes, 1971). This process may stem from a long history in Yugoslav society of collectivism—the *zadruga* for instance—rather than the individualism typical of the Western commercialized world, as well as from the need to develop a strong cohesive support base, or threshold, with a high degree of locomotion to propel a decision through the diffusion process. A similar procedure was followed in arriving at a decision to re-allocate labour among the two plants of XYZ in order to raise productivity without reducing the labour force; this time the initiative came from the director of one of the enterprise plants. Throughout, the Director of XYZ participated in discussions but never attempted to impose decisions.

As with the similarities in location behaviour that emerge from Western corporate and socialist central planning decision-making procedures, so here, too, different internal enterprise environments have produced similar plant modernization and integration patterns as a result of interaction with the external (market) environment. Different as the decision-making behaviour may be between Yugoslav enterprises of type ABC and type XYZ, there are nevertheless important common denominators without which self-management would probably be ineffective, leaving enterprises to flounder on the rocks of workers' inaction. First, a general perception of stress conditions impinging on the enterprise must permeate the collective; this will often be evident to the worker in stagnant or declining wages and during workers' council meetings to determine how wages should be paid and profits distributed among the workers. Second, an individual who can gather strong support has to be interested enough in his enterprise's future to devote the time and the effort to try to secure a decision and its implementation.

References

Adizes, I., 1971, *Industrial Democracy—Yugoslav Style* (New York: Free Press).
Andrić, S. and M. Sever-Zebec, 1969, *Bibliografija o Učešću Radnika u Upravljenju Poduzećima u Jugoslaviji* (Zagreb: Ekonomski Institut).
Bićanić, R., 1967, *Problems of Planning: East and West* (The Hague: Mouton).
Bićanić, R., 1973, *Economic Policy in Socialist Yugoslavia* (Cambridge University Press).
Danilović, R., 1968, *Radničko Samoupravljenje i Osnovi Industrijske Sociologije* (Belgrade: Textbook Printing Works).
Gojanović, J., 1963, 'Basic characteristics of the forms, measures, and methods of work of organs of workers' self-government in Yugoslav enterprises', *Seminar on Social & Cultural Problems* (Ljubljana: University), 73–90.
Gorupić, D. and I. Paj, 1970, *Workers' Self-Management in Yugoslav Undertakings* (Zagreb: Ekonomski Institut).
Hamilton, F. E. Ian, 1968, *Yugoslavia—Patterns of Economic Activity* (London: Bell; New York: Praeger).
Moore, R., 1968, *Self-Management in Yugoslavia* (London: Fabian Research Series, 281).
Stefe, T. and Shoulberg, T., 1969, *Participation in Planning* (Ljubljana: Urbanistički Institut).
Vojnič, D., 1970, *Aktuelni Problemi Edonomske Politike i Privrednog Sistema Jugoslavje* (Zagreb: Ekonomski Institut).

18

Industrial Location in Nigeria

J. Okezie C. Onyemelukwe

One basic, but sometimes tacit, assumption made by industrial location theorists is that decision-making is entirely within the entrepreneur's control—that within the bounds prescribed by market forces, and to the extent that the entrepreneur has access to relevant information, his location decisions generally tend towards rationality and profit-maximization. The quality of available information and the effectiveness of its processing for subsequent use both largely affect the resulting decision. Classical location theories also assume that, given adequate information, the entrepreneur's process of decision-making would conform to the principle of transitivity of preference: in the face of given alternatives, his approach to decisions would be logical in preferring x to y and y to z and, hence, that he should prefer x to z, not z to x. Von Thunen's (1966) 'economic rent' concept, Alfred Weber's (1909) 'material index' and 'critical isodapane', and Lösch's (1954) 'market area' and 'profit maximization' principles are among well accepted theoretical concepts in the process of optimizing place utility. While these models still remain central in geographers' analysis of spatial economic patterns, many problems surrounding location decision-making still remain largely unresolved. The entrepreneur in the average private firm, is hardly in possession of sufficient information for effective decision-making. This raises fundamental questions: is the private entrepreneur as central in location decision-making as models of industrial location give us to understand? Are there other factors that direct the individual's hand and condition his decision-making? Answers to these questions touch upon the very origin, spatial disposition and ordering of cities as the direct or indirect outcome of decision-making beyond the means of the private entrepreneur. Thus if the development, location and the socio-economic structure of the centre in which the individual entrepreneur locates his plant are them-

462

selves products of decision-making, how central is the individual or the firm in the aggregate location decision-making process? On the other hand, the factors that have significantly influenced decision-making are apparently much more numerous than is consistent with the principle of economic efficiency, even though, quite often, that principle is ostensibly declared the guideline.

A major influence on location decision-making comes from public enterprises, since the latter control the greater part of industrial investment in our case-study area—Nigeria. This chapter, therefore, attempts to shed light on some of the economic development problems of an underdeveloped land such as Nigeria. To that end, the main thesis is that industrial location decision-making is the product of large-scale group activity within the framework of which the private entrepreneur's is a mere space-filling function.

The chapter is divided into three main parts. The first discusses the stage-setting role of exogenous factors operating at extra-national, national and regional levels and setting the limits within which the private entrepreneur organizes his business. The second part examines the economic and the non-economic variables that have been prominent in decision-making by private firms in Nigeria. The third part highlights the main consequences of location decision-making processes on the performance of industrial establishments in the country.

The Exogenous Environment

The literature on economic development is explicit on the notion of externalities as a major factor in the economic growth of a region or country as an open system. Externalities imply dependency relations. Countries or regions maintain economic relationships with places outside their boundaries such that, in input–output terms, a country, as a system, finds itself in a form of power balance (not necessarily balance of power) with such external sources of influence. This form of economic interaction implies that each country (or region) in such a relationship has some economic export base (Alexander, 1954; North, 1955; Alexandersson, 1956). It is the quality of a nation's relative quantum of visible and invisible exports that best reflects its position in the power balance. The country exporting technology, expertise, capital and manufactures is usually the superior party in a bilateral relationship with the country which, because of poor technology and low *per capita* income, is essentially a primary export promoter—so long as the basic/non-basic ratio does not change substantially and the basic (export activity) largely determines the nation's growth rate and development in Keynesian multiplier fashion. Although economic base theory can be criticized (Burrows, *et al.*, 1971) for assuming that growth and development necessarily depend on only the export sector and its multiplier effects, the theory is, nevertheless, central in our proper visualization of the dependency relations of a developing country with her former colonial overlord.

British Influence

Until 1960, Nigeria was a dependency of Great Britain. Throughout the preceding three-quarters of a century, Nigeria constituted a cheap source of valuable raw materials and a growing market for Britan's manufacturing industry while British power domination was given practical expression in political control and economic exploitation. Pre-colonial Nigeria had a relatively simple economic structure dominated by primary activities, crafts and trade that, particularly with North Africa, was on a fairly wide scale. Although these interregional trade relations fostered the emergence and functional structure of an urban system (Mabogunje, 1968), only some towns (notably Kano, Sokoto, Zaria, Bida, Katsina, Ife, Ilesha, Oshogbo, Ogbomosho, Ibadan, Abeokuta and Benin) survived the nineteenth century wars and pillages dominated by the Fulani Jihad. The advent of British influence disorganized the existing urban hierarchy system by fostering the emergence of many new urban centres, e.g. Lagos, Port Harcourt, and the decline of many pre-colonial towns.

Britain's colonial objectives required an administrative-cum-military presence and a modern transport system in Nigeria to facilitate both the political control of the territory and its economic link with the home market (Taaffe et al., 1963). Lagos, as the administrative and commercial headquarters in Nigeria and main contact point with the outside world, became the logical starting point of Britain's first rail route in Nigeria (Figure 18.1) the construction of which began in 1895. This coast-to-interior railway, and the later Port Harcourt line, served to amalgamate Northern and Southern Nigeria and to engender large-scale production and export of vegetable and mineral products to Britain. It also precipitated a spatial transformation that has had far-reaching consequences for the country's economic space. A new set of urban centres emerged at the road and rail junctions. First, because the route system was the product of an extra-territorial decision-making body whose goals were not necessarily consistent with the best interest of the Nigerian pre-colonial system of towns, many of the latter were by-passed. Now that manufacturing industries occupy more prominence in national economic space, it is to those growing route centres possessing the greatest growth-generating potential—evident from their infrastructural facilities, relatively large heterogeneous labour force, comparatively high income and purchasing power—that decision-makers tend to gravitate in making plant location decisions. Pre-colonial Nigeria had eighteen towns with over 20,000 population. Eleven of them, however,

464

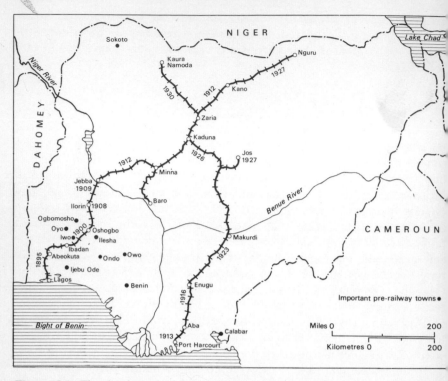

Figure 18.1. The development of the Nigerian railway network 1895–1930 and the location of major pre-colonial Nigerian towns.

were off the early colonial route system (Figure 18.1) Sokoto, Iwo, Ede, Oyo, Ijebu-Ode, Ogbomosho, Argonou, Deegoa, Kiama, Baebaegie and Dikwa. Their decline was such that, by 1952, the last five had under 5,000 population and fell below the minimum urban threshold (Population Census, Nigeria, 1952/53). Reversal in size and functional order, and thus in the spatial disposition of bargaining and decision-making power, may be illustrated as follows. Before 1850, forty years before the advent of Nigerian railways, Sokoto, the then political metropolis of Northern Nigeria with an estimated population of 120,000 was four times larger than Kano, the leading trade centre of the region. By 1952, after barely forty years of effective railway service, Kano had become three times larger than Sokoto which had declined in population to 52,000. Moreover, Sokoto's political leadership had long been lost to Kaduna, a town which ranked nowhere in Nigeria's pre-1900 urban system. Between 1952 and 1963 the population of Kaduna rose from 45,000 to 149,000 mainly because of the administrative decision-making primacy of the town in post-1945 Northern Nigeria and of the later concentration there of textile manufacture. Favourable location at the junction of the early colonial

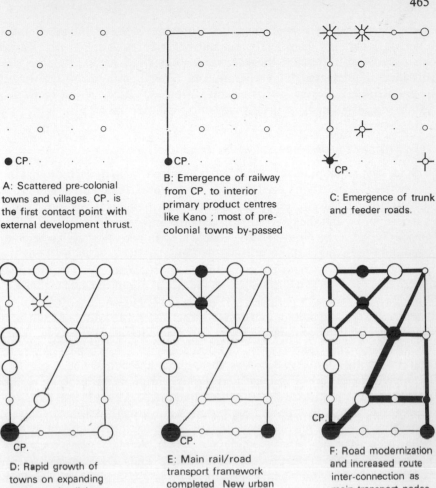

A: Scattered pre-colonial towns and villages. CP. is the first contact point with external development thrust.

B: Emergence of railway from CP. to interior primary product centres like Kano ; most of pre-colonial towns by-passed

C: Emergence of trunk and feeder roads.

D: Rapid growth of towns on expanding transportation links

E: Main rail/road transport framework completed New urban centres emerging

F: Road modernization and increased route inter-connection as main transport nodes become industrial.

Figure 18.2. The emergence of a modern industrial location pattern in Nigeria (modelled after Taaffe, Morrill and Gould, 1963, and Hamilton, 1967).

transport arteries in the case of Kaduna was an exogenously-determined environmental transformation which followed the imposition of a modern route system. This now serves as the structural framework around which a Western type of urbanization and industrialization has been evolving: This is conceptualized in the model evolutionary process shown in Figure 18.2

The Role of Central Government

The effects of the national administration, however, have been both more direct and influential on the location decisions of industrial firms than extra-national factors. The central Nigerian government has shaped location decision-making through three important media: (1) the distribution of industrial infrastructure and direct government interest in manufacturing; (2) the provision of various institutional inducements; (3) the organization of national space into regional subsystems.

(1) Infrastructure and Government Industrial Decisions

Since its assumption of political responsibility and decision-making powers in national affairs, the central government has attempted to improve industrial environment, especially transport, communications, power and water supplies, and the provision of technical and research centres. Understandably, these facilities are not evenly distributed, the few large cities invariably receiving a disproportionately greater share of them. Thus the pattern imposed by extra-national influences becomes more ossified and centripetal forces of growth centres on industrial establishments increase at the expense of the vast periphery (Myrdal, 1957; Hirschman, 1958; Friedmann, 1963). The choice of locations for the Federal Institute of Industrial Research, for nodes of the power grid that originates from the Kainji Dam and the Afam and Ughelli power stations, are central government decisions that affect other location decisions throughout the country.

Direct state influence through involvement in industrial processing and manufacture is motivated by several national needs. First, some decisions were designed to create propulsive industries at growth poles in relatively undeveloped or peripheral areas and to improve the welfare of people living there (Perroux, 1955; Boudeville, 1957). A plant using local raw materials and labour to produce intermediate and consumer goods can be effective in a predominantly agricultural area if coordination of linkage economies is achieved. The Bacita sugar factory in the Jebba area, Middle Belt, was initially designed for this purpose. Additional sugar factories have been proposed for other areas with similar socio-economic and ecologic environments: Lafiagi-Fadamas, Sokoto-Rima Valley, Baro, Numan and the Anambra-Do areas (Second National Development Plan 1970–74, 1970). The extent to which this will achieve a location pattern of paper, confectionery and other allied industries which can benefit from linkages with sugar-processing enterprises remains to be seen.

Second, the need for economic efficiency to raise Gross National Product has stimulated decisions on the basis of comparative costs rather than of regional equity. This rationale underlay the choice of Nkalagu for its first integrated cement factory. Although limestone and clay are widely available in Nigeria, Nkalagu has the unrivalled advantage of very large deposits of high quality limestone, nearness to power and direct rail and road access to both nearby coal and cement markets (Ugoh, 1964). The economic efficiency principle guided the location of Nigeria's oil refinery at Alesa-Eleme near Port Harcourt. With this decision, the central government has influenced private entrepreneurs' environment in respect of industries for which a viable refinery can be an 'industrie motrice'.

Whatever the central government objective, plants bring both social benefits and bargaining power to the area in which they are located. Government-sponsored industrial establishments are relatively large-scale and have good chances of survival or of success, considering their infrastructural facilities, their access to vital sources of information and their share of capital stocks. To the private entrepreneur their location indicates the presence or imminent creation of a favourable industrial environment and gives the small industrialist hopes for some external economies or linkage benefits. Frequently small firms move in to take advantage of such opportunities and so collectively accelerate growth.

Because of the enormous developmental implications of state-sponsored industrial projects, the central administration is often regarded as a major factor in the economic growth and welfare differentials between the regions. It is thus pressurized by regional interest groups attempting to influence decisions at the federal level. Recent central government indecision over locating a steel complex is evidence of this. Being a heavy and highly capital-intensive industry with significant export and multiplier potentials, economic efficiency should govern the location of steel production, i.e. where production costs are least and market accessibility greatest. Because of the industry's high technological threshold, only one complex is economically viable in Nigeria. A preliminary feasibility study considered that the near optimal location was Onitsha. This city is nodal in relation to nearby reserves of bituminous coal, limestone and medium-grade iron ore, and the river Niger is deep enough for large river barges to connect with Atlantic seaports, especially Port Harcourt. The alternative location is Port Harcourt whose port facilities and market proximity are expected to counterbalance distance from coal and ore sources. A third location–support for which is apparently more political than economic—is Lokoja, a river port farther inland and less accessible from seaports and external markets than Onitsha, but competitive with it in its proximity to large ore and coal reserves. Whatever decision is ultimately reached and implemented by the central government will greatly influence future plant location decisions in both public and and private sectors. Separate locations, once considered for two sub-optimal steel plants, might generate the emergence of a 'development corridor' along the main transportation route between the two steel centres.

(2) *Institutional Inducements*

Another central government mechanism shaping location decision-making is the institutionalization of several control measures and entre-

468

preneurial incentives. Import restrictions are imposed mainly to stave off competition, but many industrial activities are given special incentives through either reduced import duties on input factors or tax holidays. Spatial variations occur in wage rates. There is a lower investment limit for foreign industrial interests. Such institutional manipulations influence entrepreneurs' decisions on both the type and the location of manufacturing activity.

To the extent that such measures very widely across national boundaries and affect industrial profitability, the central government can influence decisions by would-be foreign investors in Nigeria on two levels. The first is the choice between locating in Nigeria and locating in another nation. Today, this level may be affected by national policies to nationalize foreign enterprises. Happily, this extreme measure is completely ruled out by the Nigerian government which, instead, has set an industrial investment floor, a £ Nigerian 200,000 minimum start-up capital, for foreign firms. The second level of decision-making by foreign firms becomes relevant only after an entrepreneur decided definitely to invest in Nigeria: the selection of a location within the country. At this level, foreign investors consider spatial variations in industrial infrastructure, raw material sources, demand

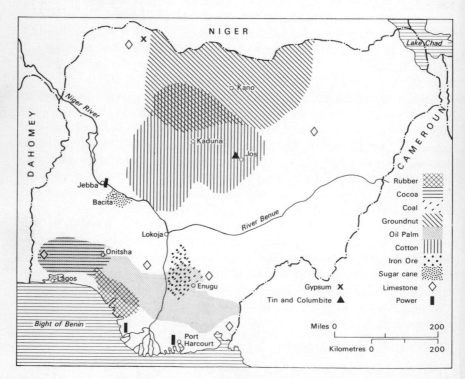

Figure 18.3. The major industrial resources of Nigeria.

potential, as well as wage rates and customs duties. Two main reasons why cotton textile manufacturing is concentrated in northern Nigeria are favourable wage rates and cotton prices. A 10 per cent duty charged on cotton lint moving from the six northern states to other Nigerian areas largely explains spatial differentiation in prices less transport cost. This is a very significant location factor, since 70 per cent of cotton production costs arise from raw cotton supply (Onyemelukwe, 1972).

(3) *Government Organization of National Space*

The Nigerian government organizes its national space into regional

Table 18.1. Total Public Sector Capital Investment in Nigeria, by Governments and Sectors, 1970–74

Sector	Total	Federal Government	All States
Economic	£Nm.	£Nm.	£Nm.
Agriculture	107,663	30,835	76,828
Liverstock, forestry and fishing	25,004	3,188	21,816
Mining	2,586	2,586	—
Industry	86,069	40,817	45,252
Commerce and finance	18,890	10,970	7,920
Fuel and power	45,325	45,325	—
Transport	242,599	167,133	75,466
Communications	42,641	42,641	—
Resettlement and rehabilitation	10,000	10,000	—
Subtotal	580,777	353,495	227,282
Social			
Education	138,893	49,122	89,771
Health	53,811	10,130	43,681
Information	10,931	4,782	6,149
Labour and social welfare	11,974	3,004	8,970
Town and country planning	19,075	5,287	13,788
Water and sewerage	51,696	—	51,696
Subtotal	286,380	72,325	214,055
Administration			
General administration	52,370	23,432	28,938
Defence and security	96,360	96,360	—
Subtotal	148,730	119,792	28,938
Financial			
Financial obligations	9,482	9,482	—
Subtotal	9,482	9,482	—
Nominal total	1,025,369	555,094	470,275

Source. *Second National Development Plan* 1970–74, Lagos, p. 273.

economies or subsystems. As usual with federal administrative structures, this also involves devolution of some decision-making powers to the regions (states). The major decision-making power lever of the central government is its treasury: its periodic fiscal regulations and financial disbursements can exert substantial control over decision-making in the regions. Out of over £N1,025 million earmarked for the 1970–74 Plan period (Table 18.1) the central government is investing over £N555 million (54 per cent) mainly in transport (30·1 per cent of federal investment), defence, education and industry in that order. Occasionally the central government experiences embarrassing power relations with the regions and seems incapable of prompt and decisive action especially over matters affecting interregional trade terms: the Northern State's Marketing Board's arbitrary cotton lint tariff and the prolonged stalemate over where to locate a steel complex illustrate clearly the magnitude of state (regional) influence.

State governments shape decision-making in their own provinces by deciding (i) budgetary allocations, (ii) direct financing specific projects, (iii) stipulating project criteria, (iv) approving project feasibility studies, (v) loans to private entrepreneurs and (vi) which parts of the region be favoured

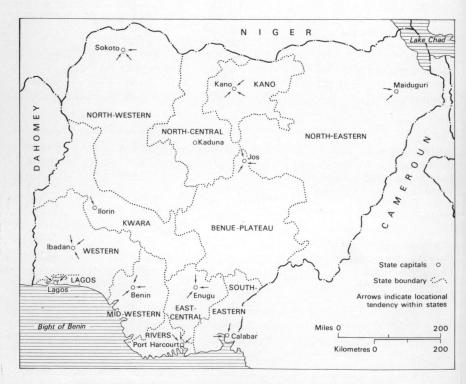

Figure 18.4. Locational tendencies within the States since 1967.

with new roads which, in effect, fill in the central government route system. Under the 1970–74 Plan state governments are spending £N72,436,000 on roads compared with £N93,858,000 by the central government. Each state government also provides industrial estates in the first and second order centres within their hierarchy of urban centres to assist small private industrial firms. Where properly planned, organized and serviced, like the Ikeja Industrial Estate (north of Lagos), such estates save small industrial firms, the effort, time and cost of site selection, acquisition and the ever-present risk of court litigation. They also assure it substantial agglomeration economies not realizable at isolated sites. By providing industrial estates, regional governments improve the growth-promoting potentials of selected centres, thereby influencing location choices by prospective industrial entrepreneurs.

With respect to public (i.e. federal and state government) *vis-à-vis* private (indigenous and foreign) industrial investment, 'the Federal Government in conjunction with the state governments, ensure that industries of basic and strategic importance to the economy are effectively controlled by the public sector' (*Second National Development Plan* 1970–74). The plan permits the Government to take a minimum of 55 per cent of the share capital in such industries. In other large-scale industries where technical partnership with overseas investors is desirable, the Government reserves the right to take 35 per cent of the equity holdings. The Federal Government controls the development of most strategic and capital-intensive industries: chemicals, oil refining and steel, for example. States complement rather than compete with the Federal Government: in addition to joint participation with the Federal Government in investing in major industrial projects, each state develops industries considered basic to its own economy and involving much more capital than indigenous entrepreneurs can mobilize. Partnership with foreign investors also exists. Thus, industrial investment by federal and state governments is generally positively coordinated to avoid state duplication of industrial projects and hence to reduce costs.

The current pattern of industrial distribution in Nigeria reflects strongly central and state government decisions. By 1966, just before the conversion of the four (Northern, Western, Eastern, Mid-Western) regions and the Capital Territory of Lagos into the twelve present states, 70 per cent of total industrial investments in Nigeria were concentrated in three areas: the Lagos–Ikeja core area, the Port Harcourt–Aba axis and the Kaduna–Kano–Jos triangle. About 35 per cent were in the Lagos–Ikeja area alone. The Mid-Western Region then still had little industrial concentration around its capital, Benin. However, the replacement of one Northern Region by six states, of one Eastern Region by three states and the annexation of former Western Region's industrial 'programme area' (Boudeville, 1957) to the new Lagos State, has created new administrative centres which are becoming the new foci for the industrial activities of the emergent states.

Figure 18.4 illustrates the spatial industrial implication of central government decisions in favour of twelve-state administrative structure.

Location Decision-Making by Private Entrepreneurs

So far, attention has focused on the main administrative framework within which private firms decide plant locations. Given its constraints, what other factors relate to such decisions by private firms? How much is consistent with the traditional industrial location theories? Given the effects of official policy decisions, are market forces all-powerful in the location of private manufacturing firms? Neither the Weberian cost-minimization approach nor the Loschian market-control principle provides a comprehensive framework for successfully considering locational optimality; nor does the 'minimax' model suggested by Greenhut (1956) and others (Dunn, 1956). Real-world situations involve non-economic and often non-quantifiable variables which influence and sometimes determine location decisions.

The size of Nigerian private firms is relevant here. Two broad size groups exist: a 'small' (workshop) industry group, comprising firms which each employ fewer than ten persons, and a 'large-scale' group of medium-to-large firms each employing more than ten persons. Employment is the best criterion for grouping industries since most firms are labour-intensive; other criteria—capital invested, power consumed, floor space used, value added—are less satisfactory measures. The few capital-intensive industries like the tobacco, brewing, cement and oil-refining industries, are so large that, in fact, they also belong to the largest employment group.

First, in 1965, some 53 per cent of all firms in the 'large-scale' group employed fewer than 50 persons each: 23 per cent employed fewer than 20 persons. Second, under 5 per cent employed 500 or more persons but accounted for 45 per cent of total value added and of receipts by manufacturing industry—compared with only 2 per cent by firms employing fewer than 20 persons. The theoretial expectation that employment correlates positively with other size indicators, such as total receipts and value added, is justified by Nigerian experience.

Third, 20 per cent of all Nigerian industrial establishments were sole proprietorship ventures and accounted for only 4 per cent of total employment. This underlines the small-scale nature of Nigerian industry.

Generalizations based on national-scale statistical aggregates may, however, have little utility since figures for the major cities that constitute the industrial foci of the country may be swamped by those of the many small service centres, each of which provides a large enough threshold to sustain several plants in the 10–19 employment group. Table 18.2, however, does not bear this out. In Ibadan in 1963 about 64 per cent of 'large' industrial

Table 18.2. Large-Scale Industries in Ibadan by Size of
Employment, 1963

Number of people employed	Number of establishments	Percentage of total establishments
		%
10–24	10	21·3
25–49	20	42·6
50–99	8	17·0
100–199	6	12·8
200–499	2	4·2
500–999	1	2·1
Total	47	100

Source. *Industrial Directory*, Lagos, 1967.

establishments employed fewer than 50 persons each: only 6 per cent employed more than 200 persons. In fact, the three largest plants were capital-intensive, including those of the Nigerian Tobacco Company and the Odutola Rubber Factory. The low concentration of industrial establishments in Ibadan in terms of the location quotient (Bendavid, 1972) is due partly to the apparent neglect of social and industrial infrastructure on the city and partly to the former Western Regions preoccupation with developing the Ikeja Industrial Area as the regional core—until it was annexed to Lagos in 1967. Tardiness by the city's decision-making body in embracing innovation and change (Mabogunje, 1968) and the 1967–70 civil war explain why the industrial outlook of Ibadan has improved significantly since the 'loss' of Ikeja by the boundary changes of 1967.

The same can be said about small firms. Mabogunje (1968) has shown that the majority of over 2,000 small-scale industrial establishments in Ibadan reportedly (Ibadan Town Planning Authority, 1963) employing fewer than ten persons each were, in fact, employing no more than five. Of 10,7228 firms in fourteen former Eastern Region towns, 38 per cent were one-man businesses, 54 per cent employed 2–5 persons and only 5 per cent employed 6–9 persons (Table 18.3).

What are the implications of these size characteristics for location decision-making?

The most significant is small firms' relatively greater tendency towards apparent 'deviant behaviour'. To a one-man enterprise, nearness to a major labour source or market, low land values for factory floor space, adequate housing or commuter transport facilities for workers and regional variations in wage rates have no mignificance and hence no locational importance.

The same applies to small industrial firms employing a handful of workers and operating in residential house frontages. Thus for a vast majority of industrial firms in Nigeria, traditional 'Western' location factors are often

Table 18.3. Distribution of Small–Industry Firms in Selected Centres in the Three Eastern States of Nigeria, 1961–62

Town	No. of firms	Total employed	Firms by number of workers			
			1	2–5	6–9	10+
Aba	2268	6243	786	1291	121	70
Abakaliki	338	737	179	139	14	6
Awka	186	329	124	57	1	4
Calabar	440	1000	166	254	11	9
Enugu	1250	2980	641	520	63	26
Ikot Ekpene	275	612	117	145	8	5
Onitsha	2259	7121	824	1165	165	107
Owerri	292	742	84	190	10	8
Owerrinta	42	107	22	20	—	—
Oron	166	347	70	90	4	2
Port Harcourt	2258	6017	801	1271	116	70
Umuahia	579	1514	169	363	31	16
Uyo	288	804	92	175	12	9
Uzuakoli	87	168	34	53	—	—
Total	10,728	28,721	4,109	5,731	556	332

Source. Kilby, P., *The Development of Small Industry in Eastern Nigeria,* March 1962, pp. 6–7.

non-issues. Socio-cultural and other non-economic factors play a prominent, if not dominant, role in the location decisions of small firms. This should not be construed to imply that the average industrial entrepreneur in Nigeria is economically irrational or non-responsive to the pull and push effects of market forces if he is aware of them. He is known for both his astuteness and positive reaction to innovations, but he must contend with very limited information, capital resources and organizational ability.

Large-scale industrialization in Nigeria, as in most developing economies, is aimed at import substitution. This implies substantial dependence on domestic markets, so that the entrepreneur's choice of location increasingly reflects the need for close contact with the market. Field investigations carried out in 1970–71 showed that the majority of private commercial companies created their own environment of industrial profitability by beginning their life as trade businesses which provided the initial capital and marketing facilities. Most large firms which moved into manufacturing did so as a matter of expediency, setting up plants to substitute domestic production for foreign imports and so retain their control of a large share of the home market. This marketing-cum-manufacturing strategy has involved location considerations quite consistent with the Löschian market-area principle. Nigerian Breweries Ltd. and Guinness Stout Ltd. (Nigeria), provide good examples of the market-control approach to location decision-making in Nigeria.

Import substitution, following in the wake of political independence

(1960) expressed in the rapid decline of beer and stout imports and in the increase of domestic production. Nigerian beer and stout output rose to 10·5 million gallons in 1963, cutting imports from 7·1 million gallons in 1961 to 1·89 million in 1963. To continue its domination of the beer market, Nigerian Breweries Ltd. has located its three breweries to match regional patterns of purchasing power: in Lagos to supply the Western, Mid-Western and Kwara States, in Kaduna to supply the Northern states, and in Aba to supply the three Eastern states. It would appear that the minimax compromise has come into full play in the company's concentration of decision-making in Lagos, close to foreign sources of malt, hop and sugar raw materials and of its bottle and crown needs, in close touch with the federal centre of decision-making in the country and for quick access to or from Britain. This is the main reason why Guinness Stout Ltd. is content to maximize its near-wharf location advantage, making up for distance to the northern and the eastern market centres with economies of scale and high product quality in one plant.

Nigeria's import substitution economy has involved locally produced intermediate inputs on a very negligible scale (Onyemelukwe, 1972) because of emphasis on processing and assembly which itself results from the generally low level of technology in, and hence low value added content of, most local manufactures. The preponderence of raw materials in the structure of industrial costs (Table 18.4) leaves grounds for a priori conclusions that industrial plants in Nigeria are more likely to be material-oriented and less inclined to seek linkage economies through agglomeration. Yet, because many industrial raw materials and intermediate inputs come from overseas sources, location decisions are more complex: all the more so as the main ports—Lagos and Port Harcourt—are also the main market centres. Locations at these contact points with foreign raw material sources blur the comparative importance of the market and the material factors

Table 18.4. General Structure of Industrial Costs in Nigeria, 1963–65, (In £N000s)

Year	Raw material	Fuel	Electricity	Contracts	Repairs	Goods for resale	Total
1963	59,822	1148	1786	620	626	17,768	81,770
	(73)*	(1)	(2)	(1)	(1)	(22)	(100)
1964	79,446	1649	2306	83	629	26,543	110,656
	(72)	(1)	(2)	(—)	(1)	(24)	(100)
1965	100,488	2194	2846	141	845	29,625	136,140
	(73)	(2)	(2)	(—)	(1)	(22)	(100)

*Percentages in parentheses
Source. Second National Development Plan 1970–74, Lagos, p. 273.

in firms' plant location selection. At any rate, that these locations were chosen because they are the principal ports and the public policy decision-making headquarters with the highest concentration of government-financed industrial infrastructure and high-income professional service class, points *a fortiori* to the pervasive influence of the state (central and regional) administration in the industrial location decision-making environment of private firms.

Two major industries—cement, and cotton textile manufacture—illustrate the location of industries which derive their raw materials from Nigerian sources.

Although essentially raw material-orientated, the *cement industry* approaches its optimum location the nearer its material sources are to the market. Limestone constitutes about 95 per cent of the finished product, gypsum 3–5 per cent. Limestone loses considerable weight and bulk in the conversion process, about 1·5 tons to limestone being used to produce 1 ton of cement. Because raw materials are ubiquitous and cement is itself a heavy commodity relative to its price per unit of weight, location near the market also reduces costs. The real situations shown in Table 18.5, however, indicate that other factors influenced the location of some integrated Nigerian cement plants-especially the Calabar factory that is 19 miles from the limestone quarry. The Ewekoro factory still depends on an adjacent quarry and uses cranes and conveyor-belts for quarry-to-factory movement of limestone and clay; quality problems, however, demanded the opening in 1971 of a quarry nine miles from the cement works. The Sokoto plant suffers from distance from its market, the Kaduna–Kano-Jos triangle, which lies over 300 miles away (nearly 10 hours by truck).

The dominant non-economic factors influencing some cement plant locations were social and political: government ownership of the plants partly explains this. The Calabar factory results from the desire to give this old and declining town a prestigious industry which would both cater

Table 18.5. Distances of Nigerian Cement Factories from Main Raw Materials Sources and Product Markets

Firm	Factory location	Distance from quarry*	Time distance to market centre
		miles	minutes
Nigerian Cement Co.	Nkalagu	0·5	50
West African Portland Cement Co.	Ewekoro	0·5 and 9·0	60
Northern Nigeria Cement Co.	Sokoto	Approx. 1·0	600
Calabar Cement Co.	Calabar	19·0	100

*The critical distance beyond which cement production becomes uneconomic is 12 miles.
Source. Onyemelukwe, J. O. C., *Cotton Textile and Cement Industries in Nigeria,* University of Ibadan, 1972, p. 37.

for unemployment in the then 'minority area' and satisfy a political sense of belonging. The former Eastern Nigerian government commissioned a fesibility study for establishing a cement factory: the study recommended Oron on a least-cost basis, but political considerations weighed on officials in favour of Calabar. Oron is almost as far from the limestone quarry and has about the same waterway facility as Calabar: its situation on the main market for the lower Cross River plain is its locational advantage over Calabar. The report recommended the aerial ropeway system for moving limestone to Oron.

Because cheap labour recruitment is easy almost everywhere, the labour supply variable can be held constant in the study of the location of *cotton textile industries*. Since it is cheaper to transport finished cloth or yarn than cotton, textile production would, *ceteris paribus*, be located near the raw material (cotton) source. However, the pull of raw material is weak on mills which finish and print cloth: for them close contact with fast-changing consumer tastes and preferences assures considerable advantages, agglomeration economies (realized mainly in plant servicing, labour training and pooling facilities) and nearness to the wharf for contacts with overseas markets, and encourages market-orientation. The major Nigerian market

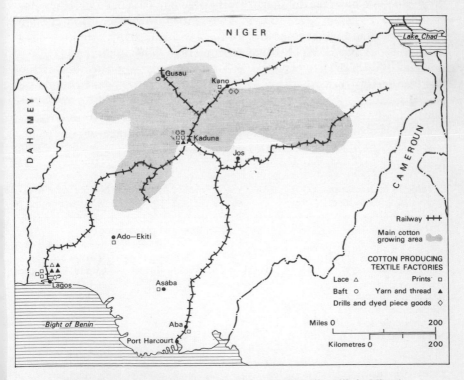

Figure 18.5. The distribution of major cotton textile mills in Nigeria.

for printed piece goods is in the south; that for grey and bleached piece goods is in the predominantly Moslem areas of the north where grey cloth is used for making traditional 'riga' (robes).

Out of twenty cotton textile plants surveyed, 6 are clearly raw material orientated and concentrated in Kaduna and Kano. Two—the Kaduna Textile Mill Limited (KTL) and the Zamfra Textile Mill in Gusau—are equally material and market orientated: their final products, grey and bleached fabrics, have their market in the Moslem north where most raw materials are produced. Another 11 market orientated plants are in the south—nine in the Lagos—Ikeja area and one each in Aba and Asaba. The Ado-Ekiti Textile Mill is more or less peripheral to both markets and materials.

If locations for Nigerian cotton textile factories were decided mainly on cost, a quite different pattern would have emerged. Plants producing grey cloth and bleached piece goods or yarn would have tended more to the material source than to the market; and those producing printed textiles would have been locationally tied to the centre of their markets. However, Table 18.6 shows that 5 of the 10 plants specializing in cotton prints are located in the raw material source region, not the area of effective demand. If production near the market is cost-reducing, then factors other than production costs, or even the market-control principle, must account for the apparent high-cost location of the five far northern printing mills— at a considerable distance from their market. The dominant factor is political: four of the five plants are controlled by the New Nigeria Development Company (formerly the Northern Nigeria Development Corporation) whose stated manufacturing policy is to confine new industry to the six northern states constituting the former Northern Region of Nigeria. Politics has also influenced the Ado-Ekiti textile mills location.

Yet such political considerations stem from the genuine need to ensure

Table 18.6. Location and Type of Cotton Textile Plants by Nature of Final Products

Location	Number of plants producing			
	Prints	Baft/piece-dyed fabrics	Yarn/thread	Other
Raw material source	5	—	1	—
Market	4	2	3	2
Raw material source/market	—	2	—	—
Neither market nor material	1	—	—	—
Total	10	4	4	2

Source. Onyemelukwe, J. O. C., *Cotton Textile and Cement Industries in Nigeria,* University of Ibadan, 1972.

effective control of production and marketing as well as to provide employment opportunities in the promoters' home area, especially if it is otherwise
peripheral in the national distribution of socio-economic welfare. Thus
plant locations are determined not by theoretical optima but by the plan
objectives of the decision-maker. It is in this context that other non-economic
influences on the decision-making of the private firm may be understood.
For example, the phenomenon of social identification (Mabogunje,
1961) is typical in Nigerian society. The industrial entrepreneur establishing
the one-man proprietorship type of business often seeks plant location
in his home community. This is done with an eye not on the developmental
effect of his enterprise on the community but mainly on the socio-political
prestige and reward that could accrue to him from the community's recognition of his contribution towards societal goals. That this form of
elite mentality has had considerable influence on location decision-making
of the private firms is not very surprising when it is realized what promise
it holds in a society where wealth and social standing constitute the passport
to political honours through the ballot box. The prestige factor is not the
same for an entrepreneur operating outside his home area. The 'home
area' can range from one's town or village-group (clan) to a wider geographical area constituting one's language group. Social recognition and
success tend to decrease with distance from the place of birth. Once outside
his home area, the entrepreneur needs another form of reference to reach
his socio-political goal.

There is thus a common tendency for private investors to set up their
industrial plants in the urban centre where they reside at the time the enterprise is contemplated. Theoretically this may not be the best choice, but
it is conditioned by three factors. The first is the investor's lack of requisite
information, which may be reflected in either ignorance about investment
opportunities outside his district of residence or an exaggerated sense of
insecurity in the few investment opportunities known to exist farther afield.
The second is the problem of capital mobilization. The initial capital for
an industrial venture is often very difficult to come by; successful capital
mobilization is frequently not through formal financial institutions—banks
—as it is in the Western commercial traditions, but through informal sources,
especially within the entrepreneur's extended family circle and among
people of the same socio-cultural background. Thus even where the entrepreneur desires to establish his enterprise in another centre which seems
to offer better promise of industrial profitability, capital immobility may
inhibit long-distance movement away from one's own people. The third
factor is the high land value in cities: promise of good investment opportunities, especially through external economies, raises the price of industrial
floor space beyond the reach of the small investor. Moreover, land acquisition or lease outside the muncipal boundaries is so susceptible to the danger
of long drawn out and costly litigation that the small investor prefers to

establish his business on his own property or where tenant–landlord relationships are on a personal level. An inquiry conducted by the author in 1972 into the location of industrial plants in Ibadan showed that out of 37 establishments employing over nine persons each, 23 (62·2 per cent) were located there mainly because the proprietors happend to be residing in Ibadan long before the enterprise was contemplated. Although almost all firms mentioned the market as a factor for locating in Ibadan, only 9 (24·3 per cent) considered it paramount. Most of the 5 which ranked 'State headquarters' factor highest were state-owned.

The importance of local ties came out as the most dominant factor among small industry, being ranked highest by 65 of the 108 establishments that cooperated with the author. Prominent, too, was the effect of apprenticeship: individuals who were apprenticed in an industrial line in which they became investors immediately after their training were most likely to establish their own business in the city where their skill was acquired and where their information surface in the business was likely to be highest. However, since the decision to undertake an apprenticeship in Ibadan was itself influenced by the factor of market attraction (ranked by 43 firms as dominant) and familiarity with the locality, the effect of apprenticeship on the location of the small firm is subsumed under these variables.

The economic and non-economic variables shown to have influenced decision-making by the private firm are not peculiar to Nigeria. They are typical generally of capitalist economies but particularly of developing nations in which cultural patterns and societal value systems still impinge upon the economy. Their effects on industrial firms in Nigeria may now be considered.

Some Consequences of Plant Location Decisions

The wide variety of experiences through which Nigerian industrial firms have passed reflects, among other factors, the influence of their location.

Table 18.7. Transfer Cost Structures for Calabar Cement Factory Products from the Factory to the Market (Nigerian currency)

Product	Location of market depot	Ferry cost per ton	Coastwise freight per ton	Handling charges per ton	Total costs per ton
Cement	Oron	15/-	—	5/-	20/-
Clinker	Lagos	—	5/-	8/-	13/-

Source. Calabar Cement Company, March 1971.

Since effects of location on overall performance are difficult to separate from the effects of other independent variables, the analysis will be limited to the few cases in which requisite data are available.

Of the four integrated cement factories in Nigeria (see Table 18.5) the Nkalagu and Ewekoro plants are best located for cost minimization and full realization of scale economies to which the cement industry is so responsive (Ugoh, 1964). By contrast, the Calabar mill is so badly located—so far from its materials and markets—that its production costs, reflected in the high transfer costs shown in Table 18.7 operate negatively on performance, including the realization of scale economies. In addition, high investment outlays on road access provision and high rates of depreciation on trucking limestone have been significant in raising production costs.

Marketing costs are high, even prohibitive. The initial plan was for production to be 80 per cent clinker to feed the clinker-grinding coastal mills, and 20 per cent cement; but high production and transport costs caused abandonment of the plan after the initial attempt in 1967. A ton of clinker cost 87 Nigerian shillings (N. Sh.) to produce; an additional transfer cost of 13 N. Sh. per ton to sypply the cement works at Apapa, Lagos, raised delivery costs to 100 N. Sh. per ton, compared with 95 N. Sh. per ton of imported clinker. Full cement production at Calabar after 1967 was, therefore, more a last resort than an intended decision. By the Elder Dempster ferry route across the lower Cross River, Calabar is 16 miles from Oron which is the nearest eastern gateway to the factory's market. Transfer costs for factory-to-depot cement movement have been as high as 20 N. Sh. per ton (Table 18.7). Despite the fact that the company has never satisfied effective demand in its market area, the Calabar factory, on account of its location, has never operated at full capacity (indeed in 1971 only at 60 per cent capacity). Similar problems, almost entirely derived from location vis-à-vis the supply sources of materials, fuel and power, and their markets, affect the Sokoto plant which in 1971 had 30 per cent excess capacity.

Cotton textile plants have had equally bitter experience largely as a result of their locations. Poor vertical integration within, or linkage between most Nigerian firms, dependence on other (especially foreign) sources for intermediate inputs such as baft or grey cloth has meant that firms located on the coast—in Lagos–Ikeja conubation—have been able to operate more easily by using their port location to procure foreign chemicals and dyes. By contrast, the five textile printing mills in the north, far away from their markets and the ports, have suffered high transport and production costs and this has enabled competing, cheaper and better quality textile imports to erode the markets of Kaduna and Kano mills but not those of Aba and Asaba. And this is despite the 10 per cent duty paid by the firms located outside the six northern states. Two textile firms in Kaduna proposed in 1971 to lay off much of their labour force because of their non-competitiveness.

The fruit canning factory in Ibadan represents another example of bad location decision adversely affecting industrial performance. The Lafia Canning Factory is a Western Region (State) Development Corporation project designed to take advantage of the local potential for fruit production and to encourage much-needed diversification in a cocoa-based agricultural economy. Although other factors, particularly bureaucratic bottlenecks, have affected performance, the major problem derives from location away from the fruit growing centre of the region: the factory has had to procure oranges, pineapples and mangoes within a radius of more than 50 miles from Ibadan, involving high transport costs on weight-losing and perishable raw materials. During the period of this survey in 1972, the factory was paying £N8 (formerly £N6) per ton of fruit within, and £N7·75 per ton beyond, 30 miles of Ibadan. The irregularity of fruit collection by the Corporation's van, one consequence of long-distance inputs, involves excessively heavy transport input by small farmers to reach the factory themselves: both tend to dampen farmers' interest. Fruit supply has thus been so variable (and seasonal) that the plant has always operated well below capacity—(as low as 13 per cent in 1966) when *maximum* average tonnages of fruit processed per eight-hour shift were 24 compared with the planned average of 80! The resulting high production costs and prices have restricted the market for canned fruit to the small population high-income group whose demand for such items is less price elastic than the majority of low-income earners whom the factory was initially meant to serve also. Thus, the Lafia Canning Factory cannot expand and encourage fruit production as a profitable and full-scale economic activity for the local farmer: the vicious poverty circle continues.

Conclusion

Powerful forces external to the industrial firm exert considerable influence on the location considerations of the Nigerian entrepreneur. Under the constraints of extreme scarcity of both capital and the right quality of industrial infrastructure, government policy decisions, responsible for (among many other things) the provision and spatial distribution of the little investment that is available, have been a critical factor. Federal and State decision-making, in selecting modern routes and port development, in choosing nodes for the new federal power grid and in providing better-equipped industrial estates in selected urban centres, are positive factors in increasing the industrial potential of the favoured centres. Such spatially concentrated provision of much-needed infrastructure strongly influences the locational behaviour of the private industrial entrepreneur. To the extent that the investor's range of choice of location is thereby narrowed down to a few feasible points in national economic space, the individual entrepreneur is not as central in industrial location decision-making as traditional location theory assumes. His is at best an attempt to fit into a spatial framework which he cannot safely ignore or possibly alter. Even within that framework, his choice is often rational but less frequently aims at optimality for the industrial enterprise: rationality must be understood from the decision-makers viewpoint of plan objectives and methods for achieving them. Thus the non-economic considerations shown to have influenced many location decisions in Nigeria are often not irrational. To appreciate this point one should view the industrial enterprise as an integral part of, rather than the whole of, the decision-maker's web of activity interrelationships. As such, the decision in favour of a sub-optimal location is rational to the extent that it promotes the attainment of overall objectives— objectives which are sometimes more socio-political than economic.

State-owned industrial ventures, which appear to have been consciously located sub-optimally, may counterbalance high plant operating costs with social benefits (including employment opportunities, accessibility and much-needed social amenities) which accrue to the area where the factory is located. They may also assure the decision-maker the political loyalty of the local population. Nevertheless, without being prejudicial to the same socio-economic and political objectives, many public enterprises appear to be deeply in debt and would have been much more effective if due regard had been paid at the decision-making phase to economic constraints on the location of particular industrial types.

The industrial structure of Nigeria is dominated by firms of very small scale. These firms, though much less able to realize economies and attain appreciable growth under normal conditions, are much more adaptable and successful in modern industrialization than large-scale enterprise that are located sub-optimally. Losses are generally less crippling and adaptations to changing conditions much easier. Nigerian experience shows that the study of plant and firm size is an essential preliminary to a meaningful appraisal of location decision-making processes in a nation's industrial firms.

References

Alexander, J. W., 1954, 'The basic-non-basic concept of urban economic functions', *Economic Geography,* **30**, 246–61.

Alexandersson, G., 1956, *The Industrial Structure of American Cities* (Lincoln: University of Nebraska Press).

Bendavid, A., 1972, *Regional Economic Analysis for Practitioners* (New York: Praeger).

Boudeville, J. R., 1957, 'Contribution a l'étude des poles de croissance brasiliens', *Cahiers de l'Institute de Science Economique Appliquée, Cahiers disponibles,* Series FO, 10, 71.

Burrows, J. C., C. E. Metcalf and J. B. Kaler, 1971, *Industrial Location in United States* (Lexington, Mass.: Heath).

484

Dunn, E. S., 1956, 'The market potential concept and the analysis of location', *Papers and Proceedings, Regional Science Association*, 2, 183–94.

Friedmann, J., 1963, 'Regional economic policy for developing areas', *Regional Science Association Papers*, 2, 44.

Greenhut, M. L., 1956, *Plant Location in Theory and Practice: The Economics of Space* (Chapel Hill: University of North Carolina Press).

Haggett, P., 1965, *Location Analysis in Human Geography* (London: Methuen).

Hamilton, F. E. Ian, 1967, 'Models of industrial location', in *Models in Geography* (London: Methuen), 361–424.

Hirschman, A. O., 1958, *The Strategy of Economic Development* (New Haven: Yale University Press).

Industrial Directory, 1967 (Lagos: Nigerian Government).

Isard, W., 1956, *Location and Space Economy* (New York: Wiley).

Kilby, P., 1962, *The Development of Small Industry in Eastern Nigeria* (United States Agency For International Development).

Lösch, A., 1954, *The Economics of Location* (New Haven: Yale University Press).

Mabogunje, A. L., 1961, *Yoruba Towns*, Ibadan.

Mabogunje, A. L., 1968, *Urbanization in Nigeria* (University of London Press).

McNee, R. B., 1970, 'Regional Planning, Bureaucracy and Geography', *Economic Geography*, 46 (2), 191–8.

Myrdal, G., 1957, *Economic Theory and Underdeveloped Regions* (London: Duckworth).

North, D. C., 1955, 'Location theory and regional economic growth', *Journal of Political Economy*, 63 (3), 243–58.

Onyemelukwe, J. O. C., 1972, *Cotton Textile and Cement Industries in Nigeria: A Geographic Appraisal of Factory Location and Production Distribution* (University of Ibadan).

Population Census of Nigeria, 1952/1953 (London: U.K. Colonial Office).

Perroux, F., 1955, Note sur la notion de 'pole de croissance', *Economie Appliquée*, 8, 307–20.

Perroux, F., 1961, *L'economie du XXme siécle*, Paris.

Second National Development Plan 1970–74, 1970 (Lagos: Federal Ministry of Information).

Taaffe, E. J., R. Morrill and P. Gould, 1963, 'Transportation expansion in underdeveloped countries: a comparative analysis', *Geographical Review*, 53, 503–29.

Ugoh, S., 1964, 'The Nigerian Cement Company', *The Nigerian Journal of Economic and Social Studies*, 6, 1, 72–91.

Von Thunen, H., 1966, *The Isolated State* (translated by C. M. Wartenberg, ed.) (Oxford: Pergramon).

Weber, A., 1909, *Uber den Standort der Industrien, I: Reins Theorie des Standorts*, Tubin ed.

19

Location Decision-Making by Firms in Japan

HISAO NISHIOKA

Japan stretches 2,600 km from north-east (45 N) to south-west (20 N) and consists of four major islands: Hokkaido, Honshu (Main Island), Shikoku and Kyushu. It lies east of the world's largest continent and west of the world's greatest ocean and belongs to the circum-Pacific orogenic, volcanic and earthquake zone. Accordingly, climatic differentiation is great, topography steep and varied, plains scaree and fragmental, and environmental hazards—typhoons, earthquakes, landslips, floods, volcanic eruptions and heavy snows—frequent. Yet the nation benefits from the long shoreline, the monsoon elimate, which provides enough water for double cropping (especially in the south-west), minerals (limestone, sulphur, coal), marine products, and from diligent people, a single language, political unity and a favourable position for trade. More than one hundred million people live in an area of 370,000 km.[2] Most people and industry are confined to small alluvial plains because of the relief and rapid post-war industrialization which followed the end of national isolation and the growth of overseas trading. Early on, the capital lay almost in the central area of Kinki, in or near Nara, Osaka or Kyoto. Advanced culture flowed along waterways mainly from the west. Central Kinki became a focus for both western and eastern Japan but, with time, the political capital alternated between Kyoto, Kamakura and later Tokyo.

Though generally the pre-war economy of Kansai (i.e. Kinki) was more advanced than that of Kanto, this relationship has been reversed since World War II. The reasons are as follows:

(1) National agricultural policies aimed at improving farming in north-eastern Japan by protecting crops from frost, by government incentives for early-season rice production.

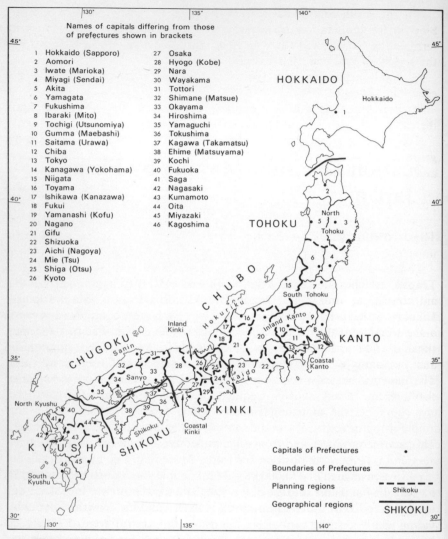

Figure 19.1. The administrative, geographic and planning regions of Japan.

(2) Rapidly increasing demand for domestic rice from Kanto came from rapid population growth and cessation of imports of foreign rice.

(3) Land reform improved agricultural conditions.

(4) Public investment developed Hokkaido and Tohoku.

(5) Production of iron ore, coal, petroleum, natural gas; coniferous forests grew in the east.

(6) Textile and coal mining industries, the backbone of the western economy, declined.

(7) The Asian continental market disappeared largely because of either Sino-Soviet cooperation or autarkic Chinese and Korean development, terminating the demand there for food and industrial products from, and the supply of raw materials to, western Japan.

(8) Trade expansion with the United States benefited all regions, but especially the east.

(9) Population pressure, especially in western agricultural villages, increased following the inflow of repatriates from abroad.

(10) The importance of the capital city (Tokyo) rose, supported by growing central government influence in decision-making, investment and economic policy.

(11) The median point of Japan's population, labour force and purchasing-power shifted eastward.

These trends are interrelated, but the seventh, eigth and tenth are particularly important.

Today, the zone from southern Kanto to northern Kyushu through Tokaido and the Seto Inland Sea coast embraces the largest metropolitan and industrial areas: Keihin (Tokyo-Yokohama), Chukyo (Nagoya), Hanshin (Osaka-Kobe) and northern Kyushu (especially Kita-Kyushu and Fukuoka). Called the Pacific Coast Belt Area, it accounts for one-third of Japanese territory; yet in 1965 two-thirds of the population and five-sixths of the manufacturing of Japan was concentrated there. The most important trunk zone, from Keihin to Hanshin, is now called the 'Tokaido Megalopolis'.

The Socio-Economic Environment and Bureaucratic Leadership in Japan

An internationally-isolated position enables Japan to maintain national identity and to make central authority prominent and effective. Long ago the Imperial Court was important in diffusing advanced culture—rice cultivation and Buddhism—into peripheral areas. After the Meiji Restoration bureaucracy became stronger both to protect the state from invasion and to promote economic development. Yet great spatial differentiation in climate and culture combined with dense population and the long-established effect of feudal policies by the Tokugawa Shogunate to perpetuate parochialism in Japanese society. Intense competition between factions is found in government offices planning for regional development. Vertically-integrated leadership and intense lateral competition, which are not successfully mixed in most countries, uniquely coexist and have assisted the rapid development of Japan especially since 1945.

Unlike Britain, the United States and the Soviet Union—which have been models for economic policy in developing countries—Japan has continued development unusally by combining modern large-scale industry, petty workshops and many very small farms. Since the Meiji era, the Government has stimulated the growth of big firms, while encouraging small firms both to render services to them and to belong to a group controlled by a big firm. Thus competition in a given industry is often more severe among groups than among firms.

Though many talented young men became central government officials, big business officials, and military officers in the pre-war period most have been active in the first two circles since 1945. Moreover, members of the central government elite are often transferred to important local government positions; they take up key posts in big companies or public corporations or they enter the political world as Ministers, Dietmen or prefectural governors. Accordingly, close interrelationships exist between central and prefectural offices and leading companies and organizations, elites of the central bureaucracy acting as the key link. These interrelationships may have been intensified by long-run government by the Liberal-Democratic Party.

Labour unions are organized, not by occupation but by companies. Thus, a strike in one company may encourage its rivals and discourage its branch or subcontracted factories. Similarly, the exodus of a firm from a major industrial area does not always result in decreased labour costs. A company, its employees, branches and subcontracted factories tends to form a 'Gemeinschaft', although this depends also upon a system of promotion by seniority, increasing salaries and retirement pensions for longer service, permanent employment and obstacles to employees' inter-firm mobility.

Location Choices by Firms in Japan

Since decisions must be made by men, not by computers alone, students of location who can 'verstehen' (in Dilthey's sense) can probably interpret firm behaviour properly. However, explanations given by Japanese firms (and often by researchers) for location decisions seem too complex to be understood adequately:[1]

Some people are convinced that problems of location are attributed to the availability of industrial sites, water and harbours. Others insist that henceforth labour, roads and airports must increase in their importance. Yet others advocate that the ability of land to support heavy weights, the availability of trunk telephone lines and lower costs of preventing or rectifying environmental disruptions are becoming the main issues. Some people feel keenly the significance of the weather, being impressed by snow damage in Hokuriku in 1963.

Some people explain that places from which Mt. Fuji[2] is visible stimulate employees' spirits, or that plants located along the Tokaido railway line can use mass-media for advertizing to boost employee morale.[3] Some businessmen think that in the largest cities the membership fee of the Chamber of Commerce and Industry is cheaper, the reputation of a firm located there is supported by the city and, because there are too many big businesses to be strictly inspected by the national tax bureau, the evasion of a tax must be easier than anywhere else. Others insist that places close to a university or to a government office are advantageous for acquiring information or specialists.[4]

Some may think that to meet future changes—such as the increased use of computers, the development of highways and new trunk railways, the automation of production the peaceful use of atomic power and the industrialization of developing countries— the present distribution of industry should be now reexamined. Yet others stress the effectiveness for regional economic development of a central factory or growth pole around which modern production may be diffused in the form of sub-contracting firms.

Each of these views contains part of the truth. To pursue such fragmentary knowledge, however, does not lead to clear systematic thought: to collect such partial knowledge is necessary but its mere accumulation may mislead one's judgment. Thus, certain Japanese regional governments constructed dams and sites for attracting industrial plants and yet, in effect, merely doubled their debts. By contrast, governments of more promising regions—which did not need to concede to firms—dangled bait which was too large and, subsequently, have become congested, run short of social facilities and suffered from public nuisances.

A systematic framework for arranging various kinds of information is necessary. Before presenting such a framework, however, the main features of Japanese corporation locational choices will be discussed, and this requires specific emphasis on the use of government help, the role of land, attention to hazards, close relations between parent and subcontracted firms, the orderly spatial evolutionary sequence of large firms and locational innovation.

(1) *The Use of Government Aid.* When a firm considers establishing a new plant anywhere, it may not only use information and advice from central and local governments or other public organizations (such as the Chamber of Commerce and Industry) but it may also demand improvement of locational conditions in an area, and so require public investment and revision of regional or urban plans. Long-term plans announced occasionally by the Government have contributed to economic growth by inspiring firms with confidence. In fact, vigorous investment by private enterprise has repeatedly made Japanese development exceed goals planned by the government.[5] This resulted in continued underestimation of tax yields which, in turn, restricted government expenditure, causing the current acute shortage of social overhead capital.

(2) *The Role of Land.* Weber excludes rent or land costs from his general location factors while recognizing it as a deglomerative force. This exclusion is right for most non-urban locations. The ratio of direct land costs to total costs for most industries is small, even in densely populated Japan[6]—contrary to the expectations of most Japanese students and government officials. However, once indirect land costs are considered, such as compensation money for farmers, fishermen or residents, land-owners' unwillingness to sell in expectation of better prices, so-called 'inhabitants' power' for protecting their community from environmental disruptions, it is often difficult for a firm to get an adequate industrial site.[7]

Land in Uchisaiwai-cho, Tokyo, owned by the Japan Broadcasting Corporation was priced at over 11 million yen per tsubo (i.e. £41,460,000 per hectare!!) by the highest bidder, Mitsubishi Estate Co. Ltd., in December 1972. Argument as to whether or not public authorities can acquire enough land in Tokyo for public use itself symbolizes both land scarcity and the appetite of big business for land.

Land reclamation has continued for centuries particularly in agriculture, where land productivity has been traditionally more critical than that of labour. Demand by industry for seashore sites has so rapidly increased with the growth of manufacturing based on imported materials and supplying overseas markets that land reclamation from the sea has had to be on a large scale and has been a critical location condition.

Eagerness by post-war central and local authorities to construct industrial areas, creating an economic miracle, has, however, been combined with a legacy of poor social infrastructure and government apathy to environmental pollution. Unfortunately, the warning by Marshall of the vital need to acquire public land[8] appears to have been forgotten by the authorities.

(3) *Attention to Hazards and Physical Environment.* The late president of Kawasaki Steel, Yataro Nishimura, provides an interesting example of the importance attached to potential disasters: in seeking a new plant site around Mizushima, he climbed a mountain to insepect damage to an old shrine and the tree shapes to assess the influence of typhoons in the area. Anxiety about specific hazards is understandably serious, especially just after their occurrence. Yet prevailing types of hazards differ spatially and seasonally: series of typhoons annually visit south-western Pacific coasts (especially southern Kyushu) in summer and early autumn, while heavy winter snow paralyses railway transport for a few weeks in some years in Hokuriku. Locally, the extent of actual disasters can vary widely. An entrepreneur from a cold north-eastern prefecture may be impressed by the warm winter climate and virile people of south-western Japan. Another, from a warm region may be impressed by the cool summer climate and hard-working people of north-eastern Japan.[9] The perception or estimation of a particular hazard or environment in a given area depends more or less

also on a decision-maker's career, personality, philosophy, interest and knowledge.[10]

(4) *Close Connections between Parent, Branch and Subcontracted Firms.* As labour unions are organized by firms, wages and working conditions are usually decided by central collective bargaining between labour and management in the firm. Thus a new branch-plant is often formed as a new, separate enterprise, especially when located in a less developed area to employ labour cheaper than in the 'parent' plant and to adjust products, technology and marketing practices. Even when located in the same area, the separate subsidiary firm can employ cheaper labour because its labour union is separate from that of the parent firm. Products are sold often through the parent company or under its brand name. Establishment of separate plants meets local approval for the economic benefits they, especially international firms, bring. Most small businesses are subcontractors and subordinate to large firms: the former have to be located generally in reference to the locations of the latter, and vice versa. Branches located at greater distances from parent firms tend to become separate subsidiary firms and those located nearer parent firms tend to become subcontracting plants.

(5) *The Orderly Location Sequence in the Evolution of Multi-Plant Firms.* The Japanese island chain extends so far distance-wise that, *ceteris paribus*, a firm will probably locate its first plant somewhere in central Japan, the Pacific Coast Belt or the Tokaido Megalopolis. If a firm requires only one plant to satisfy demand it will generally locate in Keihin or Hanshin. Once the firm expands and requires branches, its spatial diffusion is fairly predictable: a firm with one plant in, say, Kansai is likely to place its second one in Kanto, *ceteris paribus*. This *ceteris paribus* condition is, of course, unrealistic. A small firm producing and selling a product with a high price-elasticity of demand and with limited transportability will channel its efforts into securing and maintaining a certain, often peripheral, section of, and will not necessarily locate centrally in, the entire national market.[11] Agglomerative advantages may attract the firm to, and disadvantages may repel the firm from, the Belt Areas or Tokaido Megalopolis.

The core cities of the largest metropolitan area, accounted in 1968 for nearly one half of the number of depots of, and about 78 per cent of, the sales by large-scale wholesalers. Those with medium and small scales were more dispersed. However, different regional growth rate patterns occurred in wholesale sales during three periods. During 1960–64 rates were higher than the national average only in the core cities of major metropolitan areas and in the larger-sized regional cities. During 1964–66, regional cities achieved the highest rates. Between 1966 and 1969, cities around the largest metropolitan areas and local cities experienced higher growth rates. Such data on the timing of the opening and location of new establishments by wholesalers lead us to the conclusion that big wholesalers 'opened their branches first in Tokyo, Osaka and Nagoya ..., then selected larger regional central cities ... and recently have placed stress on local core and other cities'.[12]

(6) *Locational Innovation.* Innovations in the Schumpeterian sense can be spatial as well as non-spatial. In a repidly growing economy, those firms which adopt an active attitude get larger gains or suffer smaller losses than firms with fainthearted policies, *ex post facto.* They are also more likely to be 'locational innovators', an example is Kawasaki Steel. It was once firmly believed that Japan had excessive capacity and that industrial development would be confined to inland sites. That today most Japanese heavy industries—steel, engineering and chemicals—occupy seaside sites largely results from the innovative decision of President Nishiyama of Kawasaki Steel[13] to build its first furnace at Chiba on Tokyo Bay in 1953. Success stimulated other firms e.g., Yawata (now Nippon) Steel to follow suit, leading to industrialization of Tokyo Bay and subsequently many other coastal areas around Japan. The same innovativeness is evident in Case Study B in establishing industry in an underdeveloped region, Kyushu.

The Framework for Understanding Locational Choices

Location Conditions

Place is predicted by a definite position, area and other physical and cultural properties. Those characteristics of a place which exert an influence different from those in other places are termed 'location conditions'. Some location conditions—position or distance—can be continuously different. Others—climate or topography—can be similar over relatively large areas and quite different between areas, even though micro-climate or topography can vary greatly from place to place. What the local conditions are depend not only on place and on time, but on what is being located. Usually in Japan, the term 'location condition' refers to location requisites for the project being located or for the locator (entrepreneur choosing a location): the term is used in this chapter in both these meanings. Location conditions can be changed intentionally, gradually or suddenly by firms or their activities. To deepen a harbour and reclaim the foreshore is intentional, planned change of location conditions. Ground subsidence from excessive use of underground water by factories or office buildings is an example of gradual change.

Before selecting a location, an entrepreneur will, or should, undertake research into location conditions and attempt to discover their probable or possible effects on his proposed plant. Most conditions, however, cannot be quantified; yet the locator has to compare data for alternative places and evaluate them. Such evaluation is either economic or non-economic. If a location is chosen in a cold, snowy area, plant investment costs are higher because of the need for stronger building materials and heating facilities; temporary stoppages of transport as a result of heavy snow may raise operating costs which can be diminished only by larger expenditure on company housing and warehousing near the plant and product warehousing near the market. Yet costs of maintaining quality in materials or products and for air-conditioning are lower at this type of location. Favourable or not, these effects are reflected in costs and revenues. The same may be said for any condition, hence a particular condition is usually related to various factors—and vice versa. Moreover, as Aoki (1959), Esawa (1954), Isard (1956), Greenhut (1956), and Moses (1958) have shown, there are substitutions between location factors. Accordingly, a survey of location conditions does not necessarily mean a survey of location factors. Most items in such surveys are *conditions* rather than *factors* of location; and a particular condition does not correspond exactly or exclusively to a particular factor.

Non-economic evaluation is significant either for entrepreneurs who seek psychic satisfaction or a means of entering the political arena or for non-profit-seeking organizations. No firm can neglect economic evaluation if it wishes to survive in the long run.

Location Factors[14]

Location factors may also be economic or non-economic. The former are economic advantages or disadvantages, to which the latter cannot be reduced. Political considerations are often important when a foreign firm or advanced nation wishes to locate a new plant in the developing world. Even so, once politics has defined the region, responsible persons may attempt to place the plant most effectively within the region. The disposal of industrial waste can be restricted by government in the interests of public welfare; private enterprises will thus locate plants where total costs, including transport costs of waste, charges for using public facilities to prevent environmental pollution, and local taxes, will be minimized—or, rather, where the excess of total revenues, including local subsidies, over total costs will be maximized.[15] Although good climate and landscape may be non-economic *per se*, they add to or save costs, affecting demand for air-conditioning, raising productivity and attracting a large and better labour, influencing turnover.

Entrepreneurs, especially of smaller firms, frequently locate production in their native town: some consider this to be an uneconomic or irrational choice.[16] Some researchers believe the entrepreneur's main aim is the psychological satisfaction of 'returning home loaded with honour'. Ability, funds and time are usually too limited for small firms to do locational research well. An unsuccessful location will have large, long-run adverse effects on the firm, its employees and the owner's family life. To avoid this and to secure stable profits, the entrepreneur seeks a rational way to locate a plant in his town. Friends or relatives may assist him in acquiring technical know-how, a line of production, a plant site, funds materials, labour and customers. Although clear differentiation of both economic and non-economic factors is very difficult in practice, there are limits to the spatial margins within which a firm can survive in an economically competitive world if its entrepreneur takes non-economic factors into conderation.

Entrepreneurial Objectives

Generally, economists believe that business firms aim at achieving maximum profits. Some, however, prefer stable profits but others may aim at increasing their market share or monopolistic power, or at overthrowing rivals; such objectives do not necessarily contradict the attainment of maximum profits. Yet a real-life decision-maker is not only a businessman or an official, but also a husband and family member. Thus, he may take family welfare as well as profits into account. Owners of small firms usually seek a plant site within their families' action spaces. Even in larger firms the personality, career, preference or human relations of a responsible person may influence location choice.

In Japan, a person in charge of selecting a new plant location frequently becomes its manager, often with able subordinate personnel from the parent firm. A decision-maker should thus be concerned with human satisfaction because this indirectly affects his, and his firm's, success. Some entrepreneurs, in making location decisions, will consider the future possibilities of, or need for, diversifying or converting their activities at a proposed site, and possible capital gains, loans secured for land, and even the profit to be gained by reselling the site.[17]

Locational Adjustment

An entrepreneur makes a location decision with imperfect information and ability in conditions of risk or uncertainty. His goal is neither necessarily singular, nor purely economic. Short- and long-run objectives may not be identical. Even if the objective definitely is maximum profits, precise prediction of costs and especially revenues is difficult, often impossible, because of limited funds, time and information. Moreover, the optimum will shift as location conditions change.

Thus locational adjustment or adaptation will probably have to be made after the opening of a new plant, and in one or a combination of the following ways: changes in product prices; changes in operation levels and capacity; modernization or scrapping of equipment; product diversification; conversion of plant to new uses; the establishment, closure, integration or disintegration of branch-plants, branch-offices and warehouses; improvement of location conditions; intensification of after-sales servicing or advertising; forming a group of branch or subcontracted firms; amalgamation with, or takeover of, other firms or plants.

Relationships between Location Conditions, Location Factors and Stages in Selecting a Location

Location decisions made by firms are influenced by many elements: their history; scale; the number of locations of established plants; capital resources; the ability and personality of top managers; attitudes towards and of competitors, contractors, labour unions and communities; government policies; the general economic situation. However, in principle, decisions usually involve three stages: (1) choice of market area in which to sell the product; (2) choice of area from which shipments to market is desirable or competitive; (3) selection of a site. In practice, the number of stages and range of markets may vary with different industries, firms or plants, and with time: this is a neglected field in which studies on location theory, economic geography, business administration, industrial organization and economic development should be combined. Principal locational factors also vary with each stage.

Post-War Industrial Distribution in Japan

The spatial pattern of post-war Japanese industrial development has varied among three periods: recovery (1945–50), consolidation (1950–55) and expansion (1955–65).[18] Figure 19.2 summarizes the changing regional shares in the value of Japanese manufacturing output.

Economic Recovery, 1945–50

In World War II Japan lost nearly 45 per cent of her territories (cf. 1919), 30 per cent of her industrial equipment, 70 per cent of her ships and housing for nine million people. Repatriation of Japanese from abroad and a high birth rate increased the population by 22 per cent (16 million) from 1945 to 1955. Despite material shortages, inflation, disrupted transport and abandoned land, improvement came gradually. This resulted from American aid following intensification of the 'cold war', the use of concealed and hoarded goods, democratic reforms (including the establishment of labour unions, status improvements for women, dissolution of the Zaibatsu, the

496

revitalization of leaders by the purge and agricultural land reform) and increased harnessing of national resources.

Numbers of plants and industrial workers in 1945 equalled those of the late 1920s. Five prefectures, including three of the largest industrial areas, contained 43·4 per cent of all industrial labour—but this proportion was the lowest since 1909. Mining and manufacturing output did not exceed 30 per cent of that in 1934–36. Superficially, interregional dispersion of industries occurred because in most larger industrial centres, heavy industrial production was paralysed by war damage and material shortages, while consumer's goods production began in plants evacuated in wartime to areas where foods and raw materials were relatively abundant. However, recovery of major industrial regions was stimulated, first by the 'priority production system' to raise production of coal, steel and fertilizers and second, by the grant of permission by the General Headquarters of the Allied Forces to increase the numbers of spindles in the textile industries and to reopen refineries along the Pacific coast.

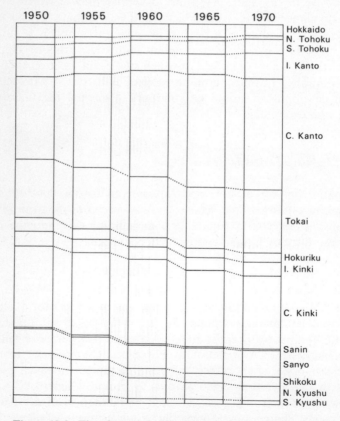

Figure 19.2. The changes in the regional shares of the value of Japanese manufacturing production shipped, 1950–70.

497

Consolidation, 1950–55

This period saw the construction and rationalization of production. Major stimuli were the military production boom associated with the Korean conflict (1950), the cold war, the consumption boom, vigorous investment (1951–52), the signing of the San Francisco Treaty (1951) and deflation and credit contraction (1953–54). Further stimuli were: the import of foreign capital and technology (especially in the steel, electronics and petroleum refining industries), the establishment of the Japan Development Bank (1951), the growth of government investment, the return of authorized reparation factories and the mitigation of the anti-trust laws.

Pre-war primary industrial regions regained their vigour through investment in rebuilding and rationalizing plants. As industrial activity increased, the need for establishing or improving infrastructure, especially roads and ports, became acute. The problem of rationalizing coal production arose as petroleum imports expanded. Significant changes began in the former four leading industrial regions. The economies of northern Kyushu, dominated by coal-mining and steel industries and dependent upon continental Asian raw materials and markets, and Hanshin, which depended heavily on textiles and Asian markets, began to decline. By contrast, growth occurred in Chukyo and Keihin, replacing Hanshin as the leading industrial area. Southern Kyushu became the least developed region, and unemployment increased. These processes, however, reduced inter-prefectural differentials in *per capita* income. The east gained predominance over the west.

Economic Expansion, 1955–65

The year 1955 'no longer belonged to the post-war period' (Economic White Paper, 1965 edition), because marked increases in exports to booming world markets induced 'quantity expansion' without inflation. From mid-1956, a capital investment boom ushered in a period of vigorous technical innovation, increased scale of production and equipment modernization leading to rapid industrial growth and diversification. Some firms making and rolling steel integrated vertically with other firms producing pig iron; others developed petrochemical industrial complexes, or *Kombinato*. They were located in coastal industrial areas to serve markets, procure raw materials and exploit limited reclaimed flat land. Yet others concentrated on components manufacturing for, or assembly of, machinery and vehicles and located principally inland, but in or near existing industrial regions of the Pacific Coast Belt. *Per capita* income differentials widened, especially between the industrial and agricultural prefectures, stimulating a major 'national' population migration, particularly toward the Tokaido Megalopolis. Yet the shares of the national value of manufacturing products shipped by the three major industrial regions began to stagnate in the early

1960s. The causes were scarcities of land and water, congestion of roads and harbours, increased industrial pollution and a growing preference (especially among machinery firms) for locating in areas neighbouring the already established industrial areas.

Location Policy in Japan

Location policy did not evolve in Japan until the early 1950s. Yet embryonic controls had existed earlier. City Planning and Street Architecture Acts (1919) restricted certain sizes and types of firms to zoned industrial areas, while permitting clusters of congested houses and stores around factories. In and after 1917 the ten Ministry of Agriculture and Commerce encouraged 'rural industries' to use resources and labour to relieve poverty in rural areas. Following successive disasters in Tohoku—crop failures (1931–34), tidal waves (1932) and flood (1935)—a Board of Inquiry for Promoting Tohoku was established in 1934 to study industries suited to conditions in Tohoku. The Tohoku Kogyo Company (later the Tohoku Industrial Promotion Company Ltd.) and Tohoku Power Development Company were set up in 1936 on the lines of the T.V.A.; by 1945, the former company had investments in 91 companies and directly managed 22 concerns.

Success in 1934 by the Kure Naval Dockyard in Hiroshima Prefecture in buying components from small factories in Kochi Prefecture stimulated the then Ministry of Commerce and Industry to establish in 1935 a Rural Industrialization Committee. It subsidized local governments in encouraging subcontracting factories to their areas; but in 1939 it announced that industrial dispersion to rural areas would (1) benefit national defence, (2) contribute to solving population and health problems and (3) promote rural development. By a simple application of Alfred Weber's theory, the committee selected types of industries suitable for rural areas.

In 1945–46 the Land Plan Basic Policy and Land Recovery Plan Outline were introduced. These were concerned with conversion of plant from military to peace-time production, and reconstruction of basic industrial production (such as fertilizers, coal and steel). However, the inadequate planning controls of this period affected long-term land use in Japan: once invested, capital determined future investments through its immobility and generation of agglomerative economies. It is difficult though to see how the government could have worked out a plan for the proper location of industry under the industrial limitation policy of the allied occupation forces that then operated.

Regional planning emerged from the work of the Comprehensive Land Development Council which was created in 1949 under the Economic Stabilization Board (the present Economic Planning Agency). Plans for the Nation and 22 Specified Areas were drawn up by central government, the Regional and Prefectural Plans by local governments and aimed at optimizing industrial location. But insufficient funds, executive decentralization of capital and parochialism existing in government agencies limited their success. However, the Hokkaido Development Agency was established within the Prime Minister's Office to coordinate and finance development. Separate treatment of Hokkaido was deemed essential because of its different history, its lower population density and its larger land reserves, and to develop effective communication channels between the central and Hokkaido prefectural governments.[19]

During this resource-development period, many government officials neglected the location problem and concentrated on using domestic resources because of severely restricted overseas trade.

Industrial location policy was finally systematized in the expansion (1955–65). Growth demanded industrial rationalization. Ministry of International Trade and Industry (MITI) began research into sites suitable for factories and in 1958 established in Industrial Location Guidance Centre. Laws to regulate industrial water use and land subsidence, to modernize harbours and airports, to construct roads and to develop the national capital region followed. Demands to stimulate development in peripheral areas were voiced by their local governments successfully: Development Promotion Acts were introduced for Tohoku (1957). Kyushu (1959), Shikoku (1960), Hokuriku (1960) and Chugoku (1961) and new enterprises there were financed by loans from the Regional Finance Division of the Japan Development Bank. Money from property taxes was used by local governments also to attract factory development. Although called the 'Belt Area' period, such policies did not formalize the 'Belt Areas' concept.

That came in 1960. Government experts had begun to question the resource-development programme and the low developmental efficiency of regional investment especially in remote areas. People in peripheral areas objected strongly to concentration of industry in the Belt Areas. In the latter regions people were equally dissatisfied with the constant shortage of social overhead capital. To meet these objections, the Plan for Doubling National Income was adopted by the Government in December 1960. Recognizing the failure of public investment to keep up with private investment, it sought to: (1) allow the Belt Areas with large markets, suitable industrial bases, subcontracting businesses, closely linked industries, spare land and water and the most efficient social overhead investment to be prominent in industrial location during the plan period, 1961–70; (2) prohibit or restrict new industrial concentration in the four old major industrial areas; (3) provide medium-sized new industrial districts in intermediate areas of the Belt region; (4) invest intensively between 1967 and 1980 in peripheral regions to create an industrialization basis there. This is the 'Pacific Belt Areas Plan'.

A vigorous protest movement developed against the plan in thirty non-

Belt prefectures in the belief that interregional income differentials would further increase. Consequently, the policy of 'channelled investment' early on in the Belt (1961–67) and later on in the underdeveloped areas (1967–70) was modified to one of parallel development in regions and regional growth poles, in a new National Comprehensive Development Plan (1962), i.e. of balanced development among regions.

In practice, the nation was divided into three regional categories: (1) the 'over-congested regions', where policy aimed at redevelopment; (2) the 'adjustment regions' which were not crowded and were outside the major three industrial centres, but which could enjoy external economies from those centres: policy there aimed at improving infrastructure to facilitate industrial dispersal from the over-congested areas and to foster medium-size cities as large industrial or regional development centres; (3) in the remaining 'underdeveloped regions' policy aimed at establishing basic public facilities to stimulate industrial development in both large- and medium-scale cities or growth poles which were selected for their higher investment efficiency and potentially greater trickling-down effects on the surrounding regions. Regions were to be developed with cities or areas as nuclei and were to be connected nationally by high speed transport net works—a strategy called 'nuclei development'.

The most important factor shaping the nuclei was government subsidy of development under the Law for Promoting the Establishment of new Industrial Towns (1962). 'An unprecedented petition battle' and a 'battle in the name of regional development' developed among 44 applicant areas in 39 prefectures, most of which had plans to attract steel or petrochemical refineries. Ultimately, 15 new industrial towns were designated. Six areas considered suitable for large-scale industrial development in the adjustment regions were designated as special areas under the Law for Promoting Designate Industrial Development Areas (1964). A research-scientific city constructed at the foot of Mt. Tsukuba was acknowledged in a cabinet meeting (1964) to be for the purpose of removing governmental institutions and universities from Tokyo. By October 1963, some 300 plants had been located in the 96 designated areas which covered about 20 per cent of Japan. Moreover, special policies for coal-mining areas, introduced and modified from 1955, succeeded in developing industrial estates, retraining labour and facilitating migration of unemployed to other regions to such an extent that from 1962 the problems confronting coal-producing areas shifted from general unemployment to either labour shortages in coal mines or persistent unemployment among older miners.

Case Studies [20]

(A) *Aichi Tokei Denki (Aichi Clocks and Electric Equipment Manufacturing Ltd.)*

(reported by Mr. Ryiochi Takajashi, Chief of the Planning Section, on 2nd October 1964, in Nagoya City)

The head office, equipment factory and woodworking shop of the firm are located in Nagoya City, with branch sales offices in nine principal cities. About 40 per cent of production comprises water-supply meters, which are sold to water-supply bureaux in many cities, and about 23 per cent clocks and 15 per cent gas meters marketed throughout Japan.

As the present site is congested, another location was required for a new factory to meet the expansion needs of the firm. In December 1963 the President defined for the managing director the principles that should govern location choice:

(1) an available site of 20,000 tsubo (i.e. about 66,000 m^2 or 16·3 acres), the same as the present site;
(2) suitability for expanding machinery and tools production;
(3) the site must be located, within a radius of 90 minutes by car from the parent factory, in Aichi, Gifi or Mie Prefectures.

A temporary committee headed by the managing director was established in February 1964 and empowered to report by March 1964. Directors from head office and some departmental managers became committee members. The manager of the General Affairs Department and the chief of Planning managed the committee's official work.

Prior to receiving the President's basic principles, the chief planner had collected research materials and advised him on general plant location ideas. Two days after the committee's first meeting, on 11th February, he visited the Research Department of Nagoya Chamber of Commerce and Industry for information about plant location in Aichi Prefecture and also prefectural and central government offices with industrial location interests. He visited several companies to hear how they had recently selected or negotiated new plant locations. On 14th and 15th February, he visited the Section for commerce, Manufacturing and Sightseeing in Gifu and the Headquarters for Comprehensive Development in Mie to hear opinions there on plant location and to obtain data. Finally at the Industrial Location Section of the Nagoya Bureau of International Trade and Industry he learned for the first time of the Law Concerning Research of Factory Location, under which MITI collects detailed data and selects 'suitable sites for factories'. Those who wish to look at the data can do so. In placing a plant at a suitable site on agricultural land, smooth conversion from agricultural to industrial use is expected; elsewhere, conversion could be difficult. Although he had thought that enterprises could select a location freely, he found that firms establishing plants with more than 9,000 m^2 area or 3,000 m^2 floor-space size had to report previously to the MITI.

At the committee's second meeting (18th February) the chief planner proposed selection of a location in three consecutive stages: the selection of communities (cities, towns or villages); selection of sites; final decision.

Seven criteria for selecting communities were agreed: that sites should (1) exceed 15,000 tsubo (46,500 m^2) in area; (2) cost less than 4,000 yen per tsubo (approx. £490 per acre); (3) be within 45 minutes by rail of Nagoya station; (4) be within 3 miles of a national or prefectural road; (5) be within two miles of electricity grid supplies; (6) not be exposed to risks of damage by water; (7) be located inland, not near the coast. The firm's committee approved these criteria. From data obtained in the Industrial Location Section of the Bureaux, the chief planner listed suitable sites in the three prefectures, marking them zero for success or X for failure for each criterion. The list was presented to the Committee on 28th February and 12 communities in seven areas were chosen from 105 communities in fifteen areas after assessing their location conditions, particulaly labour (junior high school-leavers), electricity supplies and commuting conditions.

More detailed criteria for selecting sites were established: eleven major items, mostly subdivided into two, three or four items. From these criteria, locational conditions of each community were estimated with scores of 2, 1, 0, −1, and −2, using data from offices in the 12 communities. On this basis 18 sites in seven communities were chosen. Between 18th and 24th March all committee members inspected and gave scores to each site. Eleven sites in five communities were picked at the 25th March meeting. Each committee member was asked to select the best three from eleven sites, stating the reasons. Most chose Oka in Okazaki City, Aichi Prefecture, as the best. The firm thus asked the Okazaki city office to secure the site for it. A final report was made to the firm's President on 12th April. He inspected personally the three best sites with top executive staff. On 20th May, the firm officially chose Oka as the location, on condition that Okazaki City would meet the company's requirements regarding payment for the land and road provision. The city fulfilled these requirements and the firm built its new factory on the site.

(B) *Kyushu Matsushita Denki KK (Kyushu Matsushita Electric Co. Ltd.)*
(reported by Hiroji Aonuma, Managing Director, on 15th April 1965, in Fukuoka City)

The managing director came to Kyushu with his company to spend the rest of his life. He had considered that, outside the central industrial areas, Kyushu was superior to Tohoku, Hokuriku and Sanin which are covered with snow for four months of the year, lack sunshine and are separated by sea from the centrally-located Main Island (Honshu). Kyushu is contiguous with Honshu, reached via tunnels, and warm enough for a plant to operate at almost constant conditions throughout the year. Distance from central areas, like Hanshin, is not a problem because the company exports its products.

The director thought that even private companies should help to restrict over-congestion in Keihin, Hanshin and Chukyo by locating in less developed areas. This would benefit both public welfare and firms by avoiding land and labour shortages and by optimizing plant size.

He considered it undersirable for one gigantic plant or group of plants to be localized in one region and produce many products. Specialized production at optimum scale is ideal in his view and decentralized evolution in accord with the principle of 'proper production in the proper place'. The director stated that, when he came to Fukuoka City in 1955, influential political and economic circles asked him to locate a plant there. The firm, however, spent much time deciding whether or not to locate in Kyushu, mainly because little manufacturing existed there. He stated that some entrepreneurs considered that electrical appliance manufacture had little growth prospect in Kyushu. Thus related firms, which could cooperate with the firm, did not exist. The management decided to introduce, therefore, integrated production within its own Kyushu plant. Even so, it had then to spend nearly five years encouraging components suppliers to come to Kyushu, but now 25 factories subcontract from, and 70 others are supplied by, Kyushu Matsushita Electric.

Kyushu has abundant labour, the people are honest and hardworking. The director thought that to start a new enterprise in Kyushu was very risky— it would be safer in Tokyo or Osaka—but if a firm succeeded in maintaining modern industry in Kyushu, local people would gain a good reputation and companies from all over Japan may revise their perception of the area. The director stressed that he and his firm were proud to be successful pioneers in Kyushu. He observed that it was more difficult for a firm located outside Kyushu to establish a branch in Kyushu: it would be better for firms (and for Kyushu) if they located their head offices in Kyushu, where his was, in Fukuoka City, because this would ease administration which in Japan is costly and impairs firms' international competitiveness.

The management of Kyushu Matsushita Electric thought of locating several specialized factories of optimum scale in appropriate areas of Kyushu. Instructions were received from the parent company, Matsushita Denki (Matsushita Electric Industrial Co. Ltd.), to establish a new plant to produce solely for export. The firm built a test-plant near Tosu City, Saga, to foster an internationally competitive factory run by able managers, because 'to meet demand, it may be necessary to establish our plants overseas in, say, Sydney or Hamburg. In establishing Tosu Plant, therefore, we collected and arranged data involved there in a manner suitable generally for decisions relating to the establishment of overseas branches. After the Tosu plant was opened, we built another branch in Sadohara, Miyazaki'.[21]

(C) *Kawasaki Seitetsu KK (Kawasaki Steel Corporation)*
(reported by Mr. Nobuo Shimizu, Director and Sub-manager of Mizushima Plant, on 10th December 1965, in Hiroshima City)

The company originated in Kansai,[22] but a plant was built in Chiba in 1945 to supply Kanto. Until 1950, Kansai was ahead of Kanto in industrial growth, but the situation is now reversed. In 1906 the company built a plant in Kobe where shipyards provided a market for steel products. At present the Hyogo, Fukiai (both in Kobe) and Nishinomiya plants supply Kansai, Chiba supplies Kanto, and Chita supplies Chukyo.

However, a major competitor, Fuji Seitetsu (later combined with Yawata Seitetsu into Shin Nippon Seitetsu, i.e. Nippon Steel Corporation) had plants in Muroran, Kamaishi and Hirohata, all far from central markets. Fuji Seitetsu thus planned to establish Tokai Seitetsu (later integrated into Fuji and then Nippon) in Nagoya, aiming at Chukyo markets. Production, concentrated in (and near) Yahata and using raw materials from the Asian continent in the pre-war era, was to be located in Sakai to serve the Osaka market and in Kimitsu for Kanto. Each company sought a market-oriented location for new plant.

Taking the company's (Kawasaki's) established plant locations into account, attention was first focused on Suruga Bay, especially around Shimizu, and then Atsumi Bay, especially Toyohashi. There were, however, some site disadvantages: heavy indemnification for fisheries, gravel strata which would make it expensive to dig a waterway for ore carriers of 100,000 tons, and a lack of flat land. The firm investigated Chugoku and Tsurusaki, but finally reduced the alternatives to Mizushima and Matsunaga both in Chugoku.

Company officials then went to the Ministry of Transportation to ask whether an ore carrier of 100,000 tons could enter the Seto Inland Sea. The head of Transportation Bureau emphasized that vessels of more than twelve metres draft, or an ore carrier of more than 35,000 tons, could not enter Seto Inland Sea. He went on to say, 'It may be well for Governor Miki of Okayama Prefecture to say that he will make a port with 16 metres depth, in order to advertize. The State, however, can never take responsibility for his statement'.[23] Thus executives thought again of expanding Chiba Plant, but also had the pilots of Kawasaki ships doing research throughout the Inland Sea. In the end they concluded that a 100,000 ton class ore carrier could enter the Sea. Matsunaga was ideal, being sheltered from wind, but her flat areas were too small to accommodate future expansion of a proposed new plant. So Mizushima was chosen. Kansai is the nearest market for the new plant. Considering its abilities to supply intermediate products to the parent plant and, in the future, to others along the Seto Inland Sea and to export, Mizushima was regarded as most favourable.

(D) *Tohoku Toyo Gomu KK (Tohoku Toyo Rubber Co. Ltd.)*
(reported by Mr. Masafumi Gyoten, Manager of Manufacturing
Department, on 21 March 1966, in Sendai City)

This company mass produces standard rubber tyres for the domestic
market. The parent company, Toyo Gomu Kogyo (Toyo Rubber Co. Ltd.) in
Osaka, which grew and was separated from Toyo Hoseki (Toyobo Co. Ltd.),
predicted that a new plant would be required about 1965 to meet increased
demand in Japan for automobiles. Six makers of rubber tyres were located
in Kobe or Yokohama, including the parent company. Automobile assem-
blers—Nissan, Isuzu and Prince—are located, however, near Tokyo, though
Toyota is near Nagoya and Toyo Kogyo in in Hiroshima. Toyo Gomu has
several plants, but only two produce automobile tyres in Kansai. It was
desirable, therefore, to build a third tyre plant in Kanto. People from
the branch office in Tokyo, for which the manager was then working,
examined the Kanto area. At the time, land prices were increasing rapidly,
but as the firm could not meet the prices demanded of some landowners,
no decision was taken.

The firm was then invited by Iwanuma Town, Miyagi Prefecture, to locate
a plant there. Analysis showed such a location to be suitable. As Governor
Miura of Miyagi Prefecture advised, and many other people requested,
Toyo Gomu Kogyo established the new plant as a separate company to
become a 'home-town firm'. However, its products are identical to those of
the parent company that markets the output of the Tohoku branch company.

The manager then discussed the major location conditions: transportation, related or subcontracting firms, schools, distributive organization,
labour, commuting, electricity, the prevention of public nuisances and
finance.

(E) *Tokai Seitetsu KK (Tokai Iron and Steel Corporation, later
integrated into Fuji Seitesu and finally into Shin Nippon
Seitetsu, i.e., Nippon Steel Corporation)*
(reported by Mr. Makoto Ohgaki, Manager of Productive Equipment
Department, and formerly Fuji's Sub-Manager of Construction Department, in June, probably 1960)

In selecting a plant location, the choice of area comes first. Though various
conditions—market, material sources, water, transportation, including sea-
ways, geology, topography, climate and labour—were considered, the
market factor is of overriding importance, judging from increased
dependence upon raw material imports. Such a location, however, is
necessarily expensive because of city congestion. Accordingly the firm sought
a location with land reclaimed from the sea. Southern Nagoya was finally

506

chosen because its ground geology and water supply were better than those of Yokkaichi or Kuwana.

(F) *Nihon Kogyo KK (Nippon Mining Co. Ltd.)*
    (reported by Mr. Sakae Hashimoto, Head of the temporary Office for Constructing Mizushima Plant, in June, probably 1961)

In 1946 the company required a site suitable for its second petroleum refinery. Management examined, in order, Yokkaichi, Iwakuni, Osaka, Kure, Komatsujima, Tobata and Mizushima. Finally, only in 1959 was it decided to build a plant in Mizushima. In selecting a location, the whole country was divided into eastern and western oil product markets along the western boundaries of Shizuoka, Negano and Niigata Prefectures. Since total and *per capita* demand for oil products in the west exceeds that in the east, the company decided to locate first in the west. The main locational conditions considered by the firm were the depth of sea, coast line, railways, roads, site area, ground, weather, tidal and other marine features, industrial water, electricity, sites, and facilities for the employees' welfare. Minor items were the availability of materials for construction, including sand and ballast (gravel), local labour supply, local regulations for attracting plants, cooperation provided by regions or communities, fees or charges for the use of sea-surface, roads, rivers and other considerations such as hotels for foreign vistors.

(G) *Oita Prefectural Government*
    (reported by Mr. Masharu Yamaguchi, Vice-Director of the Tokyo Office of Oita Prefectural Government, in June 1961)

In 1959, Mr. Masaharu Yamaguchi was placed by Oita Prefectural Government in an office in Tokyo to work exclusively on inducing plants to come into the prefecture, especially into the Oita-Tsurusaki industrial estate sited on land reclaimed from the sea. He succeeded in bringing in a refinery and persuading Fuji Seitetsu to establish a new plant. Subsequently, Oita Prefecture decided to meet central government demands for dispersing new factories to less developed areas to reduce interregional income differentials. Successes were achieved for three major reasons. Stated in the vice-director's words, 'these were first, "heaven-sent chance"; second, natural advantages; and third, the unity of men. A famous strategist in old China stated that heaven-sent chances are less valuable than natural advantages; natural advantages are less valuable than the unity of men!'.

At first, Prefectural officials went to the Industrial Location Guidance Centre of MITI to study trends in investment by industries and prefectures. They concluded that although investment was vigorous nationally, new firms would hardly come to an area as distant from major markets as Oita. Nevertheless, the decision to attract industry was timely because it coincided with the economic boom. Demand for petroleum increased rapidly as the energy shift quickened from coal to oil. Iron and steel industries expected to produce 48 million tons in 1970: in fact, they produced 93 million tons. Attempts to induce firms to locate plants in Oita Prefecture, therefore, matched many firms' expansion needs and searches for new plant sites.

The major natural advantage of Oita is extensive costal land—about 5 million tsubo (16,500 hectares)—available for industry. This offset disadvantages of distance to central markets. The area, however, does lie along the Seto Inland Sea and is nearer than the northern Kyushu industrial region for interaction with Kanto. Moreover, the Oita–Tsurusaki area still has access to abundant water and harbour facilities: such areas are becoming rare in Japan. The vice-director also stressed the merits of safety from typhoons (being sheltered by the Saganozeki Peninsula) and proximity to the famous spa, Beppu. According to him, the firms' officials worried about possible damage by typhoons because the decision to attract industry was taken just after seashore damage around Nagoya by the Isewan Typhoon.

Cooperation—the 'unity of men'—in organization is necessary to attract factories. The director and vice-director worked hand in glove with the Committee of Attracting Factories, related Ministries (especially MITI) and leading persons from Oita Prefecture who now live in Tokyo. He stressed that, in his experience, local planners or promoters should pay careful attention to the merits or demerits of their own areas. For example, since companies like to locate along railway lines to advertize themselves, he suggested that local governments had better attempt to attract companies to lower-priced land near transportation nodes. Companies also liked good land prices, electricity supply, roads, harbours, railway sidings, labour, favourable local regulations and political conditions, good relations between Prefecture and City, and educational facilities. Firms investigated matters which directly impinged upon the Prefecture, its laws and infrastructures: compensation for the loss of fisheries through pollution, water supply for industry and availability of land for industrial uses.

In negotiating with a firm, the following points had to be kept in mind by Prefecture officials: (1) an office or officials in charge of attracting factories to an area *had* to be located in Tokyo; (2) to keep a matter secret is very important, otherwise inter-area competition for attracting factories induced land speculation and attempts to raise indemnities for fisheries; (3) it is advisable to utilize the industrial location service of the MITI.

As the late Professor Hiroshi Sato of the department of economic geography, Hitotsubashi University, said when he saw monkeys at Mt. Takasaki in Oita Prefecture, 'the problem of how to attract industrial plants is similar to that of attracting monkeys: if one monkey of a group is attracted, the matter will be settled!'.

508

Notes

1. Nishioka (1966b), pp. 92–3; Nishioka (1968), pp. 3–4.
2. More generally, scenic beauty. One of the main reasons why the founder of Asahi Chemical Industry Co. Ltd. decided to locate a plant in Nobeoka was, according to some publications by the company, 'purple hills and crystal streams'.
3. When Mr. Riichi Ezaki of Ezaki Glico Co. Ltd. (confectioner) sought a plant location, Mitejima and Kanzaki, both in Osaka City, were the two final alternatives. Though land price and construction costs were lower at the Kanzaki site, he finally chose the Mitejima site which was on railroads and, accordingly, *at which advertisement costs could be decreased by four-fifths;* see Nihon Keizai Shimbun, Ltd., 1964, Vol. 20, pp. 49–58. This type of advertisement effect may be less significant in most European countries. At least at some time in pre-war London, however, developers seemed to place the stress on the 'publicity value of arterial road sites'; see Martin (1964), p. 138.
4. President Masaru Ibuka of Sony Corporation, established a plant for manufacturing magnetic tapes near Sendai, to keep in close contact with the Metal Materials Institute of Tohuku University, Sendai; see Nihon Keizai Shimbun Ltd., 1963, Vol. 18, p. 366. The establishment of a company for manufacturing precision machinery in 1937 by Mr. Soichiro Honda was related to the existence of a good college of industrial technology in Hamamatsu. At that time he was striving to learn how to manufacture piston rings and went to school to learn it. On the other hand, an auto-bicycle assembly plant of Honda Motor Co. Ltd. was established at Kami-Jujo in Tokyo in 1950, according to him, to stimulate his originality in an exciting large city environment. See Nihon Keizai Shimbun Ltd., 1962, Vol. 17, pp. 271–3, 283.

A senior high school owned by the Soni Atsugi School Juridical Persons is attached to the Atsugi Plant of Sony, in Kanagawa Prefecture. The school and its dormitory, combined with the name value of Sony, seems to attract girls from all parts of Japan and to reduce their turnover. The company sometimes pays school fees on behalf of students working for the company, in order to retain young labourers, despite increasing labour shortages in the area.

Japanese parents are so eager for school education for their children that many owners of small firms are likely to select a plant site within a certain radius not only of their homes but also of their children', schools. Even big business leaders have to take into consideration the existence of good schools, and universities, in order to secure able staff and maintain their families in a particular place.

5. Many scholars and central government officials were repeatedly misled into setting too low a value not only on the growth potentiality of Japanese economy but also on that of the Belt Areas, because of their lack of knowledge of location theory and practice. See also Nishioka (1965b; 1967). For example, the Design for the Proper Distribution of Industry, announced in 1961 by the Ministry of International Trade and Industry (MITI), conceived that the share for, say, Coastal Kanto in the national value of manufacturing products shipped would decline from 25·2 per cent in 1958 to 18·5 per cent in 1970 and for Kyushu would rise from 7·7 per cent to 8·0 per cent. It would be interesting for the reader to compare the 1970 target with the actual results in 1970.

The Economic Planning Agency (EPA) of the Prime Minister's Office also attempted in 1962 to predict interregional distributions of industries through: (1) determining what government specialists thought to be 'four major factors' of industrial location, (2) estimating the importance of the 'factors' in each region and (3) evaluating the potentiality of each region in attracting each kind of industry. This study by the EPA reached similar conclusions to the study done by the MITI, even though they differed in the research methods.

Obviously, such mistaken forecasting resulted partly from a political pressure by various local leaders and, in turn, misled them considerably. The reader is referred to Nishioka and Krumme (1973) for a detailed discussion on a research undertaken by the MITI and also to Nishioka (1964) for that on the above EPA's study.

6. As Weber recognized well, this does not mean that the ratio of any particular costs to total costs, rather than spatial differentials in the particular costs, indicates the locational force; see Aoki (1959), pp. 101–2.

7. According to an interesting study by Professor Keisuke Suzuki (1972), though urban population distribution in Japan does not fit the rank-size rule, her urban population *densities,* when they are classified into east and west Japan and into groups of less than and more than 50,000 population, are log-normally distributed.

8. Marshall (1961), pp. 802–3.

9. The founder of Fujikoshi Ltd., Araki Imura, who was born and raised in Nagasaki, wrote, 'But Kyushu land is most deviously situated and, moreover, Kyushu people are somewhat capricious. They are passionate, but do not keep up. Their fickleness is not desirable for a firm which in my contemplation requires precise work ... people in Toyama Prefecture have the tendency of tenacity, since they have to stand the rainy and snowy climate. Moreover, in Toyama Prefecture, foods are abundant ... and labour turnover is low. Transport costs are not serious for precision machinery industry ... Electricity is, of course, abundant and cheap. For these reasons, I decided to build a plant in Toyama' (Nihon Keizai Shimbun Ltd., 1960, Vol. 10, pp. 235–6). Compare this case to case study B.

10. According to Y. Nishiyama, who was born in Kanagawa Prefecture, 'the Japan Sea coast is not suitable for a steel maker since iron and steel are very apt to rust due to high humidity. In this aspect, the Pacific coast is better. But on the Japan Sea coast, human nature and manners are better: people are simple, steady and good-natured'. Daiyamondo Ltd., 1964, p. 107.

11. For theoretical aspects see Smithies (1941), Esawa (1954) and Greenhut (1956). I was given the following impression by a talk with an official of Aichi Clocks and Electric Equipment (case study A). The President's preliminary limitation of a radius for selecting a new plant location in the chukyo area was conditioned by the need for close connection with the parent plant and by maintaining the steady basis in Chukyo rather than advancing into Keihin. According to the late President Toshio Iue of Sanyo Electric Co. Ltd., there was ill-feeling among Kanto makers toward the advance of a Kansai maker even of household electric appliances into Kanto; see Nihon Keizai Shimbun, 1963, Vol. 19, p. 59.

12. Daiyamondo Ltd., 1967, pp. 534–5.

13. More elaborate discussions are to be found in Nishioka (1965a, 1966b, 1968). The reader is also referred to Hamilton (1967) and Krumme (1970).

14. Differentiation between (1) location conditions as used by economic geographers and (2) location factors as used by location theorists, including Weber, was clarified first in Japan by Kunimatsu (1953, pp. 36–7) and Kasuga (1958, pp. 1–5); see also Nishioka and Krumme (1973).

15. A brief explanation of the possible application of Weberian type of location theory to cases which include costs for preventing public nuisances is seen in the revised edition, p. 106 of Nishioka (1965a).

16. Most reporters on locational decisions in the case studies section do belong to this category.

17. An interesting case in the 'disguised factory'. Even if a community, which is anxious to attract plants and to check the outflow of young people, provides an enterprise with cheap or free land and buildings, the secret object for the enterprise might be to employ local youth and, when they and their parents became familiar with the firm, to send them to another larger plant far from the locality; see Nishioka (1968), pp. 15–16.

18. Because locational trends and regional policies in Japan have been very fluid, this chapter is not concerned with the period since 1965.

19. There are several other laws concerning regional development with specific aims and areal coverage such as the Outlying Islands Development Promotion Act. Many laws were enacted more or less on an *ad hoc* basis, independently of each other. Accordingly, administrative machinery for regional development, established in accordance with the provisions of these laws, is also on an *ad hoc* basis. 'Apart from some machinery such as Hokkaido Development Agency and National Capital Development Committee which are independent agencies within the Prime Minister's Office, most functions of regional development planning and coordination are assigned to the Development Bureau of Economic Planning Agency of the Prime Minister's Office' (Okita, 1965, pp. 242–4). The coordination or adjustment by the EPA, however, often goes on the rocks because of sharply divided opinions among ministries, central and local governments, industries and local people.

20. Case studies A to D are summaries of mimeographed materials edited by the Japan Industrial Location Centre (1967), which was given to the author in December 1972 by Managing Director Teiichi Iijima and Director Goro Suzuki of the Centre. The last two cases are summaries from a publication edited by the Industrial Location Guidance Centre (1962) of MITI. The final one is a speech by a local government official in charge of attracting plants into his prefecture.

510

21. A more detailed report of aspects of this company, including its circumstances at the time of its establishment, its locational policy and Matsushita's philosophy of management, is found in a speech by President Arataro Takahashi (1968).

22. Strictly speaking, the founder, Shozo Kawasaki, built a shipyard at Tsukiji in Tokyo in 1878. However, the location was shifted to Kobe after 1886 and the personally-owned shipyard was reorganized into a joint stock corporation in 1896.

23. The late Governor Miki was famous as the 'King of Inducing Plants'. Great efforts made by him, and also prefectural people including a prominent figure, late President Soichiro Obara of Kurary Co. Ltd., for the development of Mizushima can be traced in Mizunoe and Takeshita (1971). The then Chairman, Omori, of Kawasaki Seitetsu said: 'I come from Okayama Prefecture, have known Mr. Miki very well from early on, and have placed my greatest trust in him. The establishment of the Mizushima Plant or Kawasaki Seitetsu was realized by human interaction between Mr. Miki and President Nishiyama', (Mizunoe and Takeshita, 1971, p. 23); and Managing Director Yamaji said: 'The reason why our company decided to come to Mizushima is attributable to locational conditions of Mizushima and to our trust in Mr. Miki, about half and half. He performed, one by one, his promises, such as those on problems of water, port and land reclaimed from the sea, appealing to central government ... He was overwhelmingly supported by both parties in and out of power, and I really had a great admiration for his ability', (Mizunoe and Takeshita, 1971, p. 233).

24. According to Director Takeo Hirakawa of the Nippon Koyu (refinery), his plant was the first of those which emitted smoke in Mizushima and Mitsubishi Sekiyu (Mitsubishi Oil Co. Ltd.) would certainly decide to come to Mizushima 'after looking at our smoke'; see Mizunoe and Takeshita (1971), pp. 191–2. Also, the then head of the commerce and industry department of the prefectural office, Tatsuhiko Egami said: 'After the arrival of Mitsubishi Sekiyu, Nizushima became famous and other companies moved in. Mitzubishi Sekiyu was, as it were, the first guest for Mizushima and we gave it a service like the morning discount of a cinema house' (Mizunoe and Takeshita, 1971, p. 197).

References

Agency on Small and Medium Enterprises, MITI, 1972*, *White Paper on Small and Medium Enterprises,* 1972 (Tokyo: Printing Office, Ministry of Finance).

Aoki, Toshio, 1959, 'On the cost factors in the location of industry', *Annals of the Hitotsubashi Academy,* **10**, no. 1, 91–107 (original Japanese article appeared in 1957).

Aoki, Toshio and Hisao Nishioka, 1966, 'Location theory and policy in Japan', *Research Reports in Social Science,* **9** (2) (Tallahassee: Institute for Social Research, Florida State University), 17–35.

Beika, Minoru, 1958*, *Plant Location* (Tokyo: Nihon Keizai Shimbun-sha).

Daiyamondo Ltd. (ed.), 1964*, *Yataro Nishiyama* (Tokyo: Daiyamondo-sha).

Daiyamondo Ltd. (ed.), 1967*, *A Short History of Yataro Nishiyama,* Kobe: Nishiyama Commemoration Service Committee, Kawasaki Seitetsu KK.

Esawa, Dyodi, 1954, *The Theory of Industrial Agglomeration* (Tokyo: Jicho-sha).

Greenhut, Melvin L., 1956, *Plant Location in Theory and in Practice* (Chapel Hill: University of North Carolina Press).

Greenhut, Melvin L. and Marshall R. Colberg, 1962, *Factors in the Location of Florida Industry* (Tallahassee: Florida State University).

Hamilton, F. E. Ian, 1967, 'Models of industrial location', in *Models in Geography,* ed. R. S. Chorley and P. Haggett (London: Methuen), 361–424.

Hoover, Edgar M., 1937, *Location Theory and the Shoe and Leather Industries* (Cambridge, Mass.: Harvard University Press).

Iijima, Teiichi, 1964*, *The Study on Industrial Development and Methods of Developemnt and Equipping of Industrial Land* (mimeo).

Industrial Location Guidance Centre, MITI (ed.), 1962*, *Industrial Location* (Tokyo: Tsusho Sangyo Lenkyu-sha), enlarged and revised edition.

Isard, Walter, 1956, *Location and Space Economy* (New York: Wiley).

Japan Industrial Location Centre (ed.), 1967 or perhaps 1968*, *Collected example of Factory Location: Experiences of Constructing A Plant* (Tokyo: JILC) (mimeo).

Kasuga, Shigeo, 1958*, 'A reconsideration of factors determining location', *Economic Journal of Oita University,* **10** (3), 1–24.

Krumme, Gunter, 1970, 'Location Theory', in *Focus on Geography,* ed. P. Bacon (Washington D.C.: National Council for the Social Studies), 3–37.

Kunimatsu, Hisaya, 1953*, *The New Human Geography* (Tokyo: Kokon Shoin).

Marshall, Alfred, 1961, *Principles of Economics,* 9th (variorum) edition with annotations by Guillebaud, 2 vols. (London: Macmillan).

Martin, J. E., 1964, 'The industrial geography of Greater London', in *The Geography of Greater London,* ed. R. Clayton (London: Phillip), 111–42.

Mizunoe, Suehiko and Shozo Takeshita, 1971*, *Formation and Development of Mizushima Industrial Zone* (Tokyo: Kazama Shobo).

Moses, Leon N., 1958, 'Location and the theory of production', *Quarterly Journal of Economics,* **72** (2), 259–72.

Namiki, Masayoshi *et al.,* 1967*, *The Research Report on Agricultural Problems in Sparsely Populated Areas* (Tokyo: Zenkoko Nogyo Kozo Kaizen Kyokai (mimeo).

Nihon Keizai Shimbun Ltd. (ed.), 1957–*, *My Personal History,* 47 vols. upto January, 1973 (each of which contains several persons' own history published in Nihon Keizai Shimbun, a famous newspaper) (Tokyo: Nihon Keizai Shimbun-Sha).

Nishioka, Hisao, 1959*, 'On the location policies for the various types of region'. *Aoyama Journal of Economics,* **2** (2) and (3), 138–53.

Nishioka, Hisao, 1962, 'Interregional economic differences within Japan', *Aoyama Journal of Economics,* **13** (4), 37–57. (For much more detailed discussion, see his 'Regional structure and location policy',* *Aoyama Journal of Economics,* **12** (1), (2) and (3), 1–25, 83–109 and 75–93 respectively, or his *Location and Regional Economy*,* 1963 (Tokyo: Miyai Shoten), Chaps. 6 and 7.

Nishioka, Hisao, 1962, 'A reconsideration of the economic location theory', *Aoyama Journal of Economics,* **14** (1), 25–42. (Origianl Japanese article appeared in 1961.)

Nishioka, Hisao, 1964*, 'Planning and reality of industrial location', *Aoyama Journal of Economics,* **16** (1), 91–118.

Nishioka, Hisao, 1956a*, 'The analysis of economic location', in *Economic Geography,* ed. H. Kumimatsu *et al.* (Tokyo: Meigen Shobo), 46–90 (revised edition, 1971, 56–115).

Nishioka, Hisao, 1956b, *On the Industrialization of Underdeveloped Regions,* Occasional Papers 3 (Tokyo: Economic Institute of Aoyama Gakuin University). (Original Japanese article appeared in 1958.)

Nishioka, Hisao, 1966a* 'A review of Japanese industrial location policy'· *Human Geography,* **18** (1), 48–58.

Nishioka, Hisao, 1966b*, 'Regional development and locational conditions for industries', in *Regional Development and Managerial Planning,* ed. S. Takamiya and R. Ichinose (Tokyo: Daiyamondo-sha), 75–102.

Nishioka, Hisao, 1967, 'On the interregional income differentials in Japan', *Papers and Proceedings of the Second Far East Conference of the Regional Science Association,* 1965 (Tokyo: University of Tokyo Press), 169–80. (For detailed discussion, see his *A Study of the Interregional Income Differentials in Japan,* Tokyo: Kokon Shoin).

Nishioka, Hisao, 1968*, *The Introduction to Economic Location,* Nikkei Library 98, (Tokyo: Nihon Keizai Shimbun-sha).

Nishioka, Hisao, and Gunter Krumme, 1973, 'Locational conditions, factors and decision-making process', forthcoming in *Land Economics,* **14** (2), pp. 195–205.

512

Okita, Saburo, 1965, 'Regional development policy in Japan', *Papers and Proceedings of the First Far East Conference of the Regional Science Association,* 1963 (Tokyo: University of Tokyo Press), 237–52.

Okuda, Yoshio, 1964*, 'Regional trends in industrial development in Japan', in *The Study on the Regional Structure of Industrial Development,* ed. K. Oharu (Tokyo: JILC (Japan Industrial Location Centre)), (mimeo), 1–25.

Okudaira, Yashuiro, 1970*, 'A critical examination of legislative process of basic law of countermeasures for public nuisances', *Jurist,* **485** (Tokyo: Yuhikaku), 170–6.

Sato, Motoshige, 1963*, *Industrial Location Policy in Japan* (Tokyo: Kobundo).

Schumpeter, Joseph Alois, 1934, *The Theory of Economic Development* (Cambridge, Mass.: Harvard University Press). (Original German edition appeared in 1912 and 1926.)

Science and Technology Agency, Prime Minister's Office, 1961*, *The Resource Problem of Japan,* 2 vols. (Tokyo: Shigen Kyokai).

Smithies, Arthur F., 1941, 'Optimum location in spatial competition', *Journal of Political Economy,* **49**, June, 423–39.

Suzuki, Keisuke, 1972*, 'On the type of the distribution of population density of cities and the mechanism of the generation of it', *Journal of the University of Transportation Economics,* **7** (1), (Ryugasaki, Ibaraki: Ryutsu Keizai Daigaku), 25–41.

Takahashi, Arataro, 1968*, 'Thinking better of ability of young people. The social bearings of a firm are important', *Kyukinkai News,* No. 110 (under the new title), 20 August (Fukuoka: Kyushu Kinyu Keizai Kondan-kai), 2–7.

Tekko Shimbun Ltd. (ed.), 1971*, *A Life of A Leading Figure in the Iron and Steel Industry: Yataro Nishiyama* (Tokyo: Tekko Shimbun-sha).

Weber, Alfred, 1929, *Theory of the Location of Industries,* translated with an introduction and notes by C. J. Friedrich (Chicago: University of Chicago Press). (Original German edition appeared in 1909.)

Index

522

Imperial Chemicals Industries 190–3, 206–7, 219, 451
Imperial Tobacco Co. 220
Import substitution 474–6
Independent discretion 37, 457
Independent loggers 433–4
Index of importance 180–1
Index of plant linkage change 31, 328–31
Index of spatial linkage change 329–31
Indianapolis 119
Individualism 26, 55, 458
Induced amenities 172–182
Industrial complexes 61, 78, 102, 198, 341–5, 368, 371, 413, 426, 434, 441, 497
Industrial Development Act, 1966 396–8
Industrial development certificate policy 27, 30, 40, 393–409
Industrial estates 27, 257–60, 398, 471–2, 506–7
Industrial Location Guidance Centre (Japan) 499
Industrial movement 397–400
Industrial quarters 369–70
Industrial Reorganization Corporation (U.K.) 281
Industrial revolution 6, 9–10, 335, 402
Industrialization of peasant society 417, 449–51, 456–7
Inertia 55, 61, 172, 227, 270, 281, 290–1, 365, 450, 473
Infancy 6
Inflation 261, 497
Information 4, 9–10, 22, 24, 26, 49, 63, 65, 101, 105–31, 172, 175, 178, 185, 194, 214, 235, 245, 272, 287, 337, 356, 364–5, 370, 405–6, 414, 426–7, 461, 479, 489
Information components 124–5
Information economics 105–6, 124, 310, 315, 375
Information curtain 292, 412
Information feedback 9, 11, 21, 25, 40
Information flows 5, 6–7, 11–3, 17, 19, 20, 25–6, 31, 36, 37, 40, 53, 55, 58, 106, 108–9, 116–23, 124, 127–9, 130, 202, 421, 436, 455–6, 458–9, 499, 501–2
Information gaps 25, 68, 70, 290, 309, 479
Information leakage 26, 418
Information network 65, 230, 371

Information-rich agglomerations 130
Information surfaces 12, 480
Infrastructural Urbanization Economies 368, 370
Infrastructure 38–9, 56, 156, 172–86, 235, 240, 273, 375, 413, 438, 449, 452, 463–4, 466–9, 473, 497, 500
Inherited resources 29, 56, 70
Initial location 6–13, 18, 48, 53, 146, 213, 221–43, 262, 309
Initiating force 248–9
Innis, H. 146–7, 167
Innovation 11–12, 15, 18, 21, 58–9, 108–9, 114–5, 116–23, 143–66, 201, 204, 218, 246, 270, 294, 296, 427–9, 449–51, 473–5, 492, 497
Innovation centre 145, 153
Innovation potential 12
Innovation strategy 19–20, 204, 293
Innovation threshold 12
Innovative industries 106
Innovator 7, 296
Input-output 4, 107, 148, 249, 310, 314, 368, 386, 462
Input supply 18, 29–32, 36, 56, 80, 83–5, 93, 110, 124, 150, 172–82, 255–6, 297–8, 309, 311–32, 336–62, 367–89, 417, 424, 428, 430, 436–7, 440–1, 450, 454, 481–2, 503, 505
Institutional economists 48
Institutional inducements 467–9
Insurance, Factory 229
Integration, Horizontal 15, 35, 57, 61, 66, 110, 228, 230–1, 241, 354, 424, 429, 451–2, 455
   Vertical 10, 15, 17, 35, 54, 57, 61, 66, 78, 83–4, 145, 156, 158–9, 228, 230–1, 241, 261–2, 279–80, 354, 424–6, 429, 451–2, 455, 481, 495, 503
Interaction 128, 246, 371, 437
Interdependencies 78, 105–6, 113–4, 116–7, 119, 128, 130, 144–5, 154–5, 214, 415, 417, 456, 462–5
Interests, Vested 7, 9–10, 21, 24–5, 37–40, 54–5, 65, 199, 204, 247, 270, 272, 406–7, 413–4, 431–2, 434, 452, 467, 487
Inter-factor relationships 83, 87–8, 98–9
Inter-industry structure 102
Intermediary organizations 424
Intermediate areas 397
Inter-ministerial divisions 35

524

Kyushu 485, 487, 490, 496–7
Kyushu Matsushita Denki KK 502–3

Labour availability 85, 113, 119, 123,
147, 156, 172–82, 196, 229, 231,
233, 250, 254, 261, 294, 331, 341,
399, 442–3, 452, 454, 477, 502–3
Labour market 172, 375
Labour productivity 28, 172–82, 229,
417
Labour rates 172–82, 196, 234, 454,
469, 491
Labour relations 251–3
Labour resource regions 38, 442
Labour, Skilled 150, 172, 368, 371
Labour training 294, 393, 397, 399,
477
Labour-intensive industries 397, 454,
472
Lagging new-model policy 82
Lagos 463, 471–2, 475, 481
Lagrangian function 93, 98
Lake Baykal controversy 412
Lampard, E. E. 110, 135
Lancashire 9–12, 321–6, 335, 393
Land market, Industrial 33, 402–7, 499,
501–7
Land prices 33, 196, 235, 402–4, 490,
501, 503, 505, 507
Land plan basic policy 498
Land reclamation 490, 497, 505–6
Land-use planning 406–7, 490, 498–9
Land value gradient 402–3
Lanzilotti, R. F. 82, 103
Lasuen, J. R. 107–8, 116, 128, 135
Latent function 72
Law for Promoting Designated Industrial
Development Areas 1964 (Japan)
500
Leadership 196, 487–8
League of Communists (Yugoslavia)
452
Leakages 388
Learning 23, 26, 125, 190, 289–91, 309,
363, 453
Least cost location 275
Leather industry 85
Leeds 209
Legal services 373–89
Leicester 209
Leningrad 428–9, 434, 438–9, 441

Leningrad Optical Mechanical Associa-
tion 428
Leningrad Plastic and Polymerization
Materials Association 429
Leontief-type production function 77
Lever, W.F. 27, 29, 310, 333, 340,
362
Lexington (Kentucky) 19
Liberman, E. 412
Licences 248
Lichtenberg, R. M. 115, 130, 136
Liege 258
Likhachev motor vehicle plant 428
Lima (Ohio) 18
Linear programming 58, 191–3, 197–8
Linkage, Backward 5, 8, 17, 28–30, 35,
108, 110, 158, 208, 310–32, 340–62,
368–89, 423, 429, 435, 440–2, 451,
454–5, 466
Forward 5, 8, 17, 28–30, 35, 84,
108, 110, 116, 128, 158, 208, 310–32,
340–62, 368–89, 423, 429, 435, 440,
451, 454
Inherited 326
Inter-city 20, 31, 108–9, 116–18, 343–5
Inter-firm 337, 345–62, 383–4, 427,
434–5, 454
Inter-industry 4, 107, 336–62, 374
Intra-firm 8, 20, 53–5, 61, 83–4,
354–6, 366–7, 370, 383–5
Intra-Metropolitan 31, 350–4, 356–
62
Service 341, 364–90
Linkage changes 297–9
Linkage length, Mean 316–7
Liossatos, P. 79, 103
Lithuanian Republic Council of Ministers
427, 436
Livesey, F. 43
Liverpool 9–11, 209, 261–2
Living conditions 250
Ljubljana 452, 455
Loasby, B. J. 288, 306, 394–5
Local Employment Act, 1960 (U.K.)
395–6, 398
Location choice 6–13, 61–2, 65, 68,
71, 101, 106, 183, 190, 231–43, 290,
365, 399, 415, 421–2, 451, 468–9,
488–95, 501–6
Location conditions 492, 502, 505
Location factors 172–4, 254–7, 488–9,
493–4